Praise for Donald L. Miller's *City of the Century*

"Has attracted—and deserves—considerabl[e] [attention among histori]ans and in the popular press. . . . Unlike m[any in aca]demic history departments, Miller not only w[rites well,] he conceives his task as the telling of a story. And he is a superb storyteller."
—Douglas Greenberg, *Chicago Tribune*

"Perfectly blends anecdote, theory, and fact into a fascinating read."
—Gillian Engberg, *Chicago Life*

"Miller skillfully juxtaposes his stories about the fair, the university, the skyscrapers, and the other symbols of achievement with tales of the city's unbelievable filth and squalor."
—Alan Ehrenhalt, *The Washington Post*

"Remarkable . . . a model for future historians. Highly recommended."
—Boyd Childress, *Library Journal*

"A picaresque biography of a picaresque city."
—*Kirkus Reviews*

"A glorious anthem to a tumultuous city, this synthesis of industrial, social, and cultural history captures the raw, robust spirit of Chicago on every page. . . . Big, colorful, engrossing."
—*Publishers Weekly* (starred)

"Convincing . . . a solid book."
—*Booklist*

"In this spirited telling of the Chicago phenomenon, Donald Miller, one of our ablest historians, takes us to the heart of what made America tick, made us what we are. This is a book bearing directly on much that needs to be understood about the role of great cities in American life and that itself brims with life, with people, surprise, and with stories—and stories within stories—all worth telling."
—David McCullough, author of *Truman*

Donald L. Miller

CITY
of the
Century

The Epic

of Chicago

and the

Making

of America

Simon & Schuster Paperbacks

New York   London

Toronto   Sydney

SIMON & SCHUSTER PAPERBACKS
Rockefeller Center
1230 Avenue of the Americas
New York, NY 10020

Copyright © 1996 by Donald L. Miller.
First Simon & Schuster trade paperback edition 2003

SIMON & SCHUSTER PAPERBACKS and colophon are registered
trademarks of Simon & Schuster, Inc.

DESIGNED BY KAROLINA HARRIS
PICTURE SECTION DESIGNED BY BARBARA MARKS

Picture Credits

1—Rufus Blanchard, *Discovery and Conquests of the North-West, with the History of Chicago* (1880); 2, 10, 11, 17, 19, 41—The Chicago Public Library; 3—photograph by Mathew Brady (Chicago Public Library); 4, 7–9, 29, 37, 44—Library of Congress; 5—*Harper's Weekly*, 1871; 6, 35, 40, 43—Chicago Historical Society; 12, 14, 16, 20, 22, 23, 32, 36—The Art Institute of Chicago; 13—*Building News*, 1884; 15—*A History of Chicago* (Chicago: Inter Ocean, 1900): 18—Marshall Field & Co. Archives; 21, 38—Joseph Kirkland, *The Story of Chicago*, vol. 1 (1892); 24—Goodspeed Publishing Company, Chicago; 25—*Industrial Chicago* (Chicago: Goodspeed Pulishing Co, 1891); 26—*Inland Architect*, c. 1890; 27—Alfred T. Andreas, *History of Chicago*, vol. 3 (1886); 28—Hasbrouck Peterson Associates; 30—William S. Donnell; 31—courtesy of the Western Society of Engineers; 33—*Harper's Weekly*, 1889; 34, 42—author's private collection; 39—*Harper's Weekly*, 1886.

Manufactured in the United States of America

16   17   18   19   20

The Library of Congress has cataloged the Simon & Schuster edition as follows:
Miller, Donald L.
City of the century: the epic of Chicago and the making of
America / by Donald Miller.
p.   cm.
Includes index.
1. Chicago (Ill.)—History.   I. Title.
F548.3.M55   1996
977.3'11—dc30   96-4018

ISBN-13: 978-0-684-80194-0
ISBN-10:   0-684-80194-9
ISBN-13: 978-0-684-83138-1 (Pbk)
ISBN-10:   0-684-83138-4 (Pbk)

In loving memory of my father, Donald L. Miller,
and of my nephew Andrew Miller

ROUGH-AND-TUMBLE-BUSINESS CHICAGO AFTER THE GREAT
FIRE WAS A REGIONAL CAPITAL, AND IN MANY WAYS, BECAUSE
OF ITS INNOVATIONS IN INDUSTRIAL METHOD AND IN
ARCHITECTURE, BECAUSE OF ITS MIXTURE OF BRUTAL
WICKEDNESS AND REVOLUTIONARY NEWNESS, THE BLOOD OF
THE YARDS, THE SHOWPIECE GEMS OF THE LAKEFRONT, THE
SEETHING OF ITS IMMIGRANT SLUMS, BECAUSE OF ITS
VIOLENCE, CORRUPTION, AND CREATIVE ENERGY,
IT WAS ALSO A WORLD CITY.

— SAUL BELLOW

Contents

II

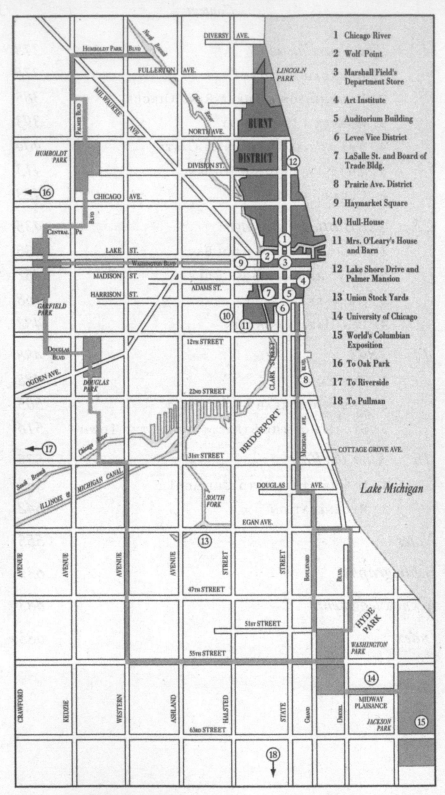

1 Chicago River
2 Wolf Point
3 Marshall Field's Department Store
4 Art Institute
5 Auditorium Building
6 Levee Vice District
7 LaSalle St. and Board of Trade Bldg.
8 Prairie Ave. District
9 Haymarket Square
10 Hull-House
11 Mrs. O'Leary's House and Barn
12 Lake Shore Drive and Palmer Mansion
13 Union Stock Yards
14 University of Chicago
15 World's Columbian Exposition
16 To Oak Park
17 To Riverside
18 To Pullman

Chicago around the time of the fair.

Preface

ON the evening of October 7, 1871, George Francis Train, a popular lecturer on moral themes, gave a talk in Chicago to a packed house at Farwell Hall. There is no record of the topic of his address, but his concluding remarks were noted. "This is the last public address that will be delivered within these walls!" he thundered. "A terrible calamity is impending over the city of Chicago! More I cannot say; more I dare not utter."

The following night, around nine o'clock, a fire broke out on the West Side of the city in the cow barn of Mrs. Patrick O'Leary. Aided by strong winds off the prairie, it turned into a one-and-a-half-day holocaust that consumed the entire core of the city of some 300,000 people, leaving 90,000 homeless and nearly 300 dead. It was the greatest natural disaster up to that time in American history. Frederick Law Olmsted, sent by *The Nation* to the stricken city, reported that many of those caught in the inferno thought they were witnessing "the burning of the world."

The morning after the fire, fear gave way to disbelief. Everything was gone. All familiar landmarks—churches, street signs, corner groceries, bars—had disappeared into thin air, and people wandered around like shock victims, lost in their own city. "For three days after the fire we walked through the streets, covered everywhere with heaps of debris and parts of walls, and could not help comparing ourselves to ghosts. . . .," one man observed. "All those magnificent streets, all those grand palaces, which but yesterday were the pride and glory of the chief Western metropolis, are today indeed a mass of scattered, shapeless ruins."

But more amazing than the destruction was the recovery. The rebuilding began while the ground was still warm in the burned district, and within a week after the fire more than five thousand temporary structures had been erected and two hundred permanent buildings were under construction. Derrick hoists crowded the main streets, and the air came alive with the sound of hammers and the shouts and whistles of draymen and carpenters. "In the midst of a calamity without parallel in the world's history. . . ," *Chicago Tribune* editor Joseph Medill wrote immediately after the fire, "the people of this once beautiful city have resolved that CHICAGO SHALL RISE AGAIN." Chicagoans were convinced they had survived a biblical test, a terrible but purifying act that had cleared the way for a vast regeneration that would transform their ruined city into the master metropolis of America.

Such inflated boosterism was standard fare in the city before the Great Fire, but the fire gave it greater urgency; and with astonishing rapidity, fact almost aligned with myth. By 1893, when the city held the World's Columbian Exposition to celebrate—one year late—the four hundredth anniversary of Columbus's discovery of the New World, Chicago had the busiest and most modern downtown in the country, with a dozen and more of the highest buildings ever constructed. Chicago would never become as big or as consequential as New York, its greatest rival, but it had made good its boast as the city that could accomplish almost anything.

•

There is in the life of any great city a moment when it reaches its maximum potential as a center of power and culture and becomes fully conscious of its special place in history. For Chicago that moment was 1893. In that year the world's first skyscraper city had a population of over a million people, and among them was an early settler who remembered it as a desolate trading post of some thirty souls living between a swamp and a sand-choked river. Without ever leaving Chicago, this old man had moved, by 1893, from the country to the city, from an agrarian to an industrial America, and had lived, in the process, through the entire history of his still-growing city.

This book is a history of Chicago in the years of its ascendency, from the first recorded discovery of the site by a missionary and an explorer in the service of France to the Columbian Exposition, the culmination of a postfire burst of physical growth and technological and artistic achievement, a civic awakening unparalleled in the history of American cities. It is about the nineteenth century's newest and most explosively alive metropolis, the city of the century, "the first of the great cities of the world," in the words of Henry B. Fuller, its first important novelist, "to rise under purely modern conditions."

The epic of Chicago is the story of the emergence of modern America. Child of the age of steam, electricity, and international exchange, Chicago "[is] the very embodiment of the world-conquering spirit of the age," an English writer observed in 1893, a city people visited to witness the forces that would shape the next century. Chicago was also, many people thought, the most typically American of the nation's big cities, a scene of boiling economic activity and technological ingenuity, American industrialism's supreme urban creation. In an unreservedly commercial country, it was, a visiting French writer noted, "the purest kind of commercial city." The novelist Frank Norris described a cable-car ride through late-nineeenth-century Chicago: "All around, on every side in every direction, the vast machinery of Commonwealth clashed and thundered from dawn to dark and from dark till dawn. . . . Here, of all her cities, throbbed the true life—the true power and spirit of America." Chicago was "the only great city in the world to which all its citizens have come for the one common, avowed object of making money," Fuller captured part of its character. "There you have its genesis, its growth, its end and object." Yet Chicago's wealth and vitality—along with its overwhelming problems—drew to it some of the most creative young architects, writers, and reformers of the time, who came there to record, interpret, humanize, or simply experience the new phenomenon of metropolitan life.

No large city, not even Peter the Great's St. Petersburg, had grown so fast, and nowhere else could there be found in more dramatic display such a combination of wealth and squalor, beauty and ugliness, corruption and reform. City of idealists and dissenters, of Jane Addams, Florence Kelley, Clarence Darrow, Mary McDowell, Thorstein Veblen, Albert Parsons, and Ida B. Wells, a young African-American insurgent who moved to Chicago in 1893 to mobilize a national crusade against lynching and racial segregation, it was also the city of thieving aldermen and plundering capitalists, of the sharp-dealing transportation king Charles Tyson Yerkes and his political procurator, Johnny Powers, and of those legendary "boodlers" Michael "Hinky Dink" Kenna and "Bathhouse" John Coughlin, aldermen who gave one dollar to the needy for every two they stole. Chicago in 1893 was the city of Marshall Field, Philip Danforth Armour, and George Mortimer Pullman, "the Chicago Trinity," the newspapers called them, and of those who wrote about them and a hundred other urban figures, in what became the first realistic American reportage and fiction about the big city—Theodore Dreiser, Eugene Field, Hamlin Garland, Robert Herrick, George Ade, Henry B. Fuller, Ray Stannard Baker, and Finley Peter Dunne, creator of the affable saloon-house philosopher Mr. Dooley. And to Chicago, after the Great Fire, came the young founders of modern American architecture, John Wellborn Root, Louis H. Sullivan, and Frank Lloyd Wright, to join such visionary builders as Daniel Hudson Burnham and William Le Baron Jenney in creating urban works of audacity and beauty. In the time of these makers and dreamers, Chicago was the site of some of the greatest achievements and failures of American urban life.

Civic boosters and chauvinistic city historians portrayed Chicago in these years as a unified community that had called together its enormous resources after the Great Fire to build a new city on the ash and rubble of the old one. But Chicago was a deeply divided, corrupt, and violent city, a place of extreme contrasts, and it was this that gave it its character. I have tried to capture the spirit of this "queen and guttersnipe of cities," to describe the historic forces that shaped its physical form and personality, and to give a sense of what it was like to live there when its leaders in business and the arts were calling it the "wonder of the world." Recalling his life in Chicago in these years, Theodore Dreiser remarked that "it is given to some cities, as to some lands, to suggest romance, and to me Chicago did that daily and hourly. It sang, or seemed to, and . . . I was singing with it."

●

With the ancient Greeks as my model, I have tried to write a city history that gives prominence to geography and personality, to the way the natural environment and human beings interact dialectically to create culture. And with Lewis Mumford as my modern inspiration, I have tried to write a "natural history of urbanization" in which the city is treated in the context of its regional economy, culture, and ecosystem. By studying the city in this way, Mumford argued, we arrive at true appreciation of the environmental consequences of urbanization—not just the impact of the spreading city on its rural hinterland but the impact of its growth on its own land, air, water, and people. Built on a windswept prairie marsh—a place so forbidding the Miami Indians refused to settle on it—modern Chicago was a triumph of engineering over nature's constraints. This was the source of the city's famous "I Will" spirit, the belief that it could surmount any obstacle nature or man put in its way. Yet when surging Chicago built shoddily or in defiance of nature's ways, it felt nature's reactive fury. The city of heroic engineers and architects, of great water supply and drainage systems and twelve-story buildings that stood straight and strong in shifting mud and against ripping winds, was also the city of natural calamities—of consuming fires, cholera and typhoid epidemics, poisoned water and air.

The great theme of Chicago's nineteenth-century history is the battle between growth and control, restraint and opportunity, privatism and the public good. Chaotic Chicago seemed to have sprung up spontaneously, without planning or social foresight, a pure product of ungoverned capitalism. Yet the city that was a sprawling spectacle of smoke and disorder had a magnificent chain of parks and boulevards, one of the best sewage and water-supply systems in the world, a Sanitary and Ship Canal that was one of the engineering marvels of the century, and a splendid complex of cultural and civic buildings along its downtown lakefront. The city that critics compared to a gigantic real estate lottery, where everything was for sale, even its streets, undertook some of the most ambitious public improvement projects of the age. In 1893 it was a place well known for both its unlicensed cupidity and its strong civic consciousness. Even if Chicago provides no easy answers, the story of its unresolved struggle between order and freedom remains instructive for our time, as we seek ways to build and maintain cities that retain their humanity without losing their energy.

The story of rising Chicago is one of big and small folk—of assembly-line meat cutters and millionaire beef barons, or five-dollar-a-week salesclerks and magnificent merchant princes, of stenographer-typists and the architects who built their new offices in the sky, of devil-may-care French Canadians and straight-living Protestant improvers who drove them from their frontier trading post and built there a perfectly gridironed capitalist canal town. The lives of these people remind us that ecological history must merge with cultural history if it is to encompass the full life of the city. This type of urban history sees the city itself as a culture-creating system of biotic relationships and as a place not only where the goods of civilization are made and exchanged but also where experience is heightened and transformed into art, ritual, and civic pageantry. "A product of nature," the city is also a product of "human nature," the pioneering Chicago sociologist Robert Park reminds us. But the city, in turn, reshapes human nature. This two-way process of people making Chicago and of Chicago making people is the dominating theme of this urban story.

Part I

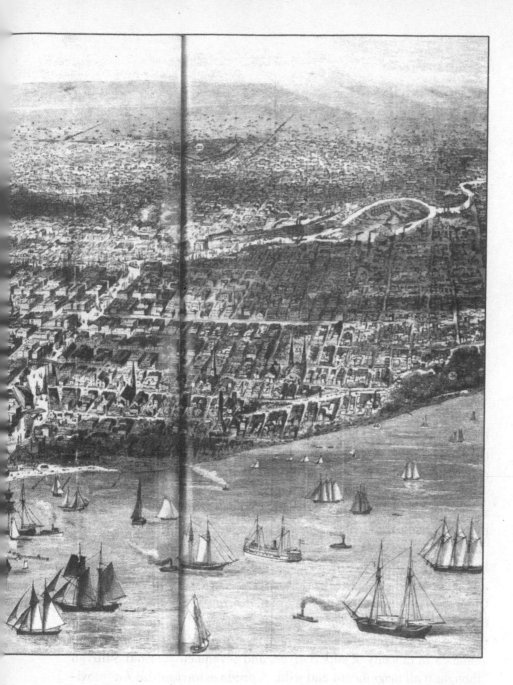

Chicago on the eve of the Great Fire.
Harper's Weekly, 1871

Introduction:
City of Dreamers
and Doers

WHEN Louis Sullivan arrived in Chicago from the East to begin his architectural career, he felt he had been chosen for a special destiny and that this rejuvenated city was "the place" for him. Ashes and debris still covered much of the city in 1873, but no one wanted to talk about the ruins. All interest centered on the rebuilding. The past seemed to have no meaning to these incessantly forward pushing people, and civic patriotism was the prevailing religion. "Big"—or rather, "biggest"— was the word on every Chicagoan's lips, Sullivan recalled in his autobiography. Chicago was the "biggest" livestock, lumber, and grain market in the world and the "biggest" railroad center. Chicagoans even boasted that theirs had been "the biggest conflagration 'in the world.'" But the Chicago "shouters," as Sullivan called them, were not spinning tales. There were powerful builders and visionaries in this city of superlatives, and seventeen-year-old Sullivan "thought it all magnificent and wild: A crude extravaganza: An intoxicating rawness."

After apprenticing for seven months in a firm headed by William Le Baron Jenney, Sullivan left for Paris to continue his studies, and when he returned in 1875, work was hard to find because the city was in the grip of an economic depression. So for Sullivan this became a time of preparation, a chance, as he put it, "to get the lay of the land." Every day he would walk twenty miles or more around Chicago and out into the yellow prairie that stretched beyond it. What explained this raw, robust place? What gave it its impelling drive, the "sense of big things to be done" and the will to carry them through?

Nature gave him the first clue. She had favored Chicago with an unrivaled agricultural hinterland, which Sullivan had first seen from the window of his inbound train from Philadelphia "stretching like a floor to the far horizon." "Here," he thought, "was power—power greater than the mountains." Then there was the inland sea, silver-blue Lake Michigan, born, like the prairie, of the slow advance and retreat of ancient ice sheets. It opened Chicago to the lumber lands to the north, to the ports of the East, and from them, to the world. On occasions when bad weather kept the lumber fleet in port, Sullivan would watch, as the skies cleared, the long lake schooners "pour in a stream" from the mouth of the Chicago River, "spread their wings, and in a great and beautiful flock, gleam in the sunlight as they moved with favoring wind, fan-like towards Muskegon and the northern ports." Without the lake, "born companion" of the prairie, there would be no Chicago, he realized. But Sullivan saw the key to it all in the old portage, a narrow ridge of marshland, long since built over, between the Chicago River—the city's busy harbor—and a prairie river, the Des Plaines, that reached the Mississippi via the Illinois. That low divide over which Indians and French traders had portaged their canoes linked Chicago to the vast, resource-rich mid-continent. Nature had thus set the stage for Chicago, "offspring," Sullivan called it, "of the prairie, the lake and the portage."

Nature had not created Chicago, however; she had merely made it possible. The city would not have been set on its course had not men of energy and empire first envisioned and then cut a canal through the portage. While Chicago's earliest historians insisted that geography had determined the city's future, Sullivan, the architect, saw city building as a supremely human art. Nature provided opportunities as well as constraints, but cities and civilizations were the work "of proud people and their power to create." If ever there was a place shaped by the actions of "big men," surely it was Chicago, Sullivan thought.

On his solitary urban surveys, Sullivan would sometimes walk from the place where the Chicago River flowed into the lake, down the south branch of the river to the "old-time historic portage," and across it (then a place of fevered commercial activity) to the "forest-bordered River Des Plaines." It was here that Jacques Marquette and Louis Joliet pulled their canoes from the river on a September day in 1673 to cross the portage to the future site of Chicago on the final leg of a historic exploration. To learn more about what happened on this spot,

Sullivan read Francis Parkman's "wonder stories" of Marquette and Joliet and "shared in mind the hardships of these great pioneers."

Chicago did not have to invent a heroic past, Sullivan discovered. It already had one, a history in which fact often read like fabulous fiction. The story of the exploration that led to the "discovery" of Chicago was a founding legend as unexpectedly true as the boasts of the Chicago shouters, a simple and inspiring tale of two men seeking new lands and souls to save.* And Sullivan must have been delighted to learn that it was Joliet, an adventurer and visionary, who first suggested building a canal across the portage to link the lake and prairie at the site of what he surmised would become a city of continental importance. He was the forerunner of the "men of destiny" who were building modern Chicago. So the story of the first Chicago became, in Sullivan's mind, a living part of "another story" just beginning, the creation of a new city on the blackened ruins of the old one. It was the approach of this "new story" that most excited him. He would "bide his time."

Sullivan arrived in Chicago in the year, and close to the month, of the two hundredth anniversary of Marquette and Joliet's passage up the Chicago River, the first white men on record to see the site of his adopted city of "dreamers" and "doers." They were not looking for it, having come upon it by accident on one of the great voyages in the history of exploration. They had set out from the upper Great Lakes in search of the Mississippi River and found it. And with them, a priest and an explorer heading home as fast as they could to report their find, the history of Chicago begins.

*It is likely that French-Canadian traders visited the site of Chicago before Joliet and Marquette, but they left no record.

1

Discovery

1. The Priest and the Explorer

THE voyage that brought them to the site of Chicago had its origins in a spectacular pageant of possession in the wilderness of the northern lakes. It was called in 1670 by the intendant of New France, Jean Talon, to establish France's claim to the entire mid-continent, an unmapped territory of unknown extent, rich in minerals and fur-bearing animals and of tremendous strategic importance. Talon had been sent to the struggling colony by Louis XIV's chief minister, Jean-Baptiste Colbert, to begin a program of economic upbuilding, part of the young Sun King's design for a French imperium. When Talon arrived in Quebec, the territory of New France extended just a few miles beyond the junction of the Ottawa and St. Lawrence Rivers, west of Montreal; and he came with orders from Colbert to strengthen the foundations of the central colony before launching any precipitous campaigns of territorial expansion. But Talon was an eager imperialist, anxious to claim for France the interior of the continent, hemming in the English on the Atlantic seaboard and challenging Spain's claims to the American Southwest. All the while, in a more contested theater of expansion, his king prepared to war on the Dutch and the Spanish in an effort to push back France's borders to the Rhine and the Alps, inaugurating an age of French dominance in world affairs.

Since the interior of the continent was still an unknown world, Talon, with no army to speak of, had to rely on French-Canadian fur traders and explorers, like Joliet, and Jesuit missionaries, like Marquette, to carry out his design. The Jesuits had already pushed across the continent to the southern shore of Lake Superior, where Marquette had a mission on remote Chequamegon Bay; and the traders had built a network of alliances with the tribes of the western lakes, who coveted glass beads, iron tools, tobacco, and if they could get it from unscrupulous traders, brandy and whiskey. Now Talon moved to consolidate these gains and establish French influence over the lands and native peoples to the south of the lakes, as far as Florida and Mexico. When he accomplished this, he intended to send an expedition in search of the mysterious river the Indians called Messipi, the Great Water. If it flowed into the California Sea, as some guessed it did, his explorers would be the discoverers of the long-sought western waterway to Cathay.

In 1670, Talon sent out messengers to the chiefs and captains of the tribes of the North to gather that following spring at Sault Ste. Marie for a council with an ambassador from the king. Talon chose a commanding and symbolic site for the occasion. Located at the head of the Great Lakes, on the explosive rapids that carried the waters of Lake Superior into Lake Huron, the sault was the nerve center of French fur trading and missionary enterprise in the Northwest. As the *grand monarque*'s envoy, Talon named Jean-Baptiste de Saint Lusson, a nobleman and soldier of fortune whose only claim to a place in history was his command of this expedition into "that far-away corner of the world."

Waiting for him at the sault were representatives of fourteen tribes. They had come, in part, out of curiosity—to see the man Talon had promised to send, "the voice" of the "captain of the greatest captains," whose "house," they had been told by the traders and fathers, contained "more families" than the largest of their villages. But they were there mainly to cement trade ties with the French, a trade the Indian tribes were becoming utterly dependent upon, to their ultimate disadvantage.

On the morning of June 14, 1671, the missionaries assembled the tribal chiefs on a hill overlooking the village, the mission, and the falls of Ste. Marie, with the pine-scented forest in the background. It was a time of great beauty in the northern woods, and the tribal delegates were greased and perfumed for what they had been told would be "the most solemn ceremony ever observed in these regions." On the ground just in front of them, at the highest point on the hill, lay a large wooden cross of fresh-cut timber and a cedar pole with some kind of plate on it.

The Indians watched in silence as the gate of the mission stockade swung open and a procession wound its way to the place where they were waiting. At its head were the "black robes," holding crucifixes in front of them and chanting a Latin hymn. Then came the traders dressed in buckskin, among them Louis Joliet, who had a thriving fur business at the sault, and a French-Canadian voyageur, or river man, who would accompany Joliet and Marquette on their journey to the Mississippi. Finally, Saint Lusson came into the Indians' sight, magnificent in his crimson uniform and glistening helmet, a ceremonial sword in his right hand.

After the cross was blessed and planted in the ground, the cedar post bearing the royal arms of France on an escutcheon was placed beside it, while the priests chanted the twentieth psalm. At this point, Saint Lusson stepped forward and in a loud voice took possession for his monarch "of Lakes Huron and Superior . . . and of all other countries, rivers, lakes and tributaries, contiguous and adjacent thereunto, as well discovered as to be discovered, which are bounded on the one side by the Northern and Western Seas and on the other side by the South Sea including all its length and breadth." Then Father Claude Allouez, the most revered missionary in New France, called the chiefs close to him and spoke to them in their tongue of what sort of a mighty man "he was whose standard they beheld, and to whose sovereignty they were that day submitting."

When members of Saint Lusson's cortege left the sault, one of them slipped a copy of the report of the annexation behind the escutcheon. After they were gone, the Indians removed it and burned it, fearing that the paper was a spell that would cause the death of all the tribes that had sent representatives to the sault. Then they returned to their people. They were not sure exactly what they had witnessed or what it portended. There was no misunderstanding in Quebec, however.

Talon saw the ceremony at the sault as a prophecy to be swiftly fulfilled. France had laid claim to the largest colonial possession in the world; now she must occupy and hold it. At the pageant there had been more talk, which reached Talon, of the river the Indians said rose in the north and flowed south to a place they had not reached in their longest journeys. No Frenchman had any idea that this was the river Hernando de Soto had crossed and claimed for Spain a century before. The memory of that find had dimmed with time and Spain's falling fortunes in Europe, and those few cartographers who knew of de Soto's river speculated that it was but one of many that flowed north to south through the continent. Without orders from Colbert, Talon formed a party of exploration and named Joliet, at age twenty-seven the colony's most accomplished explorer and mapmaker, to head it. Joliet's orders were to find the Mississippi and follow it to where it entered the sea.

Son of a wheelwright, the Canadian-born Joliet was educated by the Jesuits in Quebec, intending to enter the order until the lure of the wilderness claimed him. He had spent some time with Marquette at the mission station at the sault, where they had talked of making a voyage together to the river that several Illinois Indians had described to the priest. Marquette had promised that he would carry the gospel to their lands, which bordered the Mississippi, so he was the logical choice of Claude Dablon, his superior, to be chaplain of the expedition. Some Jesuits thought that the more experienced Allouez should be the first apostle to the Illinois, but Marquette was younger—in his mid-thirties—had skills as a geographer and cartographer, and had mastered six Indian languages since his arrival in Canada in 1666, immediately after his ordination.

Marquette had the blazing zeal of the Jesuit martyrs of the Iroquois massacres he had read about back in his native Laon. He "seems," Francis Parkman wrote of him, "a figure evoked from some dim legend of medieval saintship." But in addition to being apostles, Marquette's generation of Jesuit missionaries were explorers and men of science, eager to travel to unknown lands and send back fact-filled accounts of climate, geography, soil conditions, plant and animal life, river currents and lake tides, and the habits and customs of the native peoples they encountered. On his and Joliet's journey, which took them north, west, and south of the future site of Chicago, Marquette kept an accurate journal of the places they passed through and, with the help of nothing more than a compass and an astrolabe, drew the first reliable map of this part of the world. Joliet also kept generous records—which have been lost—gave a full account of the journey to his superiors, and made a better map than Marquette's. These records and recollections form the first picture we have of the bounteous forests and flatlands—the far-spreading hinterland—that would give rise eventually to a major market and transporting center at the site of Louis Sullivan's "historic portage." They are the first "natural history" of the Chicago region. Reading them today we understand why there became a Chicago. They are, as well, a thrilling tale of origins and adventure, a Chicago Aeneid.

•

They left for Illinois country on May 17, 1673—five voyageurs, the priest, and the explorer—in two birchbark canoes. Their jumping off point was the mission of St. Ignace that Marquette had founded in 1671 on the Straits of Mackinac, at the far northeastern edge of Lake

Michigan. Their outfit was light for so long a journey: a supply of smoked meat and Indian corn, a package of trading trinkets, powder, balls and muskets, paper and bottles of ink for taking notes, and Marquette's storage box filled with vestments, altar wine, a supply of Communion hosts, and his breviary. The first leg of their journey took them through territory already mapped and explored: across the northern rim of Lake Michigan and south to the bottom of sheltered Green Bay, where Allouez had established the mission of St. Francis Xavier, and from there up the Fox River, through its treacherous rapids and falls, to an Indian village deep in the hardwood forests that would help feed nineteenth-century Chicago's insatiable hunger for lumber. When they arrived at the settlement of the friendly Mascoutins and Miamis, twenty-two days from St. Ignace, they reached the farthest limit of French penetration into the continent. There they called a council of the elders and asked for guides to show them upriver to the portage that they were certain, from Indian reports, would take them to a western river that discharged into the Mississippi.

Their hosts had a great fear of these interior lands, the country of the hostile Sioux—"the Iroquois of the West," as the French called them—and they tried to persuade Marquette and Joliet to proceed no farther. The "Big Water" they hoped to reach was filled with "horrible monsters which devoured men and canoes together," these Indians and others they had met farther north told them, and its banks were home to bands of warriors who would "break their heads without any cause;" while to the south, if they made it that far, they would run into searing heat, which would wilt them, turn them black, and eventually kill them. "I thanked them for the good advice . . . ," Marquette records, "but told them that I could not follow it, because the salvation of souls was at stake, for which I would be delighted to give my life." On the tenth of June, with two Miami guides, they left "in the sight of a great crowd, who could not sufficiently express their astonishment," Marquette writes, "at the sight of seven frenchmen [*sic*] alone and in two Canoes, daring to undertake so extraordinary and so hazardous an Expedition."

They paddled up a sluggish stream broken by a maze of swamps and stagnant lakes, and when they reached the portage, the Miamis left them. They were alone now, "in the hands of providence," cut off from lands and people in any way familiar to them. Before boarding their canoes, Marquette called them together, and they knelt on the forest floor for a prayer to his patroness, the Virgin Mary. They then paddled down the broad and beautiful Wisconsin River, the voyageurs timing their river songs to the strokes of the paddles. On the seventeenth of

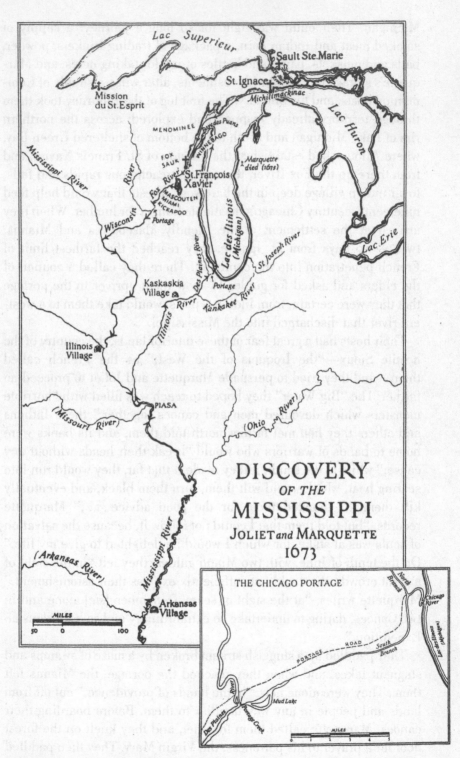

DISCOVERY
OF THE
MISSISSIPPI
JOLIET *and* MARQUETTE
1673

THE CHICAGO PORTAGE

Atlas of American History, ed. Kenneth T. Jackson and James Truslow Adams (New York: Charles Scribner's Sons, 1978).

June they entered the Mississippi "with a Joy," Marquette wrote in his journal, "that I cannot Express."*

"Here . . . on this so renowned river," Marquette and Joliet began to take more careful notes—on the current and depth of the river, on the variety of fish and game along its course, on everything that excited their curiosity. They saw wildcats, what they described as "Swans without wings," and "monstrous fish" (probably catfish), but it was the bison, or "wild cattle," as Marquette called them, that most interested them. Huge herds of them blackened the prairies, and they were the first Europeans to give eyewitness accounts of them. When one of their men killed a bison, Joliet and Marquette examined it like eager surgical students and jotted down detailed anatomic notes. From this point on, the flesh and fat of the bison was "the best dish at [their] feasts."

In this country where "we knew not whither we were going," they proceeded with great caution, on the lookout for hostile Indians. Toward evening, they made only small fires on the riverbank to cook their meals, and after supper they slept in their canoes, which they anchored in midstream, posting an armed sentinel "for fear of surprise." They traveled down the meandering Mississippi almost 200 miles without seeing a trace of a human being, the only sound on the river the splash of their paddles in the current. Then, on the twenty-fifth of June, they saw through the morning mist footprints on the west bank of the river and a path leading into a spacious prairie. Thinking it would take them to an Indian settlement, Joliet and Marquette decided to follow it, unarmed, leaving the voyageurs behind to guard the canoes. Both of them had "the courage," Dablon would write, "to dread nothing where everything is to be feared."

After walking almost six miles, they spotted a village on the bank of a river and two other settlements on a hill in the distance.† They approached so near that they could hear conversation and laughter. Saying a prayer together to summon up their courage, they decided to reveal themselves by standing in the open and shouting "with all Our energy." Their yells set off alarm in the village, and the Indians came streaming from their wigwams to gather around their chiefs. Seeing Marquette's black gown, some who traded in the North probably recognized them as Frenchmen, and four elders were sent out to greet them, two of them bearing calumets, sacred smoking pipes elaborately

*They entered the Mississippi at the present site of Prairie du Chien, on the border between Wisconsin and Iowa.

†The river was the present-day Des Moines, and they were probably the first white men to set foot on what is now Iowa.

decorated, which were a sign of peace. They walked slowly and silently toward the Frenchmen, raising the pipes toward the sun.

Marquette spoke first, asking them if they were Illinois. They said they were and escorted them to the village of their chief, where gifts were exchanged and Joliet explained the purpose of their presence on the river. A great feast followed, with the "Master of Ceremonies," as Marquette quaintly called him, feeding his guests from a spoon as if they were children. That night they slept in the cabin of the chief, and the next day six hundred Indians accompanied them to their canoes. As they pushed off, Marquette began making notes of "their customs and usages." On his lap, as he wrote, was a calumet the chief had given them. It was to be displayed, they were told, whenever they confronted danger, for even "in the hottest of the fight" warriors would "lay down their arms when it is shown." In the canoe ahead of Marquette, curled up behind Joliet, was the chief's ten-year-old son, whom he had given to them, he said, to show them his heart.

Drifting downriver at a rate of forty miles a day, they passed, a week later, a tremendous stone cliff painted with the lurid images of two monsters "which at first made Us afraid, and upon which the boldest savages dare not Long rest their eyes." They were so vividly depicted, Marquette says, that "good painters in france [*sic*] would find it difficult to paint so well." No savage, he thought, could be "their author." Was the devil in these lands? Or perhaps the Spanish? Marquette made a drawing of the monsters, and as the Frenchmen pulled their canoes together to speculate about their meaning, remembering, perhaps, Indian warnings about man-eating river creatures, they ran into real trouble.*

Coasting through calm water, they heard the sound of what appeared to be rapids ahead, and as Parkman describes the scene, before they could react, "a torrent of yellow mud came rushing at them, boiling and surging, sweeping in its course logs, branches, and uprooted trees." Marquette clung to the gunwales and prayed for his men's lives as their light canoes spun in circles and entire "floating islands" rushed by them. But they recovered control and "held their way down the turbulent and swollen current of the now united rivers."

This watery whirlwind had poured forth from the mouth of the Missouri River, which Marquette named *Pekitanoui*, an Indian word meaning "muddy." It is still the "Big Muddy" to farmers along its

---

*When Francis Parkman was doing research for his monumental work *La Salle and the Discovery of the Great West*, he found these cliff paintings just above the city of Alton, Illinois, "entirely effaced by time." Parkman, *La Salle*, p. 59.

shores, who joke that its waters are too thick to drink, too thin to plow. Marquette and Joliet were probably the first whites to see it, and Marquette speculated that it led "to the southern sea, toward California," which he resolved to discover someday by way of this angry river.

Below the desolate, forested site of the future city of St. Louis, Chicago's nineteenth-century urban rival, they passed the mouth of a stream called Ohio, or "the Beautiful River" in Iroquois. At that point the scenery and climate changed dramatically. They saw majestic cottonwoods and elms, their branches filled with flocks of parakeets, and cane growing so thick along the riverbanks that "wild cattle" had trouble pushing through it to reach their watering spots. The heat became "unbearable," as the northern Indians had warned them, and they were attacked by swarms of mosquitoes. To shield themselves from the sun and the bugs, they built canopies with their sails, and while drifting downriver under the protection of their awnings, they came into a clearing and saw an Indian village ahead. A cry of warning went out, and "savages . . . armed with bows, arrows, hatchets, clubs, and shields" raced to the riverbank. Some of them jumped into huge wooden canoes and quickly surrounded them, while others rushed into the water to try to overturn their birchbarks. Marquette, crying to his men not to fire their guns, held up high the calumet, and as he did, a club flew over his head. But just as the warriors on shore were about to release their arrows, several old chiefs standing on the water's edge spotted the calumet and stopped the attack.

When they landed their canoes with the chiefs' protection, Marquette and Joliet found an old man who could speak a little Illinois. They questioned him about the river and other matters, but he told them all their queries would be answered the following day, when they would be taken to Akansea, the chief village of their nation. This was near the mouth of the Arkansas River and not far from the village where de Soto died of fever in 1542 while searching for gold. At the main village the warriors, naked and with beads hanging from their pierced noses and ears, gathered around the Frenchmen while Joliet explained their mission and Marquette told them of his God. The Arkansas Indians said it was only five days to the sea (actually it was more than seven hundred miles) but warned them to go no farther because warlike tribes with guns acquired from Europeans infested the area. Surely this meant the Spanish, who were now at war with the French.

That evening, following a feast, a group of warriors plotted to kill the Frenchmen and steal their guns, but the chief learned of their scheme and put an end to it; and to reassure Marquette and Joliet, he danced the calumet dance and smoked the tobacco pipe with them. It was a sleepless night, however, for the priest and the explorer. All evening they debated what they should do next. Should they push on farther, risking capture by Spaniards or attacks by Indians "expert in firing guns"; or should they be satisfied with their great find: that the Mississippi flowed into the Gulf of Mexico, not into the Atlantic, near Virginia, or into the Vermilion or California Sea? They agreed that their discovery was too important to jeopardize and the next morning informed their hosts that they would head back north after resting awhile.

Nine years later, René-Robert Cavelier, Sieur de La Salle, passed through the Chicago portage in the middle of winter and reached the mouth of the Mississippi, where he took possession for his king of the lands watered by the river and its tributaries, naming the country Louisiana. It was a territory stretching from the Alleghenies to the Rockies and from the Red River to the headwaters of the Missouri. Two centuries later, Chicago would claim it as its economic domain.

"What now remains of the sovereignty thus pompously proclaimed" by La Salle, Joliet, and Saint Lusson? asked Francis Parkman in the 1893 edition of his magisterial *La Salle and the Discovery of the Great West.* "Now and then, the accents of France on the lips of some straggling boatman or vagabond half-breed—this, and nothing more." That November the Homeric historian of Anglo-Saxon manifest destiny died at his home on the banks of Jamaica Pond, near Boston, two weeks after the closing of the Columbian Exposition in Chicago to celebrate several centuries of American progress and land expansion. What did not die with Parkman was the explosive mixture of romanticism, racialism, religious zealotry, nationalism, and economic cupidity that powered French and Anglo-American expansion—for good and ill—for three centuries. That summer of 1893, another historian, Frederick Jackson Turner, had taken the podium at a gathering of his colleagues at the Columbian Exposition to announce the end of the North American land frontier, while in Congress imperialists screamed for the seizure of Hawaii as part of a new American overseas empire. Had he been alive, Talon would have smiled knowingly.

•

Joliet and Marquette started back for Canada on the seventeenth of July, retracing their steps; only now they had to battle a powerful river current in overbearing heat. The journey became a horror for Marquette, who came down with dysentery. When they reached the mouth of the Illinois River, forty days upstream, the Indian boy in Joliet's care told them to enter it, as it would greatly shorten their return to Lake Michigan.

Paddling up this wide and clear stream, they thought they had come into an earthly paradise, a land even more beautiful than L'Ile de France. "We have seen nothing like this river that we enter, as regards its fertility of soil, its prairies and woods; its cattle, elk, deer, wildcats, bustards, swans, ducks, parroquets, and even beaver," Marquette wrote in his weakened condition, which prevented him from taking fuller notes of this lush country. Joliet made a more complete record in his lost journal, the contents of which he summarized in his reports to officials in Quebec, for he was eager to return to Illinois country to plant a colony. "There are [great] prairies," he told Claude Dablon, the Jesuit superior, in a series of interviews, with grass "five or six feet high," so high that they had trouble seeing bison grazing within a stone's throw of them. These wide sweeps of unbroken grassland presented a magnificent vista, relieved by upland streams and patches of forest.

They had entered, without knowing it, an inland sea of grass more than a thousand miles long and bordered on both east and west by dense forests. They were in the part of it known today as the Tallgrass Prairie, extending, roughly, from western Indiana to eastern Oklahoma, where farther west the grass is less continuous and not as high. It was a landscape entirely alien to them, as strange as the painted monsters they had seen on the bluffs of the Mississippi. Having no word in their language for these billowing grasslands, they called them prairies, meaning "large meadows" in French. They had heard about them from the Indians, but they were the first white men to describe them, however sketchily. Later accounts of travelers coming upon the untouched prairies for the first time give a fuller indication of what Joliet and Marquette saw, of what every overland traveler to Chicago would see coming west two centuries later, before the entire prairie had been obliterated to meet the exploding needs of urban markets for agricultural products.

Some travelers found them empty and desolate—even frightening—places. But most accounts play upon their distinctive form and beauty. Many likened a journey across them to ocean travel, a recent experience for most immigrants and foreign visitors. It was not just the waving grass in the strong breeze, like the heavy swell of the ocean, or the enormous midland sky; there were no landmarks or guideposts in these endlessly open spaces, and coming upon a forest grove, or "solitary island," as Louis Sullivan had described a cluster of trees on the prairie outside Chicago, was like approaching a friendly port of call.

After traveling for many weeks under the oppressive forest cover of the east or the north, it must have been a thrilling experience to enter

this great grassland of endless horizons and wide-open sky, with ea-
gles and hawks wheeling high overhead.

Joliet had expected to see nothing but field after field of green and
brown grass, but the late-summer Illinois prairie was ablaze with colors. The new stalks of bluestem grass had reached full height by
August after spring rains, and great numbers of brilliantly colored
wildflowers grew up between them—black-eyed Susan, blazing star,
prairie dock, aster, and goldenrod. By then, the tall grasses of all vari-
eties took on a multitude of shades—bronze, copper, crimson, and
gold—colors that seemed to change and blend as the sun moved
across the sky and clouds threw off lengthening shadows.

From the Kaskaskia Indians they met in the area, Joliet learned that
the soil was so fertile that it yielded corn three times a year, and he was
sure that wheat and "grain of all kinds" could be easily grown here, in
what would later become part of the greater Chicago corn and wheat
belt. He also saw what would eventually draw waves of immigrants
here. "A settler would not . . . spend ten years in cutting down and
burning the trees; on the very day of his arrival, he could put his plow
into the ground."

His head filled with plans for a settlement in this abundant valley,
Joliet pushed his voyageurs upriver and toward home, after Marquette
promised the Kaskaskia he would return "to instruct them." A party of
Indians escorted them to the Des Plaines River, a branch of the Illinois, and through its rapids to the Chicago portage. After carrying
their canoes across the portage, they passed up the south branch of the
Chicago River and out into the lake. They were back at the mission of
St. Xavier on Green Bay by the end of September, having paddled from
there some twenty-five hundred miles in four months.

•

Joliet would never again see the Illinois Valley, or the site of
Chicago, but Marquette returned to this region the following winter in
fulfillment of his promise to the Kaskaskia. After spending the year at
the mission of St. Xavier recovering from his illness and completing
his journal, he set out on October 25, 1674, with two voyageurs,
Jacques Largillier and a man who had been with him on his first voyage, Pierre Porteret. They were accompanied by a party of Indians
heading home to Illinois country.

It was a horrible time of the year to be on the lake, and they had
trouble reaching the sheltered Chicago River in their nimble but fragile canoes. They ran into blinding snow and punishing winds and were
almost wrecked by "floating masses of ice." Huge waves, as high as
Marquette had seen on the Atlantic, forced them to shore for days at a

time, and they camped near the stone bluffs, which were "very poorly sheltered." After several weeks of this, Marquette's illness returned, and he was barely able to sit up in his canoe.

They entered "the river of the portage" on December 4 and found it frozen solid. After camping at the mouth of the river, where they killed some game, they moved six miles downstream to a spot where the portage began and decided to winter there in a makeshift cabin, for Marquette had begun to hemorrhage and could not continue. The Illinois who accompanied them went ahead to their people but alerted other Indians in the area of the Frenchmen's presence on the portage, and parties came to their cabin to trade meat, pumpkins, and "robes of ox skin" for tobacco. Marquette's voyageurs also found two French traders camped about fifty miles from them, and these men, one of whom, Pierre Moreau, had been with Marquette on his first voyage, brought them Indian corn and berries. After Christmas, Marquette told his companions that he was sure he would die soon, but he asked them to join him in making a novena to the Blessed Virgin so that he would be spared until he could take possession of his "dear Mission." His health improved the following month—a miracle, he thought—and when the ice broke on the Des Plaines in late March, flooding the portage, they paddled across it and downriver against strong winds and over dangerous rapids to the village of the Kaskaskia, where Marquette was received "as an angel from Heaven."

On Holy Thursday Father Marquette said mass in a beautiful prairie clearing carpeted with Indian mats and bearskins. His congregation, made up of five hundred chiefs and elders and several thousand younger men, women, and children, sat around him in an enormous circle. On Easter morning he called another council and preached again to the entire village, telling them that his mission would have to be carried on by other black robes who would follow him, for his illness obliged him to return to his home mission of St. Ignace. On the day of his departure, delirious from loss of blood, he was placed on a stretcher made of buffalo robes and lowered into his canoe. A band of Illinois escorted him to Lake Michigan and urged his men to head back along the eastern border of the lake, which the French had not yet explored, as this route would save them several days' travel to the Straits of Mackinac. On the lake, Marquette began to lose his sight and became so weak, his voyageurs later reported, he had to be "handled and carried about like a child." The evening before his death he told his companions "very Joyously, that it would take place on the morrow" and gave instructions for his burial. They should dig a grave in advance, he said, and as soon as he expired, they should take the little handbell he used in the mass and sound it while he was being put in the ground.

As they pushed up the line of the lake, they came to the entrance of a river, flanked by a stretch of high ground, and Marquette asked his men to paddle ashore. This is where he wanted to die. They prepared a shelter for him and carried him to it. Prostrate and too enfeebled to raise his head, he heard their confessions, begged them not to weep for him, and gave thanks that he would die as he had always prayed he would, in a wild and empty land in the service of souls. Then he told his men to get some sleep, as his hour had not yet come. He would wake them when it was time. Several hours later, he called out for them. When they came to him, he removed his crucifix from around his neck and asked one of his men to hold it before his eyes. "And so with a countenance beaming and all aglow, he expired without any Struggle, and so gently that it might have been regarded as a pleasant sleep." In this way Jacques Largillier and Pierre Porteret described his death, which took place on May 18, 1675, on the shores of the Michigan river that now bears his name. He was thirty-seven years old.

That night, they slept close to his body, and in the morning the only sound on the forest shore was Father Marquette's little chapel bell. Before they left the site of his death, the voyageurs planted a wooden cross near his grave "as a sign for passers-by."

But "God did not permit that a deposit so precious should remain in the midst of the forest, unhonored and forgotten," Dablon wrote in his own account of Marquette's death. Two years after Marquette's burial, a hunting party of Christian Indians located his grave, opened it, washed and dried the bones, put them in a birch box, and carried them back to St. Ignace, chanting their funeral songs along the way. They sent a canoe ahead, and as the funeral procession of nearly thirty canoes approached the mission, the priests, traders, and Indians crowded the shore. After gaining assurance that this was the body of Père Marquette, the Jesuits buried it in a vault beneath the church, "where it rests," Dablon closes his account, "as the guardian angel of . . . our missions."

•

In 1877, six years after the Great Chicago Fire, Marquette's grave was discovered at the site of the mission of St. Ignace. Only a few bones remained; the rest were believed to have been taken by Indians who considered him a forest spirit. His remaining relics are at Marquette University, under the care of his order. And this gentle missionary who dreamed of the glory of martyrdom in the wilderness became, in time, the closest thing to a patron saint that gritty Chicago would have. The location of the cabin in which he spent the winter of 1674–75 was officially sited in 1905 by a committee of the Chicago Historical Society and marked two years later by an impressive cross of mahogany, to which Catholic immigrants in the neighborhood came to pray for the intercession of "the saint." By standing on this site in 1905, it was possible to see, to the West, the entrance of the recently completed Chicago Sanitary and Ship Canal, which connected the city to the great river Marquette's journal disclosed to the world.*

Three years after the fifteen-foot Marquette Cross was placed in its concrete pedestal, J. Seymour Currey, a leading member of the Chicago Historical Society, published a celebratory history of Chicago's "Century of Marvelous Growth." Most of it is given over to the achievements of builders and businessmen, but Currey opens the book with the exploits of Father Marquette, "the patron saint of the people of Chicago." Marquette's story should be "told in every Chicago home . . . ," he writes, "to awaken a pride in our earliest annals." Twelve years later, Mayor William Dever named December 4 Marquette Day in Chicago.

Marquette, the missionary, was a perfect founding hero for a city at times anxious to prove that it was devoted to more than money and merchandising, but Joliet, the trader, would have had a far more secure place in Chicago history and mythology had it not been for a stroke of bad luck he suffered in the rapids above Montreal.

2. Joliet's Dream

In the spring of 1674, Joliet headed up the Ottawa River for Quebec to make an accounting of his expedition for the new governor, Comte de Frontenac. After he passed through forty-two rapids and "all danger seemed over," his canoe capsized in the fierce waters of Sault St. Louis, almost within site of Montreal. It was a near total calamity. His two voyageurs and the Indian boy who had led him to the Illinois River valley were killed, and all his papers and maps were lost. Miraculously, he managed to cling to a rock for four hours until some fishermen pulled him from the river, unconscious. When he recovered, he hurried to Quebec, informing Frontenac that he had left a copy of his journal of the expedition with the Jesuits at Sault Ste. Marie. Later that

*The location is near what is now the intersection of Damen Avenue and Twenty-sixth Street and the south branch of the Chicago River.

summer, the mission house at the sault was set on fire by feuding Indians, and Joliet's journal was never found. The loss of that journal, as one historian has said, "secured [Marquette's] fame forever."

Joliet did, however, make a full oral report of his expedition to both Frontenac and Claude Dablon, and they sent a record of it to Paris. These documents exist, as does the map he made from memory for Frontenac and a letter he sent to the bishop of Quebec, his patron, indicating his great disappointment about what had been lost. "Except for this shipwreck, Your Excellency would have had a quite interesting relation, but all I saved is my life."

While Marquette's journal provided extraordinary information about the lands and peoples they encountered, it was subtly shaped by its author and its editor, Dablon, into an argument for the founding of Jesuit missions up and down the Mississippi and its tributaries. Joliet had a different agenda, and his journal certainly would have reflected it. A government-commissioned explorer and a crack geographer, he had a farsighted understanding of the economic and strategic potential of the areas he explored, as his thin but suggestive reports show. Marquette might have been "the first recorded Chicago resident," in the opinion of one of the city's early historians, but he wrote nothing about the possibilities of the site. Just a glance at Joliet's map, however, reveals his excellent understanding that this was one of the commanding sites on the North American continent.

•

When Joliet led his tiny exploring party up the Chicago River from the portage sometime in September 1673, they passed through a flat, marshlike plain. It must have been difficult to see these featureless fields, for much of the prairie riverbank was lined with wild onion plants, which would cause the Frenchmen who followed Marquette and Joliet to this spot to call it Chicagoua, an Indian name meaning the place of the wild onion, or skunkweed. They had just been through the Illinois Valley, and the soggy, windblown plain of "the river of the portage" must have struck Marquette as a miserable location for a civilized settlement; there were not even Indian encampments there. But Joliet's inborn sense of geography and his trader's instinct told him otherwise. Modern geology tells us why he was right.

The history of Chicago's human settlement is amazingly short, but the shaping of its physical environment was an aeons-long process. Roughly a million years ago, the climate of the upper regions of the earth grew unusually cold. Winter snow remained on the ground year-round, forming itself over time into huge ice fields that drifted down from Greenland and blanketed the entire northern half of the continent, putting areas around Chicago a mile deep under layers of ice and debris. At least four successive glaciers advanced and retreated, flattening hills, filling valleys, gouging out enormous basins, polishing older, rough surfaces, and creating new ones. The last of these ice sheets, the Wisconsin Drift, receded some twelve thousand to thirteen thousand years ago—just yesterday to geologists—but not before it reconfigured the entire mid-continent.

The Wisconsin glacier swept up boulders and bedrock from the north and used them like a gigantic snowplow to scrape off thick layers of soil, sandstone, limestone, and shale, which it pulverized and blended and set down in the region to the south. These glacial flatlands are the midland prairie, its base soil rich in ground-up minerals and covered by layers of windblown silt called loess, deposited there when the glacier ebbed. When the climate warmed, deep roots from plants and grasses built a sod so thick it would break the plows of the first homesteaders.

To the north, far more dramatic geologic activity occurred. There the glaciers performed a bulldozing operation, greatly widening former river valleys into monstrous basins that became the Great Lakes. As the southern edge of the Wisconsin glacier began to melt, drainage to the north and northeast through the St. Lawrence River valley was cut off by a massive wall of ice. The glacial meltwater had no other way to go but south, where it filled a basin between the receding ice front and a crescent-shaped ridge, or terminal moraine, created by glacial drift around the southern rim of what is now Lake Michigan. This made Lake Chicago, of which present Lake Michigan was merely a part, a lake named by geologists for the place that its waters once entirely covered to a depth of sixty feet.

This inland sea receded in stages, its waters cutting their way south to the Gulf of Mexico through the Illinois-Mississippi River drainage system. When Marquette and Joliet ascended the Mississippi to the Chicago River, they came through this glacial cut-through. The mile-wide valley created by the escaping waters of Lake Chicago is known today as the Chicago outlet and has been for a century and a half one of the principal transportation corridors of the city, site of the Illinois and Michigan Canal, the Chicago Sanitary and Ship Canal, and several major rail lines and motor highways. The waters that created it, however, no longer flow southward, for as the ice sheet retreated, drainage through the St. Lawrence River reopened, and Lake Michigan again drained eastward to the Atlantic. The seemingly currentless Chicago River that Joliet and Marquette paddled up actually flowed out toward Lake Michigan.

This would have catastrophic consequences for nineteenth-century Chicago, taking the sewage of the river, Chicago's waste dump, out into the lake that supplied the city with its drinking water. The river runs southward today, toward the Mississippi, because engineers used pumps and a deep sanitary canal to pull the city's waste away from the lake and downstream, over the place of the old portage, to complaining but less politically powerful communities to the south. This was one of Chicago's great civic projects in the year of the Columbian Exposition.

The Wisconsin glacier gave the future city of Chicago another natural advantage over other future city sites farther south, such as St. Louis. When the final ice sheet gradually retreated up the St. Lawrence River valley, beyond Lake Ontario, a rushing river took the drainage of the Great Lakes, by way of the Mohawk Pass, to the Hudson River estuary, boring a gap through the Appalachian Mountains. This gap became the route of both the Erie Canal and the New York Central Railroad, nineteenth-century Chicago's two chief ways of reaching New York City. Because of the Mohawk Pass there is no mountain barrier between Chicago and New York, as there is between Chicago and other eastern ports, such as Boston and Philadelphia. New York, the busiest ocean harbor in the world, and Chicago, the busiest inland harbor in the world, became linked by nature and man, their economic destinies intertwined. Throughout the nineteenth century, as Chicago prospered, so did New York; and vice versa.

Lake Chicago created more than future Chicago's corridors of commerce. It created Chicago itself. As this glacial lake contracted over thousands of years to the present dimensions of Lake Michigan, its wave action and undertow smoothed the pliant surface of the site of Chicago to its tabletop flatness. This lake plain—present-day Chicago—is only slightly higher than the lake itself, and its level surface, and the layers of poorly porous clay that the glacier deposited, made it extremely difficult to drain. Once a prairie swamp, the early town would be a mudhole for good parts of the year, and as it grew into a city, it would be afflicted by a succession of drainage-related public health epidemics. But the level surface of the ancient glacial lake bottom had its advantages. It made it easy to lay out streets and rail and trolley tracks and placed no physical barriers in the way of Chicago's outward expansion to the north, the south, and the west.

To the east, of course, is the lake. Until the development of a sprawling industrial district along the tiny Calumet River, the Chicago River was the city's only access to the largest inland waterway in the world, highway to ports to the north and east, such as Duluth and Buffalo, to the Atlantic—through the St. Lawrence River—and to the northern forests and ore beds that would supply Chicago with timber and iron to fuel its growth. This small prairie stream is the principal reason why Chicago grew up here, on its banks. For it is a well-protected harbor, as snug and sheltered as New York's, on a long and mostly uninterrupted shoreline. Of equal significance, it led, as we know, to the portage; and this is what made Chicagoua, an Indian crossroads and summer trading spot, a truly exceptional site for a city.

When the waters of Lake Chicago withdrew from the Chicago plain, they left exposed a thin line of land that secured Chicago's destiny. It was a low, almost imperceptible morainic ridge—not over ten feet high—that Joliet, in crossing over its muddy summit, had the geographer's sense to realize was part of a great continental divide. This drainage barrier, or watershed, separated by only a few miles the two principal water systems of the west: the Great Lakes–St. Lawrence system, Joliet's familiar trading grounds, and the Mississippi system he had just explored. On the one side of the divide, rainfall drained into the Atlantic Ocean; on the other, into the Gulf of Mexico. Together these systems comprised over thirty-five hundred miles of navigable water roads traversing the continent, interrupted, as Joliet's map indicated, only at the Niagara and Chicago portages. By cutting a canal through the narrow place in the continental divide at the "river of the portage" and positioning a fort and a town to protect it and reap its largesse, New France could begin to command the continent, Joliet suggested to his governor.*

His recent voyage, he reported to the powers in Quebec, had produced "a very great and important advantage, which perhaps will hardly be believed. It is that we could go with facility to Florida in a bark, and by very easy navigation. It would only be necessary to make a canal by cutting through but half a league of prairie, to pass from the foot of the Lake of the Illinois [Lake Michigan] to the river Saint Louis [the Illinois River]." Joliet asked Frontenac to send him back across the portage to build a colony "in countries so beautiful and upon lands so fertile." In his would-be role of colonizer, he almost certainly would have taken an active part in the establishment of a garrison town on the "river of the portage," where there "is a harbor," he pointed out, "very convenient for receiving vessels and sheltering them from the wind." With this "excavation of which I have spoken," the harbor

---

*This is one of the lowest but longest of North America's continental divides. And today it is the only one with a population of over 7 million residents within a radius of less than fifty miles.

could become, he dreamed, a gateway to the fertile prairies, to what even he could not imagine would become the most productive agricultural region of its size in the world. With this prophetic plan Joliet gave the design not of Canada's but of Chicago's future economic empire. And the two great water highways he drew on his map became the main axes of settlement of the trans-Appalachian West, with Chicago situated at their juncture. It is there because Joliet's dream became the dream of others centuries later.

His rival La Salle dismissed Joliet's "proposed ditch" as vastly impractical because, except for the time of the spring freshets, there was insufficient water in the Des Plaines to make it navigable. But even La Salle saw a large future for "Du Portage de Checagou." In a prophetic letter he wrote from a log hut on the portage in the winter of 1682–83, he predicted that through this "lowest point on the divide between the two great valleys of the St. Lawrence and the Mississippi . . . the boundless regions of the West must send their products to the East. . . . This will be the gate of empire, this the seat of commerce. Everything invites to action. The typical man who will grow up here must be an enterprising man. Each day as he rises he will exclaim, 'I act, I move, I push,' and there will be spread before him a boundless horizon, an illimitable field of activity."

Joliet's report to Frontenac on the advisability of planting colonies in Illinois country was backed by the accounts of other explorers who followed him there. But in 1674 the colony of New France was too underpopulated—barely sixty-seven hundred inhabitants—to build new settlements in the far interior. Agricultural villages must be established, Colbert ordered, but in the St. Lawrence, not the Illinois, valley. In any event, Frontenac was not interested in encouraging the kind of colonization Joliet had in mind in the central colony or on its periphery. He saw greater gain for Canada, and for himself, in the lucrative fur trade. This trade depended on the cooperation of the Indians and demanded the preservation of their way of life and their lands, the source, after all, of the coveted furs and skins. The ax and plow of the homesteader threatened all of this. So Joliet's plan was set aside, and, years later, he received as his reward an island on the lower St. Lawrence. He built an estate there, made money from the abundant fishing grounds of his fief, and drew maps of the river. In 1680 his estate of Anticosti was smashed by the cannon and fire of an English fleet on its way to Quebec. After teaching hydrography for a time in Quebec, Joliet virtually disappeared from the historical record. He died in 1700, a financially broken and largely forgotten figure, his chance for greater fame, *la gloire*, destroyed years before by accidents of fire and water.

Sixty-three years later, almost all of the region he had explored with Marquette was ceded to the English as part of the peace ending the Seven Years' War. After the Revolution, it became part of the United States, and Fort Dearborn was erected by the federal government in 1803 to guard the strategic site of Chicago. When another war with Britain broke out in 1812, the fort was abandoned, its fleeing soldiers, traders, and their families slaughtered on the sands of Lake Michigan by Indian allies of the British, an event that became part of Chicago's mythology. It was rebuilt and regarrisoned after the war amid talk out of Washington of the resurrection of Joliet's plan for a canal through the portage. On the strength of these reports and rumors, the town of Chicago was born. And the man who would become its most promiment and picturesque founder arrived at the fort on the portage in 1818 from the Straits of Mackinac in a bark canoe, after visiting the site of Marquette's death on the shores of Lake Michigan and reading of the lands Joliet had revealed to the world.

2

"Didn't Expect No Town"

1. Wild Chicago

THE canoe that carried sixteen-year-old Gurdon Saltonstall Hubbard to Chicago in the fall of 1818 was not one of the light and fleet birchbarks used by Marquette and Joliet. It was a bateau, or freight canoe, fifty feet long, with a crew of five voyageurs, four of them rowing while the fifth steered from the stern. Although made of bark, it carried, in addition to its crew, several traders and clerks and over three tons of merchandise and provisions. Owned and outfitted by John Jacob Astor's American Fur Company, which had recently gained a monopoly on the Indian trade in the regions Joliet opened up for New France, it was one of twelve boats—a "brigade"—headed for the Illinois wilderness by the route Marquette had taken back from there on his final voyage.

Le Bourgeois, or "boss," of the Illinois outfit was Antoine Deschamps, a lean and aging French Canadian who was enraptured by the heroic age of French exploration in North America. Two of his heroes were Marquette and Joliet, and that summer, at the Mackinac headquarters of the American Fur Company, he had taken Hubbard, an apprentice clerk who shared his passion for the history of discovery, to Marquette's grave on Point St. Ignace. When Deschamps left Mackinac for his trading posts along the Illinois River, he asked Hubbard to join him in the head boat "and led the way," Hubbard recalls, "with his fine strong voice start[ing] the boat song, in which all the crew heartily joined."

Timing their strokes to the beat of their *chansons,* the oarsmen of the long canoes made the trip around Lake Michigan to the Chicago River in twenty days. "Nothing of interest transpired," Hubbard wrote in his old age, "until we reached the Marquette River." There they spotted the weathered cedar cross Marquette's *donnes* had erected to mark the priest's grave, and the voyageurs "paid reverence to it by kneeling and making the sign of the cross. It was about three feet above ground, and in a falling condition. We reset it, leaving it out of the ground about two feet." Though Hubbard would pass this spot often in his travels up and down the lake, he never again saw the cross. "I doubt not that it was covered by the drifting sands of the following winter, and that no white man ever saw it afterwards."

Hubbard related this story in his autobiography, which was first published two years after his death in Chicago in 1886, the year Louis Sullivan began work on his first great commission, the Auditorium Theater and Hotel. It is a captivating account of his ten years as a fur trader in frontier Illinois, taking his life up to 1829, one year before Chicago was surveyed and platted as a future canal town and five years before he moved there to align himself with its future.

Descendant of Rev. Gurdon Saltonstall, a colonial governor of Connecticut, he was also the adopted son of Waba, chief of the Kikapoo, and for a time was married to a Kankakee woman and wore his hair long, like an Indian. The Potawatomi called him Pa-pa-ma-ta-be, "the Swift Walker," for he could cover fifty miles between daylight and darkness without great effort. Fellow traders at Fort Dearborn called him "Yankee Hubbard." Both names fit the man, for his life linked two cultures and two epochs of Chicago's earliest recorded history.

•

The first draft of Hubbard's memoirs—an 800-page manuscript—was destroyed in the Great Fire, along with his ivy-covered home on the North Side and much of the fortune he had amassed as a pioneering businessman. Hubbard never resumed his commercial career, living a life of retrospection for his last fifteen years as the most revered of Chicago's remaining "old settlers," who formed a society of that name and met regularly. A big, bright-spirited man, he loved to swap stories with old friends of bygone days in Chicago, and he resumed work on his autobiography—slowly, for he was ill—writing in pencil on lined foolscap. Sickness and old age eventually stilled his pen; and in 1883 he lost sight in his left eye, and when an infection developed, it had to be removed. "True to his Indian training," his nephew recalls, "he resolutely refused to take an anesthetic or to let anyone hold his hands. He simply lay down and without a murmur or a tremor let the doctors cut out his eye." The next year he lost sight in his remaining eye, and it, too, was removed. He continued to entertain friends, however, and just before he died, he learned from one of them that Chicago's civic leaders had launched a movement to hold "a Great World's Fair" in the place he had first described in a letter to his mother as "four and a half houses, a fort, and a Potawatomi town."

Funeral services for Gurdon Hubbard, Chicago's oldest settler, were held at New England Congregational Church. "The congregation . . . was a sea of white heads," reported the *Chicago Times*, "representing the men who came to Chicago when there was no Chicago, and who have lived to see the results of the work they began." The old settlers followed Hubbard's casket in carriages to Graceland Cemetery, the resting place of the city's founders and heroes. Later, they eulogized him at meetings of the Chicago Historical Society as the man most responsible for bringing the canal to Chicago, as the city's first shipping magnate and meatpacker, and as its last living link with the Fort Dearborn days. At the "time [I met him in 1835]," an old friend reminisced, "he was the most perfect model of physical manhood, which I ever knew," a robust, powerfully built man with a strong-featured face. His biography "is the history of Chicago and the Northwest," said his friend Grant Goodrich, "and if . . . properly prepared it will be found more interesting than a romance." A half century later, Hubbard's great-nephew, Henry R. Hamilton, wrote a book about his uncle's life he entitled, he thought fittingly, *The Epic of Chicago*.

But there was more to Hubbard's life than his eulogizers were given to mention. No one spoke of his Indian wife, Watseka, niece of Chief Tamin of the Kankakees, of his brotherly ties to the Potawatomi chiefs whose lands Hubbard's fellow Yankees stole to establish legal claim to Chicago, or of his friendship with flinty, hard-drinking French Canadians and mixed-bloods who were the real first Chicagoans—not the Protestant old crowd who packed the pews on the day of his funeral. This was a part of Hubbard's life, and of the life of their city, that his old friends either romanticized or ignored entirely.

Hubbard was honored on his death as a city legend not because he was the last of Chicago's fur-trading pioneers but because he was the only one of them to have kept in step with what Chicagoans liked to call "the march of civilization." "Only a single man became identified with the modern commerce and trade of the city, who had been connected with the crude Indian traffic," Chicago historian Alfred T. Andreas wrote of Hubbard in the 1880s. Hubbard was a local Natty Bumppo who had traded in his buckskins for a collar and coat. He had lined up with the winning side—the modernizers—when most of his old trader friends stuck to their ways and, in the words of one of the only Chicago historians to write perceptively about them, raised "a defiant middle finger to the world."

His life *is* the epic of Chicago, but it takes us to a seldom-visited corner of the city's history and reveals truths about Chicago's lusty origins that are less than romantic.

Chicago's transition from fur-trading outpost to capitalist town, a cultural revolution Gurdon Hubbard lived through and helped bring forward, shows that in the city-building process in the West there were clear winners and losers. The western town did not evolve organically out of the nucleus of the trading village, as Frederick Jackson Turner suggested in his famous essay "The Significance of the Frontier in American History." In Chicago's case, town and hamlet were wholly different types of human settlements, and the explosive emergence of one meant the complete disappearance of the other. To appreciate what was gained and lost in this transformation is to achieve a fuller understanding of the urban process on the American frontier and of the larger historical importance of Chicago's beginning. The history of early Chicago is a history, in small measure, of the American frontier. To know Gurdon Hubbard is to know that story.

•

Hubbard was born on August 22, 1802, in Windsor, Vermont, a town of machinists and millwrights on a beautiful bend in the Connecticut River. His mother, Abigail Sage of Middletown, Connecticut, was from Puritan stock and his father, Elizur, son of a Revolutionary War officer, was one of Windsor's five lawyers. Sometime around 1812, Elizur lost all his money and property in some speculative ventures and took his family across the border to Montreal, where he made a bare living as an attorney for local fur companies. Gurdon was thrown into the world at an early age, apprenticing as boy-of-all-work in a hardware store, where he slept at night on a merchandise counter. He liked to read books about voyageurs and fur traders and at age sixteen signed on as a clerk with a brigade of the American Fur Company headed for Mackinac, Michigan. His contract of indenture bound him to the company for five years at pay of $120 a year. His brigade left for the western lakes in May 1818 from a place on the Ottawa River not far from where Joliet's canoe had capsized.

Working in the company's fur warehouse that summer, he had become friends with an apprentice clerk about his age named John Harris Kinzie, whose father, John Kinzie, was a trader in Chicago; and just before Hubbard left for Chicago, Kinzie had given him letters of introduction to his clan. When Hubbard's Illinois brigade reached the mouth of the Calumet River on its nineteenth day out of Mackinac, they camped for the night, dressing themselves and decorating their boats for a ceremonial entrance onto the Chicago River. The next morning broke calm and clear, "and we, in our holiday attire, with flags flying, completed the last twelve miles of our lake voyage." Passing up the shoreline, they arrived at a place where there was a break in a row of oak trees, and Hubbard asked to be let ashore. Climbing a tree, he "gazed in admiration on the first prairie I had ever seen. The waving grass, intermingling with a rich profusion of wild flowers, was the most beautiful sight I had ever gazed upon." On the horizon to the west, he could see the timber-bordered Des Plaines River, and "looking north, I saw the whitewashed buildings of Fort Dearborn sparkling in the sunshine."

Hubbard took a beaten trail to the fort, passing across the sand hillocks where the Fort Dearborn massacre had occurred just six years before. When he reached the river, a soldier ferried him across in a canoe, "and thus I made my first entry into Chicago, October 1, 1818."

His brigade had been met upon landing by John Kinzie, and when Hubbard presented his letter of introduction he was invited to stay at the family's "mansion," as locals called the modest-sized log house that fronted the river directly opposite the fort. After a few days spent repairing boats and visiting the tents of local Potawatomi women, the Illinois brigade struck camp and headed up the south branch of the river, camping near the spot where Marquette had wintered in 1674–75. There they made preparations to cross the portage, an experience that would forever convince Hubbard of the need for a canal at this critical frontier portal.

At dawn the following day, they unloaded their boats and pulled them on cedar rollers up the bed of a channel to a place called Mud Lake (more a swamp than a lake). The mud was like wet cement, and the wild rice and tall grass along the edge of the five-mile-long lake were almost impenetrable. Four men stayed in a boat and pushed with poles, while eight others, wading alongside in mud up to their waists, pulled it along. In places, the mud was so deep that the men had to cling to the sides of the boats so they would not sink over their heads. Slimy bloodsuckers clung to their bodies, and they were attacked by gnats, flies, and mosquitoes. The remaining crew members went on ahead with cargo bags weighing up to a hundred pounds strapped to their backs.

It took three days to get the boats over the portage, and when the men reached the banks of the Des Plaines, they rested their "swollen and inflamed" limbs, burned the "abominable black plagues" from their bodies with a "decoction of tobacco," and, Hubbard recalled, cursed "this miserable lake."

It took almost a month for the outfit to reach the trading station Hubbard had been assigned to on the Illinois River. The following spring, he returned with his outfit to Mackinac to deliver the furs and pelts he had traded for with the Indians. After clerking the following two seasons in Michigan country, he spent the remainder of his days as a trader in Illinois country, first on the Iroquois River, where he became head of Deschamps's trading posts after the old man retired, and later at Danville, where he established his headquarters in 1828.

Danville was about 120 miles south of Chicago and was larger than Chicago when Hubbard settled there. The settlement at the portage, however, remained Hubbard's trading base and shipping center, and he was drawn back to it regularly for business or visits to friends at the taverns and trading posts on Wolf Point, at the fork of the Chicago River, where the North and South Branches meet and form a wider stream that flows out to the lake that leads to Mackinac.

The river village owed its existence to the American Fur Company's headquarters at Mackinac. It received almost all its essentials for living and trading from there and marketed its single product there. The only business at Chicago was furs; its only inhabitants, aside from the troops and support contingent at the fort, were traders and Indians. The traders lived with their families and voyageurs on high, dry ground along the banks of the river or on the lakefront, places from which they could intercept the bateaux headed either to or from Mackinac. And there was a Potawatomi encampment on the prairie just to the west of Wolf Point. The land surrounding these clan settlements still looked as it had to Marquette and Joliet. The occasional prospective settler who wandered into Chicago in the 1820s saw at once that there was no hope of drawing a living from its marshlands and foul-smelling bogs and moved on to the drier prairie land that stretched to the south as far as Springfield.

Early Chicago had two focal points: the fort and Wolf Point. They were only a half mile apart, but the only convenient means of communication between them was by canoe or rowboat. "I passed over the ground from the fort to the Point on horseback," a visitor to Chicago in the 1820s reported. "I was up to my stirrups in water the whole distance. I would not have given sixpence an acre for the whole of it." The wet, shallow soil and the raw winds that blew off the lake for most of

NOTE—The names given on various tracts of land are those of the primary patentees, or persons by whom entry was made, entered or patented between the years 1828 and 1836. The information is taken from "Book of Original Entry." Streets as shown were laid out subsequent to 1830.

A. T. Andreas, *History of Chicago* (1884).

the year made it impossible to grow crops, and "the village . . ." wrote another traveler, William H. Keating, "consists of but few huts, inhabited by a miserable race of men, scarcely equal to the Indians from whom they are descended. Their log or bark houses are low, filthy and disgusting."

Keating might have made a single exception had he paid a visit to the Kinzie house, with its fenced-in orchard and wide, poplar-shaded piazza. John Kinzie had acquired the property in 1803 from a man who had bought it from Jean Baptiste Point du Sable, a cultivated mulatto fur trader from Santo Domingo.

The Canadian-born Kinzie had a reputation as a sharp-dealing Indian trader when he first arrived in Chicago in 1804 at the age of forty to establish a trading post near newly constructed Fort Dearborn. Until fighting broke out along the northwestern frontier during the War of 1812, Kinzie had been the head man at Chicago, fashioning a trading fiefdom. His ties with the local Potawatomi tribe had allowed his family to be spared in the slaughter on the dunes south of the fort, and they later escaped to Michigan.

In the summer of 1816, when troops and mechanics arrived to begin rebuilding the second Fort Dearborn, the only signs they saw that this had been a place of habitation were the abandoned Kinzie house, a shabby trader's cabin on the southern shore of the lake, the blackened brick magazine of the plundered and burned fort, and the scalped bodies of the massacred victims, which had been left unburied in the shifting sands, an eerie reminder of the fragility of life on the Indian frontier, where Chicago was the only white settlement between Fort Wayne and Green Bay. The soldiers buried the victims on the steep banks of the lakeshore, where the windblown waters would uncover parts of the pine coffins. It was to this desolate place that a much-aged and financially strained John Kinzie returned in 1816 to try to regain his stature in the fur trade.

He had no chance against the new power at the portage, the American Fur Company, and after trying to make it on his own, he was forced to enter its employ as a trader and an Indian interpreter. Following his death in 1828, his Connecticut-born daughter-in-law, Juliette Magill Kinzie, wife of his son John Harris, enshrined him as the city's original permanent settler in *Wau-Bun: The "Early Day" in the North-West,* her saccharine account of the Kinzie family in frontier Chicago. Juliette Kinzie was a notorious social climber who wanted to be known and remembered as part of a Chicago family dynasty; and in *Wau-Bun,* written in 1856, she portrayed her father-in-law, a hard-drinking village brawler whom she never met, as a "courtly" and successful trader, an esteemed friend of the Indians, and the man the struggling settlers looked to for leadership, Chicago's own version of Capt. John Smith, a white Protestant who had far more to do with Chicago's emergence than the "savage" French Canadians and half-breeds who were his neighbors.

John Kinzie might have been Chicago's first *white* resident, but Point du Sable has the strongest claim to being its first permanent non-Indian settler. His house at the mouth of the river is commonly referred to in early histories of Chicago as a primitive cabin, but a document listing the property he sold to Jean Lalime in 1800, before leaving Chicago for Missouri Territory, gives a picture of a man of some substance. Had he not been black, Jean Baptiste Point du Sable would not have been an embarrassment to old settlers; indeed, one historian speculates that his father was a descendant of a famous French family. That is pure conjecture, but the fact remains that "the First Chicagoan" was a proud and prosperous black man who lived at the head of the river for almost twenty years in a house that his white-skinned pretender was too impoverished in his old age to hold on to.

•

The center of early Chicago was not the place where John Kinzie's homestead faced the lime-slaked walls of the fort. It was just upriver at Wolf Point, the rollicking gathering place of a racially mixed settlement of Indians, half-breeds, French Canadians, and Anglo-Americans. There was a lot of bickering and petty crime and even an occasional murder in this wilderness settlement that hugged the river to the north and south of the Point, but its inhabitants were bound together into a community by three things: isolation from civilized society, trade in furs, and drinking and reveling at the river taverns on Wolf Point. The most popular of these makeshift hotels was managed by a devil-may-care Creole from the Detroit area named Mark Beaubien, the spirit of a long-forgotten Chicago that lived for a brief but turbulent moment in the years just after Gurdon Hubbard arrived in 1818.

Mark Beaubien was the younger brother of one of Chicago's earliest fur traders, Jean Baptiste Beaubien, who lived with his large, part-Indian brood on a government field just south of the fort and helped his brother get started in the tavern business in a building Mark Beaubien named after his half-breed friend Billy Caldwell, who was called "the Sauganash," or Englishman.

By 1830, there were three taverns in the area of Wolf Point, and the next year they were connected by a log-raft ferry run by Mark Beaubien. These taverns, and frontier Chicago itself, attracted every manner of humanity. At various times there were Frenchmen in the village who had fought with Napoleon at Jena and Waterloo, Yankees who had been with Andrew Jackson at New Orleans, and Indians, like Billy Caldwell, who had fought alongside the legendary Tecumseh. Occasionally, a gambler or a criminal on the run showed up and stayed for a bit, for there were few better spots in the Old Northwest to find a card game or a place to disappear.

At the Sauganash and its neighboring hotels, men and women of every color and class were welcome; and whiskey, song, and dance were the great democratizers. Visitors from more civilized parts were shocked to see Indian braves spinning the white wives of fort officers around the dance floor of the Sauganash to the frenzied fiddling and toe tapping of Mark Beaubien, or Indian and white women drinking home-distilled liquor straight from the bottle. To add an edge to the evenings, local white traders, usually led by the raucous Kinzie clan, would put on feathered headdresses and spring into the crowded tavern with war whoops and raised tomahawks, scaring the wits out of tight-buttoned easterners.

Years later, when the traders were long gone, old settlers, who arrived in Chicago just as Mark Beaubien's world was disappearing, would remember him as "a jolly good fellow . . . full of fun and frolic," who would play his fiddle and call out the figures for the dancers in his mangled English. "I plays de fiddle like de debble," he once told a group of eastern spectators who asked him what he did for a living, "an I keeps hotel like hell." To old settlers, he was "our Beaubien," part civilized, part savage in spirit, a reckless but lovable man who managed to spend whatever he made. But Mark Beaubien, father of twenty-three children, was not the one-of-a-kind village character of old-settler memory. He was a representative figure in a precapitalist community that flaunted progress and prided itself on its disdain for proper public conduct, a wild town with three taverns but no churches, school buildings, or meetinghouse. "Oh them was fine times," he declared toward the end of his life, "never come any more."

Mark Beaubien and his riverside neighbors ran a barter economy on the rim of civilization. Until the town was officially surveyed and platted in 1830, they were squatters on their land. They traded parcels of real estate, in what became the center of the world's first skyscraper city, for saddles and bridles, or won or lost them in noisy games of stud poker. Convivial Mark Beaubien often gave away land to people he took a liking to in an effort to get them to settle in the village that was "a mighty lonesome, wet place" when the first Beaubiens arrived from the other side of the lake. No one thought things would change as they did. After lots he gave away became fantastically valuable only a few years later, Mark Beaubien could only remark, with a shrug: "Didn't expect no town."

2. Banishing the Past

Mark Beaubien's community of traders and Indians sealed business deals with a handshake or the exchange of a tobacco pipe, preferred leisure to unrelenting work and spending to saving, put family and friends over personal advancement, and lived for today, not tomorrow. With its premodern values and easy-paced routine, this community had no chance against the get-ahead easterners who began to arrive in growing numbers in the early 1830s.

It was talk of a canal that brought them, and it was the canal project—the dream of Joliet—that made Chicago a town. The first of the barter-trade pioneers to see the future coming and the only one to successfully prepare himself for it was the Vermont Yankee Gurdon Saltonstall Hubbard.

The first sign of new times was the falloff of the fur trade. "I have been unsuccessful in trade this winter and grow more and more displeased with it," Hubbard wrote his sister from Danville in 1827. To augment his income, he began raising hogs on the open prairie and driving them to Chicago along a trail he cut himself. Hubbard's Trail, it was called on maps before it became a state road in 1834, Chicago's main artery to the fertile Wabash Valley. Its Chicago terminus, State Street, named after the state road, would become one of the busiest and most fashionable streets in the country fifty years later.

Hubbard continued to make his annual trek to Mackinac to buy winter supplies for the declining fur trade, but after 1827 he avoided the difficult portage route. On his return from Mackinac, he would scuttle his canoes in the slough of the Chicago River to protect them from prairie fires and use a hundred or so pack ponies to cart his trading goods to the string of posts he established along his trail, which he traveled alone through forest and prairie inhabited entirely by Indians, who were "[my] true honest friends," he said, "in whom I placed confidence."

His mind soon turned to more distant markets. In the winter of 1829 he drove a large number of hogs to Chicago and had them slaughtered there, intending to pack them in barrels and send them east by lake boat. The steamer bringing his barrels failed to arrive, however, and he had to pile the meat on the frozen riverbank, where it lay untouched until spring because the community "knew who owned it," as an acquaintance of his tells it. This was the beginning of Chicago's meatpacking business, in which Hubbard would play a leading part for a long time.

When settlers began to push up the Illinois River valley along the route Joliet and Marquette had taken, the legislature of the recently established state (1818) laid plans to connect this area of Illinois by canal to the East via the lakes and the Erie Canal, which was opened in 1825. In 1822, Congress granted Illinois a right of way across public land coercively purchased from the Indians between the portage and an area a hundred miles to the south and west of it; and five years later, it ceded to Illinois alternate sections of land along the proposed canal corridor, to be sold to pay for construction. In 1830 state canal commissioners laid out two towns at the expected termini of the canal, Ottawa and Chicago. With the surveying and platting of Chicago by James Thompson, whose descendant "Big Bill" Thompson would be the city's flamboyant and corrupt mayor during Prohibition, the seventy-five or so squatters at the stream on the portage gained legal title to their lands. They were capitalists now, like it or not.

When Mark Beaubien was shown the rigidly gridded town plat, he discovered that he was the victim of the cold geometry of the modernizers: His cabin was in the middle of one of the rectilinear streets. Not long after lots went up for sale, he bought two of them for a total of $102 and moved his combination house and tavern a few yards out of the way of progress.

In this way, modern Chicago was born, the creation not of the forces of the private market, as some historians claim, but of state planners, who, in laying out canal towns, became what the geographer Michael P. Conzen has called "urban strategists." Government design established what became capitalism's quintessential urban offspring, and through the portals of this publicly planned canal town came the settlers who filled up the region around it. Frederick Jackson Turner saw the rise of the western town as the final act of the frontier drama, the sign that the frontier stage of civilization had ended. However, as Richard Wade, William Cronon, and other historians have argued, western history is a story of metropolitan expansion. The settling of the American frontier was one of the most ambitious city-building efforts in all of history. Along with farmers, ranchers, and miners came merchants, lawyers, and speculators, who, in the words of an 1867 guidebook for pioneers heading west, "love the hum of crowded streets, the excitement of trade." For many of these settlers, Chicago became a gateway city connecting the new farms and towns of the West with the expanding industrial economy of the Northeast. In the Illinois of Gurdon Hubbard, the urban frontier opened the way for Turner's plowmen.

Land sales were slow at first, and not nearly enough money was raised to begin canal construction. But the canal seemed a certainty now, and that fact drew the attention of land speculators back East. They realized, however, that before a canal could be built and large numbers of settlers attracted to the area "the Indian Threat" would have to be removed. When the fabled Indian fighter Andrew Jackson took the oath of presidential office in 1829, that, too, became a certainty. "Fate," as Sophocles said, "has terrible power. No fort will keep it out, no ships will outrun it."

•

On a clear spring morning in 1832 the aging warrior Black Hawk led a band of about a thousand Sauk and Fox Indians across the Mississippi and up the green Rock River valley. They were returning to Illinois lands they had been forced from the previous year by the terms of a treaty they had not signed. Black Hawk had convinced his followers that if they returned to their homelands in peace and farmed them like the settlers who had pushed them out, they would be left alone. It was a reckless gamble, and it backfired.

As soon as they were spotted, an alarm went out all across northern Illinois, settlers fearing that this was the start of a war of reprisal against white intruders. State militia and federal troops were assembled to hunt down and destroy Black Hawk and his band. Among their ranks were Abraham Lincoln and Jefferson Davis and local militiamen Jean Baptiste Beaubien and Gurdon Hubbard, none of whom got close to the fight. When federal troops under Winfield Scott arrived in Chicago by steamer, they brought with them the deadly Asiatic cholera that was sweeping the coastal states. Fort Dearborn was converted into a camp hospital for the stricken and dying, and when young soldiers who had been in perfect health at breakfast died that same afternoon, their bodies were tossed into a lime-coated pit outside the palisade walls. It was the first of what would be a century-long succession of cholera epidemics in Chicago.

A month later, when Scott's remaining men were healthy enough to march, they headed out across the Des Plaines for a fight that was already over. Black Hawk's retreating band, slowed by the old, the young, and the half-starved, was caught in its attempt to cross back into Iowa at the mouth of the Bad Axe River and slaughtered. Many of the victims were scalped by white soldiers, and some of those killed were women attempting to swim across the river with children on their backs. Those in Black Hawk's band who made it to the west bank of the river were pursued by the Sioux, the ancient enemies of the Fox and Sauk, and killed. Black Hawk surrendered, and he and his son, Whirling Thunder, were sent on a tour of the eastern states by President Jackson to witness the spread and might of the nation they had tried to defy. Black Hawk eventually was allowed to return to his new land in Iowa, where, after writing a stirring autobiography, he died in 1838. Many years later, an impressive granite monument to him designed by Chicago's Lorado Taft was erected on lands that had been taken from his people on the beautiful Rock River.

This fifteen-week "war" had large and lasting consequences for both the winners and the losers. All of Illinois was considered pacified—safe for settlement—and the troops who had tracked down Black Hawk returned home with stories of the sweeping prairies and sparkling lakes of northern Illinois and southern Wisconsin, giving impetus to what became one of the greatest land migrations in the history of civilization. By 1833, the Potawatomi, the principal landholders in Illinois, had been forced to sell almost all their holdings. And in August of that year, word went out from the government Indian agent at Chicago to the chiefs of the United Potawatomi Nations of the Great White Father's interest in purchasing from them the 5 million acres they still held in an enormous semicircle around the village at the portage.

Charles Joseph Latrobe, an English travel writer, was in Detroit when word reached him of the upcoming treaty council at Chicago, and he hurried there as fast as the primitive open wagon he booked a seat on could carry him, convinced by those he had talked to that this would be the last important Indian treaty in the Old Northwest and a spectacle not to be believed. When he arrived at the "upstart village" six days later, he found it "crowded to excess" and counted himself lucky to find a room in the "comfortless and noisy" Sauganash Hotel. Six thousand Potawatomi were encamped around Chicago, and the interior of the village, "a chaos of mud, rubbish and confusion," was filled with what Latrobe described as a "demi-civilized" assemblage of horse traders, land sharpers, peddlers, grog dealers, confidence men, portrait painters, and Indian agents. In the afternoon, great crowds of these frontier hustlers amused themselves at horse races run by Mark Beaubien on a level track outside the village that he had equipped with makeshift booths for the sale of stimulants.

The Potawatomi headmen had seen Black Hawk's return to Illinois as the suicidal action of a deluded mystic and his fanatical followers. Reluctant realists, they favored an orderly withdrawal through treaty negotiations. Black Hawk had badly weakened their bargaining position, but they remained resourceful negotiators, determined to get as much as they could for lands surrendered. When treaty talks began at Chicago and they were told by Gov. George B. Porter of Michigan Territory that their "Great Father" had heard that they wished to sell their land, their chief negotiator replied that "our Great Father . . . must have opened his ears to a bad bird."

Porter saw this for what it was, a well-worn bargaining tactic, and informed them that President Jackson wanted them to move west of the Mississippi to lands far richer than those they presently occupied. They would be paid generously for what they gave up. When pressed to reply, the chiefs searched the September sky, spotted a few passing clouds, and announced that the day was not clear enough for so important a council. They went back to their encampments and delayed for well over a week, happy to feast on free government rations and the great quantities of whiskey that ravenous traders sold them for the promise of treaty money they had not yet received.

Unable to read, write, or relax in the "appalling confusion, filth, and racket" of the Sauganash Hotel, Charles Latrobe spent much of his time in the Indian encampment, a scene, in his words, of "desolation and decline." Drunken warriors raced their ponies, "whooping and yelling like fiends," while men barely able to stand hacked away at each other with knives over a pint of whiskey or the rights to a woman who sat blank-eyed near the action. In the coarse tents made of blankets and canvas and smelling of rotting meat and the droppings of "wolfish" dogs, he saw women seated in twos and threes who appeared "even more elevated with the fumes of whiskey than the males." Years of contact with white traders had driven these Indians "into the lowest state of degradation," Latrobe wrote, and to submerge the loss of their lands and pride, bands of them patrolled the edge of the village at night screaming war chants and brandishing their tomahawks.

After a week of delay, Porter called in the headmen with a signal fire from the fort cannons and gave them what Latrobe called a "forcible Jacksonian discourse," warning them "not to play with their Great Father." On September 26, the council fire was lighted in an open shed near the old Kinzie house, and the chiefs, at least two of them staggering drunk, drew their mark on the treaty papers in the presence of Gurdon Hubbard, an official government witness, agreeing to leave the lands they had occupied a century before Marquette and Joliet reached Chicago. Jesuit-educated Billy Caldwell, whose fur-trading patrons had arranged for him to be one of the principal negotiators for the Potawatomi, passed by his friend Hubbard on the way to the treaty table, where he signed his Indian name in his flowing script below the column of X's.

For their 5 million acres of land, the last great Indian cession in the Great Lakes region, the Potawatomi received an equal amount of land in the West and over a million dollars in goods and provisions, an unseemly portion of which went, by government order, to their clamorous creditors; and they agreed to leave for their new land within three years. This sordid transaction was the legal basis for government possession of a good part of the greater Chicago region. "Chicago, like Carthage," Edgar Lee Masters wrote a century later, "was founded by cheating the natives out of the land."

Immediately after the final signing, frame and clapboard houses were thrown up for the expected invasion of white immigrants, and Charles Latrobe left town to the sound of the "active axes and hammers of the speculators."

The Illinois Potawatomi were removed slowly at first. Then, in the late summer of 1835, they were called to Chicago for their final treaty payment, after which they were to be escorted to lands that a government exploratory expedition found "too poor for snakes to live upon." In a final act of ritual defiance, eight hundred braves staged a spectacular war dance that snaked its way through the entire village and past the Sauganash Hotel, where Gurdon Hubbard and a group of locals gathered to watch.

The braves were naked except for loincloths, and they had smeared their bodies and faces with scarlet and black paint and pulled their hair into scalp locks, a sign of hostile intent. From a second-story window of the Sauganash, John Dean Caton, a newly arrived settler and future chief justice of the Illinois Supreme Court, looked down upon the procession and later described what he saw. Led by a band of music makers banging sticks together and pounding on war drums, the dancers, "their eyes wild and bloodshot," made "the most frightful yells, in every imaginable key and note," leaping in the air as they screamed. When they reached the front of the hotel, they looked up at the white people in the windows, "with hell itself depicted on their faces," and wielded their weapons as if they were about to attack. It would be easy for them in their "maddened frenzy," Caton remembered thinking at the time, to "turn this sham warfare into a real attack . . . and leave not a living soul to tell the story," destroying Chicago at the very moment of its inception.

The following week, a train of forty army wagons, pulled by oxen, carried away the children and effects of the Potawatomi, while the adults, led by a contrite Billy Caldwell, who had decided his loyalties rested with his banished people and not with the traders who had no further use for his services, walked silently alongside. And "Chicago," as a contemporary historian wrote, "was troubled with them no more."*

•

In anticipation of the Indian land cession, a group of settlers had met at the Sauganash Hotel in August 1833 to sign papers incorporating their "mushroom" village as a town. The population numbered barely 150, and the place presented "a most woe-begone appearance, even as a frontier town of the lowest class," an early historian conceded. There was not a single steeple or chimney four feet above any roof, and the wind-torn flag that flew above the ramparts of the fort was Chicago's only emblem of civic pride. Yet many of those who had arrived that summer for the treaty decided to stay, swelling the population to around 250 by the end of the year, and hopes ran strong for the town's future now that the Indians were "removed."

With the Potawatomi went the old French fur-trading community, and Chicago ceased to be the town of "'all nations and kindred and people and tongues,' black and white and red" that a traveler in 1833 had described in his diary. In 1835 the American Fur Company closed its business in Chicago by selling its property to Jean Baptiste Beaubien, and families with names like Bourrassas, Mirandeau, and Juneau—in fact, almost all of the half-breed families—followed the Potawatomi to lands beyond the Missouri River, replaced on the voting rolls by settlers more money conscious, time conscious, and mindful of the sabbath. "Strict sobersides from the land of Jonathan Edwards," one observer called the starch-shirted easterners. That overstated it, for Chicago continued to draw its strong share of rogues and roustabouts. But the eastern migration did set in motion irreversible changes as what Lewis Mumford called the "passive endurance of the village" gave way to "urban 'civilization,' that peculiar combination of creativity and control, of expression and repression, of tensions and release."

No longer was it sufficient for the village trader to feed his family and satisfy his simple pleasures; life must be efficiently organized and nature claimed and conquered in the interest of profit and gain. Capitalism came to frontier Chicago like some new word on the wind; it didn't grow from what was already there. And the watchword of its au-

*Billy Caldwell died of cholera in 1841 in Council Bluffs, Iowa, where he had gained a reputation as a stubborn defender of Indian rights.

dacious agents was change. They left nothing untouched, not even history itself.

A few Anglo-Americans lamented the passing of original Chicago. A resident of Detroit, a town that was going through a similar cultural revolution, expressed their mingled feelings of guilt and regret: "The shriek of the steam whistle and the laborious snort of the propeller [boat] . . . announce that on these shores and waters the age of the practical, hard-working, money-getting Yankee is upon us, and that the careless, laughter-loving Frenchman's day is over."

Joseph N. Balestier, a transplanted lawyer from Vermont, spoke for the new day in the first historical lecture given in Chicago, in the year 1840. Chicago, he said, was already a city of "magical changes." The indolent village of Indians and half-breeds described by the traveler William H. Keating "resounds with the cheery echo of labor. Capacious warehouses and commodious dwellings have taken the place of the log and bark houses 'low, filthy and disgusting.' 'The miserable race of men' have been superseded by a population distinguished for its intelligence and enterprise; and all the comforts of our Eastern homes are gathered around us."*

---

*Mark Beaubien sold the Sauganash the year after the Indian treaty, when the center of Chicago moved east toward the lake, on drained land that was previously thought to be uninhabitable. He lived for a time in Chicago as a lighthouse keeper and manager of a tavern, and died in 1881 at his daughter's home in Kankakee.

3

Ogden's Chicago

1. The Founder

IN the fall of 1833, Gurdon Hubbard returned to Danville from the Chicago Indian treaty signing and began closing his trading station and preparing to move to the newly chartered town at the portage. He had a large brick warehouse under construction near the river—"Hubbard's Folly," skeptics called it—and had bought land from Billy Caldwell north of the Kinzie homestead, where he was building a handsome house on a rise overlooking the lake. He had remarried in 1831 after he and Watseka separated following the death of their daughter. And in January 1834, with the snow deep on the ground, he and Eleanora Berry, a judge's daughter from Urbana, Ohio, headed up Hubbard's Trail for what Gurdon called "the smaller town" upstate. Eleanora rode under cover, wrapped in Indian blankets, while her husband, clad in buckskin with a tomahawk in his belt, led the wagon train on his horse, "Choppy," shouting orders to the sleigh drivers in his caravan as they cleared away snow in front of the ponderous Pennsylvania wagons.

They boarded at a tavern until their house was ready, and that winter, Hubbard threw himself into the business of the town, anticipating the completion of a public improvement that he expected would make him rich.

Hubbard's experience as a trader made him intimately familiar with the geography of the Northwest, and like Joliet, he believed an important city, the center of a future inland empire, would grow up on the spot where the two great water systems of North America almost met at the Chicago River. But he realized that other places equally favored by geography had not spawned towns or cities, while two other Lake Michigan towns less well situated than Chicago—Milwaukee and Michigan City—were larger in 1833, had better harbors, and, some thought, brighter futures. He had also traveled to and from Chicago enough to realize that nature had not stacked the deck entirely in the town's favor.

The greatest obstacle to Chicago's becoming a city was its isolation. A split of sand and a low, wet prairie made it a difficult place to reach by land or water. The sandbar blocked the mouth of the river, forcing lake boats to anchor a half mile or so offshore and ferry their passengers and cargo into the harbor on lighters, while the ships' captains prayed they wouldn't be surprised by a fast-forming lake storm. When the laborious unloading was completed, the boats returned to home harbors with sand as ballast, for Chicago had nothing to sell.

It was not even self-sufficient. Food supplies came from the Wabash valley, some two hundred miles to the south, over rutted trails in prairie schooners drawn by horses or yokes of oxen and guided by long-bodied Hoosier farmers dressed in butternut-colored pants and calico shirts, their flowing hair and beards making them look like "foreign peasantry." When these wagons carrying bacon, flour, potatoes, and apples reached the outskirts of Chicago, many of them literally became stuck in the mud. For a distance of eight to ten miles around the town, water on the prairie was up to a foot to three feet deep in places, the coarse grass preventing it from running off into the lower-lying river. Crawfish would burrow holes in the ground beneath the water, and when teams of horses hit these holes, streams of water would be thrown up in the drivers' faces and the wagon wheels would sink in the mud, sometimes above the axles.

In the town it was no better. In 1836, Charles Cleaver, an Englishman who became one of Chicago's first businessmen, saw a stagecoach locked in the mud on Clark Street, "where it remained several days, with a board driven in the mud at the side of it bearing this inscription: 'No bottom here.'" Town officials used fill to try to make the main streets passable, but this proved too expensive in a place that had almost no money to improve itself.

In the stormy winter Hubbard arrived from Danville, Chicago's "inmates," as they whimsically referred to themselves, barely had enough food to make it through to spring. Even game was scarce on the ice-covered prairie, drawing in starving wolves that prowled the village at night for garbage. The town's hastily constructed cabins were "mere shells," incapable of keeping out the freezing blasts off the lake. With the temperature dropping to as low as twenty-eight degrees below zero, Charles Fenno Hoffman, a visiting New York author, found it impossible to write in his tavern room, for his ink froze in the bottle and his hands, even with gloves on, were too numb to grip a pen. With conditions like these, "we felt and knew," John Dean Caton wrote, "that wisdom and energy and industry could alone build up such a city as its geographical position seemed to require."

Charles Cleaver, Gurdon Hubbard, and most of the other recent arrivals had come to Chicago that year only because harbor improvements were under way that promised to open the town to the markets of the East and attract investors who were its only hope of making it on a frontier where many an incipient city became, in no time, a wilderness ghost town. The harbor project had been recommended by Jefferson Davis, a young army engineer from the South with whom Gurdon Hubbard had played poker at the Sauganash Hotel on Davis's only visit to Chicago. By the spring of 1834, government engineers had cut a channel through the sandbar and shored it with two long piers, making the mouth of the river look much as it does today. On July twelfth, the schooner *Illinois* sailed up this channel into the sheltered river harbor, instantly establishing Chicago as one of the leading ports on the lake, its major enterprises, among them Hubbard's warehousing and forwarding business, hugging the banks of the sluggish river, as they would for the remainder of the century. By 1893, Chicago's harbor, which the visiting writer Caroline Kirkland called the "worst . . . any great commercial city ever lived on," would be busier than New York's.

Before the harbor improvement was completed, most travelers coming from the East took a packet boat up the Erie Canal, a steamer from Buffalo to Detroit, and a stagecoach or two-horse wagon across the timbered Michigan peninsula and around the southern curve of the lake, arriving in Chicago, often as not, "sick in consequence of fatigue and exposure," as a traveling companion of Hubbard's cousin wrote in 1831. This is how New York investors Arthur Bronson and Charles Butler got there in the summer of 1833 on a visit that set in motion a sequence of events that tied Chicago to the eastern economic engine that would power land expansion and urban development in the West for the next half century.

•

Bronson, a member of New York's commercial aristocracy, had heard from his friend Gen. Winfield Scott of the verdant Illinois country and of the likelihood that Chicago would become a flourishing prairie port when its harbor was improved. In the spring of 1833, as he was making plans to go to Chicago, he happened to run into John Kinzie's son, Robert, in New York City at a specialty store that sold goods to Indian traders. When Kinzie was introduced to Bronson by the store's owner, he described prime town land his family had for sale at a price that he secretly thought was extravagant but that Bronson considered a steal. His interest whetted, Bronson invited Butler, his upstate investment partner, to join him on an excursion to the West to examine the Kinzie land and explore new fields of opportunity. This would be a chance for great gain, they thought; they would be the first eastern capitalists to assess the situation in Chicago. They took a packet boat up the Erie Canal, and onboard their steamer from Buffalo to Detroit they met the defeated warrior Black Hawk, who was returning from his meeting with President Jackson. The wrinkled chief talked with great sadness about the future of his people. Bronson and Butler, however, were improvers; while they felt sorry for their steamer-mate, they saw the western tribes standing in the way of vast civilizing changes they had in mind.

Of the two men, Butler was the more audacious, if less well heeled, investor; and he became possessed of a triumphal vision of Chicago's future. His letters, diary entries, and reports from Chicago are as euphoric about the site as those of Louis Joliet. In defiance of what almost every traveler to frontier Chicago saw, he found it a beautiful river hamlet surrounded by a magnificent expanse of grassland and lake. "If I were a young man [he was thirty-one], and unmarried, I should settle in Chicago," he wrote back home, for it was marked by nature to become "a great city." In a few years, "there will be," he predicted, "a line of steamboats, stages, and railroads the entire distance from Albany to the Fort at St. Louis." And Chicago, with the "finest backcountry in the world," will be the "commanding" city on this "great western thoroughfare," views his friends in New York found "visionary and absurd."

Bronson also saw possibilities in Chicago; and after he and Butler met with the principal men of the town, including Hubbard, he bought land on the north side of the river for twenty thousand dollars. He and Butler then helped these local expectant capitalists prepare a resolution to the governor to authorize a private company the New Yorkers promised to form to begin construction of a canal or railroad connecting Chicago to the Illinois River valley. Butler did not have the capital at the time to buy town lots, but in 1835 he formed his own land consortium and bought Bronson's Chicago land for one hundred thousand dollars, Bronson not allowing a friendship to get in the way of his earning a nice profit.

Bronson's original purchase changed everything in Chicago. Interest in the place quickened in New York when word spread that one of Wall Street's most powerful brokers had put money on its future. In the spring of 1835, Gurdon Hubbard bought eighty acres for himself and two eastern backers on a desolate spot along the north branch of the river, and when he passed through New York City several months later on a family visit to Connecticut, he found interest in Chicago land so "wild" that he drew up a crude map of his property, had an engraver prepare copies, and auctioned off parts of it for a profit of seventy-five thousand dollars on a five-thousand-dollar investment. When he returned to Chicago, news of the sale had preceded him, and he was hailed by local newspapers as a bold land speculator. He began construction at once of a new warehouse and of the town's first real hotel, the Lake House, three stories high and extravagantly appointed, with printed menus and a French chef.

That spring, the canal bill was revived in the legislature, and a land office was opened in Chicago once again to sell lots to pay for construction. This time the auction was a roaring success, for the canal was seen by many as "the only remaining link wanting to complete the most stupendous chain of inland communication in the world." Every steamer and two-masted schooner arriving in Chicago carried agents of eastern capitalists. One of them was a young country lawyer from western New York named William Butler Ogden, whose sister had recently married Charles Butler, a marriage that dramatically changed Ogden's fortunes—and Chicago's as well.

•

Ogden had resigned his seat in the New York legislature to come west to supervise the sale of Butler's land, expecting, no doubt, that his services would be smartly rewarded by his politically influential brother-in-law, who was part of Martin Van Buren's political machine, the Albany Regency. After booking a room in one of the town's overcrowded hotels, Ogden headed out to inspect Butler's property. There had been heavy rains, and as he tried to walk the unbroken field of wild grass and underbrush, he found himself sinking knee-deep in mud and marsh. "[You have] been guilty of an act of great folly in making [this] purchase," he wrote Butler. The land, he thought, was not worth the money he had paid for passage to this repulsive prairie swamp. But Ogden stayed on to carry out his charge, hiring men to drain the land, post it, and open up streets to its settlement lots. When he offered lots at auction, he was astonished at the price they commanded—$100,000 for a mere third of the property. He thought people insane to buy swampland for such prices and returned to New York immediately after the sale. But when land prices continued to climb into the following year, he became convinced that Chicago indeed had a future. In the summer of 1836 he moved there with the idea of making a fortune.

Ogden returned to Chicago as a land dealer and developer, operating independently and also as an agent for Butler and a growing group of other eastern investors. But whereas he was interested in making permanent improvements on land he bought and sold, adding steadily to its value, others came to Chicago simply to gamble on escalating land prices in what became a chapter in one of the most frenzied speculative episodes in American history. In the West, city building and land speculation proceeded hand in hand, and from its inception Chicago was, in the writer Nelson Algren's phrase, a hustler's town.

The public domain was the nation's most valuable asset, and when large chunks of it were sold in Chicago in the 1830s in conjunction with the canal lots, the entire Northwest became a speculation. "I never saw a busier place than Chicago was at the time of our arrival," the English writer Harriet Martineau remarked in the summer Ogden arrived from New York. The dusty streets were packed with speculators rushing from one sale to another. "A Negro dressed up in scarlet, bearing a scarlet flag, and riding a horse with housing of scarlet, announced the time of sale," Martineau described the scene. "At every street corner where he stopped the crowd flocked round him; and it seemed as if some prevalent mania infected the whole people."

By late June, enough money had been made from land sales to begin construction of the canal, an enormously expensive project that was supported by New York capital raised by Butler, Bronson, and Ogden. Contracts for part of the work were taken out by local businessmen, including Ogden; and advertisements went out for laborers, drawing hundreds of Irish immigrants to Canalport, on the South Branch of the river, where work was to begin. It was later called Bridgeport, and the dirt path that led to it was named Archer's Road, after the chief canal commissioner. And both the settlement and the street (as Archy Road) would be immortalized in the humor of Finley Peter Dunne at the end of the century, when Bridgeport was the central village and political camp of Chicago's Irish.

Groundbreaking was set for the Fourth of July. Three howitzer blasts from the fort opened the ceremonies, and frontier dignitaries crowded on the side-wheeler *Chicago* and its tow of two small sloops for the ride to Canalport. A large gathering of rowdy spectators followed on foot or in wagons. A fife and drum enlivened the trip upriver, and so did kegs of beer and rum onboard. When the *Chicago* came to a bend in the river, a group of Irishmen, well in their cups, demanded to be let aboard, but the captain pushed on to the site of the ceremony. After a reading of the Declaration of Independence, Col. William B. Archer turned the first spadeful of earth. Then the crowd started to chant "Hubbard, Hubbard," and the former Indian trader, now a canal commissioner, stepped forward and dug up a shovelful of earth on the spot where Marquette had wintered. Judge Theopholus W. Smith, who had apparently hoisted too many toasts that morning, followed with a "wild prophesy" as the Chicago papers called it, that the town's population would reach 100,000 within a century. When he shouted out his prediction while standing on a barrel, the crowd exploded with laughter, and a local official pulled him from his impromptu podium and told him he was making a fool of himself. After the local militia company gave a fifty-six-gun salute, one for every legislator who voted for the canal bill, the local officials and their families headed back to town on the *Chicago.* When they passed the same group of Irish "shovelmen" on the riverbank, they were met by a barrage of stones and rocks that broke windows in the cabin. The captain landed, and a gang, led by Hubbard, Mark Beaubien, and several Kinzies, rushed the Irishmen and beat up a number of them they caught. Bloodied but in excellent spirits, the local heroes joined the rest of the crowd for a night of dancing and drinking at Wolf Point. When the canal is completed "we shall see Chicago take her stand among the proudest cities of the nation," Joseph Balestier declared, "and . . . no obstacle can impede her onward march to greatness."

Years later, Hubbard would be credited by a number of prominent Chicagoans as the person most responsible for locating the canal terminus at Chicago. In the early 1830s the legislature had considered reversing its earlier decision to make Chicago the northern terminus of the canal. It would be cheaper, surveyor's reports indicated, to dig a canal through the Calumet Sag—located to the south of Chicago—to the Des Plaines River than to cut through the portage and Mud Lake. After listening to these arguments, Hubbard, a canal lobbyist for Chicago, unfolded a map and pointed out to the legislators that the "great city" that would develop at the head of canal navigation would reach into the state of Indiana if it were located on the Calumet River, although "the great expense of construction would devolve upon our state." That settled the question, according to one lawmaker, and the Chicago–Ottawa route was officially approved the next year.

But if Gurdon Hubbard is partly responsible for locating present-day Chicago where it is, the one most responsible for turning it into a flourishing city was his lawyer and sometime business associate, William Butler Ogden, "Chicago's Founder."

A friend once described Ogden's salient characteristic as his "absolute faith" in Chicago. For him, its future was "a fixed fact." But if we take Isaac N. Arnold's compliment too literally, we miss the empowering factor responsible for Ogden's—and his own—decision to move to Chicago. They were gamblers, risking their future on Chicago's prospects. They had to believe in the place; if it failed, they failed.

"I did not . . . come here involuntarily, but of set purpose," Gurdon Hubbard's friend Grant Goodrich told a meeting of Old Settlers late in his life. As a law student in Chautauqua County, New York, Goodrich pored over maps of the Northwest, decided Chicago had geographical advantages, and "resolved that when I should graduate I would seek my fortune there." Once settled in the town, he and other young risk takers became, by that very decision, mutually dependent on Chicago's future. "[We] had faith in each other and faith in Chicago. Its future greatness became [our] theme of thought and conversation, and the inspiration of great plans and deeds." But for a desperate moment, not long after Ogden opened his land office, it looked as if those extravagant dreams would come to nothing. Chicago, the town marked by nature for greatness, almost didn't make it.

William Butler Ogden was born in 1805 in a New York village on the Delaware River and was prepared for life on the northwestern frontier, he would later tell his Chicago friends, by his hardscrabble beginnings in this remote mountain community. He had planned to study for the law, but when his father suffered a stroke, he had to take over his business interests as a land developer and lumber trader. He was sixteen at the time and by his early twenties had proved to be a more successful businessman than his father, who died when Ogden was twenty. Andrew Jackson made him postmaster of his village; and at twenty-nine he was a lawyer and a state senator, having overcome, by his own account, every obstacle life had put in front of him.

Although he started in New York politics as a Jacksonian Democrat, Ogden was an advocate of government-backed internal improvements, envisioning federal support of a continuous railroad from New York to Chicago, which would be, he told his colleagues in the New York Senate, "the most splendid system of internal communication ever yet devised by man." He had run for the New York Senate on a platform of state aid for the construction of the New York and Erie Railroad, and the bill he backed passed just as he was deciding to move to a place that had staked its future on a canal.

Ogden's priority in Chicago was his land business, but no frontier businessman, he believed, could afford to stay out of politics. These new western towns depended on government assistance for their very survival—no place more so than Chicago. The federal government had removed the Indians from the area and given land to the state of Illinois to dig a canal. For a time the sale of government lots along the canal was the only business in town, while Chicago's hopes for developing active commerce with the East were based on continuing harbor improvements undertaken and paid for by Washington. And further government action—local, state, and federal—would be needed, Ogden was convinced, if the town was to amount to anything. That meant businessmen who believed as he did would have to run for office; and they did in almost every would-be western city, unlike the economic elites in older northeastern cities, who were at this time retreating from active engagement in urban politics. Ogden was one of the new species of western booster-businessmen who fused their own interests with those of their adopted cities. "He could not forget," one of his business associates remarked, "that everything which benefitted Chicago, or built up the great West, benefitted him."

The summer that Ogden made his home in Chicago he became part of a committee to draft a city charter for submission to the state legislature; and when Chicago was officially elevated from a town to a city the following year, he ran against John Harris Kinzie in its first mayoralty election. Gurdon Hubbard was Ogden's law client, but he and his old Chicago friends backed Kinzie, whom they falsely portrayed as "the first born of Chicago," while painting Ogden as a "transient speculator." But the Kinzie campaign strategy was a year or two behind the times. By 1836 the eastern newcomers formed a majority in the town, and they put their man in office by a generous margin.

When Ogden became mayor, Chicago was "a poor excuse for a city," in the words of one of his early biographers. Most of its buildings were wood shanties, it had no sidewalks or decent bridges, its streets remained unpaved, and the "waterworks" consisted of several two-wheeled carts that ran to and from the lake—hogsheads on wheels, each with "a faucet, under which the consumer's bucket received a supply for a price paid to the proprietor and driver." Imports totaled just over $370,000; exports, about $11,600. The city had no money in its treasury and no credit, and the income-earning residents in its expanding population of four thousand made their money largely by selling town lots to one another. "Men exchanged lots with each other," an early settler recalls, "very much as boys swap jack-knives. The greatest storyteller was about as big a man as we had."

Ogden's aim was to turn this mudhole into a metropolis, and that aim became a thirty-year crusade. First as mayor for one term, then as a regularly elected alderman, he pressed the city to raise tax money for new streets, plank sidewalks, and bridges of his own design. Public improvements the city could not pay for he underwrote with his own funds and those of his eastern clients and investment partners. In his first decade in the city, until Chicago could go it on its own, this was Ogden's largest contribution to its development—as a conduit for investment money necessary to start and sustain not just public improvements, like roads and a canal, but a myriad of new businesses that he and other aspiring entrepreneurs formed on their arrival in the city. Contrary to the old Turnerian notion that the frontier developed in isolation from the settled East and that farmers and venturesome town capitalists fashioned an economy on their own, the Old Northwest in the 1830s, as historian John Denis Haeger demonstrates, "was a colony into which eastern financiers poured their surplus wealth . . . in order to make profits and to build an integrated national economy." Through the natural corridor from New York formed by ancient geologic processes flowed the capital to raise Chicago from the mud.

Like other great cities that began their lives on rivers or at trading junctions—London and Paris, to name just two—Chicago began as an exchange center dealing in goods not produced or processed there— or even destined for buyers in the city. Here its strategic location was of crucial importance. But the source of its success was its versatile, risk-taking businessmen. Cities are not ordained by geography; as the writer Jane Jacobs argued, "they are wholly existential." In this process of urban building, Chicago entrepreneurs like Ogden and Hubbard had the greatest incentive possible: Having invested early and heavily in Chicago real estate, every urban improvement they supported was money in their own pockets. Even bigger money was to be made, however, by exploiting Chicago's geographic advantages.

Ogden and Hubbard, like most Chicago businessmen, focused their private investments on enterprises designed to funnel East-West trade through Chicago's portals. Hubbard joined with a Buffalo shipping company, Pratt and Taylor, to establish the Eagle Line of sailing vessels and steamers, the first regularly run East to West transportation service to Chicago, and Ogden became president of the Chicago and Michigan Steam Boat Company, which provided passenger, freight, and mail service to lake ports. By 1840 it was possible to go to New

York City by steamer and rail in a matter of six days. Every manner of commodity, from beer to baskets, was shipped to Chicago, and when the prices of eastern beer became too high for local consumers, Ogden formed his own brewery and made a steady profit from what would become one of the city's largest industries. He also financed banks in the city, including one Hubbard helped to form—the city's first—on the ground floor of his sprawling riverfront warehouse and shipping building, headquarters of Hubbard and Company. With Ogden's encouragement, Hubbard and a group of local capitalists also went forward with the construction of the city's first real waterworks. By the early 1840s, the Chicago Hydraulic Company was furnishing lake water through log pipes to portions of the town. In these years Chicago's growth can be measured by the size and scope of William Butler Ogden's investments. He is the man "who built and owns Chicago," said the French historian Guizot with only slight exaggeration.

When Ogden first arrived in Chicago on the steamer *Pennsylvania*, he was largely the creature of his financial backers. By 1848, he was the most powerful capitalist in the West. Success came so fast it seemed somehow unreal to him. When told one day by his secretary that he was worth more than a million dollars, he reportedly remarked, "By God, Quigg, that's a lot of money!"

2. A Prairie Aristocracy

Ogden, Hubbard, and their colleagues were part of a closely connected leadership group that comprised Chicago's first urban elite. Made up mostly of young, self-made men from New England and New York State, this elite dominated business, politics, and the professions and assumed leadership of the city's intellectual and philanthropic activities, founding and supporting a rich array of historical, scientific, literary, and musical associations in the 1840s and 1850s, including the Chicago Lyceum, the Chicago Historical Society, the Academy of Sciences, the Chicago Musical Union, the Orphan Asylum, and the Chicago Relief and Aid Society, the city's chief charity and humanitarian organization. They also established Chicago's common school system and its first institutions of higher learning, among them the old University of Chicago, Hahnemann Medical College, Rush Medical College, Female Seminary, and Northwestern University, in the outlying town of Evanston. Holding hard to the values of steady work and individual responsibility for success—"every man in those days stood on his own merits," one of its leaders recalled—they were also selfannointed community stewards. Ogden's friend J. Young Scammon summed up their secular creed: Since Chicago "made us what we are," he declared in his presidential address to the Chicago Historical Society, "[we] owe . . . it to Chicago . . . to see that . . . [our] public institutions, which it is our duty now to found, are placed upon a solid base."

That was not empty rhetoric; but to the Chicago elite, money remained the one and only measure of acceptance. Blood and background counted for little, since so few members of the inner circle came from well-connected families. When asked about his lineage, William Hibbard, a hardware tycoon, said that all he knew was that his father was an honest man. Most of the wealthiest members of the elite, like Ogden and Walter L. Newberry, made their initial money in real estate and branched out into an astonishing variety of enterprises. Versatility was their hallmark as businessmen. They produced, shipped, and handled everything essential to making Chicago a great city; and they moved back and forth from business to politics, even though some of them professed a strong dislike for rough-and-tumble political partisanship. Only two of the first nineteen mayors of Chicago in the period before the Civil War—a bartender and a blacksmith— were not notable businessmen. All but three of them came from New York or New England, and all were native-born Americans with clear feelings about the city's first proletariat—the "poor and vicious foreigners," as Ogden called the Irish who lived in the squalid "shanties" and "rookeries" of Canalport.

This was a frontier aristocracy, not a polished, patrician class, and it admitted into its ranks anyone who managed to push his way to the top. An excellent example is six-foot-six "Long John" Wentworth, who came ambling into town on October 27, 1836, his muddy boots hanging on a stick over his shoulder and a jug of whiskey in his hand to bathe his blistered feet. He was twenty-one years old and from Sandwich, New Hampshire, where his father had a prosperous business, but where there were few opportunities for hungry young men. A graduate of Dartmouth College, he had come West "in pursuit of fortune and fame," his letter of introduction from the governor of New Hampshire announced; and he had made his way across the country by stagecoach, canal boat, rail car (the first train he had ever seen), and steamer, walking the last leg from Michigan City behind a mud wagon that hauled his baggage. He arrived on Lake Street with his entire savings of thirty dollars, and he was carrying his boots because he wanted them to dry so he could begin looking for work that very afternoon.

By chance, he ran into one of his classmates on the street and was taken to the old Sauganash Hotel, by then renamed the United States

Hotel, and introduced to a local attorney, who offered him a chance to study law in his office. The next month, he was hired as editor of the *Chicago Democrat*, a paper he would soon own. Wentworth wrote vehement Jacksonian editorials, becoming, in time, a master of political ridicule and mudslinging. The following year, he put his paper strongly behind the mayoralty candidacy of William Ogden, receiving as his reward the post of city printer.

After being admitted to the bar in 1841, he entered politics, serving five terms in Congress and two as city mayor after switching his allegiance to the antislavery Republican Party. All the while, he made several million dollars in land investments and railroad development and built a vast estate, modeled on Monticello.

On one occasion, when running for mayor, he gave what the poet Carl Sandburg called "the shortest and most terrifying stump speech ever heard in Illinois." When a large group outside the courthouse began yelling for him to appear, he walked out, scanned the crowd with a scowl on his face, and said: "You damn fools. . . . You can either vote for me or you can go to hell."

In his retirement, Wentworth became Chicago's most flamboyant and easily recognized Old Settler and the acknowledged authority on its history and legend. He had a capacious memory and would rent halls to deliver extemporaneous lectures on local history. He would arrive for his speeches in his barouche, wearing his broad-brimmed slouch hat, a swallow-tailed coat, and high black boots, an enormous cane in his right hand steadying his three-hundred-pound frame. In the fire and storm of his lectures, he would take big gulps of water from a glass and mop his bald head with a bath towel he hung over the podium. He died in 1888 and, at his request, was buried under a sixty-foot-high granite obelisk imported on two railroad cars from New Hampshire—the tallest tombstone in the West.

As a young man, Wentworth had been something of an embarrassment to the city's antebellum elite, whose social life was family centered and temperate. He preferred to drink at the local taverns with Hoosiers and stevedores and, in a city desperately short of women, was probably one of the "desolate . . . young bachelors," mentioned in an 1837 news story, who would "flock to the pier . . . ready to catch the girls" as they landed. He was not likely to have attended many of the strawberry parties thrown in the homes of young married couples on the North Side. Entertainment in Chicago in the 1840s and 1850s was a far cry from the Sauganash days. People of all ages, trades, and professions would get together at balls or square dances where homemade refreshments were served; and household parties usually ended by eleven or twelve o'clock. Nor, as William Ogden's neighbor Isaac Arnold notes, was there much pretension or "vulgar exhibition of wealth"; there was not enough money in town for conspicuous display. During the city's first depression, there were only two carriages in town, and ladies of the leading families were not embarrassed to be seen riding to church in the back of a dung cart, "with robes thrown on the bottom on which they sat."

But an inner circle of the most prestigious families in the city did meet frequently at their homes on the North Side, laying the foundations for what came to be known as "society." "It is a remarkable thing," declared Harriet Martineau, "to meet such an assemblage of educated, refined, and wealthy persons as may be found there . . . on the edge of a wild prairie." Families from New England organized the New England Society of Chicago and observed the anniversary of the landing of the Pilgrims. They and other North Side families were polite enough to invite vulgar newcomers like Wentworth to their parties, but "when we [bachelors] had a party on the South Side," Wentworth recalls, "instead of coming themselves, the ladies would send their domestics."

The social center of refined Chicago was the North Side residence of William Butler Ogden. Not long after his arrival in Chicago, Ogden brought in the architect John M. Van Osdel from New York to design a large Greek Revival house for him on a four-acre square of the city's grid. When the porticoed house was ready, Ogden invited his mother and sister to live with him; and with them as hostesses, he threw big country-style parties. Drink in hand, he would entertain guests around a blazing fire with stories of his youth in Delaware County, where he had been an outdoorsman and a crack sharpshooter. When anyone of note was in town, he or she usually stayed at the Ogden mansion, whose guest ledger included the names of Martin Van Buren, Samuel Tilden, Daniel Webster, Ralph Waldo Emerson, and Margaret Fuller. "The guest always found good books, good pictures, good music, and the most kind and genial reception," Isaac Arnold recalls. The expatriate portrait painter George P. A. Healy, whom Ogden met in Paris and talked into relocating in ragged Chicago—perhaps Ogden's most spectacular feat as a city promoter—claimed that Ogden was "in conversation a worthy rival of the three best I ever met"—Louis Philippe, John Quincy Adams, and Dr. Orestes A. Brownson, the brilliant transcendentalist writer.

Ogden was a handsome, imposingly built man, full of energy and spirit. At parties he sat at his piano and sang old songs for his guests, encouraging them to join in; and he liked to take newcomers on tours of Chicago in his open carriage, talking with enthusiasm about its future as he drove his high-pacing horses through its dust and disorder. Toward sunset, he liked to ride alone on the open prairie, stopping to gather wild plants for his garden.

The North Side was still forestland when he settled there, and the majestic elms, cottonwoods, and oaks "gave to the neighborhood," Arnold writes, "a rural, suburban aspect, novel for a locality so near the centre of the City." The only things in the city higher than its noble trees were the masts of the sailing vessels in the river port, which Ogden could see in the distance from his rooftop observatory. In back of the house he had a glass conservatory and a forcing house in which he raised exotic grapes, apricots, peaches, and figs. His favorite writer was the poet of nature William Cullen Bryant, who stayed at his house on his visits to Chicago. Ogden hired a European-trained gardener to care for his grounds and helped organize the Chicago Horticultural Society. He considered a well-tended garden the reflection of a "cultivated mind."

Operating on a grand scale, Ogden intended as a businessman not merely to get and spend but to elevate Chicago to a city of power and consequence. He also wanted to make it a fit place to live. He had a deep-grained sense of public duty, evidenced by his generous contributions—in mid-career, not in his dotage—to the city's charities and to its cultural and educational institutions. His manner of giving was not the signing of a check. He was an active force in almost every cultural institution he endowed, and he paid regular visits to orphans and the sick, bringing them flowers and fruits from his garden. He also tried to rein in the city's acquisitive spirit, cautioning his clients not to overextend themselves in land speculation and not to let greed get in the way of ordinary decency. The rapid advance of land values in 1837, he agreed with Isaac Arnold, had "turned the heads of many sober-minded men, and produced a frenzy which unfitted them for ordinary business." Speculation and "deceptive treachery," he wrote, was being rewarded with success, raising "a precocious set of scoundrels [to] . . . positions in society." In his reflective moments, he had to agree with the dark verdict of one of his more charming houseguests, the Swedish writer Fredrika Bremer, that most people came to Chicago merely "to trade, to make money, and not to live."

The merchant John Farwell summed up the prevailing spirit: "To be busy is my delight." Still, in the privacy of his diary, Farwell wondered where all this commercial energy was driving his city. "Men are greedy for gain, and yet they are never satisfied. . . . The cry is—more—more—more—from morn til eve; from youth to heavy age." In

such an atmosphere, the influence and example of a William Ogden
was inconsequential. Portrayed by some historians as early Chicago's
representative man, he was, in fact, a splendid anomaly.

3. The Grid and the Balloon Frame

In the twin drives for profit and urban expansion, two of the most
prized values were speed and efficiency. And these—along with the
profit motive itself—were clearly expressed in early Chicago's architecture and physical design: in "the grid" and "the balloon frame."

When the surveyor James Thompson filed his half-square-mile plat
for Chicago in 1830, he determined for centuries the physical shape of
the city. His seemingly blank urban diagram also gave expression to
nineteenth-century Chicago's paramount priorities as a city and to an
expanding nation's attitudes about man's relationship to the land.

There was, of course, nothing new or unusual about making cities
by laying out straight streets to intersect at right angles, creating, in
the process, a gridiron or checkerboard of relatively uniform urban
blocks. The ancient Greeks and Romans used the grid to design some
of the handsomest cities ever constructed, and Hippodamus of Mile-
tus, the founder of town planning, saw the geometric grid as a reflection of cultural values: It symbolized the clarity and rationality of the
civilized mind. But the grid, or any other urban design, does not convey timeless, invariable meaning. It can become whatever a city-
building people want it to represent. The Romans used the Greek grid
in many of their colonial towns but did not adapt it to the terrain, as
Greek planners did. And for the Romans the grid had a unique and
powerful symbolism. The forum was situated on sacred ground near
the crossing of the two main axial streets, the decumanus and the
cardo, while local spiritual and civic centers, akin to the central meeting point, were located near key intersecting streets in the outlying
housing precincts. The square-block grids of Roman towns, moreover,
were usually bounded by rectangular walls, creating feelings of protection, intimacy, and enclosure.

William Penn drew on Roman tradition in designing seventeenth-
century Philadelphia, creating a rectilinear city organized around a
number of spacious town squares that relieved the severity of the grid.
Thousands of towns and cities in the trans-Appalachian West were
patterned on Penn's Philadelphia, but with a number of variations that
made them characteristically capitalist creations. In the Chicago of
William Butler Ogden, Penn's spacious proportioned grid, designed to

distribute population and discourage the spread of fire, became the speculative urban plan.

Western towns like Chicago were gridded because it was the easiest way to survey and divide land for quick sale and profit. "With a T-square and a triangle," Lewis Mumford wrote, "an office boy [could] . . . 'plan' a metropolis, with its standard lots, its standard blocks, its standard street widths." In Chicago, the use of the grid represented the transformation of land into a mere commodity—real estate—without sacred or civic significance. Its single value was its market value. Profit took precedence over public interest, and city planning itself became a speculative enterprise—with the major "planner" being the market itself. Land went to the highest bidder; to remove land from the market for public use—such as park space and public squares—was considered a waste of a profit-generating resource. It was hardly coincidental, then, that the only significant public spaces in Chicago in the 1850s were a small city square containing a combined courthouse and city hall designed by John M. Van Osdel; a public promenade along the lake that the federal government carved out of the old Fort Dearborn reservation; and a longer stretch of lakefront public ground created by the state canal commissioners in 1836. The remainder of the city was surrendered to the speculators. With the resulting paucity of parkland, private cemeteries charging a fee to picnickers did a booming business.

Another feature of Chicago's grid was its boundlessness. Unlike the Roman grid, it was meant to be virtually limitless. As the city grew, it grew, its only apparent constraints the size of the expansionist dreams of Chicago businessmen. This vision of an ever-growing city expressed the nineteenth-century notion that empty land was to be removed from nature and "improved" by builders and enterprisers and that, in the writer Richard Sennett's phrase, the American "powers of conquest and habitation [should be] subject to no natural or inherent limitations."

The speculative grid was also an environmentally blind approach to designing cities. It was arbitrarily imposed on all types of topography—hill sites like San Francisco, river-valley sites like Cincinnati, flat sites like Chicago. Some have argued that the symmetrical grid is aesthetically ideal for level surfaces. But while Chicago is flat, it also has a meandering river topography that its grid makes no allowances for. Downtown streets stretch right to the riverbank and then begin again on the other side, as if connected by invisible bridges, a design that created intractable traffic problems. Nor was any thought given to sun or wind conditions—those ancient considerations—in laying out city buildings. It was simply a matter of putting one building beside the other on square lots facing straight streets.

It is too easy, however, to blame the grid itself for this type of urban development. With time, imagination, and enlightened public policy, these prosaic two-dimensional diagrams can be transformed into richly attractive urban sites. It was unregulated capitalism—speculative adventuring in the absence of social regulations on land use—that created nineteenth-century Chicago, which Fredrika Bremer called "one of the shabbiest and ugliest cities I have yet seen in America."

The historian Sam Bass Warner has called this culture of unrestrained moneymaking "privatism." From roughly the mid-nineteenth century onward, the "success and failures of American cities," he writes, "have depended upon the unplanned outcomes of the private market." Its needs and demands for land, water, air space, and workers have determined the physical shape and quality of life of America's large cities. While not the creation of privatism, the grid reflected its impelling ideas about urban space. In Chicago, the individual building lot, the block, and the street were treated "as abstract units for buying and selling," in Lewis Mumford's words, "without respect for historic uses, for topographic conditions, or for social needs." Except where minimal state intervention curtailed the process, the city government lost control of land needed for proper municipal development.

But whatever its social defects, the grid provided for Chicago's explosive physical growth as no other urban design could. "Emigrants were coming in almost every day in wagons of various forms," Charles Butler said of Chicago in 1833, "and in many instances families were living in their covered wagons while arrangements were made for putting up shelter for them. It was no uncommon thing for a house . . . to be put up in a few days." That summer, Arthur Bronson himself hired out a contractor to build a house for him in a week so that he and Butler could move out of their cramped inn at Wolf Point. "The houses, with one or two exceptions," Butler wrote, "were of the cheapest and most primitive character for human habitation, suggestive of the haste with which they had been put up." But in that year a revolutionary method of wood construction was developed in Chicago that provided for durability without any sacrifice of speed, "a common-sense way," historian Daniel J. Boorstin suggests, "to meet the urgent housing needs of an impatient migratory people."

Instant cities like Chicago and San Francisco could "never have arisen, as they did," a writer in the 1860s observed, "if it had not been for the knowledge of balloon frames." No one knows for certain who invented the balloon frame, but it was first used widely in Chicago and was the forerunner of another Chicago architectural innovation: the method of hanging a skyscraper's façade on a light and strong steel frame. The first building in the country constructed in the new way was probably a warehouse at the mouth of the Chicago River erected in 1832 by a New Hampshire businessman and jack-of-all-trades named George Washington Snow, who arrived in the city that summer in a canoe paddled by an Indian guide. The following year, a Connecticut carpenter, Augustine Deodat Taylor, built St. Mary's Catholic Church with a balloon-frame method on land donated by Jean Baptiste Beaubien. It took three months and three men to build St. Mary's at a cost of four hundred dollars, roughly half the expenditure of time and money required to put up a conventional building of this kind. By the time of the Civil War, the balloon frame, one of America's first important contributions to architecture, was the standard form of construction on the treeless plains of the West, and today nearly all wooden buildings in the United States continue to be erected with a form of balloon framing.

Like the grid, the secret of the technique was its simplicity. The centuries-old method of constructing a house was to build on a frame of heavy timber posts, which were held together by cutting down the end of one beam into a tongue, or tenon, and fitting the tongue into a hole, or mortise, in the adjoining beam. If there happened to be some give on the joint, the connection was fastened by a wooden pin driven into a hole bored through the joined timbers. In place of this laboriously constructed mortise-and-tenon frame, Taylor substituted a light skeleton of pine lumber two-by-fours, called a balloon frame because it looked as if it would blow away with the first substantial wind. The two-by-fours were cut by new circular steam saws and held together by cheap, machine-cut nails, without which this construction would have been prohibitively expensive. The frame was then covered by clapboard siding nailed to the studs. As Sigfried Giedion notes: "To put together a house like a box, using only nails—this must have seemed utterly revolutionary to carpenters."

It was ordained, then, that Chicago would be a city of wood, an inviting target for prairie fire. Its hastily constructed wooden buildings, sidewalks, and bridges gave it a rough, impermanent-looking appearance, like so many other western towns of its kind. It was this insubstantial character of American communities that struck Alexis de Tocqueville, although he never got to Chicago. Houses seemed to be mere square boxes, to be lived in until luck, opportunity, or failure drove their footloose owners to move on; people were too restless, it appeared to Tocqueville, to settle in substantial houses of brick or stone.

When John M. Van Osdel arrived in Chicago in the spring of 1837 to build William Ogden's house, he had a reaction not unlike Tocqueville's. The town seemed more a real estate lottery than a permanent settlement, and although just built, it already appeared to be falling apart. Passing from his landing dock on the river to Ogden's office on Kinzie Street, he saw a block of three-story buildings, "the fronts of which had fallen outward and laid prone upon the street," he recalled years later. After inquiring, he found that the floors were not constructed in a strong enough fashion to support the south-facing walls of the buildings and that when the summer sun melted the frozen clay underneath the foundations, the front walls collapsed into the dusty street. Van Osdel's first job in Chicago was to rebuild the floors of this "frontless block."

•

The entire town—its architecture as well as its economy—seemed to rest on flimsy foundations. As it happened, the architecture held, but the economy collapsed just as Van Osdel was completing Ogden's mansion. The Panic of 1837—"the day of retribution," Joseph Balestier called it, for a national orgy of land speculation and overbuilding of internal improvements—almost ruined Chicago. "It fell on the country and the city," an early Chicago historian wrote, "like a thunderbolt out of a clear sky. . . . Men went to bed rich and awoke to find themselves worth less than nothing." The land they owned became a liability; "the more land a man had," Balestier remarked, "the worse off he apparently was."

Some Chicago businessmen subsequently became millionaires because they could not sell their land at any price during the early months of the panic. In December 1837 all money payments at Chicago ceased, and the city and the nation spun into a five-year-long depression. Almost every businessman in Chicago was either ruined or badly hurt. For a time, canal construction blunted the impact of the depression, but when the state approached bankruptcy in 1841, it stopped construction, and hundreds of contractors went under.

The crisis peaked when large numbers of the city's frightened debtors organized a mass movement for relief from their financial obligations. A public meeting was called to have "stay laws" passed for the suspension of court action on the collection of debts. "Inflammatory speeches greatly excited and made desperate many of the

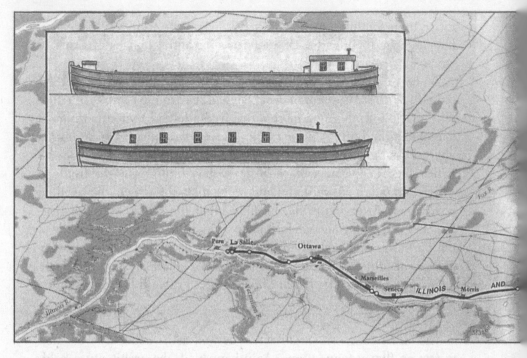

The Illinois and Michigan Canal Corridor, 1848. The much broader Sanitary and Ship Canal of 1900 runs roughly parallel to the old I&M Canal, and remains

crowd, and everything looked as if dishonor would crown the city's brow," said an early city historian. At that point, Ogden stepped forward to address the crowd, his first and only public talk as mayor. Speaking in cool, reasoned tones, he urged his fellow citizens to have the "courage of men" and to remember "that no misfortune [is] so great as one's own personal dishonor. . . . Above all things . . . do not tarnish the honor of our infant city." Ogden's measured eloquence carried the meeting. Efforts to repudiate debts were voted down, and Chicago emerged with its credit image intact. Later, this allowed Ogden to help put together a bond and loan package with Arthur Bronson and other outside investors that allowed the state to resume canal construction in 1845.

As the depression lifted, wagon-hauled and lake commerce poured into Chicago, along with settlers heading for the open prairies or for life in the resurgent city. As its hinterland filled up with homesteaders who broke the thick prairie sod with new steel plows and put in crops of yellow grain, Chicago emerged as the area's principal shipping and supply center. Hoosier wagons now arrived with cash crops—wheat and corn—and left with cookstoves, barrels of salt, ready-made cloth-

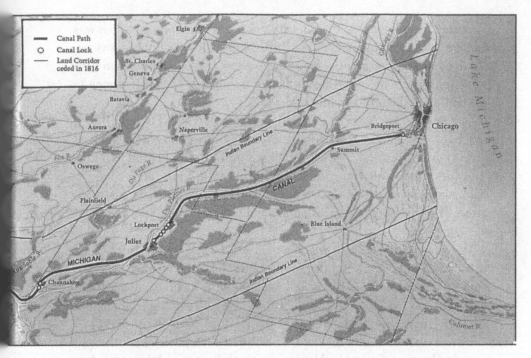

today the chief water link between the Great Lakes and the Mississippi River. David Buisseret, *Historic Illinois from the Air* (Chicago: University of Chicago Press, 1990).

ing, and pine lumber. By 1846, Chicago's population was fourteen thousand, and when William Cullen Bryant's steamer from Mackinac Island sailed into the city's busy harbor in July of that year, the poet claimed to have some difficulty recognizing the place he had seen just five years before. A "raw" and "slovenly" looking settlement had become a thriving commercial center with "warehouses and shops, [and] . . . bustling streets," he wrote in his travel letters.

After spending the evening at William Ogden's home, Bryant set out the following day in a stagecoach for Peru, Illinois, and was surprised to see how the settlement of Chicago had extended westward into the open country. In 1848 the process of digging the Illinois and Michigan Canal through the prairie from Chicago to the towns of Ottawa, La Salle, and Peru was completed. And Chicago was launched as the largest pork, lumber, and grain market in the country.

Perhaps befitting the more mature city, the canal ceremonies were not nearly as raucous as "shovel day" had been. On April 16, 1848, a big passenger packet, the *General Fry*, arrived at Bridgeport on the maiden trip up the canal, met there by a huge but orderly crowd. More significant was the arrival at Lock No. 1 a week later of the *General*

Thornton from New Orleans. Its cargo of sugar and other produce was reloaded on a steamer headed for Buffalo, and its arrival there was announced in a speech on the floor of Congress by young Abraham Lincoln. Joliet's dream of a water route from the Gulf of St. Lawrence to the Gulf of Mexico was finally realized.*

During the first period of canal operations, from 1848 to 1854, Chicago's population rose from just over twenty thousand to almost seventy-five thousand; and both imports and exports soared as farmland was opened all along the one-hundred-mile-long canal corridor. "Chicago really owes its existence to the canal," an early historian wrote. "Its advantageous location was not fully realized until the canal was completed."

The very year the canal was opened, however, Chicago hitched its future to a rival means of transportation. In 1847, the city did not have a single mile of railroad track. Ten years later, it was the rail center of America, and Ogden, who built the city's first railroad, the Galena and Chicago Union, was being hailed as the Railway King of the West.

To win charter rights for the tiny railroad that set in motion these historic changes, Ogden had had to defeat the counterclaim of his former law client Gurdon Hubbard, an action that ended their friendship and reduced Hubbard to a second-level position in the city's ascendant railroad economy. For the city of Chicago as well as for Gurdon Hubbard and William Ogden, 1848 was a decisive year.

---

*The canal, however, was not wide enough or deep enough to handle heavy, waterborne traffic.

4

The Great Chicago
Exchange Engine

1. The Big Junction

MODERN Chicago was born in 1848. In January of that year, the
first telegraph line reached the city, and in succeeding months the Illinois and Michigan Canal was opened, the first oceangoing steamship
arrived from Montreal, Cyrus Hall McCormick, the future "Reaper
King," moved to the city from the Shenandoah Valley, and construction began on Chicago's first railroad and on its first wooden turnpikes
over mud and marsh to grain farms and young market towns on the
prairie. To promote and give direction to the city's exploding economy,
merchants and commission men established the Chicago Board of
Trade in March 1848 in rooms over a flour store near the river. And
later in the year, trade in the two principal commodities bought and
sold in its "pit"—grain and livestock—was given an impetus with the
construction of "Bull's Head" stockyard, Chicago's first cattle yard,
and Capt. Robert C. Bristol's steam-powered grain elevator—a storage
house and distribution point for the golden harvests that wagons, rail
cars, and canal barges began delivering to the city. Finally, in 1848, a
man named William "Deacon" Bross, an itinerant teacher who would
become Chicago's most vigorous promoter, moved to the upstart town
on the lake from northern New Jersey. Bross had come to Chicago after
a study of geography and a tour of the West convinced him it was the
most promising place in America. Before the mud on his boots had

dried, he was predicting it would soon overtake St. Louis as the main city of the mid-continent.

For Bross, a large-built, wild-looking man with blazing eyes and thick black eyebrows, Chicago became not just a home but a crusade. But when he sang Chicago's praises to friends back East in his first years in the West, he was speaking only of its prospects. Chicago, he later admitted, was the filthiest "slab city" he had seen in his travels. Everything was covered with mud after soaking spring rains, and there were no paved streets or sidewalks and no sewers. Nor was there any drainage. Rainwater collected in rancid pools under the new plank roadways, where it was fed by waste runoff from businesses, barns, and overflowing backyard privy vaults. Occasionally, a loose piece of planking would give way under the weight of a passing wagon and "green and black slime," Bross recalled long afterward, "would gush up between the cracks." To keep a check on accumulating garbage that was simply tossed into roadside ditches, scavenging pigs were permitted to run free in the streets.

Roads in and around the city remained impassable for weeks in the spring, bringing business to a virtual standstill. Walking through the city, Bross noticed idle clerks amusing themselves by putting signs in the mud where the last dray had been dug out: No Bottom Here, Gone but Not Forgotten, or On His Way to Lower Regions. With no railroad entering the city, mail came by "propeller" boat or stage from New Buffalo, Michigan, across the lake, the farthest point to which eastern railroads had penetrated by 1848. During fierce storms or in the wet season, when outlying roads were strewn with wrecked Hoosier wagons, "we would be a week or two without any news from the outside world," Bross remembered.

In the summer, when the prairie winds dried the roadways, Chicago's air turned into swirling clouds of dust, and at night, until gaslights were installed in the 1850s, people had to use lanterns to negotiate the dangerously constructed streets, which, with growth and prosperity, began to be filled with criminals, drifters, and rowdy sailors and canal boatmen. This "is as mean a spot as I ever was in, yet," an easterner wrote in his journal, and he found western optimism as hard to swallow as the region's bad coffee. Chicago boasted of being "Queen of the Lakes," but "she sits there on the shore . . . in shabby *deshabille*," Fredrika Bremer offered her cold parting judgment, "[resembling] rather a huckstress than a queen."

Chicago's single greatest asset was the people who were drawn to it—pushing, hustling, hopeful people, many of them "wild, rough, almost savage looking" emigrants from the northern regions of Europe. Most of them arrived from Buffalo by lake boat and headed out to unseen lands after buying supplies in Chicago, but a good number of them, their hopes raised by the brassy city's air of confidence, found jobs and settled in.

John Lewis Peyton, a writer visiting Chicago in 1848, found it a small city in a big hurry, filled with a "restless activity" such as he had seen nowhere else in the West, "except in Cincinnati." After touring the mud-bound town, he had dinner at William Ogden's clapboard "mansion," and there he met a group of the city's surprisingly young civic leaders, including the new Democratic senator from Illinois, Stephen A. Douglas, who had moved to Chicago with his wife the previous year and, with Ogden and his friends, was "determined," he told Peyton, "to build here . . . the finest City of the West."

•

These were the men who had promoted and then saved the canal project, but their city's future, they agreed, was with the railroad, the invention of the age. "The modern world began with the coming of the railways," the historian Nicolas Faith argued. "They made a greater and more immediate impact than any other mechanical innovation before or since." From the time the world's first public railway was built in 1825 by George Stephenson, railroads were seen as carriers of progress—miracle workers, people called them—and they opened up entire regions of the earth—Siberia, the Argentine pampas, and the American Midwest. "The development of the [prairies] by means of a railway is such, that what was yesterday waste land is to-day a valuable district," the Scotsman James Stirling wrote in the 1850s. "There is thus action and reaction; the railway improves the land; the improvement pays for the railway. . . . There is nothing in history to compare with this . . . progress of civilization."

By the opening of the Civil War, more railroads met at Chicago than at any other spot on the globe, making it the "Big Junction," or linkage point, of the national economy. A city created by the canal, Chicago tied its economic livelihood to the locomotive, and railroads came to dominate the cityscape. Their tracks were Chicago's capillaries and arteries, and they crisscrossed the entire town, converging at the juncture of the river, the canal, and the lake—Chicago's port and central business district—where freight was carried by smoke-belching "iron agencies" to waiting grain elevators, canal barges, and lake steamers and where incoming passengers disembarked at tremendous train sheds filled with steam clouds and noise and packed with people from all walks of life and every corner of the globe—salesmen, immigrants, cattle kings, and confidence men. "Chicago does not go to the world," boasted the *Chicago Times*. "The world comes to Chicago."

England invented the railroad, but by 1840 over half of the railroad tracks in the world had been laid in America, and in that year the country was about to embark on a half-century-long program of railroad building that was the largest construction enterprise since the Roman Empire. In these decades, Americans became enthralled by the speed and transforming power of the steam engine. Locomotives could roam across the entire landscape, scaling mountains and tearing across rough country no artificial waterway could pass through. And they ran in the dead of winter, when northern canals froze up and shut down. On level land, they were also cheaper and easier to build than canals. "There seems a natural, pre-ordained fitness between the railway and the prairies," James Stirling explained, "for the prairie is as eminently suited to the formation of railways, as railways are essential to the development of prairies."

On the expansive prairies, the locomotives' speed could be truly appreciated as they rocketed across endless acres of grass and cropland, excited farm children racing to the tracks to wave to the blue-capped engineers. Through all of history, travel had never been faster than a galloping horse, but now "space is killed by the railways," the German writer Heinrich Heine noted, "and we are left with time alone."

To William Ogden, railroads meant more than power and money for himself and rising Chicago. He had a vision of railroad expansion that transcended personal gain, of a corridor through the continent that would open the West and link its development and destiny with the Northeast, creating a strong and united nation. Ogden lived to see his dream take shape when the Union Pacific met the Central Pacific at a point in the Promontory Mountains of northern Utah on May 10, 1869, completing the world's first transcontinental railroad, with Chicago as its principal eastern terminus. The driving of the famous "Golden Spike" made Ogden, the first president of the Union Pacific, a nation builder, not merely a city builder, and capped his career as the country's "first great railroad man."

•

When Ogden began his career as a railroad builder in 1848, the Chicago city government would not invest a single cent of the public treasury in railroads. Nor would it for the entire century. It didn't have to. The railroads came to Chicago, anyway.

Chicago possessed the great geographic advantage of being on the southern rim of an inland sea that penetrated deep into the continent, imposing an impassable barrier to land transport along the shortest route from the East to the far West and the Northwest. Lake Michigan—the remains of Ice Age Lake Chicago—forced railroads bound for these areas to go around its southern tip and into the city built on its smooth-bottomed basin of clay.

It was water, ironically, that guaranteed Chicago's place as the nation's railroad hub. With the completion of the Erie Canal and the Illinois and Michigan Canal, Chicago's location on the terminus of an all-water route between New York and the Gulf of Mexico, the longest inland waterway in the world, made it virtually certain the city would become a major rail center. Chicago is the ideal example of the unassailable economic combination of rail and water. Wherever nineteenth-century railroads met an important navigable stretch of water, urban growth invariably occurred, with eastern money promoting it heavily. But eastern capital did not make Chicago a national railroad hub without Chicago's considerable help. Atlantic Coast capitalists would not invest in Chicago railroads until William Ogden demonstrated to them that they could be built and run profitably. The vigorous entrepreneurial action of Ogden and his city associates, a group of men that included Walter L. Newberry, J. Young Scammon, and Isaac N. Arnold, ensured that Chicago would become *the* main railroad center of the Midwest and hastened the inevitable coming of the eastern railroads. As the *Tribune* wrote of Ogden on the occasion of his death: "No one else in the history of the city better understood its prime commercial position, and no one did more to influence the world to appreciate it." With the construction of Ogden's Galena and Chicago Union Railroad, events were set in motion that forever changed Chicago and much of the rest of the country.

In 1846, Ogden and a group of his wealthy North Side neighbors purchased the charter rights to a moribund railroad that Gurdon Hubbard had tried to revive in the late 1830s. The road was to run from Chicago to Galena, a lead-mining center in northern Illinois that was larger and busier than Chicago into the early 1840s and had therefore been put first in the railroad's name. It was, in part, to interest eastern investors in his railroad that Ogden took the lead in organizing the River and Harbor Convention in the summer of 1847, the first national gathering in what would become America's convention city.

Over ten thousand delegates and onlookers met under an enormous tent in the center of the city to press for federal aid for transportation projects in the west and to protest President James K. Polk's veto of a Rivers and Harbors Appropriation bill that would have provided money for additional improvements to Chicago's harbor. Ogden used the occasion of the convention to present his railroad plans to Atlantic Coast capitalists who had come to Chicago to assess its investment possibilities. He found them still cautious, however, about putting money in a city and a state notorious for their speculative excesses; and he discovered, to his surprise, that many of his fellow Chicago businessmen did not want a railroad. Retail merchants feared that a railroad would actually hurt the city's trade by allowing farmers to ship crops to town instead of hauling them in by ox-drawn wagon and stay- ing for a stretch of days to buy supplies and patronize the city's grow- ing number of hotels, saloons, and bawdy houses. They saw plank roads, privately built toll roads made of oak strips nailed to crossties— "the poor man's railroad"—as the answer to the city's transportation problems in areas the canal did not reach.

Unable to raise sufficient money in Chicago or in the East, Ogden and J. Young Scammon went out to solicit stock subscriptions from farmers and merchants along the proposed route of their railroad. Traveling by horse and buggy over rutted roads that were their strongest selling point for a railroad, Ogden and Scammon called on people in lead-mining towns and sleepy hamlets, convincing farmers' wives to buy single shares of stock on a monthly installment plan with money earned from selling butter and eggs and their husbands to pur- chase shares with money borrowed from Chicago grain dealers. By the spring of 1848 Ogden and his associates had sold over $350,000 worth of stock, not nearly enough to complete the road but enough, Ogden decided, to begin laying track and buying rolling stock.

A recalcitrant city council, controlled by local merchants, refused Councilman Ogden's request to build a depot in town, so construction of the line had to begin at the corner of Kinzie and Halsted, then the western edge of Chicago. Ogden did get council permission, however, to put down temporary tracks from this point to the Chicago River in order to bring the Pioneer, a secondhand "steam horse" that arrived by lake vessel that October, to the head of the road. Joseph Kirkland called it "the first of the mighty army of iron giants which have made Chicago," but it was a small, precariously built contraption weighing only ten tons and with a single pair of driving wheels; and it ran at a speed of barely sixteen miles per hour over unstable, metal-capped wooden track.

On November 20 it made its first run, a "flying trip" to the end of its eight-mile-long line, with the company's directors and lending stock- holders on board in rigged-up seats in its freight cars. When it steamed back from the Des Plaines River with a load of wheat it had picked up from a farmer traveling by ox wagon to the city, Chicago was on its way to becoming Carl Sandburg's "player with railroads"—"the big city far off, where all the trains ran."

A week later, city merchants were "electrified" to learn that more than thirty loads of wheat were waiting at the Des Plaines to be hauled into town, and the city council lifted its ban on the railroad. Ogden moved at once to build an engine house on the north branch of the river and, later, a new depot on North Water Street, with a drawbridge across the Chicago River. Chicago had its first railroad, the only one in its history controlled and backed by city entrepreneurs.

The Galena and Chicago Union Railroad made money from its first day of operation, and in the 1850s, Ogden expanded the line into the wheatlands to the north and west of the city, all the way to the Mississippi and up into Wisconsin. Eventually, he incorporated it into a vast 860-mile system, the Chicago and North Western Railway, Chicago's "great wheat feeder." By this time, Ogden was a deskbound railroad president, but local legend has it that in the early years of his Galena and Chicago Union, he would head down to the Halsted Street depot at the break of light, climb to its second-story cupola, and with a long marine telescope, sight the smoke of his train coming in over the empty flatlands.*

In succeeding years, eastern investors, operating through Ogden and other agents in Chicago, built a spreading network of rail lines to the north, south, and west of the city, into vast hardwood forests, deep minefields of bituminous coal, and the largest region of continuously fertile land in the world. William Bross boasted that all roads led *to* Chicago, but he could have just as accurately said that all roads led *from* Chicago, since the city became the center for planning and constructing railroads in the West. Low-volume western railroads ran from Chicago to all the major points in its resource hinterland, picking up business "by driblets," a government railroad report described the system, and feeding it through Chicago to high- volume trunk lines pointed to eastern port cities. Chicago became the link binding together coastal markets and western resources into a single chain of enterprise. In this capacity, it soon replaced St. Louis, as Bross predicted it would, as the gateway city to the West. Chicago "lays tribute on all the regions of the continent," a geographer would characterize the imperial city's mature economy, "and through the ports of the Atlantic, Pacific, and Gulf, on all the regions of the world."

---

*The Pioneer remained in active service on repair crews until after the Civil War and was put on display in 1893 in Louis Sullivan's Transportation Building at the Columbian Exposition.

By 1857, Chicago was the center of the largest railroad network in the world, consisting of three thousand miles of track. Almost a hundred trains entered and left the city every day, and wherever its trains went, they changed frontier to hinterland and brought to the city the multiplying products of farms and forests. As Chicago became urban, its surrounding landscape became rural. At the same time that enterprising capitalists were building factories, meatpacking plants, and gigantic grain elevators on the banks of the Chicago River, farmers were plowing up prairie sod, and lumberjacks were cutting the forests of Wisconsin and Michigan and sending their lumber by lake ships to the port of Chicago, where it was unloaded and then reshipped by canal and rail to prairie sod breakers, giving them the essential material for building civilization in the West. So Chicago, situated on one of the most treeless landscapes in America, became the busiest lumber center in the world and a city of wood as well, built of the white pine that fire and strong prairie winds—was it nature's revenge?—would ravage in the fall of 1871.

As historian William Cronon points out in *Nature's Metropolis*, his illuminating account of Chicago's place in nature, Chicago and its hinterland were one—they made each other and depended on each other for survival. Out of the interplay between country and city, metropolitan Chicago was formed. In its furious drive for markets and resources, Chicago helped create an integrated city-country system that was the most powerful environmental force in transforming the American landscape since the Ice Age glaciers began their final retreat. To feed Chicago and its tributary cities' insatiable demands, buffalo herds were slaughtered, often by shooting parties firing from the cars of moving trains, seemingly inexhaustible forests were turned into cut over and abandoned tracts of blackened stumps, dozens of wildlife species were destroyed, and magnificent prairie grass, so tall in places that the artist George Catlin had to stand up in his stirrups to look out over it, gave way to factory-like feedlots where livestock were fattened before being sent to Chicago to be slaughtered. These were the environmental costs of Chicago's expansion, costs that were considered unavoidable and necessary by most Americans at that time.

Ogden and other early investors in Chicago railroads had a clear understanding of a city's relationship with its hinterland as a symbiotic process, something that historians failed to see for many years. As the city transformed its tributary regions, these regions, in turn, transformed the city, with the railroad the principal agency of both changes. An astute observer of Illinois history in the making, John Dean Caton witnessed firsthand the mutually reinforcing process of city-country building, the "action and reaction" process that James Stirling saw at work in railroad construction on the prairie.

Caton liked to grouse hunt in La Salle County, and when work was suspended on the Illinois and Michigan Canal in 1838, he watched laid-off canal diggers pack sacks of cornmeal in wheelbarrows "and, followed by their wives and little ones," head out into unbroken prairie, where, with spades, they cut up sod to make crude shelters. Twenty years later, with the completion of the canal and the arrival of the railroad, these forlorn sod huts had been replaced by "neat farmhouses . . . fine barns, herds of cattle and horses in the pastures, and great crops of grain in the fields." And with railroad and canal building, the city grew and changed as rapidly as its "contributory areas," with pioneering urban builders, like Caton himself, overcoming physical obstacles as daunting as those that confronted the La Salle County sodbusters with whom he formed lifelong acquaintances.

Caton was one of the first men in the West to take an interest in telegraphy and in 1857 became the principal owner of all the telegraph lines in Illinois and Iowa. By 1865, when he transferred these properties to Western Union on terms that made him a rich man, the railroad, developed hand in hand with telegraph services, had completely transformed Chicago.

The railroad city of that year was not simply larger and wealthier than the canal town of 1848; it had the look and feel of modernity. "All is astir here," observed the popular writer Sara Jane Lippincott in 1871. "There is no such thing as stagnation or rest. Lake-winds and prairie-winds keep the very air in commotion. You catch the contagion of activity and enterprise, and have wild dreams of beginning life again, and settling—no, circulating, *whirling*—in Chicago, the rapids and wild eddies of business have such a powerful fascination for one." A town built on wilderness swamps and clay banks a mere four decades earlier, Chicago now had a population of over 300,000, scores of luxurious hotels and magnificent marble stores and residences, great warehouses and docks, and "street railways traversing the city in all directions, carrying annually 7,000,000 passengers," Lippincott breathlessly informed readers in her travel book *New Life in New Lands*. Lippincott called Chicago "the lightning city," pronouncing its railroad-inspired growth "one of the most amazing things in the history of modern civilization."

•

The city of Chicago may not have given a single cent of its tax revenue to the railroads, but it handed over to them something far more precious—its very land, air, and water. Railroads were the uncontrolled colossi of Chicago development, and they had an unlicensed right of way to go anywhere and build anywhere in the city. In no other American city did railroads play a more decisive economic role, or cause greater environmental and civic problems. Like modern urban freeways, railways cut right through the heart of the central city, destroying neighborhoods, fouling the air, and endangering pedestrians and horse-drawn wagons at unmarked grade-level crossings. In the absence of social planning or regulation, railroads were permitted—invited is more like it—to turn great areas of the city into a smoky wasteland of freight and storage yards that it would have made more economic sense to locate on the outlying prairie, where they are today.

The railroad that had the earliest and longest-lasting effect on Chicago's physical environment was the formidable Illinois Central. Chicago lacked the money to build it, but Chicago politicians Stephen A. Douglas and "Long John" Wentworth and Chicago publicist John Stephen Wright, a close friend of William Bross's, were greatly responsible for its creation.

•

In the fall of 1833, Stephen A. Douglas, the first Chicago politician to make a name for himself nationally, arrived in Meredosia, a struggling village on the Illinois River. A Vermont youth of twenty, he had dreams of becoming an important western lawyer and statesman, though he stepped off the stagecoach that day with only five dollars in his pocket. That June, he had left his widowed mother and, with his patrimony of three hundred dollars, "started for the 'great west,'" he later recalled, "without having any particular place of destination in view." Illinois became his new home because that's where he ran out of money.

Finding no work in Meredosia, he walked to nearby Winchester, where he had been told farmers needed a school for their children. That December, he opened a country school, reading for the law and arguing politics in the village store on lonely prairie evenings. Four years later, he was the state's attorney for Morgan County and at twenty-four was elected to the state legislature, where he had his first debate with a tall, slim Illinoisan named Abraham Lincoln. By this time, he was known locally as "the Little Giant," a squat, fresh-faced orator of volcanic energy with an inborn instinct for politics.

People thought him born to his calling. "It was as natural and spontaneous with him to reason, to argue, to seek to convince, as it is to all men to eat," a man who knew him at this time remarked. He also gained a reputation as a passionate promoter of the interests of his region. "I have become a *Western* man," he wrote his family, "have imbibed Western feelings, principles and interests and have selected Illinois as the favorite place of my adoption."

Douglas saw the railroad as the key to the future of the West and, after serving on the state supreme court and in the House of Representatives, was elected to the U.S. Senate in 1846 on a platform calling for the federal government to cede public lands to the state, as it had with the Illinois and Michigan Canal project, to help pay for construction of a Central Railroad running north and south across Illinois and extending all the way to the Gulf of Mexico. This was part of Douglas's nationalistic vision of a stupendous rail system that would bind together large sections of the country and kill off growing sentiment in the South for separation.

The first stretch of the Central Railroad was to run from Cairo, at the juncture of the Ohio and Mississippi Rivers, to Galena, but after moving to Chicago in 1847, Douglas proposed that a "branch" line be built from Centralia to Chicago. In anticipation of the branch becoming the trunk of the system, he bought extensive land in and around the city where the railroad was likely to build. Although Douglas and Ogden considered him too volatile to work with closely, no one promoted the new railroad more vigorously than John Stephen Wright. At his own expense, he distributed nationally some six thousand circulars, each bearing a petition to Congress urging support for the "Douglas Plan"; and when the bill was about to come up on the floor, Wright moved to Washington to personally lobby for it. After the legislation authorizing the railroad land grant—the first of its kind—passed the Senate, Daniel Webster, with extensive real estate holdings in Illinois, worked with John Wentworth to line up northeastern congressmen, who were also being pressured by powerful home-district investors in Chicago holdings. On September 20, 1850, a message went out over the telegraph wires from Washington to Chicago announcing President Millard Fillmore's signing of the Central Railroad bill. The following year, the Illinois Central Railroad Company began constructing what Douglas called "one of the most gigantic enterprises of the age."

In 1856 the 705-mile-long railroad from Chicago to Cairo, the longest in the world, began regular service, and Chicago immediately felt its impact. Trade on the upper Mississippi that had previously gone downriver to St. Louis was rerouted by rail to Chicago, whose boosters began calling the Illinois Central "the St. Louis cutoff." In addition, the railroad began using its two and a half million acres to create its own economic lifeline, "colonizing" the previously empty central-eastern prairie with settlers recruited from as far away as Norway. Thirty-five thousand farming families were eventually sold land along the railroad's Y-shaped corridor, and the "IC" gathered up their tribute and forwarded it to Chicago.

When the Central Railroad project was first proposed, both Galena, whose only resource was its lead mines, and Cairo, a pesthole of river mud and squalor, had dreams of becoming the leading city of the state. But when lead mining dried up in Galena, the Illinois Central established its northern terminus on the Mississippi, across from Dubuque Iowa, while downstate farmers sent their crops and livestock not to Cairo but to Chicago, where the thriving lake trade with the East guaranteed them the best prices in the region for both what they sold and what they bought. The closely contested trade war between the state's cities that was expected to break out with the building of the Central Railroad turned into a full-scale rout; and Douglas, Wentworth, and Wright, along with hundreds of other speculators in Chicago real estate, saw the value of their holdings soar in what became the city's second great land boom.

•

A railroad war of another kind occurred in Chicago itself as a result of one of Douglas's real estate deals with the Illinois Central. Douglas sold land to the railroad in the Lake Calumet area, south of the city, and when the Illinois Central's directors requested access to Chicago's inner harbor from this point along the line of the lake, they set off a hotly contested legal struggle that continued into the next century and greatly influenced the physical shape of the modern city. At issue was the preservation of Chicago's undeveloped lakeshore along South Michigan Avenue, from near the mouth of the river all the way to the city's southern boundary on Twenty-second Street. In almost every other waterfront city in industrializing America, choice land along the water's edge was appropriated by manufacturing and transportation concerns and transformed into an unsightly wall of development that closed off the city from its most picturesque natural feature and despoiled its aquatic life and drinking water with the garbage, slag, ash, and chemical runoff from its mills and refineries. By 1850, this was already happening to the Chicago River, but the lakefront had thus far been saved from this fate by three men who had refused to bow to speculative pressure: William F. Thornton, William B. Archer, and Gurdon Saltonstall Hubbard.

Back in 1836 they were canal commissioners charged by the state of Illinois with supervising the sale of canal lands, one of the more valuable lots being a narrow strip running along the lake south of Fort Dearborn, where Jean Baptiste Beaubien had built his trader's cabin.

In land-grabbing Chicago that thin parcel would have commanded a fine price, but the commissioners decided to set it aside for public use, marking the lakefront side of their real estate map with the now famous words "Public Ground—A Common to Remain Forever Open, Clear, and Free of Any Buildings, or Other Obstruction Whatever."

Chicago today has one of the most magnificent waterfronts in the world, a chain of sandy beaches, curving walkways, and generous greenswards, largely because of that decision. It was a pledge that Chicago's most valuable land "by right belongs to the people," as Daniel Hudson Burnham put it in his 1909 Chicago Plan, "[giving them] their one great unobstructed view, stretching away to the horizon, where water and clouds seem to meet." It was a pledge, however, that was kept only because concerned Chicagoans were willing to fight in the courts and the state legislature for nearly half a century for a clear and free lakefront.

The battle for the lakefront appeared lost forever in 1852 when the city council granted the Illinois Central's request to drive its line of track straight across Chicago's "front yards." At the time, however, this was seen by many Chicago taxpayers as the answer to a potentially expensive civic problem. Strong storms and currents had badly eroded the canal commissioners' Lakefront Park, a popular promenade for wealthy South Siders, who had built their houses on Michigan Avenue, directly fronting the park and the lake. In winter and spring, gales sent tremendous walls of water across Michigan Avenue and right against their front doors, but the common council was unwilling to raise taxes—already considered alarmingly high—for offshore barricades. Its recently instituted method of funding municipal works was to have the owners of real estate that derived "particular benefits" from such improvements pay for them by means of a special tax assessment. When the owners of the princely town houses facing the lake refused to pay for such a special levy, insisting that lakefront protection was a general public responsibility, the city council, on the advice of Douglas and Wentworth, cut a deal with the Illinois Central, giving it a lakefront right-of-way to the terminal and freight complex it had just purchased on the old Fort Dearborn estate in exchange for construction of the badly needed dikes and breakwaters.

Thanks to the canal commissioners' civic foresight, the land the city ceded to the Illinois Central was at the bottom of the lake, not on its shoreline. The IC would have to enter Chicago on a trestle built several hundred feet offshore, the two-mile-long stretch of stone cribs and breakwaters it agreed to build protecting both its elevated tracks and Chicago's damaged shoreline. When this deal was agreed to in the railroad's New York offices by Douglas and city officials, they tried to appease the barons of Michigan Avenue by getting the railroad to fill in the land between its seawall and the shore so that the city could create a new park and promenade. But IC officials flatly rejected the idea. The IC's attorney put the company's position in the bluntest terms: "Railroads are *not* constructed for the purpose of *building* cities, nor of *adorning* cities, nor of *repairing* the damages they may have suffered from fire and water. . . ." A lakefront promenade "would be as palpable a perversion of [company] funds," he scolded the city officials, "as though the same amount were donated to the city for . . . endowing institutions of Charity."

Writing sometime later, Joseph Kirkland echoed the feelings of many city taxpayers when he insisted that the IC, in return for transit rights through "pathless waves," had provided Chicago with a "grand benefaction"—not just the breakwater but a basin it formed between its high stone barricades and Michigan Avenue, a basin, he claimed, that was used by Chicagoans for sailing, swimming, skating, and rowing. Ungrateful Chicago "pocketed the benefit and forgot its source."

City groups in favor of a lakefront park saw the matter differently, however, and fought every effort by the railroad to extend its riparian rights, a battle that was finally won in the courts at the turn of the century, opening the way for Daniel Burnham's vast shoreline improvements. But for decades after the Chicago Compromise of 1852, the city's southern lakefront remained the principality of the Illinois Central Railroad. The trains it sent steaming across its Lake Michigan trestle, turning the lakefront into a sooty industrial corridor, were an hourly reminder of who owned Chicago. The railroad received court permission to use additional submerged land at the river's mouth to create a landfill extension of its terminal, storage, and docking facilities, and Joseph Kirkland's bucolic basin was turned into a still pool filled with industrial debris, floating packing crates, and the bloated corpses of horses and cattle.

To the south, this basin ran right up against the Illinois Central's tightly massed industrial staging area, part of one of the great economic exchange engines of the age—Chicago's river-harbor complex. The *Times* (London) reporter William H. Russell described the view from a window of an incoming passenger train in 1861: "As we approach . . . Chicago, the prairie subside[s] . . . and when the train, leaving the land altogether, dashes out on a pier and causeway built along the borders of the lake, we see lines of noble houses, a fine boulevard, a forest of masts, huge isolated piles of masonry, the famed grain elevators by which so many have been hoisted to fortune, churches and public edifices, and the apparatus of a great city; and just at nine o'clock the train gives its last steam shout and comes to a standstill in the spacious station of the Central Illinois Company."

2. The Mechanical Man

When William H. Russell stepped down from his train on the spot where Gurdon Hubbard had approached the whitewashed walls of Fort Dearborn in 1818, he could see just across the river the busy Reaper Works of Cyrus Hall McCormick, connected by a rail spur to William Ogden's westward-pointing Galena and Chicago Union Railroad. Ogden had gone into partnership with McCormick when the Virginian arrived in the city with a letter of introduction from Stephen A. Douglas. His railroad carried McCormick's shining red harvesters to farmers all along its line and brought back to the city, to the great grain houses in the river harbor, the wheat they cut with a speed that was truly astonishing.

McCormick's four-story brick factory was one of the first industrial concerns in the city and by far the largest, employing about 120 men, and much of its machinery was driven by a thirty-horsepower engine that locals considered one of the marvels of the age. A reporter for the *Chicago Daily Journal* ran a story of the factory under the headline "The Magic of Machinery": "Glistening like a knight in armor, the engine . . . works as silently as the 'little wheel' of the matron; but shafts plunge, cylinders revolve, bellows heave, iron is twisted into screws like wax, and saws dash off at a rate of forty pounds a second, at one movement of its mighty muscles." The writer went on to describe what he considered the central and most paradoxical scene in this cacophonous theater of modern machinery. "There by the furnace fire, begrimed with coal and dust, decorated with an apron of leather . . . stands the one who controls—nay, who can create the whole."

Barely ten years before this story was written, Cyrus McCormick, wearing a leather apron and standing over a much smaller furnace fire, was making his reapers, with the help of a black slave, in a log smithy shop on his father's Virginia plantation, where ten years before that he had invented the machine—"the mechanical man"—that broke the centuries-long sway of the sickle and the scythe over the harvest fields of the world.

On a steamy summer afternoon in 1831, a few Rockbridge County farmers watched a crude-looking contraption pulled by a horse carve through a field of ripe yellow grain. Its vibrating steel blade cut the stalks of wheat easily, and the machine's twenty-two-year-old builder walked at a quick pace beside it, raking the cut grain from its platform. No one in that Virginia field that day, not even Cyrus McCormick, realized that the invention on public display for the first time would work a revolution in wheat cultivation.

Cyrus McCormick's father, Robert, had been trying to invent a reaping machine for almost twenty years, and his son's invention was an extension of his efforts. Although Cyrus McCormick continued to give field demonstrations, he didn't take out a patent until 1834, after hearing that another reaper had been invented by Obed Hussey, an ex-whaler from Nantucket. It was not until the family's iron business came close to bankruptcy in the Panic of 1837 that McCormick gave his "whole soul" to his reaper, as a Virginia neighbor characterized the beginnings of a "from then to death" obsession. By 1842, he had improved his machine and was making and selling copies from the plantation on which he had been born.

Two years later, orders arrived from the West for seven reapers, and McCormick set out for the Ohio Valley and the flatlands beyond with three hundred dollars in his belt to look into the possibility of building his factory closer to the westward-shifting center of American grain production. At harvesttime in Illinois, he saw hogs and cattle turned loose to feed in fields of ripe grain for want of laborers to gather in the crop. Grain must be harvested quickly—within four to ten days—or it will break down and decay, and with harvest hands scarce and expensive, these farmers were helpless before the vagaries of nature.

The Midwest's level, labor-hungry lands seemed a natural home for McCormick's "mechanical man," and he decided to relocate his entire operation to Chicago. He had met Stephen A. Douglas through a Virginia congressman and, with Douglas, was convinced that Chicago would soon surpass Buffalo as the major grain port of the country now that rail and canal projects were under way. Chicago was also a young city, only as old as his reaper, and he thought his business would grow with it. In 1847 he began building his riverside factory, and the following year, he moved permanently to Chicago, convincing his two brothers, William and Leander (their father had died), to follow him. After buying out William Ogden, he launched a far-flung family business similar to that which Henry Ford, another midwestern farmer-inventor, would establish a half century later.

By 1860, he was making over four thousand reapers a year, and these primitive machines reoriented and greatly accelerated the settlement of the state. Until the 1850s almost all settlers in Illinois dwelled in strips of woodland along the rivers, leaving the "prairie ocean" to the most audacious pioneers, who had the greatest difficulty scouring its thick, adhesive soil with cast-iron plows with wooden moldboards. With John Deere's steel plow, invented in 1837, farmers could more easily open up for cultivation the mineral-rich prairie loam; and with McCormick's new machine, they could reap as much as they sowed.

Wheat acreage doubled in areas where the reaper was used, and the reaper stimulated investment in other farm machinery. By 1860, Illinois was the leading state in the country in grain production and the fourth largest in population, behind New York, Pennsylvania, and Ohio. And this great granary was "mowed and reaped by machines made in Chicago."

McCormick continued to prosper through and after the Civil War, improving his reaper and successfully battling waves of competitors who entered the farm-implement business. His firm's success was not due to the introduction of progressive factory technology, as historians long supposed. Cyrus's brother Leander ran the Chicago reaper works like an enlarged country blacksmith shop, depending on the skills of machinists, woodworkers, and blacksmiths. But while the production end of the business relied on traditional practices of manufacture, the selling end, which Cyrus McCormick personally presided over, pioneered new methods of doing business. Cyrus Hall McCormick invented not only the reaper but also a modern business system.

Jettisoning the ancient practice of getting what you could for your product by sharp bargaining—a system revealingly known as "let the buyer beware"—McCormick sold reapers at a fixed price—$120, "take it or leave it!" He was also among the first to use deferred payments, extensive advertising, and written guarantees. In the 1850s farmers unable to pay in cash could put down thirty dollars on delivery and were given six months to clear the balance at 6 percent interest. If crops were bad or times were hard, they were granted an extension at an interest rate of 10 percent. If the machine broke down or failed to cut one and a half acres in an hour, it could be returned for the purchase price, no questions asked. One Price to All and Satisfaction Guaranteed was McCormick's simple sales motto.

But a $120 piece of equipment was expensive for a farmer new on his land, and in the early years of his business McCormick also had to overcome skepticism about the claims he made about his machine. So advertising became important to his firm's survival. "To sell, I must advertise," he said. He ran ads in farmers' periodicals filled with the testimonials of satisfied customers and of people farmers were likely to respect, such as William Ogden, who touted McCormick's reaper as the best on the market. These ads featured a woodcut showing how the machine worked and an easy-to-follow order blank. McCormick also hired commission agents to sell reapers all over the West. They were trained to assemble and repair them and teach farmers how to use them. They were among the first of a growing army of traveling sales-men sent out wherever the railroad went to hawk Chicago products.

McCormick was a tall, heavy man with a massive head, a full beard, and an imperious manner—"a great commercial Thor," one of his bi-ographers called him. He had no hobbies or recreations and no great interests besides his business, and he took absolute joy in defeating his rivals—at "field trials" of reaper machines at county fairs and in the courts, where he was forever tied up in costly litigation over patent rights.

He didn't drink, smoke, or swear and was at his desk at dawn and was often still there at midnight. When he died in 1884, his last words, uttered in a stupor, were "work, work!" And when he lay in state in his Rush Street mansion, there was a Virginia reaper at his feet, modeled from white flowers, and on his breast a sheaf of yellow wheat.

He left as his legacy one of the great manufacturing concerns in the world, predecessor of the International Harvester Company (now Nav-istar), formed in 1902 with his son as president. When Cyrus Hall Mc-Cormick moved to Chicago in 1848, the wheat-production center of the country was just south of Rochester, New York. Ten years later, it was in the Mississippi Valley, the chief food-producing region on the planet, and Chicago was known everywhere as the Great Reaper City.

3. *Stacker of Wheat and Wood, Packer of Pork*

From the time McCormick built his factory at the point where the canal, the lake, and the river intersected, the reaper and the railroad worked in beautifully complementary fashion. Every reaper sent by rail to the country became a feeder for the city. The reaper gave farm-ers the weapon they needed to gain wealth from the tall-grass country, and by 1856 that prairie prosperity allowed Chicago, Sandburg's "Stacker of Wheat," to overtake the Russian cities of Archangel and Odessa as the greatest primary grain port in the world.

The reaper was part of a nineteenth-century revolution in cereal production that also involved a complete change in the techniques of moving, storing, and trading grain. Chicago was at the center of this transformation as well, developing a grain-elevator system that was the most important advance in the history of the world's grain trade.

The command center of the new grain system was on the banks of the Chicago River, close by the McCormick reaper factory, where, by 1858, twelve mammoth "grain houses" dominated the skyline, huge, slate-surfaced storage sheds rising higher than the steeples of the city's churches. They were Chicago's first skyscrapers, symbols of its supremacy in wheat, the commodity that catapulted the city to world prominence as a trading center. The largest of the grain elevators were the twin towers of Sturges and Buckingham and Company that William H. Russell had spotted from the rail trestle of the Illinois Central. Built under agreement with the Illinois Central, each of them was 120 feet high, with a capacity of 700,000 bushels, and could handle a golden stream of grain almost noiselessly and with little hand labor. In what was one of the world's first automated industries, four giant steam engines in each building did what would have previously taken hundreds of men to do.

Visiting the vast grain exchange and storage complex of Sturges and Buckingham in 1862, Anthony Trollope, son of Frances Trollope, author of *Domestic Manners of the Americans*, called it the home of "the American Ceres." Rail lines fed directly into the rear of each of the harbor-front buildings, and an endless power-driven conveyor belt equipped with buckets hoisted the grain from the cars to the top of the warehouse, where it was weighed and then dropped into vertical bins. It could then be fed out the other side of the building by gravity into the storage holds of lake vessels. When these long steamers and schooners set out on "the highway of breadstuffs" to Buffalo, Oswego, or Montreal, they could be seen by the new grain-exchange nobility as they shaved at the bedroom windows of their Michigan Avenue mansions.

Trollope described for his British readers only one part of the Chicago grain-elevator system. Behind the new industrial architecture was a new way of trading grain. This trading system appeared first in Chicago because the railroad and the lake, the merging of nature and technology, made it the largest inland market for grain, the mainstay of the American and European diet, and because of Chicago's role as a receiving, storage, and transfer point—not a processing center—for grain being forwarded to lake ports in the East. Before 1850, most wheat arrived in Chicago in wagons and was transported from farm to flour mill in sacks to prevent it from spoiling. These sacks were unloaded by hand and piled on the streets, where harried sellers and buyers sought out one another and made their deals. The contracted grain was then carried by draymen to warehouses, where wheat harvested in the fall waited all winter for the lakes to thaw, water-transport costs of bulk items going east being far cheaper than railroad charges until much later in the century.

Chicago's rail lines into the wheatlands changed all this. Railroads carried grain quickly, safely, and in large quantities; and by 1852 they outstripped the combined traffic in wheat of wagons and the canal, with the burden of the city's wheat shipments arriving on the cars of the Galena and Chicago Union. Great piles and "bursting bags" of wheat were everywhere around the South Water Street marketplace and warehouses, choking the streets and raising clouds of yellow and brown powder. This enormous increase in grain—from under 2 million bushels in 1850 to over 50 million bushels in 1861—created a radical need for more warehouses and for a quicker method of storing and selling it.

Here William Ogden and the railroad men led the way. To run their businesses profitably, they needed to get their cars unloaded and back into service as fast as possible. One way was to carry the wheat in loose bulk instead of in sacks and to store it in steam-powered grain elevators, which were first developed in Buffalo but perfected in Chicago by railroad companies working in tandem with powerful grain dealers. Capt. Robert C. Bristol's steam-driven elevator, Chicago's first, was a four-story building with a capacity of eighty thousand bushels, tiny by comparison with the elevators built a few years later by Sturges and Buckingham, which had the capacity to feed Chicago's population for five years. In the 1840s it had taken an Irish crew all day to load a boat with seven thousand bushels of wheat. In the 1850s that same amount of grain could be loaded in an hour by one man at the elevators of the Galena and Chicago Union.

To speed the handling process even further—time being "the great item with commercial men"—a method had to be found to store the wheat of different sellers—hitherto kept in separate bins to identify its ownership—in larger common bins. In 1857 the Chicago Board of Trade found a way, introducing a system of categorizing wheat by "grade" and setting standards of quality for each grade—"Spring Wheat," "White Winter Wheat," "Inferior Spring Wheat," etc. Now wheat of different owners could be mixed in a single vertical bin set aside expressly for one category, or grade, of grain. When the owner placed his cargo of grain in the elevator, he carried away a warehouse receipt redeemable by anyone holding it. When the holder went to pick up his grain for delivery, he received not the original lot of grain the seller had placed in the elevator but an exact amount of the same grade and quality. With this system of grading and receipts, the Board of Trade created not just a faster, more profitable way of storing grain but also a new form of currency, backed not by gold but by grain, which in Chicago was as good as gold. This new species of capital became collateral for loans that were used, in turn, to buy more mechanical reapers and build longer railroads and larger elevators.

•

Standardized grading and warehouse receipts also led to the establishment of the world's first modern commodity exchange, a place where commodities, such as grain and hogs, are marketed in the same way that stocks and bonds are on a stock exchange. Trading that had been done in the streets amid mountains of grain was now conducted with small slips of paper in the Board of Trade's long, narrow meeting room on South Water Street. After 1856, the exchange, or 'change, was packed throughout business hours with commission agents for buyers and sellers; and their frenzied trading would spill over after closing hours into the taprooms and lobbies of nearby hotels.

At first, there was no officially established way of trading. Sellers would simply bring a Board of Trade–inspected sample of grain with them, and when a quote was shouted out, the room would explode with excitement as barking, hand-signaling men bid for grain and made verbal deals with each other. When the corridor-like room was no longer able to handle the hundreds of "grain men," the 'change was moved to new quarters at the corner of La Salle and South Water Streets. The "Altar of Ceres," the *Tribune* called the market that became the pulse of the city that claimed to feed the world.

Board of Trade rules standardizing Chicago grades and guaranteeing their quality took much of the uncertainty out of long-distance trading and lured in growing numbers of eastern and European buyers. They also led to speculation on an unprecedented scale. New opportunities for speculation were made possible by "to arrive" contracts calling for delivery of grain at a locked-in price and at a specified future date. While cutting down time-related risks for legitimate buyers and sellers, these contracts brought into the market a host of speculators who were merely interested in trading paper for profit. The result was the appearance in the 1850s of a "futures market," an innovation that changed the entire grain trade.

The game was to try to predict grain prices months in advance and buy and sell on the basis of such estimates. By selling "short," as one form of this licensed gambling came to be known, speculators known as *bears* sought a profit by selling grain (which they had not actually purchased yet) for future delivery at a current market price and then making the delivery with wheat they hoped to be able to buy at a lower price when the contract fell due. Traders who sold "long," on the other hand, bought future contracts in anticipation of rising prices. If the prices went up, these *bulls* sold the contracts on the exchange at a profit.

Speculators, however, rarely exchanged the actual commodity. They simply concluded their agreement by exchanging the differences in cash between the grain's contracted price and its market price at the closure of the contract. Futures trading thus became a denatured, and to many farmers, incomprehensible, process by which professional speculators traded not property but contracts predicting the future *price* of property. The winner in the contest between buyer and seller was the one with the more accurate wager. As one historian has neatly put it: The futures market is a place where "men who don't own something are selling that something to men who don't really want it."

This fevered trading and speculation was made easier by the rapid expansion of the nation's telegraph system. In seconds, deals could be made over the "talking wire" that influenced the economies of dozens of nations, and both buyers and sellers could negotiate with accurate, up-to-the-minute information on economic conditions in markets and production regions hundreds, even thousands, of miles away. When the 'change moved to its new building on La Salle Street, a telegraph office with Morse Code operators was located adjacent to the trading floor, and traders were connected with the "nervous system" of the nation. "Over these wires," a contemporary observed, "one could hear the sharp quick beating of the great heart of New York."

During the Civil War, the Union army's voracious demand for pork and oats to feed men and animals on the move created a futures market in those commodities as well. By that time the Chicago Board of Trade was the largest speculative commodity market in the world.

The railroad and the mechanized elevator that made all this possible tightened the economic bond between country and city, with both places profiting from the relationship. But the partnership was always an uneasy one. As the scope of their operations widened, Chicago's railroad leaders and warehousemen became linked together in the rural mind as a single monster monopoly, "a grand ring," the *Tribune*'s crusading editor Joseph Medill called it, "that wrings the sweat and blood out of the producers of Illinois."

Farmers' grievances about fraud and market manipulation were overstated but legitimate. Elevator operators sometimes defrauded farmers and grain traders by classifying a grain shipment into a lower grade than it actually was, and warehousemen were often caught underweighing shipments with doctored scales. Some railroads and grain elevators also charged rates for shipping and storage that grain farmers and dealers found extortionary. Board of Trade commission men were equally affected by these cutthroat practices of the elevator ring, and in the 1860s and 1870s they joined Grange groups to demand and finally get state regulation of grain elevators, laws upheld by the U.S. Supreme Court in *Munn v. Illinois*, its landmark 1877 ruling.

These same Board of Trade "reformers," however, were attacked by farm groups as parasites and gambling middlemen who made their money on the honest labor of the producing classes. But whatever their feelings about one another, farmers, dealers, traders, warehousemen, and railroad kings were bound together in an interdependent production and exchange system that tremendously increased the market for grain and the opportunities for gain, as well as loss, for all of them.

The reform struggle against the elevators and railroads was portrayed by its aroused rural leaders and, later, historians, as a fight against rapacious monopolists who fed on the helpless farmer. In actuality, however, it was a battle between two groups of capitalists: upstart capitalists—farmers, traders, and speculators fighting for an open, competitive market with equal opportunities for all—and entrenched capitalists, who, although subjected to new regulations, proved powerful enough to resist both a return to free trade and a challenge to their control of the market system. The historian Thomas C. Cochran has called Chicago's development "one of the most purely capitalistic endeavors the world has even known." The story of the rise, the risks, and the reform of the grain-elevator system perfectly exemplifies that profit-powered process of urban—and rural—modernization. It is a story in which there are no innocents, only winners and losers.

•

Wheat was fed into the great Chicago exchange engine by rail and fed out of it by lake boat. And the grain fleets heading up the lake passed lumber fleets heading down to Chicago, where their cargoes were shipped by rail and canal to farmers whose McCormick reapers had set in motion this lucrative trade cycle. Situated on the edge of two different ecosystems, the timber-rich forests of northern Wisconsin and Michigan and the woodless prairies, and built on the water corridor that connected them, Chicago became the leading lumber market of the world by the mid-1850s.

The Chicago lumber trade began in the year the town was incorporated, when a sailing vessel from St. Joseph, Michigan, anchored off the sandbar at the mouth of the river with a cargo of whitewood. That summer, John Dean Caton arrived in the city on one of these lumber yawls. After finding a room in a tavern at Wolf Point, he witnessed the construction of the most substantial building in town with the load of lumber he had come across the lake with and later helped two men build the sawmill on the North Branch of the river that probably supplied the cut timber for Mark Beaubien's Sauganash Hotel. Gurdon Hubbard eventually bought that sawmill, which, with several others, served the local construction trade. By the 1840s, Chicago was also sending out timber by ox-drawn wagon to settlements along Hubbard's Trail. But it was not until the coming of the canal, the railroad, and the reaper—and the settlement of the Grand Prairie that they made possible—that Chicago became a major lumber distributing center.

One of the reasons that prairie homesteads in the 1840s were located almost solely along the watercourses and in occasional forest clusters was that lumber was available there. "Over . . . this great rich prairie," Caton remembered, "not one settler's cabin could be found save only along the borders of the timber. The frontier man did not then believe that the prairies would ever be settled beyond one tier of farms around the groves. The rest, it was supposed, would ever remain an open range for stock which would make it the grazers' paradise."

It was the railroad that transformed these tenantless grasslands into growing grainfields. It brought out from Chicago not only homesteaders, steel plows, and reapers but the lumber without which the prairie could not have been settled. Before 1850, wood was so scarce there that farmers heading home from the Chicago market would tear up pieces of plank board from the toll roads that radiated out from the city and load them in the backs of their wagons. Five years later, the wood-burning timber trains of the Illinois Central and the Chicago and Galena Union were carrying to these same farmers all the wood they needed to build houses, barns, fences, corncribs, schools, and churches—and to heat their hearths and repair the plank turnpikes they had torn up.

By that time, Chicago entrepreneurs were moving to control the supply as well as the distribution of lumber. One of the first of them was William Ogden. In 1856 he acquired over 200,000 acres of pineland on the Peshtigo River in northern Wisconsin and built sawmills, a loggers' village, and a mill town on Green Bay, at the mouth of the Peshtigo River. Within several years he was manufacturing for the Chicago market over 50 million feet of lumber annually.

The majestic white pines his lumbermen cut in the winter harvesting season were hauled on sleds over ice skidways to the Peshtigo

River and then floated down to his sawmills on the spring-swollen stream, with men riding the logs or running alongside them, using poles or long hooks to keep them moving. After being turned into lumber—boards of standard lengths and dimensions—the wood was shipped down the lake to Chicago. This was the way almost all of the conifers of the Great Lakes forest reached their major distribution point from mill towns along the lakeshore, many of them built on piles sunk into marshy soil, their buildings the color of sawdust.

To handle this trade, a far-flung lumber district—a city within the city—grew up along the banks of the Chicago River, extending for miles, all the way from the McCormick Reaper Works to the entrance of the canal at Bridgeport. The Chicago harbor handled the largest lumber fleet in the world, was the largest market for forest products in the world, and had the world's biggest lumberyard. Entire city blocks contained nothing but docks and yards covered with white pine heaped a dozen and more feet high. At the entrance to the canal, diagonal channels led off the river to long wharves lined with graceful schooners and stubby barges, and at the end of every wharf was a railroad siding connecting the wharf's storage yard to every railroad in the city—and from their marshaling yards to the northern, western, and southern reaches of the country and beyond. By 1870, over two hundred lumber boats were arriving in Chicago every twelve hours. They passed through a long succession of swing bridges at a rate of two per minute during peak hours and were unloaded on the docks by lumber shovers wearing leather aprons and leather "guards" to protect the palms of their hands. Even on raw, spring days, the shovers worked stripped to their waists in an industrial arena that resounded with the snorting of switch engines, the hum of planing mills, and the jolting of big lumber wagons on corduroy roads. "Scores of chimneys and stacks," a reporter wrote, "fill the air with smoke, and the breeze carries with it the finer dust of the saw-mills."

The lumber districts became the home of a host of allied industries, including furniture and piano factories, wagon and shipbuilding concerns. There was even a firm that was happy to ship cottages, schoolhouses, stores, taverns, churches, courthouses, or entire towns, wholesale or retail, to any part of the country. Out on the prairie it was not uncommon for groups of homesteaders to gather together at a desolate depot of the Illinois Central to await the arrival from Chicago of their entire "ready-made" village.

Antebellum Chicago was known as the Great Northwestern Exchange, buyer and seller on a spectacular scale but maker of few things besides reapers. By the end of the Civil War, however, almost everything of considerable size used on the railroads, in farming, or in the construction or furnishing of houses was made in Chicago. And historian Alfred T. Andreas, writing in the 1880s, would comment on "how largely the manufactures of the great city," including its flour and grist mills and its breweries and distilleries, "have sprung from the agricultural products of which it is the great mart." This was even more the case with corn and pork than it was with lumber and grain.

•

Pork itself was a by-product of corn. Until the late 1860s the canal was Chicago's principal corn feeder, helping to make the city the world's primary corn market within three years after the opening of navigation. By 1854, however, the Chicago and Rock Island Railroad was competing with the canal along its entire route, an ominous development for the future of artificial water transport. Seven years later, the expansion of the region's railroad network and the Union army's war contracts for salted pork made it more profitable for many western farmers, who were cut off from important markets by Confederate control of the lower Mississippi River, to feed their corn to their hogs and send the hogs by rail to Chicago—and from that animal killing ground to battlefields all across the South as well as to eastern and European markets. "The corn crop is condensed and reduced in bulk by feeding it into an animal form, more portable," a contemporary explained. "The hog eats the corn, and Europe eats the hog. Corn thus becomes incarnate; for what is a hog, but fifteen or twenty bushels of corn on four legs?"

The hogs processed in Chicago in 1864 alone would reach all the way to New York City if placed in single file, bragged city boosters. In that year, Chicago replaced Cincinnati as Porkopolis, the capital of western meatpacking. Meat and bread—together they made modern Chicago.

Expanding markets and expensive new technology made it impossible for pioneer city packers like Gurdon Hubbard to compete with big processing plants built by newcomers like Benjamin P. Hutchinson, or "Old Hutch," as he was called even as a young man. Hubbard and most other antebellum packing and livestock dealers were general merchants with a wide range of business interests, packing being merely one of them. Packing at that time was almost solely confined to pork, as Americans preferred their beef fresh, and it was a seasonal business, restricted to the winter months, when temperatures dropped low enough to safely handle fresh-cut meat. When November approached, Hubbard and other versatile city shippers simply converted their warehouses into pork-packing concerns while continuing to ship east by rail live cattle they received from the West.

This is how the premodern industry was organized when Hutchinson arrived in the city in 1858 from Massachusetts by way of Milwaukee, where he got his start in the packing concern that made Philip Armour a force in the trade. A failed Massachusetts shoemaker, Hutchinson opened a small packing plant in Bridgeport, then the center of Chicago's meat-processing industry, and expanded his business with money he made gambling in grain. In 1858 he bought a seat on the Board of Trade for ten dollars and ten years later was one of the most feared commodity traders in the country, the "Napoleon of Wheat," or more accurately, "The Prince of Scalpers."

> In dealing a 'Change whether little or much,
> All wholesomely fear the insatiate Hutch.

A devoted reader of the classics, he became a student of the history of wheat—the seed of civilization, he called it—and soon knew more about its role in human development than anyone in Chicago. "The very word," he said, "always stimulated my mind. It churned my imagination. Wheat seems so powerful, so vital. There is a thrill in the feel of it, in taking up a handful and letting it sift through the fingers. And if you have ever walked alone through a field of ripening wheat, you may have some feeling of its austere dignity, and its deep imposing solemnity. Wheat is powerfully close to life."

Wheat was also money in the bank if you knew how to trade it. "It was my immediate purpose," Hutchinson said of his earliest intentions in Chicago, "to create a fortune . . . and to have a fund adequate for large speculative drives."

Hutchinson lived for his hours in the trading pit. He arrived at the 'change wearing a threadbare, long-tailed coat, a blue polka-dot neckerchief, doeskin pants that barely reached his ankles, and a black broad-brimmed hat that made him look like a Catholic clergyman. When he bid on commodities, he stood off from the whirling center of action, a tall, lean, fiercely focused figure, his nose bent like the beak of an eagle. And he talked to no one. The Mysterious Stranger, other traders called him.

Hutchinson read almost everything published locally about the wheat trade, rising at 5:00 A.M. to get to the newspaper offices to collect the papers as they came flying off the presses. But it was his cold audacity more than his close knowledge of the markets that made him

a fortune—and that ruined him in the end. After failing as a speculator in his eccentric old age—his luck changed, was his simple explanation—he opened a small tobacco shop across from the Board of
Trade building, where he would sit in a back room sipping whiskey
and swapping stories with old trading cronies. He had no regrets, he
said. He had come to the 'change broke and left it nearly broke, but for
an exciting stretch of years he was as rich as Croesus.

In his prime, Hutchinson was also a business innovator. During the
Civil War he expanded his pork-packing operations and in 1867 incorporated several small firms into the Chicago Packing and Provision
Company—Hutch House, locals called it. He was the leading pork
packer in Chicago until Philip Armour came to town in 1875, and after
the "Big Three" of Armour, Gustavus Swift, and Nelson Morris began
to dominate the industry, he returned to the "pit." "My place is [there],"
he told friends. "There I find comfort. There I am at rest." But before
he retired from meatpacking, he helped make it a modern industry.

•

In 1868, Hutchinson was the first packer to move from Bridgeport to
a cleared and drained bog next to the new Union Stock Yards in the
town of Lake, four miles southwest of Chicago's city center. This gigantic enclosure had been put up by the leading railroads and livestock dealers to centralize Chicago's scattered cattle, pig, and sheep
yards and to place them where they had ample room to expand. The
land, a seemingly valueless marsh, was bought from "Long John"
Wentworth, and in seven months railroad engineers created an entire
city for market-bound animals. Like Chicago itself, it was laid out in a
grid pattern; but unlike that hastily thrown together agglomeration, it
was systematically planned and organized, and its short-term tenants
had better streets and sanitary services than most of the citizens of its
urban neighbor. When the stockyards opened on Christmas Day,
1865, a state-of-the-art sewer and drainage system had transformed
the wetland habitat of bullfrogs and reed birds into a dry and firm
plain crisscrossed by seven miles of pine plank and wood-block pavement, with a main street named Broadway. While complaining
Chicagoans lived on mudflats and drank water contaminated by the
blood and steaming tankage of riverside packing plants, cattle and
pigs at the "Yards" drank clear, cool water from deep artesian wells.

The clean, well-lighted pens were capable of handling over 120,000
animals. There was also a fifteen-mile belt line connecting the yard
with all the major railroads of the city and a canal linking it with the
Chicago River. An ornate limestone gate led to a Bank and Exchange
building with its own telegraph office and a full range of financial ser-

vices, and nearby was a well-appointed cream-colored hotel, the Hough House, where commission agents, drovers, and cattlemen from the range country could get a steak dinner for fifty cents, with another steak "on the house" if the customer still had an appetite.

If he happened to have another kind of appetite, there was, across the way from the Hough House, a string of saloons, several with expensive prostitutes as hostesses. A commuter line ran from the stockyards to downtown Chicago, and visitors were encouraged to come out and see what soon became Chicago's most popular tourist attraction. "Strangers visiting the city would as soon think of quitting it without having seen them," the *Tribune* wrote of the yards on the tenth anniversary of their opening, "as the traveler would of visiting Egypt, and not the pyramids; Rome, and not the Coliseum; Pisa, and not the Leaning Tower."

The removal of the yards to the town of Lake cleared Chicago's streets of drovers and their animals, but the smell of the Union Stock Yards reached the city on strong prairie winds. City officials didn't seem to mind this greatly, however, for it was the aroma of a burgeoning trade that had become "the backbone of Chicago's greatness."

From the high rooftop cupola of the Hough House, visitors could see, in 1868, Benjamin Hutchinson's new brick packing plant, the first of its kind in the Chicago area. Hutchinson moved to the site called the "Back of the Yards" to be close to the animals he slaughtered and the railroads that bore his barrels of cured pork to swelling cities and towns—and also to be out of the jurisdiction of city health inspectors who, in Bridgeport, had monitored the disposal of his tankage. When his plant opened, it had some of the newest equipment on the market, but other packing companies followed him to the Union Stock Yard and built integrated, streamlined plants with cooling rooms lined with natural ice that allowed them to pack pork year-round, one of the principal innovations in the industry.

These developments drove warehouse packers like Gurdon Hubbard out of the trade and presaged a new era in meatpacking, which arrived after the Great Fire with the development of the refrigerator car and the vast international market it created for chilled dressed beef. By 1893, nearly one-fifth of Chicago's population was dependent for employment on an industry that Gurdon Hubbard had begun by driving cattle and pigs from the tractless prairie to a fort at the rough edge of the country.

•

In the push for economic primacy, Chicago's chief western rival was St. Louis. Founded in 1764 by French fur traders near where the Missouri meets the Mississippi and where turbulent river currents almost ended the explorations of Marquette and Joliet, St. Louis was the "gateway" to the West before Chicago got its start as a town. The expeditions of Lewis and Clark and of Zebulon M. Pike started from there, and keelboats and, later, steamboats carried fur trappers and mountain men up the Missouri River and into the unknown country Marquette had hoped to explore. In 1848, at the height of the golden age of the steamboat, nearly all of the nonlocal trade of the Mississippi, Illinois, and Missouri Rivers passed through St. Louis, and the "Memphis of the American Nile" looked upon Chicago as a crude pretender. Cities were "the mightiest works of mankind" to western boosters, most of whom saw the day not far in the future when the central valley of North America would be filled with them, with St. Louis the supreme city and Chicago one of its many satellites. Over the next fifteen years, however, these two cities engaged in head-to-head competition for hinterland markets and resources, an imperial struggle that the railroad, geography, and assertive entrepreneurial effort decided in Chicago's favor.

Within twenty years after the Pioneer first steamed across the prairie, Chicago had driven rail lines into every part of St. Louis's trading territory. Chicago railroads crossed the Mississippi at four places and cut into Iowa, Missouri, and Minnesota, pulling into the city's orbit the wealth coveted by St. Louis river merchants; and the Illinois Central extended its line all the way to New Orleans and Mobile, a declaration of war on St. Louis's Mississippi lifeline. Three Chicago railroads converged at Council Bluffs, Iowa, opposite Omaha, Nebraska, and when the Union Pacific was completed in 1869—the same year the Suez Canal was opened—Chicago was connected to the Pacific and to the trade of the Orient.

Money for this western rail network continued to come from the East, and much more of it went to Chicago than to St. Louis because railroad conglomerates favored the northern avenue of commerce that nature, the Erie Canal, and their own railroads had established between New York and that city. Located three hundred miles to the south of this corridor, St. Louis was in a disadvantageous position, relative to Chicago, to tap into the flow of products, people, and capital coming out of the East.

It was also slow to respond to the challenge of the railroad, its conservative business leaders convinced that railroads would remain mere feeders of steamboat commerce. The only early, aggressive action St. Louis took against fast-rising Chicago was to wage war in the courts against the construction of rail bridges over the Mississippi, in-

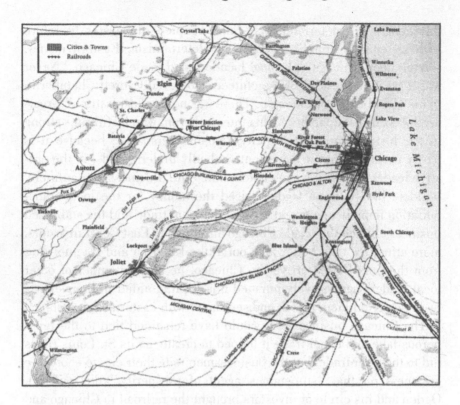

Chicago's railroads, shortly before the Great Fire.   David Buisseret, *Historic Illinois from the Air* (Chicago: University of Chicago Press, 1990).

sisting that bridge pilings created river currents that endangered steamboats. These legal obstructions were easily overcome by smart railroad lawyers like Abraham Lincoln, and it was only when it was too late to stop Chicago's drive for economic supremacy in the region that St. Louis raised a substantial amount of money for railroad development and hired Capt. James B. Eads to build a magnificent rail span across the Mississippi. When it was completed in 1874, St. Louis, "the Samson of the West," had already fallen victim while it slept, a St. Louis booster wrote, to the crafty Delilah, Chicago, "the tool of the Philistines in the East."

On the eve of the Great Chicago Fire, Chicago and St. Louis had nearly identical populations, but Chicago was indisputably the central mart of the region and the great urban portal between East and West, joining the two sections into a single market system that stretched from New York to San Francisco. Chicago had become by then what it still is today, the great "central hall" of America.

Chicago prophets from Louis Joliet to William Bross had argued that geography would make Chicago "inevitable." After the Civil War, this geographic determinism became coupled in booster literature with an equally simplistic economic determinism: Eastern money, seizing upon Chicago's physical location, had made Chicago. "Never was a great city less its own architect," observed Everett Chamberlin in his 1874 history of Chicago. "There was no local aspiration." Greatness was "thrust upon her." This interpretation, which still runs strong in the historiography of the city, remains persuasive because it is partly correct. What it leaves out, or badly underregards, is the creative leadership of Chicago's antebellum elite. Businessmen-cum-city builders like William Ogden raised the money for the local transportation improvements and created the local trade and the stabilized business climate that made Chicago attractive to East Coast investors, more attractive than better lake ports like Kenosha and Racine. And from the time Ogden arrived in Chicago, he and a number of other local leaders aggressively pursued this capital, aided in their efforts by bonds of religion, blood, and sentiment with eastern capitalists.

The Chicago business elite could have remained tied to the prosperous lake and canal trade it helped to create, as its St. Louis rivals did to the river trade; but the businessmen rode their city to economic greatness on that "stupendous agent of prosperity," the railroad. Ogden and his circle of investors brought the railroad to Chicago and then sank money in a galaxy of industries dependent on it. They created the kind of diversified economic base that modern economic theory considers indispensable to a city's long-term prosperity. They turned Chicago's promising but indeterminate position in the hierarchy of western cities into a supremacy that only in hindsight seems "inevitable."

The transplanted northeasterners who were Chicago's civic founders held to the moral code of the small-town Protestant environments in which they were reared. Hard work, thrift, sobriety, and concern for the less fortunate were bedrock principles of their personal morality. But in the West—the wide-open, speculative world they entered early in life and made their field of opportunity—the keys to success were risk taking, sharp dealing, and a survivor's talent for overcoming financial failure. Men in this city "do not mind failures," wrote Anthony Trollope, "and when they have failed, instantly begin again. They make their plans on a large-scale, and they who come after them fill up what has been wanting at first."

Capitalism on the urban frontier was a gambler's game. Caution had no place in it; shady behavior was an inevitable part of it. William Ogden and his North Side neighbors who founded the city's cultural and philanthropic institutions might warn in public occasions that

Chicago needed to develop "culture, taste, beauty, art, literature, or there was a danger that [it] will become a town of mere traders and money getters; crude, unlettered, sharp, and grasping." But in a place that offered such incredible opportunities for moneymaking, even Ogden and his friends had little time for anything but the pursuit of gain. They were also defenders and advance agents of the ungoverned capitalism that encouraged the grasping behavior they condemned at the founding ceremonies of libraries and city charities. Unfettered capitalism was, they were absolutely certain, the underpinning of their city's, their country's, and their own well-being.

It was a Frenchman, Michel Chevalier, who best described the life and spirit of this buccaneering capitalism and its self-justifying ideology: "In the midst of all this speculation, while some enrich and some ruin themselves . . . the field of railroads, canals, steamers, and banks goes on expanding. Some individuals lose, but the country is a gainer; the country is peopled, cleared, cultivated; its resources are unfolded, its wealth increased. *Go ahead!*"

To Chicago's business leaders, urban growth *was* greatness. That would be a problem. For while explosive, unregulated expansion made Chicago a place of fabulous economic opportunity, "the paradise of workers and speculators," it also created health and environmental problems that by the 1850s threatened to make the city almost uninhabitable in the opinion of many contemporaries. In moving to meet these problems while continuing to grow, Chicago revealed what would long remain its greatest strengths and weaknesses as a city.

5

Empire City of the West

1. Chicago Against Nature

NATURE, Louis Joliet argued, had favored Chicago with an ideal location for trade, but Père Marquette knew that the ground at that place was not meant for a city.

Built on a level lake plain undergirded by hard-packed, poorly porous clay, Chicago had always had drainage and waste-disposal problems. But unbounded growth transformed what had been a public nuisance and minor health problem into a full-scale environmental crisis.

In 1854 cholera hit the expanding city with devastating force, taking nearly 6 percent of its population. It was the sixth year in succession that Chicago had been visited by epidemics, including typhoid fever and dysentery, giving it what was believed to be the highest death rate of any city in the country. In the summer of 1854 people died at a rate of sixty a day, and "the death cart," wrote a Chicagoan, "was seen continually in the streets."

It was a worldwide epidemic, and Chicago, a city of immigrants, was fearfully vulnerable. Norwegian and Irish families arrived on lake steamers on which the disease was raging and were quarantined in a warehouse that the hospitalless city rented for the sick and dying. In early July, with the streets lined with coffins waiting to be picked up for burial, hundreds of people fled from the city, and witnesses claimed it was difficult to find men or boys to help undertakers lift bodies into coffins, for people feared that the "demon" would enter them if they touched its victims.

What made cholera doubly frightening was the way it struck and killed. The symptoms came on with terrifying suddenness, and they were "spectacular." People who were well at noon were in the grave by night, but only after a terrible struggle with vomiting, diarrhea, and stabbing cramps. Even their loved ones had trouble looking into their suffering faces, pinched and blue and cold. When death finally released them from their suffering, their coffined corpses were tossed into lime pits on the edge of the stricken city. The indigent were simply buried in the bedding in which they expired.

Cholera was believed to be caused by filthy water and noxious fumes—"death fogs"—produced by exposed sewage; and Chicago, like every other North American city, had no sewage system. But its drainage problems dangerously compounded its health problems, and its business-driven government was reluctant to invest in improvements that failed to yield immediate financial returns. In December 1854, however, aroused and frightened Chicagoans organized a mass meeting and demanded public action.

Entire areas of the city are "noisome quagmires," thundered the editors of one of Chicago's leading papers, "the gutters running with filth at which the very swine turn up their noses in supreme disgust." Human waste was deposited in privy vaults—mere ditches in the backyards and cellars of houses—and these were often located close to shallow wells, whose drinking water they polluted by leaching or overflowing. The roadside ditches that were the chief garbage receptacles were angled to wash into the river when it rained, but they became clogged with annoying regularity, "leaving standing pools of an indescribable liquid . . . to salute the noses of passers-by." Water, garbage, and animal dung also accumulated under plank streets, creating in hot weather a "miasma" that drifted into the shops of complaining merchants.

Even when the medieval-like sewage ditches functioned as they were designed to, they washed their filth into the tideless river, turning its water into "a liquid," said James Parton, "resembling in color and consistency a rich pea-soup." This river, which not only stank but was "greasy to the touch," made its way past tanneries, distilleries, glue factories, and packing plants that used it as a common sewer. "The river is positively red with blood under the Rush Street bridge and down past our factory!" William McCormick wrote to his brother Cyrus, who was away from the city. "What a pestilence may result from it I don't know."

The river water eventually made its way to the lake, where some of it was pumped into the intake pipe of the new public waterworks located just north of the river mouth. "The sort of mixture, by courtesy called water, because it is a little damp, which is furnished to the people from the Water Works, ought to be analyzed," wrote the *Tribune*. Along with other local papers, the *Tribune* issued angry editorials after the cholera epidemic of 1854, calling on city authorities to act in "self-defense" to clean up the stagnant waste water, river pollution, and standing filth that were believed to feed the disease. To do nothing, the press declared, was to invite yet another and more terrible epidemic that could wipe out half or more of Chicago's population.

•

Although the problem of waste disposal and the water supply were linked, Chicago tried to solve them separately and in alleviating one problem worsened the other. In 1855 a Board of Sewerage Commissioners was finally established, and William Ogden, one of its three appointed members, was instrumental in bringing in Ellis Sylvester Chesbrough, designer of Boston's water distribution system, to develop plans to save Chicago from another public health crisis. Chesbrough, a self-trained canal and railroad engineer who had no previous experience in building sewers, carried through the construction of the first comprehensive sewage system in the country and for the next two decades presided over the city's sanitary-reform movement. A visionary engineer with an incorruptible sense of civic duty and an ability to plan and carry through gigantic public projects, he became a new kind of hero to Chicagoans.

After studying firsthand the advanced sewage infrastructures of a number of European cities, Chesbrough decided on a "combined" system that carried both household waste and storm water in a single line of pipe. The problem, however, was that the new brick sewers could not be laid underground because the city lay only several feet above the lake and the river, the only possible outlets. So Chesbrough built them aboveground down the center of streets, connected them by ducts to buildings, and then covered them with mounds of dirt. As construction progressed away from the river, the sewers were elevated to a sufficient angle to allow them to drain by gravity into the river, which Chesbrough considered a regrettable disposal basin but one far preferable to the lake.

The river was dredged to handle the increased sewage load, and the dredged soil was used as fill to raise the street grades to heights where they could cover the sewer pipes. The roadbeds were then guttered and paved with either stone or cedar block.

Construction of the new sewers and streets forced the city council to raise the grade of the city by as much as ten feet in places. This meant that buildings, too, had to be elevated. Reporters from all over the world went to Chicago to see almost an entire city uprooted and raised to a new height by an engineering "miracle" of enormous cost and difficulty.

Owners of buildings were expected to pay for elevating them, but some refused to cooperate, leaving their houses and stores in "holes" beside rows of structures that had been hoisted to the new grade. For years Chicago was a city built on different levels, a town of "ups and downs," James Stirling called it. "When you walk along even the principal streets, you pass perhaps a block of fine stone-built stores, with splendid plate-glass windows (finer than any in New York), with good granite pavement in front: a few steps on you descend by three or four wooden steps to the old level of the street, and find a wooden pavement in front of low, shabby-looking wooden houses." This caused some unexpected embarrassment for women tourists, who were warned in a popular guidebook, *Tricks and Traps of Chicago,* to be on the watch for "sidewalk oglers" who loitered under steep stairs to catch glimpses of ladies' legs.

The raising of Chicago went on for two decades, and when it was completed, "men's feet," wrote Joseph Kirkland, "[were] above the place where passed the heads of their predecessors."

The process of hoisting huge buildings proved endlessly fascinating to visitors and Chicagoans alike. People would gather in the streets by the hundreds to watch four- and five-story buildings and entire city blocks at a time—including horsecar tracks, lampposts, hydrants, and even shade trees—raised as high as twelve feet.

The opportunities this vast undertaking opened drew to the city a young house mover from Albion, New York, who had heard about it from Mrs. Joel Matteson, the wife of a Chicago hotelier, who was visiting the home of mutual friends. George Mortimer Pullman ran a building-moving business along the widened right-of-way of the Erie Canal; and in 1859, at the age of twenty-eight, he left Albion for the western city that had a need for his skills. After raising the five-story Matteson House, the largest city building elevated up to that time, he set up a thriving business with his brother and another Albion man.

Pullman's procedure for raising large buildings was almost elegant in its machinelike coordination. He would have workmen dig holes into the foundation of a building and place heavy timbers under it. Each of the several hundred men was put in charge of four or more jackscrews. When all was ready, George Pullman, standing in the

Raising a Chicago hotel, the Briggs House, 1857.   Chicago Historical Society

street, would blow a whistle, the signal for brother Albert to order the
men to give each of their jacks a turn. As the building rose slowly, almost imperceptibly, it was shored up with wood pilings; and great
numbers of masons, working at terrific speed, would lay new footings
under it.

After Pullman left for Colorado Territory in the Pike's Peak gold
rush, his firm, using twelve hundred men and five thousand jackscrews,
raised the city's most famous hotel, the Tremont House, without breaking a pane of glass or cracking a plaster wall. As the building was
lifted to its new height, business went on inside it without interruption,
the guests coming and going as if nothing were happening. On his return from Colorado Territory, Pullman used the money he made in this
business to invest in a scheme for equipping railroad cars with sleeping facilities, launching a Chicago enterprise that revolutionized
travel the world over.

With its new sewage system, Chicago became a drier and healthier
city; without it, the city would not have been able to continue to grow.
But the more Chicago grew and the better the system worked, the worse
the river—and the drinking water—became. Pollution was not the only
problem. Small fish were drawn to the warm water of the city's shoreside

collecting basin and were sucked into the pipes and poured out into the drinking cups, cooking pots, and bathtubs of Chicagoans. It was not uncommon, William Bross recalled, to find minnows "sporting in one's wash-bowl, or dead and stuck in the faucets." When they got into the city's hot-water reservoir, they "came out cooked, and one's bathtub was apt to be filled with what squeamish citizens called chowder."

One newspaper ran a story claiming that the water system had turned Chicagoans into unknowing cannibals who were eating their ancestors. The city cemetery on the lakeshore just north of the pumping works flooded over during storms, and small fish, it was rumored, fed on the dead and were then drawn into the water pipes and fed to the living. "Of course this was nonsense," wrote Kirkland, "but it was the kind of nonsense that fastened public attention and made easy the next step in our civil life, the tunneling of the lake and bringing the water from the pure depths of two miles from shore."

•

It was Chesbrough, in his new capacity as chief engineer of all public works, who proposed an intake tunnel out of harm's way of the mounting river pollution. Visiting the city in 1864 to cover the Democratic National Convention and to gauge anti-Union strength for his friend Abraham Lincoln, the reporter Noah Brooks toured the tremendous tunnel system then under construction, the longest tunnel excavated up to that time in history. Descending by ladder a shaft sixty-nine feet deep, he entered a horizontal, brick-walled tube five feet in diameter and thirty feet below the bottom of the lake. There Irish immigrant excavators, using only picks and shovels and mules for haulage, worked in sixteen-hour shifts, relieved by gangs of bricklayers, who worked the other eight hours. The around-the-clock work went forward at a furious pace in an atmosphere of heat, blinding dust, thin air, and claustrophobic closeness, with large bellows providing the only ventilation.

One team of workers burrowed eastward from the shoreline and another westward from a "crib," or caisson, out in the lake. The immense boxlike crib of timber and iron had been built on shore and was then floated out into the lake and lined with masonry until its foundations were anchored securely in the blue clay at the bottom of the lake. Its purpose was to protect the intake shaft of the tunnel and control the sluice gates for the water system, but with its pitched roof and cupola it looked to lake craft like an impressive floating hotel. From the crib, excavators were lowered through an iron cylinder to their work under the keels of lake steamers and schooners. All of the work was done by manual labor, but the engineers had done their calculations so well

A diagram of the new Chicago water system designed by Ellis S. Chesbrough and completed in 1866. At the "crib" (far right), clean water was pulled from the lake bottom and sent down the sloping tunnels to the pumping station. From there it was pumped to the top of the new Chicago Water Tower (far left), with its 138-foot

that when the two teams of diggers met each other out under the lake, they were within one inch of achieving a perfect connection.

Just before the new "intake" system was officially opened in March 1867, water was let into the tunnel that led from the crib to the shoreline, and Chesbrough, accompanied by three reporters, went out to the crib and made a final tour of the underground work in a leaky flatbottom boat, the men standing up in the boat and pushing on the sides of the tunnel's walls to propel it forward. On their return to the crib the boat capsized, plunging the men, with their miner's lanterns, into cold water up to their necks. Unable to climb back into the boat in the pitchblack tunnel, they had to walk back to the ladder at the crib, dragging the boat behind them. When they ascended to safety, the floodgates of the crib were reopened, and "the water went down with a roar like that of an infant Niagara," reported a writer for *Harper's Weekly*.

Mayor J. B. Rice called the lake tunnel "the wonder of America and the world," and the press hailed Chesbrough as one of the supreme engineers of the age. When architect W. W. Boyington's Gothic-style water tower was completed in 1869, Chicago had a water-supply system that was a true triumph of technical genius.

Even Oscar Wilde was impressed. Visiting the city in 1882, he called the water tower a "castellated monstrosity with pepper boxes

standpipe, which established the water pressure for the distribution system. The pressurized water was then distributed to the municipal water mains. A second tunnel was built in 1872.   The Tunnels and Water System of Chicago (Chicago, 1874)

stuck all over it" but thought the pumping machinery "simple, grand and natural." The tower was one of the only buildings to survive the Great Fire and stands today astride North Michigan Avenue, a symbol of the city's "can do" spirit.

But the tunnel never worked as Chesbrough hoped it would. The very freshets and spring floods he thought would cleanse the river periodically drove sewage out past the crib and into the water system. This generated public support for a radical measure Chesbrough had called for when he first came to Chicago: the reversal of the river.

By making the river run backward, city waste would be sent down through the canal to the Illinois and Mississippi Rivers, whose waters, Chesbrough argued, would dilute and "deodorize" it. An alternative, or corollary, measure would have been the passage and tight enforcement of strict antidumping laws, measures advocated by progressive city health officials like Dr. John H. Rauch. But the capitalists who controlled Chicago and the audacious engineer they had hired feared that this would drive business from the city. Those limited laws that were eventually passed were only haphazardly enforced by a crusading but badly understaffed Board of Health under superintendent Rauch, a doctor in the Union army during the Civil War. Even the *Trib-*

une agreed that the river must remain the natural "main" of Chicago's sewer system and later recommended that the Board of Health be disbanded and its duties turned over to the police. So Chesbrough was asked to use technology to attack the *symptoms* of a problem whose *causes* in human behavior no city legislator was willing to confront. Public health policy, in the hands of engineers, would be remedial, not, as Rauch recommended, preventive.

With state permission and funds from a $3 million bond issue, Chesbrough deepened the bed of the canal so that the river flowed back into it with the help of powerful pumps at Bridgeport, a vast public works project that satisfied city pride and had no coercive effect on individuals or businesses. With a bond issue financing the excavation, there was no need even to raise city taxes.

Chesbrough was aware that a number of European cities had sewage farms and that many European engineers considered the recycling of waste into fertilizer the safest method of disposal. But he was convinced that Chicago taxpayers would not support the cost of building pumps to move sewage to irrigation farms, and, in any event, land speculators and other businessmen would not agree to set aside valuable acreage at the edge of the wildly growing city for this purpose.

The "river regeneration" was completed on July 18, 1871, and Sara Jane Lippincott was there, with thousands of others, to observe the event. When the temporary dam holding back the Chicago River was broken down, the ink-black waters appeared to remain motionless; but after a while people thought they could detect a current and to test their vision tossed straws into the river. After "some moments of indecision," the straws began to float southward and people began to shout and cheer. The great engineer had reversed the river!

Chesbrough was given a testimonial and eleven thousand dollars by the city's businessmen for devising a system for "purifying the river without," in the revealing language of the letter accompanying their gift, "interfering with the large and rapidly increasing manufacturing interests" or the "unparalleled growth" of the city.

Imperial Chicago's sanitary "solution," however, became its tributary communities' problem, a foreseeable outcome of the process whereby a powerful, expanding city develops a parasitic relationship with its surrounding smaller communities. The slow-running water in the canal did not clean the "monster sewer," and on hot nights in towns as far as La Salle, people reported overpowering smells coming from the canal. In Chicago the following year, heavy freshets backed up the river into the lake, forcing the construction of a second tunnel, this one an incredible six miles in length.

From its opening, the canal was prevented from operating as a cleansing channel by the maverick real estate policies of two of the city's icons, John Wentworth and William Ogden. Just months before the river was reversed, they built a twenty-foot-wide "ditch" from the Des Plaines to the Chicago River to drain swampland they owned on Mud Lake, seeing the deepened canal as a convenient way to raise the value of their land. But during spring freshets their drainage ditch diverted almost all the water of the Des Plaines into the South Branch of the Chicago River, forcing the river to backwash into the lake.

The Ogden-Wentworth Ditch also washed thick deposits of sediment into the canal, negating the entire effort of the dredging and deepening operation. One year after the river was reversed, its current slowed down and eventually stopped, and it became its old stagnant, pestilential self.

"The purifying power of the canal is limited," Chesbrough conceded only one year after the river had been reversed, and he warned that the growing city would not be able to discharge its "filth . . . into the river and its branches for all time to come without producing injurious results." Cholera struck the city again in 1873, and there were smallpox and dysentery epidemics throughout the following decade until Chicago built the great Sanitary and Ship Canal in the 1890s.

Chicago was a city made possible by the largest engineering project undertaken in an American community up to that time, the river reversal and the installation of a new sewage and water system. Now the fourth-largest city in North America, it was capable of doing big things and doing them well, and this became part of its permanent reputation.

2. City of Extremes

"I wish I could go to America if only to see that Chicago," Bismarck is said to have confided to Gen. Phil Sheridan in 1870 when the Union hero, who had moved to Chicago after the war, was in Europe observing the Iron Duke's rout of Napoleon III. In 1871, Chicago—not even forty years old—was a symbol to many of America's material might and get-ahead spirit. "Here on the shore of Lake Michigan," wrote Noah Brooks, "has risen a great and growing city, worthy to bear the title of the Empire City of the West."

Chicago is "a merchant's beau ideal of paradise," Henry Ward Beecher remarked after his visit. "It fairly smokes and roars with business." The city had produced no important writers, musicians, painters, or scientists, but it was brazenly unapologetic about such deficiencies. Culture would come later, with maturity. In its lusty youth the complete concern of Chicago was, as Beecher put it, "buying and selling, buying and selling, buying and selling."

The only one of the arts that any number of its commercial leaders expressed a strong interest in was the most practical of the arts—architecture. It, in turn, gave the spirit of the place. The legendary building boom the city experienced after the Great Fire actually began before it, when businessmen, who were fat with war profits, invested in new stores, hotels, and private palaces. "The eagerness to build pervading all classes of capitalists had become almost a mania," said Alfred T. Andreas, recalling the flush postwar years. Hotels already large enough to accommodate small armies were made larger and vastly more ornate; and many more of them appeared beside the new five- and six-story brick-and-marble-faced business buildings downtown.

In this "Parvenu period" of Chicago architecture, buildings were heavily embellished and entirely derivative in style. "Architecture appears to run riot here among all the ancient schools of design, which have been pillaged to decorate the piles of carved, fluted, and pillared stone piles which rise on every hand," wrote Noah Brooks. Crude and unoriginal as they might have been, these gaudy masonry piles expressed the pride and élan of the businessmen and architects who believed they were building the wonder city of the age.

Guidebook and booster literature described them as substantial, but excepting the works of amateur architects of integrity like John M. Van Osdel, W. W. Boyington, and Edward Burley, all of whom had worked their way up from the carpentry trades, most of the buildings of the prefire boom were speedily and shoddily constructed by speculators interested in fast returns on capital invested. In this way, too, the architecture expressed the place.

•

In 1871 a walking and riding tour of Chicago was considered "a must" for travelers coming west with some time on their hands. "To describe Chicago," the visiting writer Caroline Kirkland told her readers in the *Atlantic Monthly*, "one would need all the superlatives set in a row. Grandest, flattest . . . hottest, coldest, . . . wettest, driest . . . most elegant in architecture, meanest in hovel-propping—wildest in speculation, solidest in value—proudest in self-esteem, loudest in self-disparagement—most lavish, most grasping—most public-spirited in some things, blindest and darkest on some points of highest interest."

City of opportunity, Chicago was also a place of broken fortunes and struggling thousands. There were as many losers as winners in the

Chicago opportunity lottery, but even the winners, Caroline Kirkland noticed, worried incessantly that inexorable Fate would eventually overtake them, too, and this fed "the thirst for more." "There is, perhaps, no place in the world," she shrewdly observed, "where it is more necessary to take a bright and hopeful view of life, and one where this is more difficult."

The crowds of hurrying people in the streets were not unfriendly, but they were entirely preoccupied. And they were almost all male. In her stay in the city Kirkland did not see a single woman, other than "an ordinary domestic," walking in the streets. This, she said, gave the streets a "forlorn" aspect despite their stir and excitement.

There were two principal ways for visitors to enter Chicago: by lake boat or train. Both conveyances discharged their passengers at or near the little stream that poisoned and polluted the city, for it remained a meeting place of the land and water commerce that had made Chicago prosperous beyond the dreams of the Kinzies and Beaubiens who had originally settled along its banks.

The focal point of Chicago had not moved, but it had certainly changed. More vessels arrived in Chicago in 1871 than in New York, Philadelphia, Baltimore, Charleston, San Francisco, and Mobile combined, making it, Parton said, the "Marseilles of our Mediterranean." Ships heading for Bridgeport passed thirteen miles of docks and piers and twenty-four "swinging bridges," which pivoted on small islands in the middle of the river to let ships pass through. When bridge tenders operating huge steam engines swung these trestled bridges around, they created pedestrian and vehicular gridlock on both sides of the river, with cursing teamsters and lorrymen and dense throngs of pedestrians caught in black clouds of freighter smoke.

The river bridges "no sooner discharge one accumulation of people and teams than they fly open wide to allow the passage of some sort of lake craft, and smoking funnels and screeching steam-whistles go past in an almost unceasing stream," wrote Noah Brooks, who thought the scenes at these crossings epitomized the frenetic energy of Chicago. "As soon as the bridge closes in again, the impatient crowd rushes madly on, giving a stranger the impression that Chicagonians [sic] are an active race, given to gymnastics and slightly crazed."

To alleviate the congestion at the bridge crossings, Chesbrough had built two tunnels under the river—the first of their kind in the United States—but they brought little relief to the city of 300,000 whose businesses were concentrated in an area less than one square mile.

The difficulty of getting across the river to and from their places of business had driven some North Side nabobs to move south of the

Lake Street business district, along tree-bordered Michigan Avenue. A prewar visitor described it as "the only street fit to live in," but by the 1860s, barons of business had begun to build stone-turreted mansions along the South Side avenues that ran near the lake, Prairie Avenue being the choicest address. There were also pockets of privilege on the West Side, near Union Park and along wide and well-paved Washington Street, with its marble-fronted town houses; and old settlers continued to reside on the North Side in rambling frame houses in parklike settings. All of these neighborhoods had the advantage of being close to the heart of the downtown, yet removed—even if it was only by a few blocks—from its stink and filth. And all had paved streets, wooden walkways, gas street lights, sewers, and horse-drawn streetcar lines, the latest form of urban transit.

After the Civil War, the city began building a greenbelt of parks and landscaped boulevards on the rim of the settled area and within an easy carriage ride of every wealthy burgher's residence, making intown living all the more gracious. When it was completed, Chicagoans expected their Parisian-like park and boulevard circuit to be one of the grandest carriage drives in the world.

Lincoln Park, on the North Shore, which was improved and incorporated into the new park network, struck Sara Jane Lippincott as the most "magical of all the enterprises and improvements of the city." What had been five years before "a dreary waste" of sand and weeds "was already very beautiful with a variety of surface and ornamentation most wonderful." On Sundays it was filled with picnickers and boaters who stayed around to listen to the late-afternoon outdoor concerts. Lippincott found the present entrance to the park "a little disappointing"—being through a cemetery—but those "old settlers," she added, "are fast being unsettled and reestablished elsewhere." Even the dead had to "move on" in ever-growing Chicago.

In prefire Chicago, neighborhood segregation by income was not complete. The rich lived side by side with the "middling elements" and never far from the poor. "Miserable hovels are mixed up with the most beautiful and costly stores and edifices, such as I never saw in any other place," Rhode Island's Edward L. Peckham reported. Yet this was not the choice of the rich. It was, rather, the result of a city policy that abjured social planning. Residential segregation, however, was beginning to set in by the late 1860s, with choice land around the sites of the new peripheral parks being bought up by speculators, who sold it to families of means anxious to separate themselves from the noisome city—and from the poor who had become its unmentionable social problem.

•

"In all of Chicago there is not one tenement house," said James Parton, echoing the refusal of well-off Chicagoans to acknowledge the vast presence and wretched living conditions of the poor in their "city of opportunity." There were, it is true, no tall tenement houses like New York's in spread-out Chicago; but the poor—upward of 200,000 of them—lived in appallingly run-down pine cottages and shanties in every division of the city. Most of these were built two to a lot, one in front, the other on the alley, and they did not have the advantages of sewers, sidewalks, or paved streets, since only 88 of Chicago's 530 miles of streets had been surfaced by 1871.

Immigrants began arriving in overwhelming numbers in the 1850s—on just one day in 1857, thirty-four hundred arrived by train from New York—and most of them lived in waste-board warrens close to the riverside plants and industrial shops that employed them. In 1870 over one-half of Chicago's population was foreign-born; the largest group was the Germans, followed by the Irish, the Bohemians, the Scandinavians, and a scattering of other nationalities. There was also a shabby neighborhood of three thousand black Americans near the city's vice district on the South Side.

But the worst area of the city was the bleak stretch of forty to fifty acres on the west bank of the South Branch of the river. Here was Maxwell Street, a catch basin for the most desperate poor. A *Tribune* writer described it: "The street may be singled out of a thousand by the peculiar, intensive stench that arises from pools of thick and inky compound which in many cases is several feet deep and occasionally expands to the width of a small lake. Almost at every stop a dead dog, cat or rat may be seen, . . . the poor creatures [having] undoubtedly died of asphyxiation."

Booster literature on the city portrayed it as a place where the economic game was played on level ground and where inequality was less prevalent than in older seaport cities. But the few tax records that survived the Great Fire reveal an inequality problem of staggering proportions. In 1848–49, over 74 percent of the heads of families in the city were "destitute," with no land, no commercial wealth, and only a few personal items. The richest 1 percent owned 52 percent of the city's wealth, a figure between 10 and 15 percent higher than any major East Coast city of the day. The richest 10 percent—the picture becomes ever more depressing—owned 94 percent of the wealth; the richest 20 percent, 99 percent of the wealth; and the richest 25 percent, all the wealth.

Immigrant and native-born poor people settled all over the city, but there were concentrations: the Irish in Bridgeport, the Swedes and Norwegians on the North Side by the river, and the Germans just north of them in what became known as Old Town. Every one of these neighborhoods was an ever-changing mixture of the unemployed, the working poor, and the upward-bound middle class, all of whom met together in lager houses and beer gardens and in the social halls of ethnic societies.

Along the banks of the river there were also the infamous "patches," each made up of a floating population of vagrants, newly arrived immigrants without jobs or family contacts, criminals, drug addicts, prostitutes, and seasonally unemployed workers, mostly sailors and dockhands who had not followed their brother laborers to the northern lumber camps when the lake froze. The worst of these miserable shantytowns, Conley's Patch, run by an aging alcoholic named Mother Conley, helped excite anti-Irish hysteria in the city, which reached a peak in the elections of 1860, when "Long John" Wentworth, a virulent "anti-Hibernian," was elected mayor, and Gurdon Hubbard, no friend of the Irish, either, won the alderman race in the Seventh Ward. "Go to the polls early and vote for G. S. Hubbard and the whole Republican ticket," a handbill reminded Republicans before the election. "One more victory in the noble Seventh and the Celts will never peep again."

The patches were home to "the most beastly sensuality and darkest crimes," the rabidly anti-Irish *Tribune* described them. Pox-ridden prostitutes operated out of shanty saloons and gambling dens, and their pimps ran cockfights, dog races, and rat killings, with terriers thrown into a pit for gun-toting gamblers to wager on how quickly they massacred their prey. When William Ogden bought the lakeside land on which one of the worst of these patches—the Sands—stood (near the present site of the Tribune and Wrigley Buildings), Mayor John Wentworth, accompanied by a posse, several fire brigades, and Ogden's land agent, forcibly removed the squatters who refused to pay Ogden's offer of a "reasonable price" for their property and pulled down their shanties with horse-drawn hooks and chains. "Thus this congregation of the vilest haunts of the most depraved and degraded creatures in our city has been literally 'wiped out,' and the miserable beings who swarmed there driven away." But the *Tribune* should have known better. The enterprising former residents of the Sands simply crossed the river and were back in business within the week.

In the future, their major worry would not be the police but competition from the police-protected vice district downtown. The Chicago police force, established in 1855 with a volunteer fireman as its first chief, was badly understaffed and notoriously corrupt, and many police were under orders from their precinct politicians to leave gamblers and prostitutes alone, provided they paid protection money. Everything the patches offered—and more—was available in downtown Chicago, where a segregated tenderloin district operated around the clock within several blocks of city hall, an easy evening stroll from all the big hotels. There was no good reason, then, besides the thrill of it, for a man with money in his pocket and a healthy fear for his life to frequent the patches.

A major railroad center that was still a frontier town, Chicago was always filled with people passing through: tourists, farmers, immigrants, and businessmen—and hustlers who went there to prey on them. A city of strangers, it was a paradise for pickpockets, confidence men, and streetwalkers. Police occasionally hassled these small-time operators, but usually only when they threatened to scare out-of-town spenders away from the city's big, western-style gambling halls, concert saloons, and sporting houses.

There were Sunday closing laws, but they went unenforced, except on one occasion in 1855, when nativist politicians tried to shut down German beer gardens and taverns on the North Side, provoking "Lager Beer Riots" that resulted in one death, hundreds of arrests, and days later, a return to the status quo antebellum. The Illinois prohibition law was defeated by the voters that year, and Chicago had no further problem with the restriction of alcohol consumption until the 1920s.

Nor did anyone in city government try seriously to restrict gambling operations. Professional gamblers who had operated on Mississippi River boats before the war gravitated to Chicago during the war, riding about town in victorias, their strumpets beside them in furs and feathered hats. Gunfighters were so common on Randolph Street that it became known for decades as the "Hairtrigger Block." "We are beset on every side by a gang of desperate villains!" cried the *Chicago Journal*. But vice paid. It drew people to the city and emptied their pockets. So it stayed, like everything else that made money in the city.

•

The only effort Chicago made to alter its image in the boom years before the Great Fire was a vast, profit-inspired building enterprise by one of its boldest speculators. In 1867, the year this project began forming in the active mind of Potter Palmer, he was, at age forty-one, a retired multimillionaire vacationing in Europe. Two years earlier, he had shocked Chicago when, on the advice of his doctor, he retired from business to try to regain his health, transferring control of his successful dry-goods concern to two young, untried partners, Levi Z. Leiter and Marshall Field.

On the Continent, and later in New York City, the quiet Quaker bachelor learned to enjoy his money; and upon his return to Chicago in 1868 he bought a four-horse barouche to take his new sporting friends to the racetrack or to baseball games at the new park he helped build for the Chicago White Stockings, the city's successful touring "nine." In summers, Palmer was a fixture at fashionable Saratoga Springs, the dry-goods prince from wild Chicago, betting recklessly on the horses, entertaining lavishly in his hotel suite, tipping waiters with handfuls of bills, and riding behind four-in-hands accompanied, the society columns reported, by one or more of the local beauties.

But Potter Palmer did not have the temperament for a life of permanent leisure and, feeling reinvigorated after his European travels, began a second career in real estate development, becoming in time Chicago's largest landholder, its wealthiest citizen, and its first master builder.

Palmer always worked alone, a discreet, determined operator. Not once in his business career did he take on a partner, and he brought few people into his confidence. In 1868 he went forward with the biggest project in his life, one that lastingly changed Chicago, and for a time no one, not even his closest friends, knew what he was up to.

His plan was to move the city's main commercial district from Lake Street, which ran east and west, to State Street, which ran north and south, parallel with the lake, the way Chicago's downtown is presently oriented—thanks to Palmer. Chicago only learned of his plan when Palmer approached the city council with a request to widen State Street, where, he told incredulous aldermen, he had quietly bought almost a mile of frontage.

This seemed like a preposterous idea, and the council told him so, for Lake Street was thriving, while State Street, where Hubbard's Trail had come into the city from the south, was little more than a muddy alley, narrow, poorly paved, and lined by a squalid collection of pawnshops, saloons, boardinghouses, and blacksmith shops.

Merchants on Lake Street fought the proposed street widening, as did property owners on State Street, who balked at moving their buildings back, at their own expense, to create Palmer's Parisian boulevard effect. But Palmer—described by a friend as "a man of quiet persistence and fighting blood"—was absolutely fixed on his idea and drove the bill through the city council without resort, apparently, to threats or bribery.

When recalcitrant owners of some of the older buildings on State Street ignored the new street-widening ordinance, Palmer simply bypassed them, tearing down the eyesores he had bought along the street and putting up thirty or so handsome stores and business houses. These he placed on the new building line so there would be plenty of parking space for carriage trade and space as well on the newly paved street for the tracks of additional horse-car trolleys. Until all the main blocks were widened to a standard width after the fire, State Street, with its irregular, zigzagging building line, was one of the strangest-looking streets in the city. But Lake Street merchants soon began moving into Palmer's buildings, despite high rents, because, as Palmer had figured, they could not allow their rivals "to take possession of such splendid quarters." By 1871 the slow exodus to State Street, "that great street," had become a flight.

When Palmer began his State Street project, he had in mind more than changing Chicago's axis of development. The cosmopolitan capitals of Europe had made a strong impression on him, and he realized that if Chicago were ever to have a world-class downtown, it would need to attract women shoppers in great numbers. This is why he had given up on Lake Street. It was dirty, cramped, poorly lit, and filled with vagrants; and the nearby river gave off a smell so awful that women shoppers had to hold handkerchiefs to their noses. When they shopped at Palmer's Lake Street store, well-dressed ladies hurried home in their carriages as soon as they chose their purchases. Palmer's idea, then, was not just to create the most fashionable commercial boulevard west of Broadway but to change the entire character of the downtown shopping area, making it an extension of the refined atmosphere of the first shop he established on Lake Street in 1852, when he arrived in Chicago—a place he considered "embryonic but illuminated with promise"—from Lockport, New York.

With a five-thousand-dollar gift from his father and some original ideas about merchandising, Palmer had opened a dry-goods store that transformed the city's retail trade. He was the first city merchant to cater expressly to women, especially wealthy women, greeting them at the door, escorting them around the store, remembering their tastes and the names of their pets, and instructing his ever-courteous clerks that the customers were always right. Palmer carried the most expensive and exotic merchandise in the city and made regular buying trips to Europe for velvet and brocade, English carpets and Belgian glass, Parisian silks, gloves, and embroideries. He displayed these items in the big, brightly decorated show windows of the new Lake Street store he opened in 1858, the largest dry-goods establishment in the West; and he was the first city storekeeper to advertise extensively in newspapers and to run "sales" or "bargain days." He also introduced a new customer-service policy that spread to other cities and became known as "the Palmer System."

Customers in his store were handed little slips of paper entitling them to buy goods "on approval"—to take them home and inspect them at leisure and return them if they found them unsatisfactory. Palmer, like Cyrus McCormick, guaranteed customers a full cash refund, "without question or quibble," if their purchases "proved unsatisfactory either in price, quality or style," a practice that other city merchants considered "unthinkable" at first ("once sold, always sold" was the iron rule of merchandising) but were forced to copy if they hoped to compete with "the intruder," as Palmer had come to be known.

Palmer also introduced the practice of delivering goods to the homes of customers free of charge, which became a famous feature of the giant firm that eventually evolved from his Lake Street store, Marshall Field & Company. Macy's sent a representative to study Palmer's merchandising methods, and they soon became established practices at large stores all across the country and in Europe as well.

The key to the Palmer method was the attention he lavished on women customers. At a time when it was impossible for a woman to get waited on in a downtown restaurant without a male companion, he encouraged women to come to his store unescorted and to browse without any pressure to buy. This he hoped to make the reigning principle on State Street, whose stores would be spacious and tastefully decorated and whose sidewalks—lined with magnificent show windows—would be wide, well lit, and perfectly safe. Palmer's aim was to turn shopping, as it already was at Paris's Bon Marché, from a necessary weekly chore to a delightful daily pastime.

To set the tone of the street, Palmer built a six-story marble-faced emporium with Corinthian columns at the corner of State and Washington Streets and talked Field and Leiter into renting it for the unheard-of sum of fifty thousand dollars a year—well worth it, Palmer thought, for what he predicted would become the prime corner of the new downtown shopping area. The gala opening of "Palmer's Palace" in October 1868 was "the grandest affair of its kind which ever transpired even in Chicago, the city of grand affairs," the *Tribune* reported. Carriages stretched for blocks along the street, and as Chicago's first families stepped out of their phaetons and landaus, they were met by boys in blue uniforms with double rows of brass buttons who ushered them to the front door. There Field and Leiter greeted them with gifts—a rose for every woman, an expensive cigar for every man. The retail floor had frescoed walls and sculpted gas fixtures that threw golden light on the polished walnut display counters, which were filled with merchandise from as far away as China. "For once," said the *Chicago Times,* "the women came not so much to be seen as to see."

In the summer of 1870, Potter Palmer surprised Chicago again, announcing his forthcoming marriage to a radiant, convent-educated socialite, Bertha Honoré, the daughter of the real estate magnate H. H. Honoré, late of Louisville, Kentucky. She was twenty-one, and he was forty-four; and they had met eight years earlier when she was shopping with her mother at his Lake Street store. As an outspoken feminist, the grande dame of Chicago society, and the official hostess of the World's Columbian Exposition, she would become better known to the country than her husband, who returned to his quiet ways after their marriage. But on the occasion of their engagement she would be satisfied, she said, to be the wife of an innkeeper.

The "inn" was the much-talked-about Palmer House just nearing completion on State Street, her husband's wedding gift to her. Even by Chicago's standards it was an impressive hotel. At eight stories, it was the tallest building in the city, and with 225 rooms, one of the largest hotels in the country. It was decorated with Carrara marble, hand-woven Axminster carpets, and chandeliers and candelabra from France. And it would be staffed, Palmer was proud to announce, by several hundred smartly uniformed Negroes.

Palmer also billed it as the only fireproof hotel in America. It had telegraphic alarms in each room, hoses on every floor, and a large water tank on its French mansard roof. It looked like a fortress and was said to be impregnable.

On Sunday evening, October 8, 1871, Bertha Honoré Palmer was spending an evening alone at her country estate on the edge of the city. Her husband was on his way east to attend the funeral of one of his sisters, and she had been busy that afternoon making arrangements for their move to a permanent living suite at the Palmer House. It was the first time they had been separated since their marriage fourteen months earlier.

Late that night, she looked out her bedroom window and saw a lurid orange-and-yellow curtain hanging in the night sky above Chicago. As she rushed out to the front terrace, she could faintly hear noises in the distance—the crash of falling buildings, it turned out, and the explosion of barrels of oil and paint—and she saw flames ascending like scarlet-colored columns. The fire was burning so furiously there was almost no smoke, and she knew at once that the entire city was in peril.

From this day forward, Chicagoans would date their past with two simple three-word phrases—"before the Fire" or "after the Fire." And the city's history would be written with "the Fire" as both its major dividing point and its principal transforming event. Modern Chicago, this mythical view of the city goes, is the creation of the postfire generation, who built it on the scorched ruins of the western boom town. Seen this way, the fire was a fresh beginning, almost an opportunity— "the end of the old order." This became Chicago's own myth of progress—destruction as a cleansing prelude to greatness. "Good out of evil" is the evocative title of one of the chapters of Elias Colbert and Everett Chamberlin's *Chicago and the Great Conflagration,* published only two months after the fire, one of scores of books written at that time that saw the fire as the best thing that ever happened to Chicago.

This is "usable history," a common product of ascending cities like Pericles' Athens. It gave Chicago businessmen and architects of the postfire generation a myth of urban origins that energized and focused their rebuilding efforts by making them the heroic founders of a new and better city. It also induced the temporary amnesia one often needs in order to get on with life after a searing loss. "Not only was there no tearing of hair, or wild raving about lost fortunes," Colbert and Chamberlin said of the postfire mood in the city, "but absolutely no reference to the event, on the part of any business man, except as one might speak of a business failure in which the individual had no immediate interest." But like all usable history, its power to distort was as great as its clarifying and uplifting simplicity.

The Chicago of 1893 was not the entirely new city its local legendizers made it out to be. It was an enlarged, reconfigured, and vitalized version of William Ogden's Chicago, a city whose character and spirit had been forever shaped by its lusty origins. The city *looked* new—the scenery changed, and so did the cast of characters. Old leading actors disappeared from the stage, minor characters took on enlarged roles, and new and powerful characters sprang from the wings. But anyone who had witnessed the opening act of the Chicago drama would not have been surprised by the action, or perhaps even the outcome, of the second act, which ended with the closing of the Columbian Exposition and a spectacular fire that consumed the White City buildings erected by Potter Palmer's successor as Chicago's master builder, Daniel Hudson Burnham.

Yet the Great Fire of 1871 *was* a transforming experience. It raised or ruined men and was a magnificent and awful spectacle that time would never erase from the memories of those who were caught in it. It was *"a night of horror,"* said the *Chicago Evening Post* the following morning, *"never before equalled on the continent."*

6

My Lost City

1. The Great Fire

"CHICAGO was then built as if to invite its destruction in this manner," Alfred T. Andreas wrote fourteen years after the Great Fire. But Chicagoans were aware of this before the fire and feared for their families and property as dry winds and the long drought of 1871 emptied wells and cisterns and turned their cheaply built city of pine into a mass of combustible material.

In annual reports to the mayor and the city council, the fire department warned of "the grave defects of the manner in which our city [is] being built." Outside the central business district almost every building was constructed of wood, while many of the new marble-faced brick buildings downtown had ponderous wooden cornices, long wooden signs on their fronts, and mansard top stories of wood. And all of them had wooden roofs covered with felt, tar, or shingles. Even the roof of Ellis Chesbrough's fortresslike Water Works, Chicago's first line of defense against fire, was made of wood.

The fire department also warned that a great number of the city's impressive-looking stores, hotels, and four- and five-story business blocks were shoddily and dangerously constructed by "swindling" contractors, "firetraps pleasing to the eye," the *Tribune* declared, but all "shams and shingles."

These business buildings fronted pine-block streets and miles of raised wooden sidewalks—long lines of well-laid kindling—and were surrounded by flimsy frame saloons and flophouses and the rotting shanties of the poor, buildings put up in brazen defiance of Chicago's fire ordinances. In the fastest-growing city in the world any kind of construction was permitted as long as it made money for its builders and landlords. And in a city replete with insurance companies, owners of commercial buildings counted on policy coverage, not sound construction, to protect themselves from fire loss. That alternative was also far cheaper.

Chicago's fire department recommended repeatedly that a building-inspection department be established, that metal roofs be required for hotels and other large public buildings, and that the city install more fire hydrants, build larger water mains, hire more firemen, and purchase two fireboats with powerful pumps to patrol the river, which was crossed by wooden bridges, filled with wooden shipping, and lined with combustibles—grain elevators, lumberyards, woodworking factories, long trains of wooden rail cars, and mountains of coal for industrial and household use. But the city government rejected every one of these recommendations, insisting that higher taxes and stricter building codes would have a discouraging effect on business expansion.

By the first week of October 1871, this city of pine had been dried out by one of the worst droughts in local memory. Only an inch of rain fell between July 4 and October 9, and a northwesterly wind—the prairie sirocco that blew nine of ten days in the summer—carried the heat of the grasslands over the flat, exposed lake plain, "turning all the wood in wooden Chicago into tinder." In an ominous reminder of their city's vulnerability, Chicagoans watched their tar roofs bubble in the midday sun.

To add to the danger, there were large amounts of flammable material lying around in streets or yards or stored in the homes of Chicagoans. Most of the city's parched trees had already shed their leaves, and windblown piles of them lay on brown lawns, in the gutters of streets, or against the pine fences that acted as property barriers in the working-class warrens in the South and West Divisions. With winter coming on, household barns and sheds were stacked high with hay to feed horses or livestock and, in the poorer areas, with wood and wood shavings for heating and cooking. The cellars of the better houses were stocked with fresh supplies of anthracite and kerosene.

That fall—the second year of a drought that covered the entire Mississippi Valley—Chicagoans read of raging grass fires on the prairies and of forest fires in Wisconsin and Michigan that devoured entire townships. And every day in the first week of October, the fire bell in the courthouse rang, and there were reports in the newspapers of small fires in the city, giving rise to anxious speculation about a great consuming blaze. "The absence of rain for three weeks," the *Tribune* reported only hours before the Great Fire, "[has] left everything in so flammable a condition that a spark might set a fire which would sweep from end to end of the city."

Guarding the entire eighteen-square-mile city of 334,000 people was a fire department of only 185 firefighters and seventeen horse-drawn steam engines. On the morning the *Tribune* issued its prophetic warning, this entire fire force had just finished battling a seventeen-hour blaze south of the business district. One of the most destructive fires in Chicago up to that time, it consumed almost every building in a four-block area and "struck consternation to the hearts of those who witnessed it," Andreas recalled.

As people walked to church services that Sunday evening, they could see thin bluish flames and curling columns of smoke coming from the piles of coal along the river where the fire had been stopped. This fire had put Chicago on alert but badly weakened its defenses. The firefighters returned to their engine houses exhausted and beat up. Their clothing was burned. and blackened, several pieces of equipment were destroyed or put out of order, and many of the firemen's eyelids were so swollen and seared that the men had to be sent home to recover.

That Sunday evening, the conditions for a great fire were almost perfect: a level, drought-stricken city built of flammable materials and exposed to hot winds blowing in the direction where the fire hazard was greatest—the forest of shanties and mills in the southwest corner of town—was being protected by an understaffed and exhausted fire force. "The feast was spread," Joseph Kirkland wrote, "and only awaited the fiend."

All that was required was what fire officials insisted could never happen—a fire that would be spotted too late to prevent it from turning into a holocaust.

Chicago had not burned down before 1871 because it was lucky, and also because the fire department had arrived speedily at the scene of every fire and managed to contain it with their primitive equipment, a small steam engine being only a step above a well-organized bucket brigade. "[Strike] it before it gets the start of you," the city's fire marshal explained the success of his department up to this time. "That is the only secret in putting out fires." Early and accurate warning, not massed manpower or technology, was responsible for the remarkable record of success of a department that had been organized in 1858 after the city finally conceded that its all-volunteer fire brigades were inadequate.

In the summer of 1871 the city had just finished installing a new network of fire-alarm boxes. These automatic signal devices were supposed to be simple to operate and completely reliable. "One pull at a hook," said a fire official, "gives the signal with unerring accuracy." To prevent people from turning in false alarms, the 172 numbered boxes were locked, the keys entrusted to responsible citizens in nearby residences and businesses.

This up-to-date electrical system was supplemented by a medieval-like fire watch. A watchman was on duty around the clock on the high cupola of the "fireproof" courthouse, and each fire station had its own observation tower. When a fire was sighted and reported to the central-alarm-system operator at the courthouse, he set the eleven-thousand-pound courthouse bell tolling with an electrical apparatus and sent a signal identifying the fire box closest to the blaze to all the engine companies in the city.

Around 9:00 P.M., October 8, the watchman Matthias Schaffer, on duty in the courthouse tower, saw flames on the West Side of the city through the screen of smoke created by the coal fires along the river. Looking through his spyglass, he located the fire near Canalport Avenue and Halsted Street and called down through a voicebox to William J. Brown, night operator at the central-fire-alarm telegraph office on the first floor of the courthouse, to strike box 342. Within seconds, the courthouse bell began booming its alarm over the sleeping city, and hose companies set out for Halsted Street.

As Schaffer continued to watch the fire, however, he realized that he had mislocated it by a mile or so and told Brown to strike the correct box, number 319. Brown refused, claiming that this might confuse the fire companies and that they would pass the fire, anyway, on their way to box 342. William Brown's stupid blunder helped doom Chicago.

Unknown to Schaffer, the fire had already been spotted by the Little Giant Company, and it hurried its steamer to the scene, a cow barn at 137 De Koven Street, only a few blocks from the area destroyed by the fire of the previous night. Minutes before this, a storekeeper in the neighborhood had used the key in his possession to send in an alarm, but it had failed to register at the courthouse. Within forty-five minutes, seven fire companies managed to find their way to De Koven Street, but they arrived too late to check the swift spread of the blaze through an immigrant neighborhood "thickly studded with one-story frame dwellings, cow-stables, pig-sties, corn-cribs, [and] sheds innumerable . . . a *terra incognita*," a reporter called it, "to respectable Chicagoans."

In the first hours of the fire, a story spread that it was started by an Irishwoman named Catherine O'Leary, who ran a neighborhood milk business from the barn behind her house. Rumor had it that Mrs. O'Leary, a plump woman of about thirty-five, went to the barn with a kerosene lamp to milk one of her cows and that the unruly animal kicked over the lamp, igniting the hay on the barn floor.

No one has ever been able to substantiate this, and an official inquiry into the cause of the fire established that Catherine O'Leary, her husband, Patrick, a Civil War veteran, and their three children were in bed when they were awakened by a neighbor who first spotted the flames shooting up from their backyard barn. The "cow story," however, is the one that went through Chicago and out to the world, and "for all time," as Andreas wrote, "the legend of Mrs. O'Leary's cow will be accepted."

•

The fire tore through an entire block of shanties in less than an hour, but it might have been contained as a poor people's fire had it not been for the winds, which began to pick up around nine o'clock. It was a frightening, yet thrilling, spectacle to the great crowds of onlookers, most of them from Conley's Patch, just across the river, a good number of them so drunk and rowdy that at one point the hoses had to be turned on them. Large flaming brands were blown high in the air—as high as five hundred feet—and were swept by driving gusts of wind to points far in front of the main fire. As the fire companies lined up their engines in formation to block and battle the inferno in front of them, great windblown parts of it sailed directly over them, creating new fire centers to their rear. All the while the air was filled with sparks and burning cinders, which fell, people said, like red rain.

Within an hour, planing mills and furniture factories astride the river were on fire, and then the towering grain elevators, hit by fiery timber missiles, began burning from top to bottom. When the fire reached the area that had been burned clean the previous night, fire officials were sure it would die out. No one gave it a chance of spreading to the South Side, where anxious out-of-towners watched it from their hotel windows, assured by management that they were in no danger whatsoever.

Around eleven-thirty, a flaming mass of material was blown across the river and landed on the roof of a horse stable, and another flying brand struck the South Side Gas Works. From these two places, a new and larger fire center started. Even the grease-and-oil-slickened river went up in flames.

The "fiend" was in the heart of Chicago and heading straight for the courthouse, where men stood on its roof and the roofs of adjoining buildings, with buckets and tubs, putting out small fires ignited by cascading sparks that made the city look as if it were being hit by "an illuminated snowstorm."

But first the fire devoured Conley's Patch. The men and boys of Conley's Patch were at the fire on the West Side when word reached them that their shingled hovels and sheds were in flames. They made a frantic charge for the bridges, fighting past engine companies trying to get to the new fire front and through mobs of panic-stricken people fleeing in the other direction. As the wind-driven fire raced through this dismal slum, women and children rushed out into the streets screaming in terror and clutching rosaries, crucifixes, and what simple possessions they had managed to get their hands on—a Sunday dress, a child's rag doll, a clutch of family letters. Most of them escaped, but a few—mostly the sick and the elderly—were overrun by a moving wall of fire one thousand feet wide and over a hundred feet high. It was in Conley's Patch that the "death harvest" began.

The entire city was now imperiled, and the first of its great buildings to fall was the million-dollar courthouse, a flamboyant limestone pile set in the midst of a ten-acre square in the center of downtown. Tower watchman Matthias Schaffer was on the roof with another watchman putting out small fires when a piece of burning timber slammed into the building's wooden cupola and started a blaze that the two men were unable to control. Mayor Roswell B. Mason ordered the evacuation of the building and the release of prisoners in the basement jail, who had begun to scream in terror and shake the bars of their cells when the suffocating smoke came rushing through the air openings in the ceiling and floor. Many were released, but the more dangerous criminals were put in chains and taken away under guard.

At two-twenty, the tower on top of the courthouse cupola collapsed, and the enormous bell, tolling to the last, went crashing through the ruins of the building with a roar that was heard a mile away. What had been the storehouse became the tomb of the public records as every document establishing title to every piece of real estate in Cook County went up in flames. From the courthouse the flames spread northward to the great commercial core of Chicago. The post office, the Chamber of Commerce Building, the major banks and train stations, the city's most impressive stone churches, all of its newspaper offices, and most of its theaters, music halls, and hotels were annihilated, most of them in less than five minutes.

Witness to the first peacetime destruction of an entire American city center was fifty-eight-year-old William Bross. Part owner of the *Tribune,* he raced to his office from his town house on Michigan Avenue and later described what he saw as "the most grandly magnificent scene that one can conceive." Chicago's newest and tallest buildings "were burning with a sublimity of effect which awed me." The streets were swarming with people running in every direction, "shouting and crying in their terror," Bross recalled. When explosives were set off to blow up buildings in the line of the fire, they made the "solid earth," and even the air itself, shake, adding to the panic of the people, who had difficulty seeing several feet in front of them through the smoke and pelting cinders and sparks. Collapsing buildings fell into the streets with the sound of heavy artillery, and with flying fragments of limestone making a noise like the steady discharge of musketry, many war veterans must have felt they were back at Shiloh.

From the roof of a warehouse, a newspaper reporter looked down on the scene of terror and confusion in the streets and felt as if he were peering "over the adamantine bulwarks of hell into the bottomless pit." Horses, "maddened by heat and noise [and] falling sparks," kicked and bit each other, dogs ran in circles howling, and thick brown rats were driven out from under the wooden sidewalks and were "kicked at" and "trampled upon" by the fleeing crowds. Hovering over this theater of horrors were "flocks of pigeons" that circled in the air and then were suddenly sucked into the boiling inferno, disintegrating in seconds. All the while, the young firefighters were forced back again and again, for the wind blew so hard that it drove the water from their canvas hoses back into their faces.

Their avenues of escape to the north and west cut off by the fire, many people raced for the Basin, the section of the lakefront protected by the Illinois Central breakwaters. Many remained there all night, "forlorn creatures of all classes," sitting on the trunks and furniture they managed to drag from their burning homes. As the choking heat increased and brands and sparks "fell in thicker showers," the refugees on the banks waded into the cold water up to their waists. Most were women, and "their shrieks and moans," said one witness, "enhanced the terrors of the scene."

•

Newspaper and eyewitness accounts of the fire are filled with sensational stories of looting and drinking by "wild and dangerous" people, mostly, it was said, Irish immigrants, transients, and blacks. One reporter described "dirty," "villainous" Negroes moving through the streets "like vultures in search of prey" and "hollow-eyed" Irish women in bedroom slippers and torn dresses moving "here and there, stealing." Staggering men, some of them wearing stolen firemen's hats, were reportedly seen brandishing brandy bottles or rolling kegs of beer down the streets. Stories of looting and drinking, however, were greatly exaggerated, the product, in most cases, of deep fears of the unpropertied classes, the same motive, no doubt, behind the sensational and completely false accounts of public-spirited vigilantes hanging incendiaries—mostly, it was claimed, vagrants and "non-Americans"—from lampposts. With the center of the city a sea of flames and the fire advancing northward at a terrific rate, there was no time for wholesale looting and reveling. "There was little of either theft or robbery," Alfred L. Sewell reported in his eyewitness account of the fire, "for the very good reason that the thieves and robbers, if there were any . . . had all they could do to save their lives." The lurid reports of crime and "outrage" were largely the "inventions," Sewell claimed, of his fellow reporters, many of them vying to write the story of the century.

Worse than the behavior of the looters was that of the drivers of hacks, wagons, and carts, who charged outrageous prices to haul away the household possessions or baggage of victims trapped in the fire. The greater a person's distress, the more these vultures charged.

Alexander Frear, a New York alderman who was staying at the Sherman House when the fire broke out, gave a graphic account of the scene in the downtown streets that terrible Sunday night. Escaping from the area of the courthouse in a wagon driven by his Chicago nephew, he looked behind him into "a tornado of fire." Ahead, Wabash Avenue—his corridor of escape—was filled with expensive furniture, valuable oil paintings, railroad trunks, and other "treasures," some of them burning under falling embers. On his way to the West Side home of his brother, Frear passed through streets thronged with crying children searching frantically for their parents, and everywhere there were hurrying processions of refugees. Wealthy ladies, wearing what appeared to be all their jewelry, struggled along next to immigrant women hauling mattresses on their heads and half-naked prostitutes driven from their rented "cribs" on Wells and Clark Streets. People carried sick and crippled relatives on chairs and makeshift litters and the bodies of the unburied dead in coffins or wrapped in sheets. When Frear finally reached his brother's home, his clothes soaked and full of burn holes, he collapsed in the hallway, only to be awakened a little while later to lead a daring rescue of his sister-in-law, who was caught in the home of a friend in the direct line of the fire.

John R. Chapin, an artist for *Harper's Weekly,* was also staying at the Sherman House that night. After narrowly escaping from the flaming building, he made his way to a spot near the Randolph Street bridge, where he drew a memorable pencil sketch of the fire for his magazine. "I confess," he wrote his editor, "that I felt myself a second Nero as I sat to make the sketch which I send herewith of the burning of Chicago. . . . For nearly two miles to the right of me the flames and smoke were rising from the ruins and ashes of dwellings, warehouses, lumberyards, the immense gas-works," and on the south horizon was a great grain elevator that had been turned into "a living coal . . . sending upward a sheet of flame and smoke a thousand feet high."

But for Chapin the sounds were the most terrifying part of the scene. The low "moaning" of the wind, the roar of the advancing flames, the screams of the crowd, the tremendous din made by explosives and collapsing walls, were mingled with the "shrill whistling of the tugs" in the river as they pushed huge lumber ships out of the way of the fire. The tugs were helped in their work by bridge tenders, who swung open the two bridges across the river that had not burned as yet. As long lines of towed ships, some of them on fire, moved slowly downriver, crowds on the south bank shouted for the tenders to swing back the bridges so they could escape the fire that was then, in one man's words, "a mountain over our heads." That "frightful discord of sounds," Chapin wrote, "will live in memory while life shall last."

Later that day, when Chapin caught a train leaving the city, he made a pencil rendering of "that fabulous city of yesterday" from the window of his car. "Forty miles away," he wrote his editor, "we still saw the brilliant flames looming above the doomed city."

•

Chicago had had a number of big fires, but this was a fire like no one in the city had ever even heard of. The flames seemed to be shooting from a massive blowtorch somewhere off in the sky. The heat was so intense it melted iron and steel (which melt, respectively, at two thousand degrees and twenty-five hundred degrees Fahrenheit), turned stone to powder and marble and granite to lime, and made trees explode from the heat of their own resin. People running from the fire could feel its heat through their backs, burning their lungs.

But it was the wind, not the staggering heat, that made the most frightful impression on survivors. The official in charge of the U.S. Weather Signal Office on La Salle Street reported to Washington, D.C., that the anemometer on the roof of his office registered sixty miles an hour before he abandoned the building and that the terrific gusts almost blew him and his meter off the roof. It was these gale-force winds, almost all Chicagoans living at the time of the fire agreed, that caused their city to be destroyed in little over twenty-four hours.

"The fire," William Ogden wrote to a friend, "was the fiercest Tornado of Wind ever known to blow here."

But in the most complete technical study that has been done of the fire, H. A. Musham has demonstrated that the wind in the area of the city during the night of October 8–9 never reached a velocity of greater than thirty miles an hour. This kind of wind cannot lift heavy timbers and hurl them up to half a mile through the air, nor can it blow off the cornices of large buildings. What appeared to be hurricane-force winds to people caught in the fire were actually convection whirls, or fire devils—superheated columns of extremely hot air rising from a fire and sent in a rotating, tornado-like motion by cooler descending air.

In this way—by drawing cooler, heavier air into the vacuum left by its escaping hotter, lighter air—a great fire often produces its own wind, a whirling wind that throws burning debris far in advance of the main fire. These smaller fires sometimes burn together, trapping life between the main fire coming from behind and the new fire racing back toward it. In Chicago, many people were caught in this pincerlike fire action.

As Norman Maclean points out in his study of the Mann Gulch forest fire in the Montana wilderness, fire whirls can also be created by winds shearing off large obstacles, like cliffs, giving "the fires a spin and starting them to whirl." Though we have no hard evidence, this undoubtedly happened in Chicago's business district in the early morning of October 9. There the "cliffs" were massive four- and five-story brick buildings; and like Mann Gulch in the dry summer of 1949, these physical obstacles were in front of the advancing fire, with the wind behind the fire, pushing it incessantly.

These fire whirls are the reason the Chicago River could not contain the fire, first on the West Side and then on the South Side. When the fire spread to the largely residential North Side, built almost entirely of wood, it would not stop until it burned itself out on the prairie just beyond newly built Lincoln Park.

•

At about two-thirty on Monday morning, just as the courthouse tower collapsed, a piece of burning wood was carried by a fire devil across the main branch of the river and landed in a railroad car carrying kerosene. From this point, the fire moved in a diagonal line, west to east, across the North Side to the engine house of the Waterworks, "like a wild beast," Joseph Kirkland wrote, "intent on destroying . . . the enemy which it must either kill or be killed by."

The night crew at the Waterworks was on alert, guarding every exposed part of the building. With its walls made of heavy stone, its wooden roof covered with slate, and plenty of open space around it, the building seemed invulnerable. But when a burning timber fell on its roof and became lodged against one of the building's turrets, it started a fire that tore through the roof and turned the interior, in minutes, into a raging furnace. The water-storage tower across the street was only slightly damaged, but it held only enough water to supply the city's mains for several minutes. When it went dry, only the fire engines working near the lake and the river remained operable. Chicago was now helpless.

From the Waterworks the fire spread in all directions. Residents on the near North Side were standing at their doors watching the South Side burn when they discovered, to their horror, that the fire was behind them, driving like a cyclone. The fire moved faster through the North Side than in any other part of the city, devouring eleven blocks of houses in less than an hour, including the two-story brick home of Leander McCormick, who escaped in a company wagon with his family, accompanied by his brother Cyrus, who was staying at the Sherman House on a business trip from New York, where he had been living the past four years. The Reaper King had raced from the hotel to his brother's house to warn him that the fire was raging out of control.

The swiftness with which the fire struck is described by a North Side woman. At about two in the morning, she and her sister were awakened by thunderous explosions coming from the center of town. As they rushed to their bedroom windows, they heard a hard knock at the front door—a friend to warn them to pack what they valued most and prepare to evacuate. But there was no time. When a ball of blazing wood and cinders slammed into their door, they hurried into the street, one of them carrying a parrot in its cage, the other pulling a trunk with the help of a neighbor. They headed north, and when they chanced to look back at their house, they saw a surging "wall of fire . . . steadily advancing on our midnight helplessness."

It did not take them long to discover that they were hemmed in by fire and that there was no escape except to the Sands, the now largely abandoned lakeshore spot near the mouth of the river that "Long John" Wentworth had cleared of gamblers and prostitutes and where William Ogden had recently built a pier for his warehousing and shipping businesses. The sky was a brilliant yellowish red—it was night but as bright as midday—and the streets were filled with people dressed in nightshirts and nightgowns, many of them separated from their loved ones by the push and confusion and by wagons pulled by skittish, sweating horses, some of them being led through the fire shower by men with water-soaked blankets pulled over their heads. "Like an immense drove of panic-stricken sheep, the terrified mass ran, and rushed, and scrambled, and screamed through the streets," said a reporter of the desperate stampede to the lakefront. Local Jeremiahs stood on street corners, their hands raised to heaven, crying that the fire was the Almighty's judgment on this American Gomorrah, and people saw entire houses lifted in the air and thrown on top of other houses.

Those survivors not trapped on the Sands escaped to the open ground northwest of the city or fled to Lincoln Park and the abandoned cemetery just south of it. "The cry was 'North! North!'" recalled Mrs. Aurelia R. King, the wife of a city merchant who fled in that direction with her children clinging to her. She described the ordeal to friends two weeks later: "You could not conceive anything more fearful. The wind was like a tornado, and I held fast to my little ones, fearing they would be lifted from my sight. I could only think of Sodom or Pompeii, and truly I thought the day of judgment had come."

Her family moved on blindly, not knowing where they were headed until they entered Lincoln Park. Thousands of fugitives were already in the park, some of them huddling for protection in the yet unfilled graves of the old cemetery.

There were even more people on the prairie west of the city, as many as thirty thousand—the McCormicks and other North Side swells camped on the bare ground next to the "lowliest vagabond and the meanest harlot"—all "reduced to a common level of misery."

Some people talked in low tones of their losses, but most had been reduced to silence by the magnitude of the disaster.

•

By the time the sun rose, around six o'clock Monday morning, a great part of Chicago had been reduced to charred prairie, and thousands remained trapped on the Sands, the lake behind them, the fire still burning strongly all around them. A North Side woman, Del Moore, recalled that as bad as things had gone, she felt something still worse was coming but did not dare guess its extent. Just as this thought passed through her mind, she heard a cry: "The lumberyard is on fire!"

William Ogden's enormous lumber enclosure lay on the banks of the river just south and west of the Sands, and when it went up in flames, the fire spread to the entire Chicago exchange engine—the Illinois Central complex on one side of the river and the McCormick Reaper Works and William Ogden's railroad and lumber operations on the other. Clouds of black smoke rolled over the Sands, and at this moment, "such a scene of horror and terror as ensued I cannot make you imagine," Del Moore later wrote her parents. "The sun disappeared, the wind increased, straw blew, feather beds and blankets blazed and even the people were on fire. . . . For the only time unmitigated fear took possession of me. I begged Gus [her husband] if I took fire to put me in the Lake and drown me, not let me burn to death."

Horse-drawn wagons were driven into the lake, and some people jumped on them in desperation. Others stood in the water up to their necks, their backs to the fire, the air almost too hot to breathe. The lumberyard burned all day, "pouring . . . hot smoke on us, [but] cut off as we were by fire at the North . . . we [had] to bear as best we could." Almost as bad as the smoke and furnacelike heat "was the driving burning sand cutting us like needle points and putting our eyes nearly out. We watched each other that we should not burn. I was on fire three times but smothered the flames." Through all this, the people, Del Moore said, remained composed. "No one complained."

When the fires to the north and south of them subsided later in the day, Del Moore's family followed other refugees up the line of the lake to what seemed a safer spot, their camp that cold night lit by the glow of the still-burning ruins of their homes.

•

Small groups of desperate people had escaped the Sands earlier in the day by water either by taking rowboats out into the lake, where many craft became caught in rough water and remained stranded for days, or by being ferried from Ogden's Pier and an adjacent pier by tugs and propeller-driven ships.

The rescue of Isaac Arnold and his family is one of the most sensational stories of the fire. An esteemed city founder, Arnold was retired from law and politics in 1871 and was about to begin a biography of Lincoln, having already written a study of his presidency. He did his writing in his home, two blocks south of the Waterworks, an urban estate of fountains, statuary, greenhouses, and orchards. Arnold's library contained over ten thousand books and ten thick volumes of letters, including many from Lincoln, Grant, McClellan, Sherman, and Seward, men he knew from the two terms in Congress he served during the war as an antislavery Republican, having switched to the party of "Free Soil, Free Men" in the 1850s with his friend William Ogden. For the past ten years Arnold had also been collecting the speeches, writings, and state papers of Lincoln, and he owned some of the most valuable paintings in Chicago. Arnold was unable to save anything in his house because he tried to save everything.

When the fire spread to the North Side, Arnold's wife took their youngest daughter and went off to help a married daughter who lived not far away. Arnold remained with his three other children and a staff of servants to try to save the house. For a desperate hour or so, they were able to put out small fires on the house and grounds, but at around three in the morning, the barn, the front piazza, and the roof took fire simultaneously, and at that moment their water supply ran out. Grabbing a stack of papers in his study, Arnold called together his family and household help and headed for the Sands, the gardener riding a horse and holding on to the family cow by the horns.

Arnold led his family to the end of Ogden's Pier, where they found a rowboat and crossed to a lighthouse just ahead. There they were met by some of their North Side neighbors, including the family of Edward I. Tinkham. Tinkham, the cashier of the Second National Bank, was guarding a trunk containing $1.6 million of his bank's money in greenbacks and securities.

With the wind blowing strongly from the direction of the fire, Arnold thought that even the iron lighthouse was unsafe, but all avenues of escape by land were cut off. Late Monday afternoon, a tug steamed downriver through the vortex of the fire and tied up near the lighthouse, its deck and gunwales blistered from the heat it had just passed through. Arnold asked the pilot if he could take his party—including Tinkham and his money—back up the river, running the gauntlet of the fire to an unburned area of the West Side. The captain—his courage, no doubt, raised by a hefty bounty—said he could.

The women and children were placed in the pilothouse, with the portholes shut tight, and the men crouched on the deck behind the protection of the bulwarks. After hooking up a hose to the pumps to put out any fires that might break out onboard, the captain pointed the *Clifford* upriver into a thin opening between two curtains of smoke that appeared to reach to the dome of the sky. At the fallen State Street bridge he had to slow down to pick his way through the burning debris, and at this point, with the air filled with sparks and glowing cinders, the pumps gave out, and the boilers began to strain. Arnold pushed his young son flat on the deck and covered his face with a wet handkerchief, while the other men smothered fires on the pilothouse with their coats. Some screamed to turn back, but it would have been more dangerous to do that. Minutes later, when the tug passed the tangled wreckage of the Wells Street Bridge, the pilot shouted to Arnold, "We are through, sir," and in what seemed like seconds, the air cleared and cooled.

Arnold landed with no idea where his wife and the rest of his family were. He spent the next twenty-four hours searching for them, passing through the survivors in Lincoln Park and on the prairie, "peering into every grimy countenance." Sometime Tuesday afternoon, he heard that they were all at the house of a friend in the suburbs, and the entire family was reunited that evening.

Meanwhile, Tinkham and his family caught a train to Milwaukee, where Tinkham deposited in a bank vault the fortune he could easily have walked away with.

•

Sixty-nine-year-old Gurdon Hubbard, Isaac Arnold's Old Settler friend, also lost his house, the autobiography he was working on, and virtually all his other personal possessions in the fire. Hubbard had gone to bed at an early hour on Sunday evening after attending church services with his wife, Mary Ann, confident that the fire on the West Side would be put out. Mary Ann Hubbard was unable to sleep, however, and as she watched the fire spread to the South Side from a window near her dressing table, she tried several times to get her husband to come and have a look. When she finally succeeded in rousing him and he saw the three-hundred-foot-high flames just across the river, he swung around and yelled at the top of his voice, "My God, we are all going to be burned up." He immediately ordered the servants to tear up the carpets in the house, soak them in the cistern, and spread them on the mansard roof. While he worked with them nailing wet carpets to the exposed wood, his wife set out all the food in the house for the many fire victims who came there that night for refuge. Biscuits and coffee were put out on the front porch for refugees streaming by on the streets.

By the time the roof took fire and began to spit cinders and hot shingles, Mary Ann Hubbard and two nieces who lived with them had packed a dozen or so trunks, which were loaded on hired wagons, Hubbard instructing the drivers to take them to a safe spot and return when the fire burned out.

The Hubbards never saw the drivers, or their possessions, again. When they returned to La Salle Street two days later from the residence of their son, they found their handsome home a blackened ruin. Only a few possessions they had buried in the garden were recovered.

As the Hubbards were fleeing from their home on Monday morning, the fire was burning in two directions, northward to Lincoln Park and southward to the lakefront mansions along South Michigan Avenue.

Explosives were used successfully to contain the fire on the South Side once it spread outside the thickly built up business section, and it was stopped late in the afternoon at Harrison Street. That night, it halted at the city limits on the North Side. There was nothing left to burn.

The last group of buildings to fall on the South Side was Terrace Row, a connected block of elegant stone town houses facing the lake on the spot where Louis Sullivan's Auditorium Building now stands. J. Young Scammon, who lived at the south end of Terrace Row, was out of town during the fire, but his friend, Robert Todd Lincoln, the young Chicago corporate lawyer and eldest son of the slain president, helped Mrs. Scammon load onto wagons the contents of his magnificent library. As Mrs. Scammon, standing on the roof of her house, watched the fire strike the stables in the rear of Terrace Row, William Bross, having sent his family to safety, was sitting on the lakeshore, his neighbors huddled near him, "calmly awaiting the destruction of our property—one of the most splendid blocks in Chicago." Just before noon, flames began shooting from the windows of his home. "Quickly and grandly they wrapped up the whole block," Bross recalled, "and away it floated in black clouds over Lake Michigan."

Just before the fire began consuming Terrace Row, the hotelier John B. Drake was walking past the Michigan Avenue Hotel, a short distance up the street, on his way back from inspecting the ruins of his Tremont House. On an impulse, he went inside, found the owner, and offered to buy the hotel with a thousand dollars he had in his pocket as a down payment. The deal was made and witnessed, and as Drake turned to walk up Michigan Avenue, the seller shouted to him, pointing to the flames coming from the roofs of Terrace Row: "This building will go next." But the work of the explosives men and of firemen who had set up a relay line from the lake—each engine feeding the one next to it—made John Drake one of the luckiest men in Chicago that day.

Late Monday night, a cold drizzle began to fall. The fire had already run its course, but the rain made certain it would not flare up again. Mary Fales, a neighbor of the Hubbards', expressed the reaction of the entire city in a letter to her mother. "I never felt so grateful in my life as to hear the rain pour down."

2. Unapproachable in Calamity

On Tuesday at daybreak, a man who had been out of town during the fire arrived back in Chicago by train. Before heading home, he walked the city's streets trying to comprehend the almost unimaginable catastrophe. The damp streets were deserted and lined with bare, blistered trees, their black branches pointing to the northeast, the direction in which the winds had driven the fire. He felt as if he were in a large and ancient cemetery, the piles of fallen buildings looking, through the gray smoke, like stone vaults and mausoleums. No one was around, he guessed, because people were exhausted by the terror and suffering of the night before. "I was . . . left alone with these pitiful ruins. . . . Alone with the ghost of Chicago!"

Passing over the collapsing remains of one of the river bridges, he could see the desolated center of town just ahead. But except for the still-standing walls of a few familiar landmarks, he would not have been able to recognize his city. All "the new palaces of marble . . . were leveled in the dust, or shattered into unrecognizable fragments." A rich and magnificent city had sunk into its coal cellars and basements.

"Since yesterday, Chicago has gained another title to prominence," the *New York Tribune* reported that same morning. "Unequalled before in enterprise and good fortune, she is now unapproachable in calamity."

The first business of that new day was the assessment of the damage, the gathering up of the dead and wounded, and the search for the missing.

In thirty hours the fire had left a corridor of ruin over four miles long and almost a mile wide. But the driving wind that caused such destruction also limited its extent, keeping the "destroyer" to a channel cutting to the northeast from the O'Leary cottage, which firemen had been able to save.

It was one of the great urban catastrophes of modern times. Property worth $190 million was destroyed—seventy-three miles of streets and 17,450 buildings—and almost 100,000 persons were left homeless. (If the houses that burned had been set ten feet apart, they would have formed a row over a hundred miles long.) One hundred and twenty bodies were recovered, but the county coroner estimated the number of dead at near three hundred, most of them from the poorest classes. An accurate count was impossible because people fell from bridges into the river and their bodies were never found. Many more victims were utterly annihilated, "leaving no trace of a life or a death."

A makeshift morgue was set up in a livery stable, and over three thousand people came the first day to view the seventy or so bodies and parts of bodies that were laid out in rows on the dirt floor, a pile of coffins standing nearby for the remains of those who could be identified.

The fire could only be compared, said local newspapers, to the London Fire of 1666 and the burning of Moscow in 1812 by Napoleon. But the area destroyed by the Chicago fire, they almost boasted, was twice as great as the total area destroyed by both of these earlier fires. "It has been the greatest fire of the age," a Chicago salesman wrote an English customer, "far exceeding the great Fire of London in 1666!" Chicago, its insistent boosters believed, had to be first in everything.

On Tuesday evening, the man most responsible for building the city that fire destroyed returned to it by express train from New York. "I know of few scenes in history or fiction more thrilling," said Isaac Arnold, "than Mr. Ogden's arrival in Chicago, on the tenth of October."

After the Civil War, Ogden's business interests had caused him to spend more of his time in New York, and in 1866 he bought a magnificent villa, called Boscobel, on Fordham Heights, with a frontage of nearly a half mile on the Harlem River. He was living there in semi-retirement when word reached him by telegraph that "all Chicago is burning!"

Ogden received dispatches of the progress of the fire on his way to Chicago but was unprepared for the "utterly indescribable scene of destruction and ruin" he encountered. "When I reached the depot," he wrote a friend the next day, "it was quite dark, the burning district had no lamps, thousands of smoldering fires were all that could be seen, and they added to the mournful gloom of all around and do so yet." Seeing no one he knew, he hired a hack and started for his house. He directed the driver as best he could. "Often, however, I was lost among the unrecognizable ruins and could not tell where I was; not a living thing was to be seen."

As Ogden passed through the wreckage of the city, he must have been thinking of how bare and desolate Chicago had looked when he first set eyes on it in the 1830s and of all he had done to build it up. And now this.

When he came out of the tunnel to the North Side, he saw that everything was "in ashes." Finding his way with difficulty to his neighborhood, he got down from the hack and climbed around the ruins of fallen houses—pale blue anthracite fires burning in every exposed cellar—until "I came to the ruined trees and broken basement wall—all that remained of my more than 30 years pleasant home."

He then went in search of his brother Mahlon's house, where the Newberry Library now stands. Along the way he stopped by the Waterworks and was told that Mahlon's house was the only unburned residence between the river and Lincoln Park.* When Ogden found it, a guard was posted outside against criminals and arsonists. After identifying himself, Ogden found his brother and several mutual friends sitting in the front room. The rest of the family had been sent in a lumber wagon to Riverside, just beyond the city limits.

The next morning, Ogden was up at daybreak inspecting his properties. He had lost almost everything, he learned, except for the ground on which all that he had built in Chicago had stood, it being the only thing the fire could not destroy. Mahlon's losses were also great. "Millions will not cover the loss of our family," William Ogden wrote a friend back East.

That same day, Ogden learned of the destruction of Peshtigo, his Wisconsin lumber town. It had been consumed by a fire that began at almost the exact moment that flames were seen rising from the roof of the O'Leary barn. After spending several days helping with the relief effort in Chicago, Ogden took a lake steamer to Green Bay.

•

Approaching Peshtigo by wagon, he stopped at a high point overlooking the village, now an ash-covered clearing in a blackened forest of oak, pine, and tamarack, with the fast-running Peshtigo River coursing through the swath of destruction. Charred carcasses of horses, cows, bears, and deer lay on dirt roads radiating out into the forest, and smoke was still ascending from the wells where villagers had thrown their belongings—and in a few tragic instances, their children—in the first terrible minutes of the most destructive fire in North American history, a fire that hit the village so suddenly that many of its victims never knew what killed them.

The previous Sunday evening, at around eight o'clock, most of the townspeople of Peshtigo were walking home from evening church services when they heard a strange noise coming from a place somewhere in the forest. Then, with a deafening roar, a swirling fireball a hundred feet high swept into the town. The fire moved faster than life could run away from it, and in an instant, scores of people in the streets were reduced to ash. Those who had some warning tried to get to the river. From the western end of town about three hundred people made it, grabbing hold of logs to stay afloat, but those coming from the east were hit full in the face by the "swirling blasts. . . . Inhalation was annihilation," wrote a New York reporter who interviewed the survivors.

Over eleven hundred persons were killed in and around Peshtigo, a

*Eight or nine other buildings survived, according to a map made by a North Side man just after the fire.

village of two thousand—over three times as many as in Chicago. And these two tragedies of fire and wind were related in a cruelly ironic way. The tornado of flames that tore through the Wisconsin forest toward Peshtigo, a "frontier mart of Chicago," was fed by shavings and other debris left in piles by lumbermen cutting timber for buildings in Chicago that burned like tinder on October 8 and 9.

William Ogden, builder of both Chicago and Peshtigo, was a double loser that October evening. He would not, however, accept defeat in either place. Chicago would rise again, and so would Peshtigo. Ogden remained in Peshtigo into December directing the work of reconstruction through sleet and snow. Rising at daybreak, he worked until nightfall and then rode in an open cart pulled by mules eight miles to his harbor complex on Green Bay. From there he made one final trip to Chicago to join a delegation headed for Springfield to lobby for state assistance for the relief and rebuilding of his adopted city.

•

A week after the fire, John B. Drake stopped by the Michigan Avenue Hotel with the balance due on his new purchase. When the seller refused to close the deal, Drake walked out and returned with several large men. Placing his watch on a table, he told the proprietor he had five minutes to seal the agreement or he would be thrown into the lake. Drake renamed his hotel the Tremont House after the ruined building, and it became a local landmark, marking the southern boundary of the fire, and a symbol of the city's amazing recovery from one of the greatest disasters of modern times.

Aid for stricken Chicago came in from all across the country and from over twenty-five foreign nations. Schools and churches in the unburned area were opened to victims, and Mayor Roswell B. Mason, a former manager of the Illinois Central Railroad, turned over almost the entire relief effort to the Chicago Relief and Aid Society, a private group founded in the 1850s by the city's Protestant commercial elite. Mason and other Chicagoans of consequence were convinced that this organization of upstanding civic guardians would handle the fire relief program more honestly and efficiently than political bosses on the common council, who were beholden to the city's unruly immigrants.

At times, the society seemed as interested in maintaining public order as in alleviating suffering, seeing relief as an antidote to an uprising by a "starving, fierce, and lawless mob." But to its credit, it did a great amount of good. Society doctors vaccinated over sixty thousand people against smallpox, preventing an epidemic in the vulnerable city, and society directors raised almost $5 million worldwide to dispense relief to over half the city's population—clothing, bedding, medical care, food, fuel, and water, along with jobs for men and some five thousand sewing machines for women to make clothing they could sell to help support their families, the society's leaders believing that able-bodied victims should help themselves whenever possible.

With this in mind and with winter fast approaching, skilled workers who had lost their homes were given materials to build single-family wooden cottages, and by mid-November, there were over five thousand of these "shelter houses" scattered about the city. Crude barracks were built for former tenement dwellers. "To see the lines of rough sheds which are taking the place of all the magnificent buildings destroyed is simply heartbreaking," said a wealthy Chicago woman, her remarks as telling of her feelings about the poor as of her sadness for her fallen city.

Relief trains were organized in New York by Jay Gould and William Vanderbilt, and President Grant sent a check for one thousand dollars to the relief committee, along with an invitation to his friend George Pullman and his family to stay at the White House, fearing they had been burned out of their home. Pullman's house was untouched by the fire, but he and his wife accepted the invitation anyway.

Not everyone, however, was moved by Chicago's plight. An Indiana newspaper that had been sympathetic to the Confederacy pointed out that more lives and property were destroyed in the South by the "plundering" of Generals Sheridan and Sherman than by the Chicago fire. Chicago, which contributed thousands of men to Sherman's army, "did her full share in the destruction of the South. God adjusts balances. Maybe with Chicago the books are now squared."

Ogden's delegation was successful in getting some disaster relief from the state of Illinois, but the recovery was largely a self-help effort. The first concern was for the safety of the part of the city that had not been burned. With the Waterworks down, Chicago was defenseless against another fire. A furious around-the-clock effort got the pumps going by the end of October, and by then much of the city was supplied with gas and serviced by streetcars. Depositors and city bankers were relieved to learn that most of the money in Chicago's bank vaults and safes, which had been too hot to open right after the fire, was undamaged. Most banks were back in business shortly after the fire, and the rebuilding went ahead without official records of land title because on the first night of the fire the city's "abstract men" had managed to haul away in wagons their abstracted copies of property transfers.

The big losers in the business community were the insurance companies and, more tragically, their policyholders. Fifty-eight companies were driven into bankruptcy, ruining tens of thousands of people.

When all claims had been settled, only half of the money owed Chicago policyholders was paid.

Chicago's first insurance agent, Gurdon Hubbard, was still heavily involved in the business and felt honor-bound to sell off his own property to pay the claims of people he had personally underwritten, since many of the companies he had invested in or represented were pressed into bankruptcy. While young men like Potter Palmer were able to recover from the fire in a matter of months, for Gurdon Hubbard the fire was "a catastrophe," as a friend of his wrote later. "His resilience was gone."

•

In the first days after the fire, there were sensationalist reports in the newspapers of looting and incendiarism, and wild rumors circulated of an anticipated influx of out-of-town criminals, intent on breaking into the safes and vaults in the business district. Local businessmen hired Chicago-based Allan Pinkerton to deploy his forces of private policemen to guard the ruins of their stores, offices, and banks. Pinkerton, with his characteristic exuberance, issued a public warning that "death shall be [the] fate [of] any person stealing or seeking to steal any property in my charge." Gen. Phil Sheridan, stationed in Chicago since 1869 as commander of the Military Division of the Missouri, brought in six companies of regular infantry and positioned them in areas of the South Side patrolled by Pinkerton's men, where there were believed to be two or three vaults to every block. Two days later, Mayor Mason, at the insistence of a delegation of business leaders, placed Chicago under martial law, entrusting General Sheridan, a great friend of the most influential leaders of the Relief and Aid Society, with the good order and safety of the city.

Although he dismissed reports of incendiarism, murders, and lynchings as "the most absurd rumors," Sheridan did muster a volunteer home guard of a thousand men to protect the unburned areas of the city and enforce a curfew. Gov. John M. Palmer angrily protested Mason's imposition of martial law, insisting that it was illegal—a violation of state's rights—and unnecessary. But the mayor, a creature of Chicago's commercial community, feared its reaction more than his governor's and ignored Palmer's order to withdraw the troops.

Late the following night, Col. Thomas W. Grosvenor, a member of a citizens' group that had gone to Sheridan to urge him to take control of the city, was walking home from a party on the South Side when he was ordered to halt and identify himself by one of Sheridan's sentries, a nineteen-year-old college student who had never fired a weapon in his life. "Go to hell and bang away," Grosvenor is said to have replied, the claret he had been drinking overcoming his good sense. Seconds later, a bullet cut through his lungs.

He died that night at his home. Several days later, the mayor ended martial law and had Sheridan disband his Chicago Volunteers.

City leaders, however, remained anxious about their property, and a group from the Relief and Aid Society privately asked Sheridan to recall at least some of the troops. After clearing his decision with President Grant, Sheridan restationed four companies of infantry in Chicago, where they remained through the first of the year. City reporters Elias Colbert and Everett Chamberlin spoke for relieved property owners: "Under the shadow of the American Eagle's protecting wing, the people went . . . about their business, and at night lay down and slept soundly."

A coroner's jury declared Grosvenor's death a murder, and young Theodore N. Treat was arrested. With Sheridan supporting him, Treat argued in his defense that he did not know his victim was "an influential man" and by his uncivil language thought he must have been a "rough." Treat was released, and no further charges were brought against him.

Kate O'Leary did not fare as well. Hounded by the press and curious sightseers, she moved with her family from De Koven Street and became a recluse, leaving her home only to go to morning mass and run errands. Until her death in 1895, reporters would crowd her door every year on the anniversary of the fire to plead for a statement from the woman several of them had described as a drunken Irish welfare cheat who had started the fire in revenge for being taken off the city's relief rolls. (She never received government charity in her life.) When she refused to talk to them, as she always did, they invented interviews with her. Although she never allowed herself to be photographed, bogus photographs of her milking the most famous cow in history appeared in newspapers and magazines.

In 1892 a Chicago fire victim and prominent clergyman, Rev. David Swing, wrote that "it is probable the cow-story sprang up out of the inventive power of some man or woman who was hungry for a small cause for a great disaster." Twenty-nine years after the fire, Michael Ahern admitted to a fellow reporter, John Kelley, that he and two other reporters, James Haynie and John English, "concocted the story about the cow kicking over the lamp," their only basis for it being a broken kerosene lamp that was found in the wreckage of the O'Leary barn.

Just after the fire, a police- and fire-department inquiry placed the blame squarely where it belonged—on shoddy city construction, scandalously lax building-code inspection, and the city council's failure to properly staff and equip the fire department. Even if no other measures had been taken, the report suggested, the fire could have been contained on the West Side by two fireboats the department had repeatedly requested.

The report, interestingly, neglected to mention the department's own fatal mistake in locating the fire and promptly sending engines to it. Chief Fire Marshal Robert A. Williams unwittingly brought attention to his own department's culpability: "One great reason that the Chicago department has had such good success as they have had in this wooden city [is] . . . they have been right on their taps and on it before it got started."

But it was Elias Colbert and Everett Chamberlin who gave what would become the officially accepted version of the cause of the Great Chicago Fire. "The city was carelessly, and, with the exception of a single square mile, very badly built," they argued in their instant history of the fire, *Chicago and the Great Conflagration*, published in December 1871. The key words here—"with the exception of a single square mile"—shifted blame from the businessmen and architects who built that "single square mile," and from a city council that allowed them to build as they pleased, to the city's poor people and to the government's misplaced "generosity" in allowing them to build "inflammable" pine shanties in and around the business district. These clapboard houses, said Colbert and Chamberlin, were the "rations" on which the fire fed.

This was exactly the rationale Chicago businessmen needed to go forward with their plans for the "Great Rebuilding." The poor and their shanties would be removed from the larger and more modern downtown area, and technology—in the form of the latest fireproofing techniques—would make Chicago the safest city in the world. It would have been far more difficult for civic reconstructionists to accept the idea implicit in the fire department's official report—that Chicago's very approach to urban development, one that put physical growth over everything else, was one of the reasons this relentlessly expanding city was almost completely destroyed by a fire it could not have prevented but could have kept from causing such appalling losses of life and property. The civic optimism and unlicensed expansionism that had propelled Chicago forward and made her what she was almost did her in.

The creation of Chicago might have been a victory over nature, but nature had horribly exposed the city's vulnerability. No humbling lesson of this sort, however, was learned by the generation that lived through the fire. The rebuilding, for them, would be one more example, the greatest yet, of their city's capacity to overcome all physical obstacles and calamities and of the mastery of man—the City Maker—over nature's domain.

•

No city ever recovered from a disaster as speedily or spectacularly as did Chicago. But the accounts of its miracle-like "resurrection" minimize the punishing impact of the fire—the psychological as well as physical damage it inflicted. Joseph Medill's oft-quoted "Chicago Shall Rise Again" editorial, written while the ground was still hot, expressed the gritty civic pride that would power the resurgence. But Frederick Law Olmsted's "Chicago in Distress," the sober report he filed on special assignment for *The Nation* one month after the fire, gives a truer indication of the mixed mood of the city as it prepared to begin an urban building boom without precedent.

"For a time men were unreasonably cheerful and hopeful," Olmsted wrote. "Now, this stage appears to have passed. In its place there is sternness; but so narrow is the division between this and another mood, that in the midst of a sentence a change of quality in the voice occurs, and you see that eyes have moistened."

As much as people wanted to block out the past, the awful scale of the disaster would not let them. "We are in ruins," a young lawyer wrote his mother. "Our house tonight is like the house of death. I cannot see any way to get along here. Thirty years of prosperity cannot restore us."

Thousands of the fire victims were people like this, young professionals and salaried workers who, with their families, had to be sought out by relief committees because they would "not ask or be publicly known to receive charity." These were characteristic Chicagoans, people who had bought the notion—the Chicago "maxim," Olmsted called it—that even a fool could make money by buying a small piece of city real estate, putting a house on it, and holding on to it for a few years. To pay their mortgage and insurance bills "they lived pinchingly," Olmsted wrote, "and their houses and lots were their only reserves. In thousands of cases, they have lost their houses, their insurance, and their situations all at one blow."

The disaster, however, fell most heavily on the poor—victims Olmsted barely mentions in his report. Most of them had no family or friends to fall back on, and they had to stand in food lines and spend nearly every night searching for safe, dry places to sleep. They boiled drinking water on campfires, fearing cholera and typhoid, and fought off rats and wild dogs that invaded their camps on the cold, damp prairie. And when they applied for jobs through the Relief and Aid Society, they were investigated by society "visitors" to see if they were not pretending "want." All the while, the wealthy received special attention from the society, getting aid directly without having to go to distribution stations, where they would have had to line up with the unwashed. They were accorded special treatment, the society explained, because they "were not accustomed to exposures and hardships which were easily borne by the laboring people" and because "the change in their condition and circumstances was greater and more disastrous. They were borne in a single night from homes of comfort and plenty into absolute destitution."

What Olmsted's report does come close to capturing is the almost universal reaction of a community that has suffered through a sudden and near complete catastrophe—whether a fire, a hurricane, or a modern bombing raid. By early November, the immediate rush of energy and optimism that usually follows such calamities had given way to a hard fight for survival and the deflating realization of the magnitude of the rebuilding effort. "I for one do not expect to see [Chicago] restored to where it was a few short weeks ago," Anna E. Higginson wrote to a friend one week after Olmsted's story was published. "The men of Chicago are heroes; their energy, cheerfulness & determination are something almost sublime; but I fear many a brave heart will sink under difficulties utterly insurmountable."

Olmsted, however, cut closer to the prevailing feeling. No one could yet see "how the city is to recover from this blow," he concluded. But "that in some way it will recover, and that it will presently advance even with greater rapidity, but with far firmer steps, than ever before, those most staggered and cast down by it have not a shadow of doubt."

•

Passing through streets filled with workers pulling down ruined walls, Marshall Field found a temporary site for his retail store in a brick barn on the South Side. Several days later, as he directed the removal of hay and dung and the installation of display counters, he sketched in his mind plans for a new store back on State Street, which Potter Palmer vowed to rebuild on a grander scale. "I will rebuild my buildings at once," Palmer wired his employees from New York after the fire. "Put on an extra force, and hurry up the hotel."

In the first hours of the fire, the architect of the Palmer House, John M. Van Osdel, had buried the building's blueprints in a hole in the basement and covered them with thick layers of sand and clay. The plans were recovered and formed the basis for the new and larger Palmer House, built with millions of dollars in loans Palmer secured on his reputation alone. When Van Osdel uncovered the perfectly preserved plans, he became convinced of the soundness of a new method of fireproofing with clay tiles that he would use in other Chicago buildings.

The city's "Reaper King" also rebuilt his Chicago properties on a vaster scale. Hours after the fire broke out, Cyrus McCormick wired his wife in New York, asking her to join him. Meeting her at the station with a burned coat and hat, a local story has it, he decided, after talking with her that night, to sell their house in New York, move back to Chicago, and rebuild the reaper factory at another site in the city. When construction began in Canaltown, massive, gray-bearded Cyrus McCormick could be seen nearby on his favorite saddle horse watching the walls go up.

"Old Hutch" had observed the fire from the roof of his brick packing plant, where he watched his Corn Exchange Bank burn. The next morning he opened the bank in a basement property downtown. Hutchinson lost most of his fortune in the fire and for many weeks was absent from the "pit," which was moved to a new site. But one day he showed up unannounced, wearing his familiar black hat, and began bidding wheat for future delivery. "The day of his power lay ahead," his biographer wrote.

Even before the rebuilding of the city had begun, William Bross, Chicago's very own minister of propaganda, went to New York to buy new equipment for the *Tribune*. The first fire survivor to reach that city, he was interviewed wherever he went and used the opportunities to make sweeping pronouncements and predictions. "Go to Chicago now!" he thundered. "Young men, hurry there! Old men, send your sons! Women, send your husbands! You will never again have such a chance to make money!" Chicago, he prophesied, "will be rebuilt in five years, and will have a population of a million by 1900." (It reached that number by 1890.)*

New York papers took up the cry. "The wonder of [Chicago's] original growth will be forgotten in the greater wonder of its sudden new creation," declared the *New York World*. Even Chicago's bitterest rival conceded it would be rebuilt completely, bigger and more powerful than ever. But the "sad feature in this bright picture of future glory and greatness," said the *St. Louis Republican*, "is that [many of] the victims in the calamity will not . . . participate in it." When "a towering city [is built] on the site of the destroyed one, we shall find that [it] is in the hands of a new generation. . . . The ruined great men of Chicago will

*John S. Wright, Chicago's other great booster, began to lose his mind after the fire and had to be put in an asylum, where he died in 1874.

have given place to others." This was also the parting prediction of Chicago's founder.

Chicago "will be built up again in good time," William Ogden wrote his niece before returning permanently to New York, "[but] a great many of the old citizens who have assisted to build it up and lived to enjoy it . . . will never, I fear, be able at their more advanced period of life, to regain their former positions." Their place, he said, would be taken by "new-comers with money," men such as Marshall Field, Potter Palmer, and George Pullman, who had arrived in the city in the 1850s and amassed fortunes during and after the war.

Ogden knew these rising younger men and worried about them. Wonderfully innovative in business, they seemed, however, to live for little else but gain. Chicago had always been filled with men like this, but Ogden had seen his own circle of public-spirited leaders as a check, however limited, on their rampant acquisitiveness.

The generation of the 1850s had come from the same part of the country as Chicago's original elite, but only a few of them envisioned themselves as carriers of culture as well as commerce to the raw West. City builders like William Ogden, Isaac Arnold, and J. Young Scammon were as proud of their personal libraries as they were of their bank balances, and they linked self-advancement with civic advancement, investing in land, mills, railroads, libraries, learned societies, and charities. And unlike the newer men, they were passionately engaged in politics. Whatever influenced Chicago's future they had a hand in. Isaac Arnold evoked their deep sense of themselves as urban pioneers, New World founders of a new kind of city: "What is done here . . . in this great central city of the continent . . . is to influence, for good or evil, our whole country. . . . The responsibility of a vast future is upon us."

If Chicago was to become a truly great city "she must encourage and honor men of culture, letters and science," Arnold told his fellow founders of the Chicago Historical Society in 1868. The "merchant princes" of the city should take as their models not Liverpool or Amsterdam alone but also Athens and Florence. "It is time, I think . . . for a new advance. We have boasted long enough of our grain elevators, our railroads, our trade in wheat and lumber, our business palaces; let us now have libraries, galleries of art, scientific museums, noble architecture and public parks . . . and a local literature; otherwise there is danger that Chicago will become merely a place where ambitious young men will come to make money and achieve fortune, and then go elsewhere to enjoy it."

No one of the older generation more eloquently expressed the higher considerations this civil elite believed should accompany urban development. It was a call, to be repeated by a succeeding generation of civic builders and visionaries—the generation of Burnham and Sullivan—for Chicago to rise to what Arnold called "the magnitude" of its responsibility.

•

He would resist returning to Boscobel, William Ogden wrote his niece, if he and Arnold and their old band of friends could head Chicago's reconstruction, rebuilding their lost city and making it more than "a town of mere traders and money-getters." But the future, he conceded, was with the "money" men.

Still, Ogden left Chicago with paternal pride in what he and his fellow founders had accomplished in a mere thirty-some years—turning a log-and-clapboard village into "the great city of the interior, [and soon] . . . perhaps, of the nation."

While he grieved for Chicago, he grieved far more, Ogden said, for his aging friends, who had lost almost everything in the fire, while he at least had a fortune to fall back on. "Never before," he wrote, "was a large and very beautiful and fortunate City built by [a] generation of people so proud, so in love with their work, never a City so lamented and grieved over as Chicago. For this I do weep with those who have far greater occasion to weep than I."

Part II

Bird's-eye view of the business district of Chicago in the 1890s.
Chicago Historical Society

Introduction:
Let Us Build
Ourselves a City

THROUGHOUT most of its history, the United States has been known to the world as a nation of builders and inventors, a country that transforms itself by technology. Our most characteristic and character shaping achievement has been our talent for invention, and in no period was this more decisively in evidence than in the final three decades of the nineteenth century. In this golden age of American invention, independent inventors introduced the lightbulb, the telephone, the typewriter, the fountain pen, the railroad refrigerator car, the air brake, the electric trolley, the Kodak camera, the movie projector, the phonograph, and the zipper. The steel-frame skyscraper was also a product of these years, and this collaborative "invention," arguably the most stupendous engineering accomplishment since the erection of the Gothic cathedrals, gave rise to and became the symbol of a new type of technological city, of which Chicago was the most dramatic example.

The builders of postfire Chicago were entrepreneurs, architects, and engineers who fashioned their products, systems, conveyances, and structures not in virtual isolation, in "dream plants" and "invention factories" like those of Thomas Alva Edison and Nikola Tesla, but in the crowded public arena, where their genius, enterprise, and cupidity were shaped by pressures generated by the needs, challenges, and desires of thousands, and eventually millions, of customers, clients, workers, reformers, and common citizens. Out of this chaos of accident and individuality, chance and choice, emerged one of the most efficiently organized cities in the world, a metropolis of over a million whose internal workings were compared by foreign visitors to those of a perfectly synchronous machine. Seventy years after Chicago was surveyed as a possible frontier canal site and three decades after a great part of it was consumed by firestorms, it had an infrastructure of urban services that was the marvel of the world—fourteen hundred miles of paved streets, thirty-eight thousand street lamps (many of them powered by electricity), almost a thousand miles of steetcar lines, a fleet of 129 fire engines, a waterworks that pumped 500 million gallons of water a day, a system of fifteen hundred miles of sewers, a Sanitary and Ship Canal that was the biggest American engineering project of the 1890s, over two thousand acres of landscaped parks, and twenty and more of the tallest, most impressively constructed buildings on earth.

Chicago's reconstruction was a two-stage process. The first phase lasted little over two years and resulted in the rebuilding of the burned-out area and the recharging of the economy. The second and more momentous act of the postfire drama began in 1880, the year the city fully recovered from a long economic depression, and lasted until the closing of the World's Columbian Exposition and the onset of an economic crisis far greater than that of the 1870s.

The fire leveled the central business district but did not destroy integral parts of Chicago's great Prairie Exchange Engine—the stockyards and new packing plants on the South Side, the eighteen trunk lines connecting the city to the nation, twenty miles of wharfage, lumberyards, and mills along the river, two-thirds of the city's grain elevators, and that part of its new factory district to the west of Mrs. O'Leary's barn.

Chicago's economy actually grew at a brisker rate in the year following the Great Fire than it had in the year before it, given impetus by a new burst of railroad construction nationwide. In 1872 alone, one-half as many miles of railroad were built in the Midwest as in the ten previous years, and in that year the Union Stock Yards handled twice as many hogs as it did in 1870. It was this uninterrupted prosperity made possible by the railroad that underwrote the "resurrection" of the city.

By March 1872, with some of its smoldering grain elevators still sending black clouds of smoke over the downtown area, Chicago had nearly twenty miles of frontage of stone and brick buidings and tens of thousands of smaller buildings completed or under construction despite what had been a winter of unusual severity. When the new Board of Trade building was dedicated with a huge civic celebration on the first anniversary of the fire, the downtown area was almost completely rebuilt. And the rebuilding went forward with even greater energy the next year, when the city dumped thousands of tons of fire debris into the lake, filling the area between South Michigan Avenue and the trestle of the Illinois Central Railroad. On this new lakefront land, W. W. Boyington designed an enormous glass and iron Exposition Hall, Chicago's own Crystal Palace and the most conspicuous emblem of its recent revival.

The following summer, a tremendous fire swept through eighteen blocks on the edge of the business district, but Chicago was saved from another holocaust by the absence of strong prairie winds. Potter Palmer's rebuilt State Street was not touched by the flames, nor were any of the new marble-fronted buildings on the other commercial arteries. The rebuilt business core of that summer of 1874 looked much the same as the downtown of 1871 except that it was larger and a few stories higher. This surprised no one, for the chief architects of the new city were the designers of the old one. In 1880, however, a new generation of architects was about to begin rebuilding again the recently restored downtown area, creating in little over a decade the world's first vertical city.

Much of the money and many of the materials for the construction of the rebuilt business core came from new industrial enterprises, for in the 1880s, Chicago, the Midwest's greatest distribution center, became a manufacturing giant as well, with the largest industrial complex west of Philadelphia. The city also expanded prodigiously in numbers and land area, almost tripling in size and spreading far outward into the prairie. The old, compact walking city became a sprawling streetcar metropolis, held together by lines of iron that converged at State Street. New factories, hotels, train stations, mansions, office blocks, theaters, clubs, and department stores were built; and with all this material progress came new interest and achievement in the arts, what locals called an urban renaissance.

No city in the world grew faster in the 1880s or was more chaotically alive than Chicago, a place people went to see the shape of the future. Entering it for the first time shattered some visitors' very ideas of what a great city was; Chicago was that spectacular and awful.

7

That Astonishing
Chicago

1. *"Grander and Statelier Than Ever"*

O N a fall morning in 1887, ten years after William Ogden's death at his estate on Fordham Heights, a reporter for the *Times* (London) left Jersey City on the Chicago Limited Express, the crack passenger "flyer" of the Pennsylvania Railroad. His assignment: to file a story on the greatest urban rebuilding effort of modern times.

The train he boarded at the Pennsylvania's sprawling terminal on the Hudson River shore, reached by ferry from Manhattan, was a symbol of Chicago's postfire pride and prosperity. Billed as the most elegantly appointed passenger train on an American railway, the Limited ran daily between New York and Chicago, a distance of just over nine hundred miles, in twenty-five hours, leaving New York harbor at 9:00 A.M. and arriving in Chicago at 9:00 A.M., local time, the next morning. The fare, including a sleeping berth, was twenty-eight dollars.

The long black locomotive pulled four sleeping coaches, a dining car with a first-class restaurant, and a "composite car," which had a compartment for luggage and mail bags, sleeping berths for the train men, and a smoking and reading room with reclining chairs, a small library, writing and card tables, a telegraph service, a toilet room with full bathing facilities, and a barbershop.

This was the morning time of luxury long-distance train travel. In the dining car of the Limited, white-coated waiters served woodcock, prairie chicken, and "the best ham what am" from the Chicago packinghouse of Morris and Company on tables set with Belgian linen and fine English China. And in the passenger wing of the composite car, a traveler could have his hair cut and curled for half a dollar, a shave for a quarter, and a bath for seventy-five cents. The smoking compartment contained "an excellent selection of current literature," the daily papers of the major American cities, stacks of engraved stationery, and a discriminating stock of wines, strong spirits, and mineral beverages.

The bright green coaches of the Limited belonged to the Pullman Palace Car Company, organized after the Civil War by the former Chicago building raiser George Mortimer Pullman. Almost single-handedly, Pullman had made land travel comfortable for the first time in history, bringing the luxuries of the fashion set to ordinary travelers for a modest bump in the regular price of a ticket. In these fabulous coaches "the dreaded journey" between New York and Chicago "becomes a mere holiday excursion," a woman rider described the relieved reaction of passengers who no longer had to dash out at station stops to grab a quick meal in a crowded depot or sleep sitting upon hard, bench-back seats. The platforms between the cars of the Chicago Limited were fitted out with the latest Pullman innovation—vestibules, accordion-like covered passageways that locked the cars together, shutting out smoke and wind, steadying and quieting the ride, and making the linked palace cars seem like a long luxury ship.

Thick carpeting, bevel-edged French mirrors, tufted footstools, frescoed ceilings, and velvet curtains transformed these coaches into a chambermaid's idea of paradise, and they were lit by electricity, the wonder of the age. The expensive bed linen supplied by Marshall Field and Company (Field was one of the Pullman Company's principal stockholders) discouraged the traveling American male's practice of sleeping with his boots on, and gilded cuspidors in the smoking room curbed the western habit of spitting on the floor. On retiring, gentlemen placed their boots under their seats and found them brilliantly polished in the morning. "It is literally a first-class American hotel on wheels," the *Times* correspondent, writing anonymously, captured perfectly the aim of what had become the largest hotel organization in the world.

Running at a speed of up to sixty miles an hour, the all-Pullman express cut across the farm and river country of Pennsylvania and out over the Alleghenies into the low hills of Ohio, where, in villages and towns formed by a recent oil boom, people turned out in crowds to watch the daily "wizzer" fly by. Following dinner with wine and an hour or so of games and conversation with his fellow passengers, the *Times* correspondent watched "nimble negro 'porters'" slip into their "snow white jackets, pull . . . down the sloping sides of the coach, and quickly [make] up the sleeping berths." After an all-night run across the prairie, the first sign of city life from the big windows of the Pullman cars the next morning was the converging of networks of steel rails toward a common destination, the Boss Town of America, the Pullman porters called it.

Steaming toward the heart of Chicago, its engine bell clanging furiously, the Limited passed through an industrial amphitheater bigger and blacker than Pittsburgh—endless reaches of factories, marshaling yards, slaughterhouses, grain elevators, and iron mills, and slag heaps and coal piles that looked like small mountains. Soot-covered cable cars and long lines of freight wagons waited at crossings for the train to shoot by, and everywhere, covering everything, were wind-driven clouds of black and gray smoke, "a sky of soot under the earth of flaming ovens."

When the Chicago express roared into the downtown business section, the *Times* reporter could barely make out the tall temples of trade through the thick bituminous smoke. As he strained to catch a glimpse of the Chicago River, jammed with industrial shipping, the train pulled into a thousand-foot-long shed with a high-arching steel-and-glass roof. White arc lights were "spluttering," steam engines were "hissing," bells were "clanging raucously," and people were "hurrying to and fro," Theodore Dreiser, a fifteen-year-old boy escaping the bare-featured life of small town America, described his own arrival at the Pennsylvania Railroad's Chicago terminus that same year.

"She-caw-go! She-caw-go!" the breakman shouted as he tore open the door of the Pullman car, and the *Times* reporter stepped down into a scene of metropolitan pandemonium.

•

"This was the age of cities," Hamlin Garland wrote of his decision to move to Chicago around this time. To live in a big city was to be in "the great stream of life." Between 1789, when Gen. George Washington set out from Mount Vernon for New York City to be sworn in as the nation's first president, and 1889, when Jane Addams set out from Rockford, Illinois, to open a settlement house in a Chicago slum, America's urban population had increased more than one hundred times, while the total population had multiplied only sixteen times. The immense depots on the borders of every large American city's business district were the gateways to this new world. Imperially designed enclosures with sweeping barrel-vaulted train sheds and lordly waiting rooms, they were miniature cities in themselves, equipped with business offices, bars, hotels, restaurants, barbershops, reading rooms, laundries, fruit stands, and even small jails and hospitals. Some of them handled over thirty thousand passengers a day, enough to populate a small city.

Chicago's railroad stations were products of the new urban milieu of money and magnificence, monuments to the centralizing agency that had created that city and defined its spirit. The best of them, Grand Central Station, was designed by Solon Spencer Beman, architect of the model town of Pullman, just south of Chicago, and of the Pullman Company's ten-story headquarters in downtown Chicago. It was an imposing temple to steam, its outstanding feature being its 242-foot-high Norman-style clock tower, a Chicago landmark in its day. The brilliantly illuminated clock, the second largest in the United States, could be seen from blocks away by passengers hurrying to catch their evening trains, and the eleven-thousand-pound bell could be heard all over the city tolling the night hours.

Incoming passengers passed through the doors of Grand Central's glass-and-iron concourse into an electrically lit carriage court where their luggage was loaded onto omnibuses by smartly uniformed drivers of the Parmelee Transfer Company and where hansoms and two-horse hacks waited to take them to their hotels. "We find ourselves in the gigantic vestibule of a large city," a nineteenth-century traveler said of the experience of entering an urban train station. "The space encloses thousands of people in any single minute and then disperses them in all directions in the next." It was architecture that operated like a smoothly disciplined machine, a miracle of the combination of speed and functionalism that defined end-of-the-century Chicago to many visitors from abroad. In this way, Chicago's railroad stations, handling a total of almost a thousand trains a day, were not only the gates to the city but concentrated expressions of metropolitan life.

For many travelers, however, the first impression formed upon arriving in Chicago was not of the rail terminal as a small city but of the city as a great terminal, "the greatest in the world," wrote the New York reporter Julian Ralph. No other city had so many major railroad stations, and four of the six were located near the fork of the river harbor, within a few blocks of one another, turning that section of the city into an intrusive maze of tracks, terminals, freight sheds, signal towers, sidings, and storage halls. The activity of this area was greatly magnified by the astounding fact that no passenger railroad passed through Chicago without interruption—a pig could go through Chicago by train, a local saying had it, but not a human being. This meant that all travelers whose final destination was not Chicago had to switch trains there—and usually terminals—often necessitating an

Vicinity of Van Buren Street and Grand Central Station, one of the great railroad districts of Chicago. The two passenger stations shown here, Van Buren Street Station (no. 1, center) and Grand Central Station (no. 2, top left), are located close to two huge hotels, Gore's (no. 3) and McCoy's (no. 4), and to the Board of Trade Building, whose main trading hall was connected by a "bridge" to the upper stories of The Rialto Building (no. 5). Bird's-eye Views and Guide to Chicago (Chicago: Rand, McNally & Co., 1898)

overnight stay, an inconvenience that proved a bonanza for the city's hotels, restaurants, and sporting houses.

Unlike older cities built before the age of steam, Chicago's physiognomy was not greatly changed by the railroad. Nineteenth-century Chicago grew up around its roads of steel, just as twentieth-century Los Angeles grew up around its concrete freeways, and was a clear creation of their commerce. The railroads owned or controlled almost any land they desired in the city, and when they finished carving up central Chicago and creating a steel ring around it, they left only a single square mile of land at the center of the city free from their direct presence. "No other great city in the world," wrote the English journalist William T. Stead, "has allowed its streets to be taken possession of to a similar extent." Long, twisting freight trains blocked street intersections downtown, choking traffic and blighting entire neighborhoods; and the great railroad district on the southern end of the business center—a Chicago Chinese Wall—prevented the logical expansion of downtown in that direction, hemmed in, as it was, on its other three sides by the river, the lake, and other railroad terminals and freight facilities. This drove up center-city real estate prices and caused businesses to build into the sky to maximize land use. In this way, the railroads created the conditions for Chicago's skyscrapers. These solid rows of office towers, in turn, became part of the city's railroad environment, trapping smoke in their stone canyons, which echoed with the thunderous noises of the nearby steam trains.

The trains were not just a nuisance; they were a real physical danger. Aside from requiring trains to run at reduced speeds within city limits, Chicago's city government had made no concerted effort since William Ogden's time to make its street-level rail crossings safe for its citizens. In the late 1880s, two persons a day, on average, were killed or mangled at grade crossings. The railroad companies' failure to elevate their tracks at street intersections gave rise to angry public protests and to a spate of lawsuits by injured parties; but in their defense "the railroad officials argue that they invented . . . Chicago"— Julian Ralph neatly summed up the situation—"and that her people are ungrateful to protest against a little thing like a slaughter which would depopulate the average village in a year."

•

The terrific crowding and tumult of Chicago's downtown railroad region was frightening to many first-time visitors to the city. In Hamlin Garland's Chicago novel *Rose of Dutcher's Coolly,* published in 1895, a young Wisconsin woman arriving in the city for the first time to find work as a writer sits nervously in the waiting room of one of the city's terminals, where she can "hear the obscure thunder of the street out-side" while she awaits the arrival of a friend with whom she has arranged to stay. "It was terrifying, confusing. Shrill screams and hoarse shouts rose above . . . [the sound of steam hammers], the clang of gongs and the click of shoe-heels."

When her friend finally arrives, they head out into the roaring city, boarding one of a train of cable cars that comes "nosing along like vicious boars, with snouts close to the ground." From the outward-facing seat of the open-sided "summer" car, Rose Dutcher gets her first look at Chicago.

The streets were busy and loud beyond belief, and rows of "mountainous buildings" seemed to stretch "to the ends of the earth." Walking the downtown streets alone the next day in search of work, Rose feels at first unable to handle this full-bore assault on her country sensibilitites. But as she moves along her confidence rises. The city begins to thrill and engage her. She feels "in the center of human life. To win here was to win all she cared to have." Garland evokes what Chicago meant to him when he moved there in 1893.

•

When nineteen-year-old Frank Lloyd Wright arrived alone in Chicago from Wisconsin to begin, like Rose Dutcher, his artistic career, he found the city "murderously actual"—raw, hard, ugly, a vast "piling up of blind forces." Most of the architecture struck him as disappointingly ordinary—bold and big but not freshly thought out. But how sensationally alive the place was that cold, drizzly spring day of 1887.

Chicago's pace was dizzying. "A born New-Yorker, the energy, roar, and bustle of the place were yet sufficient to first astonish and then to fatigue me," Julian Ralph confessed in his book on the *Great West*. And while people hurried along, they talked "money through their noses," Rudyard Kipling remarked in 1889, after a quick tour of the city while on an American excursion. Others found in money-mad Chicago the vigorous spirit of young America. Twenty-four-year-old Kipling thought the entire spectacle "barbaric."

In "the City of Speed," cable cars traveled at more than nine miles an hour in heavy traffic, three miles an hour faster than New York's horsecars, still the main means of public transportation in that city in the late 1880s. Riding on these dangerously crowded cars at rush hour, with standing passengers clinging to straps from the roof or hanging by their fingertips from the platforms at each end of the car, was like a visit to "a new circle in the Inferno," wrote Eliot Gregory of the *Atlantic Monthly*. When the iron wheels flew off their axles, as they often did on the poorly laid rail lines, passengers were thrown off the platforms, and hardly a day went by when a pedestrian was not hit by a cable car. Sometimes when a big dray got in the way of a line of cable cars and was too hemmed in by traffic to move, the lead car—its gong ringing like a fire alarm—would lift it in the air and push it aside, overturning wagon and team. "The civilized man marvels," said William Stead, "and keeps on his way."

"Chicago never seems to go to bed," declared a fellow Englishman, "and the streets at night are a blaze of electric light and thronged with people. I asked a man at a saloon once what time they shut up, and his answer was, 'Well, I've been here over ten years, and it's never been closed since I've been here.'" The noisiest—and busiest—place in the city was the corner of State and Madison Streets at the height of the business day. Just crossing the street there was high adventure. "With the prairie breezes buffeting you and waltzing you by turns, as they eddy through the ravines of Madison, Monroe, and Adams Streets, you take your life in your hands when you attempt the crossing of State Street, with its endless stream of rattling wagons and clanging trolley-cars," wrote the Scottish journalist William Archer.

•

The place to feel the beating pulse of busy Chicago, however, was the trading floor of the new Board of Trade Building at the head of La Salle Street, the Wall Street of the mid-continent. Designed by W. W. Boyington, it was a chaotic symphony of virtually every architectural cliché of the age, a granite monstrosity fronted by a 310-foot Gothic clock tower. Passing in front of its formidable façade on his second day in the city on his way to apply for work at Boyington's office, Frank Lloyd Wright made a decision that influenced the direction of his career. "Boyington had done it, had he?" he later recalled his reaction to the building. "This . . . thin-chested, hard-faced, chamfered monstrosity? I turned aside from Boyington's office then and there."

The building's outstanding feature—and it had but one—was its richly frescoed second-story trading hall with cathedral windows, stained-glass skylights high above the trading pits, and a gallery for spectators. Leaning against the front rail of the visitors' gallery on one of his first mornings in the city, the *Times* reporter who had arrived from New York witnessed a spectacle that resembled, he thought, an ancient gladiatorial contest. "Upon the broad floor . . . assemble the wheat and corn and pork and lard and railway kings of the town, in a typical American life scene of concentrated and boiling energy, feeding the furnace in which Chicago's high-pressure enterprise glows and roars." The "gladiators" had their respective pits, or "amphitheaters"—one for corn, one for wheat, one for pork—and when the opening bell was struck, "a tumult was unchained." Men began to swing their arms wildly, their fingers extended, and jump up and down. "This Chicago 'Board of Trade' has witnessed some of the wildest excitements of America," wrote the *Times* reporter. Pit kings like Charles L. Hutchinson and Philip Armour were known to have made or lost millions in a single flurry of trading.

When the gong announced the end of the trading day and the brokers, traders, and clerks put on their hats and ulsters and headed out for whiskeys and corned beef in the local establishments, the emptied trading floor was littered with grain samples and thousands of torn and crumpled yellow telegraph forms, "the débris," wrote Frank Norris in his novel *The Pit*, "of the battle-field, the abandoned impedimenta and broken weapons of contending armies."

Returning to his room at the Palmer House on State and Monroe Streets, the *Times* reporter came upon a scene nearly as alive with business energy as the place he had just left. In Chicago, "a great hotel is much more than a place to eat and sleep in," explained a Rand McNally guidebook. "Its lobby is the people's club, men meet to settle political and commercial questions of vast importance." Of all of these public clubs of Chicago, the lobby arcade of the Palmer House was the largest, the busiest, and the most lavishly appointed. After a shave and a shoeshine in the hotel's famous basement barbershop, its floor inlaid with silver dollars, a businessman could walk up to the lobby and check the latest Board of Trade prices on the conveniently located "tickers" and "news bulletins"—and if he had the urge, take an immediate "flyer" in pork or spring wheat at the broker's exchange. The front lobby of the Palmer House "is a news exchange for the busy city," the *Times* reporter noted, swarming with businessmen who filled the air with cigar smoke and trade talk from early morning until far into the night. Potter Palmer, a power in the Democratic party, made his hostelry a caucusing center for the party's national conventions, which were held regularly in Chicago, and a place where Chicago ward chieftains could make connections with local men of affairs.

The hotel of the Republicans—and of the city's leading speculators—was the equally opulent Grand Pacific on La Salle Street, at the doors of the Board of Trade Building. Designed by W. W. Boyington and run by the fortunate fire victim and former owner of the Tremont House, John B. Drake, it represented, better than any other hotel in the city, the intimate Chicago connection between luxury trains, big passenger terminals, and grand hotels. Built a few hundred yards from the Van Buren Street Station with money from the railroads using that terminal, it had doormen who sent drivers around to pick up arriving guests and drop them off at its glass-domed carriage rotunda. Travelers going west from Chicago could have breakfast in the Grand Pacific's sumptuous dining room, lunch on fresh white linen in the Rock Island's Oriental Car, and dinner in a plush railroad hotel in Council Bluffs, Iowa, where their luggage was waiting for them in their rooms, along with complimentary trays of sweets and big glass pitchers of spring water.

Hotels like the Palmer House and the Grand Pacific were self-promoting Chicago's outstanding examples of conspicuous display—and architectural celebrations, as well, of the city's recent rise not only from the fire but also from its crude frontier beginnings. "Our menu was illustrated," an aristocratic English guest said of her first dining experience at the Palmer House in 1880. "On one side was depicted a pigsty and a hovel—'Chicago forty years ago.' On the other was a wonderful city—'The Chicago of to-day.'" Coming to fire-ruined Chicago, she had "expected to find traces of ugliness and deformity everywhere. . . . But, Phoenixlike, the city had risen up out of its own ashes, grander and statelier than ever."

2. America's City

"There is in history no parallel to this [meteoric growth]," Charles Dudley Warner wrote of Chicago in the 1880s, "not St. Petersburg rising out of the marshes at an imperial edict, nor Berlin, the magic creation of a consolidated empire and a Caesar's power." Warner had been to the city a number of times since the Civil War, but each time he returned, it looked like a different place, an experience his friend Mark Twain related in *Life on the Mississippi.* "We struck the home trail now, and in a few hours were in that astonishing Chicago—a city where they are always rubbing a lamp, and fetching up the genii, and contriving and achieving new impossibilities. It is hopeless for the occasional visitor to try to keep up with Chicago—she outgrows her prophecies faster than she can make them. She is always a novelty; for she is never the Chicago you saw when you passed through the last time."

People began calling it America's city, "the concentrated essence of Americanism." Foreign writers, especially, saw this raw, unfinished colossus, with its surging commercial energy, technological wonders, and absence of settled traditions as the most characteristically American of America's largest cities. Older eastern cities like Boston, New York, and Philadephia reminded the French architecture critic Jacques Hermant, of "the great English cities," while San Francisco had "a Spanish or Chinese flavor." But "Chicago," he declared, "*is* America."

His countryman, Paul de Rousiers, a prominent economist, found Chicagoans enterprising and confident "in a manner at once foolish and admirable." Most cities and nations were conscious of their physical limitations, but not Chicago, the stupendous product of American expansionism. In Chicago, the American "go-ahead" spirit—the impulse to press forward without hesitation, regret, or even foresight—"attains its maximum intensity," he wrote in his observant 1892 book *American Life.* This was the confident spirit of America, but it was also the spirit of youth, for Chicago remained, as ever, a "city of young men." The generation of the 1850s had grown gray, but it was far easier for young men—or women—to rise to positions of influence in Chicago in the 1880s and 1890s than in New York, Philadelphia, or Boston.

•

This magnet metropolis continued to attract fresh-faced hustlers eager to make a fast million, but it had recently begun to attract, as well, artists and architects, reporters and reformers, with destruction a catalyst of this new migration. Postfire Chicago was the only place in the world at the time where a young person could go and take part in an effort to reinvent the city. Architects and writers, especially, rose to the opportunity, one group to remake the city, the other to document a new kind of city in the making.

> Mamie beat her head against the bars of a little Indiana town
>   and dreamed of romance and big things off somewhere the way
>   the railroad trains all ran.
> She could see the smoke of the engines get lost down where the
>   streaks of steel flashed in the sun and when the newspapers came
>   in on the morning mail she knew there was a big Chicago far off,
>   where all the trains ran.

That's Sandburg, and that was Chicago to the Mamies and the Carrie Meebers, the Frank Lloyd Wrights and Theodore Dreisers, of the midland towns. For them, Chicago was a place of desire and dream. They came from towns and villages—Rockport, Madison, Moscow, and Cedarville—hungry for the city's excitements and opportunities, and they found Chicago "august as well as terrible," intimidating but inexhaustibly vital. "The business section so sordid to others was grandly terrifying to us." Hamlin Garland recalled his and his brother's initial walk through Chicago as they counted the stories of the tall buildings and absorbed "the drama of the pavement. . . . Nothing was commonplace, nothing was ugly to us."

We find this sense of the industrial city as a place of amplitude and opportunity most brilliantly in the work of Theodore Dreiser, who had lived in Chicago with his family briefly in the early 1880s but returned on his own in 1887 to "a world of hope and opportunity."

Dreiser is the only American writer at the turn of the century who can be compared with Charles Dickens as a renderer of urban life, a wide-awake traveler in new regions of humanity. He took in the big city in its full sweep and complexity, describing people, places, and scenes as though no one else had ever written about them. Being poor and wanting to be rich, he could write with equal insight about the "great" streets and the "bleak" streets. As a young Chicago reporter, he was also drawn to the red-light and gaming districts, where, in early evening, "the hetaerae of the city" could be seen "preparing for those gaudy make-believes of their midnight day." And he also liked the areas "crowded with great, black factories" where men hammered out the products that Chicago shipped by rail and lake steamer to every corner of the country.

Later, Dreiser went to New York and wrote the great Chicago novel, and in describing Sister Carrie, he unconsciously described Chicago itself, so close was his identification of the city with its people. Like Chicago, Carrie Meeber is desperate to rise materially, but she also feels "the drag of desire to be something better." An aspiring actress, she is a romantic seeker after deeper meaning in life. Looking back on his youth in Chicago, Dreiser writes of a city seething with energy and excitement, an unequaled place to watch "a new world . . . in the making."

But in Dreiser's Chicago novels, the big city is more than a romantic place of excitement and opportunity. It is an ungiving force of nature that ruins as many lives as it elevates, an image evoked by Carrie Meeber and her fated lover, Hurstwood, one made by the city, the other undone by it. That is the way Chicago was. Many an opportunity seeker just off the train must have paused at one or another of State Street's crowded corners and asked himself what chance he had to make it in this huge, indifferent place. Few of these ordinary men and women set down their experiences, but Rudyard Kipling spoke for many of the disillusioned in his bitter assessment of the dark side of Dreiser's Chicago Dream.

"I have struck . . . a real city," he wrote on his arrival from a tour of the far western states. "The other places do not count. . . . This place is the first American city I have encountered. . . . Having seen it, I urgently desire never to see it again."

For ten hours, Kipling wandered through the "huge wilderness" of Chicago, a hired guide filling his head with fact and fable of the city's progress since the Great Fire. "He conceived," Kipling wrote of his guide, "that all this turmoil and squash was a thing to be reverently admired; that it was good to huddle men together in fifteen layers, one atop of the other." To him, this was "proof of progress"; Kipling considered it "a great horror." And the city was ugly and filthy, he thought, beyond belief. Not even the Palmer House impressed him: "A gilded and mirrored rabbit-warren," he called it.

Kipling and Dreiser, speaking for voiceless others, described two Chicagos that were really one, a city of extreme, even violent, contrasts. City of millionaires, Chicago had some of the worst slums in the civilized world. In this the "most American of cities," over three-quarters of its residents were of foreign parentage in 1893. Garden city of parks and tree-bordered boulevards, it had most of its streets filled with uncollected horse manure and putrid animal corpses. Temperance capital of the country—headquarters of the globe-touring evangelist Dwight L. Moody and of Frances E. Willard's Woman's Christian Temperance Union—it had one saloon for every two hundred persons, its second-largest industry was liquor distilling, and its world-famous vice district operated around the clock with police protection. The most corrupt city in the country and a stronghold of antilabor sentiment, it was the center of the nation's trade-union and socialist movements and a rallying ground for urban reformers. Magnet city of the mid-continent, it was portrayed by prairie newspapermen as a place their young people should shun, where thieves, gunmen, and white slavers lay in wait. "All America," wrote a horrified German visitor, "looks with fear at this city that hurls her threat over the country."

Chicago "embraces in its unimaginable amplitude every extreme of splendor and squalor," wrote William Archer. "More than any other city of my acquaintance, [it] suggests that antique conception of the underworld which placed Elysium and Tartarus not only on the same plane, but, so to speak, round the corner from each other." Dreiser thought it "spoke of a tremendous future"; Kipling questioned whether "the snarling together of telegraph wires, the heaving up of houses, and the making of money is progress." But no matter how observers differed in their reaction to its messy vitality, few would have disputed Henry Adams's conviction that end-of-the-century Chicago was the best place to observe "the new energies" of the age.

•

This is what brought Paul Bourget to Chicago. An eminent French novelist and cultural critic, he sailed for America in 1893 to see the future of his own country and went directly to Chicago because he had heard it best "symbolized" America, "with its contrasts of extreme refinement and primitive crudity." A city ahead of its age, Chicago foretold the major conflicts and challenges of the "new universe" of science and democracy that Bourget, a deep-dyed conservative, anticipated with fascination and fear.

Bourget left New York with a trainful of tourists bound for the White City, but he was more interested in Chicago than in the instant city Daniel H. Burnham had built on the shores of Lake Michigan for the Columbian Exposition. On the autumn morning of his first day in Chicago, he went to the top of the 270-foot-high tower of the Auditorium Building on Michigan Avenue, a favorite tourist attraction. "One's first visit on arriving should be here," he wrote in *Outre-mer,* his sharp-eyed assessment of American civilization, "in order to get the strongest impression of the enormous city, lying black on the shore of its blue lake."

A city of spectacular distances, Chicago stretched for twenty-four miles along its lakefront and for ten miles and more into the vastness of its industrial suburbs, while its solid rows of skyscrapers, with their belching chimneys, reached up into a black-and-gray canopy of their own creation. It was an urban physiognomy different, Bourget thought, "from every other since the foundation of the world," an unvarying flatland of industrial neighborhoods that rolled on—backward from the horizon—for miles and miles until it climaxed in a silhouette of towers tightly wedged between river, rail lines, and lake. Entering this tall, closely packed city by rail gave some visitors the sensation of entering a walled medieval stronghold that commanded the countryside, with the river and its pivot bridges serving as the prairie bastion's moat and drawbridges.

The gray imposing sameness of its mills and neighborhoods made Chicago look to Bourget as if it had been built by "some impersonal power, irresistible, unconscious, like a force of nature." This power, he wrote, was the "business fever which here throbs at will, with an unbridled violence," and it manifested itself most magnificently in the city's austere office towers. These "cliffs of brick and iron" were the signature of capitalist Chicago, just as the high dome of St. Peter's was the signature of Catholic Rome. Standing atop a tower that was one of the supreme achievements of modern engineering, a floor above the offices of its builders, Louis Sullivan and Dankmar Adler, Bourget

1. Wolf Point in 1832, the "Wild Place" that was the center of frontier Chicago.

2. Gurdon Saltonstall Hubbard, fur trader, merchant, and town founder. His biography is the history of Chicago from 1818 to the mid-1880s.

3. William Butler Ogden, Chicago's first mayor. A land dealer and railroad builder, he, more than anyone else, turned Chicago from a mudhole into a metropolis.

4. The trading floor of the Board of Trade Building, at the end of a business day. The trading pits were scenes of wild excitement, where "pit kings" like Charles L. Hutchinson and Philip D. Armour made or lost millions in a single flurry of trading.

5. *The Great Fire. The rush for life over the Randolph Street Bridge, from a sketch by John R. Chapin, an artist for* Harper's Weekly. *After narrowly escaping from his hotel, Chapin made his way to a spot near the bridge, where he drew this pencil sketch.*

6. *The smoking ruins of Chicago, looking north from the courthouse.*

7. The pens at Armour and Company. The animals shown here arrived at the yards the previous morning and would be slaughtered by the end of the day, when the ritual of collecting, selling, and killing would begin all over again. The packing plants themselves—"Houses of Blood"—are in the background.

7–10. The Union Stock Yards, an empire of order and blood.

8. The revolving hog wheel. A live hog, about to be slaughtered, was placed on this immense wheel, which had chains hanging from its rims. When the wheel rotated, the hog was jerked into the air, upside down, squealing and kicking, and was carried by the movement of the wheel to an overhead railway, where a butcher cut its throat. The hog then passed down the "railway of death," to be dissected by teams of assembly line workers.

9. The cattle chutes. Cattle were driven into narrow chutes and were bludgeoned with sledgehammers. One side of the pen was then raised, and the unconscious animal was pulled by a chain onto the adjacent killing beds, where it was killed by a "sticker," who plunged his knife into its chest as it hung from a steam hoist.

10. Philip Danforth Armour. Armour ran the most tremendous butchering establishment in the world, a fourteen-acre "village" in the Yards with its own rail lines, fire company, and chemical laboratory. His company motto was "We Feed the World."

12

11

13

11–15. George Pullman as a
young man (11). Pullman
arrived in Chicago in the
1850s and by 1893 was "the
best known Chicago name
throughout America." His
Chicago empire included the
model industrial town of
Pullman, built in the 1880s
(12); the ten-story Pullman
Building, his downtown
company headquarters (13);
and his Prairie Avenue
mansion (14). His architect,
Solon S. Beman, also built
Grand Central Station, with
its 242-foot high clock tower
(15). Passengers boarded
Pullman Palace cars in
Grand Central's spectacular
glass-and-iron train shed.

14

15

16

16. *State Street, north from Madison, the famous "Ladies' Half Mile," the main street of the Midwest. Open-air "summer cars" pass by the entrance to Marshall Field's department store, in the center right of the photograph. The department store and the commercial skyscraper were the anchor institutions of a new type of downtown, invented in Chicago.*

17

18

17. *Marshall Field, the "merchant prince" of the midcontinent. He started in Chicago in the 1850s as a clerk and within a few decades was one of the richest men in the world.*

18. *The handkerchief and kid-glove-cleaning departments at Marshall Field's. In 1893, Marshall Field's was the world's largest department store. It was one of the first stores anywhere to install electric lights.*

19

19. *Potter Palmer, the retail and real estate magnate, built this imitation Rhenish castle in the 1880s on a stretch of dune and marsh on the North Shore that he transformed into Chicago's "Gold Coast," inviting his friends to form with him and his wife, Bertha, a community where there had been a wilderness. Located on the new Lake Shore Drive that Palmer had the city build, it was the most imposing private house in Chicago. It contrasted sharply with the lakefront downtown, only a few miles to the south (20).*

20

21. When the "Palmer Castle" was completed, Bertha Palmer became the "social queen" of Chicago and, later, head of the Columbian Exposition's Board of Lady Managers. She is shown here with her famous rope of pearls.

21

22. In this magnificent 75-foot-long picture gallery, Bertha Palmer hosted the most talked-about parties in Chicago. She left her outstanding collection of French Impressionists to the Art Institute.

looked out at the first urban skyline of the post–Classical Age not dominated by church steeples and domes.

Bourget found poetry in these buildings—and power; like ancient deities, they could hide the sun, direct the wind, and "shut out the light of day." For him, however, the most striking physical feature of Chicago that clear September morning was not its profit-inspired towers but its far-reaching, factory-like environment, the greatest industrial landscape in the world. Chicago was a spectacle of raw economic energy. There was no attempt to disguise what the city was, no fancy architectural masquerading, no effort, even, to control the noise, the stench, or the smoke. It was, as James Parton called Pittsburgh, "hell with the lid taken off."

The "whole powerful city, more extensive than London—resembles, except for the better residential areas, a human being with his skin removed," wrote Max Weber on his first and only visit there, "and in which all the physiological process can be seen going on." Bourget, a novelist with the eye and interests of a sociologist, had a similar thought, only he preferred an inorganic metaphor. Chicago presented itself to him as a gigantic machine with all its moving parts exposed, an engine that powered an economic empire of continental reach. In the Chicago River, the feed line of the machine, Bourget could see, through twisting columns of smoke, the complex commerce of empire—iron barges from Lake Superior, lumber schooners from Green Bay, grain boats from Duluth, coal scows from Erie. Rail tracks—thick webs of them—spread out from harbor terminals and piers. And through trade corridors lined with signal towers and semaphores, long steam trains bore through the plains and forests of mid-America carrying what Chicago built and bringing back what it bought.

A number of Chicago's giant industries had begun to move to the suburbs, but the river harbor was still the center of economic activity, as it had been when Gurdon Hubbard began trading furs and trinkets there. Entering the river in the summer of 1886, the year of Hubbard's death, a French traveler, fresh from a visit to Marquette's grave on Point St. Ignace, gave a picture of what Hubbard's Chicago had become in the span of a person's lifetime.

"We reached Chicago in the morning through the beautiful blue lakeways," L. de Cotton wrote in an account of his travels published in Paris three years later. "Suddenly, on a low coast, a cloud of smoke appeared. I was told it was the city." As his ship made its way slowly upriver, "stirring up the infectious and muddy waters," he saw "endless piers piled with merchandise, [and] . . . through a black cloud, huge

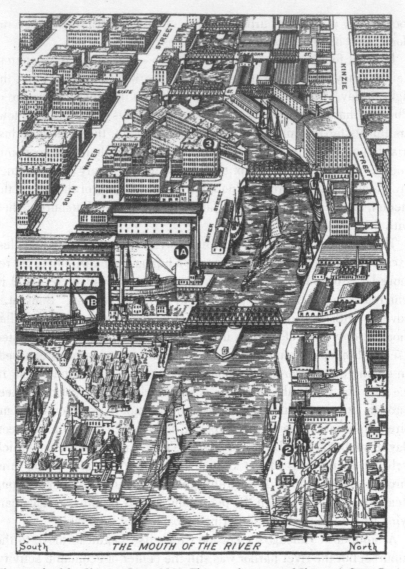

The mouth of the Chicago River, 1893. This was the center of Chicago's Great Prairie Exchange Engine. Products poured in and out of Chicago through this busy portal. The Illinois Central's trains came in from the south, and those of the Chicago and Northwestern from the west. The city's two largest grain elevators (nos. 1A and 1B), which served the Illinois Central, stand on slips at the left, near the mouth of the river, with grain ships docked beside them. (The Galena elevator that served the Chicago and Northwestern Railroad was farther upriver on the north bank.)

The light at the mouth of the river (no. 2, bottom) could be seen for sixteen miles out on the lake.

On the left stretches the South Water Street Market, the main marketplace of the city. The Hoyt Building (no. 3) occupied the site of Fort Dearborn. The Kinzie "mansion" was located just across the river from it, near what became Kinzie Street. Just upriver is Wolf Point.   Bird's-eye Views and Guide to Chicago (Chicago: Rand, McNally & Co., 1898) constructions, similar to what must have been the granaries of the Egyptians." Standing at the ship's rail, de Cotton could actually feel the smell of the city grabbing him "at the throat." One breath of Chicago's air "reeks of coal smoke," wrote another foreign traveler, "the other of boiling glue."

On the banks of the river, close to the spot where Isaac Arnold's rescue boat had been imperiled, de Cotton looked out at "huge red brick buildings with large factory-like windows, adorned with inscriptions several meters high." Even the coal-scarred office buildings in the business center had large, wide windows, "giving the whole city the appearance of a huge factory." Surrounded by assaultive Chicago, de Cotton felt a sensation of almost physical pain. "I felt an instinctive need to glance behind [at the disappearing lake], and something cold pressed my heart. Oh! What an awful city."

But where he saw Coketown incarnate, his countryman saw the design of a new economic order of "immense originality," whose "makers," Paul Bourget argued, "are examples of a more vigorous humanity." Chicago was a "summary of [America's] energy and inexhaustible impulse." But Bourget wondered where this cyclonic energy was taking Chicago and the country. "Toward what goal marches . . . America?"

Chaotic Chicago seemed to have sprung up spontaneously, without planning or social foresight, a pure product of ungoverned capitalism. "It is the most perfect presentation of nineteenth century individualist industrialism I have ever seen," H. G. Wells remarked after passing through the city on a tour of the United States. "Chicago is one hoarse cry for discipline!"

Wells got his best view of Chicago as he was leaving it, relaxing in a backward-facing seat in the open observation car at the tail end of the Pennsylvania Limited Express. He had not made the obligatory trip to the stockyards, claiming "an immense repugnance to the killing of fixed and helpless animals," but as his train passed the slaughterhouses, he smelled their "unwholesome reek" and saw "for the first time the enormous expanse and intricacy of railroads that net this industrial desolation." To the right and left of the tracks he saw nothing but industrial power and devastation. Huge freight trains thundered by his train—"long trains of doomed cattle" heading northward, and along the tracks were the slatternly cottages of workmen. "So it goes on mile after mile—Chicago."

Then, suddenly, tearing through one last field of smoke and grime, the Pennsylvania Limited was in "the large emptiness of America," and Chicago, in the retreating distance, became a "dark smear in the sky."

This was the same scene—in reverse—Dreiser had passed through on his journey of initiation from rural Indiana, but what different meanings the two writers put on what they saw: one leaving Chicago anxious about its future, the other entering the city of his desires; one a famous socialist who preached of reconceiving the industrial city, the other a town boy who dreamed of becoming famous by writing about city life as it was, not as reformers wanted it to be.

Dreiser speaks for those who insist that for a city to be great it must be big, busy, and packed with people—and allowed to grow freely and naturally, even if the result sometimes resembles mayhem. Wells, by contrast, is the voice of those who believe that urban growth must be shaped by intelligent public intervention. It was the absence of orderly planning, he argued in his book *The Future in America* (1906), that explained all that was ugly in New York, Liverpool, South London—and, most riotously, in Chicago, which had not evolved socially, he said, beyond the stage of "the prospector's camp."

Wells saw Chicago as a monstrous creation of the nineteenth century's preeminent features, runaway industrial growth and a Darwinian faith—he called it "optimistic fatalism"—that assumed that the city's problems would somehow right themselves automatically. Passing by the stink and filth of Packingtown on the Pennsylvania Limited he had a wish, he later recalled, that he could "catch the soul of Herbert Spencer and tether it in Chicago for a while to gather fresh evidence upon the superiority of unfettered individualistic enterprises to things managed by the state."

Unlike a number of present-day historians, Wells did not see this urban tradition of privativism—the hard pursuit of profit without the constraint of conscience or law—as a uniquely American phenomenon. He had, after all, been to Manchester, a city built and run, as both Alexis de Tocqueville and young Friedrich Engels described it, without "the directing powers" of government. Wells, however, did leave America convinced that urban laissez-faire had reached its purest, most capricious form in Chicago. "The dark disorder of growth" struck him as the city's supreme characteristic.

In Daniel Burnham's White City, a masterwork of neoclassical architecture and orderly urban design, Paul Bourget saw the beginnings of an effort to discipline Chicago's ill-regulated civic life. But the White City was, Bourget thought, a denial of Chicago itself, everything the actual city was not. So while Henry Adams, William Dean Howells, and hundreds of other out-of-town writers spent days touring Burnham's model city, Bourget went instead to the Union Stock Yard. What went on there, he believed, had more to say about the future of

Chicago—and of America—than Burnham's make-believe city of plaster and staff.

The big ideas of America, Bourget argued, were business ideas, and Chicago was America's capital city of big ideas. No other city had created so many revolutionary industries and commercial institutions. The Pullman car, the nationwide mail-order house, the refrigerator car, and the modern packing plant were Chicago ideas; and the originators of these ideas—George Pullman, Gustavus Franklin Swift, Philip Armour, Richard Warren Sears, and Aaron Montgomery Ward—had turned them into vast business organizations, the sum total of which comprised the main parts of the Chicago production and exchange engine that had powered the city's spectacular recovery from the fire, built the new downtown business area, and given the city the 1893 Columbian Exposition.

Chicago was much more, certainly, than a production engine, but to know how the Chicago Machine was reconstituted after the fire and how it operated both for and against the general good—its heedless growth generating civic contests that would be fought for decades—is to understand Chicago in the year of the Columbian Exposition. And an understanding of 1893 Chicago and the Chicago Machine is impossible without insight into the character and lives of the men who projected themselves so strongly in these, their proudest creations.

When Paul Bourget went to the Union Stock Yard to see its synchronized killing machine, he went with the idea of learning more about the ideas and ingenuity that would make the next century, he was convinced, the American century, with Chicago its vanguard city. As he passed by the stockyards on his way out of Chicago on the Pennsylvania Limited, H. G. Wells's thoughts ran in a similar direction. The future was in America. And in centers of energy and change like Chicago, he mused as his train passed into the prairie, the ongoing battles between order and freedom, capitalism and community, that would shape the coming epoch would be won and lost.

8

The Chicago
Machine

1. Empires of Order and Blood

"Y O U shall find them about six miles from the city," wrote Rudyard
Kipling, "and once having seen them you will never forget the sight."

The private carriage that took Paul Bourget and his traveling companions to the Union Stock Yard crossed a huge patch of the city cob-
webbed with train tracks and crammed with two-story frame cottages,
stores, and saloons—"never a hill and never a hollow," Upton Sinclair
said of that stretch of Chicago, "but always the same endless vista of
ugly and dirty little wooden buildings." The carriage stopped at what
must have seemed like hundreds of busy rail crossings and passed
over bridges spanning creeks and canals lined with factories whose
stacks sent up curling streamers of smoke, darkening the entire sky.
"But after each of these interruptions, the desolate procession would
begin again—the procession of dreary little buildings."

Then, just as the landscape turned bare and the sky grew even
blacker, there came the smell—a sickening odor carried toward the
city on high prairie winds. It was made up of mangled meat, animal
blood, dung, and urine, and it announced the end of the journey. Holding handkerchiefs to their faces, Bourget's party passed through the
imposing stone gate of the Union Stock Yard, built in 1879 by the then
fledgling firm of Daniel H. Burnham and John Wellborn Root on a
commission arranged by Burnham's father-in-law, John B. Sherman,

the first superintendent—the first mayor, of sorts—of this one-square-mile city of "order and death."

Inside the yards, the smell mingled with the sounds—the bellows, squeals, and bleating of seventy thousand and more cattle, hogs, and sheep amid the "yips" and "ki-yies" of buyers and sellers on horseback cracking long whips and riding up and down the wooden alleyways between the neatly gridded pens. Standing on the visitor's viaduct that overlooked the yards, Bourget watched deals being struck right in the open, in clouds of dust sent up by masses of moving animals, the bargains sealed "at the crook of a finger," the nod of a head. As a seller galloped off, the gates securing his sale were swung open, and gangs of mud-draped drovers led the animals to immense scales to be weighed and priced, and then herded them over ramps and viaducts to the holding yards next to the big packing factories to cool off before they were killed and cut up.

Almost every animal in the vast ocean of animals that Bourget looked out over had arrived the previous night by train and been unloaded under sputtering arc lights. And by the end of the day, almost all the pens would be empty, and the ritual of collection, selling, and killing would begin all over again.

For years the city's leading tourist attraction, "Chicago's Pride," the stockyards were on display for the Columbian Exposition of 1893. All the leading packing companies had exhibits at the fair, and exhibitors invited fairgoers to visit the yards, the second-biggest show in town that summer. They came in record numbers, as many as ten thousand a day, and were met by company guides at the Halsted Street gate or at the new passenger depot Burnham and Root had designed for the occasion of the fair. Touring the works, they were bombarded with facts and figures about Chicago's largest industry, the one that best expressed its character and spirit. The combined livestock and packing operation, an industry comprising almost a hundred separate concerns, was at that time the "greatest aggregation of labour and capital ever gathered in one place," an economic power "greater than courts or judges, greater than legislators, superior and independent of all authority of state or nation," in the words of the muckraker Charles Edward Russell. To Upton Sinclair's Jurgis Rudkus, fresh from the fields of Lithuania, "it was a thing as tremendous as the universe."

In 1893 a workforce of some twenty-five thousand men and women, boys and girls, processed almost 14 million animals a year, the value of packinghouse products equaling nearly $200 million, an expansion of over 900 percent since the Great Fire. "In Chicago," the historian

Sigfried Giedion would write a half century later, "we are dealing with dimensions for which there is, even today, no yardstick. A spontaneously growing center of force, it embodies, as few other places do, that brutal and inventive vitality of the nineteenth century." That vitality was nowhere more clearly in evidence than in the Union Stock Yard, the central symbol of this burly giant of a city. In Philip Armour's Chicago "they did it straight," Norman Mailer would write, "they cut the animals right out of their hearts—which is why it was the last of the great American cities, and people had great faces, carnal as blood, greedy, direct, too impatient for hypocrisy, in love with honest plunder."

On a tour of North America, Sarah Bernhardt retained only two impressions of Chicago—the hospitality of Potter Palmer and the "butchering of the hogs, a horrible and magnificent spectacle." No one "can be said to have a proper appreciation of the enterprise and business ability which have made the city what it is," observed the *Scientific American* in 1891, "without an investigation of the vast business carried on at the Chicago stock-yards."

Standing by the holding pens next to the pork plant of Armour and Company, Paul Bourget watched a long line of hogs being driven up an

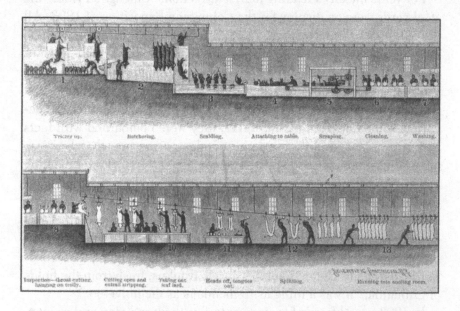

The killing and cutting line at Armour and Company. Shown here are the stages of the slaughtering operation, after the hogs have been put on the revolving hog wheel. The ground area covered by this building was 50 acres in extent, giving it a floor area of 140 acres and a chill room and cold-storage area of 40 acres.
Scientific American, 1891

inclined chute—the Bridge of Sighs, packinghouse wags called it—to a small opening in the top story of the boxlike building that, when he entered it, gave off an overpowering stench that seized him "by the throat." Walking across a sticky floor saturated with a "sort of bloody mud," he and his companions were led up several flights of stairs to a visitors' gallery at the top of the building. From there they could see the entire slaughtering operation. The tour of this "House of Blood," Bourget later wrote in his notes, "will always remain to me one of the most singular memories of my [American] journey."

Just ahead, in the catching pen, were the pigs, "alive grunting and screaming, as if they had a vision of the approach of the horrible machine, from which they can no more escape than a doomed man whose head lies on the guillotine." This killing instrument was an immense, spokeless wheel with chains hanging from its rims. As it began to move, the chains dragged on the floor, and a man fastened a hook on the end of one of the chains around a hind leg of a pig. When the wheel began to rotate again, the defenseless creature was jerked into the air, upside down, screeching and squealing, kicking and biting, and was carried by the movement of the wheel to an overhead railway that ran the length of the building on a descending angle from the top to the bottom floor. For the helpless hog, "this is the carrier from then on, and the rail is a direct sloping path to death, dissection, and the refrigerator," Theodore Dreiser described the world's first assembly line, or more accurately, disassembly line, after his tour of the Armour plant in 1898.

Hanging by its feet from the trolleys on the aerial railway, the pig was carried by gravity to its executioner, a brawny "red-headed giant" covered with blood. With a quick thrust of his knife, he cut the soft throat of the animal and a stream of blood spurted out, "jet black and thick as your arm," some of it hitting the butcher as he dodged to avoid it.

Meanwhile, another hog was pinioned to the wheel, "and then another, and another," wrote Upton Sinclair of this unchanged process a decade later in *The Jungle*, until the wheel was filled with them, "each dangling by a foot and kicking in a frenzy—and squealing. The uproar was appalling, too much for some of the visitors." The men looked at one another and smiled nervously; the women, wringing their hands, grew pale and faint.

After the butcher made his cut, the animal gravitated downward for ten yards or so, bleeding into a catch basin that preserved its contents for fertilizer. When the hog—still twitching and perhaps still alive—passed over a vat of boiling water, it was released from the guide rail and disappeared with a splash, silenced forever. The scalding water softened and loosened the hair and bristles, and the pink carcass was then scooped out of the tub by a rakelike device and lifted onto a table. An endless chain was attached to a ring in its nose and the animal was pulled through a scraping machine, emerging ten seconds later shaved from nose to tail. What hair remained was removed by teams of fast-working hands. The head was then almost completely severed, left hanging "by a thread," and the body was hitched up again to the overhead rail and carried by its own weight to a lower level of the plant, where it passed over a table flanked by a cutting gang, six workers to a side. This was highly specialized work, each man working "as if a demon were after him" to perform a series of cuts and scrapes as the carcass glided past him. Animal parts flew everywhere in this whirligig of disembowelment, and each of the cutters was "blood-red" from head to heels.

As the cleaned carcass passed down the final stretch of the "railway of death" it was cut down the middle by expert "splitters," and the halved carcasses were pushed into enormous chilling rooms—thirty or forty acres of them at the Armour works—where they were suspended for twenty-four hours to cool and become firm and "where a stranger might lose himself in a forest of freezing hogs."

The entire operation, from the killing wheel to the death locker, took less than ten minutes.

Walking past the big doors of the chilling rooms, Bourget saw carcasses being pushed out along the ubiquitous rail to a cutting-up room, where each table was a "sort of human chopping machine," as Frederick Law Olmsted described the same operation in a Cincinnati packinghouse. Two men lifted and turned the carcass, and two others did the butchering with cleavers that had glistening blades two feet long. "No iron cog-wheels could work with more regular motion. Plump falls the hog upon the table, chop, chop; chop, chop; chop, chop fall the cleavers. All is over. . . . Amazed beyond all expectation at the celerity, we took out our watches," Olmsted wrote, "and counted thirty-five seconds, from the moment when one hog touched the table until the next occupied its place."

The unerring cuts created hams, sides of pork, and racks of ribs; and these were sent through chutes to pickling, salting, and smoking rooms below. From there they were put in boxes and barrels and sent to platforms where huffing freight trains were waiting. Standing there, Bourget realized that he had come finally to the ground floor of this gigantic killing concern.

In the Beef House, where Bourget and his party went next, the "death struggle" was different. There were no shrill cries from the animals, and the work was done on one floor only, with an overhead visitors' gallery down the center of the dimly lit building, from where Bourget looked down into an inferno of blood, steam, and sweat.

The cattle were led up a lime-washed gangway by an old red "Judas" steer, and when he disappeared by an escape gate, they were driven into narrow chutes, one or two to a chute, penned in so tightly they were almost immobile. On a platform above and adjacent to the chutes, iron-muscled men in shirtsleeves guided the steers into the stalls, "caressing" them with the tips of their sledgehammers to calm them down after they had picked up the scent of blood. Then, suddenly, one after the other of the men lifted his bludgeon high in the air and slammed it with a thud into an animal's forehead, and the beast sank down "in a lifeless heap." One side of the pen was then raised, and the unconscious animal was pulled by a chain onto the killing beds, breathing heavily and bleeding from the nose and mouth. Its hind legs were shackled, and with a press of a button the huge beast was lifted up by a steam hoist, placed on an iron railway, and sent down the line to a "sticker," who plunged his knife into its heaving chest, severing in one surgical slash its principal arteries. The animal was left hanging to bleed, and then the "headman" decapitated it with two or three well-aimed blows.

"If the pig men were spattered with blood," Kipling wrote of the scene on the killing bed, "the cow butchers were bathed in it. The blood ran in muttering gutters," and the terrible stench "bred fear." The blood on the floor looked to be almost an inch deep despite the work of hard-faced immigrants who shoveled it into holes in the floor.

The cutting-up process was as quick and efficient as in the hog factory, only here there were many lines of carcasses. And instead of the animals being brought to the men, the men moved from one carcass to another, working with "furious intensity, literally upon the run." Each man had a specialized task to perform on the suspended carcass. When he was done, he would rush to the next carcass in the line, to be followed by a different kind of specialist. In this way, a gang of almost two hundred men could stun, kill, gut, scrap, clean, and cut up over eighty cattle per hour.

Here also, at the end of the line, were the chilling rooms. But whereas almost all the pork was preserved after cooling, most of the beef was sent directly to refrigerator cars, bound for butchers' cabinets and dinner tables in New York and Boston, Richmond and Savannah.

"It will arrive," Bourget wrote of the work of the refrigerator car, the decisive invention in the history of the meat industry, "as fresh, as intact, as if there had not been thousands of miles between the birth, death, and dismemberment of the . . . peaceable creatures."

•

Seated in their carriage as they headed back to town, Bourget and his party began discussing what they had seen, trying to "discern the intellectual significance" of this unsurpassed operation. "We all agreed that the first characteristic of this enterprise is the . . . stupendousness of its conception," Bourget wrote. But behind this "colossal" effort of imagination was a driving passion for order, and this union of order and vision, Bourget and his companions agreed, was the key to Armour's great manufactory. They were surprised, however, at how little this production system depended on modern machinery.

"It was all so very businesslike," Upton Sinclair wrote of the pig-slaughtering process, "that one watched it fascinated. It was pork-making by machinery." It was not actually, for almost all the work was done by skilled butchers, assisted by many more unskilled workers. "I had expected to see machinery of surprising ingenuity, almost superseding hard work, which would kill, cut and prepare an animal without the direct intervention of any workman," Paul de Rousiers said after visiting the Armour plant. But organization, not invention, explained the brutal efficiency of Chicago's packing plants, modeled after crude assembly-line operations first developed in Cincinnati before the Civil War—and later the inspiration for Henry Ford's assembly line for making Model T's. "Of all the large industries in this country," observed the *Monthly Labor Review*, "slaughtering and meat packing ranks as the one which is probably least susceptible to mechanization." This was because the raw materials—the hogs, cattle, and sheep—varied greatly in size, shape, and weight. Of all the machines experimented with by packinghouse technicians, only the automatic scraping machine could adapt itself to the organic irregularities of the animals. "Even when dead," Giedion wrote, "the hog largely refuses to submit to the machine." Meatpacking, then, became the first assembly-line industry because packers were not able to mechanize their operations, which forced them to turn from technology to the division of labor as a way of reducing production time and costs.

Chicago's slaughterhouses, however, were most definitely machines—machines made up almost entirely of human parts, like the human machines that had built the pyramids of ancient Egypt before the invention of the wheel or the pulley. Unable to mechanize operations, the packers built mass-production engines that depended, ironically, on hand labor. As the socialist A. M. Simons wrote in 1899: "That marvelous speed and dexterity so much admired by visitors is simply inhumanly hard work."

Bourget saw Armour and Company and the other big Chicago enterprises he visited as reflections of the men who ran them, businessmen with the vigor and vision of "grand seigneurs." Every important business in Chicago seemed to be "made in the image of who [founded] it . . . the visible will of that man, his energy, as it were, incarnated and made evident." These businessmen were, to him, the real makers of America, capitalist conquistadors who had tamed a continent and raised great cities in one generation, a "phenomenon" that had not "elsewhere been seen, and . . . will . . . never be seen again." They were truly the "heroes of modern times."

What Bourget found most arresting about these businessmen was their warlike combativeness—and coupled with it their taste for risk taking. "The cautious rentier mentality that betrays later generations—be they individuals or nations—" wrote Sigfried Giedion, "could have brought not a single stone to the building of these giant [meatpacking] concerns. All this called for men ready for danger, ready to win or to lose. There was no middle course. It was a staking of all against all."

In 1893 the most famous of these "Chicago giants" was Philip Danforth Armour, "the Meat King of America," a trader and manufacturer of world influence. "A map of his business," a journalist wrote, "is a map of civilization." But the real founder of the modern packing industry was Armour's dour, simple-living rival Gustavus Swift; "Stave," his family called him. In a city of risk takers, he was the most audacious gambler of them all.

Armour and Swift arrived in Chicago in the same year, 1875, and their careers as meat barons and city builders are closely linked. One was a ditchdigger, the other a country butcher, and their ascent was greatly attributable to their entrepreneurial energy, yet one enormous advantage was theirs. They arrived in Chicago at a time ideal for men with giant projects. National conditions were ripe for a historic leap forward in the meatpacking business. Both were supremely capable organizers, and in the approaching era in the industry, organization would be everything.

•

When thirty-six-year-old Gustavus Franklin Swift moved his pregnant wife and five children into a rented house not far from the Union Stock Yard, on the street they would live on until the end of the century, Chicago's meatpacking business was still dominated by the packers of pork. In the absence of refrigeration technology to preserve the product in transit, meat had to be preserved by salting or smoking; and though Americans had a taste for bacon, sausage, and smoked ham, they preferred their beef fresh. Almost all western cattle arriving by rail at the yards were shipped "on the hoof" to wholesale butchers, who, in turn, supplied retail grocers and meat shops. Swift, whose ancestors arrived in Massachusetts in the time of John Winthrop, got his start in life at the age of fourteen as a butcher's apprentice to his brother, and at sixteen he was already eager to get out on his own. Borrowing twenty dollars from his father, a Cape Cod farmer, he bought a heifer, which he killed, dressed, and sold door-to-door from a wooden cart. That small loan, he liked to tell people later, was the beginning of Swift and Company.

From butchering, Swift went into cattle dealing, and as the primary cattle market moved west so did he, first to Albany, then to Buffalo, and finally to Chicago, following geographically shifting opportunity, as Cyrus McCormick had three decades earlier.

A buyer for eastern interests, including several of his own firms, he arrived at the yards every morning at six, a tall, tight-lipped Yankee on a Texas pony far too short for him, his long legs hanging close to the ground. He preferred the pony, he said, because he could open stock gates without dismounting, saving valuable time—a prefigurement of his obsession with saving time and money in his business operations. A hard-bargaining man, he made a reputation as a crack cattle dealer, but he had the foresight to realize that the business he was prospering in was about to change, and he was determined to be a leading agent of that change, even though he had little capital of his own. It fired his blood to think that he could be in on the making of a vast new Amerian enterprise, and he wrote excitedly to his family back on Cape Cod of his "Wild West Scheme."

It was changes in hinterland production patterns that opened the way for revolutionary changes in the meatpacking business and in the eating habits of entire nations. This sweeping economic and cultural transformation was the outcome of two accidentally complementary developments. Just as population in the swelling cities of the East began to outstrip the local meat supply, there was a tremendous expansion of cattle production on the unfenced plains of the West, America's new cattle kingdom. Thundering herds of Texas longhorns, a quarter of a million in a herd, were driven in swirling clouds of dust to new railroad towns like Abilene, Kansas. The primary industry in Abilene had been raising prairie dogs before a Chicago livestock dealer named Joseph McCoy built cattle pens near the new rail depot there, at a place on the map where old Spanish trading trails intersected with the westward-pushing railroad. From the holding pens of this brawling cow town—and scores of others that grew up as fast as it did, places like Newton, Dodge City, Ellsworth, and Cheyenne—cattle were sent to Chicago on slatted cars and shipped from there to slaughterhouses everywhere. The animals, however, were badly treated in transit, many of them arriving too bruised or emaciated to slaughter. It was also expensive to feed and water them on their way to their doom. Swift, who had what one of his sons called "an eye for waste," saw an even greater inefficiency in this system, for only 40 percent of every healthy steer he bought in Chicago was edible, making over half of what he paid the railroads to ship by the pound absolutely worthless.

The answer, obviously, was to slaughter the cows in Chicago and send only the edible parts east, keeping them cool, somehow, along the way. The potential savings—and the opportunities for profit—were so great that Swift was willing to jump into the trade ahead of the enabling technology. First he sent chilled beef to Boston in the dead of winter in boxcars, with the doors slightly ajar for ventilation and cooling. A "hands-on" businessman, he superintended the loading himself, hanging quarters of beef by ropes from racks made from two-by-fours. He then sold his interest in one of his wholesale firms and used the profits to buy a small beef-packing plant, staffing it with five butchers imported from Boston. All the while he pursued the dream of George Pullman of a new kind of railroad car that would spawn a new industry—and with it, a sizable fortune for himself.

Rivals thought his scheme "insane," given the primitive state of refrigeration technology, his limited capital, and the public's strong prejudice against western chilled beef, which was widely believed to be "poisoned" by preservatives. But Swift thought the idea was too good to fail. "Commercial history has few instances of a courage more genuine," Charles Edward Russell wrote in grudging admiration of Swift in his 1905 exposé *The Greatest Trust in the World*. "The risk involved was great. The project was wholly new; not only demand and supply had to be created, but all the vast and intricate machinery of marketing. Failure meant utter ruin. Mr. Swift accepted the hazard."

In 1878, Swift hired Andrew S. Chase, a Boston engineer with experience in designing cold-storage facilities, to invent a state-of-the-art refrigerator car. Earlier cars—no more than iceboxes on wheels—stored ice dangerously close to the meat. When the cars swayed, some of the meat invariably touched the ice, discoloring it and making it unsellable. The doors of the cars also had to be opened a number of times in transit for re-icing crews, and this sometimes raised the temperature, spoiling the meat. In the car he designed one year later, Chase placed ice in ceiling bins, allowing workers to re-ice from openings in the roof. As air passed through the bunkers at the top of the car, it cooled, became heavier, and dropped to the floor, forcing warmer, lighter air out of the car through the ventilators. It was this application of elementary physics that transformed the ancient trade of beef slaughtering from a local to an international business, for refrigerator cars led naturally to refrigerator ships, which carried Chicago beef to four continents.

In Swift's integrated system, the most highly rationalized production and distribution network in the world in the 1880s, a side of beef leaving his Chicago production plant was pushed along a rail that connected the freezer to a refrigerator car; and when it arrived in New York, it was pushed into the freezer of one of his distribution houses "without being removed from the hook on which it was hung when killed," *Harper's Weekly* reported in 1882. It was this attention to detail, joined with big-scale vision, that explained Swift's success.

•

Instead of solving Swift's distribution problems, however, the refrigerator car initially created a host of new ones. Railroads refused to build refrigerator cars for him, fearing they would be making a product that would undermine their own lucrative livestock trade. Undeterred, Swift had a Detroit company manufacture Chase-designed cars for him. When the big railroad companies set rates for chilled beef as high as three times those for livestock, he made a deal with an upstart railroad, the Grand Trunk, which had not invested heavily in rolling stock and feeding pens for cattle in transit. Eventually, the major trunk lines saw that greater profits were to be made in chilled beef than in shipping live cattle and went after Swift's business. By the mid-1880s, however, the tail was wagging the dog. Swift and several other packers who followed him into this burgeoning enterprise were able to force the railroads to grant them favored rates and secret rebates on the basis of the sheer volume of their carrying trade.

The consequences of all this for Chicago were enormous. The refrigerator car was a powerful impetus to urbanization. It allowed beef butchering—now a year-round business—to be concentrated in Chicago and later in a number of other western cities, such as Omaha and Kansas City, where the big companies installed regional branches. With the refrigerator car, Chicago moved from a center for the transfer of live cattle to a center for slaughtering and packing cattle, taking a large step toward its postfire emergence as a major manufacturing center. Here, too, Swift led the way, building in 1881 the largest beef-packing plant in the country in the Union Stock Yard. By 1889, when the surburban town of Lake, where the stockyards were located, was annexed to Chicago, beef packing had surpassed pork packing as greater Chicago's largest industry, and Swift's "Wild West Scheme" had made him a millionaire several times over. Yet he remained as frugal as ever, insisting to his sons that "no young man is rich enough to smoke twenty-five cent cigars."

But this is to anticipate. Before Swift could conquer the eastern market he had to overcome the opposition of butchers and consumers and set up a network of distribution centers for his product. In doing this—in becoming the first modern packer—Swift brought to birth America's first vertically integrated business corporation, a professionally managed firm that reached out to control the supply, production, and distribution of its product, from the purchase of western steers to their delivery as steaks and roasts to the neighborhood butcher.

No Impure Chicago Beef Sold Here! signs in butcher-shop windows announced when Swift's "miracle cars" began arriving in seaboard cities and towns; and butchers organized a nationwide boycott against his western chilled beef. "How he wore down the eastern public's prejudice against western dressed beef is of itself an epic of selling," Louis F. Swift wrote of his father. It was. But power more than persuasion—power derived from rationally organized mass production—explains Swift's complete success. The whole thing was of a piece, production and distribution beautifully complementing each other.

Swift persuaded established wholesalers to carry his beef by offering them the opportunity to buy a minority interest in his business, turning them from wholesale butchers of live animals to wholesale distributors of dressed beef. If wholesalers resisted, he built his own distribution centers, with storage facilities and a professionally trained sales force—and drove them to the wall. Continuous-flow production back in Chicago made it possible for him to "sell a superior 'cut,'" as his son explained, "at a lower cost than the butcher [could] sell an inferior 'cut' taken from an animal killed in his own slaughter house." Where the opposition was most formidable, Swift dropped his prices below cost, market share being the paramount consideration for him. "If you're going to lose money," he instructed his branch managers, "lose it. But don't let 'em nose you out."

Swift's success made it impossible for other packers to stay out of the dressed-beef trade, and they, too, formed vertically integrated corporations. Five of them, "the Big Five," dominated the slaughtering business of the country by 1893, making informal pooling agreements among themselves to carve up market shares, fix prices, and discourage wage increases and a union movement. Ruthless in competition, Swift was "cunning in cooperation." It was one thing to take on the butcher; it would have been quite another to take on the likes of Armour and Morris.

"The causes of oligopoly [in meatpacking]," argues one of this industry's historians, "lay much more in prosaic, interrelated forces of technology and markets than in the workings of entrepreneurial genius. . . . As entrepreneurs, [the Chicago packers] affected the rate and pattern of change, but they themselves were not the fundamental cause of that change." Gustavus Swift and Philip Armour would have agreed with this, but only up to a point. It was largely "the growth of the West [that] did it," Armour told a reporter who asked him to explain the phenomenal growth of the chilled-beef industry. Railroads were reaching out into the cattle-rich range states, and urban population was growing, "making the creation of a food gathering and delivery system necessary." The packers, he admitted, were "the intelligent servants of a great public need." But Armour—speaking for Swift as well—made it clear to the reporter that he was no ordinary businessman elevated to importance by impersonal market forces. The "food-gathering and delivery system" he referred to was the creation of packers like himself, who were, as he fiercely insisted, instigators as well as benefactors of far-reaching market and technological changes. Armour and Swift didn't create the national conditions that opened the way for the emergence of the chilled-beef business, but they responded to the new situation with unusual foresight and skill, creating the production, marketing, and administrative innovations that transformed a struggling seasonal business into the most powerful industrial combination up to that time.

The size and complexity of these corporations forced their personalistic founders, however reluctantly, to delegate authority to salaried managers, accountants, and engineers, paving the way for the impersonal, managerial corporations of the twentieth century. "Swift and Company," Gustavus Swift said, foretelling the future, "can get along without any man, myself included." It would be wrong, however, to view the big Chicago packing companies of the 1890s as impersonal organizations. They were, as Paul Bourget saw them, images of the innovators who built them. In 1893, Swift and Company was still largely Gustavus Swift; Armour and Company, still largely Philip Armour. Both were family concerns with stock ownership and decision making resting in family hands. And their dynastic founders laid careful plans to keep them that way.

Seven of Swift's sons joined him in the business, and his daughter married Nelson Morris's son Edward, who entered his father's company along with his two brothers. "Father was very happy and, I think, proud," recalled Helen Swift, "that the boys all loved the business and had no leaning toward any other." Swift brought his brothers into the business, and so did Armour. "You must all stand together," Armour's mother used to tell her five sons. "We brothers do stand together," Armour said later. "I would rather give my last dollar before I would see any of them fail." And, like Swift, Armour expected his sons to follow him into the business as soon as they finished basic schooling, which, to Armour, meant a year or two of technical training beyond high school. One son, Philip Danforth, Jr., a mirror of the old man in physical appearance and temperament, did; but the eldest son, Jonathan Ogden, quiet and bookish, went to Yale and also to England to study architecture against his father's wishes. When Jonathan Ogden returned to Chicago from his trip abroad, he told his father of his new plans, which Armour related—along with his own reaction—to his stockyard crony John B. Sherman. "Ogden was impressed with the fact that so many Englishmen had a leisurely life on a small income, with a lot of worthwhile things to do . . . [things] he would like to do instead of grubbing for money, when we already had more than enough. He thinks he should retire. I told him to be at the Yards in his working clothes at seven on Monday morning."

Jonathan Ogden left Yale at his father's "request" to assist him "in carrying his business cares." When Philip, Jr., died suddenly in 1900, at the age of thirty-one, the first son reluctantly agreed to take over a business he never developed a feel for, the Chicago colossus his determined father had put his personal stamp on.

•

"At sixty, this marvelous specimen of American energy is the busiest soldier in the army he commands," a reporter wrote of Philip Danforth Armour in 1893. "You can always tell when the 'old man' is here . . . ," said one of his lieutenants. "He puts a zip and electricity into the air. Everybody feels it and everybody hustles."

Big, florid, and magnetic, with a large bald head and full red whiskers, Armour ran the most tremendous butchering establishment in the world from the company's main office in the Home Insurance Building, the first iron-frame skyscraper in Chicago. This office, reached from a gorgeous lobby by two flights of marble stairs, was one huge room, with no partitions, where some three hundred employees, from scribbling clerks to heads of major departments, sat in the open at small desks, "in a manner," wrote the reporter John J. Flinn, "suggestive of school-rooms."

Working alongside them at his plain flattop desk was 250-pound Philip Armour, talking, as Flinn might have seen him that morning, to one of his managers while a messenger stood at his elbow reading him telegrams from trade centers all over the world, his mind capable of handling two, three, and four streams of information simultaneously. White-shirted clerks hurried up and down aisles between the rows of desks, delivering telegraph messages and stacks of envelopes, more mail than arrived every day in a small city; and the room was alive with the rattling of typewriters, the clicking of telegraph keys, the ringing of phones, and the shouts of buyers and sellers exchanging information on the shifting prices of pork, beef, and mutton. "Such a mobilization of energy, to promote the private affairs of one man, I had never seen," Theodore Dreiser wrote after interviewing Armour in 1898.

A long line of callers, some of them there on business, some to plead for the Chicago charity they represented, waited near the doorway to see Armour. When P.D., as his friends called him, was ready for the next one in line, a young man would shout out the caller's name and point him toward the chief's desk. It was only in 1893, at the insistence of his sons, that Armour agreed to build a small, sparely furnished office in the corner of the room so that he would not be overwhelmed in his advancing years by people demanding to see him.

Armour never liked his little office and would prowl the big office outside it, checking on this or that matter in his empire of meat and holding impromptu cabinet councils with his managers around one of their paper-cluttered desks. Work was his life, and he couldn't wait to get to it, rising every morning before five o'clock to breakfast with his wife by gaslight—the news of world markets by his plate. He walked to La Salle Street from his Prairie Avenue home and was at his office by six, a matter of particular pride to him. The big deals were usually made early, he said, "before the boys with polished nails show up." Workers arriving at the La Salle Street office a little after seven were greeted by Armour with a booming "good afternoon."

He worked like a high-horsepower steam engine, stopping only for a Spartan lunch of bread and milk and a short nap, which reinvigorated him for the rest of the day. "Give me plenty of work, and it is about all the tonic I want," he would say, but his secret was that he knew how to relax. In his later years he would leave the office at around three or four o'clock and go for a ride along Lake Shore Drive in his custom-built buggy, taking the reins himself and driving his two blooded trotters as fast as they could run. Then, his head cleared of business concerns, he would stop by the Armour Institute, the technical school that was his favorite charity, to see "my boys" and on his way home pay a visit to his grandchildren. He was back at 2115 Prairie Avenue by six and in bed by nine, unfailingly. "I never think of the office until I return to it," he told Dreiser.

"Your sleep is never disturbed?"

"Not at all."

"You have your pile . . . why not retire?" a Chicago journalist once asked him. He couldn't, he shot back. "I do not love the money; what I do love is the getting of it, the making it."

A brusque, hard-edged man, Armour had a volcanic temper and was mercurial in his moods. "He had eyes that could twinkle and again grow searchingly shrewd and hard and sometimes fighting mad," said the writer Ernest Poole, whose father worked for Armour. But he possessed iron self-control, a product, perhaps, of his strict Scottish upbringing. He refused to touch hard liquor; it would set off the "cyclones" in him, he claimed.

The one weakness he never disciplined was his passion for speculation. That "weakness" made him one of the most powerful players on the Board of Trade, which was conveniently located next to his La Salle Street office. Some of his speculations were so spectacular that they became part of local lore. In 1893—in an incident related to Paul Bourget by his stockyard guide—Armour uncovered a plot by rival speculators to ruin him by buying wheat and filling all the elevators in Chicago with it in an effort to force him to buy from them at extortionist prices in order to fulfill his heavy futures contracts. Armour learned of the "corner" a month before his futures contracts came due and bought land on an island in the Chicago River and put three crews to work around the clock building the largest grain elevator in the world, which he filled with wheat brought in on monstrous grain ships in time to fulfill his contracts for May delivery. Yes, Mr. Armour did it, Bourget's guide told the Frenchman with a big smile, "working night and day."

When a reporter for *McClure's* magazine arrived in the city in 1893 to do a story of a typical Chicago figure he asked a number of people to suggest the öne person who best represented "your Western life, ideas, ability." The reply, he said, "was always, 'Philip D. Armour,'"— a "Chicago man to the backbone."

Armour liked to tell stories about his hardscrabble origins. At age nineteen, with a hundred dollars in savings, he left his family's farm in upstate New York, near the utopian colony of Oneida, for the gold fields of California. He went with three other local boys, but only he made it to the Sacramento valley—one died and the other two turned back. When his friends left him, Armour hooked up with a party of overland travelers in Iowa and crossed the Rockies with them into "the land of the Eldorado."

He panned for gold and built sluiceways for miners, saving almost $8,000 in five years. When he returned to Stockbridge and discovered that the girl he hoped to marry had found a husband, he joined his brother Herman in Milwaukee, where he sold supplies to incoming sodbusters. During the Civil War he and his brothers, Herman and Joseph, set up a grain business in Chicago. One year later, Philip became a partner with Milwaukee's biggest pork packer, John Plankinton. In 1864, gambling on an imminent Union victory that would lower the demand for pork, Armour sold pork futures "short" on the Board of Trade and made his first million.

When the Union Stock Yard opened the next year, he bet on Chicago's future, establishing Armour and Company there to pack hogs, pouring the money he continued to make on the exchange into his new business, managed by his brother Joseph. When Joseph's health failed in 1875, Philip moved to Chicago to run the business, bringing with him his wife—the daughter of a Cincinnati merchant— and their two boys. His company was already Chicago's leading pork producer, but within a decade Armour was also competing with Swift in the dressed-beef business and owned the largest packing concern in the world, a fourteen-acre "village" in the yards with its own rail lines, fire company, and chemical laboratory—and a fleet of bright yellow refrigerator cars displaying the company motto: We Feed the World.

"Through the wages I disburse, the provisions I supply"—Armour did not exaggerate—"I give more people food than any other man alive." As he would tell his sons: "Oneida is for those whose dream did not come true. Mine did."

●

Unaided ability played a part in Philip Armour's rise, but so did good luck. Both he and Swift, as Swift's daughter said, arrived when "Chicago was the place where money could be made right on the ground floor."

Armour was more of an organizer than an innovator. He used "scientific business methods"—his term—to wage remorseless warfare on waste and inefficiency. Armour found a way of using waste itself to eliminate waste by placing a value on the intestines, heads, hoofs, and other discarded parts of slaughtered animals, making a fortune on what he and other packers used to throw away.

When he arrived in Chicago, the packing companies were running gutters of blood right into the Chicago River and hiring scavengers to cart away offal and bury it in big pits on the prairie. Eventually, small businesses grew up in the vicinity of Packingtown that feasted on animal carnage like the carrion crows that hovered over rural slaughterhouses. In wooden plants along the river, they transformed the garbage of the packers into glue, oil, tallow, fertilizer, hairbrushes, and buttons. Shortly after entering the beef business, Armour began incorporating these satellite enterprises into his own, using the profits made from selling by-products to keep down the price of his dressed beef, a practice other packers soon followed.

Armour announced the new philosophy of the beef kings: "It is the aim that nothing shall be wasted." Horns, hoofs, and sinew were turned into glue; fat was transformed into oleomargarine, a new and popular substitute for butter; intestines were cleaned and salted and used for sausage casings; bladders were dried and sold to druggists; and low-quality meat was canned and marketed as new products, like pork and beans. Armour even established a laboratory at the yards where the inner linings of the hogs' stomachs were made into pepsin, a digestive aid. "I pack . . . everything," Armour boasted, "but the last breath of a hog."

In cutting down on the disposal of waste, Armour and other packers reduced the amount of blood and offal they dumped into the Chicago River. The packers had created, Armour claimed, a most ingenious method of attacking pollution, turning pollutants into profitable products.

The public soon learned, however, that there were drawbacks to using every part of the pig "but the squeal." To use everything meant to use some things that should have been thrown away. As government inspectors sent into the packing factories later testified, carcasses infected with trichinae were turned into sausage and sold to an unwary public. Canned meat was altered or adulterated or sometimes befouled by the droppings of rats that scurried over it as it was being prepared; sawdust and dead rodents made their way into sausage; and every spring, as Upton Sinclair reported, waste barrels filled with dirt, stale water, and old nails were "dumped into the hoppers with fresh meat and sent out to the public's breakfast," practices that led to tighter federal inspection standards after President Theodore Roosevelt read *The Jungle* in 1906.

There were other social costs to mass-producing meat. "Like all great industries," wrote Mary McDowell, head of the University of Chicago's settlement house in the yards, "the human being is the last factor to be considered, and he is not considered until he becomes restive or makes a protest that disturbs the equilibrium of the business."

2. A Fortress of Oppression

"Be quick, damn you, be quick," a foreman yelled at a Lithuanian immigrant as he waved him through the gate of the packing plant, one of the fortunate few among the hundreds waiting there at dusk every day for the chance to work. This man was sent that winter morning to the beef house to push blood along gutters in the floor. "They get all the blood out of those cattle," a fellow worker shouted to him from across the steam-filled room, "and all the work out of us men."

In their unrelenting effort to cut costs, the builders of these machines for making meat and money turned in the 1880s to the speedup. It was not enough to minutely divide up the work—to deskill it, as the experts would say; the work had to be done faster and faster. In the pork house this was simply a matter of a foreman pushing a lever and moving the hogs at a quicker rate along the slaughtering line; in the beef house, "pacers" were placed among the workers and paid extra to speed up the job. And in both places there were barking foremen who drove the men like galley slaves.

With this, the work grew more dangerous. Upton Sinclair explains: "Sometimes, in the haste of speeding-up, they would dump one of the animals out on the floor before it was fully stunned, and it would get upon its feet and run amuck." Men would shout warnings and scramble for the nearest pillars, slipping on the blood-wet floor and falling over one another. It was especially dangerous if a steer got loose in the winter season, when the room was so thick with steam from the hot blood and the hot water that the men, carrying razor-sharp knives, could not see more than a few feet in front of them. "And then, to cap the climax, the floor boss would come rushing up with a rifle and begin blazing away!"

The cold increased the incidence of accidents. The plants were unheated, and workers on the "lightning line" would tie up their feet in old newspaper, which would become soaked with blood and frozen. Sometimes when their foremen were not looking, the men would plunge their freezing feet into the hot carcasses of the steers, but there was no way to warm their hands. The workers were unable to use gloves because of the nature of the job, so their fingers would grow numb; and then, with the quickened pace, there would be injuries—

the severing of a finger or a hand, or a deep cut that would become infected from the grime all around the workplace.

In yet another effort to keep down labor costs, packers hired many workers only as long as they were needed—for a week or a day or even a few hours. An expanding city of job-hungry immigrants, Chicago had all the desperate laborers the packers needed to run this system. The unemployed showed up at the plant gates of the big houses every morning at dawn, and the strongest-looking ones or those who could afford to pay bribes were picked out by company guards and ushered quickly into the plant. "[Then] some policemen waved their clubs," a rejected Lithuanian worker recalled, "and we all walked on."

With a system like this, it was easier to keep down the wages of steady workers. There was always a hungry man at the gate eager to have another man's job at whatever rate they paid him. At the turn of the century, as many as one-third of a plant's workers were "casual" hands hired in this manner.

As he toured the House of Armour, Paul Bourget's sympathies went out to the doomed animals, but Giuseppe Giacosa, a visiting Italian dramatist and journalist, could think only of the workers. These men "have neither the face nor the body of humans," he wrote in his book of American impressions. A mixture of animal grease and blood—red and shiny—stained their faces, and blood hardened in their hair and beards and on their overalls, forcing them "to walk with long stiff strides." This and "the abrupt and rapid movement by which they throw severed pieces to neighboring workers . . . gave them an appearance altogether ahuman, and rather like the . . . animals they destroy with much dispatch." As a British correspondent told Upton Sinclair: "These are not packing plants at all; these are packing boxes crammed with wage slaves."

But it was not that clear-cut, as Giacosa learned to his amazement when he walked past the packinghouse gate at closing time. Out through the portals came "a lordly collection of gentlemen whom one of our country ladies would take as models of sporty elegance. They are often young, tall and blond, with well-trimmed mustaches and polished shoes. They wear handsome ties, plaid jackets in the English style, and little hard hats."

These were the "subhumans" of an hour earlier, scrubbed, dressed, and eager to spend "on the good things" what "they earned in the blood and mud." Living in "a nation which knows no ease, the Americans accept the inequality of labor in order to attain a relative equality of goods," Giacosa caught the central paradox of well-paid mass production work. The butchers did not will it this way. The skills of their trade devalued, their work degraded, they had come to depend for their self-esteem more on what they purchased than on the kind of work they did.

These craft-proud butchers, most of them Irishmen, Germans, and Bohemians, lived in well-kept cottages in neighborhoods north and south of the yards. When Giacosa visited the yards in 1898, however, the skilled workers were being rapidly replaced by miserably paid Eastern European immigrants, who made up almost two-thirds of the industry's labor force by then. Taking what they could afford, they moved into the deteriorating neighborhood just behind the yards that the butchers and their families were fast abandoning. A pastoral little settlement in the 1870s, by the 1890s Packingtown, or the "Back of the Yards," as it was also called, was the vilest slum in Chicago.

•

What made Packingtown so extraordinarily bad was not the depth and extent of its poverty—most of the heads of households were at least employed—but the nature of the industry that brought it into being. "No other neighborhood in this, or perhaps in any other city," wrote the housing investigators Sophonisba P. Breckenridge and Edith Abbott, "is dominated by a single industry of so offensive a character," an industry whose atmosphere of blood, death, and disintegration per-meated everything, having a demoralizing effect "not only upon the character of the people, but the conditions under which they live." The only open space in this squalid pile of meat mills and acid-eaten houses was the "hair field," where the hair of hogs and the skin of cat-tle were spread out to dry, drawing great clouds of bluebottle flies. When a committee was called together by Robert Hunter, Jane Ad-dams, and other Chicago reformers to document the tenement problem in the city, the Stockyard district was not included in the survey be-cause sanitary and environmental conditions there were so shock-ing—"as bad as any in the world"—that investigators thought they were unrepresentative. Even a lawyer for the packers said that the only "remedy" for the Back of the Yards was its "absolute destruction. You should tear down the district," he told his clients, "burn all the houses."

The Back of the Yards was surrounded by a circle of stench and dis-ease, smoke and slime. To the east were the yards and the slaughter mills. To the west was the largest municipal dump in Chicago; to the south, a maze of railroad tracks servicing the yards; and to the north, Bubbly Creek, a dead arm of the Chicago River named for the carbolic acid from decaying refuse that bubbled to its surface. Bubbly Creek annually took pollution equivalent to a city of a million people. In the summer, when a hard brown scum settled on its surface, cats and chickens could be seen scurrying across it.

When residents of the Back of the Yards, led by Mary McDowell, complained about the unprotected rail crossings on the forty-three lines of track that spread out from the yards, giving the names of children killed or maimed by stock trains, or complained about the loathsome creek, citing ordinances forbidding dumping, they were ignored, for city government, as everyone knew, was a branch office of the packers. And when residents lodged protests about the garbage dump, stung into action by the deaths of one out of every three infants in the households facing it, they were told by a lawyer beholden to Tom Cary, the ward boss who owned the dump, that "a place segregated for unpleasant things [was] a necessity in a great city like Chicago." In this necessarily unpleasant place lived over thirty-five thousand people in 1893.

In the summer, when the flies and mosquitoes came in like a plague, women had to close the windows of their houses, for they had no screens, and seek relief from the heat out-of-doors, dressing their preschool children in long clothing to prevent them from being bitten. Sitting on the steps of their wooden cottages on these long summer days, they could see the women of newly arrived families in Packingtown scavenging on the mountains of garbage at Cary's dump, picking around for kindling for cooking, for old mattresses, and even for edible pieces of food. "A worker ill-nourished from improper food [and] poisoned by bad air in his house and in his neighborhood . . . is an almost ideal soil for tuberculosis," reported Caroline Hedger, a heroic young physician who practiced in Packingtown. "You have but to supply the germ." At the turn of the century, tuberculosis rates in Packingtown were among the highest in the country.

But the people who lived there feared the cold more than they did this disease they never quite understood. On winter nights, families sat around the kitchen stove and ate supper in their laps and then went directly to bed with all their clothes on, including their overcoats. "The cold which came upon them was a living thing, a demon-presence in the room." It tore through the cracks in the wallboards, wrote Upton Sinclair, "reaching out for them with its icy, death-dealing fingers; and they would . . . try to hide from it, all in vain. It would come, and it would come."

The smells from the yards were overpowering, and residents were able to clearly distinguish six of them. "In the night we would be awakened by a choking sensation," recalled Mary McDowell. "One night it would be the odor of burned flesh, another of feathers, another of stys, etc." And the smoke from the trains and the plants was so impressive that children got it mixed up with their religious ideas. "Yes, He sees everything," Mary McDowell overheard a little boy tell his friend. "He can see inside of you. Why, He can see down through the smoke, God can!"

Most of the streets in Packingtown were prairie mud, and most of the houses were balloon-frame cottages and two-story tenements without sewers. Garbage and drain water collected in ditches beside the roads, and this stagnant water stood for so long that a "thick, green leathery scum covered the surface." A child that Mary McDowell knew walked into this solid-looking muck, thinking it was part of the street, and drowned in the ditch. At night, with the streets lit only by kerosene lamps, drunken men stumbling home from Whiskey Row, a solid line of saloons on Ashland Avenue, would fall into these ditches and have to be pulled out by their friends.

When Mary McDowell moved to Packingtown in 1894 from her parents' home in affluent Evanston, it looked to her like a "frontier" town. "Even the people seemed rural in their manner and customs . . . [and] there were more saloons than grocery stores, while gambling, horse and dog racing were the frontier sports." Had old John Dean Caton gone down there in the year McDowell set up her settlement house, he would have been reminded of the Chicago he settled in sixty years before, a slatternly settlement of wood on a wet and forbidding prairie. An immigrant to this new urban frontier, however, would not have the same chance Caton had to rise with his adopted town. Many Poles and Slovaks had been lured to this stinking square mile of stockyards by labor agents of the packing companies to take the jobs of those who came before them, hardly the kind of conditions that had kindled the dreams of Caton, Hubbard, and Ogden. They kept coming in—these immigrants—like the trainloads of cattle and hogs they were hired to slaughter. "Cattle and hogs from the West. Women and men from the East."

One of the chief architects of this "fortress of oppression" was thought, by some, to be the most generous man in Chicago. In 1893, Philip Armour was richer than anyone in the city, with the possible exception of Marshall Field, and he gave more than anyone else to local charities, his favorite causes being the Armour Mission, established with an endowment left by his late brother Joseph, and the Armour Institute, an excellent technical school he built in 1893 to help needy and talented boys. And for a titan with a fortune estimated at over

$25 million, he lived unpretentiously in a spacious but drab house built by a contractor, preferring to spend his evenings at home with his wife. "I am just a butcher trying to go to Heaven," he described himself.

Armour loved children and had an old-fashioned belief that they were special, the future of the country. People who knew him said it hurt him to see children disadvantaged, their potential stunted. Every Sunday afternoon he would visit the mission Burnham and Root designed for him at Thirty-first Street, a run-down neighborhood where blacks were starting to settle. As he inspected the scrubbed and brushed children, over a thousand of them sitting in the auditorium waiting to hear him lecture on his favorite topic—character—he would slip cold silver dollars down some of their backs.

Armour didn't believe in trying to reform adults; their habits were too well settled. "Take youth and train it," he preached. "Let me have young men about me." His mission, which had a kindergarten, a library, nurseries, and a free medical dispensary, performed some of the kind of work Hull-House would take on, and unlike most other missions in the city, it was resolutely nondenominational. Armour insisted on that. You can baptize them, he told his staff, but "I don't care whether the converts are baptized in a soup-bowl, a dish-pan, or the Chicago River." Nor would he go to the churches for help in paying for the mission. He built a complex of 144 apartments next to the mission, Armour Flats, and encouraged his middle-level employees to live there, using the rent to help subsidize the work of the mission and his own money to add a manual training school in 1889, the seed of a bigger idea.

Philip Armour believed "that the labor problem must be solved, not by leveling down, but by leveling up," the pastor of his church, Rev. Frank W. Gunsaulus, wrote of him just after his death. This conviction inspired the founding of Armour Institute, which Armour persuaded Gunsaulus to head, promising the young Congregationalist minister that if he would give him five years of his life, he, Armour, would give him all the money he needed for the school. For a tuition of sixty dollars a year, the first entering class of a thousand students received one of the finest technical educations available west of the Alleghenies. Armour provided scholarships for all students, black or white, who could not afford the tuition, provided they could pass the school's rigorous entrance exams. Only males were enrolled, but Armour also established a high-school-level academy that offered trade courses for young women and a circulating library for residents of Chicago's poorer neighborhoods. Young men and women of the best families were admitted to the institute, with the aim, as the *Chicago Tribune* noted, of "rubb[ing] out the line between the laboring classes and the wealthy classes. . . . The millionaire's daughter and my lady's dressmaker or laundrywoman are already standing here, shoulder to shoulder, learning to see things from the same point of view."

Aside from his business, the institute was Armour's proudest accomplishment. He was there nearly every afternoon, dropping in on classes, inspecting the facilities, talking with faculty and students in the hallways. "An American captain of industry," a reporter for the *New England* magazine noted, "could not rear for himself a more fitting monument." Or a more fitting expression of his social views. Like his company, the institute was a mirror of Armour's mind. Visiting the school only ten days after it opened, the reporter Arthur Warren described it as "a place for developing character." What young people need, Armour told Warren, is not a college but a practical education, "which will fit them for the active work of life." Armour had no use for "theories." Facts and science would solve all practical problems. A frustrated orator, he preached this to his faculty and his students—along with his own homilies about success. "Always keep at it. Don't let up," he was overheard lecturing a student at the institute. "Let liquor alone, pay your bills, marry a good wife and pound away at whatever you want—and sooner or later you'll make good." Never immodest, Armour would offer as evidence the example of his own ascent from poverty to preeminence.

•

In the first week of January 1901, Philip Armour died in his bed after catching pneumonia playing with his grandchildren in the Christmas snow in front of his Prairie Avenue home. Chicago mourned him as a warm civic benefactor, the greatest of the "Dei Majores of Prairie Avenue." And in a tough, give-no-quarter business, he was remembered by the press as a fiercely demanding but generous employer who hired good people and treated them well. That reputation, however inaccurate, survived him. "Old Man Armour . . . was a shrewd old divil," an Irish worker told the journalist Ernest Poole in 1904, "who knew how to get on with the boys! We struck against him now and then but what good did it get us in the end? Like a dog he could make you work for him and yet keep you liking him all the time! Every morning he'd get out to the Yards . . . when the whistle blew, and all day long he'd make trips through the plant, where he knew every one of us by name—for we were not so many then."

The "old personal days" that the Irishman recalled were Armour's first years in Chicago; but as early as 1879 they were gone, and Philip Armour was rarely seen in his plant. In that year, and again in 1886 and 1894, Armour entreated his fellow packers to give not an inch to the industry's burgeoning union movement. "As long as we are heads of our own houses," he announced defiantly in 1879, "we shall employ what men we choose, and when we can't, why, we'll nail up our doors—that's all." After all three of these strikes were crushed—the last two with the help of strikebreakers protected by state militia, Pinkertons, and local police—Armour made his workers sign "iron-clad" agreements not to join a union and systematically blacklisted union leaders, making Chicago the citadel of antiunionism.

There was something about the slaughtering industry, as Upton Sinclair wrote, "that tended to ruthlessness and ferocity." And since they were family concerns, built from the ground up by the men who ran them, there was the strong feeling that no one but ownership should have a voice in how things were done.

When Mary McDowell arrived in the Back of the Yards after the 1894 strike, which left the industry nonunion until after Armour's death, she found the workers "more hopeless than bitter, more conservative than radical, without courage and self-reliance." And many of them could not support their families. Two-thirds of the male workforce in Packingtown made an average of fifteen cents an hour in the early 1900s, when investigators first began studying wage conditions in Chicago, and many laborers were laid off at least two months in the summer—the slow time in the packing trade—and for shorter periods throughout the rest of the year. A 1911 study of Packingtown by Mary McDowell's settlement-house investigators found that the average weekly wage for male heads of households was just over $9.50, while the estimated minimum weekly expenditure needed to support a family of five was $15.40. So entire families were forced to work. Children were pulled from school and sent to local factories, wives took in boarders or sewed clothing at home, and husbands and older sons sought work outside Packingtown during slack times, often hopping trains to become seasonal farmworkers in the wheat and corn belt that rimmed the city. It is no wonder the workers saw a union as their only hope. "You must get money to live well," an immigrant laborer told Ernest Poole, "and to get money you must combine. I cannot bargain alone with the Meat Trust."

Ethnic and skill divisions between workers, especially Irish and German resentment against unskilled Eastern Europeans, made it doubly difficult to organize a union in the industry. And in later years, the packers would hire increasing numbers of black workers from the South, who, in return for a living wage and steady work in this racially divided city, helped the owners keep the open shop in the industry.

A good employer, Armour was convinced, was the only answer to the labor problem. He had to drive his workers as he did, he reasoned, in order to keep down production costs, which translated into lower prices for his products; and in keeping down costs and prices, he kept thousands of people at work, the most he or any employer, he believed, could do for the cause of labor. "We want to make some fine Americans out of rough material," Armour once told a reporter visiting his mission. But this benefactor of young unfortunates closed down every collective effort by their parents to raise their living standard and battle a production system "that stopped or set [them] going like so many pack-mules at the pleasure of the driver."

"[It was] certainly very good of Mr. Armour to build Sunday-schools, educate artists, buy pictures, and patronize music," wrote Nell Nelson, a Chicago reporter who took a job with Armour and Company to investigate conditions in the canning plant—where, in the paint room, Polish and Bohemian girls inhaled so much paint that their sputum was blue, "[but it] would not be wasted charity," she said, to give a little consideration to the working conditions of thirteen- and fourteen-year-old girls.

But it was Dr. Caroline Hedger who put it all into a sentence. "It must be realized in Packingtown that the workers are human beings."

Was it possible to treat workers humanely and still turn a profit? Philip Armour's Prairie Avenue neighbor George Pullman was convinced it was. "The working people," he declared, "are the most important element which enters into the successful operation of any manufacturing enterprise," and they must be decently housed and paid and surrounded with beauty and opportunities for culture and play if they are to be productive for the company. In 1893, his model manufacturing town on the prairie south of Packingtown, the biggest industrial concern in Chicago next to the stockyards, was being lauded by observers from all over the world as proof that business itself could solve the labor problem, the most troublesome social issue of the day. "No place in the United States," observed the *Times* (London), "has attracted more attention or been more closely watched than Pullman."

3. The Pullman Idea

Visitors to Pullman often arrived after touring the stockyards the previous day, and the contrast could not have been more startling. Passengers taking the Illinois Central train from downtown Chicago, a trip of forty-five minutes, stepped off the cars at a small station fronting an elm-bordered boulevard that curved down to a sparkling lake with an ornamental waterfall. Grouped around the station were a landscaped park, a picturesque hotel, a stately limestone church, and a brick-and-glass Arcade Building housing the town's post office, savings bank, library, theater, and all its shops. Across the lake and facing the station was the splendid administration building of the Pullman Palace Car Company, capped by a tremendous clock tower. Behind it stretched the many-windowed buildings of the company's car works, built of red brick to blend in with the neat rows of slate-roofed cottages and apartments on the shaded streets on the other side of the lake.

It looked like—and was—"an abnormally healthy place," the product of the vision and will of an autocratic Chicago capitalist. The operatives and their families," wrote the *Times*'s (London) Chicago correspondent, "appear in a far better condition, and look as if they were of an improved class compared with those usually seen in factory towns." Pullman had a state-of-the-art urban infrastructure. Every residence was equipped with running water, gas, and indoor toilets; the streets were paved with macadam and lit by gaslights; and the buildings and grounds were "kept in perfect repair and cleanliness by the company at its own expense," George Pullman liked to boast. Since the town was completed in 1881, not a single case of cholera, typhoid, or yellow fever had been reported, and Pullman, with a population of 12,600, was reputed to have the lowest death rate of any community of its size in the world.

The town had a free kindergarten and excellent schools, and its handsome library housed a collection of six thousand books donated by its builder. Mr. Pullman was also a great believer in the therapeutic value of sports and recreation for workers. On Athletic Island, a five-acre creation in Lake Calumet, reached by a wooden bridge, he erected one of the finest sports facilities in the country, with a boat house, a cinder track, an ice-skating rink, a rowing course, and two impressive grandstands. The Pullman Athletic Association promoted regattas, cycling contests, track meets, cricket matches, and baseball leagues. And every Memorial Day it held Spring Games modeled after the Olympics.

A London reporter called Pullman "the most perfect city in the world," and American papers invited "distressed socialists and vague visionaries of the world" to study it. "They will learn," reported the *Graphic*, in an 1893 feature on the town, "that there is not now and never has been a single person in Pullman dependent on charity; that there is not a single saloon in the town; that residents are not pledged to promises nor bound by restrictions." The town of Pullman, wrote an impressed Theodore Dreiser, "stands related to the question of how cities should be built in general—how man should live."

Pullman, however, was founded on the less than generous principle that no one should receive anything for nothing. It was run as a business, not a philanthropic, enterprise. George Pullman was one of the only entrepreneurs of his day to understand the connection between a contented workforce and rising productivity. "The manufacturing interests of the company," he wrote to his stockholders in 1882, "cannot fail to be largely benefitted by . . . careful attention to the welfare and comfort of employees." Still, he expected his town, like his company, to turn a profit. To ensure that it did, he set rents high enough to guarantee a return of 6 percent on his considerable investment in land and buildings. Nothing was free in Pullman, not even the library.

When the Columbian Exposition opened, George Pullman was "probably the best known Chicago name throughout America, as well as abroad," said the *Times* (London)—a railroad titan, a city builder, and to many, "a man truly anxious about the moral progress of his work-people." He had built his model city, he told reporters, against the determined advice of his company's board of directors, who had recommended that he turn over housing construction near the Calumet works to speculative contractors, who would have thrown up shoddy cottages and tenements like those in Packingtown. In America, George Pullman's "example of high-principled oversight is rarely followed," Paul de Rousiers wrote in defense of Pullman two years before the violent strike that ruined his reputation and his town. "The industrial chiefs of the [country] usually concern themselves very little about their employees, and do not seem to be very anxious either for their material or moral advancement."

Critics of Pullman City were correct to point out that the impressive landscaping and architecture facing the passenger· station shielded from view "rows of tenement houses known as 'the barracks'—and unsightly wood shanties near the brick yards where the brickmakers with large families live." Even so, there was no working-class housing anywhere in the Chicago area, or in the country, for that matter, to compare with that at Pullman. George Pullman's town was his proudest creation, and when prominent visitors came to Chicago, he liked to take them out to it in his special rail car, a sixty-seven-foot-long mansion on wheels with its own servants' quarters. His great hope was that these doubting Thomases would leave convinced that the labor "problem" could be solved by enlightened paternalism and that a new era in industrial relations was dawning in Chicago, "where so much that was new and hopeful for the future of America was coming into being."

•

Tourists heading out to Pullman by train passed by its founder's mansion on the rim of Lake Michigan, near the dead cottonwood tree—the Massacre Tree—where soldiers and settlers escaping Fort Dearborn were cut down by hostile Potawatomi in 1812. In the summer of 1893, on the broad lawn of his urban estate and in the presence of ex-president Benjamin Harrison and an assemblage of Chicago notables that included Marshall Field, Judge John Dean Caton, Robert Todd Lincoln—the company's chief legal counsel and future president—and Chicago's foremost historians, Alfred T. Andreas and Joseph Kirkland, Florence Pullman unveiled the bronze statue commissioned by her father to commemorate the Fort Dearborn Massacre. This former Indian campground was now "the Olympus of the great gods of Chicago," observed the visiting journalist William T. Stead after being taken to Prairie Avenue not long after the dedication of Pullman's statue. "'Methinks the place is haunted,'" he wrote, "and a subtle spell woven of dead men's bones attracts to the scene of the massacre the present representatives of a system doomed to vanish like that of the redskins before the advancing civilization of the new social era." That era would soon be ushered in, he declared, by the victims of the "trusts and combines" of great capitalists like George Pullman. In the summer of 1893, however, George Mortimer Pullman saw his model town as the guarantor of all that he and his fellow lords of Prairie Avenue had built and owned. And most holiday visitors who passed his mansion on their way to his town wished this visionary plutocrat well in his bold experiment, for the alternative, they feared with him, might be social revolution.

Passengers on the White City Express to Pullman were given souvenir pamphlets explaining that the idea behind the town they were steaming toward was exactly the idea behind the Palace Cars they had seen on display earlier that morning in the Exposition's Transportation Building. "The story of Pullman naturally divides itself into three parts, the building of the car, the building of the operating system, and the building of the town. Each of these stages is the natural logical sequence of the other. Through them all there runs the same underlying thought, the same thread of idea." George Pullman was eager to expound on this Pullman idea to reporters who regularly called on him that summer at his company's regal Michigan Avenue headquarters, a corporate tower with stylish apartments on its top three stories for

Pullman's middle managers so that they, too, like the workers in Calumet, could be close to their jobs and under the watchful eye of the company.

With its plush carpeting, heavy furniture, and extravagant Victorian bric-a-brac, Pullman's office suggested the atmosphere of one of his Palace Cars; and like his cars, it was "wonderfully neat," a *New York World* reporter wrote in 1893, "with a place for everything and everything in its place." The morning Pullman met with this reporter, he wore a perfectly pressed Prince Albert coat, a conservative vest, striped trousers, and gleaming patent-leather shoes. A stiff and formal man, he never took off his coat in the office, even on boiling-hot days, and he always wore a tall silk hat to work, just like the one his black coachman wore. Pullman was one of the few Windy City plutocrats to prefer black to British servants in his home because of their deferential attitudes toward whites, exactly the behavior he expected of his sleeping-car porters, many of them former slaves.

"He was one of the most frigid, pompous autocrats I have ever seen," a neighbor described him. "Rather a handsome man in a way, with high complexion and chin beard, tight-set mouth and very bright eyes." Around the office—and at home—he was "a regular martinet." He had little patience with his office staff or his family, except for his "model" child, Florence, after whom he named the showcase hotel in his model town. He had only a few friends, fellow Chicago kingpins he played poker with at Marshall Field's mansion or at the Chicago Club, at what was known as the Millionaire's Table. When not working, he preferred to be alone, escaping whenever he could to his suite at the Florence Hotel, to his mother's apartment in New York City, or to his isolated retreat—Castle Rest—on the St. Lawrence River, time away from home that led to arguments with his wife, Harriet, a formidable figure in Chicago society. When he vacationed with his family, it was usually at their seaside mansion in Elberon, New Jersey, which he had built in the 1870s near the summer White House of his friend Ulysses Grant.

George Pullman was only at ease when talking about himself, his vanity overcoming his tightly wound reticence. Sitting behind his big mahogany desk, his reading glasses hanging from a gold chain around his neck, he recalled for a Chicago reporter the origins of his gigantic railroad company, which gave employment to fourteen thousand workers and operated cars carrying more than 5 million passengers a year over three-quarters of the nation's railways. The idea for the Pullman Palace Car came to him, he said, while riding in one of the country's first sleeping cars on a long business trip. Lying half awake and fully dressed in his uncurtained berth—one of a stack of three wooden shelves permanently attached to the side of the New York Central coach—he began to think of ways of improving these primitive bunk cars. Back in Chicago, he took time from his building-raising work to remodel three old cars as "sleepers" for two local railroads, one of them William Ogden's Galena and Chicago Union. These cars were not much of an improvement over existing ones except that they were equipped with concealed upper berths that were lowered by pulleys and ropes from the ceiling, turning a day coach into a night coach in a matter of seconds, the beginning of the Pullman Idea.

In 1860, Pullman headed to the gold fields of Colorado to raise the capital he needed to build the biggest and most beautiful sleeping car in the world. He returned to Chicago three years later with money made in a variety of western investments and went to work on his dream car with a team of carpenters and mechanics in an old repair shed on the banks of the Chicago River. Frescoed, walnut trimmed, and richly upholstered, the "Pioneer" of 1865 was the world's first truly luxurious sleeping car, land travel's equivalent of the opulent public rooms of the western riverboats.

It was big and beautiful, but it was not, railroad companies believed, practical. It cost over twenty thousand dollars, four times that of any other sleeping car; and to make it comfortable to his exacting standards, Pullman built it higher and wider than any other car in service, so that if railroads wanted to use it, they would have to raise the height of trestles and widen bridges and station platforms. Pullman also insisted on controlling his product as completely as he would control his company town. Pullman cars were leased—not sold—to railroads; and Pullman supplied and staffed them and collected the extra cost for a night's journey, two dollars over the regular price of a passenger ticket. With such terms and with the high cost of infrastructure alterations, railroads were not interested in doing business with this thirty-four-year-old upstart with no big money behind him.

A national tragedy reversed George Pullman's fortunes suddenly and sensationally. When the funeral train carrying President Lincoln's body reached Chicago in May 1865, a local committee of businessmen that included several of Pullman's friends coupled The Pioneer to the funeral cortege for the final leg of its journey to Springfield, sending out crews to rip up platforms and tear down bridge underlayment. After the president's burial, Pullman put his car on display in several cities and made it available to carry General Grant home to Galena after the war. "Mr. Pullman's car became the subject of universal comment," recalled a company official years later. "From that moment its success was assured."

Midwestern railroads began regularly carrying his cars, however, only after experimental runs with trains pulling both his cars and sleepers costing fifty cents less demonstrated that the public would pay for greater comfort. The only travelers who rode in the cheaper cars, noted a contemporary, "were those who were grumbling because they could not get berths in the new ones." Unlike Gustavus Swift, who wiped out the small butchers by price-cutting, Pullman bested his competition by raising prices, along with quality. "[The] principle upon which I have always acted," he told a reporter in 1893, "is that the people are always willing to pay for the best, provided they get the worth of their money."

Nor was Pullman's success based, like Gustavus Swift's, on a technological breakthrough. He did not invent the sleeping car. He invented, instead, a new idea, "luxury in travel" for the middle class. And in gambling that beauty and comfort would pay dividends, he was confident, as well, that they would improve the behavior of his customers, making his cars easier and less costly to maintain. "We know now," the company's publicist wrote in its World's Fair souvenir book, *The Story of Pullman*, "that men will not climb in between the sheets of a Pullman sleeping-car bed with their boots, and that they will not regard sleeping-car carpets and upholstery in the light of convenient cuspidors. We know that the same instinct which makes people conform in their habits to elegant surroundings in homes, will make them proportionally conform to them in public vehicles." It was this faith in what Pullman called "the educational refining influences of beauty" that would underlie his conception of town planning.

Pullman's Palace Cars pushed out sleeping-car competitors as quickly and completely as Swift's refrigerator cars pushed out cars carrying live cattle. The transcontinentals began carrying his cars, and through a merger with a rival company controlled by Andrew Carnegie, Pullman got the powerful Pennsylvania Railroad to use his cars exclusively. By the late 1870s, the Pullman Palace Car Company, chartered in 1867, had but one rival, the Wagner Car Company, controlled by Cornelius Vanderbilt's New York Central Railroad. But Webster Wagner stayed in business only by copying his competitor's designs, and his company was eventually absorbed by Pullman's in 1899.

George Pullman attributed his success, as Philip Armour did, to "attention to detail." He had started out as a cabinetmaker and brought to his railroad business the craftsman's concern for superior workmanship. He was also—again like Swift—a persistent innovator. His company constantly improved its cars, introducing innovations like shock-absorbing "paper wheels" for a quieter, smoother ride, and it was always, like Armour and Company, expanding its product line, adding a dining car, a parlor car with upholstered chairs mounted on swivels, and an observation car with an outside balcony in the rear, a favorite with travelers bound for the White City. He also built private cars for princes and plutocrats equipped with sunken marble bathtubs, gold-layered clerestories, chandeliers of Venetian glass, and immense pipe organs.

•

In the 1870s, Pullman was manufacturing his cars in Detroit, but toward the end of the decade he began looking for a Chicago-area site for a greatly enlarged and modernized plant that would make his adopted city the largest manufacturer of sleeping cars in the country. "The development of the sleeping-car project," wrote the Chicago correspondent of the *Times* (London), "shows the possibilities of the Great West, both in the effect of the growth of a city and a business in the expansion of a man, and the influence of a man in building a city."

The site Pullman chose was an empty stretch of marshland on the northern shore of Lake Calumet, which was connected to Lake Michigan by the shallow Calumet River. The unpromising-looking location had advantages that would make it, by the end of the century, one of the most tremendous manufacturing districts in the world. Trains coming into Chicago from the east and south passed directly through it; the federal government had begun dredging the river and improving the harbor site on Lake Michigan, making it possible, eventually, to land big ore and lumber boats; and the land was vastly cheaper than real estate in Chicago. This isolated place far from the squalor and vice of Chicago would also be ideal for an experiment in industrial living George Pullman had been fashioning in his mind for some time.

Onboard a ship for England in 1873, Pullman had read with fascination Charles Reade's *Put Yourself in His Place*, an antilabor novel set in an English industrial town. The book's hero, an inventor turned factory owner, transforms his plant into a model of worker-management cooperation—once terrorist-minded unions have been eliminated. Touring the English countryside, Pullman undoubtedly visited Saltaire, a planned industrial village in Yorkshire that embodied the social ideas of Reade's Victorian melodrama. The creation of Sir Titus Salt, a manufacturer of woolens, Saltaire was built with the intention of "breaking down the barrier which has existed between the sympathies of the labourer and the employer." A friend of Pullman's would later claim that the Palace Car Prince borrowed freely from the example of Saltaire in designing his town, but there is no direct evidence of this in Pullman's correspondence. What is almost certain, however, is that the instigating incident for the creation of Pullman City was the labor upheaval that shook Chicago in the summer of 1877.

•

For three terrifying days in June, the streets of the city's rowdy riverfront wards were taken over by thousands of angry workers who paraded from business to business, closing down packinghouses, lumberyards, rolling mills, and foundries, attacking strikebreakers, setting fire to railroad property, and fighting pitched battles with police, local militia, and federal troops. "TERROR'S REIGN," a local headline screamed. "The Streets of Chicago Given Over to Howling Mobs of Thieves and Cut-Throats." With "dresses . . . tucked up around the waists" and "brawny sunburnt arms brandish[ing] clubs," groups of "Bohemian Amazons," a Chicago reporter wrote, attacked a door-and-sash manufactory and stoned police who were rushed in to try to disperse them. The women then raced to Halsted Street, where lumber shovers and packinghouse workers carrying carving knives battled police and cavalry until they were beaten back by volleys of gunfire.

These organized street riots were part of a railroad strike that had broken out a week before in Martinsburg, West Virginia, and had swept across the country with explosive suddenness in the fourth year of a national economic depression. By the time the violence spread to Chicago, 100,000 workers nationwide had joined the struggle, bringing America closer to class revolution than at any time in its history, then or later.

In Chicago, the strike was spontaneous and leaderless—"the grand army of starvation," a local socialist called the roving bands of workers—making it all the more frightening to authorities, who searched in vain for organizers they could imprison. With the city close to "Mob Rule," in the opinion of the press, Mayor Monroe Heath deputized and armed thousands of "men of high standing," closed the city's saloons, cabled for more federal troops, and rang the city's fire bells, summoning militia companies to duty in the "Battle of Chicago." Marshall Field and his partner Levi Leiter armed and drilled their employees and lent their company's delivery wagons and horses to police to transport riot squads. Field and his Prairie Avenue neighbors also formed neighborhood patrols, as they had after the Great Fire, expecting the mobs to fan out in an assault on privilege dangerously reminiscent of the Paris Commune of 1871. "Squelch them out, stamp them out, sweep them out with grapeshot," the *Inter Ocean* demanded.

The conflict, which began on Tuesday morning, was over by the following Friday, crushed in Chicago, as it was in other cities, by massed troops and canister shot. A hundred workers nationwide were killed, thirty in Chicago, where another two hundred were wounded. Amazingly, no Chicago police were killed or wounded seriously. The strike was a siren call for a nation that had believed itself immune to European-style class warfare. Although in most cities the violence was blamed by the press on "bummers, ruffians, loafers, bullies, vagabonds, . . . [and] loud-mouthed orators," it "opened the eyes of the American people," conceded the conservative *New York Times*, "to the order of things which has grown up among them so gradually as to be unobserved. . . . Beneath the vicious elements which produced the riots, the country traces evidence of hardship, of suffering, of destitution to an extent for which it was unprepared."

The Great Uprising, as it was called, was the prelude to a quarter century of labor violence culminating in the Pennsylvania Anthracite Strike of 1902. "The Social Revolution began last July," warned the young Chicago socialist Albert Parsons in 1878. "The issue is made, and sooner or later it must be settled one way or another." By the early 1880s, Chicago had become the headquarters of the nation's socialist and anarchist movements and a center of strength for moderate labor organizations such as the Knights of Labor, which began its rise to power as America's largest labor union in 1878. "The railroad strike of 1877," Samuel Gompers wrote fifty years later, "was the tocsin that sounded a ringing message of hope to us all."

It sent a quite different message to Chicago's capitalists. Immediately following the strike, the Citizens' Association, an influential group of law-and-order businessmen headed by Marshall Field, donated money to the city's police force to buy an arsenal that included four twelve-pound Napoleon cannons, some lighter artillery pieces, and a Gatling gun; and at its urging, the city began constructing impregnable armories to house National Guard units. George Pullman was a member of the Citizens' Association, but his answer to the violence of 1877 was not bluecoats and thick-walled armories but an industrial paternalism that would mask social control so effectively it would appear even to friends of labor as a product of enlightened capitalism. The model community he unveiled in 1880 spoke less of his concern for his workers' welfare than of his prideful confidence in his capacities as a social engineer, a proven molder, in his Palace Car business, of human behavior.

•

The master builder of Pullman, Illinois, was a twenty-six-year-old architect without a reputation. George Pullman first heard about Solon Spencer Beman, a New Yorker, from Nathan F. Barrett, the landscape architect of his summerhouse on the New Jersey shore. Beman and

Barrett had worked together on some estates in the New York area, and Beman came highly regarded as the former apprentice of Richard Upjohn, a leader of the Gothic Revival in America. In 1879, Pullman hired Beman to remodel his Prairie Avenue mansion and was so delighted with his ideas that he asked him to submit sketches for his factory town. When he named Beman chief architect, he appointed Barrett as his collaborator, the first time in America that an architect and a landscape designer would work in concert to build an entire city from scratch.

It was the beginning, as well, of an architectural collaboration between Pullman and Beman that lasted until Pullman's death in 1897. Beman became the architect of his patron's vast Chicago empire—his redesigned residence, his model town, his company's downtown headquarters, the dining club Pullman liked to spend time in at fashionable Washington Park racecourse, Chicago's Grand Central Station—a showcase for Pullman's Palace cars—and Pullman's final memorial in Graceland Cemetery.

"The building of Pullman," historian Hugh Dalziel Duncan wrote, "was one of the great architectural and engineering dramas of Chicago." Special trains ran to and from Chicago every day bringing in men and supplies and crowds of reporters and curious spectators. The entire country "watched the dream of [the town's] founder take form," and Pullman himself was on the site every chance he could get, directing everything, "a captain of industry acting as the city builder."

Pullman's motives might have been founded in self-interest, but this big project brought out the idealist in him, and as it unfolded, Beman and his staff "caught fire from his enthusiasm." Solon Spencer Beman built Pullman City, but he did so as the appointed agent of his client's intentions and ideas. "Mr. Beman's association with Mr. Pullman to me is typical," Louis Sullivan would write of their collaboration, "for I always agree that it takes two to make a building. An architect alone cannot make a building. . . . The impulse for the creation of [it] . . . comes through the client."

Construction began in May 1880 with the draining of the marshes and the installation of a water and sewage system, work familiar to the great capitalist who had helped raise Chicago out of the mud so that it could install its first efficient waste-disposal system. A fortresslike brick water tower was constructed, and sewage pipes were laid to carry human waste from the residences to an underground collecting pool at the base of the tower. From there it was pumped to a company-run sewage farm, where it was treated and spread on the fields, helping to raise cabbage and corn that were sold in the market square in Pullman. "This is the best sanitary system employed in the world," declared the *Architectural Review*.

George Pullman himself hired most of the fifteen hundred laborers who built his town, and he procured his own building materials. Like the Pioneer, this would be his personal creation from first to last. Millions of bricks were made on the spot from clay dug from the bottom of Lake Calumet, and carpentry shops, fed continuously by Pullman's lumber trains, did all the woodwork. Work continued through the following winter, and in June 1881 the first permanent resident moved in. A few months later, eleven-year-old Florence Pullman turned the wheel that started up the giant Corliss engine—the central exhibit at the Philadelphia Centennial of 1876—that provided power for the shops that became that very month America's largest single producer of railway rolling stock. In 1884 a substantial town of eight thousand residents stood on the site that had only recently been a swamp. And no one apparently caught the contradiction that a great capitalist had built the only industrial city in America that was not the unplanned result of the workings of the private real estate market.

Some visitors to Pullman City were as impressed by its car shops as by the town itself. The company manufactured not just "sleepers" but freight cars, ordinary passenger cars, and streetcars, along with the steel that went into them. Its shops could turn out a freight car every quarter of an hour in surroundings that "were light and airy so as to improve morale and health, and consequently production," wrote a British visitor. The Pullman works was virtually self-sufficient. Almost all materials used in construction were manufactured on the premises, which contained an iron-and-steel mill, a paint company, a foundry, a screw company, a brickworks, and a lumberyard that sprawled over sixty acres of land. The main manufacturing complex, with its tremendous steam hammers and forges, was a model of machine-age rationalization. "Everything is done in order and with precision," wrote Paul de Rousiers. "One feels that some brain of superior intelligence, backed by a long technical experience, has thought out every possible detail."

The work process de Rousiers described gives the clue to George Pullman's decision to build a town in conjunction with his plant. Making expertly engineered twenty-five-thousand-dollar Palace Cars required a workforce of a high order, many more skilled laborers than were needed, for example, on Armour's killing lines. Recruiting and keeping such men became George Pullman's paramount priority.

His employment philosophy was to get well-trained, sober artisans—family men, preferably—and keep them productive, contented, and loyal to the company by providing attractive living and working conditions. To ensure that he got the "best class" of workers, he had every applicant for a job take a "formidable written examination involving a great deal of personal history," as the *Chicago Herald* reported. "Among other things [the applicant] must tell whether or not he has ever been married or divorced, whether he is in debt, and if so to whom, and how much, how long he went to school, whether he has any physical deformities, why he was discharged from or voluntarily left his last position, ... whether he uses intoxicating liquors, [or] plays games of chance."

The town of Pullman was designed and administered to reinforce and refine the character of already good men—and of their families as well. In this effort, its isolated location, with a *cordon sanitaire* of company-owned land around it, was almost as important as its physical design. It "was to the employer's interest," a reporter explained George Pullman's philosophy, "to see that his men are clean, contented, sober, educated and happy," and this was not possible in a tumultuous city with its "temptation[s] and snares." These included, in Pullman's opinion, not just saloons, brothels, and gambling dens but political bosses and labor agitators—and even meddling parish priests and ministers. The town of Pullman was the only working-class community in Chicago where politics and labor organizations, the principal instruments available to workers to improve their lives, were forbidden.

Although Pullman was originally part of the sprawling village of Hyde Park, its governance was entirely in the hands of its founder, who ruled unopposed through a town agent serving at his pleasure. The only elections were for the local school board, and they were often rigged by the company; the only newspaper, the *Pullman Journal*, was edited by the company publicist, Duane Doty; and the company-appointed pastor of the town's high-steepled church placed his employer, he told his congregation, just "below the angels." George Pullman even censored plays and musical entertainment in the town's eight-hundred-seat theater, allowing only such dramatic productions as he could invite his family to enjoy. He also personally supervised the workings of his vaunted sewage farm, making sure it, like everything else in his town, made money. As investigators for *Engineering News* pointed out in 1893, the main purpose of the Pullman farm was "profit," not "purification." In the summer, when vegetables had received sufficient fertilizer, crude, stinking sewage was "turned directly into Lake Calumet, from which quantities of ice for Chicago are cut."

Union organizers were kept out of town by denying them licenses to speak in public places, and rumblings of discontent were reported to company officials by paid eavesdroppers, called "spotters." The Florence Hotel did sell liquor, but its high prices and intimidating decor discouraged even the best-paid workers from patronizing it. Thirsty laborers had to go across the railroad tracks to the village of Kensington, where a row of rowdy groggeries, called "Bumtown," catered to them. "There," said a worker, "the moral and spiritual disorder of Pullman was emptied, even as the physical sewage flowed out on the Pullman farm a few miles farther south."

Residents dissatisfied with such close paternal control voted to annex their town to Chicago in 1889, but even after annexation, the town remained the personal fiefdom of George Mortimer Pullman.

The great patron cracked down hard on dissent in the workplace. In 1886 his employees—many of them secretly members of the Knights of Labor—joined a nationwide strike for an eight-hour day, but Pullman moved swiftly to end the stoppage by bringing in strikebreakers under police protection. To guard against future stoppages by ungrateful workers, Pullman placed company spies in his shops, firing and blacklisting any union sympathizers they uncovered.

George Pullman's chief instrument of control, however, was his power as landlord of all he surveyed. No one owned his place of residence in Pullman, not even company executives. "We will not sell an acre under any circumstance," Pullman proclaimed in 1881, "and we will only lease to parties whom we are satisfied will conform with our ideas in developing the place." All leases, moreover, had a ten-day clause, which allowed Pullman to get rid of undesirable tenants on short notice.

On several occasions, George Pullman announced his intention to open a subdivision of his town where workers who had proved their loyalty to the company could buy land and build their own cottages. But there is no evidence he intended to act on this plan. While admitting that it was unfortunate to force workers to be permanent tenants, he could not afford to "run the risk," he told Paul de Rousiers, "of seeing families settle who are not sufficiently accustomed to the habits I wish to develop in the inhabitants of Pullman City."

Touring Pullman in 1888, Charles Dudley Warner called such restrictions on property ownership "un-American." Yet when he contrasted Pullman with Packingtown, he was "glad," he confessed, "that this experiment has been made. It may be worth some sacrifice to teach people that it is better for them, morally and pecuniarily, to live cleanly and under educational influences that increase their self-respect." Warner spoke for a growing number of propertied Americans so alarmed by labor violence that they were willing to see democratic rights curtailed in the interests of social order. "Those who prefer the kind of independence that gives them filthy homes and demoralizing asssociations," he wrote with stern condescension, "seem to like to live elsewhere."

To Warner and de Rousiers, George Pullman was a miracle-working molder of men. The Pullman worker, George Pullman told de Rousiers, had developed into a "distinctive type—distinctive in appearance, in tidiness of dress, in fact in all the external indications of self-respect." Touring the town on a Saturday afternoon, a "half-holiday" for workers, de Rousiers failed to see a single laborer on the streets in shirt-sleeves, evidence to him of a higher sort of behavior; and he and Warner found it amazing that all this had been done "with no compulsion at all." Charges of medieval-style paternalism at Pullman were "all humbug" in the opinion of Rev. Charles H. Eaton, a friend of George Pullman's. But another of Pullman's friends, Stewart Woodford, warned prophetically—in an otherwise effusive appraisal of the town—that "it will be strange if the serpent does not hiss, even under the rose leaves of this Eden."

In 1885 a young economics professor from Johns Hopkins University arrived in Pullman to do a story for *Harper's Monthly*. Richard T. Ely was impressed with the town's architecture and "all pervading air of thrift and providence." Interviewing a number of workers, he found no complaints about wages; and inspections of the clean and tidy interiors of several homes convinced him that Pullman's plans to uplift the taste and behavior of working-class families were working wonderfully. Pullman "is becoming," he wrote, "a great school, elevating laborers to a higher plane of wholesome living."

Ten days in the town convinced him, however, that if like experiments were imitated, it would be to the everlasting detriment of democracy. "Here is a population of eight thousand souls," he wrote in his widely influential article, "where not one single resident dare speak his opinion about the town in which he lives. One feels that one is mingling with a dependent, servile people." Pullman, he concluded, was "a well-wishing feudalism, which desires the happiness of the people, but in such a way as to please the authorities."

Ely found Stewart Woodford's lurking serpent in a secret desire by residents "'to beat the company.'" One way was to move out. As soon as they could afford to, many families bought houses in nearby communities—at considerable risk, for in times of trouble, workers who were town residents were the last to be laid off and the first to be re-hired. Residents enjoyed their town's amenities, but "nobody," a local dissident minister said, "regards Pullman as a real home." In 1892 the average length of residence in the town was a little over four years, and over 13 percent of Pullman workers owned homes outside the town, many of them escaping high rents and intrusive company regulations.

In the end, Pullman's land-use and surveillance policies under-mined the very values he hoped to encourage in his town: stability, order, and company loyalty. "A large number of home owners," as Richard Ely noted, "is a safeguard against violent movements of social discontent." In Pullman the problem was not planning but paternal-ism. George Pullman, who had the habit of referring to his workers as his children, expected them to look to him as their "true and only mas-ter." He wanted them to be happy, as Ely said, "but desired their hap-piness to proceed from him, in whom everything should centre."

At a time when middle-class reformers were calling for American cities to be run like businesses, the town of Pullman already was—and the results should have been instructive. What would happen, Richard Ely speculated, if the great Palace Car maker's dream of a nation of Pullmans was realized? It would mean "the establishment of the most absolute power of capital and the repression of all freedom. It matters not that they are well-meaning capitalists. . . . No class of men are fit to be entrusted with unlimited power."

As dreadful as conditions were in Packingtown, workers were at least free from the scrutinizing eye of the discipline-driven capitalist at the end of the workday. Urban life can be made more regimented in single-purpose towns under the direction of unchallengeable ideo-logues—like ancient deified kings—with their own ideas of the good life. In the end, however, human beings will resist regimentation, even though they might desire the stability and material comforts that be-nign autocrats sometimes deliver. The ideal city is the story, through-out history, of determined dreamers who want what *they* see as the finest features of urban life, without its messy problems and complex-ities. "In dreams," writes historian Spiro Kostof, "we expect this sort of gratification without dues or consequences. In real life, we know better."

•

From the top story of the Pullman Water Tower, the highest building in the world when it was completed, sightseers could make out in the distance the Union Stock Yard and, just to the north, the tremendous chimneys and smokestacks of Chicago. If the stockyards were the raw expression of plundering Chicago, green and orderly Pullman was its antithesis. Pullman and Chicago stood side by side in 1893, opposing representations of the urban future.

Yet their histories merged in an interesting way. The year, 1880, that George Pullman's engineers began draining the Calumet swamp was "the zero hour," as Louis Sullivan called it, "of [Chicago's] amazing expansion," a physical transformation powered by its mighty economic engine and impressively expressed in its new skyscraper architecture. Behind Chicago's zero-hour growth was what had always driven that city forward—not a grand plan or an encompassing idea but the simple "passion to sell," the "impelling power in American life," Sullivan called it. Unlike the all-controlling George Pullman, Sullivan had an appreciation for the haphazard process by which interesting cities often evolve; but both he and Pullman envisioned city building as a field for soaring personal achievement. In 1880 he and a number of other visionary Chicago architects and businessmen saw themselves—as George Pullman and Solon S. Beman did in that same year, standing ankle-deep in the Calumet mudflats, blueprints in hand—as would-be makers of a new kind of American city.

4. Steel Rails to Country Kitchens

The Chicago that emerged after Louis Sullivan's zero hour was a city of steel, the supreme structural material of the industrial age. Dependent for its operation on coal—the fuel of industrialization—Chicago's steel industry, along with a host of related industries driven by coal, powered the economic expansion that raised up the "miracle city." Chicago's two distinguishing man-made features were its steel-frame skyscrapers and its sprawling suburbs and subdivisions linked to downtown by sinews of steel. The flat city and the tall city that together made up modern Chicago were made possible by the wonder material of the age.

•

After losing his job at the stockyards, Upton Sinclair's Jurgis Rudkus finds work in the steel mills of South Chicago, fifteen miles away. As his trolley car moves through the night toward the big steel city at the mouth of the Calumet River, Jurgis looks out at a sky "flaring with the red glare that leaped from rows of towering chimneys." A steel mill going full force at night was industry's most spectacular sight, but to be inside one of these thundering infernos was the real experience. As Jurgis enters for the first time the black building housing the towering, steel-jacketed blast furnaces, all around and above him "giant machine arms are flying, giant wheels . . . turning, giant hammers crashing; traveling cranes creaked and groaned overhead, reaching down iron hands and seizing iron prey"—it was "like standing in the centre of the earth, where the machinery of time was revolving." Only it was impossible to focus one's attention, for the noise was earsplitting and the entire floor of the mill rocked and shivered.

It was the sounds that most impressed Hamlin Garland when he entered a steel mill for the first time in 1893: the "wild and animal-like" cries of the men, the clash and slam of machinery, the exploding furnaces, the screaming steam-driven saws and the high whistles of the moving cranes. Yet the noise and activity of the machinery were nothing compared to the heat and fiery spectacle of the Bessemer converters, which turned molten pig iron from the blast furnaces into silver-white liquid steel, which had a casting temperature of almost three thousand degrees Fahrenheit, about one-quarter the surface temperature of the sun. From a gangway high above the work floor, Jurgis sees cauldrons "full of something white and blinding, bubbling and splashing, roaring as if volcanoes were blowing through it. . . . Liquid fire would leap from these cauldrons and scatter like bombs below," although the men working there seemed oblivious to the tremendous steel splashes.

Then a whistle blows, and one of the kettles begins to tilt, pouring "a jet of hissing, roaring flames" into a huge, bucketlike ladle. Sparks fly everywhere and hide everything from sight, and the heat is so fierce that Jurgis has to cover his face with his hands. As he looks through his fingers, he sees a stream of leaping white liquid rushing out of the cauldron, and above it are shimmering waves of heat and rainbows of blue, red, and yellow, a sight of awesome "beauty and terror." Then the cauldron swings back again, empty, and Jurgis turns and walks out into the day, where the gray smoke hangs over the mills so thick that sunlight cannot burn through it.

These black endless mills—regions of miracle and terror—were heralds of the approaching century of steel. And here on the lakeshore of South Chicago was the second-largest steel complex in America, the Pittsburgh of the prairie.

•

Chicago entered the steel age on May 24, 1865, the second and final day of the grand review of 200,000 Union soldiers in the capital of the newly reunited nation. Early that day, the first steel rail made in America was produced at Eber Ward's North Chicago Rolling Mill Company on the North Branch of the Chicago River. Steel production, however, played no great part in Chicago's economy until 1880—the year ground was broken at Pullman—when this same North Chicago Rolling Mill Company opened a plant at the head of the Calumet River, a place where land was cheap, rail connections were excellent, and there was a fine natural harbor.

The mill's proximity to Pullman and other car shops that had relocated in the area was not accidental, for the early steel industry was a creature of the railroads. The 1880s was a decade of record railroad building, and Chicago's steel mills specialized almost exclusively in rail production. By 1890, the Calumet region, home to a busy complex of iron and steel mills, was on its way to superseding the Chicago River as the most important harbor complex in the Great Lakes region. In that year, the Illinois Steel Company, formed in 1889 by a merger of the North Chicago Rolling Mill Company and two other steel concerns, was the largest, most modern plant in the Chicago region, covering 260 acres of what had recently been a desolate fishing village. In 1901 this company became part of a new colossus, the United States Steel Corporation, whose plants came to dominate the entire lakefront, from the Calumet River to the sand dunes of Indiana. In 1906, U.S. Steel, with Marshall Field as one of its major stockholders, began building on these dunes the industry's equivalent of Pullman, a company town named after the company's chairman, Chicago lawyer Elbert H. Gary.

Chicago's steel industry had an imperial reach. It had to, for it was forced to overcome daunting geographic disadvantages. Limestone, a flux for making iron and steel, was found in abundance in the Chicago area, but Chicago's supplies of iron ore were located in the Lake Superior region, almost a thousand miles by water to the north, where Minnesota's rich Mesabi range supplied 85 percent of Illinois Steel's ore. Great beds of bituminous coal lay in southern Illinois, less than a hundred miles away, but this coal was inadequate for smelting iron, forcing Chicago steel companies to buy and operate mines and coking ovens in Pennsylvania, West Virginia, and Kentucky.

To bring together iron ore and coking coal to make steel, Chicago relied on its unsurpassed water and rail transportation. Some ore was brought directly to the city by rail, but most arrived on enormous carrier ships that steamed down through Sault Ste. Marie—where a canal had been built in 1855—and docked right in front of the mills. There, feeder railroads carried the ore to insatiable furnaces. Appalachian coal was transported by rail to the Ohio lake ports of Toledo, Sandusky, and Ashtabula and shipped by freighter from these points to South Chicago. And men to make steel—a swelling army of job-hungry Poles, Lithuanians, and Slovaks—arrived in Chicago fresh from immigrant processing centers in New York in the same way the coal arrived, by lake vessel or rail. Most of them saw their first steel mill, as Jurgis did, from the greasy window of a trolley car as it made its way down the long lakefront.

By 1893, Illinois Steel owned over forty-five hundred acres of coal lands and had over eleven hundred coking ovens, four Bessemer converters, and four rolling mills employing over ten thousand men. In that year the United States was the greatest industrial power on earth. Its steel industry, the biggest in the world, made the strongest steel rails and the most powerful steam locomotives.

America's—and Chicago's—industrial economy, however, was a creation of incredible diversity, making everything from straw hats and pianos to bridges and boilers. The key to it all was coal. Coal is a city-forming material. The coal supplies of Southern Illinois, first discovered in the 1850s by geologists of the Illinois Central Railroad, made possible Chicago's fantastic industrial growth between 1860 and 1890, when the number of workers employed in the city's industries rose at least thirtyfold. Cheap, accessible fuel, the first requirement for mastery in manufacturing, allowed Chicago to maintain its transportation advantages over both water and land and induced scores of industries to locate in Chicago—including the railroads that ran on coal. "The tendency is to make here the goods sold here," the *Tribune* announced in 1884, in a terse, perfectly accurate report.

Coal attracted two types of industries to Chicago: those, like the iron industry, that used coal for heating purposes, chief among them brewing, canning, and baking, and those that used it to feed steam engines that ran rows of fast-moving machinery, such as plants for making shoes, ready-made clothing, and printed material of all kinds. Coal for generating plants also allowed Chicago to make the transition from gas to electric lighting after 1880, the year Thomas Edison's incandescent lightbulb was demonstrated in Chicago and the year strip mining—with a recovery rate twice that of deep mining—was begun in southern Illinois.

Still the great exchange engine of the mid-continent, Chicago was the second-largest manufacturing center in the country by 1890, surpassing Philadelphia in gross value of goods produced, although still trailing well behind New York. In 1890, Chicago employed 170,000 workers in manufacturing and turned out products worth $500 million, one-half the entire production of the nation in 1850. Manufacturing did not fundamentally change Chicago's ties to its hinterland; it only tightened them. The McCormick Company's reaping and cutting machines were, by 1890, made almost entirely of steel—"McCormick's Machines of Steel" is how they were advertised—and in that year alone over 150,000 of them were sent out to farmers all over the country and abroad.

The 1880s and 1890s were years of farmer protest on the plains and prairies, but midwestern farmers enjoyed the highest standard of living of any agriculturists in the world. They had money for Chicago-made machinery from the McCormick and the William Deering plants and a little extra for household goods they paid too high a price for at country stores. There was a promising market for household items out there—two-thirds of Americans in 1870 still lived on farms or in towns of fewer than twenty-five hundred persons—and back in Chicago a fast-growing manufacturing base to supply it. And linking the two was "a web of steel whose radii," a contemporary wrote, "reach[ed] the ocean in three directions, and to the northward touch[ed] the limit of civilized life." In the years immediately following the Great Fire, one man capitalized on this situation to create something entirely new—mail-order shopping. Using steel rails to reach country kitchens with shopping catalogs that revolutionized the buying habits of millions of Americans, Aaron Montgomery Ward made Chicago the mail-order capital of the world.

•

In 1893, almost 300,000 persons took a free guided tour of the seven-story headquarters of Montgomery Ward and Company on Michigan Avenue, many of them farmers and their families in town for the fair and curious to see the inner workings of the fantastic selling machine that had altered their lives. After a tour of the vast warehouse—stocked with over twenty-five thousand different items—and the bustling mailing room, where thirty clerks did nothing but open letters, visitors were invited to relax in the Customer's Parlor, built especially for the fair. Sitting in rocking chairs or on soft-pillowed sofas, as if they were in their own living rooms, they could leisurely page through copies of the company's latest catalog and place orders right there for ready-to-wear Sunday dresses or winter underwear. A visit to Montgomery Ward's, the department store without a store, was more interesting for many rural folk than a stroll through Marshall Field's vast State Street emporium, for Ward's "Big Book" had been for some time their very own Chicago shopping palace. Arriving once a year by railway express—a greatly awaited event—it brought nearly everything for sale on State Street to Main Street.

Aaron Montgomery Ward was thirty-three years old when he arrived in Chicago in 1865 to take a position as a clerk in the retail emporium of Field, Palmer, and Leiter. He had had a tough upbringing, leaving his parents' home in Niles, Michigan, at the age of fourteen and working in a barrel factory and a brickyard before becoming a boy-of-all-work in a general store in St. Joseph, Michigan. He worked at Field's for two years and then went on the road as a salesman for a St. Louis dry-goods wholesaler, an experience that changed his life.

Ward sold his wares out of a big sample trunk to country stores, where farmers gathered around the cracker barrel or the big iron stove to swap stories or to fume about the high rates charged by grain elevators and railroads to store and ship what they produced. There were also complaints about the stores themselves. Most country stores stocked a meager and shopworn inventory, and, because they were at the mercy of big-city suppliers like Ward's employer, charged prices that locals found "extortionist." Ward, the target of these complaints when he arrived in town by buggy or rail, listened sympathetically to the locals, agreeing that there had to be a cheaper way to get goods from the factory to the farmer. Riding the rails through the Mississippi Valley, he met agents of the Patrons of Husbandry, or Grange, as it was called, a league of farmers organized against the railroads and the metropolitan middlemen. One of the Grange's ideas was to establish cooperatives that sold at wholesale to members, eliminating the hated middleman, an idea much like the one Ward's own experience was leading him toward.

In 1870, Ward quit his job and returned to Chicago to start a business that would buy merchandise in volume, for cash, and sell it by mail, for cash, to the disgruntled customers of the country stores. Selling by mail and dealing only in cash would keep prices down by eliminating the need for salesmen, a store, and a credit department; and the cost of reaching a customer, and of that customer placing an order, would be a mere three cents, the price the United States postal service charged to deliver a one-ounce letter anywhere in the country that the railroad went.

In the fall of 1871, Ward was ready to open his business from a loft over a livery stable on Kinzie Street when his entire stock was destroyed in the Great Chicago Fire. Undeterred, he and his partner, George R. Thorne, rented a twelve-by-fourteen room on North Clark Street, and with a capital investment of twenty-four hundred dollars were back in business six months after the fire. Their first "catalog" was a one-page sheet, printed on a foot-power press, listing items for sale and information on how to place orders, and their only employee was a boy they hired for a few pennies an hour to help wrap packages and run them to the post office. It was not the first mail-order business; manufacturers of specialized items, from seeds to firearms, had been selling small quantities of goods by mail for some time. It was, however, the first to offer a generous assortment of merchandise, from barbed wire to paper dolls, and to sell exclusively by mail, turning federal postal employees into its very own sales force. It was an American innovation, born of rural isolation and determined efforts by government and business to overcome it; and nowhere else did the catalog business thrive as it did in this country.

It was the toughest kind of business, one based entirely on trust, with notoriously skeptical rural customers dealing with a faraway big-city seller they never saw for prices that struck many of them as "Utopian." You Can't Go Wrong When You Deal With Montgomery Ward became the company's slogan, but in 1873 the *Chicago Tribune* warned its readers not to patronize Montgomery Ward and Company. They were "Dead-Beats" and "swindlers," the editors charged, who sold "trash" to "credulous fools." After Ward convinced the *Tribune* to take a closer look at his company, however, the paper apologized, declaring it a "bona fide firm" run by "respectable persons." The customer was completely protected from fraud, the *Tribune* pointed out, by Ward's guaranteed return policy—"Satisfaction or your money back!" When a C.O.D. order arrived at the local express office, the customer could open the package and return the merchandise at the company's expense if it was broken or otherwise unsatisfactory, a policy similar to the one that had helped make Ward's former employer, Potter Palmer, the first great merchandiser in the West.

The *Tribune*'s endorsement helped the struggling business, but the breakthrough for Ward came later that year when the Grange began buying stock from him for its cooperative retail stores, eventually designating Montgomery Ward and Company "the official Grange Supply House." That helped melt rural fears about buying "sight unseen," and for years Ward dealt almost exclusively with Grange members, a potential market of over 800,000 customers. Ward wrote the catalog copy himself, determined to be as folksy as the country storekeeper, while offering prices no storekeeper could beat. When Ward expanded his business, his clientele included tens of thousands of black people in the South, who were forbidden to try on clothes in regular stores.

Ward treated his customers like his friends, writing to them for advice on what to include in his ever-expanding catalog, which had 150 pages by 1876, and answering almost all letters that came in, even those asking for personal advice. There were more and more of these personal letters in the second decade of his business, for he had become a symbol of trust and fair play to rural people living great distances from neighbors in forbidding places with "alarming amount[s] of insanity." Letters arrived from parents asking help in finding runaway boys or babies to adopt and from lonely men looking for wives. "As you advertise everything for sale that a person wants," a man from Washington State wrote, "I thought I would write you, as I am in need of a wife, and see what you could do for me." Ward wrote back explaining that it was unwise to select a bride by mail, but if he did marry and happened to need household goods, he told this lonely bachelor, "we feel sure we could serve both you and her to good advantage."

By 1893, Montgomery Ward and Company was receiving over fifteen thousand orders a day through the mail, and its catalog of more than five hundred pages reached over a quarter of a million people, making the company one of the biggest merchandising organizations in the world. Beginning in that year, however, it was no longer the only general mail-order business in America. Just after the closing of the World's Fair, the Minneapolis firm of Sears, Roebuck and Company, incorporated that year, opened a trial branch office in Chicago. The war of the catalogs was on.

•

Aaron Montgomery Ward started in the mail-order business in Chicago after careful study and with money saved at great personal sacrifice. Richard Warren Sears fell into it almost by accident and with no money whatsoever, beginning his business at a railway express station in the middle of nowhere. In 1886, when Ward's annual sales were approaching $1 million, Sears was a twenty-two-year-old freight agent in North Redwood, Minnesota, a hamlet of three houses. Sleeping in the station loft and selling venison and berries he bought from local Indians to make extra money to support his widowed mother and sisters, Sears found his life forever changed when a package of watches from a Chicago wholesaler arrived at his rail office. After the jeweler they had been sent to on approval refused to claim them, Sears dreamed up a scheme to make some money for himself. He got permission from the Chicago house to merchandise the watches and offered them for sale by mail, for a two-dollar profit, to freight agents along his telegraph line, suggesting to them that they could easily resell the stylish, gold-filled timepieces for ten dollars over his price. To allay their suspicions, Sears borrowed an idea from Ward, promising to send the watches C.O.D. and subject to refusal.

Sears sold out the shipment and in six months, drawing on new stock from his Chicago supplier, made five thousand dollars, enough to quit his job as an express agent and start his own mail-order watch company from a rented room in Minneapolis. In 1887 he expanded his line of jewelry, began advertising in magazines and newspapers, and moved to Chicago, closer by rail to his leading buyers, the station agents—twenty thousand of them nationwide—who could serve indirectly as field representatives for the R. W. Sears Watch Company. When people began to write asking to have their watches repaired, Sears hired the company's first employee, a thin, shy Hoosier about his own age, Alvah Curtis Roebuck.

Sears's watch business was aided by the establishment of standard railroad time in 1883. This replaced hundreds of local sun times with four time zones, all clocks set exactly the same in each zone, a change the *Chicago Tribune* compared to Joshua's having made the sun stand still in the sky. Now farmers who depended on the railroad—the only way in and out of the desolate wheatlands—needed accurate timepieces, which Sears offered at prices and in a variety of styles the country stores could not match.

In 1889, after only two years in business, Sears sold his company for seventy-two thousand dollars and, at age twenty-five, retired from the mail-order trade to pursue a number of other business interests. But selling was Richard Sears's passion, and he was back the next year with Roebuck in Minneapolis merchandising watches and an expanding line of other items through the mail. He was barred from doing business in Chicago for three years by the agreement he had made when he sold his original watch company, but as soon as that time restriction expired, he set up his company as the national competitor of the Ward empire, claiming his was "the Cheapest Supply House on Earth." His catalog was a booklet of 196 pages. One year later, when he moved his company permanently to Chicago, it was over five hundred pages, "a vast department store boiled down."

Like Montgomery Ward, Sears wrote almost every word in his catalog, dictating his tendentious copy on the quick from notes he had hanging from his pockets when he arrived at work in the morning. The P. T. Barnum of merchandising, he could sell anything, he boasted, even the air people breathed. It was his "generous spirit," one of his biographers claims, "that created the good will which became the most valuable possession of the firm." But Richard Sears began to bank on honesty and dependability only after he came to realize it was the true way to wealth in the mail-order business. In his first years as a catalog merchandiser, he was not averse to using base trickery to move a product. One advertisement of his in a rural paper featured a drawing of a sofa and two chairs "upholstered in the finest manner and with beautiful plush," which he offered for sale—but only for the next sixty days!—for ninety-five cents. Gullible buyers who failed to read the word "miniature" in the ad's fine print received a set of doll's furniture in the mail. By the time he formed Sears, Roebuck and Company, Richard Sears had cleaned up his sales style, although he continued to sell soothing syrup for a child's cough that had opium in it, bottled cures for drug addiction, deafness, and paralysis, tonic hair restorer, and the famous Heidelberg Belt, an electrified waist corset guaranteed to cure impotency. "Honesty is the best policy," Sears once said. "I know. I've tried it both ways."

By the early 1890s, a Sears, Roebuck guarantee was, a New York magazine noted, "as good as a government bond." It was a sign of people's unquestioning trust in Richard Sears that only three customers ever returned a Heidelberg Belt.

The Sears, Roebuck catalog, the one-man creation of one of the supreme promotional geniuses in American history, was written, like Montgomery Ward's, for an audience that the author knew intimately. Always friendly and assuring, Sears told customers never to be afraid to make a mistake in ordering. "Tell us what you want in your own way, written in any language, no matter whether good or poor writing, and the goods will promptly be sent to you." And "Send No Money," he instructed. All goods would be sent express C.O.D., to be "examined at express office in presence of the agent."

With the establishment in 1896 of rural free delivery, "the greatest revolution in farm life before the coming of radio," the fantastic wish books of the great catalog competitors arrived right in the farmer's roadside mailbox and were placed permanently in the kitchen, where the family spent most of its time. To make sure his book received priority, Richard Sears cut its dimensions so that when the Sears and Ward catalogs were neatly stacked on top of each other on the kitchen cupboard, his would be on top. Children learned to read in one-room schoolhouses from the Chicago catalogs and learned geography from their maps of the nation's postal zones. When the new catalogs arrived in the mail, the old ones were put in the outhouse for family reading, but not before little girls made cutout dolls of big-city women modeling dresses and corsets.

Alvah Roebuck sold out to Richard Sears in 1895 for $25,000, in what may have been the worst investment decision in American business history. He was in poor health and nervous about the gambling nature of his go-getting partner, who expanded advertising and inventory during the worst depression in the country up to that time.*

---

*Roebuck was hired back by the company for promotional purposes when he went bankrupt during the Great Depression. Asked, when applying for the job, if he was related to Sears's former partner, he said in his quiet way that he *was* Roebuck.

Roebuck's place was taken by a Chicago clothing merchant, Julius Rosenwald, and his brother-in-law Aaron Nussbaum. They gave the company the financial and managerial stability it would never have had under Sears's volatile direction; and in one of the fastest expansions in the history of American business, they pushed it ahead of Montgomery Ward and Company in sales after 1900. But until his retirement in 1908 at age forty-four, after a series of run-ins with Rosenwald, Richard Sears was the presiding spirit of the firm whose motto remained We Sell Everything.

The company's thousand-page catalog is a "compendium of everything to be had, except live animals and fresh fruit and vegetables," wrote a German visitor to the Sears plant at the turn of the century. "You can even order a one-family house. Give dimensions and the number of rooms, and the whole farm house is delivered to the last nail, needing only to be erected." Around 1900, Sears advertised that enough balloon-frame houses had been built "according to our plans and with our materials to shelter a city of 25,000 people."

These orders, and orders for every other manner of merchandise, were sent out with "the greatest efficiency I have ever seen," this German visitor noted. Beginning at 9:00 A.M. sharp, an average of thirty-five thousand orders a day was sent through an eighteen-mile-long system of copper tubing to the desks of thousands of clerks working nonstop at typewriters. By four that afternoon all orders were filled and sent to waiting baggage trains, their long locomotives lined up in the company's rail yard, stacks smoking, eight and nine abreast, as if poised for a race. At a signal, they steamed out to "all corners of America."

In this way, Sears and Ward drove out of business thousands of country stores. "Mail-order," an article reprinted in a Montgomery Ward catalog announced, "has solved the problem [of the tyranny] by the country merchants and released [the farmer] from serfdom. He can now buy his supplies as cheaply as can the country merchant, and by the mail can annihilate the distance between himself and the great centers of trade." But the country stores did not go down without a fierce fight, backed by powerful wholesale suppliers like Marshall Field & Company, whose stepped-up sales campaigns in the 1880s helped make rural merchants competitive for a time with the Chicago catalog houses.

After the Great Fire, Marshall Field and Levi Leiter physically separated the two parts of their dry-goods business, building a wholesale warehouse at the corner of Madison and Market (now Wacker) and rebuilding their retail palace on its original State Street corner, the latter business appealing primarily to Chicago women, the other to entire families in the territories. In 1880, Field bought out Leiter after they had disagreements over business strategy, and he reorganized the firm under his name. He then put his ace salesman, John Graves Shedd, whom he had hired a decade earlier as a stock boy, in charge of a drive to bolster rural sales in an arc of influence extending west from Chicago to the Rockies and south to the Gulf. "Are you a salesman?" Field had asked the twenty-two-year-old farmer's son when he first approached him about a job. "Yes, sir." "What do you sell?" "Anything," Shedd declared with a confident smile.

Field, whose signature was personalized service, had been reluctant to send sales representatives into his trade territory, preferring that his country customers come directly to his warehouse, where they could inspect the merchandise and place their orders in person, with the help of his solicitous staff. But Shedd, the future head of the company, convinced him that selling "on the road" was the only way to stay competitive with other wholesalers, who were sending battalions of drummers into Chicago's railroad empire; and in the 1880s the company's budget for "country traveling" increased more than tenfold.

His suit was "cut of a striped and crossed pattern of brown wool, very popular at the time. . . ." Dreiser, in portraying Charles Drouet, also described any number of railroad drummers like him. "The low crotch of the vest revealed a stiff shirt bosom of white and pink stripes, surmounted by a high white collar about which was fastened a tie of distinct pattern. From his coat sleeves protruded a pair of linen cuffs of the same material as the shirt and fastened with large gold-plate buttons set with the common yellow agates known as 'cat's-eyes.' His finger bore several rings . . . and from his vest dangled a neat gold watch chain from which was suspended the secret insignia of the Order of Elks. The whole suit was rather tight-fitting and was finished off with broad-soled tan shoes, highly-polished, and [a] grey . . . 'fedora.'"

These "whizbangs," as rurals called them, would arrive in a railroad town with their big sample trunks and set up miniature trade shows in the lobby of a local hotel, having informed the town's merchants in advance of their arrival. To reach smaller stores off the rail line, they traveled over dirt roads by one-horse buggy and by bobsled in some remote areas of the mountain states. "No place is too remote for him to penetrate, no hardship too great for him to endure, if he can only sell goods," a contemporary wrote of these mostly young, fast-talking hustlers who seemed never to forget a name.

To make their job easier, Field slashed his prices, liberalized credit terms, and expanded his product line, setting up branch purchasing offices in three European countries to bring to the American West the best that London, Paris, and Berlin could offer. And to house his flourishing business, he commissioned the country's leading architect, Henry Hobson Richardson, to design a new wholesale store on an entire city block he had purchased piecemeal over the years. With the completion of the seven-story Marshall Field Wholesale Store in 1887, one year after Richardson's death at the age of forty-seven, "modern commercial architecture was born."

Dark and enormous, with rough-cut stone walls, the building stood not far from the Chicago River like some grim medieval fortress of commerce. At once monolithic and magnificently sculpted, it was, Louis Sullivan thought, the first great building in Chicago. Its plain brown exterior mirrored the understated manner of Marshall Field himself, a coldly reserved, unpretentious merchant: "Silent Marsh," his fellow clubmen called him. In keeping with its owner's character, the building was also severely functional. There were no frills; everything had a purpose. Its interior light court and big, close-set rows of windows let sunlight into the offices and storage areas of what was described in a city guidebook as the "largest and best arranged building for mercantile purposes in the world." The interior, with its thirteen elevators and 500,000 square feet of floor space, was organized as a wondrously efficient merchandising machine to expedite the two-day buying trips of country merchants, whom Field continued to lure to Chicago almost in defiance of the efforts of John Shedd's drummers.

An Iowa store owner taking the night train would arrive in the big city first thing in the morning and head straight for the Marshall Field Wholesale Store. Entering the Adams Street lobby, he would be met by an official "greeter," and with a snap of his fingers, the greeter would summon one of the "on the bench boys" seated near the door and have him take the gentleman to the company representative he was scheduled to meet. There followed an all-day tour—punctuated by lunch at a local beef house—of the endless aisles of merchandise, as neatly and systematically arranged as Mr. Field's own private office. There was nothing else quite like it in the West. There were carpet sweepers, baby buggies, dining-room sets, tricycles, boxes of rubber diapers, baseballs, bats and gloves, harmonicas, thermometers, teething rings, and toothpicks. "Probably under no one roof," the guidebook writer John Flinn remarked, "is gathered so vast a quantity of material designed to meet the general wants of mankind." By four o'clock the customer was ready to finalize his order in the big "counting room" on the main floor, where hundreds of white-shirted clerks, seated in rows of desks, kept the books of the great establishment.

If the customer had an itch to go out on the town that night, his sales representative would serve as his escort. It was a familiar Chicago sight: a hayseed with a rumpled Sunday suit, straw hat, and high brown shoes entering a gorgeous gaslit nightspot with one of Field's smartly dressed salesmen, who was expected to wear a frock coat and a silk hat and to carry a polished walking stick. If the customer wanted gamier entertainment later in the evening, the Field man would point the way to the Levee and excuse himself with a warning about hustlers and thieves, for that kind of entertainment was not in keeping with the image of a company that refused to advertise on Sundays and lowered the curtains of the display windows of its retail store from Saturday night until Monday morning. But whatever the nocturnal pleasure of the Iowa merchant, he was on the first outbound for his hometown the next morning, his purchases to follow within the week.

Massive, functionally designed wholesale houses like that of Marshall Field & Company catered to specialists in buying, not to the general public. They were, as historian Neil Harris has suggested, the abbeys and chapter houses of the economic faith, "where members of the order gathered on professional business." The temples and cathedrals, works of spectacle and show open to all the faithful, were the department stores on State Street, a few blocks east of the main wholesale district. There, Marshall Field's sumptuous retail mart, rebuilt after a fire in 1877, stood preeminent in the year of Louis Sullivan's zero hour, a symbol and leading institution of a new kind of city made possible, like the wholesale empires of Montgomery Ward and Richard Sears, by radiating lines of steel.

9

The Streetcar City

1. Palaces of Desire

"THE nature of these vast retail combinations, should they ever permanently disappear, will form an interesting chapter in the commercial history of our nation," Theodore Dreiser wrote of Chicago's first department stores. "Such a flowering out of a modest trade principle the world had never witnessed up to that time."

They were big and busy places, thronged from morning until night with customers, as many as a quarter of a million a day, more people than lived in any other city in Illinois; and some of them had workforces larger than steel mills. Emphatically urban creations, they in turn expressed the spirit and mood of the modern metropolis: its size, scale, and congestion, its commercial energy and hypnotic allure. Marshall Field's, the largest retail store on earth at the end of the century, was itself like a small city, its entrance adorned with "the highest monoliths in the world," the store's publicists boasted, "except those in the temple of Karnak." Employing nine thousand workers in peak season, it had fifty-three high-speed elevators, a medical dispensary, a post office that handled more mail than the city of Joliet's, a delivery system covering an area of over three hundred square miles, and the largest private telephone switchboard in the world. More than shopping marts, these palaces of desire were alluring tourist attractions with eye-catching display windows, splashing fountains, electrically

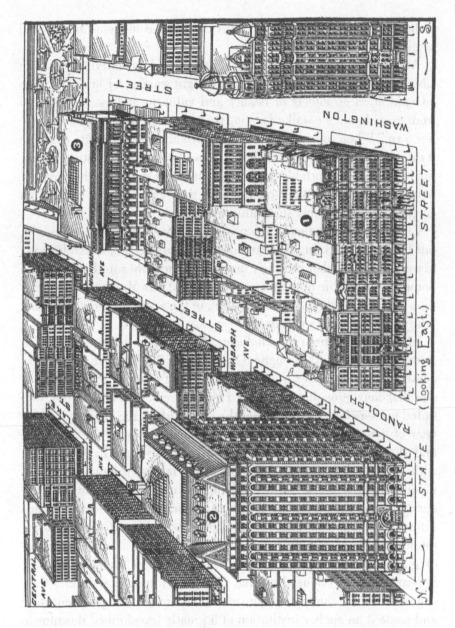

From State Street, looking east. Marshall Field's Department Store (no. 1) stretches from State Street all the way along Washington Street to Wabash Avenue. The old building, in the Parisian style, faces State Street. The new building, built for the occasion of the Columbian Exposition, is directly to its rear, at the corner of Washington and Wabash. Burnham and Root's twenty-one-story Masonic Temple (no. 2), the tallest building in the world in 1893, was just up the street from Marshall Field's. The classically designed Chicago Public Library (no. 3) fronts on Michigan Avenue. Bird's-eye Views and Guide to Chicago (Chicago: Rand, McNally & Co., 1898)

lit floor displays, brilliant light courts, and miles of aisles as crowded as city sidewalks.

At Marshall Field's a woman "found herself in fairyland," wrote Chicago's Thomas Goodspeed. "[She] might wander for hours through an exhibition of objects of beauty and value in endless variety and from every land. She walked among them as freely as though they were her own." When something caught her eye and she wished to examine it more closely, a punctilious clerk "showed her every attention," making her feel as comfortable in his department as she was in her favorite neighborhood shop. What chance had the "call of thrift," asked an English writer, "against such allurement?"

Chicago's dark-walled, Cyclopean warehouses were a man's world, but the city's sparkling department stores catered almost exclusively to women and symbolized their new place and power in the American home and in the life of the metropolis. And it was Marshall Field's genius as a merchant that made his store, in the words of a contemporary, "the modern woman's paradise."

In 1881 profits from his wholesale division greatly exceeded those from retail and would throughout the decade. But Field, the great successor to Potter Palmer, saw his company's future in urban retail. It was that conviction that had caused him to break with Levi Leiter, who failed to share his enthusiasm for the retail side of the business. In the year of their split, Field was the "Merchant Prince of the Midwest" and already, at age forty-seven, one of the richest men in the country, with a $25-million-a-year business—the largest purely mercantile business in the world—and investments in steel and iron, railroad cars and streetcar lines, banking and urban real estate—enterprises intimately connected with his dry-goods business. His greatest triumphs lay ahead of him, however. He was one of a number of merchandising pioneers nationwide, among them John Wanamaker, A. T. Stewart, Edward Filene, Rowland H. Macy, Jordan Marsh, and Chicago's Ernest J. Lehmann, who invented the American department store and made it an anchor institution of a greatly transformed downtown.

Field did this with a two-part strategy of tradition and innovation: by continuing the proven "Chicago ideas" of Potter Palmer—low, fixed prices and a liberal return policy—and by hiring and promoting audacious innovators in retail, who helped gain him a reputation as a merchandising revolutionary. At the base of it all, however, was the store's carefully cultivated image. Already in 1881, the name Marshall Field was synonymous with commercial integrity. Mr. Field built his future, declared the *Chicago Tribune,* on "the block of probity." And in the public eye, the company and the man were one and the same. Marshall Field's was Marshall Field, and what Chicagoans saw in that association was summed up by one of Field's fellow clubmen, Franklin MacVeagh. "All of Mr. Field's money was fairly made, and he was conspicuous among the immensely rich for the fairness of his competition and the cleanness of his methods. He made no money through oppression and monopoly." It was part of Field's permanent reputation that in the conduct of his business he never stooped to anything that conflicted with his unassailable personal rectitude.

This is the Chicago legend of Marshall Field. The real story is vastly more interesting.

•

What he was, what he had always been, was a supersalesman. "He had the merchant instinct." John V. Farwell recalled the fresh-faced farm boy from Conway, Massachusetts, who worked as a clerk in his Chicago dry-goods firm: "He lived for it and it alone. He never lost it." Beginning with his first paying job as a clerk in a Pittsfield, Massachusetts, general store, the position he left four years later, at age nineteen, to seek "money and advance" in Chicago, Marshall Field had an inborn ability to inspire trust, with women customers especially, and without "the old-timers' tricks, the little compliments, the slick niceties, the fawning and exaggerated graciousness." He had a low, soft voice and impeccable manners, and was painstakingly courteous. But he was also a young man of inflexible resolution. "What drove you to become successful?" Theodore Dreiser asked him late in his life in an interview for a story on "Successful Men." "I was determined not to remain poor" was the unhesitating reply.

In his prime he was a trim, elegantly dressed man with emotionless steel-gray eyes, close-cut chalk-white hair, and a full mustache. In his spotless linen and hand-tailored suits—and with the white gloves he wore even in summer—he looked more like a dashing Continental diplomat than a boom-city merchant. When he was dining at his Prairie Avenue table, "you were never forced to listen to long-winded tales of [his] early struggles and subsequent successes," recalled the writer Hobart C. Chatfield-Taylor, a young member of Field's select circle, "nor were you over-awed by any manifestation of his riches." He was, said Chatfield-Taylor, "entirely free from the ostentation that impairs so frequently the man of newly made riches." Field rarely spoke or appeared in public, and interviewers seldom got from him more than a sentence or two. Nor did he have to raise his voice to command the attention of his clerks and managers. "At work he had only to lift his eyes from his desk for chills to run down the spines of brave men."

His daily routine was as unvarying as that of his neighbor George Pullman. In 1881 he lived with his wife, son, and daughter in a three-story redbrick mansion designed by Richard Morris Hunt. Hunt had designed an arrogantly ostentatious New York home for William Henry Vanderbilt, but with the Field commission, he had been ordered to keep it simple. Field liked to walk to work, his English coachman driving a few hundred yards behind him in case of foul weather. Sometimes he would wait at the end of the block for Pullman, and the two titans would stroll up Michigan Avenue to the Pullman Building, where Field would stop for coffee and a discussion of their shared business interests. Then Field would head over to his retail store and spend the rest of the morning there, walking the aisles and demanding instant correction if anything seemed out of line.

Field's company motto—drilled into his salesclerks—was: The customer is always right. If he saw a customer arguing over a purchase, he would gently pull on the clerk's coattail and whisper to him, "Give the lady what she wants," the title of a popular book written about Marshall Field's. The store's character, wrote the journalist John Dennis, was a "reflection of the man whose brains gave it birth. Every nerve in the establishment leads back to the farmer's boy."

After spending the morning in his retail store, Field would have lunch at the Chicago Club in his reserved seat at the "millionaire's table," next to George Pullman. Sometimes Robert Todd Lincoln and Gen. Phil Sheridan would join them there, or later in the evening at Field's mansion, for a game of poker, Field's only diversion until he took up golf with avidity toward the end of his life. If the conversation turned to labor unions or radicals, Field could be counted on to take a hard line. He had complete faith in the openness of the Chicago economy. In this city of boundless opportunity "merit did not have to wait for dead men's shoes." If he, the son of a struggling hill farmer, could make it in Chicago on his own, anyone could. In line with his rigid homilies, he paid high salaries to rising men in his firm and low ones to clerks, expecting the most talented among the bottom ranks of his business to rocket to the top and gaining the loyalty of the rest with generous vacation benefits and workplace amenities that included a gymnasium, a music room, and a cut-rate employees' restaurant.

Field's workers, like Pullman's, were watched on and off the job. They were fired if they were known to drink or gamble or if they were simply seen in the company of a labor-union official. Field issued orders that customers known to belong to unions were to be escorted from his store by house detectives, and his own company records show that he even fired children—badly overworked cash boys—who dared to complain about working conditions. "Over all is a covering of soft, genial beauty," John Dennis wrote of both the store and the man, "and always underneath the steel of a rigid, undeviating system, . . . perfectly working, cold, absolutely certain."

After taking lunch at his club, Field would go directly to his wholesale store, spending the rest of the afternoon in his spartan office next to the counting room. At four o'clock sharp, he would roll down the top of his desk, the signal to his office staff that his, but not their, day was over. "I have never believed in overworking," he told Dreiser. "It always paid with a short life."

He played poker in the evenings mostly for the companionship, for his first wife, Nannie, was sickly; and they had, in any event, a stormy marriage. Nine years after her death in France, where she had been living for some time apart from him, Marshall Field, at age seventy, married Mrs. Delia Spencer Caton, widow of Arthur Caton, son of Judge John Dean Caton. She and her former husband had been neighbors and friends of the Fields', and it was whispered about in Chicago society that Marshall Field had been seeing her secretly for almost three decades; there were even rumors of a hidden tunnel connecting their mansions. Field didn't live long enough, however, to enjoy her company in marriage and didn't have a single close friend with him when he died of pneumonia in 1906; he had never, in fact, had a close friend. From his arrival in Chicago, "the store and the stock," as Farwell recalled, "was his life." After his children married, his empty mansion became a chilly monument to his complete attention to trade, the gilded successor to the cheerless household he had been raised in on Field Hill, deep in the Berkshires.

He had started out in the Chicago dry-goods business as a clerk making four hundred dollars a year and sleeping on a shelf in the store to save half his earnings; and when he had his own store, he would keep an eye out for young men in his own mold to groom as future partners. But he never got close to any of his wonder boys, and he kept his partners and managers in a state of perpetual apprehension and fear. At his annual company dinners, he would announce, in his cold and exact way, bonuses and promotions—and sometimes the name of at least one unpleasantly surprised guest who had just "resigned" as a partner in Marshall Field and Company.

Field never referred to his State Street emporium as a department store. The Fair, at the other end of Chicago's Ladies' Half Mile, was a

department store, he would testily insist; his store, like New York's
A. T. Stewart's, was a dry-goods establishment. The difference was that
German-born Ernest J. Lehmann's capacious variety store, the first department store in Chicago, went after the commerce of the common
crowd, its merchandising motto, Everything for Everybody, while
Field stocked a discriminating selection of goods designed to appeal
to the domestic needs of upper-class and middle-class women—veil-
ings, linen handkerchiefs, Parisian-made kid gloves, and designer
gowns for society occasions. Not until the late 1880s did the "Cathedral of All Stores" diversify its stock to compete with bargain bazaars
like the Fair and its scaled-back equivalent, the Boston Store. In the
words of a popular end-of-the-century ditty, sung to the tune of "Ta-ra-
ra boom-de-ay":

> All the girls who wear high heels
> They trade down at Marshall Field's
> All the girls who scrub the floor
> They trade at the Boston Store.

Marshall Field made his store the fashion center for women whose
consumer appetites had been whetted by travel in Europe, where
Paris's Bon Marché, the world's first department store, set a standard
of subdued elegance Field tried to emulate. Every Monday morning, a
double row of carriages lined up outside the store's Washington Street
entrance, each carrying a "lady of the mansion" in town for the first of
what might be three, four, or even five shopping excursions that week.
Inside the entrance to the store, where Field himself had stood in the
first years of his business, were his official greeters, who were expected to know the names of every important customer. When a lady
finished making her purchases, a bundle boy would carry them to her
waiting carriage. Larger items would be brought to the customer's door
in one of the store's brightly painted delivery wagons. If madame
didn't feel up to a trip to State Street, she could call in her order by
telephone and have it dispatched to her that day by a delivery man, a
system Field set in place to retain the carriage trade when the rich
started to move to the suburbs.

Making the store itself, not just the merchandise, irresistibly attractive was Field's master aim as a merchant. When it was brought to his
attention that women were leaving his store to go home for lunch, he
installed a small tearoom next to Women's Furs, the first of what became an entire floor of elegant restaurants. By the time of the Columbian Exposition, he had equipped his store with modern lounges and

rest rooms, writing rooms with complimentary stationery and pens, a customer's parlor and library, a nursery, meeting rooms for women's organizations, a stenographic service, telegraph and telephone offices, and a checkroom for coats. Marshall Field's became a woman's equivalent of her husband's downtown club, a place where she could spend her entire in-town day in comfort.

The store became world famous for its unhurried atmosphere. The Field customer was served, not negotiated with, and was encouraged to browse and dream without pressure to buy. Aside from Field himself, the person most responsible for maintaining this atmosphere was Harry Gordon Selfridge, a former company stock boy who was made head of retail in the 1880s and who moved to London after Field's death to found the English house of Selfridge & Co. A brilliant and beautifully dressed showman, Selfridge had fashionable sideburns, a round, youthful face, and vaulting ambition. By 1889 he was a junior partner in the firm, and in rising within the company, he changed it forever.

Selfridge was "a fountain of spectacular and imaginative ideas." It was he who convinced Field to go after customers who shopped at the fair by turning Marshall Field's small bargain basement into a separate, self-contained store, advertised as having the largest sales floor in the world. He also persuaded Field to spend more on newspaper advertising—almost a quarter of a million dollars a year by the mid-1890s. Selfridge saw urban newspapers as "streetcars of the mind," in Daniel J. Boorstin's apt phrase, putting the desires of city people on tracks and drawing them to new consumption centers.

When shoppers arrived for Selfridge's "special sales," they found the big show windows decorated by Selfridge himself to look exactly like his full-page ads in the *Tribune* and the *Daily News*. And at night Selfridge lit up the entire store—inside and out—with electric lamps and bulbs, giving it a festival-like atmosphere. Marshall Field's was the first of Chicago's big stores to make use of the magic of electricity, helping to inaugurate an energy transformation in the American city.

•

On a chilly April evening in 1878, a crowd gathered around W. W. Boyington's castellated Water Tower, the city's proudest monument, to watch a "long talked of experiment" by John P. Barrett, a city engineer. When the gas lamps in the square were shut off, the hushed crowd saw a flickering but brilliant light at the top of the tower, more light than was produced by over six hundred of the city's gas street lamps. That night, Chicago entered the age of electricity.

Barrett's two illuminating devices were arc lamps, named for the battery-powered electric current that leaped back and forth in an arc between two glowing carbon rods, creating a bright, severe light—and with it, a sharp-smelling gas. Within a decade, arc lamps had replaced thousands of blinking gas lamps on Chicago's downtown streets.

They proved to be merely a transitional technology, however. One year after Barrett's demonstration, Thomas Alva Edison invented the incandescent bulb. The arc lamp produced too much light and heat for small interior spaces, and it was a fire hazard. Edison's lamp gave off a soft, warm glow from a filament heated to an orange-colored incandescence by an electric current. And this little show took place safely under a sealed glass globe. It was an invention all the more astounding because it seemed to defy the order of nature. Before Edison, light and fire were synonymous, and all illumination was based on burning hydrocarbons in the open air. With Edison's enclosed lamp—cut off from the very oxygen that fed fire and producing none of the smoke that had always been the by-product of light—"fire and light would never again be identical."

Whereas Edison's lamps burned for hundreds of hours, the filaments of arc lamps lasted only eight or nine hours, and Edison's salesmen would flamboyantly demonstrate their safety by breaking them just after lighting them. But incandescent lamps required their own generating plants, making them expensive to install and burn. Into the 1890s only wealthy Chicagoans like Marshall Field, a director of the Chicago Edison Company, who shared a backyard generating plant with two of his Prairie Avenue neighbors, could afford to "burn the electrics" in their homes. Edison's globes were at first used primarily for decorative effect in fashionable department stores, hotels, theaters, and restaurants, while arc lamps continued to be used to light the downtown streets and sidewalks with a brilliant orange-yellow glow.

"They walked north on Wabash to Adams Street and then went west," wrote Dreiser of Carrie Meeber's first night at the opera with Charles Drouet. The yellow arc lights shined brightly overhead, "and high up were the lighted windows of the tall office buildings." The tops of these skyscrapers were ringed with necklaces of colored lights that seemed to "be suspended in air," said the *Tribune* of the winter night scene Carrie and Drouet walked through; and the show windows of the stores were bordered with double rows of electrics. Over the entrance to McVicker's Theater, where Carrie and Drouet were heading to see *The Mikado*, "a big shield of yellow, red, white, and blue attracted attention," while at Marshall Field's the "arc lights," reported the *Tri-*

bune, "were resplendent . . . giving delight to the crowds that walk[ed] the streets."

On the sidewalk, Carrie and Drouet pass "shop girls" heading home in "pairs and fours, chattering, laughing." Carrie had first encountered confident, smartly dressed department-store saleswomen when she applied for work at the Fair her first week in Chicago, and they had made her—a drably clothed Wisconsin girl—feel both envious and inferior. "Whenever she encountered the eye of one, it was only to recognize in it a keen analysis of her own position—her individual shortcomings of dress and that shadow of *manner* which she thought must hang about her and make clear to all who and what she was."

There is so much of the new metropolitan world in *Sister Carrie,* the greatest of all American urban novels. Dreiser presents the oncoming consumption culture and the "drag of desire" it stimulated in shoppers like Carrie, who wanted what they had never seen before at the very moment they set eyes on it in the new emporiums of enticement. It was a culture, as Philadelphia's John Wanamaker described it, that spoke of the "pleasures" of life. "It does not say, 'Pray, obey, sacrifice thyself, respect the King, fear thy master.' It whispers, 'Amuse thyself, take care of yourself.'" Dreiser was the first American chronicler of this culture of desire; and there is also in *Sister Carrie* a brilliant sensitivity to the changing nature of dress as an indicator of class and station.

Throughout history, clothing has always been an insigne of status. In Dreiser's Chicago, however, a salesgirl making six dollars a week could save her earnings and buy one or two ready-to-wear outfits that placed her on a level with her middle-class customers—at least until she began speaking—and that separated her from "common" women who worked in shoe factories and sewing plants and who came to socially intimidating State Street only for special purchases unavailable in neighborhood stores or from pushcart vendors. H. Gordon Selfridge claimed to cater to the "shawl" trade as well as the carriage trade, but the wives of Italian-American street sweepers were rarely seen on Chicago's fashion avenue. The department store may have democratized shopping, as Emile Zola observed in his novel of Paris's new shopping empóriums, *Au bonheur des dames* (1884), but for the urban poor it remained the equivalent of the Florence Hotel for George Pullman's factory hands.

In *Sister Carrie,* Dreiser describes better than anyone before him the fast-changing character of the big city downtown. A large part of it had already become a woman's world, for an estimated 99 percent of purchases at State Street department stores were made by women. Women came downtown to shop or to work, the well-off to shop and the less well off to work, usually either in department stores or as office help in the new commercial skyscrapers. Shopgirls who lived away from home were compensated barely enough to buy their clothing and pay their keep in cheap rooming houses. Annie M. MacLean, a Chicago social investigator who joined the sales forces of several department stores to collect data, reported some women making only three dollars a week, "starvation wages" that caused an alarming number of them to work in the evenings as escorts or common prostitutes. But most of Chicago's women shop clerks lived at home, and their jobs released them from the constricting routine of domesticity and put those who worked at places like Marshall Field's in glamorous surroundings and around women such as they dreamed of becoming someday.

The presence of these female salesclerks made shopping all the more pleasurable for women, especially in departments that specialized in intimate ladies' items; and the lighted shop windows and streets made the downtown shopping area safer and more inviting, the crowning accomplishment of changes set in motion by Potter Palmer, who had turned State Street into Chicago's Fifth Avenue. In the 1880s Chicago women began to be seen for the first time on downtown streets without male escorts, sometimes into the early evening. Women no longer remained caged at home, wrote *The Nation*'s editor E. L. Godkin. Wearing long, clinging dresses and black button shoes and carrying muffs in the cold weather, they could be seen on "the streets, in horse-carts, omnibuses, excursion boats, railroad trains, and hotel corridors," making city life "so much more down-towny," in Henry James's euphonious phrase.

Shopping was required work for a middle-class woman, but it also became a form of urban entertainment. Some women shopped incessantly, one spasm of buying succeeding another; and when not buying, they "window-shopped," a new urban pastime. Whether they were buying or just looking, their new behavior became the subject of considerable commentary. An 1881 editorial in the *New York Times* called attention to "the awful prevalence of the vice of shopping among women," a "purse-destroying [addiction] . . . every bit as bad as male drinking or smoking." Yet the accepted place of Victorian women in a male-dominated society—in the home all day taking care of children, sewing, cleaning, cooking, and entertaining, work that was difficult even with a domestic helper—made shopping a liberating escape from both convention and domestic drudgery. With so many callings closed to her, the middle-class woman "acknowledged the call of the shops."

•

A suburban woman's day in the city might begin at Marshall Field's, with lunch with friends in the tearoom and an ice-cream soda at Kranz's Viennese confectionery just across the street, followed, perhaps, by some window-shopping and a last-minute stop at the South Water Street Market to pick up a delicacy—a leg of mountain sheep or an antelope steak—for the next day's dinner. Then it would be back to Marshall Field's to catch a cable car or one of the store's own omnibuses, which ferried shoppers to the main suburban railroad stations. It was a longer, more pleasant ride for those taking suburban steam trains to big houses with generous lawns on the edge of the city, where the family gardener might be waiting in a pony cart at the gabled village station. For those taking the crowded, rattling cable cars, "it was a long way to home," wrote a Chicago reporter, "no matter where they lived."

"All of the principal street car lines, which formerly had been drawn by horses, were now pulled by cables," Dreiser wrote of this frenzied four o'clock scene, "and threaded the downtown thoroughfares in clanking rows. The very sight of them envisioned always the far-flung suburbs of the city."

2. The Loop

On a January morning in 1882, a train of ten small cars packed with city dignitaries and decked out with flags and streamers made its way down State Street from Marshall Field's store to Twenty-first Street, four miles south, the end of the first stretch of tracks of Chicago's first cable-car system. A crowd estimated at three hundred thousand in a city of five hundred thousand lined the tracks of the Chicago City Railway Company to watch local history being made. Five years later, this and a parallel line on Cottage Grove Avenue reached all the way along the line of the lake to the once-secluded village of Hyde Park. And by the time of the Columbian Exposition, Chicago, the farthest-spreading city in America, had the largest cable-car system in the world tying it together, with eighty-six miles of track, eleven power plants, and over fifteen hundred cars.

Marshall Field was a director and leading stockholder of the Chicago City Railway Company. The great merchant put his money into it because it made money for him, bringing shoppers from outlying neighborhoods directly to the doors of his retail store. Mass transit concentrated the city tremendously, creating the downtown congestion that turned dry-goods outlets like Marshall Field and Company into fabulous shopping emporiums. By Christmas of 1882, the South Side cable lines converged near Field's State Street store to create a loop, or turnabout, that the cars swung around "on the fly" before heading back to the fringes of the city to pick up more holiday shoppers. The term "Loop" became synonymous with downtown Chicago fifteen years before the completion of the elevated railway system around the central business district that still remains a defining Chicago land- mark. The overhead ring of iron formed by the Union Loop would make the already concentrated downtown area one of the most densely packed commercial cores on earth. In 1910, the one-half-square-mile Loop contained nearly 40 percent of the total assessed land value of the 190-square-mile city. "The man who has no business in this sec- tion of the city had better look about and arrange matters so that he has," declared one visitor, "or he has no business in Chicago."

Like Caesar's Gaul, Chicago was divided into three parts—the North Side, the West Side, and the South Side—whose inhabitants rarely mingled. The Loop was Chicago's "neutral land, however, where [Chicagoans] transact business by day and enjoy themselves by night," wrote Hobart C. Chatfield-Taylor. They came into the Loop to work—upward of a quarter of a million people a day—and left at dusk for their outlying houses and flats, "but no sooner is the soot washed from their faces than a goodly proportion of them hasten back to the Loop again, for here are the clubs, theatres, restaurants, and hotels." A workplace by day, a pleasure spot by night, the Loop "is literally, as well as metaphorically, the heart of the city," Chatfield-Taylor contin- ued, for here "is found everything material or aesthetic which the in- habitants of our three 'sides' enjoy in common."

By the 1880s, the cable cars that created the first Loop had replaced horse-drawn streetcars as Chicago's principal intracity transit technol- ogy, although into the early 1900s some horsecar lines continued to operate as short-haul feeders to the main transit tracks. The Chicago City Railway Company and a rival company had begun running horse- car lines just before the Civil War, more than twenty years after east- ern cities had begun licensing them. They were a great improvement over the slow, dangerously unstable omnibuses, or urban stagecoaches, that were the city's first form of mass transit. The rails reduced surface friction and allowed horses to pull larger vehicles while providing a smoother ride. But no sooner were they introduced in Chicago and other American cities than inventors began searching for better ways to move masses of urban people who had begun to acquire the "riding habit."

The problem with the horse was not unlike that of the modern automobile: It was a heavy noise and air polluter. In Rochester, New York, health officials estimated that the fifteen thousand horses on the city's streets in 1900 produced enough organic waste a year to create a one-acre-wide, 175-foot-high mountain of manure capable of breeding 16 billion flies. And in that year Chicago had over five times as many horses at work on its streets, pulling conveyances of all kinds, as Rochester. On rainy days, gutters became rank-smelling brown streams; in dry weather, pulverized manure blew into the faces of downtown shoppers; and throughout the year, iron-shod horses created an around-the-clock cacophony. Horses were also overworked and miserably treated, and many died in the streets. Over ten thousand of them a year were removed from Chicago's gutters by municipal carts.

Steam power looked to be the logical alternative to horse power, but steam had a disabling disadvantage. Locomotives had to build up a head of steam to move their driving pistons, making them inappropriate for frequent stops and starts. They also produced tremendous soot and noise, and the sparks they threw off were a fire hazard. But in San Francisco, where crowded horsecars had difficulty climbing the city's steep hills, a local wire-rope manufacturer invented a steam transit system that could stop and start trains of cars at every corner while moving them along at twice the speed of horsecars—and without the pollution. Andrew Smith Hallidie ran his first experimental cable car in 1873. Seven years later, a group of Chicago investors headed by Marshall Field formed a consortium to introduce San Francisco cable cars in the flattest big city in the country. Moving on dead-level, gridded streets, where difficult turns were infrequent, cable cars were ideally suited to Chicago's topography and urban form.

The system was expensive to install but simple to operate. A tourist visiting the engine house of the Chicago City Railway Company described the working machinery of the cable network. "The street cars are propelled or rather drawn along by means of endless [steel] cable, which runs along under the road between the rails. In the centre of the road between the rails is a slot or opening . . . which runs the whole length of the two tracks. Through this slot an iron lever passes from the car to the cable. . . . The street cars . . . run coupled together in 3's or 4's. The front car is called the 'grip' and is open all round. The grip-man stands in the centre and works the brake and grip lever." When he pulled the huge lever, or "steel hand," the clamps of the grip closed on the cable and the cable pulled the cars along with it. "By loosening the lever the cable is freed and then stopped by means of the brake." Inside the powerhouse were "the two largest boilers in the world."

They fed stationary steam engines that drove the cable, moving surface cars at speeds of over ten miles an hour "without any visible means of propulsion"—a "very odd" sight to a stranger from out of town but a gold mine to Marshall Field, as an estimated one hundred thousand passengers a day in the 1890s passed the big display windows of his store. In New York, which installed a much smaller cable system in the late 1880s, "shopping hours are confined to the late forenoon and afternoon and early evening," observed a Scottish visitor to Chicago in 1890. "Here, from early morning until dark, there seems no halt in the procession."

Chicago soon found that there were disadvantages to being ahead of its eastern rival. Its complete commitment to cable cars was one reason it was slower than New York and other large American cities in adopting the far less expensive and more efficient system perfected for commercial use in Richmond in 1888 by Frank Julian Sprague, a former assistant to Thomas Edison. What Edison's incandescent bulb was to urban illumination, Sprague's electric trolley was to urban transportation; and it was adopted with equal alacrity. By 1890, the electric railway track of the United States was nearly three times that of cable, and after 1892, nearly every stretch of streetcar line laid in Chicago and other American cities was electrified, for the advantages of electric over cable cars were by then indisputable. Called trolleys for the "trollers," or four-wheeled cages, on their roofs that were pulled, or trolled, along overhead electric wires, they were capable of speeds of up to twenty miles an hour. Their small but powerful motors also allowed them to carry more passengers than cable cars. Electric systems were cheaper to install than cable lines, and they, too, were pollution-free, with the extra advantage that their cars were lighted and heated by the humming copper cables. Perhaps no other invention in history, not even the automobile, was put into general use more quickly than the electric trolley.

In 1893, the "Cable Czar" of Chicago was an ex-convict from Philadelphia, Charles Tyson Yerkes. He arrived in the city in 1881 with his reputation in question and left it under pressure less than two decades later, the most vilified public figure in Chicago's history. But Yerkes was a maker as well as a manipulator. In building a fortune through crooked stock dealings and political thievery, he fashioned the world's greatest urban transportation system.

Son of a Quaker bank president, Yerkes came to Chicago after serving part of a prison sentence (he was pardoned by the governor) for misappropriation of Philadelphia bonds and after being ostracized by the city's social elite for leaving his wife, who had borne him six children, for a younger woman. A financial genius who had his own banking house and brokerage office before he was twenty-two, Yerkes made a fast fortune in the banking business and on the Chicago Board of Trade, but the truly big opportunities, he became convinced, were in mass transportation. Backed by two powerful Philadelphia traction speculators, he moved to gain control of the major street railway companies of the North and West Sides, the Chicago City Railway Company remaining firmly in the hands of South Side financial giants. "Street cars, he knew, were his natural vocation," Dreiser writes of Frank Cowperwood in *The Titan*, part of a "Trilogy of Desire" based on Yerkes's life. "Even more than stockbrokerage, even more than banking, . . . he loved the thought of street cars and the vast manipulative life it suggested." It was a nearly fail-safe business, Yerkes thought, its growth guaranteed by the unstoppable spread of this bursting western city.

The hub of the world's largest and most efficient overland transportation system, Chicago had a miserably inadequate streetcar system when Yerkes arrived there. It took more time to reach the city center from the city limits by horse power than it did to reach Milwaukee by steam power. Yerkes brought about a massive expansion and modernization of this archaic system. He began by replacing horsecars with cable cars in the North and West Divisions, bringing them into the downtown area through two formerly water-soaked, rat-infested tunnels under the Chicago River that he leased from the city, renovated, and lined with electric lights and white-glazed tiles. When he reopened these tunnels, he eliminated in one stroke what had been the chief obstacle to the expansion of mass transit in these parts of the city—the frequent delays at the swing bridges caused by river traffic.

Even before his integrated cable system was completed in 1893, Yerkes had begun introducing electric trolleys, a change many Chicagoans resisted. There were exaggerated fears, played upon by Yerkes's enemies in the press, of the dangers of hanging high-voltage lines over crowded streets—"Death in the Air," the *Tribune* called the sparking trolley wires—and there was concern that the thick network of poles and wires would interfere with the work of firefighters. Overhead wires were also unsightly, one reason European cities were slow to adopt trolleys in their historical cores. The major opposition, however, came from middle-income property owners who wanted trolley lines near, but not on, their residential streets, an obstacle Yerkes partially overcame by bribing taxpayers to sign agreements allowing him to proceed with construction. Still, public opposition kept "the deadly trolley" outside the perimeter of the downtown area until the end of the century. Commuters taking the trolleys into town were deposited at horsecar stops on the edge of the Loop, where they paid an additional fare to get to work.

To meet demands for faster transportation in the clotted downtown, Yerkes built elevated rail lines with cars pulled by mini–steam engines, a system such as New York had had since the 1870s. And he electrified many of these lines just before he constructed his Union Loop, at a time when over one-half of Paris's streetcars were still being drawn by horses. When Yerkes's Union Loop was completed in 1897, many people were reluctant to ride it, and not just because of fear of accidents. The New York Academy of Medicine warned that "el" (elevated) trains "prevented the normal development of children, threw convalescing patients into relapses, and caused insomnia, exhaustion, hysteria, paralysis, meningitis, deafness, and death." Chicago's new elevated Loop was also a brain-numbing noisemaker. It was built down the middle of the streets rather than in alleys or through right-of-ways cleared for it because Yerkes thought it would be too time consuming to buy up property and demolish buildings to clear a path for it. Its tremendous iron framing darkened streets below it, and it gave off a roar like thunder when trains came boring into the heart of the city.

The builder of this vast system was a corpulent, white-mustached dandy with a fortune of $29 million, a half-dozen mistresses, and unaccountable political influence. In addition to his Chicago mansion, he owned a Renaissance-style palace on New York's Fifth Avenue, complete with a glass-and-iron conservatory, an eight-thousand-dollar bedstead that had belonged to the king of Belgium, and two sumptuous art galleries, one for his expanding collection of modern art, the other for his rare Persian rugs, said to exceed in value and splendor the holdings of the shah of Persia. Yerkes donated a fantastic lighted fountain to Lincoln Park—a shrewd bit of philanthropy that increased ridership on his cable cars to the park—and a sixty-two-foot-long refracting telescope—still the largest in the world—to the University of Chicago, an instrument that revolutionized the study of astrophysics in the United States. Before it was shipped to the new observatory Yerkes paid for in Lake Geneva, Wisconsin, it stood on display on its twenty-ton supporting stand at the World's Columbian Exposition. But despite these benefactions, Yerkes was denounced in the local press as a predator and a plunderer, "a fellow who uses Chicago for a milch cow."

Dreiser romanticized him as a Nietzschean superman who scorned conventional morality in his drive for domination. But it was not Yerkes's power that turned power-worshiping Chicagoans against him; it was his defiantly dishonest way of using it. That and the important fact that he was an "outsider," a transient who was in Chicago merely to grind nickels out of its people, as one newspaper put it. When he had consolidated his transit empire, he intended to return to the greater luxury and leisure of his New York mansion, he brazenly announced to the press. In *The Cliff-Dwellers* Henry B. Fuller describes a character modeled after Yerkes: "He had no friends—none even of the poor sort known as 'business' friends. . . . He had no sense of any right relation to the community in which he lived. He had next to no family life. . . . But none of these considerations disturbed him very much. . . . He could rub along without the sympathy and respect of the community—while he and it held the relative positions of knife and oyster."

So while there were service problems on all Chicago transit lines, the Yerkes system was singled out for special censure by the city's two most powerful publishers, Joseph Medill of the *Tribune* and Victor Lawson of the *Daily News*. They filled their papers with customer complaints about poorly heated and ventilated Yerkes cars that were packed to "the guards" at rush hour, seventy to eighty passengers stuffed into a cable car designed to seat thirty. When concerned stockholders pressed Yerkes to put on extra cars during the rush period, he threw back the challenge to them: "It is the people who hang to the straps who pay you your big dividends."

Yerkes was also attacked for the way he went about building his streetcar empire. "The secret of success in my business," he once said, "is to buy old junk, fix it up a little, and unload it upon other fellows." Yerkes was a master manipulator of stocks and bonds and entire companies. "His bookkeeping methods and business tactics were so complicated," claims one historian, "that a clear account of how he captured control of Chicago's street railways can scarcely be made." He watered down the securities of the companies he controlled, overcapitalizing his total holdings by a conservative estimate of $62 million, but he kept his stockholders contented by paying dividends of between 12 and 42 percent. To build his cable lines, he hired a construction company he covertly controlled with Peter A. B. Widener and William L. Elkins, his powerful Philadelphia backers. Together with these two traction kings, Yerkes built the first North Chicago cable line at a cost to the construction company of $3 million but charged the cable company's stockholders over $10 million, the three partners pocketing a neat $7 million in profits.

"Mr. Yerkes is not a safe man," Marshall Field announced one afternoon to the other titans at his table at the Chicago Club. That terse remark alone would have sunk many a Chicago millionaire, but Yerkes was heavily backed by eastern capital, making him impervious to the power of the Chicago business aristocracy and, he thought mistakenly, to hostile public opinion. "Whatever I do," he declared, "I do . . . to satisfy myself." He was also rumored to be capable of the most extreme measures. When told that the *Chicago Dispatch* was preparing to publish an exposé of his personal life, he sent word to the editor that he would gun him down if the story was published. It never was.

But there were local powers with whom Yerkes was forced to work on a give-and-take basis. He needed franchises from the city council to operate transit lines on public streets, and to get them, he had to bribe more aldermen than he cared to. By the early 1890s, he controlled a sizable block of councilmen, chief among them Johnny Powers, the so-called Prince of Boodlers, and with their help he extracted from the city council the monopoly rights he wanted for far less, the press screamed, than he should have rightfully compensated the city. But his reach for more eventually brought him down.

Yerkes was a transportation visionary. Chicago sorely needed the consolidated transit system he dreamed of creating, but to have him build it would have meant surrendering control over an indispensable public service to a "Goliath of Graft." In 1897, Yerkes moved toward complete control of the city's transit network, attempting to get the city council to extend his traction franchises for fifty years. This needed state approval, and to get it, Yerkes used the full force of his influence, bribing state legislators and buying a newspaper, the *Chicago Inter Ocean,* to issue lacerating countercharges against his opponents. One of his henchmen in Springfield, an ancient, badly nearsighted state senator, offered twenty-five hundred dollars to a Chicago reporter who happened to be sitting in the seat of a member of the body whom Yerkes had targeted to be bought. The story of that grafter's pathetic mistake was circulated, but the Allen Bill passed the legislature and was signed by the governor. Yerkes's stock soared on the exchange, but "revolutions," a Chicago paper warned, "are caused by such rapacity."

Indignation meetings were convened all over the city, and when the city council met to do Yerkes's bidding, a mob brandishing guns and clubs surrounded city hall and pushed its way into chambers, tossing nooses over the rail of the visitors' gallery. Hired rowdies wearing miniature nooses on their lapels shouted for the aldermen to come out of chambers. When they did, a photographer set off his flash powder, and several of them dove underneath their desks, thinking they were being shot at. The "eternal monopoly bill" failed to carry, and the legislature repealed the Allen Bill, with only one dissenting vote, Sen. Charles Allen's. Yerkes was finished in Chicago.

He sold his local holdings, part of them to Widener and Elkins and another part to Marshall Field, whose loathing of the traction king did not prevent him from dealing with him in his decline. Then Yerkes emptied his Michigan Avenue mansion and moved to New York, and later London, where he took charge of the construction of that city's Underground. In the year of his death, 1905, he was rumored to have lost much of his fortune and to be preparing to divorce his second wife for the daughter of a famous madam from Louisville, Kentucky, a young woman he had maintained for years "in Oriental splendor."

Chicago owed him a great debt for his transportation reforms, Yerkes told reporters when he left the city. But Finley Peter Dunne's Mr. Dooley said that commemorating the day Charles Yerkes arrived in Chicago would be like "celebrating the coming of cholera."

Speaking on the occasion of his death, a friend of Yerkes's gave a different view of his importance to the city. "Mr. Yerkes was not ambitious to be a millionaire," he told a *Tribune* reporter, "but he was ambitious to be known as the foremost traction magnate in the country, and I think it will be conceded that he was. When he came here there were about 100 miles of horse car lines in Chicago," and it cost eight dollars for a rig to go to the outskirts of town, a place of forlorn farms and prairie market gardens. Yerkes "transformed those isolated vegetable gardens to valuable real estate by the lines he built" and the cars he ran. In joining town and country, this insolent powerhouse helped bring into existence something entirely new—and now long gone—the Streetcar City, perhaps the most livable of all historical urban forms.

3. City and Suburb

"Its streets and houses were already scattered over an area of seventy-five square miles," Dreiser writes of the city he entered by rail in 1890, returning from a year at Indiana University. "Streetcar lines had been extended far out into the open country in anticipation of rapid growth. The city had laid miles and miles of streets and sewers through regions where perhaps one solitary house stood out alone—a pioneer of the populous ways to be." In the summer of 1889, Chicago had annexed the huge suburb on its southern border that Dreiser's train sped through, a recklessly growing region that embraced Packingtown, Pullman, and the fashionable village of Hyde Park. On that single June day, the city added 220,000 to its population and 125 to its existing 43 square miles of territory, making it the largest municipal land area in the country and a colonizing power of the first order.

The transit technology that helped create the most concentrated downtown in the world also made possible the sprawling city that most Chicagoans lived in then, as they still do today. And in Chicago and other Anglo-American cities, improved transit inaugurated the most sweeping reconstruction of the urban settlement pattern since the advent of cities over forty-five hundred years ago. Until only recently in human history, to live in the center of town was a mark of status and privilege, while to live on the outskirts was to be confined to a "place of inferior, debased, and especially licentious habits of life," in the old *Oxford English Dictionary* definition of a "suburbe."

Urban elites have been escaping from the city since the city first appeared in ancient Egypt and the Fertile Crescent, erecting rustic villas on its verdant periphery, but they were traditionally tied to the town by duty, occupation, and preference, retreating to their pastoral enclosures for only part of the year or part of the week. For thousands of years, the poor and the pariahs had been pushed to the outskirts of town, while the rich lived at the center in great urban estates. For almost all of urban time and in almost all places on earth, wealth and power have put on their most spectacular show near the center of the city, site of citadels, temples, palaces, cathedrals, and skyscrapers. The first American cities were never this segregated by class, but in these cities, too, the rich resided near the center, and "the word suburb suggested," as historian Kenneth T. Jackson notes, "inferior manners, narrowness of view, and physical squalor."

Beginning in the mid-nineteenth century, however, mass transit, coupled with changing attitudes about both the city and the country, began to turn Chicago, New York, and other large American cities "inside out," shifting the center of population, prestige, and power from the center to the borderlands. Dispersal, not concentration, has been the dominant note of modern American urbanization despite the jutting towers of Manhattan and the Loop.

This decongestion has been a lengthy process, however, and few people who lived through its first stages—before the automobile—saw where it was taking the city. When Dreiser returned from Indiana in 1890, Chicago was actually becoming both more concentrated *and* more dispersed, with concentration promoting dispersal. And there was little concern that the exploding suburban movement would have an injurious impact on the city. Suburbs would relieve the city of its suffocating congestion and allow people to live country-style lives close to the throbbing activity of the urban center, reformers like Frederick Law Olmsted argued. City and suburb would complement each other; and for a time they did. Chicago's first suburbanites returned to the downtown sections to work, shop, and be entertained far more frequently and in far greater numbers than suburban commuters do today.

It was the Great Fire that set in motion the changes that completely altered Chicago's social geography. The rebuilt city of the mid-1870s was a greatly transformed place. In the summer before the fire, Chicago was still a walking city. Over twenty-five thousand of its citizens lived in or near the business core, people of all economic classes, ethnic backgrounds, and occupations. Spectacularly rich grain barons resided within spitting distance of miserably paid Irish mill hands in neighborhoods that contained a mixture of commercial, industrial, and cultural buildings—warehouses, foundries, churches, groceries, orphanages, schools, and corner saloons.

After the fire, retail and financial concerns returned downtown but clustered in highly specialized districts, a process begun on State Street by Potter Palmer before the fire. The entire central business district then spread southward, driving the rich farther down Michigan Avenue or to neighboring Prairie Avenue, covered by a canopy of handsome elms. The fire and the postfire downtown expansion also drove out the desperately poor of Conley's Patch and the Wells Street vice district. The resilient traders in sin were not much affected by this, relocating farther south in a much-enlarged vice district, the infamous Levee; but the Irish were prevented from returning and rebuilding their cheap cottages and shanties by new fire codes outlawing the construction of frame structures downtown.

A decade after the Great Fire, almost no one lived in the heart of Chicago, a shopping, trading, and entertainment zone that depended on transients to bring it to life from morning until well into the night. Expanding factories also left downtown for larger and cheaper tracts on the West Side or in new outlying industrial districts like the Calumet region. In 1893 the center of Chicago was surrounded by a solid, seven-mile-long wall of factories and workers' cottages. Beyond this wall, a green semicircle of suburbs stretched from luxurious Lake Forest on the North Shore all the way to Hyde Park on the South Side. Chicago, by this time, was an intensely centralized, economically segregated city with a belt of despair rimming the Loop. There, newly arrived immigrants lived in horrific poverty, surrounded by ring after ring of rising affluence, a settlement pattern shaped by the city's transit system. Those who couldn't afford mass transit lived where they could walk to work; more prosperous workers lived a short streetcar ride from foundries and factories; the middle class lived farther out along the trolley and cable lines; and the rich, with the exception of those like Pullman, Field, and Armour, who remained committed to downtown living, lived farthest from the center, easily able to afford the cost of a daily round-trip rail ticket to the Loop. In this way, the city's new transit grid described its growing class divisions.

Ideas were as important as transit technology in shaping the new urban order. Fueling the suburban movement was a new Anglo-American conception of the good life. In his postfire book *Chicago and Its Suburbs*, Everett Chamberlin put this idea in the form of an unwritten municipal guarantee: the right of every Chicago family that had pulled itself out of poverty to a cottage and a garden plot in a sylvan suburb, away from the squalor and stink of the city.

Mass transit made possible the "inside out" city, but it did not make it inevitable. Paris had an efficient system of omnibuses and a number of steam railroads in the middle of the nineteenth century, but Parisians of means chose to remain in the thick of the city, in courtyard-style apartment buildings bordering the tree-shaded boulevards built by Baron Georges-Eugène Haussmann, Louis Napoleon's master planner. The authoritarian builder's reconstruction "saved" the center of Paris for the bourgeoisie, who greatly preferred to live there if it could be made livable. And making it so—Haussmann read their mood exactly—meant demolishing the neighborhoods of paupers and the working poor and driving these unfortunates to new industrial suburbs on the urban periphery.

Similar precincts of center-city privilege were created by urban planners in Vienna and other Continental capitals, but not in London, Manchester, New York, or Chicago, cities in countries with a strong anti-urban bias. Following radiating rail lines, Americans of sufficient means, like their counterparts in Britain, began escaping the inner city in what would become the greatest internal migration in urban history, rather than trying to recapture it for themselves through direct government intervention. In Chicago, as elsewhere, the rich led the way, heading first for the North Shore in the 1850s, where a string of picture-pretty villages was built on high ground looking out over the blue-green lake, in an area connected to Chicago by steam railroad. The great stage for Chicago's postfire suburban drama, however, was the prairie to the west and south of the city.

Chicago's glacially flattened topography—easy to subdivide and build on—was ideal for suburbanization. There was not a city in all the world "more given to suburbs," Everett Chamberlin wrote. But in noting this, he had in mind more than Chicago's terrain. Chicago, unlike New York or Paris, prided itself on being a "city of homes." "The fact is thoroughly established," Chamberlin declared, "that ninety-nine Chicago families in every hundred will go an hour's ride into the country, or toward the country, rather than live under or over another family, as the average New Yorker or Parisian does." Affluent New Yorkers who preferred to remain in the city began renting French-style apartments in the 1870s; the poor of that city had been packed into high-rise tenements since the 1830s. But middle-class and upper-class Chicagoans preferred the privacy and propriety of a one-family house, while the working poor found in this land-rich city plenty of space to build their simple homesteads, even in squalid Packingtown.

The city council's efforts after the Great Fire to outlaw frame buildings everywhere in the city were defeated by an aroused coalition of immigrant laborers who stormed city hall and threatened riots and bloodshed if the law was passed. The proposed ordinance mandating brick and stone construction, they declared in a petition, would prevent "laboring people" from rebuilding the only kind of houses they could afford, forcing them "into those terrible tenement houses which are the curse of eastern cities." The bill that eventually became law did enlarge the city's fire zone but left enough land outside it, and inspection lax enough inside it, for the tinderbox shacks of the working class.

When Boston's William Dean Howells spoke against apartment living, he did so for almost all of Chicago as well. An elevator flat encouraged social pretension and provided "no room," he wrote, "where the family can all come together and feel the sweetness of being a family." This was also how "women with lovers lived in the wicked old societies, in apartments with all the rooms on one floor, and all the indecent propinquities that [French] novels described," wrote Edith Wharton, capturing the sentiments of Victorian traditionalists. The apartment, in this view, was an architectural incentive to adultery—a place like the three furnished rooms facing Union Park where Drouet installed his lover, Carrie Meeber.

But Chicagoans had their own special objection to apartment living: Families without front porches could not engage in the cherished town custom of sitting outdoors on pleasant summer nights. A city of cold transactions by day, Chicago became an enlarged and friendly village in the evening. On balmy June nights, when it was still too early for the summer exodus to the Wisconsin lakes, families of Chicago traders would sit "upon the front 'stoop,'" wrote Frank Norris. "Chairs were brought forth, carpets and rugs unrolled upon the steps. From within, through the opened windows of drawing-room and parlour, came the brisk gaiety of pianos. The sidewalks were filled with children clamouring at 'tag,' 'I-spy,' or 'run-sheep-run.' Girls in shirt-waists and young men in flannel suits promenaded to and fro. Visits were exchanged from 'stoop' to 'stoop,' lemonade was served, and claret punch. In their armchairs on the top step, elderly men, householders, capitalists, well-to-do, their large stomachs covered with white waistcoats, their straw hats upon their knees, smoked very fragrant cigars in silent enjoyment, digesting their dinners, taking the air after the grime and hurry of the business districts." Just a few blocks away, neighbors of lesser means could be seen relaxing in similar fashion—without the claret and the pianos, however.

"Once out of the thicket of the business . . . district the dwellings of the people reach mile upon mile along pleasant boulevards and avenues, or facing noble parks and parkways, or in a succession of villages green and gay with foliage," New York's Julian Ralph said of Chicago in 1893. "They are not cliff dwellings like our flats and tenements; there are no brownstone canyons like our up-town streets; there are only occasional hesitating hints there of those Philadelphia and Baltimorean mills that grind out dwellings all alike, as . . . man makes pins." Outside the downtown area, Chicago was a city of detached cottages and "villas," with a surprisingly suburban look.

•

The city's suburban movement was never exclusively a middle-class phenomenon. As early as the mid-1870s, well-paid workers were, as Chamberlin indicated, "flocking into the suburbs to live." Most of these instant suburbs, with "their tens of thousands of labor-bought homes," were located between the belt of industry surrounding the downtown district and more exclusive communities farther out on the prairie. Some subdivisions were sponsored by ethnic building societies that loaned money at low interest to members, but most were laid out by private builders appealing expressly to the working classes. They would buy land on speculation along rail lines on Chicago's borders, put in utilities, plant a few trees, and throw up a crude wooden station to induce the railroad to make scheduled stops there. Before it did, Sunday excursion trains would take laborers and their families to far-out prairie property with nothing for miles around except a big circus tent, a polka band, and a wagon stacked with beer barrels. The taps would be opened, the band would start playing lively marches, and the group would head out toward the lots, where they would be given a hard-to-resist sales pitch. When a number of families purchased lots, then or later, private contractors—often the very owners of the original land—would sell them the single-family houses of their dreams. In this way, the inner suburbs of Chicago and other American cities were built, the products of cheaper land, housing, and transportation than anywhere else on earth.

The Chicago impresario of the suburban quick sell was Samuel Eberly Gross, who is the model for the character Samuel E. Ross in Dreiser's novel *Jennie Gerhardt*. Gross built more houses than anyone in Chicago's history. By 1893, he had sold over forty thousand lots, put up over seventy-five hundred houses, and planned and developed more than sixteen suburban towns and 150 subdivisions, almost all of his holdings, as he prominently advertised, being "Outside Fire Limits!" His "great wooden signs," Dreiser wrote, "might be seen everywhere on the windy stretches of prairie about the city."

Born on the banks of the Susquehanna near Harrisburg, Pennsylvania, in 1843, Gross arrived in Chicago after serving with distinction in the Civil War. He took a law degree from the Union College of Law and went straight into real estate, settling into the business of his life, turning scrubland into lawn and garden. When the building boom collapsed after the Panic of 1873, Gross, a multifaceted man, practiced law, read science and the classics, invented mathematical instruments, dabbled in cartography, and penned a comedy of manners, *The Merchant Prince of Cornville*, which a federal judge later ruled was pirated by Edmond Rostand in writing *Cyrano de Bergerac* in 1897. With the revival of the construction industry, Gross went back into real estate in a far bigger way—and into city transportation as well, becoming a director of an electric commuter railroad that serviced one of his subdivisions and a partner with Charles Yerkes in a plan to expand another subdivision. Like Marshall Field, S. E. Gross saw mass transit as a way of funneling customers to his primary business and raising the value of land he owned. A Chicago businessman described this close connection between residential and transit expansion: "Only let me know six weeks in advance where the City Railway intends building a cable line, and I will make an independent fortune every time."

Like Chicago's catalog kings, Gross wrote his own advertising copy, featuring his pleasing countenance in his splashy ads, his personal guarantee that the sales offer was exactly as it was described. He even published his own *Home Primer*, contrasting penny-wise Andrew, who saves to buy a Gross homestead, with "hard-up" Benjamin, who runs into debt and must board with a tyrannical landlady. And like Richard Sears and Montgomery Ward, he believed he was providing something otherwise denied to ordinary people. Lewis Mumford has called the building of houses "the major architectural work of any civilization," but in Chicago there were almost no architects who were willing to design working-class housing, aside from Solon S. Beman, the agent of an extraordinary patron. Gross entered an area of opportunity that Chicago's architects surrendered to him and made himself a millionaire five times over in the process.

Gross was so popular with city wage workers that he was nominated as the Joint Labor Party's candidate for mayor in 1889. He refused to run, however, claiming he was too busy providing homes for working people, "which but for him," declared an appreciative labor publication, "they never would have had." Though other Chicago speculators built balloon-frame cottages for workers, Gross became the working man's hero because he seemed to care about his products and the people who bought them—the secret of success, as well, of Sears and Ward. Taking advantage of Chicago's position as the country's main source of raw materials for housing, Gross offered as many as four hundred house plans to break up the standardized look of a typical subdivision; and he sold houses on agreeable terms and had a reputation for straight dealing. A worker could own a Gross "model" cottage for a hundred dollars down and payments of ten dollars a month, with additional financing available if he ran into trouble. Gross rarely foreclosed, shrewdly preferring to help families pay off cottages so that they could be induced to "trade up" someday to a more spacious Gross house in a landscaped suburban village like Grossdale, complete with a wide, gaslit boulevard. A good many of his first customers were, like Montgomery Ward's, his for life.

Gross was a housing hustler with a social mission. Into his last years, when he was ill and nearly broke and living in Battle Creek, Michigan, with his second wife, the seventeen-year-old daughter of a local contractor, he believed that providing homes for workers was a capitalist strategy for equalizing America. With a good number of other Chicagoans of status and means, he saw standard-plan suburbs like his own Gross Park, built for German workers around the time Pullman City was built, but without Pullman's restraints and land-holding restrictions, as both incentives to temperance—"Beer and whiskey are forgotten," a local writer noted, when the down payment on a lot is made—and antidotes to social upheaval: "A city of such houses is safe from anarchy." No one in the city was doing more to make industrial workers self-respecting citizens, the local papers declared, than Samuel Eberly Gross.

Gross believed equally in the socially therapeutic value of city parks, places that would also encourage a sober, law-abiding work-force. But like almost every city housing speculator in the years be-tween the Great Fire and the fair, S. E. Gross became a proponent of parks primarily because they were surefire promoters of the real estate around them; and he built two of his biggest subdivisions near Hum-boldt and Garfield Parks on the West Side. In no other American city did the creation of public parks play a greater role in encouraging sub-urban development than in Chicago.

•

In 1849, John S. Wright, city booster and real estate operator, made a prediction. "I foresee a time, not very distant, when Chicago will need for its fast-increasing population a park, or parks, in each divi-sion. Of these parks I have a vision. They are all improved and con-nected with a wide avenue, extending to and along the Lake Shore on the north and south, and so surround the city with a magnificent chain of superb parks and parkways that have not their equals in the world."

Twenty years later, Chicago began building a crescent of parks and boulevards extending all the way around the city; and by 1893 it had largely fulfilled Wright's prophecy. On what had been sandhills, swamp, and desolate prairie, carriage roads carried families to greenswards, gardens, and ornamental lakes, where they picnicked and played lawn games in summer and skated and sledded in winter. Chicago's park founders built these public pleasure grounds on the edge of the city, hoping to draw the rich and the upper middle class to land they owned near them. On shaded streets bordering the new parks and on land along the regal boulevards leading out to them, families of substance could create residential islands of privilege, not unlike those that ad-joined London's St. James's Park and Paris's Bois de Boulogne.

Like nearly everything else built in nineteenth-century Chicago, parks were built mainly to make money. There were reformers who campaigned for parks for health and recreational reasons, but it was the city's real estate interests, led by Paul Cornell, the rich man's S. E. Gross, who inaugurated Chicago's parks program—and with it a great suburban movement to the South Side. Cornell was one of a host of hopeful boosters who had it in mind, as George Ade wrote, "to go out into the country and begin a town and then permit the city to 'build to it,' buying lots from him."

The two parks Cornell was largely responsible for creating on the South Side—Washington Park and Jackson Park—helped turn the neighboring village of Hyde Park, founded by him as a speculation a few years earlier, into one of the first and most exclusive suburbs of Chicago. But Paul Cornell was more than a building speculator. With his fellow park promoter J. Young Scammon—the friend of William Ogden—he had a deep interest in the city's betterment and the hope, originally planted by Ogden, that parks and cultural institutions would act as restraints on Chicago's runaway materialism. Cornell's career as a town and park builder is an example of the combination of high and low motives, of risk taking in the interests of both personal and civic gain, that had been behind nearly every major municipal improvement since the time young John S. Wright first looked out at the huddle of miserable shacks called Chicago from a schooner anchored off the town's sandbar. The park program Cornell initiated was Chicago's first effort to shape a development process dominated by unruly improvisation and to plan entire areas in advance of settlement for public, not private, use. It was also the first successful effort in the city's history to break the monotonous spread of the grid.

•

Twenty-five-year-old Paul Cornell arrived in Chicago from frontier Illinois in 1847 with all his earthly possessions: a new suit of clothes, a package of business cards advertising his freshly awarded law degree, and a dollar and fifty cents in currency, which was stolen from his hotel room on his first night in the city. With the help of his former law instructor, he set himself up as a collector of accounts for eastern capitalists with investments in Chicago and was soon a partner in one of the city's leading law offices. A New Englander of distinguished pedigree, descendant of the first settlers of Rhode Island and cousin of Ezra Cornell, founder of Cornell University, he gained easy access to Chicago society, dining at the table of William Ogden and striking up a friendship with Sen. Stephen Douglas. It was Douglas who advised him to invest all he had—as the senator himself was doing—in the Calumet region, which stood directly in the path of what Douglas anticipated would be a great southward expansion of the city, growth to the west and north hindered by crowds and delays at downtown bridge crossings.

For two years, Cornell surveyed the area south of the city on horseback almost every Sunday afternoon. It was land as unpromising looking as the soggy North Side plots William Ogden had sold for his New York partners at the time of Chicago's birth, but Cornell thought it the best place in the spreading city to secure his future. In 1853 he bought three hundred acres of uninhabited marsh, scrub oak, and sand dunes along the lake, eight miles from the city center, in a place he named—with hope in his heart—Hyde Park, after London's famous stretch of pleasure grounds and boulevards. There he planned to build a sanctuary and summer resort for Chicago's best families. After platting his town, he made arrangements to provide it with daily transportation to and from Chicago, deeding a corridor through it to the Illinois Central in return for the railroad's promise to build its first commuter station on his acres.

With his own money, Cornell then built a rambling resort hotel, a lakeside commons with a landing pier for excursion boats, and a pavilion where bands could play on summer nights for hotel guests decked out in their seasonal whites. It was the first place near Chicago where people of means could go for a weekend outing, and guests would be likely candidates, Cornell thought, to buy lots he began putting up for sale as soon as he drained the rest of his land, some of it three and four feet under lake water.

Cornell sold his first lots to his Chicago friends, who built fair-season houses around his hotel. Among the first residents were J. Young Scammon, Benjamin Hutchinson, Sen. Lyman Trumbull, William Ackerman, soon to be president of the Illinois Central, and young Paul Cornell and his family. When the Illinois Central's chief engineer, George B. McClellan, a hero in the Mexican War, completed the Hyde Park Station in the summer of 1856, the first round-trip train to Chicago didn't carry a single passenger either way. But the settlement of seven houses soon became Chicago's most fashionable resort as well as a place of tranquil retreat, where Mary Todd Lincoln escaped with her family after her husband's burial in Springfield.

Ten years after rail service opened to Chicago, the village of Hyde Park, part of the greatly larger township of the same name covering forty-eight square miles, had nearly a thousand year-round residents; but Cornell had even bigger plans for it. He hoped to make it the South Side equivalent of Evanston, Chicago's largest and wealthiest railroad suburb, with a university modeled after Northwestern as its anchor institution. Unable to attract a college, Cornell hit upon another way to enlarge his village and, with it, his own bankroll—public parks.

The success of New York's Central Park, designed by Frederick Law Olmsted and Calvert Vaux, was the immediate impetus for the Chicago park system. From the day it opened, Central Park attracted big crowds. More to Cornell's interest, however, it raised the value of land surrounding it tremendously. With the help of J. Young Scammon and Scammon's North Side law partner Ezra B. McCagg—gentlemen gardeners with an eye for the dollar—Cornell submitted a bill to the state legislature to create a South Parks Commission empowered to tax property and float bonds for the purpose of buying and improving parkland in the Hyde Park area. A supreme persuader, Cornell spent the winter of 1867–68 in Springfield steering the bill through the legislature. When it was voted down in a referendum by South Siders living in inner-city wards far from the site of the prospective parks, Cornell formed an alliance with sanitary reformers and real estate interests in the West and North Divisions and launched a publicity campaign for a citywide system of parks that would put every Chicagoan within a half hour's horsecar ride of a "people's garden."

The sanitary reformers' position was put forward most suggestively by Dr. John H. Rauch of Rush Medical College in a widely circulated pamphlet, *Public Parks: Their Effects Upon the Moral, Physical, and Sanitary Conditions of the Inhabitants of Large Cities.* Rauch's inspiration was to put the familiar ideas of Olmsted, the country's leading advocate of urban parks, into arguments the city's real leaders—its business leaders—might find persuasive. The parks' shrubs and trees would, he said, disinfect and screen the city's "contaminating" air, making new affluent neighborhoods around them all the more pleasant; and their pastoral surroundings would counteract the pull of the saloon and the gambling den, refashioning the behavior of ordinary "toilers." But civic pride is the Rauch report's strong note. While other cities were fast following the lead of Olmsted's New York, Chicago, with designs of becoming the metropolis of America, had only 125 acres devoted to park purposes, with barely one-third of these "improved." It was time for Chicago to overtake its rivals in the East, Rauch appealed to the businessmen's urban chauvinism, "in those arts which embellish and render cities attractive as places of abode; in other words, we want, not alone, a place for business, but also one in which we can live."

When Rauch published his booklet, Chicago's most popular picnic spots were its new parklike cemeteries, Rosehill, Calvary, and Graceland, which together replaced the dangerously overcrowded City Cemetery on the North Shore. These semirural cemeteries on the outskirts of the city had become so attractive for Sunday outings that one of them began charging admission to families failing to produce a buriallot certificate. To get some peace and quiet, to breathe pure and wholesome air, the citizens of the city of the living had to visit the gardens of the dead.

In Chicago it was money, not ideas about man and nature, that moved things. With Chicago's big real estate dealers solidly behind it, the revised park bill became law in 1869, and three independently chartered park commissions, armed with powers of eminent domain, began acquiring land for what skeptics thought were exorbitant prices. Park development instantly became big business, and Cornell and other influential park supporters got themselves appointed to park boards.

Over the next three decades the autonomous parks boards—minigov-
ernments made independent of city government supposedly to guarantee their integrity—spent over $46 million on parklands, some of it
going by indirection or corruption to board members and their friends
in banking and real estate who owned land where the new parks were
located.

But a great public improvement came out of this inflamed desire to
get rich. And Chicago got a superb park system because Cornell,
McCagg, and a number of other park commissioners associated with
John Rauch insisted on hiring the best design talent available. Swain
Nelson, a Swedish landscape gardener of note, was hired to continue
improvements begun in Lincoln Park before the passage of the Cornell
bill; William Le Baron Jenney, the skyscraper architect who started
out in Chicago as a landscape planner and Olmsted disciple, was appointed chief engineer of the West Parks; and Cornell persuaded Olmsted and Vaux, who were in Chicago in 1870 building a planned
suburb called Riverside, to design the South Parks system.

•

On the site of a gentleman farmer's estate on the forested banks of
the Des Plaines, nine miles from the center of Chicago, Olmsted and
Vaux fashioned what some historians still regard as "the Greatest
American Suburb." Like the city's park system, it was a speculation
raised to a conscious work of art, the brainchild of a consortium of
eastern investors led by Emery E. Childs. The Riverside Improvement
Company gave Olmsted virtually free reign to plan its investment community. It was to be a rustic retreat for the stressed-out businessmen to
whom Dr. Rauch had pitched his appeal for public pleasure grounds.
It already had a rail connection to Chicago, but Olmsted considered a
noisy steam railroad "an unsatisfactory means of communication between a rural habitation and a town." In their planning prospectus for
Childs's group, Olmsted and Vaux urged the building of a paved carriage road on which Riverside's barons of business could ride in style
to their marble-faced office blocks, shielded from bleak prairie wasteland by a continuous border of "villas and gardens."

The boulevard would symbolize the interdependence of town and
suburb, one of Olmsted's pivotal ideas. The trend of the century was
townward, Olmsted argued, but concentration had already created its
own countertide of deconcentration; and it was being powered by the
very technological conveniences that were pulling people into the
urban vortex—new energy, transit, water, and sewage facilities. These
urban amenities were now available to people of means who chose to
live outside the city, creating the possibility of a "middle landscape"

between city and country that blended the best of both lifestyles, allowing its residents to live in two places at the same time.

But they were to be distinct places—city and suburb—interlinked yet different in physical appearance and lifestyle. Riverside's distinguishing mark—the very key to its design—was the layout of the streets. The *Tribune* spoke for Chicago's nineteenth-century commercial community: "Give us straight, broad streets running uninterruptedly from one extremity of the city to the other and through the suburbs *ad infinitum,* if necessary, in the same manner." Olmsted, by contrast, proposed that the grid stop where the businessman stepped off his carriage or commuter car at the close of the workday. The gracefully curved lanes and irregular open spaces of Riverside would announce his entrance into a place of romantic shelter and enclosure, geared to "leisure, contemplativeness, and happy tranquility."

To Olmsted, the grid was as much a psychological as a physical concept. It signified "an eagerness to press forward, without looking to the right hand or the left." In Riverside there were to be no straight lines or sharp angles. "All that favors movement," Olmsted insisted, "should be subordinated." This was to be a place of settlement. And in defiance of principles that had guided economic development in Chicago since the arrival of Ogden and the Yankees, the best property in Riverside—along the wooded borders of the Des Plaines—was set aside for "village-greens, commons, and playgrounds," with walkways, pavilions, rustic bridges, and a dammed-up millpond for skating and pleasure boating.

Riverside was built to Olmsted's lofty specifications except for the carriage run to Chicago, a prohibitively expensive idea in Childs's view. "None of the planning done within the nineteenth century, not even that done under Haussmann," wrote Lewis Mumford, "compares in freshness of form and boldness of design with . . . Olmsted's Riverside." Maj. William Le Baron Jenney, who had met Olmsted at the siege of Vicksburg when he was serving on Grant's staff and Olmsted was heading the U.S. Sanitary Commission, supervised the landscaping and infrastructure work and designed a chaletlike resort hotel, a Swiss-style water tower with a wooden observation deck, and exuberant gabled houses for himself, Childs, and a number of prominent businessmen. Jenney built in harmony with the terrain and in line with Olmsted's idea that competing needs of privacy and congregation be nicely balanced. Houses with big porches and wide windows were placed at some distance from each other and from the road and had privacy trees on their front lawns; but in the early evenings, their residents spilled out into the village's public spaces, playing croquet and badminton, rowing skiffs on the slow-flowing Des Plaines, or walking along the waterside commons.

While Olmsted saw the grid as synonymous with capitalist calculation, gridironed and curved streets were actually related parts of the same process of capitalist urban growth, "superficially opposed in taste but only because in the one case," as the modern critic Raymond Williams suggests, "the land is being organised for production, where tenants and labourers will work, while in the other case it is being organised for consumption—the view, the ordered proprietary repose, the prospect." Like the parks he built all over the country, Riverside was organized by Olmsted for the passive enjoyment of pastoral surroundings. Here the hard-edged severity of commerce gives way to sweeping curves, fine views, and a countrylike serenity. Chicago's architects built offices in the air on the city's grid for the production part of the capitalists' day; Olmsted built for them an exclusive escape from the burdens of running these gigantic enterprises. Rested and recharged, Chicago's Gradgrinds and Bounderbys could return the next morning to the fight for gain.

Feeling, perhaps, morally uneasy about how he distributed his work, Olmsted insisted he never lost an opportunity to urge the "ruralizing of *all* our urban population," especially those in "the dense poor quarters of our great cities." In his more self-reflective moments, however, he confessed that the "laws of supply and demand compel me to work chiefly for the rich and to study rich men's wants, fashions, and prejudices." That is what Riverside was: the nearest thing the nineteenth century has given us of a businessman's utopia, a place where he could "withdraw like a monk and live like a prince."

Although Riverside turned out to be everything its first residents had hoped for, from its beginnings it was plagued by financial troubles. The abode of sharp-dealing capitalists, it was managed with embarrassing incompetence. Just as construction began, Emery Childs defaulted on cash payments to Olmsted and Vaux and, under pressure from his cost-cutting investment partners, made plans to build houses, including his own, on the protected riverside commons. Childs jettisoned his building proposal only when Olmsted and Vaux threatened to resign and take their case to the newspapers. It was at this point that Paul Cornell approached the partners with an offer to design the entire South Parks system; they immediately resigned their commission at Riverside, leaving the supervision of the village's completion to Major Jenney's engineering company.

The Riverside Improvement Company went bankrupt in the Panic of 1873, but a "resident park" of forty or so houses had been built by then. The planned village still stands today, surrounded by checker-boarded Chicago, a gem of the town makers' art. It was the first of sixteen suburban communities designed by Olmsted, and it influenced the development of Britain's garden-city movement, whose founder, Ebenezer Howard—a proponent of combining the advantages of town and country in greenbelt communities—was a stenographer living in Chicago when Riverside was being developed.

Riverside never became, however, a model for Chicago's suburban-land-use pattern, as Olmsted hoped it would. Except on the showpiece North Shore, the city's suburbs continued to be built as the great park planner feared they would, "little by little," as he himself described the process, "without any general plan, the only aim being . . . to extend the town streets over the suburb . . . and of thus giving a town value to the lots upon them." But the *idea* of Riverside, that of a sheltered community of single-family houses amid green and pleasant landscape, remains to this day the American idea of the good life.

Olmsted had thrown himself into this project, but the South Parks Commission would give him the opportunity he was seeking to build pleasure-time environments for all the citizens of the city, for the railroad mogul as well as his Swedish gardener and his Irish cook.

•

In designing his Chicago parks, Olmsted hoped to build in harmony with the city's only distinctive natural features: the treeless prairie and the "limitless expanse of lake." At the site of Jackson Park, along Lake Michigan, he proposed an aquatic park with lagoons, peninsulas, and wooded islands—and a thousand-foot-long "gateway" pier for excursion steamers bringing the "toiling population of Chicago . . . by many tens of thousands at a cost of a few cents." At the water entrance to the park, a channel would be cut inland from the lake and run down the Midway Plaisance, a green strip connecting Jackson and Washington Parks. Pleasure boats could descend from the lake down this prairie canal to a thirteen-acre sheet of water in Washington Park.

Washington Park was a bleak field of wind-stripped trees when Olmsted first surveyed it on foot, but he suggested that it maintain its original character, with a long meadow bordered by groves of trees and a curving carriage way, the grass to be kept short by unfenced herds of sheep. Olmsted was pressured to provide playing fields for vigorous recreation, but sporting activities were still subordinated to the passive enjoyment of scenic surroundings.

Olmsted's excursion pier for the masses was not built, but the approachways by land he called for in his plan were, and they determined the character and usage pattern of the South Parks for their first two decades. Olmsted's plan called for two boulevards of the type he had recommended for Riverside, wide and smooth and free from industrial traffic. Formal accessways to the parks, they would also create park corridors within the city that would become fashionable neighborhoods, homes of purse-proud merchants who would build their town houses behind columns of noble elms. Carriage riders coming out from the city on the boulevards would know at once they had entered a world in, but not of, Chicago when they swung their light and springy phaetons around the curving lanes leading into Washington Park, the curve being here, as at Riverside, a symbol of a different sphere of living, a different category of values.

Building parks in Chicago would be far more difficult and expensive than building them in cities like Boston and New York, Olmsted warned the park commissioners, because the proposed sites were "unoccupied for the most part" not just by people but "even by a tree or a shrub, a hill or a stone," as Horace Cleveland noted in his own survey of Chicago's possible park sites. This bare land could not simply be reshaped; almost everything would have to be "manufactured"—woods, hillocks, knolls, streams, and ponds. And deep artesian wells would have to be dug to feed the watercourses and maintain the lawns and vegetation.

Olmsted and Vaux's plan was never completely realized. After the Great Fire, public spending was directed to the rebuilding of the burned area. Horace Cleveland, who had worked with Olmsted on Brooklyn's Prospect Park, oversaw the direction of his mentor's design but was put under a cost-shaving mandate not to make major changes in the natural scenery, and that killed hopes for a water park and a canal, over Paul Cornell's determined objections. Except for a pleasant stretch along the shoreline, most of Jackson Park remained unimproved until Olmsted returned to Chicago to lay out a wondrous waterside city for the Columbian Exposition, with lagoons, basins, a wooded island, and a temporary gateway pier for steam excursions from the city. In Washington Park, however, Cleveland was given enough funding to build Olmsted and Vaux's Open Green, their sweeping carriage runs, their artificial lakes with island bird sanctuaries, and their Haussmann-like boulevards.

On the more built-up and less affluent West Side, Jenney had less money and space to work with than Cleveland, but he made his three smaller parks masterworks of the gardener's art, adding his own touch in the form of naturalistic architecture—refectories, conservatories, palm houses, children's playhouses, and fantastic floral displays in the shapes of animal and human figures.

The gem of the park diadem, however, was the abandoned city cemetery two miles north of the Loop. Lincoln Park had the city's most beautiful artificial lakes and its most impressive collection of civic and memorial statuary, including a haunting rendering of *Lincoln, the Man* by Augustus Saint-Gaudens; and it had a lakeside promenade, a carriage drive, and a splendid zoo.

On Sunday afternoons, the park's lakes and lagoons were filled with canopied swan boats and with canoes "paddled by gentlemen in high stiff collars, their ladies holding dainty parasols and trailing fingers in the water." And on dirt diamonds young men in shirtsleeves played the "American Game." As many as twenty thousand people would be in the park on sunny Sundays, many walking with their big wooden picnic baskets from working-class neighborhoods that had begun to appear north and west of the park. Electric lights were introduced in the 1880s, and summer crowds that stayed on into the evening would gather around Yerkes's electric fountain to see the colored water display, young couples discreetly breaking away to walk hand in hand along the gaslit lake promenade, the moon throwing a silver trail across the black water. "No Chicago millionaire," wrote George Ade, "has such a magnificent front yard."

When they were first laid out, most of the parks were located too far from the working-class wards of the city to be anything but pleasure grounds for the privileged. But by the 1890s, public transportation, the reduction of carfares from fifteen to five cents, and the construction of workers' subdivisions near the borders of the city made it possible for skilled laborers, clerks, and their families to use them with some frequency. All the parks, however, remained alien territory to the city's inner immigrant neighborhoods. A round-trip car ride for an entire family could have easily eaten up half a Polish mill hand's daily wage. Even upward-advancing German families from S. E. Gross's outlying communities often stayed away from the parks on Sundays because beer drinking, dancing, and cooking out were forbidden, as were political gatherings and speechmaking. And during the daylight hours the carriages and mounts of the wealthy dominated the scene, especially in Washington Park, which had the most extensive carriage runs and the best-kept paths for equestrians.

It was Olmsted's boulevards that drew "the horse crowd." In the evenings, the "jam is such," Horace Cleveland wrote to Olmsted just after Washington Park opened, "that stringent police regulations are necessary to prevent disorder." Hobart C. Chatfield-Taylor dubbed these years just before the fair Chicago's Hippic Age, an observation more revealing, perhaps, of Chatfield-Taylor and his crowd than of Chicago at that time. Erect, clean-shaven English coachmen replaced Afro-American or Scandinavian drivers, and in a raw western city unsure of its social bearings, "to merit the approval of one's English coachman," Chatfield-Taylor writes, "became an obsession, . . . for oh, what a deal of scorn lay in the curl of that supercilious fellow's lip, if one chanced to call a 'trap' by the uncouth name of 'rig,' or to speak of a pair of horses as 'a team.'"

On two evenings a week, the park commissioners waived the eight-mile-an-hour speed limit on the boulevards, and hot-spirited sports engaged in hack-racing contests on the macadamized roadway. For horsemen on steeds there was a firm, well-sprinkled driveway along Drexel Boulevard. The boulevards also became, as Olmsted had hoped they would, a pleasant way to travel to and from work. Between five and six o'clock in the afternoon, men of wealth rolled homeward on roadways closed to industrial traffic. Dreiser evoked the scene along Michigan Avenue in one of his novels of Charles Yerkes, an ardent horseman. "Smart daughters, society-bred sons, handsome wives, came downtown in traps, victorias, carriages, and vehicles of the latest design to drive home their trade-weary fathers or brothers, relatives or friends. . . . Lithe, handsome, well-bred animals, singly and in jingling pairs, paced each other down the long, wide, grass-lined street, its fine homes agleam with a rich, complaisant materiality."

Washington Park Race Club, adjacent to Washington Park, was an integral part of the new culture of the boulevards. Built in 1884 by a group of Chicago horsemen headed by Gen. Phil Sheridan, it was one of the finest Thoroughbred tracks in the country, with a grandstand that could seat ten thousand. Its clubhouse, designed by Solon S. Beman, was one of the social centers of the Prairie Avenue set. It had sleeping quarters, a billiard room, and big sitting rooms with stone fireplaces, ideal for sledding parties returning from a ride on the boulevard. The club's membership embraced the workaday deities of Chicago—Pullman, Palmer, Field, and others. On the annual June running of the American Derby, the first call of summer to the fashionable set, they would gather with their families at the Hotel Richelieu on Michigan Avenue and form a cavalcade of shining carriages that would make its way out the boulevards to the racecourse, the walkways lined with spectators straining to catch a glimpse of a famous Chicago beauty or businessman.

In the grandstand, before the betting began, all eyes would be on the line of landaus, stanhopes, drags, victorias, and tandems that rolled off the boulevards onto the club's carriage drive. Potter Palmer was always the scene-stealer, arriving one year in a French charabanc, with leopard skins covering its seats, the tails of his slim and majestic horses fashionably blocked, their heads reined high, their curried bodies shining.

•

On the lawn on Derby Day were newly rich families that had moved into stone piles on the avenues near the racecourse. But these pockets of affluence were soon surrounded by the overspill from the city. The parks and new transit lines connecting them to the Loop turned Paul Cornell's hamlet of fine drives and high society into a flourishing, mixed-income suburb with a growth rate greater than Chicago's. In the 1890s, the village proper still possessed neighborhoods as exclusive as adjoining Kenwood, but good parts of it—and all of the surrounding township with the exception of Kenwood—had become home to middle-class and working-class Chicagoans escaping the city for cheap wooden cottages. Most of them were built by speculators on cross streets off the parklike avenues or on the carved-up prairie south of Hyde Park village, which the novelist Robert Herrick described as "the refuse acres of the earth, . . . half swamp, half city suburb."

Rows of towering telephone poles stretch along the streets of the South Side subdivision that Herrick's main character in *The Web of Life*, Dr. Sommers, visits on his rounds; and on the avenue, car tracks have been laid that reach all the way back to the Loop. Railroad tracks are in the near distance, the trains making a frightening racket as they flee "the roaring cavern of the city," while to the far south, the orange-red discharges of the furnaces of the South Chicago steel mills light up the sky. But there is a meadow nearby covered with blooming prairie flowers and a small brick schoolhouse for the children of the hard-working Swedes in the factories of Grand Crossing, an industrial town Paul Cornell created after he laid out Hyde Park. "Many of the children can scarcely understand a word of English," a local teacher tells Dr. Sommers, "and their habits!" But they and their parents "are better [off] than the Poles, in the Halsted Street district, or the Russians, [on the] West Side." Here people owned their own cottages with garden plots and tended little groves of stunted oaks that must have seemed to them like forest preserves. And the electric cars passing on the avenue were quarter-hourly reminders that this hamlet of mud and weeds was part of Chicago, a small but hopeful start upward for those able to flee inner-city slums miles to the north.

•

Hyde Park village, surrounded by greatly larger and heavily industrialized Hyde Park township, was a very different place, solidly settled and comfortable, with an active civic life. "Political meetings were well attended," writes Hyde Park's first historian, "[and] church members worked together to raise building funds, establish Sunday schools, and open missions, both in this country and in faraway lands." There was a Mendelssohn club for those with an interest in music; a Shakespeare club, which met in the homes of its members and put on plays; and a much-used Lyceum and library, which invited prominent locals to speak, including Louis Sullivan, a resident of Kenwood, who gave a talk about the Auditorium Building just before it opened.

Some years later, when the automobile suburbs of Chicago and elsewhere turned their backs on the city's problems, it became fashionable to argue that the suburban movement was, from its inception, a retreat from civic responsibility. Not able to conquer the city's problems, the rich ran from them; and "the suburb served," in Lewis Mumford's stern judgment, "as an asylum for the preservation of illusion. Here domesticity could flourish, forgetful of the exploitation on which so much of it was based." While this hits the mark, Mumford misses the almost utopian fervor that fueled the first migration to the urban borderlands and gives the false impression that suburbanization was an exclusively middle-class and upper-class migration.

The suburb would contravene the redemptive hopes of Olmsted and other nineteenth-century reformers. Instead of blurring class lines, as S. E. Gross and others had anticipated, it greatly worsened both class and racial segregation, a phenomenon already in evidence in the time of the Streetcar City, when railroad villages on Chicago's North Shore fought the introduction of the trolley, with its democratic five-cent fare, fearing the influx of "the dangerous classes." The suburb was both a creation of urban expansion and a refuge from it. From its beginning, it was based on fear as well as hope, hope for a better life far from feared newcomers to the city. "It is more pleasant in a small community," said a Riverside resident, "where people are of similar backgrounds, know manners, and wash themselves." But the virus of prejudice was not confined to the comfortable classes. One ethnic group after the other moved as far toward the urban periphery as their incomes would take them to escape the "incursions" of more recently arrived immigrants.

With the coming of the automobile, urban transportation corridors became escapeways from the city, not linkages, as they had briefly been, between two separate but interpenetrating social worlds. And the linear logic of the railroad suburbs—placed along the tracks a good distance apart, like beads on a string—was broken, giving rise to the formless Spread City of highways and strip malls. But for a promising moment at the end of the nineteenth century, city and suburb were part of a single interlaced metropolitan region; and the suburbs strengthened the downtown areas on which they were entirely dependent.

No matter how far suburban families moved from the Loop, double lines of steel linked them to it. In the exploding American city it was not public planning but mass transportation—a creation of the marketplace—that unified urban space. Indeed, without mass transportation, ever-spreading Chicago, with its sharpening divisions of work, residence, and shopping and its growing class and ethnic segregation, would not have been a real city at all but what it always seemed threatening to become—*had* become in the opinion of some of its oldest Protestant settlers—a "queer conglomerate mass," in Jacob Riis's words, "of heterogeneous elements."

Just the experience of moving around the city in a cable car or trolley—"speeding sightseeing platforms"—gave many Chicagoans a sense of belonging to a community wider than their neighborhood or suburban village, a big and interesting place with its own emotional pull. Seeing their city from the window of a moving streetcar made them proud to be part of it, the kind of reaction Americans traveling west on the transcontinentals reported having.

Mass transit, the great unifier and centralizer, also opened up the city. By the time of the fair, all but the desperately poor could go anywhere cheaply: to ballparks, racetracks, public parks, theaters, and cemeteries. And for lonely young clerks and shopgirls living in cramped boardinghouses, a Sunday outing to one of the fascinating places served by the streetcars was an opportunity to connect with others, the kind of chance encounters and meetings that make cities enlivening. It was the streetcar that gave young working people in the city their first real taste of personal freedom and young lovers their first chance to be alone together on Sunday, the great getaway day for Chicagoans, when the clanging yellow cars were packed from morning until midnight.

4. Sunday in Chicago

Sophie Johnson, a young house servant in one of George Ade's stories of little people in the big town, is Mrs. Hamilton Jefferson's girl for six days a week. But on Sunday afternoons, as soon as the gleaming dinner dishes are stacked in the china closet, she walks out the door, free for a half day, with the savings of a week in her pocketbook. Walking by herself on one of these Sundays, wearing a bright hat, a pink dress, and shoes so new you can hear them squeak, she meets a young man she has had her eye on, Carl Lindgren, a frugal factory hand, his coat pressed to a shine, a dandelion stuck in his buttonhole. After exchanging "good days," he says something about Humboldt Park, and Sophie smiles and nods her head. They walk together to North Avenue, board a streetcar, and through the big window watch the procession of Sunday strollers on this perfect spring day.

In the park, Sophie drops her handkerchief, and Carl, returning it, forgets to let go of her hand. They buy a sticky five-cent popcorn ball and eat it while sitting on the grassy bank of a lagoon filled with boaters. Then they head for the park's greenhouse, stopping for a moment to put some pennies into a fortune-telling machine, "a gypsy with pointing finger and a knowing look." Toward the end of the afternoon, they walk over to North Avenue to have their picture taken in a photographer's tent. Sophie sits in a big chair, folding her hands, and Carl stands behind her as stiffly as a statue. Just before the camera clicks, he puts his big hand on her slim shoulder.

On the ride home, it begins to rain, and Sophie and Carl huddle together under Sophie's parasol as they hurry from the car stop to Mrs. Hamilton Jefferson's house, Sophie clutching a card the Gypsy had handed her—"AN UNKNOWN LOVER ADORES YOU." They pause in the entry where no one can see them. Then Carl comes out "with his face beaming and walk[s] away regardless of the rain."

On another Sunday, Carl might have taken Sophie to one of the city's fantastic cycloramas, where wraparound, floor-to-ceiling paintings reproduced memorable historical events and places—Niagara Falls, the Battle of Gettysburg, the Crucifixion, the Great Chicago Fire—or to the Eden Musée, a waxworks show advertised as second only to London's Madame Tussaud's, or to a concert on the North Side in Turner's Hall, where young Louis Sullivan became "an ardent Wagnerite" on Sunday afternoons "in this raw city by the Great Lake in the West." And if Carl Lindgren were alone and feeling in need of improvement, there were lectures at the city's theaters, music halls, and independent churches by unconventional preachers and brilliant iconoclasts like Rev. Frank Gunsaulus, head of the Armour Institute, and Prof. David Swing, whose heresy trial in the 1870s before the Chicago Presbytery held the attention of the nation. These halls and churches were packed to the doors on Sundays with knowledge-hungry Bohemian, Swedish, and German artisans and with "youths from the country towns," recalled Edgar Lee Masters, a young Chicago lawyer living in a boardinghouse in 1893. "Quite every Sunday morning it was to one or another of these independent churches or thinkers that I hurried," wrote Theodore Dreiser. "It was such an intense relief, after a week of dreary economic routine, or slavery even, to find men in pulpits . . . , unshackled of dogma, . . . suggesting the fullness and richness of life, its possibilities and opportunities for the cultivation of the intellect. . . . And ever since then I have identified the Chicago of that day—its rare, youthful, inspirational quality—with these men, and per contra, these men, their intellectual dreams of a happy, perfect world, with Chicago."

"Why is it," George Ade asked, "that the middle class has a monopoly of the real enjoyment in Chicago?"—the middle class, as he defined them, being those persons who "are neither poverty-stricken nor offensively rich." It was a particular "advantage," Ade wrote, to belong to this class on a beautiful summer night. "A middle-class family may sit on the front stoop all evening and watch the society people go to the weddings in their closed carriages." Father didn't have to wear a tight-fitting dress coat or a collar that choked him, and if he and mother wished to have some ice cream, they could go around the corner to get it or send one of the children with a pitcher. The rich, on the other hand, would never be seen in so common a place as an ice-cream store, and "the idea of sending a pitcher would be shocking."

On weekend evenings, double-decker steamers with electric lights and "resounding" orchestras left from the Clark Street bridge on nightly trips out on the cool lake. The passengers—waltzing on the deck or hanging on the rail to catch the breezes—were office clerks in summer whites and stiff straw hats, "tired husbands and smiling wives," and young servants and laborers like Sophie and Carl. All of them belonged to the "fortunate middle class," for society "could not patronize cheap excursions on the lake."

On Sunday nights, the high stairways along the "boardinghouse belt" on Dearborn Avenue became amphitheaters, as Ade called them, where young people gathered to listen to the concerts of street musicians, some of them pushing street pianos on wheels and "grinding out [Il] Trovatore." And Dearborn Avenue led directly by streetcar to the "lights and shadows and cool depths of Lincoln Park." In the park, a smooth walkway led across a bridge to a small clear lake. On its shores—quiet now that the rich, in their intrusive rigs, have headed home—the young man who drives a delivery wagon for Marshall Field sits holding the hand of the young woman who addresses letters for Aaron Montgomery Ward.

•

The Sunday activity that the rich and the middle class did enjoy equally was "wheeling," the sporting craze of the nineties. In the mid-1880s, the dangerously unsteady highwheeler with its six-foot, hard-rubber front wheel and tiny rear wheel—a conveyance for acrobats and the intrepid only—was replaced by the English "safety" bicycle, with two smaller wheels of identical size and pneumatic tires for a more cushioned ride. These sleek steel bikes could be bought from Chicago's Arnold, Schwinn, & Company for anywhere from fifty to one hundred dollars, too expensive for most unskilled factory workers but affordable to George Ade's middle class, especially with the spread of installment buying. Chicago sportsmen formed cycling clubs, fast riders, called "scorchers," meeting on Sundays in front of the big hotels on Michigan Avenue and heading out, as many as three hundred "steel steeds" in close formation, to their clubhouses on the border of the city, to one of the outer parks, or to one of the new roadside inns that had begun catering to "wheelmen." By the mid-1890s there were at least five hundred such clubs in the city, each with its own colors and with tight-fitting uniforms and spoon-billed caps for competitions, the most popular being the Chicago-to-Pullman road race on Decoration Day.

Some of the clubs became powerful political organizations, pushing for improved streets, elevated tracks, and laws to curb bike theft, a thriving black-market business. "This club and its associates control 1,500 political votes," the Vikings Bicycle Club announced, "and will support those candidates favorable to wheelmen and wheeling." Some of the clubhouses were impressive affairs, two- and three-story brick buildings with parlors, billiard rooms, sanded floors, and restaurants; and their officers invited aldermen to come and speak to them, the more astute ward heelers arriving on bicycle.

Like lawn tennis, introduced from England in the 1870s, cycling was open to both sexes, and like the streetcar, it allowed young couples, some of them on side-by-side bicycles, to go about the city unchaperoned. Cycling also liberated women from uncomfortable Victorian clothing. The preferred outfit of the woman cyclist was a soft hat, bloomers or a divided skirt, and low shoes, a "get-up" that prompted Mr. Dooley's remark that the only time "whin a woman's not a woman [is] . . . whin she's on a bicycle, by dad."

Traditionalists issued alarmed warnings that "scorcher's flush" would permanently damage a woman's complexion and that vigorous pedaling would overdevelop a woman's leg muscles, and some insisted that pedaling a sewing machine was a better and more appropriate form of exercise for women. But in 1893 the *New York Times* reported that a doctor could not be found in all of Manhattan who did not think that wheeling was a healthy form of exercise for both sexes. Some doctors even recommended cycling as a therapy for nervous disorders—for hysteria, hypochondria, and neurasthenia. The Evanston temperance reformer and suffragist Frances E. Willard was one of the first women in the country to take up cycling—when in her fifties—and she wrote a best-selling book touting cycling's health and moral benefits for women.

Cyclists were rarely seen in Bridgeport, nor did the residents there crowd the streetcars on Sunday afternoons. The five-cent fare was too great an expense for a family outing; and, in any event, most of the Sunday activities of interest—religious parades, family dinners, street festivals, meetings of local clubs and organizations—were centered in the ethnic colony. There was no Sunday escape for these people from the suffocating smoke of the city, which caused throat infections and lung diseases, or from the stomach-turning stench of the neighboring river, a smell to rival Packingtown's. And to escape the walled-in heat of the city there was only the street. Boys played stickball there, and girls played tag from corner to corner or joined their mothers for visits to family and friends after the men had drifted off to the local drinking shops. There were more bars in Chicago in the 1880s than in all fifteen southern states combined, and almost all of them remained open on Sunday despite an Illinois closing law that had been on the books since the 1840s. In their one-room workingmen's clubs, men and older boys played cards or pool or just shot the breeze, while some of the bigger saloons staged illegal boxing matches and had tenpin alleys in their basements.

In German neighborhoods on the North Side, brightly lit mahogany and brass gasthauses—so different from the bleakly severe Irish stand-up saloons—were family gathering places, with oompah bands and vaudeville-style acts, some of them just for children. And in Polish, Ukrainian, and Slovak enclaves there were polka parties on Sunday evenings in the back rooms of saloons or in the big halls of ethnic benefit societies. Jews on Maxwell Street met in coffeehouses, and in the tiny African-American community on the near South Side there was a big "resort," Chateau de Plaisance, with dancing, roller-skating, food, and drink, "the only amusement park and pavilion," it advertised itself, "owned and controlled by Negroes in the world."

In the Loop, all the theaters were open on Sunday evening. Country-born clerks and stenographers would queue up at the box offices an hour before showtime or head out on the cars to popular dance halls like Baum's Pavilion on the South Side, a raucous two-story concert hall with an adjoining beer garden illuminated by colored lights. The stage show was the attraction at Baum's—that and Saturday and Sunday night dances. On summer nights "all classes of men and women are represented there," reported a published guide to Chicago night life—"the well-to-do club man," the "hard-working and respectable mechanic," and "young girls of quite independent standing—servant girls, saleswomen and others, many of them strangers in the city, perhaps, possessed of no sterner guardians than their own consciences. . . . They see no reason why they should not spend at least one evening in a little uproarious festivity."

The dancing at Baum's ended around midnight. Then the sweaty clerks and stenographers would take open-air summer cars back to their cramped boardinghouses and flats in the neighborhoods that stretched along the transit lines raying out from the Loop. At seven the next morning, they would board the inbound cars that carried them from the Spread City that steel rails had created to the Tall City steel masters made possible, in the back-and-forth flow that was the circulating lifeblood of the Streetcar City.

It was the combination and interconnection of these two forms of expansion—outward and upward—that created modern Chicago. "The phenomenon of the CBD, the central business district, should not be taken for granted," writes Spiro Kostof, "however familiar it has since become. There was nothing quite like it in Europe, especially from the moment the tall buildings came of age [in Chicago] in the 1880s." These buildings gave the downtowns of Chicago and New York a monumental quality that rivaled the ancient structures of faith and state in Europe. In the 1880s there were many more of them in Chicago than in New York; and they were jammed more tightly together there, making them all the more impressive.

Newspapers complained about "the sunless canyons of the streets," but the Chicago Loop was a place of color and life, "an array of wonders" and "unbelievable things," the reporter Robert J. Casey wrote of his youthful impressions of the city of Yerkes, Field, and Sullivan. "There were the ornate rigs of the rich, filled . . . with beautiful and handsomely gowned women. . . . There were unending streams of drays, hauled by steaming Percherons and directed by a cavalry of police." There were men dressed as clowns carrying advertising boards, "dentist's signs in which sets of teeth six feet wide opened and closed and clacked and clacked, opticians' signs out of which amazingly large eyes looked at you and winked, red-coated Hussars in front of hotels, oddly costumed sandwich men," bobtailed horses, intrepid bicycle riders, brightly painted waffle wagons, burly, red-faced cops, "coachmen with fawn topcoats and high silk hats," and endless numbers of peanut vendors, flower girls, newsboys, bootblacks, and drifters hawking "Shoestrings—5 cents a pair."

There were dime museums, as Edgar Lee Masters remembered, with "flaunting flaps showing snake women and fire eaters, fat and skeleton men." And when the circus was in town, there were fantastic parades of elephants, acrobats, and clowns, the immense draft horses of Barnum and Bailey pounding and slipping on the granite blocks as they pulled cages holding roaring lions and leopards.

But the most thrilling sight of all to young Casey was the new stone-and-glass skyline. People would go downtown and "gaze for hours," he recalled, at shouting workmen raising colossal building frames into the city's swirling coal smoke. "The noise of the hammer men and riveters was the most inspiring thing in town."

10

Stories in Stone and Steel

1. Something New Under the Sun

"WHEN I came from Sweden [in 1881] I found America busy building," recalled the Chicago masonry contractor Henry Ericsson. "The country, it seemed, had adopted building as a national exercise by which to" show off its newfound power to "tame the ageless hostilities of gravity, decay, and fire." The America that Henry Ericsson arrived in was known to the world as a nation of builders, makers of roaring steel mills, long-reaching railroads, wondrous suspension bridges, entire new cities and regions, and its most remarkable single construction feat was the skyscraper. "The skyscraper is the most distinctly American thing in the world," wrote Col. W. A. Starrett, whose family of contractors and engineers helped define the country's urban skyline. "It is all American and all ours in its conception, [and] all-important in our metropolitan life." America's preeminent contribution to world architecture, it is, like the Gothic cathedral, an urban achievement and a symbol of the ideas and aspirations of a new civic culture that appeared with its development.*

The main business of this culture was business itself, and the skyscraper, built solely for commercial use, was its most expressive build-

---

*Architectural historians continue to debate what exactly constitutes a skyscraper. The term is used here, as it was used in Chicago in the 1880s, to describe an elevator building of ten stories or more.

ing form. "The [tall] office building is as typical of the life of our age," declared the architecture writer Barr Ferree, "as the sumptuous baths and great palaces were typical of the life of imperial Rome, or the cathedrals of the religious fervor of the Middle Ages." A purely secular building, it was nonetheless a testimony to faith, the American "faith in the dollar," as the noted New York critic Montgomery Schuyler wrote.

After visiting Chicago in the early 1890s, Schuyler thought it curious that the image of downtown that remained fixed in his mind was made up "exclusively" of skyscrapers. "Not a church enters into it . . . scarcely a public building enters into it. . . . The 'business block,' entirely utilitarian in purpose . . . is the true and typical embodiment in building of the Chicago idea." Unlike the downtowns of New York, Boston, or Philadelphia—cultural as well as financial centers—there was no architectural indication in the Loop of a "division of interest" or of purposes other than making money.

New York was the birthplace of the skyscraper, but the most brilliant achievements of early high-rise construction and design occurred in Chicago. Chicago was the nurturing ground, as well, of the first important theorists of the skyscraper: William Le Baron Jenney, John Wellborn Root, and Louis H. Sullivan. In the years between 1880 and the Columbian Exposition, Chicago's architects and engineers developed the basic structural system—called Chicago Construction—of the modern steel-and-glass office tower and found ways to align art and engineering to express great height with power and grace, turning the ungainly, tall building, laughed at by critics—its size too great to disguise its imperfections—into an elegantly integrated whole. "It all started in the long grass of the Prairies," Frank Lloyd Wright said of modern architecture.

Sheerly as a work of engineering, the urban skyscraper was a staggering achievement. Its construction, as John Wellborn Root noted, presented architects with problems for which there were no "preexisting" architectural or structural solutions. Chicago's architects developed not just a new kind of building but also a new American architecture, one that spoke the native language and expressed the national culture. It was a style confined almost exclusively to one building type—the commercial skyscraper—but the results were revolutionary. As Pullman, Swift, Field, and Armour made over the economy of Chicago, Jenney, Sullivan, Burnham, and Root transformed the city's physical appearance, bringing to birth the American vertical city.

The very idea of what a great city is changed forever with the appearance of the skyscraper. As the president of the American Civic

Association said in 1926: "It is noticeable that every American city and town that aspires to metropolitan importance wants to have at least one skyscraper—one that can be illustrated on a picture postcard and sent far and wide as an evidence of modernity and a go-ahead spirit."

"The towers of Zenith aspired above the morning mist," wrote Sinclair Lewis of George F. Babbitt's midwestern metropolis, a city that dreams to be as big as Chicago, "austere towers of steel and cement and limestohe, sturdy as cliffs and delicate as silver rods. They were neither citadels nor churches, but frankly and beautifully office-buildings."

Cloud-reaching structures were certainly not new to the city. From the Babylonian ziggurats to the domes and steeples of imperial Europe, height had been used throughout history to celebrate secular and spiritual power. But with the exception of the baronial residents of the tower houses of medieval Italy, no one had lived in these earlier urban eminences, whereas to have one's place of business in a tall office building in New York or Chicago in the 1880s—to be a "cliff dweller"— became a mark of modernity and status. And these office behemoths themselves became public symbols of corporate might—billboard architecture. Great wealth gave the capitalists who financed the first skyscrapers the confidence that they could alter the age-old image of the city as a place bound by earth and sky; and the architects in their employ came to believe that the supreme test of their talents was to build a skyscraper "so tall," in the words of Carl Sandburg, they would have to put "hinges on the two top stories so to let the moon go by."

In Chicago, these tradition-shattering aspirations were more forcefully expressed than anywhere else. Chicago's first skyscraper architects had a strong regional consciousness and the sense that they were making history in a part of America only recently claimed from the wilderness and in a city not much older than they were—the average age of the Chicago architect of 1880 was just under thirty. "At no time in the history of the world has a community covering such vast . . . territory developed with such amazing rapidity, and under conditions of civilization so far advanced," John Wellborn Root wrote of Chicago and the West. In the period of conquest and initial building there had been no time for art. It was a "long time full of deadness, except of physical force, then a sudden bursting of art into exuberant flower," the awakening of the building arts in the 1880s that Root saw as the beginning of a golden age of Chicago achievement.

•

The Great Fire is commonly seen as the necessary prelude to this architectural revolution, complete destruction clearing the ground for the new and the better. That is not how it was, however. The conditions created by the fire were, if anything, an obstacle to Chicago architects coming of age in 1880. The new Chicago was built almost instantaneously after the fire by the architects who had built the old Chicago "and who took even less thought the second time than they had the first," Montgomery Schuyler wrote, "by reason of the greater pressure upon them." This totally rebuilt city of "old fashioned" five- and six-story buildings was the Chicago that John Wellborn Root and his partner, Daniel Hudson Burnham, confronted when they began to receive important commissions with the revival of the economy after the depression of the mid-1870s.

Skyscraper Chicago was constructed building by building, one taller and more innovative new building after another rising out of an older city that was itself new, in a process of ceaseless demolition and construction that made all of Chicago appear to visitors like an enormous construction site. This is what is amazing about Chicago's post-fire recovery. In less than two decades, not one but two new cities were built, with the builders of the 1880s, in the words of one of them, "completely junking the false ideals . . . of the seventies."

Yet in one important way the Great Fire did directly influence the building of the second new Chicago. There was a lot of talk in the 1870s of constructing a fireproof city, but the hastily built business houses of that decade were firetraps. Chicago capitalists like Pullman, Field, and Armour would not finance tall buildings like those New York had begun constructing until they could be assured that such expensive investments were fire resistant; nor would fire-insurance companies underwrite them. The Great Fire actually postponed the building of skyscrapers in Chicago, but the delay worked to the ultimate advantage of local architecture. The warnings of insurance companies and the caution of investors put pressure on Chicago architects and engineers to develop new fireproofing methods and materials. When they became widely available in the early 1880s, the tall office buildings that went up were the safest against fire in the world. In the 1880s, Chicago capitalists finally began fashioning a city that would last, depending on sound construction, not fire insurance, for the protection of their property.

In his influential history of modern architecture, Henry-Russell Hitchcock expresses puzzlement as to how Chicago, with "no established traditions, no real professional leaders, and ignorance of all architectural styles, past or present," produced some of the finest architecture of modern times. But John Root and his colleagues saw the city's absence of architectural tradition as an opportunity, not an obstacle. In an atmosphere conducive to experiment and improvisation, Chicago's architects—few of them academically trained and many of them with only engineering backgrounds—invented one revolutionary method of construction after another and made the best of their buildings consummate artistic achievements as well, the equals, in many ways, of the cathedrals of the Ile de France and the palaces and churches of Quattrocento Florence. By 1886, Chicago—a place almost without architecture in 1880—was the world center of architectural experimentation.

•

If proud Chicagoans likened their city to any other in history, it was usually to Renaissance Florence. Dreiser called his adopted city "this Florence of the West, . . . this poet in chaps and buckskin." Both cities were flourishing commercial centers whose leaders combined success in business with civic philanthropy and patronage of the arts. When Daniel Burnham and other members of the city's elite compared their city to Florence, they spoke of a Chicago yet to be; but in more ways than even they realized, it already was like the arrogant city of Cosimo de' Medici the Elder, an architecture aficionado who was also one of the most cunning capitalists of his day.

If such a comparison is not to be dismissed as a modern historian's version of Windy City hyperbole, we need to remember what fifteenth-century Florence was really like. A great art capital, it was also a lusty, aggressive city, hated and feared by urban rivals it put down in its furious drive for commercial supremacy in Tuscany. Its economic might, like Chicago's, came through its near total domination of its *contado*, or hinterland. In this battle for economic empire, St. Louis was Chicago's Siena.

Like Renaissance commercial tyrants, Chicago's business barons combined "cruelty and culture," "plunder and patronage." And like Cosimo the Elder, a number of them, Marshall Field and George Pullman most notably, rarely appeared in public and cared little about toleration or free expression. Had Pullman been a student of history, he would surely have sanctioned Cosimo's dictum that "men are not led by paternosters."

Florence was also a booster city. Florentines were tireless promoters of their city's greatness, and Jakob C. Burkhardt is not the only historian to note their penchant for measuring their city's superiority with the use of statistics, a favorite tactic of Chicago boosters.

One of Florence's greatest glories was its architecture. The Florentine elite had a passion for building, and their best buildings were constructed, like Chicago's, with rational clarity and often by architects who had little formal education and were therefore open to new ideas. Civic pride launched the ambitious public building programs of both cities, and in both cities buildings became the occasion for adventures in art and technology.

The challenge of the skyscraper—how to build tall and beautifully—was equal to that faced by Filippo Brunelleschi in designing the enormous dome of Florence's cathedral. And when Florentine patrons commissioned architects to design their new palaces, they sometimes demanded utilitarian structures, not extravagant urban showpieces—Cosimo instructing Michelozzo, the architect of his new palazzo, to provide spacious offices, storage rooms, and counting-houses for his family's burgeoning business. The architects of Chicago's first skyscrapers worked under similar client constraints, and the result, in both cities, was a new conception of architectural beauty.

This is not to say that Chicago produced a culture as sinuous and enduring as Florence's or even that Chicago and Florence were similar types of cities. They might have been alike in some interesting ways, but the real point of these parallels is to emphasize that in great cities crudity and commerce have often been accompanied by memorable advances in the arts. One has to wonder whether the architecture of either Florence or Chicago would have been possible in places less prosperous, prideful, and vital. John Root's Chicago, like Brunelleschi's Florence, was built in an age of élan by merchants and visionaries fired by the resolve to make their city the marvel of its age. The architecture of both places mirrors what went on in them, as these cities built their biographies in the buildings they created.

•

"No creation proved more challenging to the human spirit or gave men such a feeling of power and sense of achievement as the spread of two dozen and more skyscrapers around . . . the Loop . . . ," Henry Ericsson recalled Chicago's pride in its new commercial architecture. But the skyscraper was a Janus-like creation. A symbol, for Ericsson, of the city's "conquest" over the "hostile" forces of nature, it also epitomized its unbalanced approach to its own development: its untrammeled individualism, its love of sheer size and magnitude, its absolute faith in technology, its passion for land grabbing. "[In] the repelling region of 'skyscrapers,'" Henry Fuller wrote of 1890s Chicago, "the abuse of private initiative, the peculiar evil of the place and time, has reached its most monumental development."

It has become commonplace to argue that the skyscrapers of Chicago were built because rising land values and rents in the constricted Loop forced investors to build upward rather than outward. But the opposite soon became equally true: Skyscrapers raised urban values in a process in which the effect became the cause. The skyscraper—a great urban instrument of concentration—promoted profits in downtown land that dwarfed those piled up by suburban speculators like Paul Cornell. Marshall Field was the richest real estate investor in Chicago, and most of his holdings were in the thick of the city, where the biggest gains were to be made. The skyscraper was as much a machine for turning land into money as it was a new silhouette on the urban sky.

"Tear down that old rat trap and erect a sixteen-story building" became the sales pitch of Chicago's new real estate hustlers. This manner of creating a city—by unending demolition and reconstruction, building higher and higher—was one of Chicago's and New York's chief contributions, for both good and ill, to the American urban heritage. Both cities went about remaking themselves in this way because American municipal governments, unlike those in Europe, were reluctant to place restrictions on the height of buildings or on the ownership and use of downtown real estate. This American style of city building had scant respect for tradition or for anything else that stood in the way of what George Ade called "the greed of 'improvement'"; and it was Ade, a sensitive interpreter of urban change, who raised some of the most probing questions about Chicago's expansion into the sky.

In the summer after the fair, Ade went down to Wolf Point, the juncture of the river where Chicago was born, to find the old Green Tree Inn, built there in 1833 by James Kinzie. It wasn't where he first searched for it, having been moved a block or so away, but it looked, he thought, much as it must have back in Kinzie's day, a weather-beaten wooden building with "square-paned little windows." The Scandinavian who now owned the saloon knew that it was the oldest standing building in Chicago, but it would do him no good, he assured Ade, to advertise its historical significance. People in Chicago were not interested in history, even their own. His customers, he said, "would go where they could get the largest glass of beer."

Yet the history of the Green Tree Inn, an ancient building by Chicago standards, only went back sixty years, so short a time that one of its builders, Silas B. Cobb, was still living and had an office on Dearborn Street, a downtown artery becoming known for its skyscrapers. Ade paid a visit to the gray-bearded builder, and later that summer he ascended to the top of a skyscraper near Cobb's office for a bird's-eye view of the great city that had sprung up around the old hickory-framed tavern, named for a solitary oak that had stood near it. As he looked out over the "downtown confusion" of "destruction and construction," he wondered when "unfinished" Chicago would "reach the era of stability."

It was claimed that from the top of Burnham and Root's twenty-one-story-high Masonic Temple "one could see Council Bluffs, Iowa, 230 miles distant," Edgar Lee Masters wrote in his memoirs. "I had to try that out, and Uncle Henry took me to the Masonic Temple." The tallest building in the world when it was completed in time for the Columbian Exposition, the Masonic Temple was demolished a half century later to make way for yet another Chicago "improvement." "Not for many years at least," Ade observed prophetically, "will this great business center of Chicago be improved to its limits and thoroughly satisfied with itself."

The men who built the first Chicago skyline were not guided by a broad civic vision, as Baron Haussmann had been in remaking Paris. In New York and Chicago "the individual is supreme," Lincoln Steffens wrote in *Scribner's Magazine,* "and thus far, unchecked. . . . Each man builds for himself, according to his own taste," in a process of chaotic creativity that for many critics was the great problem of American metropolitan development. Chicago's architects and real estate developers fought public pressure to restrict the height of buildings as fiercely as Pullman and Field fought labor unions, and for the same reason—as an obstruction to their self-sanctified right to do as they wished with their own talents and resources.

Giving support to their position was the power of the building itself. In guidebooks of the late 1880s, the skyscrapers vied with the stockyards as Chicago's chief tourist attraction, and the raising of one of these monoliths from the city's pavement became a civic event. Unlike the interworkings of a slaughter house or a steel mill, the construction of a steel-frame skyscraper was a technological show that took place— like the building of a medieval cathedral—out in the open, in the heart of the town. When one of these notable new skyscrapers was finished, thousands of sightseers in a single week would crowd its public spaces for a peek into the coming age. "Men passengers clung to the bars and women shrieked in hysteria when one of the lightning elevators made a rocket leap for the roof," said George Ade of a skyscraper opening. "There was a restaurant in the basement, a cigar-stand in the main lobby and a barber-shop on the eleventh floor, to say nothing of mail-chutes, [and] a telegraph office." Tenants left behind musty rooms with dim yellow gaslights for square towers "where the elevators flew, [and] where the walls were of white marble and the electric lights were turned on by the snap of a button." For such improvements, Chicagoans happily permitted their downtown streets to be torn up until they resembled parts of the Bad Lands.

•

It was the construction of one of Chicago's least original buildings, designed by one of its oldest architects, that opened the way for the revolutionary innovations of the 1880s. The Chicago Board of Trade's decision in 1881 to award W. W. Boyington the commission to design its new headquarters at the head of La Salle Street led almost immediately to the appearance of Chicago's first skyscraper quarter in that undeveloped area of the city. Eager to locate close to the resituated nerve center of the midwestern economy, insurance and real estate companies, bankers and brokerage concerns, packers and provision dealers, supported the construction of a cluster of the finest commercial buildings in the world, including William Le Baron Jenney's Home Insurance Building—the world's first iron-skeleton skyscraper—and five "monster" business blocks by the firm that had lost the Board of Trade commission to Boyington. The most physically impressive of these Burnham and Root buildings, the Rookery, was located in the shadow of the Board of Trade's three-hundred-foot-high clock tower, and another of them, the Rialto—headquarters of some of the city's leading stockyard traders—was connected by an iron bridge to the Board of Trade's big-windowed exchange hall.

Turning onto La Salle Street from Monroe and walking south on a sunlit morning, a person would find the effect "awe-inspiring," wrote the Boston architect C. H. Blackall. Here one did not find, as in Manhattan, one or two tall, isolated buildings jutting out of an old skyline of five- and six-story structures, but solid rows of ten-story powerhouses, blocklike, not towerlike, in appearance, "the work," it seemed to Blackall, "of giants." To understand how these buildings were constructed, Blackall argued, was to come to a closer understanding of the merger of technology and profit seeking that was making modern Chicago.

The enabling technology of the skyscraper was the elevator: no elevator, no skyscraper. In all buildings before the skyscraper, altitude was limited "by the power of ascension of the unassisted human leg." These were the first high buildings in history in which the stairs had almost no use whatsoever.

•

In a great glass-and-iron exhibition hall crowded with people and inventions, a black-bearded man stood on a platform that had been raised to the ceiling. Pausing at the top for a dramatic moment, he shouted an order to his assistant, who pulled out a knife and slashed the rope that held up the platform. Some astonished onlookers turned away, not wanting to see the lunatic crash to his death. But the platform held, slipping only a few inches; and the showman cried out triumphantly, "All safe, gentlemen, all safe!"

It was a defining moment in architectural history, although no one in the hall, not even the showman himself, realized it. He was Elisha Graves Otis, a Yonkers, New York, bedstead maker and inventor. The device that saved his neck that day in 1853 at New York's Crystal Palace, site of America's first world's fair, was an automatic "safety hoist," a braking instrument for the steam elevators Otis had begun building the year before at his workshop on the Hudson River but had had difficulty selling. It was a device of astonishing simplicity. When the rope that raised and lowered the platform broke, the weight of the elevator forced a long steel wagon spring to uncoil and lock into the notched guardrails on the elevator's shaft, stopping the platform's fall with a bone-jarring jerk.

Steam-powered hoists were being used at the time in warehouses and grain elevators, but their cables had a habit of breaking. Otis's machine was the first elevator safe for passenger use—once, that is, its safety system was improved, making the cab stop less abruptly. In inventing a new form of vertical transportation, Otis opened the way for vertical architecture. What the electric streetcar was to suburbanization, the elevator car—an aerial railway—was to the downtown high-rise.

Otis died in 1861, before he had an opportunity to see the cultural consequences of his hoisting machinery, the most sudden and stunning change in the historic city's physical appearance since the raising of the first temple towers by the ancient Assyrians. His two sons, however, carried on the family business, and by 1868 they had perfected a steam passenger elevator with a half-dozen safety features and a car of "Babylonian elegance" for use in hotels and office buildings.

Elevators, however, did not lead immediately to high-rise office buildings. They merely made it easier for owners to get better rents for the top floors of five-story office lofts, whereas before, "as the stairs marched upward," so the saying went, "they met rental values coming down." Architects were slow to see these clumsy hoisting appliances as a way of taking buildings to unprecedented heights. The first office building with an elevator (some historians consider it the first skyscraper) was the 130-foot-high Equitable Life Assurance Company Building, completed in 1870 in Manhattan. But the first truly tall buildings—George B. Post's Western Union Building and Richard Morris Hunt's Tribune Tower—were not built in New York City until five years later. They rose to 230 and 260 feet, respectively, nearly to the top of Trinity Church's 284-foot spire, which was not exceeded by a skyscraper until the early 1890s, at which point "the enterprise of business," as Lincoln Steffens noted, "surpassed the aspiration of religion."

Montgomery Schuyler called Manhattan's elevator buildings of the 1870s "tentatives." The only thing that made them skyscrapers was their unusual height, for they were built with traditional construction techniques, their interior plans were not efficient for office use, and their façades were strongly derivative. They were awkward buildings, many of them topped by stupendous Victorian towers, and with their heavy ornamentation, they looked more like fantastic urban palaces than houses of modern business.

Just as the elevator made the tall office building possible, so improvements in elevator technology made it possible to double their height. In 1878 the hydraulic elevator, patented in Chicago by C. W. Baldwin, was introduced simultaneously in that city and New York by the Otis Company and the Chicago firm of William E. Hale, one of the two men Louis Sullivan credited with being "responsible for the modern office building." Hydraulic elevators were faster than steam elevators and gave a smoother ride. Their elaborate internal mechanisms, driven by pressure in municipal water mains, made it feasible to raise buildings to the limit of brick-bearing walls. The problem was that no one knew how to build such buildings in 1878.

Architecture is a profession strongly dependent on precedent, but the skyscraper, as Sullivan said, was "something new under the sun," calling for construction techniques never before used. This was Chicago's great contribution to architectural history. In less than a decade, in "one of the most concentrated bursts of creative energy in nineteenth century technology," it showed the world how to build truly tall buildings, buildings held up by light frameworks of steel, their outer walls transformed into thin curtains with no structural function, much like the glass-and-iron-framed Crystal Palace in which Elisha Graves Otis first demonstrated his safety hoist.

•

"Not since man began to pile one stone upon another," wrote Barr Ferree, "has so difficult a problem been offered to the architect as the design of a high building." For one thing, the skyscraper was the first building to depend on machines for its operation. It needed machines to light, heat, and ventilate its interior spaces, parts of which would have been, without the aid of these machines, as dark and cold as a cave; and without elevators—the building's own hydraulic or electric rail system—the upper stories of a skyscraper would have been as "inaccessible as a mountain-top." Communication machines like the telephone and the telegraph put "tenants in the air" in touch with the city below, while pneumatic tubes carried messages and parcels to other offices in the building. And architects gave older materials like steel and fireclay new machine-age uses in order to make their new buildings fireproof, earthquakeproof, and hurricaneproof.

These were the costliest and largest habitable structures ever erected on American soil, huge not just in height but in mass, some of them housing daytime populations equal to those of considerable towns, two to three thousand tenants in a fifteen-story building. "A great office building is really a city under one roof," wrote the Chicago journalist Ray Stannard Baker. "It has its own electric lighting plant . . . ; it has its own water works system, with a big stand pipe at the top to supply the upper floors . . . ; it has its own well-drilled fire department, with fire plugs on every floor, and hose lines and chemical extinguishers; and it has its own police department, for every great building is now supplied with regular detectives who watch for petty thieves and pickpockets, and prevent peddlers and beggars from entering their domain." It even had its own mail system, "a long glass and iron tube through which a tenant on any floor may drop a letter to the big box in the basement." An English friend of Baker's, on his first visit to America, stood transfixed for a half hour watching the letters float downward through one of these glass tubes. "That is the most wonderful thing I've seen in America," he told Baker, "that, and the little tube with red oil in it which tells when the lift is coming."

One architect could not handle a tall-office-building commission. It was the skyscraper that gave rise to the modern' architectural office, with its greatly enlarged staff of draftsmen, architects, and engineers, who were forced to learn by trial and error, from building project to building project, how to make these colossi safe and sturdy, comfortable and convenient for the conduct of business. It was in these matters that Chicago architects and engineers led the world at the end of the nineteenth century. After 1880, Chicago surged ahead of New York in skyscraper construction, not only in the number of tall buildings erected but in their quality and structural inventiveness. As a New York trade publication conceded in 1891: "It is a common remark in Eastern and foreign cities among those actively engaged in building that Chicago today erects the best built structures ever known." That so many of these great buildings survive today, in excellent condition, is testimony to the genius of those who designed and built them.

Chicago had the best modern office buildings because it had the best modern architects—and also because it had progressive businessmen who were willing to spend money smartly to build them well. "The 'modern office building,'" as Louis Sullivan wrote, "is the joint project of the speculator, the engineer, the builder." The very idea of the skyscraper—the vision itself—was the brainchild of the real estate man, not the architect.

In "Tall Office Buildings—Past and Future," one of the most insightful essays ever written about the skyscraper, Dankmar Adler, Sullivan's partner, explained why Chicago real estate investors were prepared not just to build tall buildings but to do so excellently. It was, he said, a creative convergence of engineering science and capitalist cupidity. When the price of structural iron dropped and Chicago's architects developed new methods of fireproofing, local real estate investors became eager to push buildings to new heights, convinced by the popularity of five- and six-story elevator office lofts that tenants would pay good rents for bright and noiseless offices "high in the air." Investors came to see, at the same time, that it made greater economic sense to build big rather than small. "Within certain limits," Adler explained, "the proportionate cost of high-grade, first-class modern buildings diminishes with their size. To erect a small fire-proof building, and to equip it with boilers, engines, dynamos, pumps, tanks, elevators, and so forth, involves an outlay relatively greater than that required for a larger building." Thus, if the owner of a small office building wished to equip it with the same thoroughness of a skyscraper, "he will be at a disadvantage, even supposing that he is satisfied with a smaller margin of profit."

That was a reason to build big; but why build well, especially in Chicago, where business buildings had notoriously been thrown up on the cheap? It was simple, Adler said: to make money. Or perhaps he should have said, not to lose it. The unprecedented cost of a skyscraper made its investors anxious to fortify themselves against "total failure of their enterprise," failure being the inability to fill the building with tenants willing to pay higher rents than they paid for offices in low-rise buildings. Luring such attractive tenants required giving the architect leeway to design a building that was safe, comfortable, well lit, and impressively modern in its appointments and equipment. To get first-rate tenants, by Adler's logic, you had to get first-rate architects; to get big returns on investment, you had to spend big money on the investment. The business principle on which these buildings were based was the identical one that had made George Pullman the world's "Sleeping Car King": the proven idea that the customer will pay more for a superior product.

But spending money on the product did not mean spending it foolishly. Successful investors in Chicago skyscrapers supervised the design and construction of their buildings as scrupulously as George Pullman had supervised the building of his first Palace Car. And, like Pullman, they watched costs with an eagle eye, cutting back on expensive exterior decoration to make handsome additions to the interior, that part of the building—as was the case with the sleeping car—that would finally determine its profitability. Sensitive artists like Sullivan and Root often complained about cost-shaving clients, but they became better architects because of the disciplining pressure of the capitalist.

Such a convergence of architectural talent and entrepreneurial savvy produced Chicago's first skyscraper, the ten-story Montauk Block, the collaborative creation of a cost-conscious speculator, a visionary real estate manager, and two up-and-coming architects, one an artist who was also an engineer, the other a builder who was also a businessman.

2. Burnham and Root

Daniel Hudson Burnham, the greatest builder in Chicago's history, arrived in the city in 1855 at the age of nine with a struggling family seeking a fresh start in the rising American West. His father had been a failure in business in western New York, but in surging Chicago he prospered in the wholesale drug business and became the first president of the city's Mercantile Association. During the Civil War, Burnham was sent back east to prepare for Harvard. Hard-muscled and ruggedly good-looking, he was a crack athlete with a talent and passion for drawing. "He was never without a pencil in his hand," a friend remembered him, "and . . . was the . . . leader in all [the boys'] efforts for physical improvement." But schoolwork didn't interest him, and he surprised none of his friends when he failed the entrance examinations for both Harvard and Yale, sitting through several of the Harvard exams frozen with fear, unable to put down a single word.

After working briefly as a salesman in Chicago, he decided, half-heartedly, he wanted to be an architect and found work as a draftsman's apprentice in an office headed by William Le Baron Jenney. Always eager to gain favor with his mother, the dominant influence on his development, he wrote her in 1868 of his determination to be "the greatest architect in the city or country." The following year, however, he was on a train bound for Nevada mining country with his schoolboy friend Edward C. Waller, later the great patron of Frank Lloyd Wright. "There is a family tendency," he wrote years later, "to get tired of doing the same thing very long."

The two sanguine adventurers failed to strike silver or gold, and Burnham failed to make it in local politics when Waller's money ran out. After his narrow defeat for the Nevada state senate, he and Waller hopped a cattle train headed back to Chicago, where Waller went into real estate and Burnham made a second try at architecture. Determined to cure his son's "roving disposition," Edwin Burnham got him a position in the office of Carter, Drake, and Wight, a firm established just after the Great Fire. With Peter B. Wight's sympathetic encouragement, Burnham honed his drawing skills, learned the inner workings of a successful architectural practice, and finally found his direction. And here, on his first day on the job, he met his future partner.

John Wellborn Root had been called to Chicago by Peter Wight, who had been impressed with his "original designs" when they were both working in New York City. "After my visit to Chicago to see the ruins [of] the Great Fire . . . I asked him to call at my office in New York, which he did, and then told him I would send for him as soon as there should be an opening." Root had a "great desire to go West," Wight recalls, to take part in what promised to be the greatest urban rebuilding effort of modern times.

Four years younger than Burnham, Root had never known failure. He was the son of a transplanted northern businessman who married a Georgia belle, Mary Clark, and made a fortune during the war financing blockade runners for the Confederacy. From infancy, young Root was prodigiously gifted in a number of directions. He could sing before he learned to talk, began drawing almost as soon as he could hold a pencil, and could play the piano as well as his teacher when he was barely twelve.

Sent on one of his father's blockade breakers to Liverpool, England, after William Tecumseh Sherman sacked Atlanta, where his family was living in 1864, Root had just passed the entrance exams to Oxford when his family called him home in 1866, to New York City, where they had relocated and his father had begun to slide into bankruptcy. Blessed with equal talents in drawing and music, Root entered the civil engineering program at New York University, there being no school of architecture in the entire United States. After graduating with honors, he worked as an unpaid apprentice to James Renwick, Jr., architect of St. Patrick's Cathedral, and at age twenty became superintendent of construction in a Manhattan firm engaged in building the first Grand Central Terminal, one of the engineering marvels of the time. It was from there that he went to take part in building a city like none ever built before.

Burnham and Root became friends the day they met, though they were nearly opposite in talent and temperament. Root was a natural. "[He] was essentially a self-taught man," said Wight, "possessed in his youth of the greatest acquisitiveness I have ever witnessed." Root impressed everyone he encountered with his brilliance not only in architecture but in nearly everything to which he turned his ferociously active mind. Trained by one of England's supreme music teachers, he could have been a concert pianist. He read widely in art and architecture history, European politics, natural science, philosophy, and religion, and shortly after arriving in Chicago, he began writing art and opera criticism for the *Tribune,* where he made friends among the writers and editors. "His conversational powers were extraordinary," Chicago journalist Eugene Field wrote of his friend's vitalizing influence; "there seemed to be no subject which he had not investigated and in which he was not profoundly learned." And he wrote with power, lucidity, and wit.

Root carried his learning lightly. He was a natural charmer, with a soft southern accent and faultless manners, a bit shy but ever so sure of himself. He also had a delightfully mischievous sense of humor. To supplement his income as a struggling architect, he played the organ at the First Presbyterian Church, and one Sunday during services he broke into a rendition of the black minstrel song "Shoo, Fly," playing it "with such solemn slowness and with so many variations," wrote his friend and biographer the poet Harriet Monroe, "that no one noticed the indecorum." Years later, at the cornerstone ceremony of one of his most celebrated Chicago buildings, the headquarters of the Woman's Christian Temperance Union, Root turned to his friends after enduring a children's chorus performance of "The Saloons Must Go" and suggested that they cut away for a drink.

Burnham lacked Root's quick wit, his parlor-room polish, and his sparkling demeanor, but the two friends had much in common, and each needed the other to bring his talents to fruition. Root, with close-cut reddish hair, a full mustache, and flashing blue eyes, was as handsome as Burnham and, with "arms of iron," his equal as an athlete. Burnham, too, loved music, and both liked to swim and sail, to fence and lift barbells, and to court eligible young women at Chicago parties.

Together at social occasions, they made a striking impression. A Chicago society woman remembers Root as "the most . . . iridescent, radiant thing in the world. . . . When he and Mr. Burnham were together I used always to think of some big strong tree with lightning playing around it."

They were two of the most sought after bachelors in Chicago, and they had a "magnetic power over men" as well—Root with his brilliance and Burnham with his splendid plans and dreams, backed by a fixity of purpose now that he had put behind him his early failures. "He always lacked application," Burnham's mother had written of him as a student, but not long after meeting Root, application became his supreme attribute. Burnham came to be known as a young man capable of getting things done, of moving projects forward, whereas Root lacked discipline, often escaping into his music or his musings when he might have been doing architecture. It was Burnham's qualities of persistence and determination, says Monroe, that "saved Root from dilettantism." But it was Root, as Burnham never failed to acknowledge, who was the original one. "My partner . . . is a wonder, a great artist," Burnham described him to Sullivan before Sullivan had ever heard of him. "I want you to meet him some day; you'll like him."

•

Enticed by the prospect of designing homes in the suburbs for one of their friends, a young real estate broker named George Chambers, Burnham and Root formed their own partnership in the spring of 1873, their first office a small room they rented for twenty dollars a month. They could not have gone out on their own at a worse time. The Panic of 1873 put an end to the "Derrick Days" in Chicago, and to keep their firm afloat, they divided time working for better-situated architects. "With a couple of pencils, a piece of rubber, a few boards, two stools and a dozen thumb tacks, we did business," Burnham recalled, "Between us, we had a full color box and one stick of India-ink." Then, as fast as bad fortune had struck them, good luck came marching through the door—in the form of the very same George Chambers. A friend of John B. Sherman, the "father of the Union Stock Yards," Chambers convinced Sherman to hire Burnham and Root to design a mansion for him at 2100 Prairie Avenue.

It was the turning point in the young firm's fortunes. Passing by the Sherman house on one of his walking surveys of the city, eighteen-year-old Louis Sullivan thought it "the best-designed residence" in town, and well-connected Chicago families had begun asking about its designers. When the house was under construction, Burnham was always at the site, joined there for an hour or so every afternoon by Sherman's radiant daughter Margaret. She had fallen in love with him the day she met him and "used to hang around the new work in order to see him." The couple were engaged before the house was finished, and the wedding took place in sumptuous Prairie Avenue style in January 1876. That brilliant morning ended Burnham and Root's "starving time."

Sherman put his new son-in-law and his winsome partner in touch with the biggest names in the livestock and packing business, and commissions began to come in—to build a water-tower observatory and a stone entrance gate for the Union Stock Yards (the first two of many structures the partners built at the yards) and to design homes for barons of beef and pork once the depression lifted: for the Hutchinson family; for Sidney A. Kent, one of the founders of the Union Stock Yards; and for James M. Walker, president of the Union Stock Yard and Transit Company and general solicitor of the Chicago, Burlington & Quincy Railroad.

While Walker's house was under construction, Root fell in love with and married Walker's daughter Mary Louise. She died of tuberculosis only six weeks into the marriage, but Root lived for several years with the Walkers on Prairie Avenue, and later Walker got Burnham and Root the commission to design a huge new Chicago office building for his railroad. All the while, Sherman, despite concern about his son-in-law's drinking habits, helped him land the commission to design the Rialto Building on La Salle Street for Sidney Kent and Philip Armour; and several years later, Armour hired the firm to design his mission on the South Side. With both partners securely planted in Chicago society, other clients came their way. It was a two-way process: Friends became clients, and clients became friends, most of their new friends and clients belonging to either the Chicago Club or the Calumet Club, whose clubhouse on Michigan Avenue Burnham and Root designed in the early 1880s, its façade strongly echoing the Sherman residence.

It was an architectural partnership of unusual amicability, "and the work of each man," Harriet Monroe wrote, "became constantly more necessary to the other." Root was the designer and Burnham the businessman; that is how the partnership is conventionally seen. It was a more interactive arrangement than that, however. Root had a strong interest in the engineering aspect of a building and a sharp eye for figures, and Burnham was a fine architect in his own right, a master at laying out the ground plan for a building. He would sketch it in a few hours—sometimes a few minutes—once he knew his client's needs. He would then pass on this rough plan to his partner, who would refine it until it satisfied his own fiercely exacting standards. "He could really see it," said Burnham. "I've never seen anyone like him in this respect. He would grow abstracted and silent, and a faraway look would come into his eyes, and the building was there before him—every stone of it."

While Root worked alone at his drafting table, Burnham handled what Root called the "jaw work," meeting with clients in the office or at his club, ever mindful of what Henry Hobson Richardson identified as the first principle of architecture: "Get the job."

The firm's first chance to do something big came in 1879 when Root met a young, Yale-educated real estate lawyer named Owen F. Aldis at a Chicago reception. Both men had had classical educations and had studied in Europe, and after being introduced, they drifted into a small room and talked until one in the morning. "No other man," Aldis recalls, "ever impressed me so quickly and so deeply." Neither of them so much as mentioned architecture that evening, and Root apparently had no idea that Aldis's job was to recommend promising architects to his wealthy clients, but "from that night I knew he was a genius," Aldis said later, "and the next day I brought him a building."

It was the commission for the Grannis Block, a seven-story office building on a Dearborn Street lot owned by Aldis's most important client, Peter Chardon Brooks III, a young Massachusetts investor whose family had accumulated a fortune in the shipping-insurance business. "Here our originality began to show," Burnham said of the firm's first office building. "We made the front of the building all red, the terra-cotta exactly matching the brick. It was a wonder. Everybody went to see it, and the town was proud of it." When it was completed, Burnham and Root moved their offices to its top floor, and it was here, in 1881, that Aldis came to them with a commission that would begin the transformation of the entire cityscape of Chicago. "What Chartres was to the Gothic cathedral," wrote a Chicago architect and historian, "the Montauk Block was to the high commercial building."

•

Owen Aldis was that other person Louis Sullivan named as being "responsible for the modern office building." William E. Hale's high-speed hydraulic elevators made tall buildings feasible, but it was Aldis who convinced wary investment clients to build them. By the end of the century, he was managing almost 20 percent of Chicago's downtown office space for real estate speculators. He had a commanding influence—amounting almost to a veto—on the layout and design of high office buildings, a greater influence, in many instances, than that of the architects.

His power arose naturally from the character of the buildings he supervised. They were speculations, and the business that was conducted in them, it must be remembered, could easily have been conducted elsewhere, as it was, for example, in London or Paris, in three- and four-story "walk-ups." Tall buildings were built in Chicago because real estate property managers like Aldis were able to convince speculators organized into investment pools that they could bring tall profits. And these risky investments eventually became profitable because these same property managers were able to convince companies, small and large, that the most convenient and efficient way to conduct their affairs was in a building of ten or more stories, where they could share space with firms with whom they did business. The skyscraper, Aldis argued, made it far easier to do business in Chicago than in London, where much time was wasted in going from firm to firm all over the sprawling city and climbing the steep stairs of run-down buildings to small, poorly lit offices that were dusty and foul-smelling.

Descended from a distinguished Vermont legal family, Aldis arrived in Chicago in 1875 at the age of twenty-four and set up a law practice that specialized in managing local property for eastern investors, including his father, Judge Asa O. Aldis. Two of his clients, Peter Brooks and his brother Shephard, had invested in Chicago real estate as early as the 1860s, but when the national economic depression lifted in 1880, they were ready to sink much more of their family's fortune into growing Chicago. And Peter Brooks, a far more audacious investor than his brother, was ready, after the success of the Grannis Block, to commission a building to rival the tallest in Manhattan, for Aldis had convinced him that the time for such skyward structures had arrived in Chicago.

The skyscraper was the symbol of a new form of capitalism—centralized, specialized, and thickly bureaucratic. As a number of Chicago's primary businesses became gigantic national and global operations, the size of their office staffs grew tremendously. At the same time, these firms became interested in relocating the managerial-administrative side of their businesses—originally situated right at the production site—to the downtown area. There they would be close to legal, clerical, and financial services they had come to depend on and to centralized transportation facilities for their growing number of white-collar workers, who lived all over the chaotically expanding city. In the 1880s the firms of Pullman, Armour, and McCormick, along with a host of other businesses, moved their central headquarters to the Loop, a physical transfer made possible by the invention in 1876 of the telephone, which kept the two sides of the business—production and management—in instantaneous contact. Bureaucratic capitalism, along with centralized retailing and mass transportation and communications, created Chicago's downtown concentration, and this concentration made the skyscraper almost a creature of necessity.

But conditions peculiar to Chicago also influenced architects to reach for the sky. The *Tribune* summed up the situation: "Since water hems in the business centre on three sides and a nexus of railroads on the remaining, the south, Chicago must grow upward." It was this telling fact—that the business district could not move—that Owen Aldis surely impressed upon Peter Brooks, who rarely if ever visited Chicago, preferring—because of his frail health—to manage his investments from his family's three-thousand-acre estate in Medford, Massachusetts.

•

"Limited as to the ground, business sought the air," wrote an early observer of high-rise construction. "It had to be done; but how? That was the question." When Peter Brooks had Owen Aldis hire Burnham and Root to design the Montauk Block, his greatest concern, however, was not how to build tall but how to hold a tall building safely in Chicago's soft, shifting soil. He wanted to build a high office building, he wrote Aldis, "if the earth can support it in the opinion of the architects." This was a problem that intrigued Root, whose talent lay in construction as well as design. "As an engineer," wrote Harriet Monroe, "he was always venturesome: because a thing had never been done before was no reason, in his mind, why it could not be done safely." He was fortunate as well to be in a city whose astonishing growth "made such great demands upon both architects and engineers," as one of these engineers observed, "that they have been forced to be progressive."

Chicago's foundation problems "[are] probably not equalled for perverseness anywhere in the world," wrote C. H. Blackall in 1888. Bedrock—a layer of thick limestone from 90 to 150 feet below the Loop—could not be safely reached, through water and caving soil, by existing digging techniques, and above the bedrock was a sixty- to seventy-foot layer of sand and soft clay that would not support foundation piles. The water level of Chicago, moreover, was only fifteen feet or so below ground, making it impossible to construct buildings with big two- and three-level basements, such as was common in New York, where bedrock was far closer to the surface.

It was difficult to make a building of any size stand up in this Chicago quagmire. "More buildings tumbled over in the early days than there is any record of," Henry Ericsson wrote of antebellum Chicago. It was through the trial-and-error "tussle to conquer the problems of foundations," he added, "that men of Chicago came to make contributions to the art and science of modern building, quite outdistancing . . . those of any other single group of men in modern times." The Chicago skyscraper, like Chicago itself, was a triumph of technology over natural circumstances.

Frederick H. Baumann, a brilliant German immigrant, was the first engineer to find a way to solidly support five- and six-story masonry buildings in Chicago soil. His procedure, as outlined in his influential 1873 pamphlet on "pier foundations," was to dig down to a shallow layer of dry clay, called hardpan, and to build great pyramids of stone on beds of concrete in the building's basement to support the tremendous weight of the walls. These pyramids had to be broad enough to evenly distribute the building's load, allowing the structure to settle uniformly, a system of support as old as the Eskimo and his snowshoes.

Root used Baumann's system for part of the Montauk's foundation but ran into trouble at the heaviest side of the building, a wall that was to hold a high stack of fireproof vaults. Here pyramidal foundations would have had to be built so wide and high that they would have taken up almost the entire basement, leaving no room for the dynamos and central heating system. Ordered by Aldis to somehow provide more space in the basement, Root—in a mere day or two of focused thought—came up with an idea that revolutionized the system of foundations for tall buildings.

Root instructed the contractor to put down a thin bed of cement on the level clay and place on it a grillage of crisscrossed steel rails, covering this with Portland cement to prevent the steel from rusting. The process was repeated until the builder had a wide and smooth pad with "great transverse as well as crushing strength." The pad was then fitted with large cast-iron "shoes" into which the base of the columns of the building's frame were placed. This concrete-and-steel raft—a "floating foundation," Root called it—spread a column load safely over a large area of subsoil.

Root's lightweight steel-and-concrete footing of less than two feet of thickness was found to be as strong as a stone pyramid seven feet high. In later buildings, Root used floating foundations to support the entire structure, and this system was used by other architects for some of Chicago's greatest buildings until caisson-created foundations reaching all the way to hard rock were developed in the 1890s. Even today, however, grillages of steel and concrete set on bedrock are used to help support some of the tallest buildings in the world.

"In carrying out [Root's] plan," Aldis wrote, "we were surprised to find that the new kind of foundations was cheaper than the old." This news was particularly pleasing to Peter Brooks. The recklessness of these first skyscraper ventures—where staggering sums of money were put up for buildings that had yet to prove they could pay— caused developers like Brooks to be superconscious about cost considerations, a concern that translated into close client supervision of every aspect of the building's design and construction. The clean-featured Chicago Style that powerfully influenced Bauhaus architects of the next century was originally more the result of economizing pressure placed on architects by speculators than of the aesthetic ideas of the architects themselves, which is why Chicago skyscraper architecture cannot be understood simply through the ideas and plans of its architects.

In all such strictly utilitarian buildings, architects worked under tight financial requirements. But in the no-nonsense business environment of Chicago, these requirements were applied with unusual severity, and that is what made Chicago's commercial architecture distinctive and original. In New York, as Montgomery Schuyler observed in 1895, architects would try "to persuade or to hoodwink" their clients into "sacrificing something of utility to 'art.'" When they were successful, the result was business buildings that looked, incongruously, like Greek temples or Roman baths. Peter Brooks was not a Chicago capitalist, but he thought like one. He exerted such financial pressure on Root on the Montauk project that the architect, in a rage after several of his designs were rejected as too ornate, made one in frustration that he called a "sugar-factory." This was the design Peter Brooks finally approved.

"I prefer to have a plain structure of face brick . . . with flat roof," Brooks had instructed Aldis even before the architects submitted their preliminary sketches. "The building throughout is to be for use and not for ornament. Its beauty will be in its all-adaptation to its use"— words that antedate Louis Sullivan's architectural dictum that form must follow function. Brooks wanted, he told Aldis, no ornamental "projections . . . (which catch dirt)," and "the less plumbing the less trouble. It should be concentrated as much as possible, all pipes to show and be accessible, [and] . . . if necessary painted well and handsomely." After Burnham and Root submitted their first sketches, Brooks sharply reprimanded them for not taking into account the costs of their ideas, and he flatly rejected the use of tile—except for the showcase first floor—and stained glass. "Colored glass is mere nonsense," wrote this scion of New England Puritans, "a passing fashion, inappropriate in a mercantile building and worse than all, it obstructs the light. Strike it all out." Although the building was wired for electricity, Brooks understood that his potential renters needed light as much as space to conduct their businesses and that artificial lighting, then in its infancy, provided insufficient illumination.

The result of these requirements was a ten-story building as austere and tightly functional as a machine, all the floors, except the first two, identical in style. To Brooks, it truly was a machine, a money-generating engine by the fact that all parts were subordinate to the instrument's primary purpose: the provision of efficient space for the conduct of capitalist work. Peter Brooks was no penny-pincher; he spent money where money would make him even more money. The money saved on—to him—frivolous façade decoration was used to provide state-of-the-art heating, plumbing, and elevator systems, gas as well as electrical lighting, and the most advanced system of fireproofing up to that time.

•

The interior of the Montauk was supported by an iron frame, which could have been cause for concern. Before the Great Fire, iron—a noncombustible material—was assumed to be fireproof, but the decorative cast-iron fronts and iron-supporting members of Chicago's newest downtown buildings gave way in the devouring heat of the holocaust, bending, buckling, and collapsing into tangled heaps or else splintering and fracturing when exposed to the cold-water blasts of the fire hoses. This experience threw iron under suspicion as a building material. By the time the Montauk was under construction, however, Peter B. Wight, Burnham and Root's old employer, had perfected a system of fireproofing iron with terra-cotta, an ancient earth-colored clay used for pots and tiles. Aldis hired Wight as the fireproofing contractor on the Montauk building, and Wight clad all metal structural parts with hollow blocks of terra-cotta, the air spaces acting as an insulator. He also installed a subflooring of hollow tiles in the form of arches, a variant of a method experimentally used after the Great Fire by a New York contractor, George H. Johnson, in John Van Osdel's Kendall Building of 1873, but ignored by most Chicago architects of the 1870s in the reckless drive to rebuild hastily and cheaply.

Wight's extensive use of terra-cotta sheathing made the Montauk the most completely fireproof tall building in existence. It also greatly lightened the building's weight, ensuring—with Root's floating foundations—a secure settlement in Chicago's treacherously moist soil. By demonstrating a way to make big buildings lighter, safer, and less expensive—the savings on fire insurance alone being considerable in a fireproof structure—Wight and other Chicago fireproofing contractors opened the way for a burst of skyscraper construction in the city in the next ten years. Real estate developers were convinced that tall buildings were, at last, structurally safe investments.

After the completion of the Montauk Block, Chicago architects began using greater amounts of fireproofed iron to help support the walls of tall office buildings, a combined iron-and-masonry wall being much lighter than an all-masonry one. This allowed architects to safely build skyscrapers over twelve stories, the height previously considered the upper limit of masonry buildings constructed on Chicago's soil. To the list of Chicago's legendary builders, then, should be added the name of a forgotten architect who never designed a skyscraper but who, in taming fire, allowed others to reach for the clouds. By the mid-1880s, terra-cotta—the product of fire—had made downtown Chicago more secure against the spread of fire than any other business center in the world. So before the sky over Chicago could be filled with a forest of buildings, the city's architects had to conquer gravity and fire, and this was accomplished for the first time in one building with the Montauk Block commission.

•

Although John Root never liked the bleakly utilitarian Montauk Block, Burnham saw it as a prototype for the commercial structures his firm would gain a reputation for building. Burnham was especially proud of the speed with which it had been built, an essential consideration to the impatient speculator, whose money realized no returns until the offices were painted and ready to rent. Burnham had pushed the work through the punishing Chicago winter, making the Montauk the first commercial building in that city to be constructed year-round. Salt was added to mortar to make bricklaying possible in subfreezing temperatures, the concrete was insulated with straw, and a heated canvas tent was draped over the site. Electric lights under the tarpaulin made it possible to complete the foundations and basement in rain and snow and far into the night, making it the first building in the world constructed with the aid of artificial illumination.

"From the hour that the ground for a new building is put at his disposal the work of construction must go on at the highest rate of speed," said Montgomery Schuyler of the time pressures on Chicago architects. "And so the successful practitioner of architecture in Chicago is primarily an administrator." And that is what Daniel Burnham became. "My idea is to work up a big business," Burnham had told Louis Sullivan when they first met, "to handle big things, deal with big business men and to build up a big organization, for you can't handle big things unless you have an organization." Peter Wight would later describe his former draftsman as "one of the greatest businessmen of all time. . . . As an organizer and promoter he stands with the commercial and financial giants of the day."

Even as he worked on the Montauk project, Burnham was putting together the largest, most professionally run architectural practice in the city, with an extensive research library and a team of draftsmen and consulting engineers, a growing practice he housed in the top story of the Montauk. "He was the dictator," an associate captured him in his prime, "who organized the work of various mechanical and technical experts who contributed to the making of tall buildings."

The first Chicago skyscraper, the Montauk was also the first building in the city to shatter the notion that the street floor of an elevator office building was more desirable than the top floor. "There are men called 'high livers,'" wrote Lincoln Steffens, "who will not have an office unless it is up where the air is cool and fresh, the outlook broad and beautiful, and where there is silence in the heart of business." On every elevator ride to the top of the Montauk there was an invisible passenger, the value of land in the Loop.

After Owen Aldis rented out all 150 offices of the Montauk, Peter Brooks was eager to invest further in Chicago office buildings, and Burnham and Root became his architects of preference. In the next half decade, the young partners designed some of the biggest and finest office buildings in the world, most of them on or near La Salle Street. The best of them was the red-faced Rookery, a breakthrough building for Root as a designer.

•

The eleven-story Rookery, in the shadow of Boyington's Board of Trade Building, was commissioned by a consortium of investors, including Peter Brooks, the major stockholder; William Hale, the elevator tycoon; Edward Waller, Burnham's boyhood friend; Owen Aldis; and Burnham himself, by this time a rich man. The group organized itself as the Central Safety Deposit Company—president, Owen F. Aldis—incorporated for the ostensible purpose of building a structure to house fireproof safety vaults. The company was a legal subterfuge, a phantom organization called into existence—like many others similar to it in 1880s Chicago—to dodge an Illinois statute prohibiting speculative building by limited-liability corporations.

The site of the Central Safety Deposit Company's "banking" building was city-owned land designated for school purposes. But Edward Waller had influence with the mayor, Carter Harrison, a fellow Kentuckian and former real estate speculator who had been a neighbor of the Wallers in Chicago's Kentucky "colony" on the West Side. Harri-

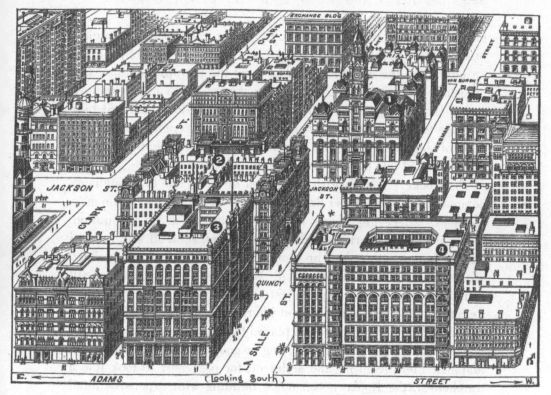

Vicinity of the Board of Trade. Here is where the first group of Chicago high build-ings was erected in the early 1880s. The nine-story Board of Trade Building (no. 1, center), completed in 1885, was at the head of La Salle Street. The trading hall, "the marketplace of the world," was located on the second floor, with its eighty-foot-high windows. The Grand Pacific Hotel (no. 2), a famous meeting place of traders, was right next to the Board of Trade Building. The eleven-story Rookery's central light court (no. 3) can be seen from this angle. Burnham and Root's offices were on the upper floor. Burnham and Root's ten-story Rand-McNally Building (no. 4) was the first skyscraper in the world completely supported by an all-steel skeleton frame. Natural light in this building also came from an interior court.
Bird's-eye Views and Guide to Chicago (Chicago: Rand, McNally & Co., 1898)

son was prohibited from selling school property to Waller, but he did the next best thing, leasing it to the Central Safety Deposit Company for ninety-nine years—an eternity in Chicago time.

The building, completed in 1888, was named for the one that was torn down to make way for it. After the Great Fire, a temporary city hall and water tower had been built at La Salle and Adams Streets. There was a horse barn in the rear that attracted droves of pigeons and crows, and Chicagoans began calling their ramshackle municipal building "the rookery." But a "rook" is also a name for a cheat and a swindler, and the moniker called to mind the corrupt aldermen who "roosted" at 209 La Salle Street. Brooks wanted a more dignified name, but Chicagoans would accept no other, Aldis informed him. Perhaps to make certain the name stuck, the irreverent Root had two pairs of laughing rooks—Old World birds akin to the North American crow—carved into the building's granite entrance arch.

The Rookery is a Moorish citadel set down on one of capitalism's commanding streets. Peter Brooks requested a building of "plain massiveness," suggesting Henry Hobson Richardson as an inspiration. Root gave him his dark, formidable exterior but set it off with fanciful Islamic minarets that shoot up over the building's flat, sharply defined roofline. Like Richardson's Field Warehouse, the Rookery—still standing today after an inspired restoration—has tier after closely set tier of high and wide windows. But whereas the lowest row of windows of Richardson's warehouse were placed too high for passing pedestrians to look through them (there being no good reason, one can picture Marshall Field lecturing the architect, for passersby to look into a warehouse), the Rookery—an office building with expensive retail space on its ground floor—has big sidewalk-level bay windows. These are separated by columns of highly polished granite that break up the block-long front wall into what looks like a row of friendly London shops. These "shops" flank a cathedral-like archway that welcomes the city walker.

Burnham, with Aldis's assistance, laid out a ground plan for the efficient conduct of business and gave Root virtually free reign in the design of the interior. Root had the gift of being able to see a finished building in his mind's eye even before he sketched it, a total "architectural prevision." With this fresh in his mind, he would begin sketching "like lightning" on big sheets of heavy brown paper, gripping the pencil so close to its lead that it looked as if he were drawing with the tips of his fingers. The public spaces of the Rookery, the outflow of this fevered process, are as fine as anything Root ever set to paper.

The Rookery's La Salle Street archway led into a high, white-marble vestibule. Passing from here through a low, dark elevator lobby, the visitor came into a light-filled courtyard two stories high, its roof of translucent glass set in a carved cast-iron frame, which was painted pure white. Everything in this magical space glowed with a golden hue, the light pouring in through a central light well that opened the interior of the building to the sky. Standing in the middle of the courtyard with the sun high in the sky was like standing under a fabulous silk tent.*

Entering the light court from the lobby, one saw straight ahead a double staircase of ornamental iron leading up to an open mezzanine of glass-fronted shops and offices that encircled the courtyard. If the visitor turned completely around before climbing these stairs, he would see an architectural oddity, a cantilevered double staircase that hung from the mezzanine like a giant butterfly, its iron wings—two identical staircases—meeting at "a landing in the sky." From this landing a second run of stairs led back into the building through the light court's glass roof. These sculpted iron stairs—the building's elegant fire escape—rose in a spiraling fashion all the way to the top of the building. Ascending them, one was actually outside the walls of the building in an oriel of glass and brass, a tower, of sorts, that ran up one of the inside walls of the light well. Stopping on the top landing of the oriel and looking through the windows of decorated iron, one could see eight stories down to the iron-and-glass roof of the light court, or across into the big-windowed offices on the other side of the light shaft, the building being designed like a square doughnut, the light well the hole in the doughnut.

The white glazed bricks and gold terra-cotta trim of the light well's walls were designed to reflect light into the interior offices. In this way, valuable rental space sacrificed to the light well was more than made up for by the high rents Aldis could command for these well-lit offices deep in the building, which were also far quieter than offices fronting on turbulent La Salle Street. The beauty of Root's plan, in the minds of Peter Brooks and Owen Aldis, was that it had shown a way for art to augment commerce.

While there is no available evidence to prove it, Aldis surely had a large role in laying out the interior of the Rookery and other Chicago office buildings he managed for investment companies. "The real estate man . . . is coming to be the chief of builders," wrote Lincoln Steffens in an essay on the skyscraper as a collaborative effort. "Indeed, it is he who often suggests the whole enterprise." He was the principal adviser to the investors, making recommendations on what land to buy, what to build on it, and what amenities were needed in a building to make it attractive to business firms. Aldis pressed his clients to install lavish appointments in the lobbies and other public spaces of their skyscrapers. "Build no second-class space," he advised Peter Brooks. "The parts every per-

---

*The court was remodeled after 1905 by Frank Lloyd Wright, and its recent restoration is in sympathy with Wright's, not Root's, original plan.

son entering sees must make the lasting impression." So elevator cages were decorated with carved bronze and wrought iron, and marble-columned lobbies came to resemble the regal staterooms of Europe.

By the mid-1890s, New York was building skyscrapers as visually stunning as Chicago's, but Chicago's were better designed for business use. After inspecting several Manhattan towers of the 1890s, Aldis wrote: "The truth is that many of them have been built for advertise-ment—a mere rage to spend stockholders' money. They are the most gorgeous things I have ever seen, and the combination of carved gran-ite, lavish marble, gilding, mahogany (carved), with bad light, narrow and deep elevators, and awkward halls is amazing. You see, no company there ever builds two buildings, so their acquired experience is useless."

New York, a wealthier city than Chicago, was headquarters to many more giant companies, and they built skyscrapers largely as corporate advertisements. Most Chicago skyscrapers of the 1880s and 1890s had the advantage of being built by investment consortiums composed of players who were in the game for the long haul, not just for a single splashy project—as Aldis indicated—and whose cupidity and fear of failure aligned them with real estate managers who advised them on how to build handsomely yet gainfully.

•

Speaking to an audience of his fellow architects while the Rookery was under construction, John Root predicted that the time was fast ap-proaching when American architects would begin designing "trade palaces . . . whose splendor will be phenomenal in the history of the world." That year, he had on his drawing table the rough sketch of the Chicago building that would fulfill his own extravagant prophesy.

The Monadnock, sixteen stories high, with masonry walls six feet thick at its base, is actually two interconnected structures, built on Jackson Boulevard, with similar but subtly different designs and with radically different construction techniques. The north half of the building is the work of Burnham and Root, with Root as chief designer, while the southern extension, completed in 1893, a year after Burn-ham and Root's building was opened, is by the firm of William Ho-labird and Martin Roche, architects of the Marquette Building, still one of the finest office buildings in the Loop. Holabird and Roche's ad-dition is partially supported by a steel frame, then an advanced engi-neering innovation, and it is a simply decorated building whose somber brown brick walls and gently projecting window bays blend beautifully with those of Root's building. In Root's building, however, the walls carry the weight of the structure; they are not just a decora-tive shell. This masonry support system was considered technically outmoded by Chicago engineers even as the building was on the drafting board; but the structurally dated Monadnock was audaciously modern in its complete absence of external ornamentation. A freestanding structure of great power and simplicity, it is as austere and beautifully adapted to its purpose as the streamlined lake steamers that serviced the port of Chicago in the 1890s. A prominent Boston critic pronounced it "an achievement unsurpassed in the architectural history of our country," and it continues to inspire visitors to the city in its perfectly restored form.

The Monadnock is the first modern building in which the architect rejected ornament completely and expressed his vision sheerly through mass and structure, in the manner of later modernists like Le Corbusier. And what is intriguing is that there is almost no hint of it in Root's previous buildings, with the possible exception of the Montauk. The Montauk, however, is a short building made tall by an inelegant accretion of stories; the Monadnock's sculpted walls rise right up from the pavement to the sky in uninterrupted fashion.

So how did Root, an inspired ornamentalist, come to design this handsomely understated building? The long-accepted explanation was that of Harriet Monroe, his adoring sister-in-law, who published her biography of Root just four years after the Monadnock was completed. Monroe hated the "brick box" face of the Monadnock and insisted that the design had been pressed on Root, as the Montauk had been, by Peter Brooks. This story, however, is undermined by the correspondence between Aldis and Brooks, which shows that Root conceived a design, largely on his own, entirely without ornament. The purely business intentions of Brooks might have disciplined the artistic vision of Root, but Brooks, it turns out, was asking him to design the type of office building that Root himself had begun advocating in his luminous essays on American architecture.

Root, one of the great writers on architecture of his time, was one of the first of his countrymen to call for a fresh and purely American architecture, "a new spirit of beauty [that] . . . springs out of the past, but is not tied to it, [that] studies traditions, but . . . is not enslaved by them." The American architecture of his day found its inspiration in the works of the Renaissance, the Middle Ages, and classical antiquity; and Chicago had perhaps the single worst representation of this historical eclecticism, Boyington's Board of Trade Building. "It was very ungrateful of them," Montgomery Schuyler wrote of the anarchists who demonstrated in front of the building on its commemoration day, "for one could go far to find a more perfect expression of anarchy in architecture."

Interesting styles are never made, Root wrote with this popular building in mind, by copying from the past. They emerge "by the careful study of all the conditions which lie about each architectural problem," influences as general as local climate, soil conditions, and geography. A Chicago newspaper editorial of 1879 mirrored Root's sentiments exactly: "The conditions of Chicago are so unlike those of any part of the union or of the world that what had been learned elsewhere is of no great value when applied to this city. . . . Before Chicago attains a complete success in its architecture, it must have a school of its own." To which Root later added: "There never was a picture that people loved, nor a building that they went out of their way to see, which was not essentially local," a view of art akin to Mark Twain's idea that all great literature is regional literature.

"Michelangelo did not paint Spanish beggars; nor did Jean-François Millet paint Alpine mountains," Root noted. While Millet was inspired by peasants and harvests, Root thrilled to the energy and material feats of metropolitan industrialism. He wanted American architecture to express the spirit and adopt the new materials and methods of machine technology, as great American bridge builders like James B. Eads and the Roeblings, father and son, already had. Architecture for too long had been dissociated from engineering. It was time to bring together the prose and poetry of the building arts.

Root lived in a business-driven city and designed his office buildings as "enduring monuments to the broad and beneficent commerce of the age." He admired the boldness and civic religion of Chicago's merchant princes, and in his finest office buildings—and above all in the Monadnock—he expressed in masonry and glass what he considered the ideal attributes of modern business: "simplicity, stability, breadth, dignity"—but above all, stability.

John Root's Chicago was a city of violent class and labor discontent, the volatile center of American socialism and trade unionism. We know little of Root's politics, but he was certainly a conservative, fearful, as were his well-placed clients, that labor agitation would escalate into social revolution. While putting the finishing touches on the design of the Monadnock, he was also working on the First Regiment Armory, commissioned by the city after the Haymarket Riot and located near the South Side homes of Chicago's wealthiest families.* Both

---

*Root also designed the pedestal for the monument commemorating the policeman killed in the Haymarket Riot. The monument itself was designed by his friend, the sculptor Johannes Gelert.

buildings gave public emphasis to the social values Root felt Chicago needed most at the time: order and civic discipline. Modern business buildings "should . . . by their mass and proportion," he wrote, "convey in some large elemental sense an idea of the great, stable, conserving forces of modern civilization." This strongly stated sentiment might be the reason he took as a model for the façade of the Monadnock the Egyptian pylon, a piece of stately public architecture embodying the ideas of the permanence of kingly power and the unchanging nature of ritual.

This is not to suggest that Root was an apologist for the capitalist status quo. On the contrary, he tried to humanize crude, tumultuous Chicago. This comes through clearly in the essays on architecture that he wrote while he worked on the design of the Monadnock. To convey stability and permanence, he favored "grave and simple treatment." As he told a gathering of young Chicago architects in 1887, in words that further challenge Harriet Monroe's interpretation of his role in the design of the Monadnock: "The value of plain surfaces in every building is not to be overestimated. Strive for them, and when the fates place at your disposal a good, generous sweep of masonry, accept it frankly and thank God."

To produce the kind of plain but imposing office buildings most Chicago capitalists wanted, the architect had to exercise "self-denial," especially in the application of ornamentation. If he didn't, Root noted, the client would intervene. Factors such as profits and "per cent. [have] always been considered foreign to art," yet they "may sometimes guide art, if not positively foster it." This is a long way from Root's complaints about Brooks's pinchpenny interference in the Montauk project. This time, when Brooks asked for a design that used "solidity and strength"—not ornamentation—to produce an effect, Root was eager to go in that direction.

When Root started making sketches for the Monadnock in 1884, it was almost universally assumed that lofty business buildings—monstrosities, people called them—could not be made into works of art and that the only way to improve their appearance was to "mercifully cloak" them with heavy ornament. But Root "refuses to give up the problem," Aldis reported to Peter Brooks that year, "and declares that if he fails to make a harmonious and massive and artistic building this time, he will never build another Office Building."

The Monadnock, named by Brooks for the New Hampshire mountain Melville loved, was completed in 1891 to less than favorable local reviews. Lunatic architecture, outraged Chicagoans called it—a packing box with holes punched out of it. But several important eastern

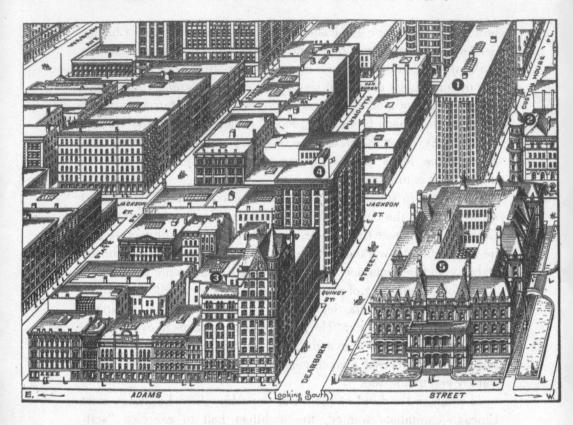

From Adams Street, looking south. "The scene before the reader," said the Rand McNally guidebook from which this drawing was taken, "portrays some of the most remarkable buildings in the world." Among the most significant were the Monadnock (no. 1), the palatial Union Club (no. 2) next to it, the fourteen-story Owings Building (no. 3), the Great Northern Hotel (no. 4), and the Post Office and Custom House (no. 5), which never closed and where an estimated 50,000 persons went every day.   Bird's-eye Views and Guide to Chicago (Chicago: Rand, McNally & Co., 1898)

critics thought it a precedent-setting building, the first expression of a genuinely American style of commercial architecture. Montgomery Schuyler spoke for them: "This is . . . the thing itself."

"An amazing cliff of brickwork," in Louis Sullivan's famous description, the Monadnock is a forbidding building when seen from some distance. As one draws close to it, however, it is not the tremendous wall—the full length of a city block—that impresses, but the windows, hundreds of them, set in rounded bays that appear to grow right out of the wall. These vertically set bays of glass are the skyscraper's equivalent of the horizontal bays of glass in Frank Lloyd Wright's prairie houses. They open the offices on both sides of the narrow building to light and air and provide splendid urban views. This is an architecture of humanism, a building designed to serve the people who use it.

Root made it even more handsomely functional by turning the lobby, a spinal corridor running the length of the building, into a light-filled urban arcade flanked by attractive shops and restaurants that opened on both sides—to the street and to the lobby itself—through plate-glass windows and doors. A visitor walking through the lobby was in the building but also on the street—in the city. There was nothing like it in Chicago, and it is still a model for architects seeking to give gracious ground-floor treatment to their office towers. In the Monadnock, John Root achieved a union of beauty and utility, street-level intimacy and skyscraper monumentality.

While the Monadnock expressed its height better than any other tall building in the country, its structural system brought architecture to what Louis Sullivan called "a crisis, a seeming *impasse*." To take masonry, gravity-bearing walls any higher would have necessitated an impossibly wide and ponderous base, one that would have turned the first floors of the building into a squat, slit-windowed fortress, almost impossible to rent. John Root's Monadnock was the last of the tall buildings erected in the ancient manner of wall-bearing construction. William Le Baron Jenney's Manhattan Building, constructed by twenty-nine-year-old Henry Ericsson, pointed architecture to the future.

The Manhattan Building didn't look tall; a weighty, block-shaped monolith, it simply looked big. Yet holding up this monster pile was a thin, lightweight metal frame, a skeleton, architects called it. This riveted-together and wind-braced frame was a great improvement over the less stable, bolted-together metal cage Jenney had used to support his Home Insurance Building of 1885. When Jenney completed the Manhattan Building, he brought to a climax the architectural revolution he had begun with the Home Insurance Building, the most important transformation in the structural arts since the age of cathedrals.

3. The Major's Birdcage

William Le Baron Jenney was the only classically trained architect-engineer in Chicago when he arrived there after outstanding service in the Civil War. The mentor of Louis Sullivan, Daniel Burnham, William Holabird, and Martin Roche, all of whom worked in his atelier, "he gave young architects the preparation they needed to tackle new problems for which the schools could offer no solutions," wrote Sigfried Giedion. A deeply passionate man, he urged his young apprentices to put all they had into their work, for in these buildings later generations, "[will] read the feelings and aspirations," he would say, "of those who erected them."

He also introduced his draftsmen to the life of the city, encouraging them to take evening courses in architectural history, to frequent the theater and the opera, and to spend Sunday afternoons at the noisy German beer gardens where he was a greatly loved regular. "The Major," recalled Louis Sullivan, "was a free-and-easy cultured gentleman, . . . a *bon vivant*, a gourmet." Educated in Paris, he "knew his vintages, every one, and his sauces, every one; he also was a master of the chafing dish and the charcoal *grille*." Leaving the office for his home in Riverside, the suburban village he had helped Olmsted design, he could be seen carrying "by their naked feet, with all plumage, a brace or two of choice wild ducks, . . . or a rare and odorous cheese from abroad."

Jenney liked to host big dinner parties at his rambling Swiss-style house, his bright-spirited wife hiring for entertainment the finest concert musicians in Chicago. Seated at the head of the table, champagne glass in hand, he would spin wonderful stories of campaigning with Grant and Sherman and of his racy student days in Paris. He was known for his graciousness and generosity to "the least of his draftsmen," said his partner, William Mundie, and for his eccentricities and absentmindedness. One evening, as he was reading by the fireplace in his home library, his wife and son looked on from the next room without comment as he put "a lump of sugar in his pipe and a spoonful of tobacco in his tea cup, not discovering the mistake," his son Francis told the story, "until he tried to light the lump of sugar."

In an unfair judgment that has stuck to Jenney, Sullivan insisted he was "not an architect except by courtesy of terms." Trained as an engineer, Jenney concentrated on the structural problems of a building, but this absorbing concern was actually his strength as an architect, for he believed that the beauty of a building arose organically from its structure and function. Teacher, author, town planner, and landscape architect, Jenney was as versatile as John Root and, like Root, one of the outstanding innovators in the history of building technology. "Today William Le Baron Jenney's imagination and courage are not sufficiently recognized," Giedion wrote three decades after Jenney's death in 1907. They still are not.

•

The son of a prosperous whaling fleet owner whose ancestors helped found Plymouth Colony, Jenney grew up by the sea, in Fairhaven on Buzzards Bay, and had sailed around the Horn to the California gold-fields and on to Manila before entering Harvard's Lawrence Scientific School to study civil engineering. Finding the curriculum stale and unchallenging, he transferred in 1853 to Paris's Ecole Centrale des Arts et Manufactures, a prestigious engineering school, passing the entrance exams after being tutored in French by a Harvard professor hired by his family.

Jenney later described his three years at the Ecole Centrale as so difficult an ordeal that "I was obliged to deny myself the theatre and opera, balls and receptions." After graduating with honors, he became a railroad engineer in southern Mexico, and when that didn't work out, he returned to Paris, where he learned "to draw from life" in the studio of his friend James McNeill Whistler, the beginning of his serious interest in architecture. To support himself, he joined a company that was promoting European investments in American railroads. When he was sent back to the United States in early 1861 to meet the firm's new president, William Tecumseh Sherman, Sherman told him that "war is upon us" and that he should "get in the army as soon as you can. Use my name in any way you like but get in."

Jenney enlisted a short time later and was assigned to Grant's staff at Cairo on the Mississippi, taking part in the capture of Forts Henry and Donaldson. He later served as Grant's liaison with his troops at the slaughter at Shiloh and played a pivotal role in the siege of Vicksburg, building corduroy roads, pontoon bridges, and siege fortifications that allowed Grant to break loose from his base, live off the land behind enemy lines, and eventually take the "Gibraltar of the West" in one of the most spectacular marches in military memory. Following the surrender of Vicksburg, Jenney marched with Sherman to Atlanta (but not, as Sullivan claimed in his autobiography, "to the sea"). At the war's end he was serving as chief of engineers of the Army of the Tennessee, and in 1866, after making maps of all of Sherman's wartime campaigns, he was discharged as a major, a title he always bore with pride.

Jenney's Civil War experience had a direct bearing on his practice of architecture. "The engineering corps of the army during the war," he recalled, "was an excellent school to learn expedients." Grant and Sherman fought "engineering wars," moving great numbers of men and matériel over tough terrain with lightning speed, in campaigns that called for quick and often astounding feats of both destruction and construction. The skill of Sherman's engineers was legendary, none more so than their ability to rebuild bridges almost as fast as the Rebels destroyed them. They carried interchangeable parts of bridge trusses on flatbeds pulled by oxen, and one foreman boasted he could build a bridge "about as fast as a dog could trot." Few of the Union engineers had prior military experience. They had to be jacks-of-all-trades, relying on inborn good sense and ingenuity, experience that prepared Jenney, Dankmar Adler, William Sooy Smith, and other Chicago architect-engineers who served with Sherman and Grant to take on the challenge of the skyscraper.

After marrying Elizabeth H. Cobb in Cleveland, Ohio, Jenney moved to Chicago in 1867, where opportunities for a formally trained builder were almost limitless. After working at Riverside and on the West Parks, he became a full-time architect, a profession he trained himself for by writing about it, coauthoring a book with his first partner, Sanford E. Loring, called *Principles and Practice of Architecture*. It covers architecture from the Greeks through the Renaissance, but its centerpiece is an assessment of the Gothic cathedral. In Paris, Jenney had come under the spell of the renowned neo-Gothicist Eugène Emmanuel Viollet-le-Duc, who saw the cathedrals of thirteenth-century France as essays in engineering science as well as religious faith.

Gothic builders used the ancient materials of wood and stone to achieve transcendent height, along with a feeling of lightness, the pinnacled towers of their cathedrals appearing to float in the air over the morning mist, the "weightless expression" of the divine spirit. Viollet-le-Duc was the master restorer of his day of Gothic cathedrals but was no mere copyist in his independent architecture. He pressed his fellow builders to study closely the "organic" principles of medieval skeleton construction—where the structural skeleton is braced by an exterior cage of flying buttresses—and to adapt these principles to modern structural materials like machine-fabricated iron to produce a new machine-age architecture, with vaulting enclosures of glass framed in iron.

Jenney's French-inspired ideas on structure had a decisive, if little noticed, influence on Chicago architecture. His book and the English translation of Viollet-le-Duc's *Lectures* became available just as Chicago architects began struggling with the structural problem of the tall office building. "A practical architect," Viollet-le-Duc remarked in his *Lectures*, "might not unnaturally conceive the idea of erecting a vast edifice whose frame should be entirely of iron, . . . preserving [that frame] by means of a casing of stone." Although the Frenchman never proposed such a frame for a business building, through the impact of his ideas on Jenney, the French cathedral became an inspiration for the Chicago skyscraper.

The cathedrals were the skyscrapers of their day, rising to a precarious height, their enclosing curtain walls so filled with glass that they looked transparent. "Bright," said Abbot Suger of St. Denis, the originator of the Gothic style, "is the noble edifice that is pervaded by new light," words that prefigure by almost a millennium the aspirations of early skyscraper architects. The Gothic style arose, as did the steel-frame skyscraper, at a time of furious urban and economic expansion and achieved its most sublime form in Chartres, an out-of-the-way—some might say frontier—commercial center. Chartres's merchants poured gold accumulated in the grain trade and manufacturing into a sky-aspiring structure that reflected the power and reach of their newly rich town.

Gothic cathedrals, like Chicago's skyscrapers, were at odds with accepted ideas on civic symbolism, and the opulence of both building forms offended enemies of the ascendant material spirit. Abbot Bernard of Clairvaux, an earlier-day leveler, lashed out at the powerful Order of Cluny for the "immense height" of its churches and their "sumptuous decoration," much as Chicago anarchists of the 1880s attacked the Board of Trade Building as a vanity of the local lords of commerce. And to take the comparison between Chicago and the Gothic one step further, it might be remembered that the Gothic cathedrals appeared after tremendous fires consumed the old wooden-roofed churches, along with the carelessly constructed wooden towns in which they once stood.

•

The Great Chicago Fire presented Jenney with his first important architectural commission, the Portland Block, an austere four-story office building with two elevators—some say the first passenger elevators in Chicago. It was commissioned a year after the fire by Peter Brooks and was the Chicago building that most impressed young Louis Sullivan when he arrived from the East. After seeing it, Sullivan inquired about its architect and found work in Jenney's office.

Jenney filled the wall areas of the Portland Block with windows and gave all the offices in this commanding-looking corner edifice street views, the beginning of his interest in filling big buildings with natural light. The Portland Block was one of the best business buildings in the rebuilt city, but the one that made Jenney's reputation as an architect was the five-story warehouse he designed in 1879 for Levi Leiter, Marshall Field's partner. Stylistically the most advanced building in the city, perhaps in the country, it was a virtual glass box, the walls of narrowly separated windows supported by cast-iron columns in conjunction with thin brick piers. It marked the arrival of a new spirit in Chicago architecture, an emphasis on simplicity and structure "largely influenced," Peter Wight pointed out in 1880, "by the study of medieval Gothic architecture and the works of Viollet-le-Duc."

In the First Leiter Building, as it would later be called, Jenney came close to achieving complete skeleton construction, where the walls support none of the floor loads. Such a structural system, however, wasn't a radical departure from engineering practice, as Jenney well knew. Cast-iron framing had been used as early as the 1790s in English cotton mills and warehouses; and in New York in the 1850s, James Bogardus and his rival, Daniel Badger, had made iron-framed industrial buildings, manufacturing the prefabricated parts in their casting shops. Bogardus had also built a 175-foot-high shot tower for the McCollough Shot and Lead Company of New York City with a cast-iron frame of skeletal construction that supported the masonry enclosure. By using an iron-framed structure with bolted connections, it was possible to build a tower, he had written prophetically, "many times the height of any other edifice in the world, which would be perfectly safe to visitors, in the face of storm or tempest."

He had not mentioned fire; and it was American iron's calamitous experience with urban fire that had allowed the less cautious French to push ahead of the Americans in iron-framed construction, mostly of industrial buildings and department-store atriums. But when Peter Wight and others found new ways to fireproof metal columns and beams, Jenney and other architects began throwing more of a tall building's load on the iron, lightweight cast iron being a material with tremendous compressive strength. This became imperative in Chicago, as we have seen, where, unlike in New York, there was no easily reachable bedrock to anchor heavy buildings. Facing greater natural obstacles than their New York colleagues, Chicago architects were forced to think more daringly in terms of structure, making their walls—with the aid of iron—lighter and thinner. But while the iron helped hold up both Jenney's First Leiter Building and Burnham and Root's Montauk, it was the formidable masonry piers that still did most of the bearing work in tall commercial buildings when Jenney was awarded the commission that altered the course of architecture.

Jenney entered the architectural competition for the New York Home Insurance Company's Chicago headquarters in 1883, the year of the gala opening of the Brooklyn Bridge, the world's supreme achievement up to that time in iron-and-steel construction. Like the Roeblings' bridge, his history-altering design sprang straight from the requirements of his commission. It was a practical solution to the architectural problem he was presented with. That problem was not how to build tall but how to bring natural light—before the widespread use of electricity—into the deep interiors of a massive business block, not just to a stack of offices facing an interior light well, as in the Rookery, but to every rentable space in the building. "It was actually in the quest for light, not height," as a modern historian has written, "that William Le Baron Jenney made the decisive move in the development of the fully framed modern skyscraper."

The Home Insurance Company wanted a tall building with a "maximum number of small offices above the bank floor." As Jenney saw it, this called for reducing the piers (the building's vertical support system) between the windows to "a size too small to carry a load above" if the walls were built of masonry. Jenney's answer was to design a completely new kind of building, as he explained later, "with an iron column in each pier, the masonry only used to *fireproof* the iron." The "outside walls and floors were to be carried, story by story, independently on [iron] columns."

Henry Ericsson, whose company did the masonry work on several of Jenney's skyscrapers, gave a different version of the origin of the metal skeleton frame, a story that, even if apocryphal, explains in a clear way its basic structural principle. Leaving work on the Home Insurance Building early one afternoon, Jenney surprised his wife, who, rising to greet him, put a heavy book she was reading on top of a birdcage that was sitting on a table by her chair. "At that an inspiration struck Jenney," writes Ericsson: "if so frail a frame of wire would sustain so great a weight without yielding, would not a cage of iron or steel serve as a frame for a building?"

This sounds like a story the major might have told his Swedish friend over snifters of brandy. The truth is undoubtedly more prosaic. Jenney had seen light but hurricaneproof huts of bamboo frame in the Philippines, where he had first decided to become an engineer when he was only seventeen years old; he was also familiar with the iron-framed constructions of Bogardus and the French. It is even possible that he got the idea of the metal cage from Chicago's very first architectural innovation, the balloon frame, which employs the principle of light skeleton construction, albeit with nailed-together two-by-fours.

Jenney's contribution, then, was not the skeleton frame but, rather, the use of a frame of iron to support the walls of a large civilian building without the help of masonry. When he presented his plan to the

The steel frame of William Le Baron Jenney's Fair Store (1890–91) under construction.   Industrial Chicago (Chicago: Goodspeed Pub. Co., 1891).

New York Home Insurance Company he was asked: "Where is there such a building?" To which he replied: There was none.

Lunchtime workers passing by the construction site of the Home Insurance Building could not have been aware in the first months of construction that they were seeing architecture history being made. With its heavy stone base arising out of its pier foundations all the way up to the second floor, it looked like any of the other nine office buildings then under construction in the Board of Trade area. But when construction pushed upward beyond the immense granite base, a new thing appeared in the September sky, a lacy network of bolted-together iron columns, piers, girders, and floor beams. "Here, for the first time since bricks were burned in history's early dawn," wrote Ericsson, "men were [about to lay] . . . brick walls that were only curtains."

Skeptics said the frame would collapse when the heavy masonry walls were put on it. Fearing for its investment, the Home Insurance Company stopped construction and called in an outside expert to examine Jenney's frame. Jenney found him a nuisance around the construction site and got rid of him; his replacement was Daniel Burnham, Jenney's former draftsman. When Burnham pronounced the design sound, the inquiry ended.

Jenney's adventurous clients approved yet another breakthrough in construction history. As the architect was assembling his iron frame, a load of Bessemer steel beams arrived in the city from Pittsburgh's Carnegie Phipps Works, and Jenney was persuaded by the company's local salesman that lightweight structural steel could be used as effectively in skyscrapers as it was being used in bridges. After receiving permission from his clients, he substituted steel for wrought-iron beams above the sixth floor of the nine-story building.* When the new beams were put into place as support for the floors, they "wrote against the sky" the future of the American steel industry.

•

Jenney's reputation as the originator of the metal skeleton skyscraper has always been in dispute. His was only a partial frame, critics have correctly pointed out, supporting merely the upper floors of the building's street façade; the party walls at the back of the building were masonry bearing. And although a panel of experts who examined the construction of the Home Insurance Building when it was being razed in 1931 concluded that "it was unquestionably the first building of skeleton construction," Jenney's critics and rival claimants—and more recently revisionist architectural historians—have insisted that his metal skeleton was not self-supporting. Jenney himself was aware that the metal frame by itself would not hold up the Home Insurance Building, several modern historians maintain; he placed the building's iron columns in heavy masonry piers not simply "to fireproof the iron," as he claimed, but also, these historians argue, to reinforce the iron frame, helping it support the building's loads. "Without the rigidity of the two rear masonry bearing party walls and the masonry piers [Jenney's] iron frame, with its loosely bolted together and clamped connections could not have resisted any wind loads," two of his critics point out. Doubts have even been raised as to whether the "idea" of the iron-frame office building was originally Jenney's. In the year construction began on the Home Insurance Building, Frederick Baumann, Chicago's pioneering theorist of foundations and a loser to Jenney in the architectural competition for the Home Insurance Building, published a pamphlet outlining a complete system of iron framing for a tall business building. His pamphlet appeared months before Jenney began constructing his metal skeleton.

Historians have produced no hard evidence, however, that Baumann had the idea before Jenney; indeed, William Mundie, Jenney's draftsman at the time, insisted that Baumann stole the idea from Jen-

*Two stories were added in 1890.

ney, and that he—Mundie—was the unwitting accomplice, innocently answering questions Baumann put to him one day about his rival's plans for the Home Insurance Building.

In the absence of corroborating documentation, it is impossible to prove either Baumann's or Mundie's claim. Rather, the point to be made is that whoever had the idea first, it was Jenney who actually *built* a skeleton frame, albeit a partial one, and a frame to support not a shot tower, a warehouse, or a department-store atrium but a massive masonry building in one of the most congested downtown areas in the world. That took engineering daring and real structural skill. Moreover, Jenney had wanted to build a complete metal frame but was prevented from doing so by Chicago's building code, mandating that he use solid masonry piers to support the building's party walls. "This principle of carrying the entire structure on a carefully balanced and braced metal frame, protected from fire, is precisely what Mr. William Le B. Jenney worked out," wrote Daniel Burnham in 1896. "No one anticipated him in it, and he deserves the entire credit belonging to the engineering feat which he was the first to accomplish."

Jenney himself never claimed to be a revolutionary. "Mr. Jenney," Mundie pointed out, "was always opposed to any statement that spoke of the skeleton construction literally as an invention, or that it just 'burst forth' somewhere." He considered it "nature's child," a product of an evolution in structure going back at least as far as the primitive huts he had seen in Manila, shelters the local people had probably been putting up for a millennium or more. Jenney's modesty aside, it is unpersuasive to argue that he didn't know what he was doing when he built his metal frame. He had a vast knowledge of the history and current practice of iron framing, and when he was presented with, as he put it, a "simple engineering problem" of bringing light into a big building on a thickly developed street—exactly the structural problem that presented itself to builders of Gothic cathedrals—he knew what to do. And that was to take iron architecture to the next step, to turn what had been an evolution into a revolution, "the most extraordinary revolution in the construction of buildings ever recorded in history," in William Mundie's opinion.

•

Jenney's frame opened the way for stunning architectural breakthroughs as Chicago architects, Jenney prominently among them, developed in a mere seven years the true skeleton construction that allowed twentieth-century towers to go to ten times the height of the Home Insurance Building, the mother of them all. Chicago architects, however, did not follow Jenney's lead immediately. Most big buildings constructed right after the Home Insurance Building was completed, including three of the masterworks of the Chicago School—the Rookery, the Monadnock, and the Auditorium Theater and Hotel—were structural hybrids, with a combination of metal framing and load-bearing walls. The new structural steel coming out of Pittsburgh was more expensive than iron and less resistant to corrosion, and it was feared that atomic changes might occur in steel under tremendous lateral and vertical stresses, dangerously weakening a building's main structural support. "Disaster was predicted for years," wrote Colonel Starrett, "by men of technical knowledge." This helps explain Peter and Shephard Brooks's decision to build the Monadnock with masonry-bearing walls. Although these fears proved baseless, architects who experimented with steel in designing the new urban monoliths were taking what many thought were wildly reckless chances.

The first step in the evolution of the metal cage after the Home Insurance Building was the twelve-story Tacoma Building, completed in 1889, the first big project by the small but soon-to-be-important firm of Holabird and Roche. The young, Jenney-trained architects used a steel-and-iron frame with some conventional masonry support but hung on the frame a thin wall of terra-cotta and brick, the first true "curtain" wall in an urban building since the Middle Ages. Stylistically sleek, with its gossamer finish, the Tacoma made all other Chicago business blocks look overbuilt by comparison.

Two years after construction began on the Tacoma, Burnham and Root designed a breakthrough building, the Rand McNally (1890), the first tall structure in the world completely supported by an all-steel frame. Root had experimented spectacularly with iron framing in the Rookery's light court, but in the Rand McNally project he went all the way, using the very latest materials and construction innovations. Root's experimental temper drove him to the cutting edge and beyond of engineering knowledge. "The devices by which his sky-scrapers were tied together vertically, horizontally and diagonally, against all possible resistance of weight and fire and cyclones, were always an engrossing study with Root," his brother recalled. "When I resented one day his preoccupation with these commercial buildings, he replied, 'But I rather like to make them stand up.'"

To build truly tall buildings would require, Root realized, the use of steel, which has far greater tensile strength than iron. Not only that; the frame would have to be stiffer, and hence more stable, than Jenney's bolted-together cage. All connections between columns and beams would have to be tightly fastened so that they could transmit bending forces without the assistance of stiffening provided by ma-

sonry walls. This would have to be done by new rivet guns; and to further strengthen the frame, making it "absolutely trustworthy," Root
used the steel Z-bars columns invented by one of Andrew Carnegie's
remarkable engineers, Charles Louis Stroebel, who, as Carnegie's
Chicago sales representative, might have been the person who convinced Jenney to use steel in the Home Insurance Building. Although
only ten stories high, the Rand McNally was the first building to employ modern skyscraper construction. All that was needed for buildings to scale the heavens was a reliable system of wind bracing. When
Jenney installed such a system in the Manhattan Building, he capped
the transformation in structure he had begun.

The Rand McNally Building demonstrates why property investors
were willing to experiment with "bird-cages" even before steel prices
dropped 50 percent and more after 1892. High-strength steel made it
possible to space columns even farther apart than Jenney had in the
Home Insurance Building, giving buildings cathedral-like window
panels. Rental space was greatly augmented now that there was no
need for interior structural columns. Office space also became more
flexible, as nonbearing room partitions could be moved or even removed to suit the occupant's needs. Because they could be built faster,
steel buildings were also cheaper to construct than masonry fortresses
like the Monadnock, since the difference between the cost of iron and
steel was more than made up for by savings in labor costs. Chicagoans
looked on in amazement as the frameworks of skyscrapers were pieced
together by fearless "high iron men" as fast as a story a day. And because the frame alone supported the loads, the thin brick walls of steel
and terra-cotta could be constructed from the top downward, presenting pedestrians with a most unsettling sight, Alice in Wonderland constructions that looked as if they were being built upside down.

"The life of the buildings constructed with steel cages will be
short," New York architect George B. Post confidently predicted in
1894. But there was no stopping developments begun in Chicago in
the mid-1880s. "We have entered upon a new age," said Jenney, "an
age of steel and clay."

With the perfection of the steel frame, it remained only for Chicago
architects to give it artistic form, to express outside the building what
was inside holding it up. Here, too, Jenney led the way—not with the
somewhat cumbersome looking Home Insurance Building but with the
Second Leiter Building of 1891. This State Street emporium—still
standing today—is the steel-age equivalent of Root's masonry-age
Monadnock. Both of these buildings foreshadow the minimalist aesthetic of the founder of the Second School of Chicago Architecture,

Ludwig Mies van der Rohe, but Jenney's building, while not a sky-scraper at all (it is only eight stories tall) is closer in plan and detail to Mies's elegantly sculpted steel-and-glass boxes.

The Second Leiter Building was designed to house the department store of Siegel, Cooper, and Company, which rented it from Levi Leiter. The building was said to have the largest retail floor area in the world, and every part of this one-half-million-square-foot selling area was bright and airy without the aid of an interior light court. The skeleton frame that made this possible was also the deciding factor in the de-sign of the building's block-long State Street façade, this in line with Jenney's French-inspired conviction that function and structure should determine form. It is a classically proportioned building of white Maine granite, with a plain surface that allows us to focus on how the building works as a structural composition. The frame's rec-tangular pattern is carried to the outside walls in the form of large, glass-filled grids, separated by widely spaced granite columns, deco-rative additions that suggest their interior metal supports. The art mir-rors the engineering, much as the flying buttresses articulate the supporting system of a Gothic cathedral. Jenney's supreme achieve-ment, it is one of the most original and impressive works of modern American architecture, a true cathedral of commerce.

4. Factories in the Sky

"Fifteen years ago, there was no such thing as an office building known in Chicago," John Flinn declared in one of his popular guide-books to the World's Fair city. "Today . . . the stranger in his travels about town is impressed with the idea that the business of Chicago is done in offices . . . known as 'Sky Scrapers.' . . . What all the people who occupy the [skyscraper] offices do," Flinn added, "will be a source of wonder to the visitor."

Flinn's guidebooks took visitors to Chicago where insistent elevator captains would not permit them to go—into the business heart of the skyscraper. Peeking over the transoms, so to speak, he gave many of his readers their first glimpse of modern office work, with clerks and managers, their desks set in long, closely spaced rows—as at Ar-mour's headquarters in the Home Insurance Building—working at a nonstop pace, the air alive with the clicking of telegraph keys, the ringing of telephones, and the unfamiliar clatter of a machine new to American business.

The typewriter was both a response to and a cause of a transformation in capitalist office procedure that began about the time the Montauk Building was designed, an "office revolution" that accompanied the architectural revolution that gave America the tall business building. As businesses expanded tremendously and consolidated with other firms, they had need, as we have seen, for larger and more centrally located offices. In turn, the increased size, scope, and complexity of business operations led to an extraordinary increase in paperwork—a veritable "paper empire"—and increased the need for faster communication and more efficient means of record keeping. Two new pieces of office technology—the typewriter and the vertical file cabinet—helped answer these needs and, with the skyscraper itself, symbolized a break with older forms of capitalism and the beginning of what historian Oliver Zunz has called "bureaucratic rule and hierarchy."

In the skyscraper offices of big corporations readers of Flinn's guidebooks could see, through the author's practiced eye, a system of getting out the product not unlike the killing line at Armour's pork plant. An architectural expression of the new separation of factory and office, the skyscraper also became a new kind of factory, with a white-collar proletariat made of young unmarried women, who, like their earlier factory-floor counterparts in the textile mills of Lowell, Massachusetts, expected to work only a few years before marrying and becoming homemakers.

As at Armour's plant, the originating agency of change was the division of labor necessitated by the increased size and scale of modern business and the competitive pressures to keep down prices and labor costs. But while there was almost no labor-saving technology in the packing plant, new technology, principally the typewriter, had a transformative role in the operation of the skyscraper office. By the turn of the century, this innocently intentioned machine had helped bring about a division of labor almost as destructive of workers' independence and aspirations as Philip Armour's "disassembly" line. Built by famous architects for empire-aspiring capitalists, the skyscraper was also the nine-to-five home of the new "office girl." As Carl Sandburg wrote:

> Smiles and tears of each office girl go into the soul of the building
>   just the same as the master-men who rule the building.

The first efficient typewriter was invented in Milwaukee by Christopher Latham Sholes and put on sale in 1874 by E. Remington and Sons, the arms manufacturer, for $125. It was primarily intended for the "literary man," Mark Twain being one of the first to purchase what he called the "new fangled writing machine." But in the 1880s it became a ubiquitous office feature, especially with the development of five-finger touch typing and the widespread use of carbon paper, patented in 1869. "Five years ago the typewriter was simply a mechanical curiosity," reported a business journal in 1887. "Today its monotonous click can be heard in almost every well-regulated business establishment in the country. A great revolution is taking place, and the type writer is at the bottom of it."

When the typewriter entered the capitalist business office, so did women, their first full-scale entry into what had been a male province, a small, cigar-scented place of hardwood and metal finishings, the clerks dressed in shirtsleeves, their visors hiding their faces as they worked with their pens and books, the owner or manager—his space separated from theirs by a low wooden rail—dressed in a frock coat and seated at a high rolltop desk, a gilded cuspidor within spitting distance. The first women typists were trained by typewriter companies and sent with the machine, like some inseparable part of it, to its new destination. Both machine and operator were, in fact, called typewriters. Seated at their work, typists looked almost like machines in their posture and motions: their backs ramrod straight, their wrists arched, their fingers bent rigidly over the keys, and their eyes locked on the text and not on the keys, so as not to waste any time, motion, or energy.

Women's slim fingers and middle-class women's experience with the piano, it was argued, made them natural typists, and in the business office this "literary piano," as sellers came to call it, became almost exclusively a woman's machine. Christopher Sholes used his daughter to demonstrate his typewriter, and pretty young women showed it at trade expositions and in the hotel lobbies of big cities.

At first, there was some opposition to employing young single women in offices. Women were incapable of separating business from social life, declared a woman's journal, and were by nature oversensitive, "expecting the same little delicate attention from a gentleman during business hours as [they] are accustomed to receive in the parlor." And they weren't committed to permanent careers; most were only looking, it was claimed, for some "pin money" or an upstanding man to marry. On the job, these "flowers in the office" spent most of their time, said the *Chicago Journal,* with their "powder puffs, . . . munching on chocolates."

There was also the moral issue of mixing sexes in tight quarters. "In the cozy den or private 'studio' of her employer, temptations and opportunities are constantly arising, and the susceptible employer is easy picking for the girl of brilliant plumage with tender glances that fascinate and lure." The impressionable office girl, this Victorian moralist insisted, was all too willing "to kiss and to be kissed, in order to secure special favors . . . from her susceptible employer." "Here I sit," vaudeville comedians joked, "with my typewriter on my knee." No young woman "can live a consistent Christian life," said one writer, "and hold a business position."

But women were in the office to stay. In the early 1880s, the number of women in clerical work increased tenfold. By 1890, there were thirty-three thousand stenographer-typists (the two tasks soon became interlinked) in the country, 9 percent of all clerical workers, whereas twenty years before, there were no stenographer-typists, and fewer than 1 percent of women in the workplace held clerical jobs. This was only a harbinger, however. By 1920, over 50 percent of the clerical work in American business firms was being performed by women. Sandburg told the story in his poem "The Skyscraper": "Ten-dollar-a-week stenographers take letters from corporation officers, lawyers, efficiency engineers, and tons of letters go bundled from the building to all ends of the earth."

Women were accepted into the office because they didn't threaten men's jobs. They took new ones created by advancing office technology and streamlined paperwork procedures. With the typewriter came a plethora of other office machines—accounting machines, addressing machines, calculating machines, dictating machines, and in 1890, a mimeograph machine. These machines greatly speeded up office work and, together with new operational methods, rationalized and standardized it. Office work became as factory work already had, more routinized and mind dulling, requiring concentration more than skill, and there was an equivalent division of tasks in the interest of speed, efficiency, and reduced operating costs. Tasks once performed by a single clerk, the office equivalent of the packing plant's old master butcher, were divided among a number of less skilled workers: typists, stenographers, file clerks, mail handlers, and billing clerks—a growing preponderance of them women. Women worked all the machines and performed much of the assembly-line-style work in the new factory offices of the 1880s and 1890s.

Chicago's new stenographer-typists were overwhelmingly young (under twenty-five), white, native born, and unmarried, and most of them came from lower-middle-class families and worked to support themselves and sometimes to help support their families. They were not at their machines for "pin money" or a husband. Since they had to work, doing so in a clean, light-filled office with men who wore shirts and ties was greatly preferable to domestic or factory labor, or even to sales work at Marshall Field's. In the late 1880s, a saleswoman at Marshall Field's could expect to earn about eight dollars a week, while typists made up to fifteen dollars a week. (For a time, Chicago typists were paid more than public school teachers.)

Even so, typists were paid less than male clerks who did equivalent work, and that, in the end, is why women were hired. That, and what was widely believed to be their attitude toward work and their so-called natural bent. Women were thought to be "especially suited as typists and switchboard operators because they were tolerant of routine, careful, and manually dexterous." Young women office workers were also believed to lack ambition to rise in the company, an important consideration for work offering no hope of advancement. A woman might make an ideal filing clerk, declared a popular textbook on office management, but the head of a filing department "should preferably be a man." In the new business office, separate hierarchies were created for men and women to keep women from being promoted into managerial positions.

There was only one potential problem with hiring young unmarried women to do routine clerical work: They would leave the firm—in fact, were expected to leave the firm—when they married. There was a huge turnover of unmarried clerical workers in the 1880s and 1890s, but management tolerated it because the replacement personnel came to the job already trained for it in the new commercial schools that had begun to spring up over the country or in the new commercial courses offered in public high schools.

There was a world of difference in skill level and training between the all-around male clerk of 1870 and the female clerical worker of 1890. The master record keepers of the firm, clerks were expected to come to the job with solid skills in penmanship, composition, and arithmetic—and with "energy," tact, and abstemious habits. Once hired, they received extensive training in the internal workings of the business house, for an apprentice clerk's job was the first step toward possible promotion to a managerial position or even to partnership in the organization, as it was for Marshall Field, John Shedd, and Harry Selfridge—and for John D. Rockefeller, Andrew Carnegie, and Jay Cooke. By the 1890s, however, modern office work had become so routinized and deskilled that it could be done with only general training offered by clerical courses and without the rigorous company-specific training Shedd and Selfridge received at Marshall Field and Company.

Women hired for clerical work were expected already to have all the training necessary to do their jobs within a week, at most, after being hired. A nationwide increase in women high school graduates in the 1880s, coupled with an absence of attractive job opportunities for these women, created an available pool of inexpensive, easy-to-replace workers, white-collar capitalism's equivalent of the Lithuanians at the gates of the Union Stock Yards.

Since most clerical workers were hired for the short term, they were—as the women at Lowell had been—less likely to press for wage increases or to complain about the work. Their very impermanence made them that much more attractive to employers. They proved to be as easy to replace as the interchangeable parts of the business machines they operated. "The alienating conditions of modern work now include the salaried employees as well as the wage-workers," the sociologist C. Wright Mills would write a half century later, a condition Melville anticipated in "Bartleby the Scrivener."

Mechanization and systemization also eroded the status and skill level of male clerks. By 1900, they had become, in many firms, little more than process workers with scant hope of advancement, as colleges and universities provided companies with their new managerial prospects. Even the pens the clerks worked with became standardized, one company-ordained nib being used for all dip pens. The technology of writing and record keeping came to mirror the more hierarchical structure of business firms. While male clerks wrote with dip pens exclusively, executives used the new fountain pens perfected in 1883 by Benjamin Waterman. The clerks didn't need portable fountain pens, it was reasoned, for they never left their desks. Women employees never even picked up a pen. A wooden pencil and her noisy machine were a woman's exclusive office instruments, marking her place in the firm's new chain of authority.

Manual office work inched ever closer to factory work when the Self Winding Clock Company introduced an electric synchronized clock system for both factories and offices. At the World's Columbian Exposition the company regulated two hundred "slave" clocks from its main pavilion, the master clock—eerily called the Autocrat—programmed to ring bells and to start and stop machinery. The time clock was advertised as a cure-all for workers' tardiness and a guarantee that they wouldn't leave early if the boss wasn't around. And in the office's equivalent of the factory speedup, managers began to use clocks to measure the amount of piecework performed in a specified time, typists punching in at the start and finish of each job.

23. *William Le Baron Jenney's Home Insurance Building (1884–85). This was the first skyscraper built with a (partial) metal skeleton, an engineering innovation that altered the course of architecture. The frame supported the walls without the help of masonry.*

24. *William Le Baron Jenney.*

25. *Jenney's Second Leiter Building (1891). Built as a department store, it foreshadowed the minimalist aesthetic of Mies van der Rohe, founder of the Second School of Chicago Architecture. The art mirrors the engineering, as the skeleton's rectangular design is carried to the outside walls in the form of glass-filled grids, separated by granite columns, which suggest their interior steel and wrought-iron supports. Jenney's greatest triumph, it still stands on South State Street.*

27. Burnham and Root's Montauk Block (1881–82), Chicago's first skyscraper.

27

26

26. Daniel Hudson Burnham and John Wellborn Root in their office in the Rookery.

28. The eleven-story Rookery (1885–88) on La Salle Street in the financial district. Recently restored, it is one of Burnham and Root's handsomest skyscrapers, a Moorish citadel set down on one of capitalism's commanding streets.

28

29

30

29. The skylighted lobby of the Rookery Building, circa 1895. It was redesigned by Frank Lloyd Wright in 1905.

30. Burnham and Root's Monadnock Building (1889–91) as it appeared in 1896. This plain-walled masterwork remains, in its restored form, one of the great buildings of Chicago.

31

31. Louis H. Sullivan.

32

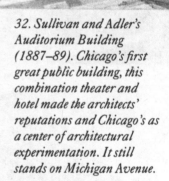

33

32. Sullivan and Adler's
Auditorium Building
(1887–89). Chicago's first
great public building, this
combination theater and
hotel made the architects'
reputations and Chicago's as
a center of architectural
experimentation. It still
stands on Michigan Avenue.

33. Opening Night, the
Auditorium Theater,
December 1889. The
completion of this great civic
project marked Chicago's
cultural coming of age. The
theater became the gathering
place for Chicago's elite.

34. Sullivan and Adler's
Schiller Building (1891). Of
all of Sullivan's skyscrapers,
this came closest to being a
"proud and soaring thing."
Its "set-back" design allowed
light and air into the offices
of the tower.

34

35

36

35–37. The Art Institute, c. 1892 (35). Charles L. Hutchinson (36), its founder and longtime president, turned it into one of the great art museums of the world. A millionaire banker and Board of Trade speculator, Hutchinson was nineteenth-century Chicago's greatest cultural benefactor. With his friend and fellow trustee Martin A. Ryerson, he helped make the new University of Chicago (1892) a distinguished research university, open to both men and women (37). The orderly Gothic quadrangles they commissioned architects to design were a "wonderful contrast," H. G. Wells remarked, to the gross "disorganization" of commercial Chicago.

37

38

38. *Carter H. Harrison I, the former Kentucky plantation owner who was a five-time mayor of Chicago. The* Chicago Tribune *called him "the most remarkable man that our city has ever produced."*

39

39. *An artist's drawing of the Haymarket Riot, May 4, 1886, the most divisive event in the city's history.*

40. *Harrison was assassinated on October 28, 1893, during the last week of the World's Columbian Exposition. His funeral was the most impressive pageant in the young city's history. Over half a million people gathered on the streets to view his casket as it passed by carriage through the city to Graceland Cemetery.*

41. *Jane Addams—"Saint Jane," as the press called her—arrived in Chicago in 1889 to found Hull-House, which became the leading laboratory of urban reform in the United States.*

42

43

42. *Taking in the spectacle of the Columbian Exposition's White City from the roof of the Manufactures and Liberal Arts Building.*

43. *The light show in the Court of Honor, demonstrating the new power of electricity.*

44

44. *Black leaders such as Frederick Douglass and Ida B. Wells denounced the fair's exclusion of the accomplishments of African-Americans. Douglass and Wells wrote and distributed to foreign visitors to the fair an impassioned broadside explaining why "the Colored American" was not included in the World's Columbian Exposition. Wells remained in Chicago after the fair to battle for civil rights.*

At about this time, the century of the chronologically organized press book, indexed alphabetically by correspondence, was replaced by the file cabinet, with all the correspondence of a client or an account in one easily reached manila folder. This part of the business office now came to suggest the style of the building that housed the firm, file cabinets being vertically organized and their drawers framed in iron or steel. Filing cabinets in the sky is how Patrick Geddes described the new capitalist skyscrapers, an image that resonates in Louis Sullivan's description of how architects organized skyscraper office space—two showcase lower floors and above these "an indefinite number of stories of offices piled tier upon tier, one tier just like the other, one office just like the other office—an office being similar to a cell in a honey-comb, merely a compartment, nothing more." Seated at his desk in one of these high-rise cells, a clerk in a George Ade story looks out the window and wonders if the dense network of telegraph, telephone, and electric wires atop the neighboring building have been spun deliberately into cobwebs "to keep buzzing, toiling flies as himself . . . from escaping."

The great promoter of business interaction, the skyscraper discouraged the face-to-face meetings in street-side places that George Ade saw as the blood and bones of a living city. For Ade, the skyscraper was the cause of an erosion of civic values, a decline Chicagoans mistook for progress.

That was certainly not the view shared by Louis Sullivan and John Root, who, in the absence of high achievement in the other arts, were Chicago's greatest artists in the years prior to the fair. While both believed that this "sterile pile" could be made a thing of great beauty, it was Sullivan (if only because he lived longer) who became the prophet and poet of the American skyscraper. The architect, he said of his self-appointed role, "[is] not a merchant, broker, manufacturer, businessman, or anything of the sort, but *a poet who uses not words but building materials as a medium of expression.*"

It was in this spirit that he took on the Auditorium project, his first and biggest-ever commission. In this square-shaped, bearing-wall building, the businessman's cost considerations and delight in simple construction combined with the architect's vision to produce the blending of sentiment and commerce that would become the defining feature of Sullivan's steel-framed skyscrapers. The Auditorium dramatized, as no other building did, the shift in leadership of American architecture to Sandburg's "coarse and strong city."

11

Sullivan and Civic Renewal

1. The Auditorium

THE construction of the Auditorium marked Chicago's cultural coming of age. Beginning with this tremendous civic enterprise, the merchant kings of Chicago began commissioning architects to design not just office skyscrapers but a host of new cultural institutions: libraries, museums, concert halls, a new Art Institute, and a distinguished university. The crowning achievement of this building and beautification effort was the White City of 1893, the Chicago elite's vision of what a great city could be like at a time when the country's large cities were almost universally thought to be ugly, dangerous, and ungovernable. In these years between the launching of the Auditorium project and the completion of Daniel Burnham's celestial city for the Columbian Exposition, Chicago's makers and millionaires set out to prove to London, Paris, and New York that their town was "something more than a centre of pig-sticking and grain-handling."

These parvenus saw patronage of the arts, and of architecture especially, as a way of enhancing their own fame and making Chicago a more pleasing and profitable place to do business. If you're going to give something to your city, a character in a Henry Fuller novel advises one of her rich friends, "make it something that people can see . . . something solid and permanent; it must be a building. . . . Nothing can bring you more credit." Yet while their motives were not always unselfish, these self-anointed modern Medici were genuinely proud of their city and became generous givers to its civic causes.

There was also in Chicago a close alliance of artists and entrepreneurs. Writers, musicians, architects, and sculptors dined at the tables of reaper and railroad magnates, and Daniel Burnham and John Root were not the only two artistic talents to marry into the ruling commercial families of the city. The remarkable exfoliation that Chicago experienced at the end of the nineteenth century was, like Vienna's *fin-de-siècle* renaissance, led by a cohesive coalition of civic-spirited capitalists and culture makers bound together by intermarriage and membership in the same clubs, churches, and charitable organizations.

This close association between capitalists and artists was a new phenomenon in American culture, embracing Boston, New York, and other large eastern cities, and it produced some of the greatest cultural and educational institutions in the country. But the alliance was tighter in Chicago than in any other American city, in part, perhaps, because there was already a precedent for it in the collaboration between architects and businessmen in the building of office skyscrapers. And in Chicago, as opposed to established eastern cities, the civic uplifters included a group of activist women, the wives of traders and packers, who became figures of real importance in the life of the city, not just hostesses of charity balls and glittering literary evenings. Edith Wharton would have been hard pressed to find material for her novels of women of the idle elite in Gilded Age Chicago.

This civic movement had as much to do with what Chicago had become as with what its best families hoped it would become. Alarmed by escalating labor violence, massive immigration, and the capture of city government by Irish "boodlers," these business families and their artist allies saw cultural reform as a way of creating a shared civic patriotism in which museums and musicals would perform the same socially redeeming function as landscaped parks: bringing people of all classes together in surroundings designed to refine and uplift. Many Chicago leaders agreed that their city had become the victim of its own cyclonic growth, that it was less a city than an industrial camp, loud, filthy, and brutishly money hungry. It was time for civic patriots, Daniel Burnham proclaimed, "to bring order out of the chaos incident to rapid growth."

There was "only one city in the world having a population of half a million along whose streets no traveler or citizen can find a single structure built by local benevolence," declared the minister David

Swing in the early 1880s. "Chicago has the honor of being that city." The Auditorium was Prairie Avenue's answer to the challenges thrown down by Burnham and Swing.

But Gilded Age Chicago was not entirely bereft of culture. The Auditorium was built, in fact, because the city already had a burgeoning cultural life, a strong theatrical tradition, and a record of supporting both serious and light music, especially operas, oratorios, and concerts by German-American orchestras and choruses. What Chicago lacked, however, was an architecture to house and encourage its new cultural activities: galleries and schools for its young sculptors and painters, museums to display the growing art collections of its world-traveling capitalists, and a great central hall for music and theater.

At the 1885 Chicago Opera Festival, over a hundred thousand persons attended twelve operas by a touring company featuring the renowned prima donna Adelina Patti at the Inter-State Exposition Building on the downtown lakefront. This ungainly barnlike building had been renovated and made acoustically sound—"to the faintest pianissimo"—by the newly formed architectural firm of Dankmar Adler and Louis Sullivan, but the enormous turnout for the festival convinced its sponsor, Ferdinand W. Peck, that the time had arrived for Chicago to build a permanent music hall "larger and finer" than New York's Metropolitan Opera House, a "public auditorium" that could be converted into a ballroom for charity affairs and a hall for political conventions, mass meetings, and Civil War army reunions.

At a May 1886 meeting of the Commercial Club, the tribal gathering spot of the city's chieftains of commerce, Peck unveiled his plans for a temple of music for all the people, not just the fashionable few, and soon had the financial backing of five hundred of Chicago's leading businessmen. Among them were the men who would come together in the next decade to form and run the city's new cultural institutions. Some of them were of the generation that had made Chicago the capital of the mid-continent, including George Pullman and Marshall Field. But their leaders—as cultural reformers, that is—were younger men, several of them sons of the commercial fathers of the city: Martin A. Ryerson, art impresario and graduate of Harvard Law School, whose rough-edged father, a former Indian trader in the Michigan forest, had amassed a $3 million fortune in the lumber business; Charles L. Hutchinson, Ryerson's devoted friend and fellow art collector, the son of Benjamin Hutchinson, "Old Hutch," the legendary commodities speculator; Cyrus McCormick, Jr., son of the late Reaper King; and Peck himself, scion of a Chicago founder and sharp-eyed land dealer, Philip F. W. Peck. In "older communities" these young men "might have been fops and idlers," wrote a reporter for the *New England Magazine,* "but . . . in this atmosphere of enthusiasm and abounding life [they] are among the most public-spirited citizens, acting upon the theory that relief from the necessity of labor entails upon them the obligation to devote time and energy to the promotion of the public good."

The Chicago elite was close-knit and family centered, and this gave the sons influence with the fathers and with family friends and relatives in Chicago's equivalent of New York's famous "Four Hundred." Thomas W. Goodspeed, the Baptist fund-raiser for the new University of Chicago, expressed the situation perfectly when he remarked, after recruiting support for the project from Hutchinson, Ryerson, and Peck: "[These three young men] can raise more money than any three men in Chicago." But it wasn't that difficult to sell the idea of cultural patronage to the older generation. They were easily made to see that the town they had turned into a colossus with their sweat and money would never be a world-class city unless it changed its image and appearance. Their pride of accomplishment as city founders is captured by Robert Herrick in his novel *The Memoirs of an American Citizen.*

His main character, Van Harrington, arrives in Chicago broke and rises to become a stockyards giant through plunder, stealth, and driving will. By the end of the novel, he has lost all his friends and even the love of his family, but in a final scene he takes solace, at least, in what he has accomplished in Chicago. Standing at a busy bridge crossing while a tug pushes a tremendous lumber boat through the draw, he looks down at the river, rimmed with material might, and thinks to himself: "I, too, was part of this. The thought of my brain, the labor of my body, the will within me, had gone to the making of this world. There were my plants, my car line, my railroads, my elevators, my lands. . . . Let another, more perfect, turn them to a larger use; nevertheless, on my labor, on me, he must build."

The creator of this character, however, believed that Chicago needed more than the Van Harringtons of the city had given it. Herrick, a transplanted New Englander who had come West to teach at the new University of Chicago, was friendly with Hutchinson, Peck, Ryerson, and Burnham, and agreed with them about what raw Chicago lacked. He had no faith, however, that it would ever be anything other than what it was, a place where everything was measured by money. Whereas his Chicago novels are about the irreconcilable conflict between art and commerce, Burnham, Hutchinson, Peck, and Ryerson combined their cultural reformism with pride in Chicago's business accomplishments. Chicago could be culturally transformed, they were convinced, without challenging or even deeply questioning its commitment to commerce and cupidity. "The past shows plainly enough," Burnham grandiloquently declared, "that the great flowers of fine arts are born on the stalk of commercial supremacy. It has been so from Athens to Chicago."

•

The Auditorium was as important a building for nineteenth-century Chicago as Brunelleschi's cathedral cupola had been for fifteenth-century Florence, and like that stupendous dome, it was an engineering as well as an artistic challenge. It was the biggest architectural commission in the history of the city, and Burnham and Root, it was expected, would get it. But the job went to the much smaller firm of Adler and Sullivan because it was Peck's project and he considered Adler the best acoustical engineer and theater designer in the country. And to get Adler he had to take the untried Sullivan, "a pleasant gentleman," a local reporter described him, "but somewhat troubled by large ideas, tending to metaphysics."

In Adler, twelve years older than his partner, Peck got exactly what he expected, an engineer of proven excellence; in Sullivan he unexpectedly got someone like himself, a self-described "dreamer for the populace." Peck's dream was to erect a great musical hall for all Chicagoans; Sullivan's was to create an architecture for a democracy, one that would break through European precedent and become, in his words, "an art that will live because it will be of the people, for the people, by the people." As Adler's chief designer, he would be given a large say in the creation of the Auditorium, and if he did it right, this "enormous, unprecedented work" would move him strongly in the direction of his desires. With the Auditorium Building, the reputation of Louis Sullivan, and of Chicago itself, as historian Carl Condit has written, "was made and secured."

•

"There are many men whom nature has made small and insignificant, but who are so fiercely consumed by emotion and ambition that they know no peace unless they are grappling with difficult or indeed almost impossible tasks and achieving astonishing results." Writing in the sixteenth century of his fellow Tuscan Filippo Brunelleschi, Giorgio Vasari might have been seeing ahead to Louis Sullivan, another "genius . . . sent by heaven," in Vasari's phrase, "to renew the art of architecture." From an early age, both men had thought themselves marked for greatness, and they underwent their apprenticeships in advancing cities where they were confident their destinies would be filled out. Both were civic dreamers, and each of them, interestingly, had a life-transforming epiphany in Rome.

"Only the heroic scale measures Louis Sullivan," writes one of his biographers. "The titanic task he set for himself was to shape his society through architecture, as the Parthenon did for Athens, the Cathedral for Paris. He was the first prophet to build for the American condition."

The son of artistically inclined immigrant parents who encouraged his sense of being special, Louis Henry Sullivan had dreamed of being an architect since he was eleven, when he became entranced with buildings in his walks around his native Boston. When his struggling family moved to Chicago, where Patrick Sullivan, a fiddler and dancing master, opened a dancing academy, Louis persuaded his father to let him remain in Boston with his French-speaking grandparents to continue his studies. At sixteen—without finishing high school—he entered the Massachusetts Institute of Technology, the first American school of architecture. Disappointed with its constricted curriculum, he dropped out after one year to "see what architecture might be like in practice." He worked briefly in Philadelphia with Frank Furness, that city's most original architect, until the economic panic that almost ruined Burnham and Root put him out of work. In the fall of 1873, he joined his parents in Chicago, finding employment in Major Jenney's office, where he met the only intimate friend he would ever have.

John Edelmann, Jenney's brilliant young foreman, introduced Sullivan to German metaphysics, to Richard Wagner's thunderous music, and to the Lotus Club, a group of young athletes who exercised on weekends near their boathouses on the banks of the Calumet River. Ideas flew off Edelmann like sparks from a fireball; just being around him was an awakening education for Sullivan, and he began to read Darwin, Taine, Rabelais, Shakespeare, and Swinburne. But Sullivan decided he needed further formal training in architecture. In 1874, dipping into his modest savings account, he sailed for Paris to study at the Ecole des Beaux-Arts, the world center of architectural thought; "headquarters," he called it.

Here, too, he quickly grew impatient with classroom instruction. When he returned to Chicago after less than a year abroad, he was alive with excitement, not about what he had learned at the "Great School" but about what he had seen in Rome on a student trip. Sitting for two days in the Sistine Chapel studying Michelangelo's ceiling, "alone there, almost all the time," was the transfiguring event of his young life. In this magnificent space he met his first "Dreamer [and]

Adventurer," he later recalled in his rushing prose: "a Super-Man" who had transformed the world with the power of his vision.

The lesson Sullivan took from Rome was the same one that the "thunder-struck" Brunelleschi had on "seeing for the first time," as Vasari tells the story, "the grandeur of the [ancient Roman] buildings": to create in the spirit of earlier giants, not to imitate their work. Back in Chicago, Sullivan set out to be an artist-hero in the mold of Michelangelo, not through the study of dry texts and ancient canons but by reaching within himself and out to the world around him, especially to nature, his emotional identification with nature rising over the years to "almost a pantheistic adoration." "Imitation cannot go above its model. The imitator dooms himself to hopeless mediocrity." This credo of Ralph Waldo Emerson, another of Sullivan's growing galaxy of heroes, became his own. That and the "germ" of an idea that had entered his mind at the Ecole and that later, after studying "nature's processes," he would formulate as a law: Form follows function. "The function of a building," he would write, "must . . . organize its form . . . as, for instance, the oak tree expressed the function oak, the pine tree the function pine," a theory that allowed for both structural and emotional expression.

With the Chicago building trades still depressed, Sullivan worked as a freelance and studied engineering on his own, fascinated by great American bridge builders like Capt. James B. Eads. To his splendidly romantic mind, they were dreamers "who *did* things. . . . Their minds were trained to deal with real things, . . . while the architectural mind lacked this directness, this simplicity, this singleness of purpose." For a time, Sullivan considered becoming a bridge engineer. "The idea of spanning a void appealed to him as masterful in thought and deed," he wrote of himself in his autobiography. But Chicago's unrivaled building opportunities seduced him back to architecture, where he could, like his engineering heroes, join science to feeling in triumphant civic works.

His first opportunity came when Dankmar Adler took him on as a junior partner in 1882, promoting him to full partner the following year. With Chicago booming again, the firm got plenty of work, especially from leaders in the Jewish community, for Adler's father was a prominent local rabbi. While he produced nothing of great note in these formative years, Sullivan began the course of experimentation he had had in mind for some time: "to make an architecture that fitted its functions" and that expressed these needs "frankly and freshly," without reference to any "architectural dictum, or tradition, or superstition, or habit." To this end, he worked on a succession of commissions until, at age thirty, he was given the chance to create something large and important in the life of the city. "[My] heart went into this structure," Sullivan said of his work on the Auditorium Building. And when it was completed after three years of incessant, nerve-racking labor, he suffered a physical collapse and speculated that the project had shortened his partner's life.

•

Work on the Auditorium began in early 1887, with two hundred men and thirty teams of horses breaking the frozen ground for the great pit that would hold the largest private building in America. And it went forward with incredible speed, into the night with the aid of electric floodlights and through two hard Chicago winters. It proceeded uninterrupted even as the Republican Party held its national convention in July 1888 in the still-uncompleted theater—a smaller brick building erected inside the shell of a larger, unroofed one—the orations of the delegates competing with the shouts of iron men and masons putting up the building's tremendous tower, whose rooftop observatory was the highest point in the city when it was completed.

The Auditorium was planned to be three buildings in one, and this influenced the design of the façade, with its walls of spartan simplicity—a warehouse to house a grand opera house, a modern critic has unkindly called it. Unlike in Europe, there was no government support of the arts in the United States, so the Auditorium would have to pay for itself. To ensure that it did, Peck and the Chicago Auditorium Association, the stockholding directors of the operation, decided to enclose the forty-three-hundred-seat theater in a multiuse building containing a four-hundred-room luxury hotel and a complex of rental offices. Since the theater was surrounded by a shell of hotel space and offices, the commercial needs of these determined the expression of the exterior. As Sullivan would have said, the form expressed the function. In designing this façade, Sullivan's exuberant imagination was also disciplined by the cost consciousness of the building's financial backers, who rejected his suggestions for a richly decorated façade for what Peck called a more "severe treatment."

Much attention has been given by scholars to Sullivan's struggle for an appropriate artistic form for the skyscraper, but with the Auditorium commission, he had to design another type of revolutionary building: a cultural hall that was also a profit-generating business building. Sullivan wanted a civic building that was truly American— and expressive of Chicago—not a knockoff of a baroque opera palace. In this effort, he had inspiration directly at hand, for nearing completion in 1887, only a few blocks from the barely cleared site for the Au-

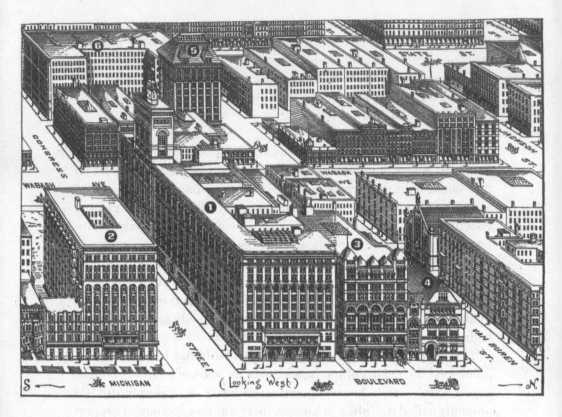

Looking west from Michigan Avenue, 1893. Facing Michigan Boulevard, the most fashionable street in Chicago, is Sullivan and Adler's enormous Auditorium Building (no. 1) with its eight-story tower. Its tower's rooftop observatory, for a brief time the highest point in the city, was a favorite tourist spot. Sullivan and Adler and their young apprentice, Frank Lloyd Wright, had their offices in the top story of the tower. Beneath the tower was the entrance to the 4,300-seat theater; the main hotel entrance was on Michigan Avenue. The building had an office section along Wabash Avenue. The Auditorium Annex, later the Congress Hotel (no. 2), was erected in 1893 as an extension of the Auditorium Hotel and was connected to it by a tunnel under Congress Street.

Solon S. Beman's Studebaker Building (no. 3) was built in 1885 by the famous wagon masters from South Bend, Indiana. In 1898 it was renovated and became the Fine Arts Building. The Chicago Club (no. 4), designed by Burnham and Root, originally housed the Art Institute, which moved up the street to its own building in 1893.

William Le Baron Jenney's Isabella Building (no. 5) was completed in time for the fair. Jenney's masterpiece, the Second Leiter Building (no. 6), housed Siegel, Cooper & Co.'s department store. It later became the Sears, Roebuck and Co. store.
Bird's-eye Views and Guide to Chicago (Chicago: Rand, McNally & Co., 1898)

ditorium, was the building that worked a spell on nearly every Chicago architect of the time, Richardson's Marshall Field Warehouse, the Brancacci Chapel of Chicago architecture. Like Richardson's building, the Auditorium was a massive yet sublimely simple structure of bearing-wall construction. Only, like the proud builders of Florence's Palazzo Vecchio, that city's civic center, Sullivan put a commanding campanile on his granite prism to lend it greater majesty.

This note of rugged simplicity is not, however, carried to the inside of the building, which is so luxuriantly ornamented that Sullivan was regarded for some time by his "professional brethren," Montgomery Schuyler tells us, "as a decorator only." A triple arched entrance on Michigan Avenue opened into a fabulous lobby with marble mosaic floors and a hand-stenciled ceiling. A grand staircase led to a second-floor reception parlor with a panoramic view of the lake through an open loggia. On the tenth floor there was a main dining hall that ran the entire length of the Michigan Avenue front, its barrel-vault ceiling springing right up from the floor. There was also a banquet hall and ballroom built right over the theater, its six-hundred-ton load carried by enormous bridge trusses engineered by Adler. And back on the ground floor was the handsomest barroom in Chicago and, next to it, an intimate street-side café.*

The building's showpiece, however, was the theater, the largest and finest music hall in the country, surpassing in size by twelve hundred seats New York's Metropolitan Opera House. The entrance was through a lobby at the base of the tower—the building's office complex—and as one entered the theater, one's eyes went straight to the ceiling, its majestic arches decorated with gold leaf and plaster reliefs and inlaid with carbon-filament lamps that gleamed like "dull, mellow gold." This room—superbly restored today—remains the best essay in existence on Sullivan's theory of design, inspired by nature but also organically integrated with the structural and functional requirements of his buildings. The elliptical arches are nonsupporting, but they are not appliqué, something added on only for artistic effect. They are keyed to Adler's acoustical plan—the smooth panels between them acting as sound reflectors—and to the theater's heating and ventilation system. The concealed ducts in the arches were designed to carry steam heat in the winter and cooled, dehumidified air—which was carried over blocks of ice and sprayed with water—in the summer, the first air-conditioning system in a large building. As a writer, Sullivan was impossibly florid; as a designer, he was more disciplined. "He

---

*In 1952, the bar and café fell victim to the widening of Congress Street.

may have been ridiculous when he wrote," Frank Lloyd Wright said. "He was miraculous when he drew."

The sight lines of the great golden room are perfect; the acoustics, magical. Adler would take dignitaries on tours of the building and, leaving them high in the theater, hurry down to the stage and begin speaking in a low, conversational tone, his voice carrying with perfect clarity to the upper gallery, half a city block away. Then he would show off his spectacular hydraulic stage mechanics for special effects— rocking and wavelike motions, elevations, disappearances—and his ingenious system of movable floors and ceilings for reducing seating capacity to twenty-five hundred for a more intimate effect. When necessary, however, the holding capacity of the hall could be greatly enlarged. The stage could be pulled out over the parquet to form a mammoth floor for charity balls, political conventions of up to eight thousand people, and games of softball, or "Chicago Ball," as it was called in the 1890s.

The Auditorium's official opening was preceded by an ancient masonic rite designated only for great civic edifices, the laying of the copestone, the topmost and final stone in the building's tower. The downtown streets were lined five and six deep with onlookers on the brisk morning of October 2, 1889, as members of the Masonic Grand Lodge of Illinois, wearing their official white aprons and led by the Second Regiment Band, marched to the front of the Auditorium, where city dignitaries, including the architects and the "promoter," Ferdinand Peck, were waiting on a flag-draped platform. In accordance with the rituals of the Freemasons, Sullivan presented the last stone and three of the tools of the mason's trade to the lodge's grand master, who then consecrated the building "according to ancient usage." After thunderous applause, thousands of spectators, led by the plumed and aproned masons, pushed their way into neighborhood saloons to raise their glasses to this "stupendous monument of western enterprise."

In the audience that morning was twenty-two-year-old Frank Lloyd Wright, who had worked on the interior of the Auditorium with Sullivan after landing a job with the firm not long after his arrival from Wisconsin in 1887. Wright was also at the grand opening of the Auditorium Theater a week later, the biggest event in Chicago between the Great Fire and the fair. The sidewalks around the building were carpeted, gaslit, and covered with a canopy, and the crush of the crowd was "terrific." The *Inter Ocean* described the five thousand invited guests as "the most brilliant audience ever assembled in Chicago on any occasion." In attendance were the mayor, the governor, and the president and vice president of the United States, Benjamin Harrison and Levi Morton, returning to the site where they had been nominated by their party eighteen months before. But the "man of the hour" was the slim, dashing land baron who had carried through this $4 million project.

There were several standing ovations for Ferdinand Peck that evening, but neither Peck nor anyone else publicly acknowledged the architects by name. It didn't matter; their reputations were made, especially Sullivan's. "A great genius had appeared in the world of architecture," Wright wrote of that cultural moment. Wright had designed, he later claimed, the Auditorium's magnificent bar "owing to last-moment pressure on L.H.S. himself," and it was there that Sullivan—no teetotaler—probably spent the last hour of that lustrous evening while his partner was in the basement adjusting the boilers.

Speakers and guests high on wine that evening compared the Auditorium to the Parthenon, the Pantheon, and as a "temple of *practical* service," to the "useless" pyramids. Most of the rhetoric, however, was self-congratulatory. The Auditorium, Mayor DeWitt C. Cregier noted, had been built by men whose chief aim was "not percent but public spirit." They backed this project for "the honor and glory of their city."

•

The opening of the Auditorium Theater was front-page news in all the leading papers of the country. A number of years later, the country read about another gala gathering in Sullivan and Adler's Theater, the opening night of a performance of Italian grand opera. "Such a crowd . . . every one you ever knew or heard of," murmurs a character in Frank Norris's novel *The Pit* as she and her sister, Laura Dearborn, recent arrivals from the East, wait for the rest of their party in the lobby. When the audience is seated and the performance begins, Laura is annoyed by the distracting whispers of the men sitting near her, who are discussing the failure that day of a trader ruined in an effort to corner the wheat market. But to her surprise, she finds herself growing excited by the talk of this colossal business failure; the drama of the wheat pit strikes her as more exciting than the operatic drama she is seeing that night, "equally romantic, equally passionate; but more than that, real, actual, modern, a thing in the very heart of the very life in which she moved," Norris wrote of her reaction.

This is Norris's vision of Chicago. Traditional art forms were no match for the drama of power being played out in the city of his birth by businessmen who were to him, as they were to young Theodore Dreiser, epic heroes and even artists in their own way. This led Norris to an unconventional view of Chicago architecture. When Laura Dearborn and her party leave the Auditorium Building, their carriage takes them through the financial district, where all the office buildings are lit "from basement to roof," except one—the Board of Trade Building, "black, grave, monolithic, crouching on its foundations, like a monstrous sphinx with blind eyes, silent, grave,—crouching there without a sound, without sign of life under the night and the drifting veil of rain."

This building symbolized for Norris the "giant strength" of Chicago and seemed to him a more fitting representation of this resolutely commercial city than the Auditorium Building. "It's like a great tidal wave," Laura Dearborn remarks of the power of business that Norris sees in the strong, dark walls of Boyington's building. "It's all very well for the individual just so long as he can keep afloat, but once fallen, how horribly quick it would crush him, annihilate him." By the novel's end it has destroyed even her husband, Curtis Jadwin, once the king of the Provision Pits.

How different is young Louis Sullivan's conception of Chicago! Crude and avaricious, Chicago could still be humanized by the creative artist. His description of Richardson's Marshall Field Warehouse is as clear a statement as we have of his own architectural faith. "A monument to trade, to the organized commercial spirit, to the power and progress of the age," it represented, as well, an effort to control and discipline these forces. Richardson's mind was "large enough, courageous enough," Sullivan wrote, "to cope with these things, master them, absorb them and give them forth again, impressed with the stamp of large and forceful personality."

This faith in the power of art puts Sullivan in the company of Burnham and Root—the rivals he is rarely paired with—and also of young men of culture and fortune like Peck, Hutchinson, and Ryerson, all of whom had a deep faith in the ability of architecture to restore a sense of beauty and order to modern urban life. Sullivan's purposes were often at odds with those of the capitalists he built for, but not on the Auditorium project. "The Auditorium Building"—Adler spoke for both himself and his partner—"illustrates how the versatile Western American can combine sentiment with thrift, and demonstrates how he can endeavor to cultivate the service of Mammon simultaneously with an effort to attain his higher artistic ideals."

2. A Proud and Soaring Thing

As soon as the Auditorium Building was ready for occupancy, Adler and Sullivan moved their offices to the top story of its great square tower. The firm now had all the commissions it could handle and employed a team of thirty draftsmen, supervised by its rising star, Frank Lloyd Wright, who that year married eighteen-year-old Catherine Lee Tobin of Chicago and moved with her into a wood-shingled house of his design in suburban Oak Park. Sullivan was often away from the office, with clients in faraway cities—for Adler hated to travel—or at his new seashore cottage in Ocean Springs, Mississippi, caring for its eleven acres of grounds and rose gardens, complete with a pond stocked with Gulf crabs. At Ocean Springs, alone in nature, he did his "finest, purest thinking," bringing his rough sketches back with him to Chicago in the private Pullman Palace Car of his brother Albert, an Illinois Central railroad executive who had also bought land in this Biloxi Bay paradise.

When Sullivan entered the Auditorium office in the morning, he "paid no attention to anyone," Wright recalled. There were "no good mornings, . . . no words of greeting as he went from desk to desk" hastily inspecting the work of the draftsmen. He always wore a dark suit that perfectly fit his athletic frame, and his appearance was impeccable—his beard sleekly brushed and neatly trimmed, his collar of the purest white and freshly starched, his expensive shoes polished to a glare. And he walked like a dancer, his gait bearing a "dangerous resemblance," Wright thought, "to a strut."

He couldn't have been more different from his partner, the "big chief," as the draftsmen fondly called Adler. Wright captured Adler wonderfully: "Short-built and heavy, like an old Byzantine church," he had enormous feet that "spread flat like the foundations for some heavy building," and he walked with long, ponderous steps. A family man, gregarious and approachable, he would move through the drafting tables "like a barge making its way between river craft" and sit for hours with his young draftsmen, the sleeves of his rumpled shirt rolled up, making suggestions "in a fatherly sort of way." These apprentices feared the other partner, an absorbed and often arrogant man who made it known he preferred to be alone. A bachelor with few friends, Sullivan worked alone, walked the city's streets—his favorite form of relaxation—alone, and drank alone. Around the office during business hours the only person he seemed to have time for was Adler; the thirty or so others might as well have been office furniture and fixtures.

The German-born Adler was self-taught. Inspired by his father's anti-slavery sermons, he had enlisted in the Illinois Light Artillery on his eighteenth birthday and learned engineering in the field during the war and architecture in the offices of the Chicago firms he worked for after the war, before opening his own practice. After their breakup, Sullivan would dismissively describe Adler—as he did Jenney—as "essentially a technician, an engineer." But while they worked together, he had the greatest respect for Adler's skill with structure, learning most of what he came to know about how buildings are put together from his richly talented partner. They had a partnership, like Burnham and Root's, that was entirely amicable, with an agreed upon division of responsibilities. Adler handled the business and engineering side of things, and Sullivan did the designing; like Burnham, Adler pushed his younger partner "to the front." Adler was the "sturdy wheel-horse," Sullivan wrote without modesty, "of a tandem team of which Louis did the prancing."

Sullivan and Adler, however, never became intimate friends. The only person in the office that Sullivan would open up around after business hours was his long-haired, foppishly dressed assistant, who also had a belief "in his own unique illuminations." Sullivan loved to talk, Wright recalled, but only late at night, after the office had cleared out and the two men were left alone. Sitting on Wright's drawing table in the office next to his, with "wide windows overlooking the vast lighted city," he would talk, often in a monologue, about books and music and large ideas—a play he had just seen, a French novel he was reading, or a suggestive thought he had uncovered in his never-ending excavations of the work of Herbert Spencer, his favorite philosopher. But mostly Sullivan loved to talk about Whitman, whose *Leaves of Grass* he first read while working on the design of the Auditorium— and about the incomparable Wagner. After attending a Wagner performance, "he would often try to sing the leitmotifs for me," Wright remembered, "and describe the scenes to which they belonged." His eyes agleam with passion, he would sometimes read his mystical prose poems, filled with feeling but utterly incomprehensible. Wright also "adored" Whitman but didn't care for Wagner, had trouble with Spencer's *Synthetic Philosophy,* which he loyally read at Sullivan's insistence, and thought his master's philosophical musings "a kind of 'baying at the moon.'"

But when Sullivan's talk turned to architecture, Wright couldn't get enough of what he had to say: about how nature must infuse architecture, how buildings must be made to live and breathe like creatures of the earth, how they were mirrors not just of a civilization but also of the souls and hearts of the men who built them—"Every building you see is the image of the man whom you do not see"—and how art and the poetic architect must take on the challenge of the steel-frame skyscraper.

•

Chicago's revolutionary metal-cage engineering demanded, Sullivan thought, "an equally revolutionary architectural mode." The "old ideas of superimposition," he would tell Wright, "must give way before the sense of vertical continuity." A steel-cage skyscraper need not express its system of construction, Sullivan argued; it was more important that it express its nature, that it be exactly what it was—tall, "every inch of it tall, . . . a proud and soaring thing.

The Auditorium commission ended what Sullivan called his "masonry period." Having successfully experimented with plain surfaces in the Auditorium commission and with two structures he built for the Ryerson family—a sharp-featured, blue-black tomb in Graceland for Martin A. Ryerson, Sr., and the clean-lined Walker Warehouse for Ryerson's son—Sullivan was ready in 1890 to carry to the exterior of a big building the highly personalized system of "organic" ornamentation he had applied in the interior of the Auditorium.

In the Monadnock, Root had expressed both height and function through structure rather than ornamentation, the plain walls sloping inward and upward from the wide and thick granite base, wide and thick because it held up the building. But because Sullivan wanted to work with the steel frame, he confronted a design problem few historians of his work have emphasized.

The steel frame is not actually a vertical system of construction. It is a system of cubes, and the base of the frame is flush with the stories above it, making it a square box. There is no natural structural slope to give the building a feeling of upward energy other than the sheer height of the stacked floors, making this type of building more difficult to look impressively tall than a bearing-wall one, at least at a time when skyscrapers were no higher than twenty or so stories. Louis Sullivan was the first architect to make the box-shaped metal-frame building *look* tall. He accomplished this with artistry rather than engineering, making his skyscrapers authentic civic sculptures.

He did this first in the ten-story Wainwright Building in St. Louis, one year after completing the Auditorium. Thin, closely ranked piers—which have no structural function—shoot skyward from the building's two-story base to its highly decorated cornice, which caps the column's vertical thrust. Frank Lloyd Wright called this "picturesque verticality," the use of "mere facade" to achieve the look and feel of great height. The form does not follow the function if by function we mean—as Jenney and later modernists did—the building's system of construction. But function never meant exactly that to Sullivan. Function, in his view, included the ideas and aspirations of both the architect and the age, and height was, for Sullivan, an emotional and an artistic idea. As one stands beside the Wainwright, one's eyes follow the red pierlike bands right up to the top of the building; these piers are there to reveal the building's true nature as a towering thing. But the lush ornamentation Sullivan added has a different function: to counterbalance the city's sharp-edged rationality with "poetic imagery" drawn from nature.

Frank Lloyd Wright refused to see this as true organic architecture, where the "countenance" of the building is "authentic of structure." But even he saw the Wainright as a revolutionary building, one that broke with all the academic styles of its day and expressed the idea of verticality in an entirely new way.

The Wainwright and the Guaranty Building in Buffalo, completed five years after it, are almost universally considered Sullivan's finest skyscrapers, but the Sullivan building that came closest to being a "proud and soaring thing" was the Schiller Building in Chicago, completed in 1892.* Like the Auditorium, it was a multipurpose building with rent-generating offices constructed around and above a sumptuously decorated theater, and it was topped by a tall tower. But here the tower was the centerpiece of the composition, and unlike the Wainwright, the building was made to seem taller than it was less through artistry than structure. The flanking walls of the building's wings, or shoulders, stopped at the ninth floor, and the clean, straight tower rose above them eight more stories into the Chicago sky. This was not "picturesque verticality." It was closer to the modernist meaning of form follows function than any other of Sullivan's skyscrapers, and the reason is undoubtedly because Adler—the real originator, in Frank Lloyd Wright's opinion, of the "dogma" of form follows function—had a dominant voice in its design, theater construction being his signature.

The Schiller Building was a sensation in its day. Barr Ferree thought it "one of the most beautiful and impressive high buildings in the world," and it was the American skyscraper that most impressed the noted British architectural historian Bannister Fletcher. The Schiller Theater "is in the same relation to the new style of tall building," he wrote, "as the Parthenon bears to the architecture of Greece."

The Schiller was a new and prophetic type of skyscraper, anticipating by twenty-five years New York skyscrapers built to comply with a zoning law intended to prevent all of Manhattan's thoroughfares from becoming dark and drafty canyons. The upper stories were "set back" from the lower ones, like so many steps. This setback design allowed

*The Schiller was demolished in 1961 to make way for a parking garage.

light and air into all the offices on the upper portion of the tower and into the streets below and prevented what could have become a wall-like block of high, interlocked buildings.

Adler employed this design sheerly for its commercial advantage: Only well-lit offices commanded good rents. But in a suggestive essay written as the Schiller was under construction, his partner took his idea—claiming it as his own—and transformed it into a vision of a futuristic city of setback skyscrapers, his only and little known venture into the field of urban design.

"The High Building Question," considered by some scholars an illustration of a social concern rare in an architect, might actually have been a calculated effort by Sullivan to stop the passage of a law limiting the height of Chicago buildings. Pressure for height limitations was building fast at the time Sullivan's article appeared in a popular Chicago magazine. There were those who favored restrictions for purely business reasons: owners of property on the edge of the Loop who wanted the downtown district to expand laterally; owners of existing skyscrapers who wanted to maintain a monopoly of office space; and owners of three- and four-story buildings in the Loop who saw their stores and offices turned into "damp and dark basements" by neighboring monoliths. But others saw skyscrapers as a menace to public health and safety. In the early 1890s one elevator passenger was killed on average every twelve days, and neither the ladders nor the water from the hoses of fire engines could reach the top stories of skyscrapers, raising fears of towering infernos. But the principal public complaint was about the "canyonizing" of the streets. Chicago's streets, critics argued, belonged to the people; they should not be made into smoky, crowded corridors to satisfy the unquenchable greed of the city's land gamblers.

To calm these critics, Sullivan urged a twin strategy of design and regulation that would supposedly balance the interests of the speculator with those of the public. There must be no mandated ceiling on height, he argued, but if a builder went above a "prescribed limit," the size of the additional stories should be reduced by law to 50 percent of the size of his lot. At twice the height limit, the building should be reduced to 25 percent of the area of his land, "and so on indefinitely, restricting the area as he progresses upward."

In an illustration accompanying his essay, readers were presented with an urban panorama of such broad-shouldered skyscrapers—many of them with dazzling towers—lining a street that is wide and clean and open to the sky. For some unknown reason, however, the sketch did not include Sullivan and Adler's own unexecuted design for the Odd Fellows Temple, a near-perfect example of the setback principle. Although the Illinois Order of Odd Fellows was unable to raise the funds to build their stupendous Chicago temple, this was the most radical skyscraper proposal of its time, a thirty-six-story powerhouse with a succession of deep setbacks surmounted by a pyramidal tower that would have been by far the highest point in Chicago, visible on a clear day from the far suburbs, yet throwing no consuming shadows on the streets below it.

"The High Building Question" is a testimony to Sullivan's fear that the skyscraper could become a "social menace and danger." But it is even stronger evidence of his conviction that it should be the commanding architectural form of the modern city—and of his allied belief in the folly of shackling its creators. No individual should have the "license [to] . . . disregard the public welfare," Sullivan argued, but "here in Chicago the freedom of thought and action of the individual should be not only maintained, but held sacred." Chicago had risen to "greatness by virtue of its brain men, who have made it what it is and who guarantee its future. These men may be selfish enough to need regu-

Louis Sullivan's vision of the skyscraper city of the future. It accompanied his essay "The High Building Question." The Graphic, 1891.

lation, but it is monstrous to suppose that they must be suppressed, for they have in themselves qualities as noble, daring, and inspired as ever quickened knights of old to deeds of chivalry." No local booster could have made the point for the Chicago businessman more extravagantly.

•

Sullivan might have written of an "architecture of democracy," but it is difficult to locate the democratic associations in his buildings or to place him comfortably in the company of Emerson and Whitman, his cultural heroes. A solitary, self-absorbed man, unengaged in the civic life of Chicago, he seemed "untroubled by a social conscience," as Frank Lloyd Wright noted, and "accepted the economic situation as he found it." He never questioned, nor did he write deeply about, the economic conditions that gave rise to skyscrapers or the motives of those for whom he designed them. "It is not my purpose," he declared in "The Tall Office Building Artistically Considered," his most famous essay, "to discuss the social conditions . . . that result . . . in a demand for the erection of tall office buildings . . . ; I accept them as the fact." Sullivan thought of himself as a living link to Walt Whitman, his spiritual kinsman, but his verses in stone and clay represent less the spirit of ascendant Democracy (he always capitalized it) than that of rising Chicago. Chicago was the nineteenth century's consummate industrial city, and Sullivan, with his Spencerian faith in automatic progress through science and invention, was one of its most representative types.

Portrayed by his most worshipful admirers as an unsullied artist who struggled against the commercial tide, Sullivan admired the energy and élan of Chicago's businessmen and hoped to harness their talents to produce a new American architecture—and with it, a new American city. Not a city of chaste, classical buildings such as McKim, Mead, and White were designing in New York and Boston, but a thoroughly modern metropolis abreast, even ahead, of its age, tall and technically sophisticated, with its buildings expressing the synthesis of capitalism and culture, emotion and reason, science and the spirit that he saw as the hope of his age. With his friend John Root, Sullivan wanted to use the hand of art to try to express and discipline the city's commercial spirit, not suppress it. The source of the anti-business Sullivan is the aging and angry man who, unable to get commissions to build, turned to writing to express his genius—but also his frustration. The productive artist of the 1880s and 1890s found himself in a city and an age wonderfully suited to his talents and inclinations. In Chicago, he wrote of his youth, "there was stir; and energy that made [me] tingle to be in the game."

Sullivan's confidence in science and technology cannot be understood apart from his ideas about democracy. They went together—science and democracy—and had been advancing in tandem, he believed, since the overthrow of feudalism, a pageant of progress thrillingly told in one of his favorite books, John William Draper's intellectual history of Europe. On one point, however, Sullivan, an inconsistent thinker, broke decisively with Draper. Democracy, for Sullivan, was not a political system or even a political ideology. In his misty writings it is a romantic belief in the power of the human spirit to grow and create, a power he associated, however, more with great men like himself and his capitalist sponsors—builders and visionaries—than with the common crowd, a Nietzschean but also a very "Chicago" idea. Every page of his autobiography declares his belief in the power of an inspired few to bring important change—a notion he would have found support for in Emerson—and his equally strong faith in the power of art as an instrument of reform. "To the artist has been given the command to go forth into all the world and preach the gospel of beauty. The perfect man is the perfect artist." These words of Whitman's describe the spirit in which Sullivan went at his work in the 1890s. Yet this architectural revolutionary, this "Poet of Democracy," raised to the level of classic art the headquarter buildings of the masters of an economic order he himself found selfish and socially blind in his failing years, when he was living alone and drinking heavily in a seedy Chicago hotel.

Adler and Sullivan built one more Chicago skyscraper after the Schiller Building, the thirteen-story Chicago Stock Exchange Building, for an investment group headed by Ferdinand Peck. Designed in 1893, it proved to be a culminating structure, one of the last of the skyscrapers of Chicago's golden age of tall buildings. The building's most striking visual feature was Sullivan's magnificently decorated trading room, which was restored by architect John Vinci at the Art Institute after the building was demolished in 1972.* The Chicago Stock Exchange's most important legacy to skyscraper history, however, is Adler's daring foundation work.

John Root's floating raft was only a partial solution to Chicago's soil problems. The greatly taller buildings that the steel frame made possible needed stronger foundation supports, lest they settle with alarming unevenness. In the Schiller Building, working with the Civil War hero Gen. William Sooy Smith, one of the nation's foremost bridge builders,

*The building's entrance arch was also saved. Sitting on the grounds of the Art Institute, it has become the "Wailing Wall" of Chicago's preservationists.

Adler had supported his tremendous tower on a raft foundation that was locked in place by fifty-foot-long timber piles—over seven hundred of them—driven to hardpan clay by enormous pile drivers. The building settled perfectly, but on the Stock Exchange job Adler feared that the earthquake vibrations caused by pile driving would damage the printing presses and shatter the adjoining walls of the Chicago Herald Building. The engineering solution he came up with was the Chicago caisson. Deep wells were sunk to hardpan, one for each column of the building's west wall. To prevent water seepage and cave-ins, these wells were lined, as they were dug, with waterproof wood sheathing and steel rings—similar to barrel hoops. As the wells reached deep into the earth toward dense blue clay, they were strung with electric lamps for the digging crews. When "suitable bottom" was reached, buckets of cement were sent down, and the wells were filled, making solid concrete piers.

These were the first caisson foundations in Chicago. No longer would new skyscrapers settle unevenly or excessively, there or in other cities. In finally solving the problem of foundations, the Stock Exchange Building "unleashed the ultimate possibilities of the skyscraper," Henry Ericsson wrote in 1942, allowing the Major's Birdcage "to climb to the dizzy heights that it has since attained."

But not immediately in Chicago. Just as local architects acquired the final piece of technical know-how to build defiantly tall skyscrapers, the city enacted laws in 1892 and 1893 limiting the height of buildings to 130 feet, or about ten stories, the height of the Montauk Block, the building that started the city's race for the sky. The Stock Exchange, the Marquette, and a number of other skyscrapers built just after 1892 went up under permits taken out before the law went into effect. Historians have argued that these height restrictions had no practical effect in Chicago, since skyscraper construction ended, anyway, with the financial Panic of 1893. But when the economic depression lifted, the law—albeit with a slightly more liberal allowance—was still there, and it prevented Chicago from competing with New York in skyscraper construction. Until 1911, Burnham and Root's Masonic Temple remained the highest building in Chicago, a scantling—at twenty-two stories—compared to the majestic Woolworth Tower, sixty stories high from subbasement to Gothic tower, Manhattan's, and the world's, tallest building when it was completed to Auditorium-like civic fanfare in 1913.

•

Late in his life, Louis Sullivan described a sea change that he saw beginning to take place in American architecture in the year he started work on the Chicago Stock Exchange Building. Just as Chicago architects began transforming the tall office building into an artistic triumph—when "the future looked bright" and "the flag was in the breeze"—a "small white cloud" appeared on the horizon. "The name of this cloud was eighteen hundred and ninety-three." In that year Daniel Burnham unveiled his make-believe city for the Columbian Exposition, its stunning white palaces inspired by the classical architecture orders. This was the most admired ensemble of buildings in the history of the country, and it provoked, Sullivan argued, "a violent outbreak of the Classic and the Renaissance," a "bogus antique" that cut short the promising movement toward an original American architecture begun in Chicago in the 1880s. "Thus Architecture died in the land of the free and the home of the brave."

This idea of "the lost cause" is one of the great romantic myths in architectural history. Modern architecture did not die in 1893, the victim of the public's sudden fascination with the White City's shimmering palaces and turrets. Neoclassical architecture, which had thrived in the early nineteenth century, experienced a strong revival at least a decade before the Columbian Exposition, while Chicago modernists continued to do important work after 1893. The firm of Holabird and Roche designed some of the finest office buildings in the country, including the Marquette, after 1893, and Sullivan himself built his most stylishly modern Chicago building, the Carson Pirie Scott Department Store, six years after "the appalling calamity" of the World's Fair. Frank Lloyd Wright, America's seminal modern architect, was just beginning his career in 1893, the year he opened his own practice in offices he helped design in the Schiller Building. After the breakup of his partnership with Adler in 1895, Sullivan continued for a time his preoccupation with the vertical, designing the beautifully proportioned Bayard Building in New York, while his worshipful "student" became the great prophet of the horizontal, designing ground-hugging houses for prairie suburbs, an architecture even more original and adventurously American than Sullivan's.

Nor was there a "violent" public reaction in Chicago against the commercial aesthetic, as Sullivan claimed. Chicagoans continued to point with pride to their deliberately utilitarian skyscrapers even as they lauded their new neoclassical libraries and museums inspired by the work of the New York firm of McKim, Mead, and White. Burnham was one of the only Chicago architects to insist that all new buildings echo the ancients, but he never urged, as Sullivan's account intimated, a mindless retreat to Boyington-like eclecticism.

The neoclassical impulse coming out of the East was an effort to purge American architecture of the wilder excesses of historical revivalism by returning to fundamental architectural principles. The ideals this architecture sought to express were the very ones the most inventive Chicago architects were trying to embody in their own work—order, harmony, and repose, values that both eastern historicists and Chicago modernists agreed were necessary to tame the modern city's turbulent energies and counterbalance its barren materialism. And McKim, Mead, and White thought that they, too, were developing an architecture for an American democracy, one founded on the classical sources that had nourished the work of Thomas Jefferson, the first great American architect.

Although Louis Sullivan saw the new direction in architecture as the abandonment and ruin of all he stood for, the civic resurgence that prepared the way for what he called Chicago's "Columbian Ecstasy" began, ironically, with the public excitement surrounding the opening of his Auditorium Theater. The architect who lost that commission was in the audience when the theater was dedicated. Daniel Hudson Burnham, dreamer of big dreams, would play a far larger role in the remaking of Chicago than the indrawn genius sipping whiskey that evening at the hotel's sumptuous oak bar.

12

The New Chicago

1. Burnham's White City

SPEAKING at the gala opening of the Auditorium Theater, Mayor DeWitt Cregier said he regretted that this princely building stood alone. But Chicago, he added, was seeking to secure "a mate," and he invited President Benjamin Harrison to the "wedding which will occur in this city . . . in 1892." If the dedication of the Auditorium "was the first act of a metropolitan drama, the city was already preparing to raise the curtain upon a more ambitious second act," wrote Harriet Monroe. That second act was cast and directed by the men who had backed and built the Auditorium, a vast collective project that announced that Chicago had the money, the organizational talent, and the civic unity to put on the most impressive World's Fair up to that time.

Chicago's cultural awakening began just before the city entered the national competition for the Columbian Exposition, but once it joined that fight, every major civic event and undertaking, beginning with the Auditorium project, was influenced by its driving desire to be America's host to the fair that would commemorate Columbus's landfall in the New World. The fair is easily the most widely written about event in Chicago history, but the preparations for it were far more important for the city's future than the fair itself. These preparations spawned or broadened the work of a host of new civic organizations and institutions that were part of what Henry Fuller called "the Upward Movement in Chicago," an elite-inspired effort at civic regeneration that continued well beyond the closing of the exposition.

•

The citizens' committee that was formed in the summer of 1889 to head the city's campaign to secure the World's Fair was a veritable who's who of the local commercial aristocracy: Marshall Field; George Pullman; Potter Palmer; Philip Armour; Charles T. Yerkes; Ferdinand W. Peck; Charles L. Hutchinson; Martin A. Ryerson; Cyrus J. McCormick, Jr.; Joseph Medill, publisher of the *Chicago Tribune;* Edward T. Jeffrey, president of the Illinois Central Railroad; Lyman J. Gage, the city's leading banker; and Harlow W. Higinbotham, the Marshall Field partner who would head the committee that was eventually formed to oversee the planning and administration of the exposition. The absolute resolve of these business titans was expressed in a motion they passed at the initial meeting of the chartered corporation formed to raise money for the fair. "The men who have helped build Chicago want this fair and . . . they intend to get it."

But this effort engaged the entire community. Clerks and salesmen bought ten-dollar shares in the World's Exposition Corporation, and the local papers published the names of subscribers and the amounts pledged. In all, nearly thirty thousand Chicagoans bought subscriptions, and the city's energies were mobilized in a military-style campaign.

A handful of cities competed for the fair, but by the time the 51st Congress convened in December 1889, it had come down to a fight between Chicago and New York. Each city established an impressive Washington-based lobbying committee, and each city's newspapers poured scorn on its rival city, but in the end, it was Chicago's reputation as a convention center, its unrivaled rail connections, its proven capacity for carrying through big municipal projects, and its pledge of an additional $4 million that decided the issue in Congress. In April 1890, President Harrison presented the Auditorium her mate, signing the bill naming Chicago the host city of the international exhibition. The date of the fair, however, was pushed back one year to allow Chicago the time it would need to put on what its newspapers called a "jumbo" event.

"Make it the Greatest Show on Earth," P. T. Barnum advised the World's Fair committee, "—greater than my own . . . show if you can." And to bring in the crowds he suggested borrowing the mummy of Ramses II from Egypt. But the fair's Chicago organizers had other ideas, hoping to dispel the belief, trumpeted in the New York press, that they would embarrass the entire nation by putting on a "cattle

show on the shore of Lake Michigan." Believing that the artistic reputation of the country was in their hands, they had already sent a delegation to study the Paris Universal Exposition of 1889, which featured
a neoclassical Cour d'Honneur framed by monumentally large exposition buildings and by two of the most celebrated civil engineering
feats of the century, the Eiffel Tower and the Machinery Palace, with
the largest clear-span roof ever erected. Chicago considered itself the
new world capital of architecture and engineering and was determined
to outdo Paris's fair as a building achievement.

•

   The Columbian Exposition was one of the most spectacular construction efforts of the century. To help it pick a site for the exposition
and prepare a ground plan, the Chicago committee commissioned
Frederick Law Olmsted. The bent, white-bearded old master arrived
in Chicago in August 1890 with Henry Codman, his young assistant,
to begin work on the culminating achievement of his career on the very
spot, eight miles south of the Loop, where he had prepared a park plan
before the Great Fire. Jackson Park, with only a few improvements on
its northern border, was a water-soaked flat, bare except for a scattering of oak trees stripped of their foliage by gales that swept in from
Lake Michigan. But in its favor, it was on the lake, the most beautiful
natural feature of the region, and was bordered on the west by the
tracks of several major railroads, connecting it with the downtown area
and, from there, with the country. Its very state of undevelopment provided Olmsted, an inspired "painter" of natural landscapes, a clean
canvas to work with.

   That fall, Burnham and Root were named supervising architects of
the exposition and began collaborating with Olmsted and Codman to
sketch in pencil and on brown paper an American Venice of interlinked canals, basins, and lagoons, with all the major exposition halls
touching water and with an architecture court—an obvious Parisian
derivation—surrounding a reflecting basin decorated with symbolic
fountains and statuary. The Court of Honor fronted the lake on an east-
west axis and was to be the "entrance hall" to the exposition for travelers arriving by either boat or train, while Olmsted's canals and lagoons
ran north from the court on an axis parallel to the lake. In the middle
of the largest lagoon, Olmsted placed a wooden island, to be kept free
of "conspicuous buildings," its natural landscaping supplying "an
episode in refreshing relief" to the grandeur of the main exhibition
halls. A quixotic combination of the stately and naturalistic, the landscape plan was a stunning visual achievement. Remembered best in
history as a spectacular architectural show, the Columbian Exposi-

tion's most impressive design accomplishment was actually Olmsted and Root's artful reshaping of an unsightly split of sand and swamp water.

In November, Burnham was appointed director of works and given the primary responsibility of choosing the architects. He and Root, by common consent, would design none of the buildings, confining their work to supervision and overall planning, work that prepared Burnham to become one of the supreme urban planners of his day. Four of Burnham's five choices to build the principal buildings on the Court of Honor were easterners: Richard M. Hunt, Charles Follen McKim of McKim, Mead, and White, and George B. Post, all from New York, and the Boston practice of Robert Swain Peabody and John Goddard Stearns. The fifth, Henry Van Brunt, was a Bostonian who had been working in Kansas City with Frank Maynard Howe since 1887 and was a student of Hunt's and the mentor of Howe, Peabody, and Stearns. All had been indelibly influenced by Hunt, a graduate of the Ecole des Beaux-Arts who had been recently using his position as founder and president of the American Institute of Architects to campaign for a national return to classical styles.

Van Brunt immediately wired Burnham his acceptance, but the eastern architects were hesitant, fearing that time-draining work on "architectural screens" built of plaster and only for a summer season would not be worth their effort. In late December, Burnham headed for New York on a Pullman car to meet with them at the Players Club and convince them to join his design team, which would erect, he confidently told them, "a dream city" that would shape the future course of American architecture. The apparent terms of their acceptance were that Burnham agree to a common style, the classical, and a common cornice line, making the buildings around the reflecting pool a harmonious composition. Burnham had no trouble with this, for he wanted, he had told a friend before leaving for New York, a "monumental" architecture to give the buildings the "splendor which an exposition of this magnitude demands."

The fair's Beaux-Arts architects were the leading style makers of American architecture at a time when Chicago's architects were still seen by most of their eastern colleagues as advocates of a crude regional vernacular. Burnham felt he needed them to give the fair prestige and to ensure that it would be seen as a national, not just a Chicago, event. On his return from New York, however, he was greeted by a firestorm of criticsm for bypassing Chicago architects, and he agreed to add a group of local designers, including Sullivan and Adler, William Le Baron Jenney, and Solon S. Beman. But only Beman—perhaps due to George Pullman's influence—was assigned a building on the Court of Honor.

When the out-of-town architects met in Chicago for the first time, Burnham drove them out in carriages for their initial look at Jackson Park. It was a raw, overcast day, and as the easterners walked the desolate site, shaking their heads in dismay, one of them climbed on a pier and shouted to Burnham. "Do you mean to say that you really expect to open a fair here by '93?" To which Burnham shot back, "That point [is] settled!" That Saturday night, at a dinner for the architects, Burnham gave a stirring speech calling for the same spirit of "teamwork" and "self-sacrifice" that had won the Civil War, and "the men left the banquet hall," a friend of Burnham's observed, "united like soldiers in a campaign."

The following Monday, when the architects met at Burnham and Root's office-library in the Rookery, a call came in from Root's wife: Her husband had come down with pneumonia. Burnham rushed to his partner's bedside and remained there, night and day, until Root expired three days later.

The night Root died, one of Harriet Monroe's aunts secretly watched from the high corner of the stairway as Burnham paced the living room, alone, between intervals of restless sleep on the couch, punching the air with his fist and talking to himself in low, despairing tones: "I have worked, I have schemed and dreamed to make us the greatest architects in the world—I have made him see it and kept him at it—and now he dies—damn! damn! damn!"

Burnham hired Charles B. Atwood of New York to replace Root as consulting architect, but the building of the fair became almost solely Burnham's responsibility.

The "Beaux-Arts boys," as Burnham called them, remained in Chicago for a week and then returned in a private car at the end of February with their completed sketches. Unrolling them on the walls of Burnham's library, a blazing fire in the hearth, they explained their ideas to the fair's grounds and buildings committee. As the winter afternoon drew to a close, the sculptor Augustus Saint-Gaudens, who had been brought to Chicago to advise on artistic matters, approached Burnham, took him by the hands, and declared: "Look here, old fellow, do you realize that this is the greatest meeting of artists since the Fifteenth Century."

•

Construction of the White City began in the early winter of 1891 with the job of dredging and filling, an operation that required moving millions of tons of earth. Giant steam dredges cut their way inland from the lake, making channels through which they could float. By summer, the network of waterways had been completed, and with incredible speed a new city rose out of the swamp and sand.

When the buildings began to go up, as many as ten thousand visitors a day paid an admission charge to see the largest construction site in modern memory. On any given week, there were as many as twelve thousand workers on the grounds, teams of them toiling into the night under electric floodlights. Railroad tracks crisscrossed the 685-acre site, and freight engines hauled in thirty-six thousand carloads of materials for the two hundred and more structures that had to be built. Henry Codman was on the site directing the most gigantic landscape scheme ever attempted in the country, a project that involved the transplanting of over a million plants, shrubs, and trees, and Charles B. Atwood, wearing a bowler hat and a flowing cape, could be seen rushing from building to building superintending the construction of an entire city of palaces. In temporary shelters scattered about the grounds, groups of the country's finest artists, including the Impressionist painter Mary Cassatt and the sculptor Daniel Chester French, creator of the Lincoln statue in Washington, D.C., worked furiously on frescoes, statuary, and bas-reliefs. Never in the country's history had so many renowned artists and architects been brought together on a single project.

The exhibition halls were framed with wood or iron, then covered with a combination of plaster of paris and hemp fiber, called staff, and spray-painted pure white, giving them the effect of solidity and splendor. But however impressive they might have looked from the outside, almost all of them were merely decorated sheds with their interior framing exposed. It was only to the trained eye that these imitations of the ancients could be recognized as products—like Chicago skyscrapers—of the most advanced iron-and-steel engineering.

Directing the entire operation was forty-four-year-old Daniel Burnham, "one of those magnificent egoists," Harriet Monroe said, "who rule their world." His men called him "Commander in Chief," and he built a large shack, his command post, on the grounds and lived there for part of every week with his black servant, supervising his army of workers, most of whom lived in barracks on the construction site. On Sunday afternoons, Burnham brought in Theodore Thomas, the director of the Chicago Symphony Orchestra, to conduct recitals in the sitting room of his official headquarters, and he had Charles Dudley Arnold, the fair's official photographer, show lantern slides of the buildings in progress to his staff in their quarters. Burnham's chief lieutenants dined together and slept on cots, and every morning at dawn—reveille—a big wagon appeared at their dormitory door, and everyone made a tour of the grounds with the Director of Works. To provide security and keep out labor agitators, Burnham built an eight-foot fence with barbed wire around the grounds and posted guards at the gates. He saw his commission as a supreme civic duty and tried to instill that spirit in his workers.

Walter A. Wyckoff, a Princeton graduate who worked his way across the country taking odd jobs to see life from a laborer's perspective, was hired as a construction worker on the fairgrounds in the spring of 1892. In his book *The Workers*, he described living with hundreds of his fellow laborers in a wooden "hotel" on the site of the future Court of Honor. "Guarded by sentries and high barriers from unsought contact with all beyond, great gangs of us, healthy, robust men, live and labor in a marvelous artificial world. . . . Work . . . is well paid and directed with the highest skill. And . . . we work our eight hours a day in peaceful security and in absolute confidence of our pay." One of Wyckoff's fellow "soldiers" was a man named Elias Disney, father of the builder of two of the next century's greatest fantasy worlds.

But Wyckoff failed to give the full picture. Burnham drove his crews relentlessly, even in the winter, when freezing lake blasts and swirling snow made work on the scaffolding spectacularly dangerous. No one working under these pressures and in this brutal weather thought himself in a worker's paradise. Burnham honored the eight-hour day but refused, until the last month of construction, to accede to union requests for a minimum wage, and when labor organizers infiltrated his crews, he moved at once to tighten security. Though he insisted on tight safety precautions, there were over seven hundred accidents and eighteen deaths in twenty months of labor, making work conditions in the Burnham compound less safe than those in a Pennsylvania coal mine. A great number of these casualties involved the architectural ironworkers, most of them Great Lakes seamen hired for their skill in working on rigging and their obliviousness to the perils of standing on iron beams a hundred feet in the sky, with the Chicago wind blowing a gale.

As the stately plaster pavilions took form, Burnham became increasingly attached to neoclassical architecture, as did important Chicago sponsors of the fair like Charles Hutchinson, who regularly visited the construction site, sometimes staying overnight with the director in his cabin in the compound, with its country-style fireplace and splendid stock of wines. Burnham's enthusiasm for Beaux-Arts classicism came to be shared by a number of prominent Chicago architects, among them William Le Baron Jenney, designer of the Horticultural Building, a sumptuous Renaissance palace on Olmsted's main lagoon. Of the important Chicago architects, only Henry Ives Cobb, with his Romanesque-inspired Fisheries Building, and Louis Sullivan, with his polychromatically decorated Transportation Building, broke decisively with the classical consensus, a consensus strengthened by Burnham's budding friendship with Charles McKim, his chief guide on the fair project "in matters of order, fitness, and taste."

It came as no surprise, then, that when the directors of the exposition announced plans to place the fair's only permanent building—one hosting a summer series of congresses on world issues—on the lakefront in downtown Chicago, they awarded the commission to an eastern firm proposing a building in the Italian Renaissance style of the Court of Honor. This palace of culture, now the world-famous Art Institute, would influence Chicago's architecture well into the next century, when a growing taste for Beaux-Arts classicism produced a group of buildings that remain local landmarks, among them the Field Museum of Natural History, the Shedd Aquarium, and the all-white, floodlighted Wrigley Building, still downtown Chicago's most dazzling night scene.

The partners of the Boston firm of Shepley, Rutan, and Coolidge, while at work on their drawings for the fair's Michigan Avenue building, won the commission for the city's new public library. These two imperially scaled buildings constituted the beginnings of what would become an encompassing design by Daniel Burnham to transform a lakefront still cluttered with train tracks, squatters' shacks, and mountains of garbage into a forum of parks, public statuary, and stately civic architecture. Burnham's Chicago Plan of 1909, the greatest municipal project in Chicago's history, would take its inspiration directly from the dream city he had built in Olmsted's lakeside park. It was the crowning achievement of an impressive succession of civic improvements begun during the "Columbian" season, none of them more important for the city's cultural reputation than the Art Institute.

2. Hutchinson's Three-Ring Circus

The land for the Columbian Exposition's downtown headquarters was secured from the city in an agreement engineered by Charles Lawrence Hutchinson, president of the Commercial Club, head of the Art Institute, and—with Burnham—the most aggressive promoter of the New Chicago. Under the terms of the deal, the Art Institute was to take over the building as soon as the fair closed, the institute having already outgrown the handsome brown building Burnham and Root had designed for it in the mid-1880s. In this way, Hutchinson made certain that the city's cultural life would be immediately enhanced by its hosting the fair, with part of the funding for the new building coming, at his powerful urging, from the exposition's coffers. It wasn't the last big Chicago art deal Charles Lawrence Hutchinson would pull off.

With a revolution going on in Chicago architecture, some critics saw the new Art Institute building as a squandered opportunity. Recent breakthroughs in construction technology would send civic buildings of the future to heights taller than the tallest business towers, a New York architect predicted, but most Chicago architects and their sponsors preferred that their new cultural centers be built close to the ground in styles expressive of the supreme civilizations of human history.

The Art Institute and the Chicago Public Library offended Frank Lloyd Wright, the apostle of innovation. "The Art Institute," he wrote, "is a stupid building with no countenance and elaborate flanks; the Public Library, two buildings, one on top of the other, is a disgraceful quarrel." But these two "gray ghosts" were widely admired when they were completed and were built, like Chicago's best modern skyscrapers, for use as well as for show, in styles at once monumental but subdued, with ornament kept to a tasteful minimum. The vertical plan and elevator technology of the skyscraper moved customers and clients arriving in twos and threes to their destinations quickly and efficiently, while the Art Institute's horizontal plan, with its spacious hallways and wide, sweeping staircases, moved great numbers of people arriving in a steady flow to, and efficiently through, the exhibit galleries. And like almost all of the skyscrapers managed by Owen Aldis, the extravagance was saved for the interior. The Art Institute's design called for a central stairway in a magnificent skylighted space, while the Public Library's interior was that of a Florentine palace, with a profusion of Carrara marble, hand-wrought iron, and beautiful mosaics.

If architecture is language, the collective expression of the ideas and aims of a community, the skyscraper and the Palace of Culture conveyed what Chicago aspired to be at the time of the fair, a city of art as well as commerce, the low, classically inspired cultural buildings hugging the lake line and the high, confidently modern business blocks rising above and behind them on the smoky skyline, the entire architectural ensemble mirroring the local hierarchy of power. Chicago was still more about business than anything else; the difference was that influential businessmen had recently become interested in subsidizing culture in a big way.

For Chicago's capitalists, promotion of the arts was part of an effort to maintain control of their city. Frightened by the direction of urban change but unable to shape it through direct political action because they had withdrawn from active engagement in city government, they sought to augment their economic power through privately managed boards and committees dedicated to civic causes, organizations born in the cigar-scented parlors of their downtown clubs. These elite clubs began to appear with the passing of the founding generation, men like William Ogden, Isaac Arnold, and Gurdon Saltonstall Hubbard, who, though rich and powerful, had remained intensely political. Through their control of self-selective civic organizations, Chicago's postfire clubmen exercised a strong influence on the culture and social character of their city, building armories and military installations to suppress labor disturbances, training schools, orphanages, and hospitals for the "deserving poor," as well as cultural institutions designed to encourage civic patriotism. A great art museum might also convince common workers of the superiority of the culture of the local elite, which would be exclusively on display in its galleries, "high" culture being differentiated from "low" culture—whose aim was to entertain, not to uplift—by the mere fact of its being in a consecrated place staffed and stocked by self-anointed cultural guardians.

Yet while the desire to impose moral order encouraged cultural benefaction, more disinterested motives also came into play. Charles Hutchinson, the institute's president for some forty years, was a man of his class, suspicious of labor unions and an ardent advocate of the doctrine of self-help. In his capacity as president of the Art Institute, however, Hutchinson was as democratic as his background and upbringing would permit him to be. "We have built this institution for the public," he told a reporter at the opening of the institute's Burnham and Root building in 1887, "not for a few. . . . We want the people of Chicago to feel that it is their property." Nor was the institute an agency of deliberate cultural indoctrination, as some modern historians argue. How patrons reacted to paintings and statuary on display in the galleries was, Hutchinson believed, their own business. His task, as a self-styled cultural entrepreneur, was to supply the product and open the doors. And he went at his work as if he were saving souls.

For Charles Hutchinson, public service was a private religion. He was one of the great urban benefactors of his day, "the expression and the product, . . . even the creator," of Chicago's civic idealism, a friend described his reputation on the occasion of his death. His father, the feared trader who read Shakespeare between world-shaking grain deals, raised him for business. But his deeply devout mother, whose family had arrived in Massachusetts Bay in 1629, carved into his character a sense of his public responsibilities as a member of a well-placed family, people who were equipped and expected to lead.

Bookish and pious, he wanted to go to college in the East after graduating from Chicago's only public high school in 1873, but his unyielding father had his way, pushing him into his world as a three-dollar-a-day clerk in his Corn Exchange Bank. Charles Hutchinson might not have had a taste for business, but he was exceedingly good at it. By the time he was twenty-seven, he was president of the bank and richer than his more famous father and, like him, a feared commodities trader, although not nearly as reckless as the man who became the "Wheat King of the World" after running a corner on September wheat in 1888, the year his son, at the age of thirty-four, was elected president of the Chicago Board of Trade.

His father's career collapsed soon after this, and when he lost his fortune, he began to lose his sanity and was finally committed to a Wisconsin sanitarium. But well before the onset of his father's financial and physical troubles, Charles had decided not to give his entire life to business.

With his inborn inclination for trade, he could easily have been far richer than he became, but "in his youth and early manhood," a friend identified the great turn in his life, "he became enthralled by a vision of a man of independent means devoted to the service of the community." At age nineteen, he began spending almost all his free time as a volunteer in a church mission, and not long after his marriage in 1881 to Frances Kinsley, daughter of the city's most famous caterer, he began giving at least half of his time—and eventually half of his yearly earnings—to philanthropic causes. "Everybody should put into the city in which he lives," he declared, "as much as he gets out of it." To name the organizations he headed or was active in is to call the roll of Chicago's principal charitable and cultural associations. At one time or another, he was treasurer of the Auditorium Association, a member of the Board of South Parks Commissioners, a director of the Chicago Public Relief and Aid Society and the Chicago YMCA, a trustee of Hull-House and the University of Chicago, and an officer or controlling figure in over sixty other organizations, among them hospitals for young women, old people's homes, orphan asylums, and centers for the manual training of boys.

But the passion of his public life was the Art Institute, the organization he helped found in 1882 and remained president of until his death in 1924. "In the deepest sense," one of his friends said, "Charles L. Hutchinson *was* the Art Institute."

Hutchinson was an art enthusiast, not just an art philanthropist, and his work for the Art Institute grew straight out of his own life experience and fit perfectly into his thought-out conception of civic stewardship. "We live," he said in an 1888 address at the Art Institute, "in a materialistic age . . . and . . . in one of the most barren cities," where most men were in "a state of slavery, . . . mere machine[s] devoted to business." For Hutchinson and other young men of fortune who had seen their fathers physically broken and morally diminished by business, art became the great counterforce of materialism, its cultivation the key to creating more balanced men and a more balanced civilization. But Hutchinson was also a cultural missionary: What was good for the select few would be even better for the masses. Art museums would raise the level of public taste and, with it, public behavior, but only if they welcomed everyone, not just the "carriage class" that many eastern museums catered to. How, after all, could cultural leaders hope to raise up those beneath them unless they brought them under their saving influence in institutions of their own creation?

This preacher of the "Democracy of Art," however, had little faith in the everyday workings of political democracy. For him, the appeal of cultural reform, as opposed to political and economic reform, was that the better classes could safely control it. "The real work of this world," he wrote, "is done by the minority." And it was done, he added tellingly, not by individuals, as it had been in the past in Chicago, but by "organized effort, working through . . . institutions" formed and led by "hard-headed businessmen." In this spirit, working with hand-picked trustees, Hutchinson turned to the "business" of bringing high culture to the most professedly uncultivated city in America.

•

After moving the Art Institute into its Burnham and Root building in 1887, Hutchinson's first task was to expand and upgrade its permanent collection, which consisted mostly of plaster-cast reproductions and some appallingly bad family portraits that Old Settlers had bequeathed to it. In this effort, he had the financial help and judicious counsel of his closest friend, Martin A. Ryerson. Quiet and scholarly looking, educated at private schools in Paris and Geneva before heading off to Harvard, Ryerson traveled incessantly, training himself on the go to be a world expert on art and religious architecture while continuing to run his family's vastly successful lumber empire. He also became a "keen trader of works of art," writes historian Wayne Andrews, "dickering for them with something of the shrewdness of his father in the Michigan woods."

Hutchinson had Ryerson appointed vice president of the Art Institute, and their two families—both of them childless—traveled together from Spain to the deepest reaches of Asia searching for rare finds to haul back to Chicago. On their first trip together in 1890, Hutchinson and Ryerson learned of the impending sale in Paris of a fabulous collection of Old Masters by the widow of Prince Demidoff, who lived in a villa near Florence. Racing to Tuscany by train and rented carriage, they convinced the princess, who had squandered her inheritance, to sell them part of her late husband's treasures, including the Rembrandt workshop's *Young Girl at an Open Half-Door*, before the canvases went on the Parisian auction block. Cables from Hutchinson to wealthy Chicago friends brought pledges covering half the cost of the paintings, and he and Ryerson reached into their deep pockets for the other half. "The princess needed money," Hutchinson described this Windy City art hustle to a reporter, "and the price was too tempting to resist."

On his return to the states, Hutchinson—in a scene right out of Twain's *Innocents Abroad*—called the paintings "corkers, every one of them," to the delight of Chicago-bashing New York reporters. Hutchinson, said one New York paper, "probably paid $1,000 a foot for his Rubenses, Rembrandts and Van Dykes and we presume the citizens of Chicago will give him a triumphal procession along the lakefront when they arrive, carrying them and him in huge floats, drawn by a team of milk-white Berkshire hogs." But Hutchinson was nonplussed. "We have made our money in pigs," as his family truly had, "but is that any reason why we should not spend it on paintings?"

Hutchinson got Charles T. Yerkes, Potter and Bertha Palmer, and other Chicago collectors to scout European capitals for canvases for the Art Institute. Bertha Palmer bought a collection of Monets in 1892, which she eventually donated, along with the work of other Impressionists, to the Art Institute, and Ryerson used his personal friendships with Monet, Renoir, and Mary Cassatt to locate some spectactular finds. He filled the walls of his Drexel Avenue mansion with Renoirs when they were not thought to be secure investments and helped purchase for the institute El Greco's *Assumption of the Virgin,* one of the greatest paintings ever. Ryerson had the gift of the true collector—an unerring eye. It is said he made only two mistakes in buying paintings, when in both cases he went to art experts for advice.

A few of Hutchinson's stuffier associates on the board of trustees would have turned the Art Institute into a shrine, a place so solemnly proper it would have intimidated all but the comfortable classes. But Hutchinson insisted that "the Institute should be measured by the service it rendered to the community in which it stands." Its central location, close to where all transit lines met—not in some remote park—made it accessible "to the great masses of the people," and in the 1890s it charged no admission on three days of the week, including Sunday, the workingman's only day of rest and recreation. On the first free Sunday, barely nine hundred people showed up, but within a few years the museum was drawing up to three to four thousand on Sunday afternoons, and the crowds included people of all classes. "Workmen," one reporter noted, "go stumping over the mosaic floor with their hob-nailed boots, and women, with no head covering but a shawl, stare respectfully at rare Old Masters." One regular Sunday visitor was a Polish immigrant worker, his face cracked and worn, who walked to the institute along the Illinois Central's tracks from Packingtown.

Hutchinson organized all kinds of activities to draw in people: concerts, lectures by popular speakers, flower shows, even an aquatic display with sixty thousand fish in tanks. "I want all Chicago here," he would bellow to his staff. Better, he said, to have the museum a "three-ring circus" than a "mausoleum."

Although the galleries were his first interest, he expanded the art school and made sure that it, too, was "a Community House for all Chicago." His allies in this effort were the institute's director, William M. R. French, a New Hampshire surveyor turned art enthusiast, and Lorado Taft, a tall, bearded sculptor trained at the Beaux-Arts, who was the most inspiring teacher at the institute. French pushed the institute in ever more democratic directions until it began exhibiting priceless works of art in the field houses of city parks and organizing noontime lectures for industrial workers right at the plant. With Taft, he made the institute the largest art school in the world, a true art university whose students later included Georgia O'Keeffe, Claes Oldenburg, and Red Grooms.

●

Hutchinson's daily routine was unvarying. He would arrive at the institute at nine o'clock sharp and leave promptly at eleven for his Corn Exchange Bank in the Rookery. There, seated at a big desk out in the open, he would administer to his far-flung businesses, always keeping time available, however, for those who came to plead for help for this or that charitable or civic cause or for friends who would drop by for personal advice. "Time and again," Ernest Poole recalled, "he would coax and plead like a Dutch uncle with some young couple to keep their marriage off the rocks. Fathers came for help with their sons, for they knew that he liked the young and could feel their points of view."

Later in the day, Hutchinson would head back to the institute roaming the halls, looking in on the classrooms and galleries, a big, round-faced man, straight as a ship's door, humming Christian hymns as he walked. His work often carried over into the evening—conferences, receptions, or student dinners—and there were always socials at his Prairie Avenue home for likely donors. At the institute he seemed forever in a hurry; at home he was the very picture of composure. He loved to sit with his wife and read, and he always had time for his brood of nephews and nieces. "Terribly fond of children and having none of his own, on Sundays he'd ask us all to his house for an enormous breakfast of corned-beef hash and waffles," recalled one of his nieces, "and after that he would lead us in a wild romp over the house. At first he would chase us and then we him, upstairs and down, our shrieks of laughter answered by his whoops and shouts! At last at the piano he'd hammer out *Onward, Christian Soldiers* while we sang, and then he would take us to Sunday school."

Every Thanksgiving he would show up at Hull-House with a dozen or more turkeys, carving them to the cheers of the children. And in summers he would take his nephews and nieces to his seventy-acre forest retreat and bird sanctuary on the shores of Lake Geneva, near the Ryersons' vacation home. He would teach them to fish, for he was an avid outdoorsman who held a number of local fishing records, or, dressed in flannels and wearing a black slouch hat like the one his father had worn, he would show them how to care for and identify wildflowers. "I could write a book upon the joy and inspiration to be found in a garden," he said in one of his talks as president of the Lake Geneva Horticultural Society. He never had the time to do so, but his wife did publish a delightful pair of volumes about the pleasures of country gardening.

A quarter of a century after the Art Institute opened its doors in rented commercial space in the Loop, Charles Hutchinson said he was no longer ashamed of his city's cultural reputation. Few cities had accomplished as much in the arts in so short a time, and "in no other city," he declared, "is the influence of art more directly felt by the masses." The figures bore him out. By then the Art Institute was drawing almost a quarter of a million more visitors than Boston's Museum of Fine Arts and 150,000 more than New York's Metropolitan Museum of Art.

But the institute was "simply in its infancy," Hutchinson later told a friend from the hospital bed on which he died. "I love to lie here and think of it—of all it will do for the people in the years to come!"

3. Harper's University

"Like the cathedral of the Middle Ages, [the Art Institute] is the one place in the city that should never be closed to the people at any time, even if it took three shifts to keep it open," declared Frank Lloyd Wright in his essay "Chicago Culture." If the University of Chicago's first president had had his way, his school, backed by the Chicago millionaires who founded the Art Institute, might have followed Wright's advice. As it was, William Rainey Harper announced that the university—which welcomed its first class as the Art Institute's Michigan Avenue building was nearing completion—would be open the entire year, classes to be held right through the summer. And Harper himself, one of the most extraordinary figures in the history of American education, maintained a ferociously demanding schedule, one person running three punishing shifts.

Up at dawn, he bicycled before breakfast, pedaling slowly so that his assistant—walking beside him—could take notes, and by nine A.M. he was in conference with his leading administrators with one of his impossibly crowded agendas. "Gentlemen," he would typically announce at the start of a meeting, "I have forty points to be discussed this morning." Taking cat naps in an office chair between endless cups of coffee, he worked at this pace well past midnight, fashioning a university unlike any other in the world.

He called it the university of the future, an experiment in both democracy and higher learning. But though he had the fortunes of some of the richest men in America behind him, not many people thought this son of a village storekeeper could fulfill his dream.

"A short, broad man with thick black hair, fat swarthy face . . . and firm chin, with eyeglasses behind which . . . sharp eyes glistened, he was altogether unlike anything I had ever seen in the academic world," Robert Herrick, one of his English instructors, described him, "[a] professor [who was also] a man of force. He was an example of what the great uncharted west was going to do when it broke into 'culture.' A man of indomitable force."

At about the time Chicago won the battle in Congress to hold the Columbian celebration, word reached Herrick and his Harvard circle of professors and writers that a young Hebrew scholar from Yale, only thirty-four years old in 1890, was preparing to build a world-class uni-

versity in Chicago "overnight so to speak, as they build grain elevators. Cambridge, skeptical and critical, affected to receive the news in
a humorous spirit," Herrick recalled in his unpublished memoirs,
"but as one after another of considerable persons in the academic
world fell before Dr. Harper's persuasive methods and aligned himself
with the new enterprise . . . even Cambridge pricked up its ears and
ceased to scoff."

When Herrick was invited to join the faculty of the new university,
he packed a bag and took a train to Chicago to look it over. Stepping
off the cable car that had brought him from the Loop, he stood on the
Hyde Park prairie Paul Cornell had platted and drained, between
Olmsted's Washington and Jackson parks, gazing with disappointment
at the "unfinished gray stone buildings scattered loosely over the immense campus which was nothing more than a quagmire with a frog
pond at the south end." Just a few blocks east of this chaotic construction scene, he could see the vastly larger building site of the great
fair Chicago would host. They stood next to each other, connected by
Olmsted's Midway Plaisance, two miniature cities in the making,
Burnham's White City and Harper's Gray City, both of them planned
by "ardent, ambitious businessmen eager to change the city's image
from one of barbarous materialism to one of refinement and culture."
There was even a sharing of executive leadership, with Hutchinson,
Ryerson, and Peck serving on both the exposition committee and the
university's board of trustees, and a sharing of architectural talent as
well. Henry Ives Cobb, designer of the university's English-Gothic
campus, was the architect of the fair's classically imposing Fisheries
Building. In that twin capacity, he worked for a time "on both sides of
the Midway."

But while there were interesting parallels between the fair and the
university, the one was temporary, Harper would impress upon Herrick and other faculty recruits, the other eternal, "witness to a still
higher and more enduring idealism." And he would commission an
alma mater to carry home this point:

> The City White hath fled the earth,
> But where the azure waters lie
> A nobler city hath its birth—
> The City Gray, that ne'er shall die!
> For decades and for centuries
> Its battlemented towers shall rise
> Beneath the hope-filled western skies.

"The whole thing," Herrick recalled, "was the strangest travesty of a university I had ever dreamed—something between a broiler house, the celebrated grain elevator, and an intelligence office." When he dropped in on Boston friends who were already living in "the wilderness" of temporary buildings around the World's Fair, they cautioned him to be sure "to get everything in writing" in his negotiations with Harper. Harper's zealotry seemed to Herrick to savor of "quackery," but the young president broke through Herrick's skepticism, convincing him that he would "carry his purpose through, build his elevator university and open on time."

•

"Harper's university," as the press began to call it, was the second University of Chicago, both of them Baptist institutions, the initial one founded in 1856 on land donated by Sen. Stephen A. Douglas. When it went bankrupt in 1886, Thomas W. Goodspeed, its most committed trustee, asked John D. Rockefeller, the world's richest Baptist, to back the building of a new and more intellectually prestigious University of Chicago, a training center for graduate and undergraduate scholars of all denominations—women as well as men—that would also house a Baptist divinity school.

Some Baptist leaders wanted their new university to be located in a wholesome rural setting. But Goodspeed, working with Frederick T. Gates, a nationally prominent Baptist who would eventually become Rockefeller's adviser on philanthropy—convincing him that good works were "a passport to heaven"—impressed on the oil emperor the importance of placing it in a city, "with its condition of highest mental activity and growth." Chicago's mix of idealism and corruption offered unexcelled opportunities, he told Rockefeller, for intellectual investigation and moral reform. "If some Christian denomination does not go in and capture the city," Gates wrote Rockefeller, "infidelity will." Shortly after this, the pious plutocrat pledged six hundred thousand dollars to a school in a city he had never set foot in.

His gift, however, was contingent on Chicago's Baptists coming up with another four hundred thousand dollars. When Goodspeed failed to raise that amount, he turned almost despairingly to the city's non-Baptist business leaders "to save the undertaking from failure." He and his fellow fund-raisers "made anxious inquiries," he recalled, "as to what man in Chicago, among its leaders in business, we could first approach with some prospect of securing a sympathetic hearing. Everybody said, 'Begin with Charles L. Hutchinson.'" So they went to see him at his Corn Exchange Bank. Hutchinson heard them out, gave them a subscription, and said he would help in any way he could, for Chicago, he believed, would remain an incomplete city without a university of the highest rank, its own Harvard or Columbia. "We used Mr. Hutchinson's name with every man we subsequently approached," Goodspeed wrote later. "It was a name to conjure with. It opened minds and purses to our appeal."

When the four hundred thousand dollars was secured, Goodspeed went to Marshall Field, a man not known for his civic generosity, to ask him to donate land he owned in newly annexed Hyde Park. This was an ideal place, Goodspeed thought, for the university, easily accessible to the Loop by rail, yet protected from the clamor and soot of Chicago by the cordon of exclusive neighborhoods Paul Cornell had laid out years ago to surround the college he had hoped to lure there. After assurances from the Baptists that Hutchinson and Ryerson would be appointed to the board of trustees, Field acquiesced, opening a new phase of his life, as several years later he gave $1 million to establish the Field Museum of Natural History, an enterprise he was closely involved with for the remainder of his life. Even William B. Ogden, from across the grave, played a part in creating the university. Remembering his devoted service to the old university as president of the board of trustees, his executors donated a generous portion of his estate for a graduate school of science.

By the time the university was prepared to open, Ryerson was president of the board and serving with Hutchinson, the university's treasurer, on the committee charged with planning and overseeing the construction of the Gray City. It was Hutchinson and Ryerson who hired Cobb, an architect of rising reputation, and persuaded him to jettison a Romanesque plan for a Gothic one, the battlemented buildings of Bedford limestone to be set in Oxford-like quadrangles. For the remainder of their lives, they oversaw every detail of campus architecture and landscaping and used their fortunes and financial talents to help carry the university through one financial crisis after another brought on by Harper's often heedless expansionism. They had no desire, however, to intrude in academic matters, contrary to the famous opinion of one of the university's most controversial professors.

•

In what is perhaps the most devastating academic exposé ever written, *The Higher Learning in America: A Memorandum on the Conduct of Universities by Business Men,* Thorstein Veblen excoriated the businessman's interference in the academic affairs of the American university, drawing most of his evidence from the University of Chicago, where he taught for fourteen years. A lean, laconic Norwegian "with smoldering eyes in a pallid, usually unshaven face," Veblen came to the university a year after Robert Herrick arrived, and the two young instructors became friends and fellow critics of many of Harper's policies. Herrick, however, was outspoken, publishing his views and expressing them with eloquent force at faculty meetings, while Veblen, a low-paid lecturer hired at the insistence of his mentor, J. Laurence Laughlin, whom Harper had brought from Cornell, operated in the shadows, never taking on the university or Harper directly. He published *The Higher Learning* in 1918, a dozen years after he left the University of Chicago, not wishing, perhaps, to further damage a career already in jeopardy because of indiscreet womanizing. When Harper had expressed to Veblen his concern for the "moral health" of his colleagues' wives, Veblen is said to have replied almost in a whisper: "I've tried them all. They are no good"—a remark, if he indeed made it, that surely eased his exit from the university.

In reading *The Higher Learning*, it is difficult to tell whom its author despised more, the captains of commerce on the university's board of trustees or the "captain of erudition"—William Rainey Harper—who supposedly did their bidding. Whereas in the past the clergy or the state threatened the intellectual integrity of the university, the principal threat to the modern university, Veblen argued, came from the plutocrats who controlled its purse strings. Responding directly to the outlandish claims of Edward Teller Crane, Chicago's crusty iron and elevator manufacturer, that higher education was completely useless for those seeking a career in business and that most colleges ought, therefore, to be burned down, Veblen declared that a good rule usually worked both ways. "If the higher learning is incompatible with business shrewdness, business enterprise is, by the same token, incompatible with the spirit of the higher learning," and businessmen ought, therefore, to resign from the boards of trustees of American colleges and universities.

Veblen moved from vicious attack—the original subtitle of his book was "A Study in Total Depravity"—to incisive analysis of the governance and interworkings of the modern university. But his controlling argument remained unsubstantiated. Businessmen-trustees did not take over the "direction of the pursuit of knowledge" at the University of Chicago. If some faculty members were treated as "subalterns," with no decisive voice in academic policy, it was Harper's doing, not the board's. The trustees gave Harper almost unchecked authority over the day-to-day running of the university (even Veblen refers to him derisively as "The Great Strong Man"), and it was Harper who set in place and maintained a two-tiered hierarchy of Head Professors and all others, the "all others" being paid embarrassingly less than the great scholars and scientists Harper used Rockefeller's millions to bring to Hyde Park. Veblen himself started at $520 a year, less than one-twelfth of what J. Laurence Laughlin made, a salary that surely had something to do with the level of his annoyance.

A young man in a hurry, Harper ran the university like a combination Christian missionary and Chicago ward boss, working through his handpicked department heads—the equivalent of the bosses' precinct captains—to give the rest of the faithful what he felt was best for them. But what was remarkable about the University of Chicago in its first decades—a time in the country of often outrageous trustee interference in university affairs—was the board's hands-off policy in academic matters. Rockefeller asked that the university not be named after him and visited it only twice in ten years for ceremonial occasions, leaving administrative matters to Harper and his academic kitchen cabinet. The main concern of the trustees all the while was raising enough money to pay for the president's imperial building program.

"No one can testify with better right than I," observed the radical writer Robert Morss Lovett, a colleague of Herrick's in the English Department, "to the fact that no other institution in the United States ever exhibited such tolerance of unorthodox opinion and behavior as the University of Chicago." The creation of powerful capitalists, it was a haven where Thorstein Veblen could publish with impunity the most savage of all attacks on corporate plunderers, *The Theory of the Leisure Class.*

In *The Higher Learning,* Veblen took special delight in ridiculing the campus's architecture, a symbol to him of what Harper's university represented. Why revert to a form of "bastard antique," with lancet windows and gabled and gargoyled fronts, he asked, when Chicago's skyscraper architects had demonstrated that a "framework" building of plain design met the needs of researchers, teachers, and students for light, space, and air? Why should "the quest of truth" be housed in "an edifice of false pretenses"? The trustees chose Gothic grandeur, Veblen insisted, because it "advertised" the university as a place of status, power, and "conspicuous waste," like their own horribly pretentious mansions. This expensive "monastic real estate" would, they hoped, impress other prairie philistines, persuading them to open their purses for many more turreted monstrosities, all of them to be named after those who banked them, memorializing economic predators as great patrons of learning. An "architecture of notoriety," Veblen called it, a phrase that would have delighted Louis Sullivan.

These buildings were, as Veblen indicated, expressions of the "cultural hopes and ambitions" of businessmen on the university's governing board, but not in the way he suggested. Hutchinson and Ryerson's preference for Gothic architecture arose from their belief in the influence of architecture on the formation of taste and behavior. Gothic buildings set in cloistered quadrangles would, they believed, create an atmosphere conducive to student-faculty interaction and to intimate, seminar-style learning, class size being fixed by Harper at no more than thirty students. The architecture would convey to undergraduates, especially, that they were in a place of high seriousness that was part of an ennobling tradition. It seemed especially important, they thought, to emphasize the values of tradition and permanence at an instant university located in a city not yet sixty years old.

Although John D. Rockefeller Jr., a trustee, complained on one occasion about putting a cathedral-like façade on a college gymnasium, Hutchinson and Ryerson never considered experimenting with a modern idiom. A consistent architectural plan would make the campus "safe," they thought, contra Veblen, "from the whims and caprices of individual donors." The orderly quadrangles, brought to full glory by some of the country's finest landscape artists, also gave the university the form and definition that the featureless prairie could not lend it. They were a "wonderful contrast," H. G. Wells remarked on his visit to Chicago, to the gross "disorganization" of the modern mercantile city.

That was the intention. With their unified designs, both the Gray City and the White City symbolized the civic cooperation Burnham and Hutchinson believed was as responsible for Chicago's growth as its unsheathed competitiveness. These paired "cities" were built at the same time to inspire a new Chicago, not to mirror what the present city was, as the skyscrapers in the Loop did. Condemned by modernist critics at the turn of the century and today, the quadrangles of the University of Chicago, historian Neil Harris wrote, "survive as one of the country's most remarkable expressions of commitment to a scholarly or priestly dream."

•

That founding dream was William Rainey Harper's. There had never been any doubt that Harper, the preeminent Baptist educator in the country, would be offered the presidency of the new University of Chicago. A child genius, he had entered Muskingum College at age ten and worked after graduation as a clerk in his father's general store in New Concord, Ohio, before heading for Yale, where he received his Ph.D. at age eighteen. Several years later, he accepted a chair at the Baptist denomination's Union Theological Seminary in Morgan Park, outside Chicago, where he met and greatly influenced Thomas Goodspeed, teaching Hebrew and biblical scholarship, though he was also trained in Assyrian, Arabic, Aramaic, and Syriac. All the while he remained active in the Chautauqua movement in New York State, lecturing in summers to adult audiences hungry for learning.

Just before the old University of Chicago closed, Goodspeed had tried to get Harper to assume the presidency and make a final effort to save the place. Harper, however, had been called back to Yale as a professor of the Bible. But when Rockefeller himself approached him about fashioning his own university, he agreed to return to Chicago. "I cannot conceive of a position," Rockefeller wrote him, "where you can do the world more good."

Doing good was exactly Harper's intention. He drafted a sweeping plan to create a university, like Johns Hopkins, dedicated primarily to graduate-school research and training, but also, like Chautauqua, to the spread of learning for the service of "mankind wherever mankind is, whether within scholarly walls or without those walls and in the world at large." It would be a university that would conjoin rigorous scholarship and cultural evangelism, an extension, in other words, of Harper himself, who, like Charles Hutchinson, was both an elitist and a democrat.

Harper's vehicle for reaching the community was a program called University Extension, modeled after highly successful outreach efforts at Cambridge and Oxford. There would be evening lectures for college credit in locations all over the Chicago region and correspondence courses for students in almost every country in the world. If students couldn't get their hands on books, the books would be shipped to them in brown paper packages—like the products sent from Montgomery Ward's warehouse—from the collection of 200,000 volumes Harper purchased for the university before he had a library in which to house them.

Some university faculty remained dubious, believing it was outside the mission of a university, in Veblen's snobbish opinion, "to comfort and edify the unlearned with lyceum lectures, to dispense erudition by mail-order, and to maintain some putative contact with amateur scholars and dilettanti beyond the pale." But Harper, an evangel without a collar, pushed the University Extension program with vigor, hiring as his prize lecturer Robert G. Moulton, son of an English Methodist circuit preacher and one of the most famous extension teachers in Britain. Living like Marhsall Field's drummers, traveling and sleeping on trains and eating at cheap lunch counters, badly paid lecturers became William Rainey Harper's agents for "the cultural redemption of America."

But it was light teaching loads and high salaries—the "hire learning," Veblen called it—not the lofty aims of the University Extension program, that attracted first-rate academic talent to the university. Veblen must have felt the floor drop from under him when he learned upon arriving in Chicago that Harper had added nine former college presidents, nine "captains of erudition," to the faculty. They included Colby's Albion W. Small, a former Baptist minister who established the first department of sociology in the country, a program of study that would use the city of Chicago as its social laboratory. Harper himself traveled around the country by train, recruiting talent for his university on the Midway. Clark University, a distinguished new graduate center, had run into financial problems, and Harper swooped down on it like a marauding hawk, carrying back with him to Chicago almost half its faculty, including future Nobel laureate physicist Albert A. Michelson.

The University of Chicago was perhaps the only institution of higher learning in history to begin its life with a world-renowned faculty. Gathered there by the mid-1890s were James H. Breasted, the Egyptologist who founded the university's famous Oriental Institute; Ferdinand Schevill, the Renaissance scholar; John Dewey, founder of the university's Laboratory School, which aimed to test education theory in light of new demands placed on it by high-change urban society; Jacques Loeb, the physiologist who became the model for the hero of Sinclair Lewis's novel *Arrowsmith;* William Vaughn Moody, the poet-dramatist; and, from the University of Freiburg, the historian Hermann E. von Holst, author of a magisterial constitutional history of the United States. "Titantic-looking . . . with his immense forehead and eyes that seem always to be gazing at the departed spirits of the founders of the Constitution," a Chicago reporter said of him, von Holst led the faculty fight for the most exacting academic standards, while the younger instructors bore the burden of undergraduate teaching.

•

The founding of the University of Chicago was front-page news in the Chicago dailies. But the most closely covered academic department of the university in its early years was one that some of its faculty protested had no place on a college campus, the Department of Physical Culture, headed by young, powerfully built Amos Alonzo Stagg, the university's soon-to-be-legendary football coach.

Upon accepting the presidency, Harper had written Stagg, his former student at Yale and the athletic director at Chautauqua, requesting an urgent meeting. Stagg, who had been named to Walter Camp's first all-American football team, left a record of that meeting. "Dr. Harper . . . unfolded his plan for the University and broached the subject of my heading the athletic department, first offering me a salary of $1,500. The whole idea was new to me [there had never been such a position as this in the history of American education] and I kept still and just thought." Harper then offered him $2,000 and an assistant professorship; and when Stagg remained stone-faced, Harper increased the offer to $2,500 and an associate professorship, "which means," he almost shouted at Stagg, "an appointment for life." Not long after their meeting, Stagg wrote to his old professor, accepting the first tenured college coaching appointment ever. Later, he confessed that he would have taken Harper's first offer. His silence reflected his incredulity, not his reservations. "The question of salary . . . was furthest from my mind."

Promoter of "muscular Christianity"—the union of athletics and morality—Stagg was coming west, he told the *Chicago Tribune,* to "spread the gospel of football throughout the land." The program began with afternoon practice on the opening day of the university, October 1, 1892. Stagg could find only a dozen young men willing to go through his body-breaking drills, but when he lightened the regimen, a few more students showed up, although Stagg himself had to play in games to steady his nervously inexperienced team. After victories over several local high schools, Stagg's eleven played Northwestern to a 0–0 tie, with almost no one in attendance. But a big game with the University of Michigan, which Stagg picked to be his school's chief rival, drew over five hundred people, and football was off to a flying start in Chicago.

When Veblen and other faculty objected to the presence of football at a research institution, Harper countered that "the university of Chicago believes in football. We shall encourage it here." And not merely for sporting fun or as a character builder. "If Chicago University places a team on the field, it must be a winning team," declared Stagg, who became a combination coach and chaplain to the students and easily the most popular "professor" on campus.

Harper got the trustees enthusiastically behind the sport. Marshall Field gave land for a practice ground—called Marshalls Field—and Saturday games became gathering events for the campus community; soon the University of Chicago's touring team was the most feared football power in the West.

•

It was difficult trying to run a school that tried to do a hundred and more things, including publishing over a dozen scholarly journals.

"Harper's Bazaar," critics called it; and Harper, like Hutchinson, was accused of being a P. T. Barnum of culture. But in less than a decade he turned a paper college into a distinguished university, one with a distinctive character and tone.

Little known to the world outside its gray quadrangles, the University of Chicago was engaged, Robert Herrick wrote in an essay at that time, in a bold experiment, an effort to create "an absolutely sexless university education." A handful of the faculty and administrators and a quarter of the students were women, and no distinction was made between the sexes "in most things" despite the objection of some faculty from the East to the "Western" practice of having men and women in the same classroom.* Many of the women were from wealthy midwestern families who wanted to keep their daughters close to home, but most of the men, and some of the women, earned their own keep, taking jobs as lamplighters, tutors, and itinerant reporters. The poor person "is the dominant person; to be rich and idle," Herrick noted, "would be most unfashionable." The average student was industrious, resourceful, driven, and students "felt a responsibility to construct a great university as much in their own way as the faculty and the trustees in theirs."

President Harper was largely responsible for this almost religious college patriotism, Herrick thought. "I believe that nowhere in the United States is a college president so thoroughly known and heartily liked and admired by all students as President Harper." Harper made personal loans to students to help them with their tuition; and he set an example for faculty by continuing to teach and do research and by attending classroom lectures by his faculty, a practice he tried to encourage, for he wanted every professor to become a student in at least one discipline other than his own.

When Harper learned at the age of forty-nine that he had incurable cancer, he refused to cut back his schedule despite periods of almost unbearable pain. He continued to work on a book he was writing and he announced bold new academic initiatives, further alienating faculty opponents who considered him a liar for not delivering all that he had previously promised. "[But] there were bigger things about this big man than telling the truth and keeping promises," Herrick wrote in his memoirs, "—his faith in other men . . . and his almost pathetic faith in the good of education, its salvation to the common man. He

*In 1905, after fierce faculty fighting, male and female students were separated in the Junior College, as it was called, which enrolled all freshman and sophomore undergraduates.

was the great heart of the small man of the Mississippi Valley throbbing to rise, to accomplish, to enjoy the best in the world."

Just before he died, a greatly weakened Harper called in, one by one, the faculty he had personally hired and discussed with them their research plans and his own hopes for the university. "His death on January 10, 1906," Robert Morss Lovett wrote, "brought out a great tribute from the city. It realized that another of the titans who had made its history, and the most unselfish of them all, was gone."

4. The Social Defense of Caste

While Harper and Hutchinson were making the University of Chicago and the Art Institute instruments of public betterment, some of their more conservative friends were turning civic institutions they controlled into exclusionary preserves of the local elite. From its beginnings, the Upward Movement was riven by disagreements reflected in the competing character and aims of the University of Chicago and the Art Institute, on the one hand, and the Newberry Library and the Chicago Symphony Orchestra, on the other.

The Newberry Library opened its massive Romanesque building, designed by Henry Ives Cobb, the year the University of Chicago concluded its first academic year. Its donor, Walter Loomis Newberry, a prominent early settler, had left $2 million at his death in 1868 to establish a "FREE PUBLIC LIBRARY." By the time his complicated will was finally executed, however, the city was laying plans for its new library building on Michigan Avenue, so Newberry's trustees decided to build a noncirculating reference library for a select circle of users in an exclusive North Side neighborhood.

The library's board was dominated by former New Englanders from solid families, and it chose as head librarian the formidable William Frederick Poole, a graduate of Yale, compiler of Poole's *Index to Periodical Literature*, one of the founders of the American Library Association, and a historian of some note. Poole had headed Chicago's public library system, formed immediately after the Great Fire when a group of distinguished English writers and statesmen, including Disraeli and Tennyson, donated several thousand volumes, many of them signed, to the stricken city. These donors thought Chicago had lost its library in the fire, but Chicago had never had a public library. Embarrassed by the British gift into establishing one, the city housed its splendid new collection in an abandoned water tank behind the old Rookery building. A skylight replaced the iron top of the tank, gaslights were hung from it, and bookshelves were built to the tank's contours. Poole eventually found a succession of barely more suitable locations and went about expanding the collection to reflect Chicago's dramatically changing ethnic composition, filling the shelves with foreign-language volumes and establishing delivery stations all over the city.

As the head of a tax-supported public institution, Poole had been under great pressure to serve the entire Chicago community. At the Newberry he was given an opportunity to establish a library to his own refined inclinations. A scholar, he assembled a first-rate research collection. A bookman, he began building one of the finest rare-book collections west of Boston. The Newberry, he declared, was to be a library to "satisfy the wants of scholars." Since there were few real scholars in Chicago before William Rainey Harper began buying them with Rockefeller's millions, Poole was probably referring to amateur gentlemen historians, history buffs from Old Settler families, and sons of the newly rich with a passion for genealogy.

The Newberry's architecture reflected what went on there. The strong-willed Poole got the board to reject Cobb's plan for a large central reading room serviced by stacks for an alcove design, a series of small, cozy nooks, each of them resembling the library of a gentleman's estate. Although three-quarters of Chicago's population was either foreign-born or the children of foreign-born parents, no effort was made to purchase volumes of special interest to these people, and the princely surroundings intimidated the occasional curious workingman who happened to wander in. There had been some discussion of putting the Newberry in Lincoln Park, but a faction on the board, led by Robert Todd Lincoln, the chief counsel for the Pullman Palace Car Company, objected. Placing a gentleman's library on public ground might subject it to unseemly popular pressures. The Newberry was run in the spirit of Robert Todd Lincoln's opinion on its possible location. It was built at a time, as Edith Wharton wrote, when "decent people fell back on sport and culture" to seal themselves off from the oppressive industrial metropolis.

By the time of his death in 1894, Poole had built a collection of 120,000 books, adding immeasurably to Chicago's cultural riches. But the treasures he assembled, a local paper noted, were only for "the better and cleaner classes."

Not long after Walter Newberry's will was violated in spirit by the creators of the library that would carry his name, the will of another Chicago founder was changed to create an equally restrictive enclave. Rich and pious John Crerar had wanted part of his estate to be used to erect a general-circulation library that would include works of literature but not "dirty French novels." But his trustees, working in cooperation with the Newberry's board, established a noncirculating reference library in the sciences, the Newberry, by agreement, to be devoted exclusively to the humanities. Both libraries maintained hours of operation—closing in the evenings and on Sundays—deliberately designed to exclude common workers, and neither established Hutchinson-like programs to draw in great numbers of patrons. They were part of a national movement for what one historian has called "the social defense of caste."

•

On November 7, 1890, as construction of the Newberry Library began, newspapers all across the country ran headlines announcing that Theodore Thomas, America's most famous conductor, was moving from New York to Chicago to head the newly organized Chicago Symphony Orchestra. Leaving the New York Philharmonic Orchestra would be difficult, Thomas was quoted as saying, but the Philharmonic performed only a dozen concerts a season, not enough to keep his musicians together, as they had to take work at dances and weddings to support themselves. In Chicago, Thomas would have his own permanent orchestra, which would perform at least two concerts a week over eight months. And he would have available to him all the money he needed "to produce the greatest music in the greatest way."

With the arrival of conductor Thomas, the Auditorium would have a musical celebrity equal to the magnificence of its architecture and acoustics, and Chicago papers began predicting that their city would soon surpass New York and Boston as a national center of symphonic music. No artistic performer ever arrived in Chicago with more fanfare or goodwill than Theodore Thomas. His famous touring orchestra, made up in part of Philharmonic musicians, had been delighting local audiences for twenty years. Now he was Chicago's alone.

Thomas had been a giant figure in the American musical world since the Civil War, the father of American symphonic music, some critics called him. Son of a struggling German musician, he arrived in New York with his family in 1845 at the age of ten and had to fiddle in waterfront gin mills to help pay his family's rent. Before he was fourteen he was touring the southern states on his own as Master T. T., his violin strapped to his saddle. He would hang his own concert posters, take tickets at the door, and then race backstage to dress for his solo performances. He didn't hear his first full orchestra play until he was eighteen, but soon after this he was first violin in the Philharmonic, America's first symphony orchestra.

A few years later, in 1863, he organized his own orchestra and began taking it on tour "from sea to sea." His aim: to educate the American people to an appreciation of the best instrumental music in the world. For the next two decades, while conducting a number of other orchestras, including the Philharmonic, he took the Theodore Thomas Orchestra to as many as thirty-eight cities in a season, the "Thomas Highway," the press called his urban circuit. At first, the audiences were embarrassingly small, but soon Thomas was a hit wherever he went, spreading the gospel of music as William Rainey Harper would spread the gospel of higher learning. He became so popular that P. T. Barnum asked him to tour under his management.

His method of reaching his untutored audiences was based on the way his father had taught him to appreciate fine music. He would begin by playing popular music, polkas, waltzes, even marches—"lollipops," in his words; then he would graduate to the soaring magnificence of Mozart, Bach, Handel, and Beethoven, "the sons of God," he called these titans. And in the summers he gave wonderful garden concerts in Chicago at the big, airy Exposition Building by the lake. It was "the only cool place in town," a Chicagoan recalls the atmosphere of these light concerts, "[with] palms and . . . little tables, [and] dim sequestered reaches at the sides and back of the floor, where quietly glowed the cigar and foamed the beer," while from the stage came the strains of "The Beautiful Blue Danube." In this way, Thomas educated countless thousands of people, in delicious small portions, to the masterworks of symphonic music. He did this without cheap tricks or theatrics, his back always to the audience, in a gesture that seemed to say, "Shut your eyes and hear the great music of the world."

But the exhausting railway tours took their toll on him, and in 1888 he disbanded his orchestra. He was too old, at fifty-three, he said, to be "a music merchant." He had also become frustrated by New York's failure to turn the Philharmonic into a full-time orchestra, and his own vitality began to ebb when his wife became terminally ill. It was then, at the lowest moment in his life, that he ran into his friend C. Norman Fay on Fifth Avenue, and Fay asked him to join him at Delmonico's. Fay, a Chicago utilities magnate who came from an amazing musical family, had been trying for nearly ten years to get Thomas to come to Chicago permanently, aided by his sister Rose, who was corresponding with Thomas and would marry him shortly after his wife's death. Now, in the master's desperation, Fay saw his opportunity. Over dinner and a light Moselle, he asked the "worn and worried" conductor if he would come to Chicago if he were given his own orchestra. The answer came back so fast it startled Fay: "I would go to hell if they gave me a permanent orchestra." Right there, at the table, the two friends roughed out the agreement that resulted in the creation of the Chicago Orchestra.

The contract Fay later mailed to Thomas made him not just conductor of the orchestra but virtual dictator of the Orchestral Association Fay established to fund it, with the backing of Hutchinson, Ryerson, Peck, Field, Daniel Burnham, and others. Thomas was given "absolute control of orchestra and programme-making" and was to carry on his "lifelong campaign for good art without reference to box-office receipts," the association putting up a guarantee against deficits of up to fifty thousand dollars a year. "All my life," Thomas wrote Rose Fay, "I have been told that my standard was too high, and urged to make it more popular. But now, I am not only to be given every facility to create the highest standard, but am even told that I will be *held responsible* for keeping it so! I have to shake myself to realize it."

So the rejuvenated musical director arrived in Chicago with a vastly different agenda than he had had in mind for his old summer concerts—not to slowly raise musical taste by a mixture of light and serious music but to bring audiences up to the highest musical standards through a full dose of symphonic music. This would be more difficult than he thought.

•

Problems arose immediately and unexpectedly. The hall was too large, Thomas protested, for his orchestra to be completely effective, even with Adler's excellent acoustics. The reverberation period was so long that his musicians couldn't depend on the hall's echoes to tell them how loud they were playing. "Sullivan, nothing comes back, nothing comes back," Frank Lloyd Wright remembers hearing Thomas shout in frustration after a performance. "I can't play in the place."

The size of the theater created another problem. "The seating capacity—nearly five thousand—is so great that many people will not buy season tickets," Thomas told his wife, "knowing that they can always get seats for single concerts when they want to attend." The single concerts that proved most popular, moreover, featured either the music of a lighter character that Thomas hoped to discourage or Wagner performances, always hugely popular with Chicago's large German community. Wagnerian operas packed the hall, but Thomas's concerts drew only an average of twenty-five hundred at best, plunging the Orchestral Association into perpetual debt.

After his first season, Thomas grudgingly added more concerts billed as "popular" and put on a short series of "Workingmen's Concerts." But he would not give up his effort to substitute his refined taste for that of his untutored audiences. Thomas saw great music, as

Charles Hutchinson saw great art, as a moral force capable of influencing behavior. The difference was that he was no longer interested, he told his wife, in "missionary work." As Rose Fay wrote her friend Frances Glessner, wife of the Chicago farm-machinery titan John J. Glessner: "Mr. Thomas is here to establish a great art work, and to make Chicago one of the musical centers of the world—not to provide a series of cheap musical entertainments for the riff-raff of the public. The highest forms of art . . . are not within the comprehension of the masses. . . . It is a useless task to attempt to produce the highest form in any art, in such a way that it can be appreciated by the ignorant. All that can be done is to produce it, and let it stand till the ignorant acquire a little education and begin to understand it."

Unfortunately for Thomas, the musically ignorant of Chicago included many of his Prairie Avenue backers. Still, he stubbornly went on trying to change not just their taste but their public decorum as well. When he heard loud whispering in the hall or saw people getting up to leave early, he would sometimes stop the music and remain standing absolutely still, his baton frozen in the air, until order was restored; and once he began a symphony, he would have the doors closed until intermission. "When you play . . . Yankee Doodle, you can keep the doors open," he admonished an audience. "When I play Handel's 'Te Deum,' they must be shut." He saw great music as a sacred rite, the musical hall as a cathedral, and the conductor as a consecrated priest. The religion of symphonic music demanded complete dedication from audience, players, and conductor.

Thomas's heavy symphonic programs, along with the association's high ticket prices and refusal to hold Sunday concerts—over the protests of Hutchinson and Peck—transformed Peck's "Hall for the People" into an upper-class preserve, like New York's Metropolitan Opera House. The exclusive boxes became scenes of high-society intrigues by women wearing décolleté gowns and elaborate ostrich feathers. Attendance at Thomas's concerts became socially obligatory for the best families, and the conductor was lionized by Chicago's elite. "We had to take our symphonies whether we liked them or not," recalled Norman Fay, for "the 'old man' . . . was a sort of stern deity, who had to be appeased with sacrifice and burnt offerings." As Rose Fay wrote of him on the occasion of his death in 1905: "He not only disciplined his musicians, but he disciplined the public, educating it sometimes perhaps against its will."

•

Thomas's concerts were the occasion for the weekly gatherings of Chicago's first true literary society, The Little Room, as the group called itself after a Madeline Yale Wynne story of a haunted chamber in a New England house that magically appears and disappears. This circle of polite bohemians included Henry B. Fuller, Lorado Taft, Hobart C. Chatfield-Taylor, Harriet and Lucy Monroe, the sculptor Bessie Potter, the novelist and *Chicago Tribune* journalist Elia Peattie, the writer Edith Wyatt, the drama coach and director Anna Morgan, and Francis Fisher Brown, editor of *The Dial*, the literary journal he had launched in 1880 to promote culture in the barbarous West. "If you do not like it now," his magazine chillingly admonished critics of Thomas's music, "pray that you may learn to like it, for the defect is yours."

Fuller and his friends met for tea and light conversation in Bessie Potter's studio following Thomas's Friday afternoon performances, a disparate bunch united by the pompous conviction that they were the only artists of note in this provincial city. Sometimes rich society women interested in the arts joined them, as did Jane Addams. Most of the Little Roomers were excited by the fair, seeing it as emblematic of Chicago's passage to a higher state of civic development. Their fragile optimism was bolstered by an exciting new writer in town, Hamlin Garland, who joined them in 1893.

The celebrated author of *Main-Travelled Roads,* a collection of haunting stories of the hardships and emptiness of the prairie life of his boyhood, Garland arrived in Chicago from Boston (where his career had been aided by William Dean Howells) demanding a literature drawn not from books but from life. What Howells was promoting as realism, Garland called Veritism. But Garland had had it with Howells's Europeanized East; commercial as well as artistic "supremacy" was passing, he was convinced, to the West and to its cultural and economic capital, Chicago. "The rise of Chicago as a literary and art centre is a question only of time, and of a very short time," he announced in *Crumbling Idols,* a book of literary essays he published shortly after settling in what he called this "splendidly American" city.

Garland arrived in Chicago determined to head the movement to transform it into a temple "to art and song." "This is where I belong," he wrote from his room in a cheap boardinghouse by the lake, "here in the great Midland metropolis," for a writer's genius, he believed, could achieve its true form only in his native region. Lecturing on "Impressionism in Art" in the library of a Chicago banker, he ran into Lorado Taft, and Taft brought him into his "artistic gang."

Brawny, explosive, and willfully ill mannered, a writer whose "heroes," in Eugene Field's phrase, "sweat and do not wear socks," Garland was at first painfully ill at ease in the company of the Little

Room's polite aesthetes, but he soon found himself strangely drawn to Henry Fuller, his near opposite in appearance and tone.

Garland was then a fervid political reformer, campaigning for Populist candidates and for land reform for hard-hit midwestern farmers like his parents up in desolate Dakota Territory. He was a "sufferer," Fuller described him, who felt the world was against him. When he preached his rural radicalism in crowded Chicago halls, his eyes would glow like hot cinders and his voice would tremble with rage. He felt completely out of place at Thomas's concerts—gathering occasions for the fashionable—and only went to other society affairs at Fuller's urging, refusing, however, to dance or to wear "fancy togs." When offered rum by silk-bonneted Chicago socialites, he would brusquely refuse, declaring that he never used it "except as a hair tonic."

Fuller, by contrast, mixed easily with the "right people," whom he then savagely satirized in his novels. A lifelong bachelor who lived alone in a succession of rooming houses, he hungered for the weekly companionship of The Little Room. Short, of meager frame, and perfectly tailored—a "wraith in pantaloons," Garland described him in his journal—he was so coldly sarcastic in his judgments of people and things that Garland doubted he valued anything very highly.

Fuller was from an Old Settler family that traced its ancestry back to the *Mayflower*. A substantial inheritance had allowed him to travel widely in France and Italy, where he gathered material for two historical romances that gave him a small literary reputation. He had a full, sleekly brushed beard when Garland met him and "carried himself with fastidious grace, a small alert gentleman who resented the mental and physical bad smells and the raucous noises of his native town."

Fuller thought Garland's enthusiasm for Chicago naive. The grandson and the son of local capitalists, he knew his city's commercial culture too well to think that it could be challenged and corrected. The cultural patronage of his Prairie Avenue friends was propelled, he suspected, less by deep interest in the arts than by a nervous desire to elevate their own and their city's reputation, a high-toned form of the crude boosterism of William Bross.

What did bring Fuller and Garland together, however, was a common, albeit fleeting, commitment to realistic urban fiction. Although he found his new friend's outlook for the town excessively dark, Garland thrilled to Fuller's exposé of Chicago's worship of wealth, *The Cliff-Dwellers*, which he read in one sitting just after he arrived from Boston. "What an awful thing"—a businessman from the East speaks for the book's author—"to have only one life to live and to be obliged to live it in such a place as this!"—as Henry Fuller's declining inheritance forced him to do. Yet Fuller had an amazing knowledge of the city he felt imprisoned in, an urban education that was "kept up," as Garland recalled, "by the most minute and constant study. He knew the boundaries of every park, and the size and character of every addition. He spent many days . . . surveying raw urban developments, a small lonely figure walking swiftly but eccentrically along weed-grown avenues."

Just after *The Cliff-Dwellers* was published, he began a novel that called together his immense understanding of modern Chicago. *With the Procession*, a sharp-eyed study of the city's imperially wealthy families, left a strong mark on young Theodore Dreiser, who would insist that it was Fuller, not Stephen Crane, "who led the van of realism in America."

A year later, Garland completed his only Chicago novel, *Rose of Dutcher's Coolly*, which deals, as we have seen, with a young woman's sexual and intellectual awakening in the city, where she comes into contact with a group not unlike The Little Room and becomes, at last, a published poet. Rose, in a sense, conquers Chicago, but Chicago would conquer Hamlin Garland. Not the Chicago of smoke and boisterous energy he described in *Rose of Dutcher's Coolly*, but the small slice of the city Henry Fuller introduced him to, the exclusive world of *With the Procession*.

Chicago grandees like Charles Hutchinson and Martin Ryerson altered Garland's image of the businessman. They were amiable, cultivated, and civic-minded, not the bloodsuckers who had been the target of his populist harangues or the Philistines he had read about in *The Cliff-Dwellers*. The angry "Son of the Middle Border" soon found himself wearing "fancy togs," eagerly attending dancing parties in splendid granite mansions, and promoting the cultural causes financed by new friends like Charles Hutchinson. The "pomp and luxury of the plutocracy inwrapped him," Fuller wickedly satirized his friend in his novella *The Downfall of Abner Joyce*, and he "reached an understanding with the children of Mammon." With this, an "original American voice" became a writer of Wild West adventure stories, the Walter Scott of the high plains, proof to Henry Fuller of the difficulty of an artist living a life of integrity in a city dominated by a business class determined to control everything it took a strong interest in.

While Garland succumbed to social striving, Fuller became the victim of his own aggressive pessimism. After his two Chicago novels failed, in his words, "to raise this dirt pile [i.e., Chicago] to some dignity and credit," he returned to escapist romance, travel writing, and critical essays. But Chicago's fiercest critic managed to find one thinly promising aspect of what his friends, in their eagerness, called a cultural renaissance—the civic energy of the city's powerfully placed women, the most influential group of women in any American city at the time.

Henry Fuller's most unforgettable fictional character is Susan Bates of *With the Procession.* A woman of ferocious ambition, she has climbed out of poverty, married a fast-rising capitalist, built a collection of modern French paintings, and made herself the unchallenged queen of Chicago society, "the most desirable of all the desirable people." As she tells her young friend Jane Marshall, she and her husband "have fought the fight . . . and we have come out ahead. And we shall stay there, too; keep up with the procession is our motto, and head it if you can. I do head it, and I feel that I'm where I belong." A perfect snob, she is, however, surprisingly interested in social reform and wants to be a force for civic change, not a beautiful trophy for her rich husband.

Susan Bates is a fictional representation of "the New Chicago Woman" visitors to the city had begun to notice around the time of the fair. The women's organizations she belongs to run orphanages, asylums, and homes for wayward women, and they battle against child labor and for better wages for factory women. "There are no butterflies in this town," she insists. "We are all workers." By the end of the novel, Susan Bates seems to be hesitating between a career "as a Society Queen and a self devotion to the Better Things; perhaps she was happy to combine both," as was, equally, Fuller's friend Bertha Palmer, the model for this wonderfully realized fictional woman.

5. The New Chicago Woman

Born into an aristrocratic Louisville family that had relocated in Chicago in 1855 when she was six, Bertha Honoré Palmer, unlike Fuller's Susan Bates, never knew poverty; nor did she live on the exclusive near South Side. Bertha Palmer didn't need a Prairie Avenue address to lend her legitimacy. When she and her husband moved in 1885 from the Palmer House to the North Side mansion Henry Ives Cobb designed for them on ground that had recently been an untenanted slough, they permanently altered the axis of Chicago society life, as years earlier Potter Palmer, the "Father of State Street," had altered the city's commercial axis. By the turn of the century, to live on Potter Palmer's Gold Coast, far from the invasive industrial expansion that had set Prairie Avenue on its course of decline, was to reside at the center of Chicago elegance and social power.

Potter Palmer had bought this stretch of dune and marsh in the early 1880s, pumped in clean sand from the lake bottom as fill, strong-armed the city to build a through street—later called Lake Shore Drive—and invited a group of his friends to form with him "a community where there had been wilderness." When his imitation Rhenish castle was completed, the *Inter Ocean* opined that "the Age of Pericles seems to be dawning." A more clear-eyed French visitor called the Palmer pile "sumptuous and abominable."

It had taken three years to complete, with the aid of an imported village of Italian craftsmen and at a cost so fabulous that a despairing Palmer asked the architects to stop showing him the bills. It had fantastic turrets, towers, and minarets and was easily the largest, most expensive residence in Chicago, although Palmer himself never liked living in it, preferring the company of his racetrack cronies in the noisy lobby of his hotel. The massively defiant exterior was the architect's idea, but the interior mirrored the grandiose taste of Mrs. Palmer, who might have done better had she followed her own theory of dress. Art is like fashion, she once explained to a women's group: "The more you put on, sometimes, the worse you look, and the more you take off, the better you look."

The interior centerpiece of her home was a spiral staircase that rose eighty feet into a tower and was completely unnecessary, it turned out, as there were two private elevators, the first ones installed in a Chicago residence. There was a Spanish music room, a Turkish parlor, a Flemish Renaissance library for Mr. Palmer, a Moorish bedroom of ebony and gold for Mrs. Palmer, an English dining room that seated fifty, a sixty-foot-long conservatory, a Louis XV drawing room, and a rooftop ballroom and picture gallery with an overhanging balcony. It was in this magnificent room in the sky that Bertha Palmer, a regally beautiful woman, dazzling in her Parisian gowns and diamond tiaras and collars, would host the most talked-about parties in Chicago.

In 1893, Bertha Palmer became the nation's, not just Chicago's, hostess, and many out-of-town guests responded to her invitations just to see the Palmers' art collection. Working through their agent Sara Tyson Hallowell, who introduced them to Mary Cassatt, Claude Monet, and the best Parisian dealers, she and her husband started their collection in 1889 with a Renoir and a Degas. They began buying in earnest two years later, when Bertha Palmer was named chairwoman of the Columbian Exposition's Board of Lady Managers, which was charged with overseeing the building of a pavilion in Jackson Park to display the accomplishments of women from all over the world. Young Sophia G. Hayden, the first woman graduate of MIT's architecture school, won the competition to design this, her first building. As it went up, Bertha Palmer sailed for Europe to encourage interest in the women's exhibition and while in Paris went on an art-buying spree, bringing back to Chicago for her private gallery, and to loan to the fair's Fine Arts Pavilion, the most extensive collection of Impressionists in the New World, along with works from the Barbizon school. Her staggering collection soon included Pissarros, Corots, Sisleys, and over thirty Monets, paintings she could not bear to part with despite the good-natured solicitation of her friend Charles Hutchinson, who was not able to acquire them for the Art Institute until a year before his death through the terms of Mrs. Palmer's will.

As Chicago prepared to host the fair, Bertha Palmer set out to remake the city socially, as her powerful husband had remade it physically. This meant challenging Prairie Avenue. Chicago's commercial kings drank and gambled like Russians at their in-town clubs, but Prairie Avenue social life was stuffy and exclusive, the same families getting together for an exchange of gossip and a night of formal dancing in the private ballrooms that had been added on to most South Side mansions in the "elegant eighties," when even George Pullman, Robert Todd Lincoln, and Gen. Phil Sheridan felt the need to take dancing lessons. In their reminiscences, a number of society women of that time described the conversation at these gatherings as all about books and "ideals," but led by the men, it invariably swung around to business. The daughter of a Prairie Avenue tycoon recalled a supper party where the guests were taken in a big, rattling omnibus to a new steel-rolling mill owned by a friend of the family to see its furnaces tapped and the white-hot pig iron poured into sand molds.

Raised in a bright and lively southern family in which French was spoken and books and politics discussed, Bertha Palmer was bored with Prairie Avenue life. In her new castle on the lake, she opened the windows and let in a little of the modern world, inviting to her soirees settlement workers and labor leaders, journalists and politicians, struggling artists and new luminaries in town like Hamlin Garland. But Bertha Palmer also liked her privacy. On her instructions, there were no outside doorknobs on her home. One could enter only by presenting one's card, which had to pass through twenty-seven servants, maids, and social secretaries before coming under the censoring eyes of the mistress of the mansion.

Mrs. Palmer could also play the snob. "I once heard her comment," a friend said, "upon the unforgivable folly of the marriage of a beautiful friend to a man without fortune as if it belonged to the category of moral delinquency." In his most unusual will, Potter Palmer left a generous sum of money to his successor in the event his wife remarried. When asked why, Palmer dryly replied: "He'll need the money."

But the "Gold Coast Queen" had that other quality Henry Fuller spoke of: She was a dauntless do-gooder, and a feminist as well. She held meetings for female factory workers and women activists in her French parlor, helped millinery workers organize a strike, and pressed her son Honoré to run for alderman in an immigrant ward, managing his campaign and hosting a reception for several hundred of his Italian supporters—including their neighborhood band—in the ballroom of her mansion.

•

The reforming energies of women like Bertha Palmer were channeled through the Chicago Woman's Club, "the Mother of woman's public work" in Chicago, Julian Ralph called it. By the mid-1880s, this club, with five hundred members, had progressed from a polite reading and self-study group to an aggressive organization for municipal betterment. Led by self-assured wives of plutocrats like Ellen Martin Henrotin, wife of the president of the Chicago Stock Exchange, it became a force in the civic life of the city. "I have said that Chicago combines all sorts of contrasts," remarked Marie Thérèse de Solms Blanc in her sparkling travel commentary *The Condition of Women in the United States,* "but nothing is more unexpected than the dominion of woman in that great centre of vigorous manhood." Far more than in New York or Boston, "women are everywhere to the fore in Chicago," and the work of the Woman's Club was all the more effective, Blanc learned, because its leaders controlled and managed their own money, thanks to a progressive Illinois statute.

The club's work was directed toward the protection of women and children. In its pathfinding investigative work in asylums, hospitals, poorhouses, and prisons, the club always asked the disarming question "What are you doing with the women and children?" Not without struggle, it was successful in having a woman physician appointed to care for female patients in the county's primitive insane asylum, where the inmates were drugged by whiskey and sedatives, forced to eat pigs' heads with the bristles still on, and slept three to a steel bed. And club leaders pressured the city to put night matrons in police prisons to stop the practice of allowing the male inmates to sexually assault the women, some as young as twelve or thirteen, who were incarcerated with them.

The club's Protective Agency, headed by the wife of a Chicago banker, provided legal advice to mothers in danger of losing their children, to housemaids and shopgirls defrauded of their wages, and to battered wives. It pushed for heavy sentences for rapists, found homes for foundlings, and set up offices in train stations to take care of "waifs" trying to get back home. Dressed in their rustling silks and jewels, its leaders tried to ensure, by their mere presence in the courtroom, that women received fair treatment at a time when it was commonplace to discredit a woman's testimony by showing her "bad character." Dr. Sarah Haskell Stevenson, president of the Woman's Club, and another crusading physician, Gertrude Gail Wellington, investigated conditions in the slums and got the city to build its first public bathhouse, arguing, disarmingly, that "the free public bath will inspire sweeter manners and a better observance of the law."

A number of Woman's Club reformers had been raised in homes in which care for the indigent was considered a religious obligation. "I had been brought up with the idea that some day I would inherit a fortune," recalled Louise de Koven Bowen, a banker's wife whose grandfather had lived in Fort Dearborn and whose mother was born inside its palisades, "and I was always taught that the responsibility of money was great, and that God would hold me accountable for the manner in which I used my talents." While still in finishing school, she taught a church class for deprived girls and later hired a Swedish woman to help her on charity rounds, work that brought her, in the early 1890s, to Hull-House, where she became a lifelong associate of Jane Addams and a generous underwriter of her causes.

•

It was to get support from just this class of women that Jane Addams had joined the Woman's Club when she arrived in Chicago in 1889 to open a social settlement, a new idea in America, in an immigrant neighborhood a mile west of State Street. Only twenty-nine years old, she struck a chord of sympathy with these privileged women because she was one of them, an educated, well-traveled "young girl," Mrs. Bowen said of her, who had been raised in a pious and prosperous Christian home and "had sympathy for her fellowmen."

She had been born and brought up in the pleasant prairie village of Cedarville, the sickly, pampered daughter of John H. Addams, the wealthiest merchant in town and a powerful figure in the Illinois legislature, a fierce opponent of slavery and a friend of Lincoln, who called him in correspondence "My Dear Double-D'd Addams." She gave her imposing father "doglike devotion" and felt embarrassingly inferior in his presence. An attack of spinal tuberculosis had left her permanently stooped and pigeon-toed and caused her to carry her head to one side. Growing up, she would pray with all her heart, she recalled, that strangers coming to town to hear John Addams teach Bible class in the village Sunday school would not recognize her as the daughter of this erect and handsome man. She wanted more than all else to be like him, a pillar of rectitude and a friend of man, and his sudden death in the summer after her graduation from Rockford Female Seminary compounded a nervous depression brought on by her inability to find a suitable career.

Jane Addams belonged to the first generation of American women to graduate from college, but she entered a world that seemed to have no use for her. Other than medicine, a career she trained for briefly before succumbing to illness, the only accepted outlets for her talents were teaching and some form of charitable or missionary work, and Addams was drawn to neither field. She also found it increasingly difficult to live with her stepmother, who pressed her to marry and start a family. Locked in mental turmoil for almost seven years, "filled with shame," as she wrote, "that with all my apparent leisure I do nothing at all," she used her inheritance to travel about Europe in a desperate search for "culture" and a cure for her mounting malaise. By the end of her second grand tour of the Continent she had begun to tire of cathedrals and galleries and finally found in a London slum a focus for her unused moral energies.

With Ellen Gates Starr, her traveling companion and college friend, she spent time in Toynbee Hall, a settlement—the world's first—in the Dickensian warrens of Whitechapel. There, young, morally earnest university men came to live, using their education to try to lift the lives of the poor. Although they pushed for social reforms, residents of Toynbee Hall seemed more concerned with cultural than with economic deprivation. Through lectures, university extension classes, and art exhibits, they brought a touch of Oxford and Cambridge into the spiritually cramped lives of their new neighbors, attempting, all the while, to break down the barriers between the classes.

Reform through "picture parties and pianos," a critic called it, which is exactly what made it appealing to Jane Addams. Here was a way to put to use her "useless" learning and to be a liver of life, not a spectator. Nor was the work of Toynbee Hall a form of charity in her view. It was help given in a spirit of mutuality, neighbor to neighbor, the Christian ideal of Cedarville. "The dependence of classes on each other," she wrote, "is reciprocal," and class conciliation would remain the great aim of her life.

On their return home, Addams and Starr moved into a Chicago

boardinghouse and began laying plans for an educated woman's equivalent to Toynbee Hall, to be established in the run-down Halsted Street mansion of Chicago pioneer Charles J. Hull, which Addams and Starr rented from Helen Culver, his surviving cousin. In her fundraising campaign in the city, speaking in pulpits, mission halls, and the parlors of wealthy Woman's Club leaders, Jane Addams admitted that her "idea" was "more for the benefit of the people who did it than for the other class." A settlement was a chance for young women whose "uselessness hangs about them heavily" to engage in morally purposeful work in a fellowship of like-spirited idealists.

After taking up social work in Chicago, the heroine of Elia Peattie's novel *The Precipice* finds "that shame at being merely a woman, with no task, no utility, no independence" has been lifted from her. But most women came to Hull-House in future years not to find solutions for inner problems but for a reason as old as humanity: the simple desire to do good. "Twenty years ago," a Chicago reporter wrote in 1908, "a young woman who was restless and yearned to sacrifice herself, would have become a missionary or married a drinking man in order to save him. Today she studies medicine or goes into settlement work."

At Hull-House, residents would be living with young women exactly like themselves and in a manner they would find comfortingly familiar. Addams did all she could to make it an idealized middle-class home. On the September morning they moved into the old Hull mansion, she and Ellen Starr hung framed pictures they had collected in Europe and furnished the place with a few pieces of "family mahogany" and new furniture in character with the high ceilings, French windows, and carved mantelpieces. "Probably no young matron," said Addams of that decisive day in her life, "ever placed her own things in her own house with more pleasure than that with which we first furnished Hull-House." The first group of twenty or so residents worked busily to keep the place as Marie Blanc found it on her initial visit—"clean, bright, [and] homelike." And in the early years of the settlement, the day ended with common prayer in the living room.

Hull-House was there to provide a mode of living to emulate. If the wary wives of Italian and Greek workers who first came to the settlement—which some of them had initially thought was an expensive bordello—didn't get the point, Jane Addams brought it directly to their doorsteps in the form of "friendly visitors" like Louise Bowen, who tried to teach them how to care for their homes and families. This smothering paternalism was the most troubling aspect of the settlement-house impulse, and it did not escape Thorstein Veblen's cold eye. "The solicitude of settlements," he wrote, "is in part directed . . . to the incubation, by precept and example, of certain punctilios of upper-class propriety in manners and customs."

Hull-House was by design a woman's place. Men from the neighborhood were welcome, but many of those who occasionally came to Hull-House functions felt uncomfortable; it is no wonder, for Addams never disguised her belief that women had superior moral qualities. Middle-class men helped at Hull-House, but in subordinate roles. Beatrice Webb remarked after visiting there that "the residents consist, in the main, of strong-minded energetic women, bustling about their various enterprises and professions, interspersed with earnest-faced, self-subordinating and mild-mannered men who slide from room to room apologetically."

Some of the women volunteers at Hull-House did little to advance its mission of class communication. Hilda Satt, a Polish immigrant woman who worked at Hull-House and wrote a book about it—the only account we have of the neighborhood's reaction to the settlement—described a "queenly looking" lady who pulled up in front of Hull-House in a gorgeous carriage, with the footman dressed in purple livery. "On her head rested an enormous hat with several ostrich plumes sort of dripping down. She turned to the footman and said: 'James, take the horses home. The air is very bad for them down here. You may return for me in two hours.'"

Jane Addams would grow and change. Experience would turn her into a tough-minded idealist concerned as much with attacking the causes of poverty as with helping its victims cope with it by leading more enlightened lives. But in its initial years the spirit of Charles Hutchinson, an early supporter, hung heavily over Hull-House, whose "line of thought and action" was directed, Addams explained, to the "higher life." And the settlement's work in the neighborhood was not all that different from that of the Woman's Club. That is why Addams found such enthusiastic support for Hull-House from Chicago's established families, including the Pullmans, and that is why the initially suspicious Helen Culver stopped collecting the rent when she discovered what her two young tenants were up to. Culver eventually donated the land on which Hull-House grew into a thirteen-building complex, a veritable department store of social welfare.*

●

*By 1894, the principal contributor to Hull-House was Mary Rozet Smith, the daughter of a wealthy Chicago businessman. Lifelong friends, Addams and Smith were quite likely lovers as well.

In its first years, Hull-House served as an informal neighborhood extension center of Chicago's three most important agencies of cultural betterment: the Chicago Public Library, the Art Institute, and the University of Chicago. It brought the advantages of these institutions to many immigrants who didn't even realize that the city had a library, an art gallery, or a university. The first physical addition to Hull-House was a gallery donated by an Art Institute trustee; the first official city agency established on the premises was a branch center of the Chicago Public Library; and two of the first extension courses offered by the University of Chicago were given in the Victorian drawing room of Hull-House. Jane Addams and Ellen Starr also shared with the trustees of these city institutions the belief in the power of culture to remake character and the related conviction that the struggle to implant culture must be led by the "better elements." In their first years in the city, they were firmly part of its elite-sponsored Upward Movement.

The first activity of Hull-House was a weekly reading party to discuss a George Eliot novel, and the working people's lecture series, organized by Addams, included speeches on "The London City Council" by Percy Alden, "Savonarola" by Rev. F. W. Gunsaulus, "Marcus Aurelius" by Prof. J. H. Tufts, "The Conscience of the State" by Bayard Holmes, and "The Economic and Social Condition of India" by Swami Vivekananda. "The blessings which we associate with a life of refinement and cultivation," said Addams in an attempt to justify such heavy intellectual fare, "can be made universal and must be made universal if they are to be permanent"—whether the audience liked it or not, she might just as well have added, echoing Theodore Thomas.

It was Ellen Starr, however, who took the lead at Hull-House in cultural matters. She set up art classes, gave slide lectures on Florentine architecture, organized guided visits to the Art Institute, worked with the Woman's Club to place paintings in the public schools, and loaned reproductions of masterworks to her immigrant students to hang on the mud-smeared walls of their tenements. Addams and Starr were careful about the kind of art they introduced to their neighbors, hanging on the walls of Hull-House only such reproductions thought to be "helpful to the life of mind and soul" and choosing for their gallery shows only those paintings offered on loan to them by Chicago collectors that combined "an elevated tone with technical excellence." It was in democratic Hull-House, not in the elite-run Art Institute, where art was used for a time as a form of cultural indoctrination.

On the occasion of a Hull-House art opening, Starr would have Edward Burchard, the settlement's first male resident, guard the pictures at night and walk through the Nineteenth Ward's wooden streets with a big placard announcing the exhibit. Neighbors would come by the hundreds to see the pictures, some out of curiosity, others just to get out of their wretched surroundings for a few hours, always one of the main reasons Hull-House was filled with activity, drawing as many as two thousand visitors a week. For many immigrant women, it was where they were coming from, not where they were going to, that mattered most.

There was something naive—almost unreal—about this cultural outreach, but enough Halsted Street immigrants were hungry for knowledge of the arts to sustain a Plato Club, a Dante Club, and a Shakespeare Club and to get enthusiastic audiences at Sunday afternoon concerts, the performances designed, like the Chicago Symphony's, not to entertain but to develop "musical taste and understanding." There was even a popular Hull-House Women's Club that was called together, like The Little Room, "for purposes of tea-drinking and friendly chat." Hilda Satt described a reading group at Hull-House conducted by "a fragile, ethereal" woman who read to the class the sonnets of Elizabeth Barrett Browning. The group was assigned a book a week, and Satt found the mind-dulling monotony of making cuffs in a shirtwaist factory "eased by thinking of these books and looking forward to evenings at Hull-House."

"The one thing to be dreaded in the Settlement," Addams wrote in her autobiography, "is that it lose its flexibility, its power of quick adaptation." When Addams and Starr discovered, soon enough, how difficult it was to study Titian after a day spent on the factory floor, they cut back some, but never all, of their cultural programs, substituting activities more in line with their neighbors' backgrounds and immediate needs. But Hull-House never ceased to be an intellectual oasis, a place where a Polish girl with dreams could meet and learn from the likes of John Dewey, Henry Demarest Lloyd, Susan B. Anthony, Clarence Darrow, and young Frank Lloyd Wright, whose wife and mother did volunteer work for Jane Addams and whose uncle and surrogate father, Rev. Jenkins Lloyd Jones, was an electrifying speaker at the settlement.

Hull-House was not the first settlement house in America. Unknown to Addams, one was established in New York City in 1886, and soon hundreds of others would be founded, sixty-seven in Chicago alone by World War I. But Hull-House was easily the most famous, due largely to "Saint Jane," as the Chicago press began to call Addams, by 1900 the best-known woman in the world, after Queen Victoria. Addams was a lifelong learner, her most imaginative social initiatives inspired by problems she confronted in her Halsted Street backyard. The neighborhood needed a kindergarten, a day nursery, a playground, a gymnasium, and a bathhouse, so she raised money to build them. She also began systematically to investigate conditions in local factories and tenements and to move into the male-dominated worlds of politics and economics, stung into more radical action by the economic depression that hit Chicago with ferocious force in the winter of 1893. But this is to anticipate. In her first years at Hull-House, Addams concentrated on "protective" reforms for women and children, often working in tandem with the Chicago Woman's Club. Behind these modest measures, however, was a new conception of urban community, a reform philosophy that viewed the city as an extension of the home and the homemaker as a municipal housekeeper. It sounded terribly tame, but it inspired constructive action and helped settlement workers, in cooperation with other urban reformers, to refashion American liberalism.

Addams and her fellow women reformers saw their work as a natural outgrowth of women's traditional responsibilities as mothers and homemakers. Women, they argued, were the "natural housekeepers" of the modern city. Through their efforts, the "city of dreadful night" would be made as clean, supportive, and morally healthful as a middle-class home in Cedarville. "May we not say," said Addams, "that city housekeeping has failed partly because women, the traditional housekeepers, have not been consulted as to its multiform activities."

Although Addams would continue to believe that women were endowed with a special insight into social injustice, she had what Elia Peattie called a "genius for inclusiveness." She was "the sister of all men," reaching out to everyone who needed help, responding to "the city's cry of distress." An adopted daughter of Chicago, she was also driven by the same impulse that powered its civic renewal of the 1890s. A character in *The Precipice* echoes Addams's urban pride: "Are n't [sic] women to serve the city as well as men? It's a practical form of patriotism, according to my mind."

6. Cleansing the City

For many middle-class Chicagoans, industrial pollution was the single most embarrassing feature of their World's Fair city. Chicago on the eve of the fair remained one of the most abysmally filthy cities in the industrial world. Most of its streets were unspeakably dirty, the horrible-smelling river remained its sewer, and thick gray smoke from locomotives, river tugs, and factories discolored its new skyscrapers, stung people's eyes, clogged their lungs, and soiled their clothing— and reduced visibility in the Loop to little more than a city block. "The smoke nuisance must go," Chicago newspapers demanded.

The city had a Society for the Prevention of Smoke, a citizens' group formed in 1891 by prominent downtown businessmen, including Owen Aldis. Using inspections by civil engineers, newspaper publicity, and aggressive legal action, it managed to persuade or pressure some businesses to substitute clean-burning anthracite for Illinois soft coal and to install new smoke-abatement technology. But after a promising beginning, it ran out of money and disbanded in 1893. Nor was it able to convince the city government to carry on its work, for the city, which burned bituminous coal in all its facilities, was the most flagrant violator of its own pathetically enforced smoke ordinance of some ten years' standing.

"The World's Fair city should spare itself the righteous indignation of the world," the *Graphic* fumed, "by doing . . . what can be done, and this at once." But convinced, as most city officials were, that laws mandating the use of expensive Pennsylvania hard coal would have an injurious impact on business growth, all its aroused editors could fall back on was the long-standing local faith in technology as the solution to the city's public health problems. "The longed for desideratum is a perfect smoke-consuming appliance. . . . Although every experiment has proved a failure, . . . the work of invention will yet accomplish its perfect work."

The city did improve its street-cleaning services in preparation for the exposition, but only in areas where tourists were expected to go. Nowhere were street conditions worse than in Jane Addams's ward. In some of its alleys putrefying rubbish was piled a story and more high; its rotting wooden streets were clogged with manure, decaying garbage, and the bloated corpses of dogs and horses; and its plank-board sidewalks were lined with large uncovered garbage boxes filled to overflowing because of erratic pickup service by city-licensed scavengers. Neighborhood children played their games in and around these breeding boxes for rats. "They were the first objects that the toddling child learned to climb," Addams remarked in her autobiography, "their bulk afforded a barricade and their contents provided missiles in all the battles of the older boys; and finally they became the seats upon which absorbed lovers held enchanted converse."

As an example to the city, Addams installed a small incinerator at Hull-House and had the settlement house's Woman's Club investigate garbage conditions in the ward and report their findings to city hall.

But to no avail. Finally, in desperation, Addams applied to become the Nineteenth Ward's garbage collector. Her bid was never considered, but the publicity it provoked led the city to appoint her the ward's inspector of garbage.

Every morning at 6:00 A.M., neighbors trudging to work would see a bent woman as pale as candle wax following the city's garbage wagons to the dump to see that they did their work thoroughly; and in the evenings Jane Addams would supervise the burning of mountains of alley refuse, the hundred-foot-high flames drawing crowds of curious onlookers. The foreign-born women of the neighborhood were "shocked," Addams recalled, "by this abrupt departure into the ways of men." But some of them came to understand "that their housewifely duties logically extended to the adjacent alleys and streets" where diseases spread by filth put their children at deadly risk.

The unflagging pressure of Addams and other settlement workers—most prominently Mary McDowell in Packingtown—forced the city to take measures to improve sanitary conditions in some immigrant wards. But not until after 1900, and not very satisfactorily.

•

"They can balance high buildings on rafts floating in mud," Lincoln Steffens wrote of Chicago, "but they can't quench the stench of the stockyards, [or] . . . solve the smoke nuisance, [or] . . . pave and clean the streets." The city did, however, take decisive action in the 1890s to combat at least one of its long-festering environmental problems, not because it was pressured by reformers like Addams and Steffens, but because it was confronted—as it had been in the 1850s—by a public health crisis of potentially catastrophic sweep. Fear and "absolute necessity," as reporter Theodore Dreiser wrote, were the inspirations for the Chicago Sanitary and Ship Canal, "the greatest feat of sanitary engineering in the world."

The most audacious engineering achievement in Chicago's history was built because its predecessor, the city's first great engineering wonder, was unable to do what its builders had tried to make it do—turn nature around. When the Illinois and Michigan Canal ceased to be a carrier of what civilization produced, it had been turned into a carrier of what it discarded, pulling sewage from the Chicago River and transporting it down the Des Plaines and the Illinois, polluting these waters and bringing "sickness and death to [our] citizens," residents in the river valleys complained. The outraged civic leaders of Joliet threatened to block the canal with dirt, forcing it to back up and causing Chicago to "stink herself to death." There was no need to do that, however, for nature was already accomplishing the deed. As silt

accumulated on the river's bottom, it negated the effects of Ellis Chesbrough's deepening and dredging operation of 1871, and the river became again a foul-smelling bayou, its greatly heralded reversal—a
mere yearlong phenomenon—short-circuited.

Then came unprecedented rain, the most concentrated downpour in
Chicago's early recorded history. In the summer of 1879, it rained for
thirty consecutive days, turning the ordinarily shallow Des Plaines
into a swollen torrent. Its flood waters poured over the historic portage
and into the Chicago River, forcing that carrier of nearly all of Chicago's sewage to back up into the lake beyond the intake pipes for the
municipal water system, causing Chicagoans to boil their drinking
water.

Indignation meetings were held all over the city, angry crowds
marched with torchlights in the streets, and the Citizens' Association—a group of businessmen smart enough to discern the connection
between public health and continued urban growth—came forward
with a bold plan for a new canal, a wide and deep channel that would
permanently reverse the Chicago River. Five dry summers, however,
limited the city's response to stopgap action—the reinstallation of the
pumps at Bridgeport to try to pull the river water into the canal. Nature
struck again in 1885, emptying six inches of rain on the city in less
than a day, and this time the contamination of the water supply set off
deadly outbreaks of typhoid fever, cholera, dysentery, and other waterborne diseases that killed an estimated 12 percent of Chicago's
population.

Public panic finally forced action on the Citizens' Association plan,
which politicians and local engineers turned into a grand design for a
combination drainage and steamship canal that would give Chicago its
long-sought water highway to the Mississippi and New Orleans. In
1889 the state legislature created the Sanitary District of Chicago, one
of the first regional authorities in the country, to build and run the new
canal and its ancillary projects, investing the authority with the power
to tax, issue bonds, and exercise eminent domain. Voters then carried
the bill into law through a referendum. The count was an overwhelming 70,958 to 242.

The new canal was to run parallel to the old one, cutting through the
low drainage divide at Summit between the Great Lakes and the Mississippi Basin and swinging down to Lockport, twenty-eight miles
southwest of Chicago, just above Joliet, where the Des Plaines met the
Illinois. With the help of a widened and deepened Chicago River, it
would draw from Lake Michigan a far greater volume of water than the
shallow Illinois and Michigan Canal. It was expected that this strong-

running stream would purify itself by a natural process of oxidation and dilution by the time it reached Joliet. It would not be a canal precisely, for it had no water-controlling locks. It would be a "ditch," not unlike the half-mile-long ditch Louis Joliet had suggested to connect the Des Plaines and Chicago Rivers. Some Chicago boosters preferred to call it a river, a new man-made river that would counteract nature itself, making the old river flow southward, as it had eons ago, when the site of Chicago lay at the bottom of Lake Michigan.

Engineers were ready to begin work the day the canal bill became law. But there were bureaucratic logjams that were not cleared away until another devastating typhoid epidemic struck the city in 1890 and lasted for two years, giving Chicago the highest death rate from typhoid fever among the principal cities in Europe and America.

On the morning of September 3, 1892, a special train carried Chicago dignitaries to "Shovel Day" ceremonies at the town of Lamont in the valley of the Des Plaines. There was the usual congratulatory oratory, but one speaker, a sewage authority trustee named Bernard A. Eckhart, cut to the truth. "I have heard, I am sorry to say, a few well meaning persons express surprise that an enterprise of such magnitude should be undertaken; rather should the wonder be that we were not forced to something of this kind years ago. No other civilized community would be guilty of such prolonged and continuous contamination of its water supply." With that, the first spadeful of dirt was overturned and work commenced on the greatest earth-moving and quarrying project in the history of cities.

•

The Chicago Sanitary and Ship Canal was built at the conclusion of a century of tremendous engineering projects, some of which totally transformed the face of nature, uniting countries that had been divided and opening up entire continents through railroads, canals, bridges, viaducts, and tunnels. It was the century of the civil engineer, "the great leveler of the age," in the words of the *Tribune*. But even the *Tribune* thought this vast and difficult water project, cutting a gorge through the backbone of the continent and turning around a river, would be a Herculean challenge for its chief engineer, Isham Randolph.

Machines and men—the largest, most technically advanced earth-moving machines in the world and over eight thousand unskilled immigrants and blacks—blasted and channeled through almost forty miles of ground, fifteen miles of which was solid rock, more land excavation than was later required for the Panama Canal. If the whole volume of rock and earth taken out of the ground of Illinois had been deposited in Lake Michigan in fifty feet of water, it would have created an island one mile square, with its surface eight feet above the water level. "The Chicago Drainage Canal is the most important public work now being executed in the world," declared *Harper's Weekly.*

It was an astounding feat of labor. The muscle work was brutally difficult, and the men, making fifteen cents an hour and living in stinking pine-board canal camps, were driven unrelentingly until, in frustration, they struck for higher wages in the summer of 1893, creating what a Chicago reporter called a "reign of terror" in Lamont. "The thirty-eight saloons are crowded with 2,000 striking quarrymen and canal laborers. Last night they marched through the principal streets demanding higher wages and cursing [and physically attacking] their bosses." When blood was spilled in a pitched battle between strikers and a sheriff's posse, Gov. John Peter Altgeld called in the militia to restore order, and the men were forced to return to work with no change in their wages. When peace returned and the work was further advanced, excursion parties from Chicago would go out to the site and descend by wooden ladders into the deep channels of the rock sections, their perfectly perpendicular walls as high as thirty feet. Only by standing at the bottom of the excavated canal bed could a person appreciate the magnitude of the digging and quarrying operation, a 160-foot-wide cut through the land that ran straight and true as far as the eye could see.

When the work was nearly completed in late 1899, Sanitary Authority officials learned that the state of Missouri would seek a court injunction barring the opening of the canal, claiming the raw sewage from Chicago would pollute the Mississippi River, the source of St. Louis's drinking water. Seeing their entire effort threatened, sanitary trustees acted quickly and quietly, not even informing the governor of what they proposed to do. At the break of dawn on January 2, 1900, they went with two reporters to the South Chicago site where a small wooden dam prevented the Chicago River from spilling into the newly completed canal. They tried to shatter the dam with dynamite. When that failed, they set it on fire and gathered near the blaze for a group picture. Then they called in a dredge, which completed the work by noon.

Chicago River was permanently reversed, making it the first river in the world to flow away from its mouth. "Though it was accomplished without any flourish of trumpets," the *Tribune* declared, "it was one of the most important events in the history of Chicago," the beginning of the "pure water era."

St. Louis still took Chicago to court, but the case was eventually dismissed when a report by scientists concluded that the canal's dilution process worked: the Chicago River's wastewater was clean by the time it reached Joliet. The transportation channel to the Mississippi, however, was not completed until the 1930s, when dams were built along the Illinois to make the river navigable for deep-water craft. The new canal, along with the St. Lawrence Seaway, which opened in 1959, would make Chicago the nation's fifth-largest port and give the continent, at last, the inland water highway from the St. Lawrence River to the Gulf of Mexico that had excited the imaginations of dreamers since the incredible journey of Joliet and Marquette.

In 1955 the American Society of Civil Engineers named the Chicago Sanitary and Ship Canal one of the seven wonders of American engineering.

"The achievements of government in Chicago," a modern historian has written, "at times rivaled the feats of the Old Testament God." But Chicago's spectacular works of sanitary engineering were necessary because the city's water disposal system was more primitive than that of biblical Jerusalem, where city engineer Hezekiah at least put in a dung port outside the walls of the city, on the leeward side of prevailing winds. In Chicago, people had been forced to drink from the same vessel in which they evacuated, slowly poisoning themselves.

In addressing these problems, Chicago's canal engineers claimed to have outwitted nature, restoring through human effort the prehistoric outlet nature had capriciously closed off with a small alluvial barrier. Man broke through that vulnerable six-foot-high spot in the continent in what can be seen as an act of heroic chutzpah. But Chicago's new sewage river flowed to the sea through the valley outlet the "Mighty Engineer," in Carter Harrison's words, had carved out long before man arrived in North America. Without that natural flow channel, the Chicago Sanitary and Ship Canal would have remained an engineer's pipe dream.

The presence of this channel—nature's gift—made Chicago the only Great Lakes city that could divert sewage from the source of its water supply. But this proved a mixed blessing, causing Chicago to emphasize sewage disposal and largely neglect water purification.

•

The drainage canal cut back dramatically the death rates of typhoid and cholera in Chicago, but it did not completely solve the city's sewage and water problems. Claiming that the water level of Lake Michigan was being dangerously lowered by the canal, states bordering on the lake brought legal action against Illinois, forcing Chicago to limit the supply of water it drew from the lake. This made dilution less successful and compelled the state to build a series of treatment plants along the sewage canal. But it wasn't until Chicago began chlorinating its drinking water in 1912 and filtering it thirty-five years later that the water was rendered absolutely safe.

Chicago had first experimented with filtration in preparation for the Columbian Exposition. When the typhoid scourge tore through the city in the early 1890s, exposition officials feared it would keep people from attending the fair. Their concerns turned to alarm when the leading British medical journal, *Lancet,* published a report based on water samples taken in the river and the lake warning visitors not to drink Chicago tap water unless it was boiled first.

Public health officials mounted an immediate and all-out publicity campaign, declaring that the city's water was the cleanest it had ever been, a statement that would not have given comfort to anyone familiar with the history of Chicago's water problems. Chicago's public health servants, moreover, had been suspected in the past of being pressured by city officials to manipulate their data to make it appear that the city was far healthier than it was. And they were arguing, anyway, from outmoded medical science, which put the cause of typhoid on noxious vapors emanating from accumulated dirt and trash—"the filth theory" it was called. This theory placed part of the blame for the spread of typhoid on indigent immigrants.

In the 1880s, a new field of medicine, bacteriology, emerged from the discovery of the cholera vibrio by the German physician Robert Koch and from kindred but independent experiments by Louis Pasteur, who demonstrated decisively that living things, such as diseases, could come only from other living things, such as virulent microorganisms, and not, as had been thought, from dirt. The epoch-making experiments of Koch and Pasteur brought about an end-of-the-century revolution in medicine that resulted in the discovery of the germs responsible for the great urban killers of the age: tuberculosis, cholera, bubonic plague, diphtheria, typhoid fever, and pneumonia. With discovery came equally epic breakthroughs in immunization.

Several Chicago researchers were among the first in the United States to publicize the new germ theory of disease, but the city's health department remained a prisoner of discredited science. Officials of the exposition, however, could not afford to be swayed by old biology and booster reassurances. They would be held responsible if a massive health epidemic broke out at the fair, as one almost had at the centennial celebration in 1876 in Philadelphia, where a sewage discharge into the Schuylkill River was believed to have caused a typhoid outbreak. In the fall of 1890, even before he selected his architects, Daniel Burnham appointed a sanitary engineer, William S. MacHarg, and had him build a purification plant in Jackson Park to provide sterilized water for his construction army. At the same time, Burnham went ahead with plans to equip drinking fountains on the grounds with the new Pasteur filters that a number of first-class hotels had begun to install in order to reduce bacteria in the drinking water. Burnham also set up a chemical laboratory on the grounds to continually test the fair's drinking water and drove a pipeline to prairie farmland to the south to carry off waste from Jackson Park's toilets to a Sewage Cleaning Works, where it would be chemically treated, solidified, and burned so that no crude sewage would be discharged into the lake. In a capping effort to allay the fears of visitors, he put a hustling Chicago operator by the name of James E. McElroy in charge of a plan to pipe in pure mineral water from a spring in Waukesha, a Wisconsin spa known for its health-restoring bottled water.

When residents of Waukesha protested the building of an ugly pipeline through their fashionable resort, McElroy descended on the spa in the middle of the night with a trainload of three hundred Chicago workers under orders to install a pipeline before the village awoke the next morning. News of his gambit reached Waukesha before he did, however, and he and his crew were met by a mob of villagers with shotguns. McElroy was arrested and jailed briefly, but there was no stopping him. Months later, he bought a spring twelve miles from Waukesha and built his 101-mile-long gravity pipeline to the White City. Since the new spring was conveniently located within the boundaries of Waukesha County, fair officials could continue to claim in their publicity that they would be piping in crystal-clear Waukesha spring water.

When the fair opened, Burnham dismantled his purification plant and put the Wisconsin water on sale at concessions and from coin-operated machines at a penny a glass. Fairgoers, however, preferred the free water from the fountains, and when long lines developed at the fountains as the crowds increased in size over the summer, Burnham rebuilt the purification plant and dispensed its water free of charge from barrels placed at convenient locations. These precautions made the Columbian Exposition a public health, as well as an entertainment and architectural, triumph. There was not a single case of typhoid reported at the fair, and its clean-water policy had an influence on city government as health officials began attributing typhoid to contaminated water, not to slum conditions. Chicago entered the era of modern medicine as it completed its White City, and the additional purification measures it took after this gave it, by 1920, the lowest death rate from typhoid fever of twenty of the nation's biggest cities. Today the largest city on earth located on a freshwater lake has the most extensive water-filtration system in existence, the indirect legacy of the Columbian Exposition.

•

On the September morning that Chicago dignitaries boarded a train to Lamont for Shovel Day ceremonies for the Sanitary Canal, Daniel Burnham was supervising the completion of the White City's most spectacular structure, George B. Post's Manufacturers and Liberal Arts Building. It was the largest building in the world, three times larger than St. Peter's Basilica and four times larger than the Roman Coliseum. "If the great pyramid of Cheops could be moved to Chicago," the exposition's publicity department boasted, "it could be piled up in this building with the galleries left from which to view the stone." Its roof, a clear-span structure of iron and steel with eleven acres of skylights, was built by E. C. Shankland of Chicago, Burnham's chief engineer, and was held up by three-hinged iron trusses, the largest and strongest ever built. It took six hundred rail cars to bring the twenty-one main trusses to Chicago from their place of manufacture.

High-speed Hale Company elevators ran to the roof, where there was an observation platform with a magnificent view of the grounds, the lake, and far-spreading Chicago. The first person other than a construction worker to ascend to the top of the newly completed roof was the Director of Works. Burnham didn't go up in an elevator, though one was then in operation. He had a rope wrapped around him and ascended with the aid of a pulley used to haul up beams for the roof crews. "It took nerve to make the trip," said the *Tribune*, "but Mr. Burnham treated it as an everyday matter."

Burnham had taken a special interest in this building, for it was to be the site of the fair's dedication ceremonies on October 21, four hundred years to the day, by the revised calendar, following Columbus's sighting of the New World. Working his crews night and day, he had the building ready on time, although there were still upward of ten thousand workers in Jackson Park on the week of the dedication preparing it for the official opening the following May. Burnham also took a close interest in the preparations for Dedication Day, which he wanted to be "the greatest ceremonial of all time."

"Dedication Week" began with a grand inaugural ball at the Auditorium hosted by Bertha Palmer. Gowned in yellow satin and puffs of velvet, with diamonds as big as grapes in her tiara, the "Queen of Chicago" led a procession of "patronesses" into Sullivan's great golden hall to the "Coronation March" played by the John Philip Sousa Band. The next morning, Chicago staged the largest civic parade in its history. All business was suspended that morning, and over eighty thousand marchers formed a procession that wound its way through the scrubbed and swept streets of the Loop, the skyscrapers decorated with colorful bunting and high-flying flags and the streets and rooftops packed with over half a million spectators. There were hundreds of military and civic bands, and the marchers—common citizens mostly—stepped smartly to the "blare of patriotic melodies."

In the crowd that day was ten-year-old Hilda Satt of Jane Addams's neighborhood. Her father, a tombstone carver, had brought his family from Poland that year after hearing stories in Warsaw of a world's fair to be held in a city called Chicago. "This would be a good time," he told them, "to go to this new world." Hilda stood on the sidewalk all morning with her eleven brothers and sisters and watched the civic parade pass by. "Each float depicted some phase of the discovery of America," she wrote years later. "We had come to America in a truly historic time."

The following morning, the city was awakened by the sound of artillery, and at exactly nine o'clock, Gen. Nelson A. Miles, who had served under Grant in the Civil War, wheeled his large horse in the street in front of the Auditorium, the U.S. Fifth Cavalry behind him, and led a parade of dignitaries, including Vice President Levi Morton (President Benjamin Harrison was at his dying wife's bedside) to Jackson Park. More than 140,000 people waited in the Manufacturers and Liberal Arts Building. There was a five-thousand-member Hallelujah Chorus, a five-hundred-piece orchestra under the direction of Theodore Thomas, and the usual barrage of holiday oratory. Bertha Palmer spoke for the Board of Lady Managers, saying it was fitting that she was part of the day's ceremonies, as it was a woman, Queen Isabella, who was largely responsible for Columbus's voyage. Then Burnham presented the buildings to the official president of the exposition, Harlow Higinbotham. As he did, the white-gowned chorus— "rising with a flutter of handkerchiefs that looked like lilies in the wind"—broke into Mendelssohn's "Sons of Art." It was, said the *Tribune,* "the day of days in the life of this city." The paper failed to mention, however, the mad rush for the food after the ceremonies were ended, in which a number of people were almost crushed to death.

•

In preparing for the fair, Chicago showed that it was more than a center of hog killing and grain gambling, but the Upward Movement would not be complete, its leaders were convinced, without an all-out effort to transform another side of the city's image—its justly deserved reputation as the most vice-ridden and politically corrupt city in the country. Chicago was still, in Lincoln Steffens's famous opinion, "first in violence, deepest in dirt; loud, lawless, unlovely, ill-smelling, irreverent, new . . . the 'tough' among cities."

Those who ran Chicago's vice trades and poisoned its politics would have to be flushed from the city, the local elite began to insist, like the stinking sewage the new canal promised to remove; and this cleansing must begin before the fair opened. That winter of 1892–93, Chicago would hold an election campaign to choose its World's Fair mayor, its representative to the world, and the businessmen-builders of the White City would do all in their power to prevent the election, for the fifth time, of Carter Henry Harrison, backing the candidacy of one of their own, a Prairie Avenue packer named Samuel W. Allerton.

Harrison represented everything Allerton and his friends believed was wrong with Chicago. As mayor, he had maintained close ties with Michael Cassius McDonald, the lord of the city's vice empire; he favored segregating, not eliminating, prostitution and gambling; he allowed the concert saloons and cheap dives to remain open on the Sabbath and after legal closing hours; and he fraternized with, and had the political support of, labor leaders and socialists as well as Irish voters and their aldermen, who were more interested in political patronage than in art museums and symphony orchestras. He was a threat and an embarrassment to Chicago's businessmen-reformers, the worst possible person to represent their city in the year of its "greatest glory."

For Burnham and the civic elite, the fight against Harrison was a fight for Chicago. The fair would be their show, an expression of their urban ideals. But they also began to see it as the opening wedge of a campaign to shut down the vice trade, reduce the power of the neighborhood bosses, and run municipal government, as the fair itself was run, like a modern business corporation. In many ways, the fair was the unofficial beginning of what became popularly known as the Progressive movement.

The election and the fair were the central acts of the Chicago drama of 1893, and the dialogue that grew out of this drama centered on the most important question that citizens of a city can ask about the community they live in: What kind of city should this be? Would it be Carter Harrison's Chicago or Daniel Burnham's? Much of the city's future would depend on the outcome of this Battle for Chicago, whose origins go back to the beginnings of Carter Harrison's political career and whose most passionately contested issues were the ones he confronted in the 1880s as mayor of this wildly growing, volatile, and violent place.

13

The Battle for Chicago

1. Politics "Ain't Bean Bag"

IT was the most impressive funeral in the young city's history, a grand pageant and moving tribute to the man whose supreme ambition had been to be mayor of the "World's Fair City." Almost two hundred thousand mourners filed past the open casket in the black-draped rotunda of city hall, and the next day, tens of thousands of Chicagoans— forming a procession that stretched nearly halfway across the great city—followed the remains of Carter Harrison from the steps of city hall to a small stone chapel in Graceland Cemetery. The business of the town was stopped, and a half-million people blackened the sidewalks all the way to the bordering buildings, creating immovable walls of humanity that the vast procession passed through.

Bands playing dirges and militia marching to muffled drums followed the black-and-gold hearse, while behind them rolled the splendid carriages of the honorary pallbearers, the business titans of Chicago. Then came the aldermen and high officials of the city, and trailing off from them was a long, disorderly column of humanity, Carter Harrison's political army. Dressed in the colors and costumes of their native countries, there were Irish, German, Polish, Bohemian, Italian, Greek, and Norwegian societies and parade row after parade row of police, firemen, letter carriers, and municipal clerks, most of whom owed their jobs to their fallen generalissimo. There were also representatives of the city's leading labor unions, for Harrison had been a staunch friend of working people, having appointed a number of socialists and trade-union leaders to municipal positions. "I never knew a man," said Victor Lawson, publisher of a stridently anti-Harrison newspaper, "who possessed in such a marked degree the politician's prime quality of keeping in touch with the masses and commanding their affection. . . . Realizing fully the extent to which the population of Chicago is foreign born he devoted himself to gaining the support of men of every nationality." Yet Carter Harrison was a millionaire real estate king who had enjoyed the support of some of the city's most substantial businessmen, friends he played poker with in his free time.

The route to the cemetery took the cortege past every place connected with the mayor's assassination. The procession passed Harrison's stately home on Ashland Boulevard, where, on the evening of October 28, 1893, after delivering a spirited speech at the closing of the Columbian Exposition, the sixty-eight-year-old mayor—still a robust and physically powerful man—was gunned down in the hallway to his parlor by a deranged office seeker named Patrick Eugene Prendergast. Here carriages containing Harrison's relatives joined the procession; and on the high porticoes of the Harrison mansion stood the servants of the household, the women weeping as the hearse came into sight.

Then the mounted parade marshal led the march past the Des Plaines Street police station, where the quiet young assassin had surrendered to police, and finally the procession passed by the county jail, where Prendergast was in custody, preparing to be defended on a plea of insanity by, among others, young Clarence Darrow. In the neighborhood of the jail there was a strong detachment of police, a precaution in the event the crowd rushed the prison and tried to give Prendergast a taste of the people's rancor.

As the funeral train passed the jail at three o'clock, a cry went up from cell to cell to "Kill Prendergast," to "Lynch the Killer," until all the prisoners were shaking the bars and screaming for vengeance. The crowd on the street heard the shouting inside the jail, and someone started a rumor that the prisoners were killing Prendergast. "For a moment the throng swayed as if undecided," the next day's papers reported. "It looked like there would be violence," but the presence of so many police cooled the mood, and the crowd dispersed after the cortege passed.

In places, spectators waited for over three hours along the sidewalks for the hearse to reach them, restlessly pushing and shouting, but when the first band playing a funeral march came into hearing, they fell silent. Men lifted their hats in respect, and some women fainted and had to be carried away. Badges sold through the crowd were labeled "Our Carter," and people spoke of him as Carter or "the Old Man," as if he had been a neighborhood friend.

As the one-and-a-half-mile-long line of carriages carrying dignitaries passed by, one person and then another in the crowd would recognize and point out Daniel Burnham, Ferdinand Peck, or Philip Armour, but not one person of privilege or position "was given that quick and general recognition which Carter Harrison always commanded in the presence of a Chicago multitude," noted a local reporter. "This was the most significant fact of the day. The only man known to all Chicago had passed away."

At points along the line of the march, people broke through the police barricades and rushed into the street, surrounding the funeral carriage, touching it and kissing it. The cortege had set out in morning sunlight but was unable to reach Graceland until early evening, as a mist began to form on the green-shaded ground. A crowd made up mostly of women and children had been waiting for hours near the cemetery gate, and they looked on as the black casket was carried into the darkened chapel, where the last rites were performed by the light of a single, smoky oil lamp. Then the casket was lowered into a crypt, and the marchers returned to the city in a cold, drizzling rain.

Carter Harrison had loved to ride through the city on his big Kentucky Thoroughbred, and the proud old mare had followed behind the hearse with stirrups crossed on her empty saddle. "We kept her out on the farm after that," recalled Harrison's oldest son, "and nobody ever rode her again."

•

Just after Harrison's death, a *Los Angeles Times* reporter caught up with the *Chicago Tribune*'s editor and publisher, Joseph Medill, at his winter home in California. The interview he filed was remarkable for its candor and surprising revelations. Medill had been Harrison's bitterest public enemy, heading a campaign of vilification against him in the 1893 election that was almost unprecedented in American urban politics. One of the founders of the Republican Party, Medill had never forgiven Harrison for voting Democratic in the 1860 elections—a Jefferson Davis disunion man, he branded him, even though Harrison had strongly supported the union cause. But Harrison's greatest political sin, Mcdill thought, was his pandering to newly naturalized immigrants, especially the Irish, a race of criminals, priests, and whiskey dispensers. A teetotaler who detested gambling, Medill also believed that Harrison had soiled the city's reputation by refusing to close down its gambling halls and enforce the state's Sunday closing law for taverns.

Harrison had also appealed, said Medill, to the most dangerous classes in the city, allowing anarchists to parade in the streets, taunting police and the local establishment "in the most diabolical and incendiary language." By granting these revolutionaries free speech and the right to assemble, he was directly responsible, Medill told the *Los Angeles Times* interviewer, for the killing of seven Chicago policemen by an anarchist bomb thrower in Haymarket Square in May 1886, in what was the most sensational labor incident in the country up to that time.

Then Joseph Medill said two astonishing things. Carter Harrison, he told the *Times* man, had always been his friend. It was almost impossible, he confessed, to dislike Harrison; he bore no grudges and was engaging, witty, and big-hearted—a "magnetic man," physically and morally courageous, and with magnificent vitality. Summing him up for posterity, Medill then said that Harrison "was the most remarkable man—and I believe that will be the popular verdict—that our city has ever produced. . . . We have had a good many strong men, I know, but no one equal to him; and among all the Mayors ever produced in the United States there never was a man equal to him in . . . power over the masses, at the same time maintaining a strong personal popularity across party lines."

Some years after this, another prominent Chicago Republican, Charles E. Merriam, a University of Chicago professor who ran for mayor unsuccessfully against Harrison's son Carter Harrison II—who would also be a five-time mayor—gave an appraisal of the elder Harrison that echoed Medill's: "Born a Kentucky gentleman, educated in Yale, migrating to Chicago and entering actively into its political life, Harrison was one of the most interesting urban figures of his time, important not only in the history of Chicago but in the history of urban development and in the history of democracy itself." He was, Merriam thought, a "novel type of a powerful leader, . . . neither a boss on the one hand nor a demagogue on the other. He was not primarily a product of the spoils system nor a personal participant in it, nor yet did he make his appeal primarily to the ignorance and prejudice of the community. In this respect he stands unique among early types of significant political leaders developed in urban American communities."

If ever a person embodied the character and spirit of his city, it was Carter Henry Harrison. A lusty, prideful, imposing man, an urban expansionist who loved the diversity and drive of big-city life, he "personified in himself," said a Chicago paper, "all the restlessness, the energy, the ability, and the ambition which have built the World's Fair city into the greatest metropolis in the Nation."

"My acquaintance with him extended over a period of nearly forty years," Joseph Medill recalled in 1893. "He arrived in Chicago a few months after I did [in 1855]. He came from the blue-grass region of Kentucky, a young, vigorous, hearty, rosy-cheeked man . . . fond of riding horseback in the city and wearing a Southern soft slouch hat." And Medill remembered his being immensely proud of his family heritage. "He made it understood that he belonged to one of the great historic families in the United States; that . . . the Harrisons of whom he was a descendant furnished" a president [later, with the election of Benjamin Harrison, two presidents] and governors of Virginia and territorial Indiana; that "a Harrison had signed the Declaration of Independence . . . and fought in the Revolution."

He belonged to the Kentucky wing of the illustrious Harrisons of Virginia and was born in 1825 in a log house on a frontier sugarcane farm near Lexington, a circumstance he would turn to political advantage, as had his most famous relative, President William Henry Harrison, in his famous "Log Cabin Campaign" of 1840. "I was born in a canebrake," Carter Harrison loved to tell Chicago audiences, "and rocked to sleep in a sugar trough." But his family had owned land and slaves, and after his father died when Carter was only eight months old, his proudly independent mother supervised the clearing of their timbered farm, turned it into a prospering plantation, and educated her only child at home until he was fifteen.

After being tutored in Lexington by the brother of Chief Justice John Marshall, he was sent to Yale College, taking his favorite Thoroughbred with him. He wasn't much of a student but acquired a campus reputation for gallantry and florid, impromptu oratory, two of his golden political gifts. When he returned home, he went at life at a leisurely pace, reading for the bar, helping out with the plantation, and—after his mother remarried—traveling in Europe, North Africa, and the Near East for two years. He learned to speak French and German fluently, and in Paris he befriended socialists, veterans from all over Europe of the failed revolutions of 1848, ardent, bearded men he sipped wine with in smoky cafés by the Seine.

Back in Kentucky, he studied for the bar at Transylvania University and, after graduating, married a distant cousin from his native Fayette County. Following the wedding, they set out for Illinois to look for a new place to settle, for Harrison had developed a loathing of slavery, publicly favoring emancipation with compensation, a position that put him in deep disfavor with his Kentucky neighbors. The young couple found Chicago filthy beyond belief, but Harrison saw it as a wonderful place to make money. After touring the dusty town on a beat-up buckboard, he told hotelier John Drake that it was "destined to be the greatest city on this continent. I have decided to cast my lot with her."

Three weeks after settling in the city, he sank the money from the sale of his land and slaves—and additional funds he borrowed from William Ogden—into local real estate, improving his valuable lots and becoming, after the war, a rich man with an estate on Ashland Boulevard (named after Henry Clay's Lexington farm) in Chicago's Kentucky colony on the West Side. When he bought this gracious house, with a commanding cupola, from his sometime real estate partner, Henry Honoré, father of Bertha Honoré Palmer, he purchased the entire city block and built a small prairie version of his bluegrass plantation, with stables and big country gardens and a smokehouse to cure Kentucky hams for his family of four children.

"He would work in the gardens till tired," his son Carter recalled, "and then lie with a book to read in a swinging seat under the trees. He read Dickens, Thackeray and Scott, histories and biographies in English, French, and German." He liked to impress people by quoting Shakespeare from memory, and he enjoyed talking science with friends who knew the work of two of his favorite writers, Darwin and Huxley. Sometimes he would sit up all night devouring a book. He read just as he ate, he once told a friend, feeding himself until he couldn't hold any more. He liked to read while sipping a bourbon and puffing on a briar pipe, yet he was disciplined enough to try his hand at writing a novel.

He was a man without pretensions, preferring band music to Mozart and the circus and the minstrel shows to serious theater. When he went to a show, he liked to laugh, he said. "It's my idea of happiness." He had a tailor, but his son doubted if he ever had a suit pressed. His only personal extravagances were a pair of high knee boots of the best soft leather and a gold ring with a diamond sparkle that he wore on the small finger of his left hand, a Harrison trademark, as were his white mare, his slouch hat, and his long cigars, the best ones carried in a pocket inside his coat and the others—his "campaign cigars"—in a conspicuous outside pocket.

But Carter Harrison's true trademark was talk. "He made himself the center of all his conversations with anybody and on every subject . . ." Joseph Medill recalled. "Yet it was done in a way that seemed to be unconscious and not unpleasant. . . . His friends all noticed it; they would laugh or smile about it, and called it 'Carter Harrisonia.'"

He entered politics just after the Great Fire, persuading Joseph Medill to head a citizens' ticket pledged to rebuild the city. While campaigning for Medill, he was elected to the Cook County Commission and from there went on to serve two terms in Congress. But his heart was in Chicago, not Washington, and in 1879 he ran for mayor on the Democratic Party ticket and broke the two-decade-long hold of the Republicans on the top office in the city. Chicago would never again be a predominantly Republican city.

An unapologetic believer in the spoils system, Harrison filled low-level city offices with his ethnic following but appointed qualified men to positions of real responsibility. While holding on to his working-class support, he won over hesitant businessmen—"silk-stocking" Democrats and some Republicans—with his record of economy and efficiency in the administration of municipal funds and by promoting improvements in the downtown area that merchants and real estate dealers like Owen Aldis considered essential. When he campaigned, he referred to himself, not disingenuously, as a "business-style" mayor.

But Harrison's power was rooted in his relationship with the Irish, Chicago's most politically powerful ethnic group. They had been an ascendant force in local politics since the 1850s, and under Harrison they took over the city's Democratic Party. Yet as much as Harrison needed the Irish, the Irish needed him, for he established himself as a proven winner at a time when almost all big-city mayors came from the Protestant patrician class. He was a different kind of patrician, willing—for his own survival—to play the game of patronage politics the Irish depended on to hold their own and advance in the Darwinian scramble that was Windy City politics.

The Irish came to Chicago in the 1830s to dig the Illinois and Michigan Canal and settled in a waste-board shantytown, Chicago's first slum, on the mudflats where the canal met the South Branch of the Chicago River, a place called Bridgeport, to this day the emotional center of Chicago's Irish community—home of Richard Daley, senior and junior, and three other twentieth-century Chicago mayors. When the canal was completed, the Irish shovel crews—who worked for whiskey and a dollar a day—took railroad construction jobs and employment in the brickyards, slaughtering mills, and glue factories that began to blanket the banks of the river, joined there by kinsmen escaping the Great Potato Famine, which drove over 2 million destitute Irish from their country between 1845 and 1850.

In Chicago, the Irish faced, yet again, a desperate struggle for survival, living in vermin-infested shacks not unlike their old cotters' cabins and in a city ruled by Anglo-American Protestants, some of whom traced their ancestry back to the reign of Oliver Cromwell, the scourge of Catholic Ireland. Bridgeport became a name synonymous with cholera, alcoholism, and violence, and its tenants—many of them forced to forage for food in the city's garbage holes—became targets of vicious attacks by Whig, Free Soil, and nativist parties, predecessors of the Republican Party. To the Protestant press, led by Joseph Medill's *Tribune*, they were "paddies"—coarse, loud, hard-drinking, and clannish, smelling of whiskey and boiled cabbage. And they were invidiously compared to the Scandinavians, who were seen as temperate, industrious, and frugal.

In 1890 approximately seventy-two thousand immigrants from Norway, Sweden, and Denmark resided in Chicago, which had the largest Scandinavian settlement in the United States. They were portrayed in the local press as a model ethnic group, people who kept their homes and places of business spotlessly clean and who were eager to embrace American ways. Thousands of unmarried Irish women—most of them traveling alone or with young relatives or friends—found work in Chicago as domestic servants, but Scandinavian girls arriving with their parents got the most coveted jobs in the city's households.

It was their faith, more than anything else, that turned native-born Protestants like Gurdon Saltonstall Hubbard against the Irish. There were weekly street brawls between gangs of Irish Catholics and local Protestant toughs, both sides armed with butcher knives and carpenter's awls. The Protestants believed that these tractable but explosively volatile peasants—thought to be under rigid Roman rule—posed a threat to the Protestant republic. A person could not be a papist and a true American, Medill and other nativists insisted, for a Catholic's true allegiance was to church rather than country.

But there was no stopping these incredibly resilient people. The Irish fanned out and built communities in other parts of the city, most prominently on the near West Side, where the Great Fire would break out in Mrs. O'Leary's cow barn. At the opening of the Civil War they were the city's second-largest immigrant group, next to the Germans, constituting 20 percent of its population. With growing numbers came political power, for the Irish were an intensely political people. They didn't learn modern big-city politics from Americans; they created it.

Irish-American urban politics was a transmuted form of home-country vigilantism. Forming clan-based secret societies led by feudal-style chieftains and demanding oath-bound loyalty, the Irish peasantry mounted a campaign of terror against resident English officials and landlords. An Irish woman put it best: "Ten o'clock in the morning and not a blow struck yet!" In Chicago the Irish continued to support terrorism by secret societies for the cause of a free and united Ireland, working through organizations like the Fenians, their hatred of the British fanned by the experience of their "exile" from their homeland. Politics, however, became their chief means of achieving protection and power in a new country where the vote was a more wonderful weapon than the rope and the rifle.

William Ogden and Stephen A. Douglas, whose wife and children were Catholic, welcomed them into the Democratic Party, believing they could be manipulated for party advantage if thrown a few scraps of patronage. But already by the 1850s, the Irish were a power in the city's Democratic Party, holding several council seats and filling the ranks of the police and fire departments. By 1865, one-third of Chicago's police were Irish, and by 1900, the Irish would have six times as many men on the force as the next largest ethnic group. In that year Chicago was the fourth-largest Irish city in America, after New York, Philadelphia, and Boston. Still, the Irish were far outnumbered in Chicago by Germans, most of whom also voted Democratic, especially if they were Catholic. The Irish gained control of the Chicago Democratic Party, then, not on the basis of numbers but by playing the cards they were dealt, using to maximum effect their home-country political savvy and ethnic cohesiveness. Unlike the Germans, they spoke the English language upon arrival in America, and their common faith and experience with poverty and religious oppression on both sides of the water made them a fiercely focused ethnic group, far more united than they had been back in Ireland.

The Irish did not settle in large ghettos made up predominantly of their fellow countrymen, as did the Germans and, later, the Italians and Poles. Even Bridgeport was a mixed ethnic community. But the Irish did group together in neighborhoods around their Irish-controlled parish churches, the nuclei of the Hibernian community in urban America. The Irish quickly gained control of the local Catholic church (between 1844 and 1915 only one of Chicago's bishops was of non-Irish birth or descent), and wherever they lived, they established interlocking neighborhood-based organizations for unity, self-help, and defense: parochial schools, immigrant aid societies, nationalist organizations, armed and uniformed self-defense societies, and political clubs, many of them operating out of Irish saloons and city firehouses manned by Irish political appointees. But unlike the situation in a number of eastern cities, Irish political control of Chicago was delayed until the twentieth century because of what locals called the Harrison phenomenon. The Carter Harrisons, father and son, used personality, not disciplined organization, to run Chicago as no previous mayors had.

•

No politician in Chicago history, with the possible exception of the elder Richard Daley, appealed to as broad a spectrum of the citizenry as Carter Harrison. Workers, including a good number of socialists, voted for him because he appointed union leaders as factory and health inspectors, supported labor's right to organize, strike, and demonstrate, and refused, on several occasions, to use police against strikers despite heavy pressure from powerful capitalists. Harrison's labor policy earned him the enmity of industrialists like Pullman and Armour, who employed thousands of disgruntled workers eager to join unions. But many Republican businessmen with smaller operations and big investors in downtown real estate continued to back him because he remained committed to infrastructure improvements that fueled urban growth and rising real estate values, creating thousands of new jobs for people in all walks of life.

It was as an urban imperialist, not as a social reformer, that Carter Harrison believed he could be of greatest assistance to the average Chicago workingman. He vigorously promoted annexation of adjoining communities, and these annexations created new jobs building and running streetcar lines, laying sewer pipes, hanging electrical wires, putting in new roads and sidewalks, and erecting fire and police stations and new bungalow developments. If Chicago continued to expand while guaranteeing labor's right to organize, it would become, Harrison believed, the best place in the world for a working-class family to settle.

As mayor, Harrison made himself available to everyone. The door to his office at city hall was always open, and on several mornings a week he would hold "open court" for two hours behind a long bar in front of his office, meeting with people who arrived without an appointment, hearing them out, learning their concerns, and doing what he could for them. After his morning conferences, he would ride through the city on his spirited mare, checking on street-cleaning and paving crews and stopping to talk with people, who would easily recognize the bearded horseman with the black slouch hat. If he didn't wear the hat, people noticed. When a Spanish princess—a descendant of Columbus—was scheduled to arrive in Chicago for the World's Fair, a crowd gathered to meet her train. Harrison came riding up in a carriage wearing a silk "topper," and the people went wild. Poised to play "Hail to the Chief," the band broke instead into the popular song "Where Did You Get

That Hat?" Then Harrison rose up from his seat, swept the air with his topper, and walked jauntily into the train station, tapping the marble floor with a Kentucky walking cane of his own cutting.

Visiting writers from Europe might have seen Chicago as the most typically American city, but Harrison also saw it as a "foreign city," its mixture of races and ethnic groups its most American characteristic. At one time or another he claimed to be a kinsman of nearly every race and nationality in the city. Speaking to Norwegians, he was the descendant of Vikings; to Germans, he was the friend of Bismarck, having had breakfast with the "Iron Chancellor" while in Berlin; to blacks, who represented only a tiny fraction of the city's population in 1890, he was "Marse Catah," nursed at the breast, he said, of a "colored mammy"; and an Indian chief he met at the fair claimed that Harrison told him they were brothers by blood. As one of his amazed critics wrote: "On St. George's Day, Harrison blooms out like an English rose. St. Andrew's Day he is stuck full of thistles. St. Patrick's Day he looks like a clover field. He is covered head to foot with shamrock. . . . Harrison is an American only through an accident of birth."

The opposition press saw these base appeals for the ethnic vote as the antics of an old and gregarious fool, but this fool knew exactly what he was doing. Historians have only recently caught up with his acute insight into the voting behavior of nineteenth-century Americans, his understanding that religion and ethnicity were more important than economic issues or class interest in determining party affiliation.

The Protestant pietists, made up mostly of Scandinavians, English, and Scots-Irish, wanted to save their neighbors' souls as well as their own, using the state to enforce Christ's law by crushing the vice trade, closing saloons, dime museums, cafés, concert halls, and public parks on Sundays, prohibiting foreign-language instruction in the schools, and keeping non-Protestants out of office and off the public payroll. Catholics and German Lutherans, the targets of the Protestant purifiers, believed that the state should steer clear of moral legislation, leaving personal behavior to the strictures of church and conscience, and allow immigrants to freely practice the customs of their country of origin, especially the drinking of alcohol on Sunday social occasions. It was a struggle, as novelist Nelson Algren would later say, between "The Live and Let-Livers" and "The Do as I Sayers," or as Irish alderman "Bathhouse" John Coughlin put it: "A Republican is a man who wants you to go t'church every Sunday. A Democrat says if a man wants to have a glass of beer he can have it."

German and Irish businessmen voted with German and Irish workingmen, bonds of culture and religion overshadowing economic differences when nativist pressure was strongest. This cultural identification was reinforced by kin, family, and neighborhood loyalties. Nineteenth-century Chicagoans rarely married across "ethnic boundaries," and changing parties was considered a form of ethnic treason.

When the "purifiers"—led by Frances Willard's Chicago-based Woman's Christian Temperance Union—went after the saloons, they attacked the workingman's club. German, Bohemian, and Irish workers feared—correctly, it turned out—that the effort to restrict the saloons' hours of operation was merely the opening campaign of an all-out moral war to close them down entirely, as the liquor trade had been shut down in suburban "dry" towns like Oak Park and Evanston. This is why Harrison became their true champion.

•

The working-class saloon was a neighborhood institution second in importance only to the family and the parish church. In Jane Addams's Nineteenth Ward, where E. C. Moore, a University of Chicago graduate student, conducted a survey of saloons, there was no place but the saloon, he argued, for the men "to meet their social needs." There were forty-eight thousand residents but no coffeehouses, music halls, or theaters and only a few small trade-union halls.

The saloon's daily routine was keyed to the rhythms of the neighborhood. Sleepy workers stopped there as early as five in the morning for an "eye-opener," and at the screaming sound of noontime factory whistles, dirt- and blood-caked men rushed out of foundries and slaughtering mills to neighboring rows of saloons for five-cent drafts, ten-cent whiskey chasers, and a free lunch of cold meats, cheese, pickles, and rye bread. Workers unwilling to fight the crowds handed over their big, empty lunch pails, called growlers, to boys at the factory gates, who charged a penny a pail to race to the nearest saloon and fill them with beer. "Rushing the can," it was called. There was a lull in the saloon's business after lunch; then the place filled up from the time the factories began letting out until last call. Some saloons stayed open all night to catch the business of workers on the late shift who stopped on their way home for a "bracer" and some conversation.

In neighborhoods where up to three-quarters of the residents were illiterate, the saloon was the local newspaper, the chief source of information about the world and, more important, about employment and lodging-house openings. For those who could read, newspapers were available, including foreign-language dailies, which some customers would comb before slipping off to a union or a political meeting in the saloon's back room, the very place where many of them had celebrated the baptisms, birthdays, and weddings of their sons and daughters.

"The saloon is a very wholesome discussion center," said a Bohemian immigrant. "Here men bring their ideas and compare them. It helps to get at the truth in a situation and fight manipulation by unscrupulous men."

Immigrants arriving fresh from the home country often came first to an ethnic saloon to inquire about a room or a job, the saloonkeeper himself sometimes being a landlord or an employment agent for a local mill. It was not unusual for a Lithuanian greenhorn stepping off a train at Dearborn Station to be clutching a note with the address of a Chicago watering hole scribbled on it, the place where he was to meet a fellow villager, perhaps a brother or a cousin who had written to him with the help of a saloonkeeper.

Saloonkeepers—successful ethnic businessmen themselves—became advisers to Polish steelworkers living in boardinghouses and saving their earnings for passage money for their families or to start a small business. They were happy to cash the paychecks of their customers, part of the money going right back into their cash drawers, and it was to them that many regular customers went first for a small loan. An immigrant's bank, the saloon was also his post office, where he picked up mail and left and received messages. When saloons began installing telephones in the 1880s, regular customers and their families were welcome to use the phone to call the hospital or the doctor in case of emergency. The local bartender was also the neighborhood pharmacist, dispensing stale beer for an upset stomach or a concoction of his own creation for a hangover or a bad cold. On sweltering summer nights in the closed-in neighborhoods of the river wards, the saloon, with its fans and big windows, its polished bar and gleaming plate-glass mirrors, was the only cool and clean place to be found. Instead of returning to their clammy rooms, some immigrant boarders would pay the saloonkeeper a nickel to sleep on his wooden floor. By 1915, Chicago had one licensed saloon for every 335 residents, and many working-class neighborhoods had up to one for every fifty males sixteen years of age or older, the age at which a boy was usually welcome to join the men at the bar. On any given day in the 1890s, more than half a million customers might find their way into Chicago's saloons.

It is no wonder that so many saloonkeepers found their way into politics. (In 1900, half the Democratic Party's precinct captains were saloonkeepers.) They built up their businesses on the basis of neighborhood trust and became local men of respect. Running a saloon was also a way to move up in the world. In the 1880s the city's big breweries, following the British "tied-house" system, began to buy out privately owned saloons and turn them into retail outlets, where only the company's product was sold. This drove out many small entrepreneurs but opened opportunities for cash-starved immigrants who wanted to avoid the factory floor. As one Chicago barkeeper said, a saloon was "the easiest business in the world for a man to break into with small capital." With two hundred dollars, he could get a brewer to set him up in business; the brewer paid the rent and the license fee and supplied the bar fixtures and the beer.

Protestant purifiers complained that there were too many bars in the city, but Carter Harrison thought there were not enough of them. He depended on the money from the license fees to pay for the urban services the middle-class reformers who were trying to close the saloons were pressuring him to provide. The rural-dominated Illinois legislature put tight restrictions on Chicago's ability to raise taxes or float bond issues, and township tax assessors kept property assessments ridiculously low in order to stay in office or to please big interests, which kept the assessors in their pay. In 1893 the total assessed value of all Chicago property was actually *less* than it was in 1871, even though the city had more than quadrupled in size; and the average assessment of real estate was only a little more than 10 percent of its actual value. This left the government heavily dependent on saloon-license revenues, which in 1886 accounted for over 12 percent of all city income. "While much has been said about the evils of saloons, . . . the fact is that we are dependent on the saloons to enable us to eke out a municipal existence," remarked one observer. "The taxpayers of Chicago ought to take off their hats to them."

As mayor, Harrison used his control of the police force to protect saloonkeepers from Protestant reformers. With the advice of Democratic Party officials, he appointed all policemen but left control of the force largely to the ward bosses, who allowed saloons to stay open on Sundays and after the legal midnight closing in return for a payoff. So ethnics had to pay to protect their lifestyles but were willing to do so, even though it sometimes meant tolerating gambling and prostitution in their neighborhoods, trades also protected by the enterprising aldermen.

This was the real source of Harrison's popularity. He understood that Chicago was a city of neighborhoods, each with its own unique customs and folkways. Whereas cultural uplifters like Charles Hutchinson and Joseph Medill had a citywide orientation and a desire to see all of Chicago's people brought up to an Anglo-American standard of taste and behavior, Harrison was willing to let people in the precincts lead their own lives. As Willis J. Abbot, one of his advisers, wrote of him, he "consistently held that the masses are better judges of their own needs than are the constituted censors of the press or of 'citizen's associations.'"

But the working people of Chicago wanted more than this from their government. They wanted politicians who were willing to defend the right of labor to organize and demonstrate for better wages and benefits. Modern urban historians like Richard Oestreicher claim that in most American big cities there was "no meaningful difference" between Republicans and Democrats on "the rights of labor." Most big-city mayors were not "spokesmen of workers," Oestreicher writes. But Carter Harrison was. And he aligned his party with the city's organized labor movement, giving Catholic and German Lutheran workers an additional reason to vote for him. Harrison offered his own view of the differences between the city's two main parties: "The Republican Party is made up of the rich and monopolistic classes, while the Democratic Party is the party of the people."

•

Harrison's stand on personal liberty was the reason, of course, he was enthusiastically supported by the city's liquor and vice interests. Laws against prostitution and gambling were, he argued, unenforceable in a "city of the world" like Chicago. "You can't make people moral by ordinance and it is no use trying. This is a free town." Harrison's policy was to segregate most of the vice trades in a small but conspicuous area at the edge of the Loop, where the police could monitor them, making sure that minors were kept out of gambling halls and whorehouses and that innocent customers were not cheated by con men.

There is no evidence that Harrison ever took money from vice lords for his personal use, but he did look the other way when money from them was used to support his campaigns. Yet it was the brazen openness of his policy on vice, not his secrecy, that most infuriated his enemies. When a delegation of ministers demanded to know if he was aware that "gambling hells" were running in plain view on Clark Street, he said that he was. He had been to several of them the night before and had a fine time.

The head of the city's gambling trade was Michael Cassius McDonald, "King Mike," as he was known in the city. Fleeing the "Great Hunger" with his Irish Catholic family, he had his baptism in crime as a plug-hatted sharper hawking half-filled boxes of candy and phony jewelry on trains running in and out of Detroit and Chicago. During the Civil War he had a lucrative Chicago business as a bounty broker and used the profits to establish a string of small gambling dives near downtown railroad stations. After the Great Fire, he opened what became the most fabulous gambling palace in Chicago, the Store, in a big four-story brick building within sight of city hall.

For twenty years, McDonald's casino-style gambling hall was the leading "sporting house" of Chicago, the meeting place for Democratic politicians and high rollers in the vice trade. McDonald organized and ran the first of Chicago's crime syndicates, an almost exclusively Irish operation, the progenitor of the coalition of criminals, politicians, and cops that Al Capone headed in the 1920s. McDonald's croupiers, faro dealers, and cardsharps swindled gullible customers by the thousands, and he hired gangs of spectacularly convincing con artists—bunko men, they were called—to comb the lobbies of hotels and train stations, trying to lure farmer boys and drummers into one of their slickly conceived confidence games.

But the backbone of McDonald's business was his "protection" racket. No gambling establishment in Chicago was free to operate unless it paid tribute to King Mike, who greatly augmented his power by gaining control of the Cook County Democratic Party in the late 1870s, using his influence to have police who were part of his organization assigned to neighborhoods where his dens were located. One word from "Mike" and the cops would shut down a place that day.

In 1879, McDonald put his powerful syndicate behind the candidacy of Carter Harrison, and while Harrison was in office, the great gambler "ruled the city with an iron-hand," Chicago papers insisted. "He named men who were to be candidates for election, he elected them, and after they were in office they were merely his puppets." The formidable Chicago historian Bessie Louise Pierce described him as "virtually the dictator of the City Hall." McDonald's influence over Harrison has been hugely exaggerated. Harrison needed McDonald's support and, to maintain it, allowed him to operate with virtual immunity from the law, but he was never "a close friend and chief advisor" of Harrison, as Herbert Asbury claimed in his popular history of the Chicago underworld, nor was he the near-dictator of city hall. Harrison loathed McDonald and would have nothing to do with him personally, and when the gambling boss stepped out of line or public pressure against gamblers proved too difficult to evade, he came down on him hard, closing his biggest operations. Two prominent Chicago historians have called McDonald the "Boss Croker of a Chicago Tammany," but nineteenth-century Chicago never had a dominating city boss like New York's Richard Croker or a centralized city machine like Tammany Hall. Neither Mike McDonald nor Carter Harrison nor anyone else "ruled" Chicago a century ago, in the heyday, nationally, of the urban political machine.

What Charles Merriam called Chicago's "feudal" structure of government made it all but impossible for a centralized machine to emerge. In 1893, Chicago did not have one government; it had at least eight, all with independent taxing powers. Eight major governing bodies—among them three park boards, a board of assessors, and an overlapping county government—were joined by innumerable minor ones distributed among the almost three hundred precincts of Chicago and Cook County. Chicago had over twenty different taxing bodies in addition to thirty-five wards, each ward represented on the city council by two aldermen, whose political orientations were almost exclusively local. These aldermen represented political parties that were neither united nor disciplined; both parties were made up of warring factions whose allegiances were incessantly shifting. And although the Republican Party won only three mayoralty elections in the twenty-eight years after Harrison was first elected, local elections were generally close and aggressively contested, while Republicans tended to carry the city in national elections. This scrambled governing system was "a greater obstacle to machine rule," a Chicago historian has written, "than all the reformers and their laws put together."

Personal loyalty took precedence over organizational loyalty in the messy world of nineteenth-century Chicago politics. Voters threw their support—but never permanently—to powerful figures who represented their values and interests. It was a situation ready-made for someone like Carter Harrison. Immigrants with peasant backgrounds were familiar with personalistic government, and Harrison's colorful, warmly human style won their hearts and votes. "He knew the whole town," Willis J. Abbot wrote of his friend, "as a Tammany leader knew his district."

Harrison's hold on the city was further strengthened by the way he used the powers of his office to maximum political advantage. He was a supreme practitioner of what Max Weber called "charismatic" leadership—the leadership of the chieftain whose power depends on his ability to reward his followers directly. Every one of the almost fifteen thousand city employees was his appointee, and he shrewdly dispensed this patronage to build his own political organization, rewarding loyal lieutenants in the precincts and steering rebellious machines into line. Patronage was meat and drink to Chicago's ward leaders. Cut off from it, they died. By distributing patronage among the aldermen, Harrison infused life into local political machines, and these organizations, in turn, could be counted on to bring in the vote for him.

In New York, Tammany Hall controlled Democratic mayors; in Chicago, Mayor Harrison governed the city, with the help of a fractious

Democratic Party organization dividing the spoils of office among his loose, unlikely coalition of ethnic aldermen, labor unions, businessmen, gamblers, grafters, pimps, saloonkeepers, and police. To get anything done in deeply divided, chaotically governed Chicago, he needed to compromise and to close his eyes to more than a little skullduggery. Rich, Yale-educated Carter Harrison understood that Chicago politics, as the saying on the street went, "ain't bean bag."

2. Why the Ward Boss Rules

Quid pro quo was the operating principle of Chicago politics, and the master deal makers were the aldermen. They were first and last the tribunes of the neighborhoods, less concerned with governing than with dividing the largesse of government among themselves and their constituents. Most of them dealt with what they called "the small stuff," particular favors for their ward. When an alderman rose in council chambers to speak for a "courtesy" for his district, he invariably got the support of his fellow political chameleons; "aldermanic privilege," it was called.

Cooperation came easily, for the aldermen were a common breed. Most of Chicago's nineteenth-century mayors came from old-stock American families and were comfortably situated and well educated (between 1870 and 1900 none of Chicago's twelve mayors was foreign-born, and only one was a Catholic), but the average alderman was a small-time businessman of foreign birth or parentage and not infrequently a saloonkeeper. The quickest way to clear the city council chamber, a joke of that time went, was to stand at the door and shout: "Your saloon's on fire!" In the 1880s and 1890s, saloonkeepers held approximately a quarter of the council seats, and most of their other colleagues were independent proprietors like 'themselves—butchers, printers, coal dealers, druggists, contractors, and plumbers. They tended to dress with flair and without taste and to smoke bad cigars and chew tobacco while conducting the city's business. "During lulls in the voting or speech-making," a veteran alderman recalled, "you could hear the steady drip or the explosive precipitation of saliva in the spittoons." And the atmosphere was less than respectful. When the Lord Mayor of Dublin visited the council, someone passed around exploding cigars.

The aldermen were out for themselves, and few of them tried to disguise that fact. "Anybody who goes into politics for some other reason than making money is a fool," declared George Dunne, one of Chicago's most infamous machine lords. Protection money was the small change of ward politics. The big money was in dealing with business-men who were both the recipients as well as the targets of political double-dealing. When a businessman wanted something the city could provide, whether it was a building permit or a tax "adjustment," he went directly to his local alderman, "squaring" him with a cash kickback or a piece of one of his commercial ventures. The hand-somest profits for aldermen, however, were in "boodling," selling their votes to grant municipal franchises to streetcar, gas, and electric com-panies. To get favorable action on lucrative city franchises, business giants like Charles Tyson Yerkes had to buy an entire "ring" of alder-men. Yerkes's man in city council, Johnny Powers, was a sensationally talented grafter who brought a measure of discipline to illegal transac-tions by making sure his more enthusiastic fellow thieves didn't sell their votes to more than one bidder. "If he speaks, it is with a low and somewhat diffident voice with a distant Hibernian twang," the jour-nalist Ray Stannard Baker said of him, "and yet every machine Dem-ocrat in the Council hangs on his words as the voicings of an oracle."

Powers was a master at covering his tracks. All deals were made by "go-betweens"—usually lawyers—and everything was done by word of mouth; there was never a paper trail. As Mr. Dooley said, "Ray-formers, . . . is in favor of suppressin' ivrything, but rale pollyticians believe in suppressin' nawthin' but th' evidence." Powers made only three dollars a session for serving in council but lived in one of the most substantial houses in his ward, owned two downtown saloons, and was "never about," said Baker, "without several Aldermanic dia-monds flashing about him."

Powers and his colleagues in crime were "gray wolves," as the press portrayed them, at loose on the urban estate. In a popular vaudeville skit of the time, city officials are sleeping off a heavy night of cele-brating at the Mulligan home. "Will I wake them?" Mrs. Mulligan asks her husband.

"Leave them be," he replies. "While they sleep the city's safe."

In 1892, when Edward F. ("Foxey Ed") Cullerton ran for reelection to council, he told the Ninth Ward voters that it was "better [to] send back the man who has stolen enough already than to send in . . . a new man."

In doing well for themselves, aldermen did well for their wards. It took a naive Jane Addams some time to realize why so many of her neighbors in Powers's Nineteenth Ward were streetcar employees and "telephone girls." Powers's price for pushing a franchise through council was something for himself as well as jobs for his supporters and their families with the business concerns with which he dealt. "We soon discovered," Addams wrote in her autobiography, "that approximately one out of every five voters in the nineteenth ward at the time held a job dependent upon the good will of the alderman." Powers sold his vote to get these jobs, and those who got the jobs, in a sense, sold their votes to him as a thank-you. "The people come cheap," Lincoln Steffens wrote of the boss's power over his flock, "but they are interested."

In the newspapers Powers was "the Prince of the Boodlers"; in his own neighborhood he was "the Great Mourner," attending at least a dozen funerals a week and providing impressive floral arrangements and private carriages that no immigrant family could possibly afford to rent. He also saved indigent families from the unimaginable horror of having one of their own buried by the county. When a sick child who had been abandoned in the Hull-House nursery died, Jane Addams had the county take care of the burial. The morgue wagon was to arrive around eleven in the morning, but by nine o'clock word had circulated through the neighborhood of this "awful deed," and a group of angry residents came to protest and took up a collection to pay for a funeral. New to the neighborhood, Addams had no idea she was "shocking a genuine sentiment of the community." It was a mistake Johnny Powers would never have made.

When the ethnic composition of his ward began to change from Irish to Italian in the 1890s, Powers learned a little Italian and encouraged his neighbors to call him Johnny de Pow. Short, barrel-chested, and dressed to the nines, with a cardboard-stiff shirt and a diamond stickpin in his tie—his hair combed into a flaring gray pompadour— "Johnny da gooda boss" visited the ward's police courts almost every day, offering bail money and jobs to young men picked up for minor infractions. He provided free railroad passes to neighbors who wanted to visit relatives in distant cities, distributed thousands of turkeys and geese at Christmas, gave generous gifts at weddings and christenings, covered the rent and coal deliveries for down-on-their-luck families, and organized neighborhood bazaars and block parties for widows and the sick, appearing in person and throwing around money extravagantly but never touching a drink. All the while he kept his nose out of people's private lives. "Votes, like babies, require both time and labor to produce," a ward leader in another city said. "Neither are dropped down chimneys by storks."

Addams got to like Powers personally but went on fighting him, anyway, organizing two unsuccessful campaigns in the 1890s to unseat him. "We had election polls here in the house," a woman who worked at Hull-House recalled. "In his big bandwagon Johnny would drive up throwing nickels to the kids with his band playing 'Nearer, My God, to Thee.' Then into our polls he would come and hand out his cigars to all voters. He'd smile at Miss Addams and she at him. . . . A wonderful woman, he said, and often he'd call her a saint from the skies." If Addams needed a permit for her ward work, she would send someone to Powers to ask for it, and "always he'd give what she wanted." She was a friend of the people, and so, Powers claimed, was he. But as Jane Addams's housekeeper said, "He'd done it in a way to roll up a fortune for himself."

If settlement workers were to compete successfully with neighborhood bosses like Powers, Addams had begun to believe as early as 1892, they would have to attack the disgraceful conditions these aldermen ignored, chief among them the infamous "sweating system"— where subcontractors, or "sweaters," hired immigrants, many of them children, to make garments on foot-powered sewing machines in their own homes—and living conditions in these tenements that were as appalling as anywhere in the civilized world.

In 1893, Hull-House workers began a series of on-site investigations of tenement sweatshops in the Halsted Street neighborhood. These pioneering sociological surveys were directed by the formidable Florence Kelley, who in her lifetime would do more for the cause of exploited women and children workers than anyone else in the country. She arrived at Hull-House with her three young children and two trunks of clothing on a snowy December morning in 1891, fleeing a husband who had begun to abuse her physically. From that day, Hull-House was never the same.

Older and more aggressive than most of the other women there, Kelley was an outspoken socialist who corresponded with Friedrich Engels, whom she had met in London. The brilliant, driven daughter of a Philadelphia congressman and former abolitionist, William "Pig Iron" Kelley, the political protector of Pennsylvania's iron-and-steel industry, she was reading in her father's library and debating public policy with him when she was only ten. Educated at Cornell, she went on to do graduate work at the University of Zurich after being denied admission to the University of Pennsylvania because she was a woman. While in Europe, she converted to socialism, married a Polish-Russian physician who was also a Marxist, and translated Engels's first and finest book, *The Condition of the Working Class in England in 1844*.

Explosive and irreverent, Kelley laughed at Hull-House's decorous tea parties and art receptions and ridiculed its evening prayer sessions. She began urging Jane Addams to alter the direction of the settlement's work from moral uplift to social change, helping to turn her into a fiercely committed public activist.

Boarding her children at the suburban home of Henry Demarest Lloyd (and later with Frank Lloyd Wright's mother), Kelley took up residence at Hull-House and began divorce proceedings against her husband. With Lloyd's help, she landed a job heading a state-government investigation of sweatshop conditions on Chicago's near West Side, the city's "port of entry" for immigrants arriving from Eastern and Southern Europe, most of them Slavic and Italian peasants and Russian Jews escaping pogroms and escalating government persecution. Her searing reports led to a landmark Illinois Factory Law outlawing the sweating system, mandating an eight-hour day for women in manufacturing, and making it illegal for employers to hire children under fourteen. She was then appointed by Gov. John Peter Altgeld as the state's first factory inspector and given a staff of eleven deputies, five of them women, to oversee its enforcement. "Nowhere else in the Western world," writes her most recent biographer, "was a woman entrusted to enforce the labor legislation of a city, let alone of a large industrial region the size of Illinois."

Operating out of offices directly across the street from Hull-House, she pulled the settlement into her investigations, which broadened in the spring of 1893 to include housing conditions in the neighborhood, part of her agreement with the U.S. Commissioner of Labor to head the Chicago segment of a national study of the slums of four American cities. In 1895, Addams and Kelley published the results of these surveys as the *Hull-House Maps and Papers,* the first comprehensive study of an American working-class neighborhood. It was a book that would influence the University of Chicago sociologists who invented modern urban sociology, with its grounding in exhaustive field studies of metropolitan life.

The aim of the Hull-House surveys, and a later survey of the entire city by Addams's friend Robert Hunter, was to present an unchallengeable case for tenement reform—sociology in the service of social action. Chicago's spread-out prairie location, which allowed the erection of freestanding wooden cottages, had for decades saved its poorest residents from the suffocating congestion of New York's slums, with their high-rise rookeries stacked next to one another in long, dismal rows. But Hunter, Kelley, and other settlement-house investigators showed that this situation was fast changing. Taking advantage of increased immigration, landlords had begun to cover almost every square foot of their slum lots with rentable space, packing three or more families into cottages meant for one and putting as many as four cottages on a single, small lot. Congestion in Chicago's slums was also beginning to produce New York–style tenements—five stories high and housing up to 150 people in six flats. In one of the city's Polish quarters, Robert Hunter reported a ground density three times that of the most congested area of Calcutta. If all of Chicago were as thickly settled, he argued, the city could house the entire population of North America.

The new brick tenements, or double-deckers, as they were called, formed a solid masonry wall along the worm-rotted pavements of many slum streets, shielding from view the most wretched of all the slum-housing types, the rear tenement. This was merely the old street-front pine cottage moved to the back of the lot, facing an alley, to make room for a new style double-decker, which was built directly up against it. The rear tenements housed the most desperate of Chicago's immi-grants, a great number of them employed in the garment industry, "Columbus tailors" who learned their trade in America. These for-eigners "look dwarfed and ill-fed," reported Agnes Sinclair Holbrook, an assistant to Florence Kelley. "They walk with a peculiar stooping gait, and their narrow chests and cramped hands are unmistakable ev-idence of their calling."

Crowding and filth made these West Side tenements a public health menace to the entire city. In the 1890s over a quarter of a million Chicagoans had no bathing facilities. Most slum residents did not take baths in the winter, the dirt accumulating so thickly on the children that it formed what looked like scales. In summer, they used the four overcrowded municipal baths, while many workers on their way home from the factory simply stopped by the local fire stations for "a spray." Sickness was rampant in these places of unimaginable filth: smallpox, cholera, consumption, tuberculosis, and scarlet fever. Although Chicago's municipal water was cleaner in the 1890s' with the comple-tion of new intake pipes, running water remained a luxury in the slums, and milk arriving in unrefrigerated wagons was often danger-ously spoiled. Customers were not always aware of this, however, as milk companies sometimes added a coloring agent to hide the deteri-oration. This led some Italian mothers to feed their children beer from the local saloon, which at least was pasteurized.

At the end of the nineteenth century, between 300,000 and 400,000 Chicagoans in a city of 1.7 million lived this way, according to Hunter's exhaustive investigations. Lincoln Steffens had it wrong: Its slums, not its rampant political corruption, were "the shame of Chicago." Nor were these conditions the result of an absence of proper values or an unwillingness to work hard, as many of those in respectable society continued blindly to insist. "The condition of the sweaters' victims," declared Florence Kelley, "is a conclusive refutation of the ubiquitous argument that poverty is the result of crime, vice, intemperance, sloth, and unthrift; for the Jewish sweaters' victims are probably more temperate, hard working, and avaricious than any equally large body of wage-earners in America. . . . Yet the reward of work at their trade is grinding poverty, ending only in death or escape to some more hopeful occupation."

In their efforts to improve these conditions, Hull-House workers confronted opposition from the people they tried to help as well as from entrenched interests. Immigrant parents would bribe city officials or intercede with local bosses to obtain working papers for their underage children so that the family could have fuel and food for the winter. In some families, fully a third of the total income came from the wages of children under fourteen—newsboys, bootblacks, cash runners, button sewers, and makers of cigars and artificial flowers for women's hats.

•

Florence Kelley's experiences during the smallpox epidemic that broke out in Chicago at the end of the World's Fair point out the day-to-day difficulties she and other settlement workers faced. What started in the fall of 1893 as a minor outbreak of smallpox, beginning with an undetected case on the fair's Midway, had turned into a full-scale epidemic by the following spring. The scandalously mismanaged smallpox hospital, or pest house, was filled to overflowing, and tents were pitched on the prairie to take care of victims as the death rate climbed.

The disease took its heaviest toll in the garment district on the West Side, and the infected immigrants of the area made the situation worse by refusing to go to the pest house, where more died than lived. Jewish and Italian mothers would wrap their dying babies in blankets and carry them through alleys to neighboring houses to escape county wagons that were sent to take them away, and doctors who tried to vaccinate people who had no understanding of modern medicine were attacked and even shot, leading some settlement workers to proclaim in frustration—as Addams did—that the "pathetic stupidity" of Italian immigrants was almost insurmountable. Since they could not adjust to urban life, the best hope for them, Addams said, was to colonize them in farm areas of the Deep South, not realizing that most Italian immigrants came not from isolated rural villages but from heavily populated hill towns where they lived in cavelike urban dwellings as tightly packed together as Chicago's tenement houses.

Florence Kelley's duties as factory inspector required her to protect buyers of ready-made clothing purchased in sweatshops contaminated by the smallpox contagion. But on her staff inspections families would hide sick or even recently deceased children as well as potentially contaminated garments, which Kelley was ordered to burn on the premises. For a tailor to surrender a coat that he had made on his sewing machine was to give up a week's food and shelter for his family to prevent the spread of germs he did not believe existed anyway. When Kelley tried to get local manufacturers to help her locate and destroy contaminated garments, she got no cooperation at first. Nor would the press help because of what health reformer Dr. Bayard Holmes called its "utter servility . . . to trade." The Chicago Board of Health was enmeshed in this "conspiracy of silence," Kelley wrote in her official report, ignoring calls for wholesale vaccination until the epidemic almost got out of control and concealment was impossible. Only after Governor Altgeld threatened to place a regional embargo on products of the needle trades going out of Chicago did garment manufacturers join forces with the health department in a massive vaccination drive.

When the epidemic began to subside, the Illinois Association of Manufacturers stepped up its campaign against the Illinois Factory Law of 1893. Anticipating court challenges to her work, Kelley had taken a law degree from Northwestern University. She battled the state's big manufacturing interests in the courts and in the legislature, but in 1895 the Illinois Supreme Court struck down the eight-hour provision of the law. The *Chicago Tribune* explained the decision: "Labor is property, and an interference with the sale of it by contract or otherwise is an infringement of a constitutional right to dispose of property." This ended yet another skirmish in the city's long-standing battle between the right of business to do as it pleased and the public's right to protection from the dangers of unchecked commercial growth, the defining civic debate of nineteenth-century Chicago.

Florence Kelley returned to New York in 1899 to become general secretary of the National Consumers' League, a powerful political lobby for the causes she had battled for at Hull-House. Her Chicago work was carried on with defiant determination by Ellen Gates Starr, Mary McDowell, and other settlement reformers, but their accomplishments were limited not only by the kind of opposition Kelley had run up against but by their own restricted social vision. Subsidized by rich benefactors like Charles Hutchinson and committed to reforms aimed at humanizing but not fundamentally challenging capitalism, they rarely went as far with their recommendations as their own field surveys might have taken them. Robert Hunter's report on Chicago's slums—more shatteringly believable than Upton Sinclair's *The Jungle*—concluded with a thin set of recommendations for reform of the city's housing codes.

Neither Hunter nor anyone else connected with Hull-House proposed that the city build public housing for the poor. Government housing, they argued, would lead to a bloated bureaucracy and discourage private capital from flowing into the housing industry. So code reforms were passed while slum conditions worsened. And Hull-House workers never stopped trying to impose the settlement's idea of correct behavior on those they tried to help. Despite all they had to endure, the residents of Chicago's poorest neighborhoods refused to see themselves, as Hull-House reports made them out to be, as helpless victims with no control over their own lives. They supported neighborhood bosses, like Johnny Powers, not out of ignorance or helplessness but out of self-interest. But even the influence of the urban bosses has been overemphasized by historians. Self-help, not the aid of social settlements or heart-of-gold Irish aldermen, was the way out of overwhelming poverty for most of Chicago's immigrants. And the irony is that well-meaning settlement volunteers wanted to take from these people the most effective weapon they possessed in their struggle to move up in the world—their Old World customs and heritage, the ancient ways that shrewd and successful urban politicians like Carter Harrison supported, defended, and successfully played upon for political advantage.

Much has been written about Jane Addams's efforts to encourage immigrants to take pride in their history and folkways, but ethnic solidarity, she always insisted, must give way as quickly as possible to social assimilation. The University of Chicago sociologist Louis Wirth, author of a classic study of Chicago's Jewish ghetto, spoke for Addams as well when he wrote that "the ghetto is a closed community, . . . provincial and sectarian, . . . the product of . . . prejudices and taboos. . . . Not until the Jew gets out of the ghetto does he really live a full life." The ultimate goal of the settlement, Addams argued, was to break down barriers of class and ethnicity and help Americanize immigrants.

Americanization took place more slowly than reformers like Addams hoped it would or University of Chicago sociologists claimed it did, and without ethnics losing their sense of distinctiveness. Remember, you have two fatherlands, Poland and America, Chicago's Polish press instructed its readers. Upon arriving in Chicago, emigrants from Eastern and Southern Europe discovered soon enough—as the Irish did—that to survive and advance in a hostile urban environment they would need to stick together "like a swarm of bees from the same hive" and hold on to the culture that had kept them together in their historic struggles with poverty and persecution.

•

The Jews are perhaps the best example of this. Chicago had a well-established Jewish community before 1880, but it was made up mostly of prosperous German-speaking Jews, many of them prominent in the city's philanthropic and cultural affairs and residents of the South Side "Golden Ghetto," among them the architect Dankmar Adler, the Sears, Roebuck partner Julius Rosenwald, and commercial families that established such thriving concerns as the Florsheim Shoe Company; B. Kuppenheimer and Company; Hart, Schaffner & Marx; and the Mandel Brothers Department Store. The "new" Russo-Polish Jews who settled in the Maxwell Street area, near Hull-House, however, spoke Yiddish and were coarse and uneducated, and their dress and demeanor made them easy targets of ridicule. The married women wore shawls and wigs, and the men had long beards and wore long black coats, broad-brimmed black hats, and high black boots. When peddlers from the Maxwell Street neighborhood fanned out over the city every morning to sell notions and dry goods they carried on their backs, they were often attacked by gangs of street toughs who threw stones at them and pulled their beards. As one Jewish greenhorn recalled: "No one was safe."

It was this kind of reception that led new immigrants—Catholics as well as Jews—to develop a defensive communalism even stronger than they had established in the Old World. Italians, Jews, and Poles customarily emigrated as a group from the same town or village and settled together in the same neighborhood, a process known as chain migration. It was not uncommon, as Jane Addams observed, to see a tenement house filled "with the people from one village."

In America they reconstructed the life they had left behind. "Emigrating, the Italian working class brings away with it from the mother country all the little world in which they were accustomed to live," an Italian writer noted, "a world of traditions, of beliefs, of customs, of ideals of their own." Among the Italian *contadini*, or peasants, this was known as the spirit of *campanilismo*, where a townsman never wanted to be out from under the shadow of his town's campanile, or bell tower, while among Russian Jews, the most powerful communal attachment was to fellow landsmen, Jews from the same Old World district or ghetto. "A *Landsmannschaft*," Louis Wirth wrote, "has its own patriarchal leaders, its lodges, and mutual aid associations, and its celebrations and festivities. It has its burial plot in the cemetery. It keeps the memories of the group alive through frequent visits, and maintains a steady liaison with the remnants of the Jewish community of the Old World."

One of the first organizations to emerge in the ethnic colony was the mutual benefit society, which provided financial and moral support in times of great family need. Members would contribute monthly dues— as little as ten cents—and in return receive insurance benefits for sickness and death, the services of a lodge doctor and lawyer, and admission to lodge social, cultural, and athletic events. In the Italian community, the mutual benefit society became the leading social center for the men, the New World equivalent of the home-country *piazza*, a place to meet and play cards and sip Chianti; and women in all of the city's ethnic enclaves organized their own fraternal and benefit societies, most of them attached to a church or synagogue. For many immigrants, the existence of one or another of these self-help organizations meant the difference between survival and defeat. In the Jewish community, free loan associations were formed to provide small loans at no interest to community members in time of "personal or business need."

The most important ethnic institution, aside from the family, was the church or synagogue, which kept an uprooted people in touch with their history and language and kept them together as a community through struggle and pain. It was only with the formation of a religious center that an active ethnic community came into existence. Even Italian Catholics, who were far less loyal to the American church than Eastern Europeans, resenting its cold, formalistic rituals and control by the hated Irish, fought as a community for the assignment of Italian priests to their neighborhood churches and gathered together at the church for the most important ritual in Italian-American life, the feast day of the village patron saint.

Around these houses of worship clustered the principal institutions and businesses of the ethnic community: foreign-language newspapers, marriage-arrangement bureaus, circumcisers, kosher-meat shops, matzo bakeries, sausage markets, saloons, soda fountains, *Volktheaters*, and bustling open-air markets, the largest and busiest of them all the Maxwell Street market, which every morning took on the appearance of a sprawling medieval fair.

Community attachments did not prevent large numbers of the ethnic community from moving to better neighborhoods as soon as they were able to, frequently with the help of community institutions. To have a home of their own, immigrant families transformed themselves into small-scale savings banks. Children were pulled from school and sent to work, wives took in sewing and washing, extra space was rented to boarders, and the money that was accumulated was hidden away under the floorboards. Through such self-denying savings, Slavic immigrants soon outdistanced almost all other ethnic groups in the city in homeownership.

When members of the ethnic colony moved outside the neighborhood, it was often to a smaller version of it in another part of Chicago, where others from the original settlement had bought homes in advance of them. Arriving in the ethnic enclave in groups, immigrants generally moved out of it in groups, and in these reconstituted neighborhood clusters many Old World ways burned strong, even into the third generation. Every Saturday or Sunday and on every important feast day, there was a parade of families back to the mother settlement, where they attended religious services and shared a ceremonial meal with kinsmen and compatriots who were Chicago's ethnic pioneers.

Neither Hull-House nor any other settlement could hope to compete for the allegiance of immigrants against the tidal pull of ethnic communalism. Settlement volunteers sometimes made their own work more difficult by taking a patronizing attitude—the "Pullman spirit," a historian has called it—toward newly arrived immigrants.

In 1893 middle-class German Jews established a Maxwell Street Settlement, but young Yiddish-speaking workers, alienated by the settlement leaders' missionary-style approach, formed their own Self-Educational Club, run by people from the neighborhood in a "truly democratic" manner. Even after Hull-House built a gym and a playground, Italian and Jewish boys continued to prefer unsupervised recreation in the streets, organizing stickball games, throwing dice in dark alleys, hanging around pool halls and candy stores, and meeting working girls dressed in their best clothes and "ball shoes" at the neighborhood dance halls that became the rage in turn-of-the-century Chicago. "It is a startling fact, but a fact nonetheless, that two-thirds of the girls who are ruined fall through the influence of dancing," a Chicago moral reformer wrote, echoing Jane Addams's views on dance halls.

Hull-House investigators exposed conditions that many Chicagoans had refused to believe existed in their World's Fair city. Whereas boosters saw one Chicago, proud and united, the reformers saw two cities growing more dangerously apart. And they described more graphically than anyone else had before them the social deterioration and moral callousness that accompanied Chicago's rapid growth. But what is missing in their reports from the underside is the energy and institutional vitality of the city's newest ethnic colonies, and the uncrushable spirit of their people, who, living in squalor and surrounded by walls of hatred, still believed they had opportunities in this surging city denied them in the places they had left behind.

Never sentimental or patronizing in his descriptions of poverty—perhaps because he had been poor—Theodore Dreiser found a "hard, constructive animality" in the rawest regions of the city, whose streets he walked in his "Newspaper Days." In the can-cluttered yards of broken-down cottages, "you could find men who were tanning dog or cat hides, or making soap, or sorting rags, or picking chickens." Poverty had not broken its victims. "Nowhere was there any blank indifference to life. People cursed or raved or snarled, but they were never heavy or old or asleep. In some neighborhoods the rancidity of dirt or the bony stark bleakness of poverty fairly shouted, but if such neighborhoods were here, they were never still, decaying pools of misery." Even in the Halsted Street forest of unpainted pine shanties, Dreiser found hope, eagerness, desire.

"Ours is a cosmopolitan city," Mayor Carter Harrison had said to the city council upon first taking office in 1879, in a warning against both intolerance and paternalism, "aggregated from many nationalities. . . . Each of the several elements has its own ideas of social and religious life, its own civilization. They have one bond of union, devotion to republican institutions and energy and pursuit of fortune. Each should . . . accommodate itself as much as possible to the social life and prejudices of each of the others, and of the whole. For any one to attempt to make a Procrustean bed, to which the others should be forced to fit, would be both ungenerous and unwise. Time alone can make them all homogeneous."

●

Jane Addams eventually developed a grudging admiration for Chicago's political bosses, even though she could never quite integrate her own self-education into her work for the settlement. "The Alderman is really elected," she wrote in her famous essay "Why the Ward Boss Rules," "because he is a good friend and neighbor." If reformers wished to win over the poor, they could learn a lesson, she argued, from such men of "low ideals and corrupt practices [who] stand by and for and with the people."

Although she was referring to Johnny Powers, she could just as well have been writing about William Lorimer, Chicago's "Blond Boss."

When Russian Jews began moving into the West Side in great numbers in the 1890s, Lorimer, a Republican who separated himself from his party's "Protestant Puritans," organized them politically, provided protection from thugs when they went to the polls, and helped them get peddlers' licenses and jobs with the city. "It got so," he recalled toward the end of his life, "they came to my home at night and talked over their little troubles. . . . I helped them always." As he once boasted: "No man can go among those people . . . as my enemy and live politically." Looking back at his years as a reporter in Chicago, Brand Whitlock said that perhaps Lorimer and Powers were "more nearly right after all than the cold and formal and precise gentlemen who denounced their records in the council. For they were human and the real problem is to make the government of a city human."

But immigrants paid a heavy price for having such men as their emissaries. Tax assessments favored the rich, prostitution was planted and protected near schools and churches, unqualified police could not be counted on to pursue and arrest criminals, political appointees in the health department ignored dangerously unsanitary housing conditions, and boss-appointed city scavengers, as Jane Addams learned, were more interested in collecting their pay than collecting the garbage. Nor was ward patronage divided evenly. The Irish controlled the city's Democratic Party and took care of their own first and disproportionately. Although they were a numerical majority in only a handful of wards and were outnumbered by Germans by more than two to one in the city in 1890, almost three of four members of Chicago's Democratic Committee and twenty-four of twenty-eight of the most powerful ward bosses were Irish. The result was a Hibernianization of the public payroll.

The Irish attributed their rapid political rise to organizational energy and sagacity—and to the comparative political apathy of the Germans. The Irish did have much higher naturalization and voter registration rates than the Germans, but the energy-versus-apathy theory doesn't explain this accurately. Language barriers lengthened the process of naturalization for Germans, who were also divided by class, regional, and religious differences. In addition, most German workers arrived in Chicago with mercantile or industrial skills. Irish immigrants, by comparison, were united by their poverty, their absence of industrial skills, their religion, and their passionate hatred of the British. Low-level jobs in the public sector were far more appealing to former Irish peasants than to skill-proud German artisans. For many Irishmen, these city sinecures were the only way out of poverty. And to get and hold them they had to get and hold political power, giving the

Irish a greater incentive to be politically active than the Germans and an additional incentive not to share power once they got it. In 1893 the city's Democratic Party nominated twenty-one Irish Americans and only four German Americans as aldermen.

Irish bosses in ethnically mixed wards had to distribute political favors broadly, but the old "Rainbow Coalition" thesis, the idea that urban machines were supported by a number of ethnic groups, each of them receiving a fair share of the patronage pot, is a myth. The Irish bosses in Chicago and other American cities never controlled enough jobs to satisfy the voracious employment needs of immigrants pouring into these cities. So bosses had to make choices, had to decide who got what. In Johnny Powers's ward, the Irish, as one Italian complained, got "the four-dollar-a-day 'jobs' of sitting in an office," while the Italians got the "dollar-a-day 'jobs' sweeping the streets." When Chicago reformers were finally able to defeat a number of ward bosses in the late 1890s, they did so by appealing to ethnic groups cut off from a fair share of ward power and city services. There was considerable Italian opposition to Johnny Powers when Jane Addams challenged him, and she might have made a stronger showing against him had she not stolen a page from Powers and run Irish Catholics, instead of disgruntled Italians, against him, revealing, perhaps, her own ethnic bias.

Election day was the day of accounting for all machine politicians, and it was an article of faith that you had to cheat in order to win. Naturalization requirements were waived by machine-controlled magistrates, and approximately half of the city's polling places in the 1880s were in saloons, where a man's vote could be won by a "liquid reward." "Floaters"—tramps, drunks, and flophouse tenants—were raked together by both Democratic and Republican ward workers, given lists of false names and addresses, and sent out to vote early and often, being paid the next day at a rate of fifty cents a vote.

In the municipal elections of 1883, George Washington cast his ballot in the Ninth Ward, and so did Thomas Jefferson, James Madison, and Abraham Lincoln. Ballot boxes were stuffed, and votes were miscounted or simply dumped into the Chicago River. In the 1893 election Carter Harrison and his eldest son voted at a barn owned by Mike McDonald in a narrow alley. The barn's doors were closed and bolted, and the Harrisons had to walk past a gang of thugs to push their ballots through a slot in the door only large enough to permit the passage of a man's hand. "Who took it and what became of it was a secret," Harrison's son recalled. If a voter had a gold ring, the ward worker inside sometimes tried to pick it as he took the ballot.

"Th' lads . . . set up all night tuckin' tickets into th' box f'r him," Mr. Dooley proudly tells a customer of his precinct work for a local candidate. "They voted all iv Calvary Symmitry an' was makin' inroads on th' potther's-field." There were street riots, stabbings, and shootings in every Chicago election, and drunken squads of Irishmen packing six-shooters traveled in flatbed wagons from precinct to precinct, assaulting the opposition with bare knuckles, baseball bats, and straight razors. "You had to have a fist like a ham in those days," recalled alderman Jimmy Quinn, "no parlor politicians then." Almost everyone "who wore a clean collar" was intimidated or assaulted, the *Tribune* reported of an election in one ward. In that same election the police arrested twenty-five leading Polish Republicans and kept them hidden until the polls closed.

Irish Democrats did not use intimidation and fraud exclusively against Republicans. They used them with equal energy against rival Democrats, often Germans, or supporters of the German-dominated Socialist Labor Party, which elected five aldermen, three state assemblymen, and a state senator in the late 1870s, at the peak of its influence. Voting places were changed in the middle of the night without notice so that German laborers could not vote on their way to work, and Germans supporting antimachine candidates were driven from the polls by Irish police and had their ballots challenged by Irish election officials.

In 1880, Frank Stauber, a socialist candidate for alderman, had victory stolen from him by ballot-box stuffing. He went to court and proved he had been the victim of massive fraud, but the election officials were acquitted because they had supposedly acted "in good faith." "We [are] fully justified in saying that the holiest institution of the American people, the right to vote, [has] been discredited and become a miserable farce and a lie," a German newspaper fumed.

Widespread electoral cheating convinced many members of the Socialist Labor Party, the majority of them Germans, to abandon electoral politics in the 1880s for a combination of militant trade unionism and revolutionary agitation. It was the Stauber affair, along with his own experience of being "counted out" in a race for alderman, that caused Albert Parsons, one of the leaders of the Great Strike of 1877, "to realize," as he wrote later, "the hopeless task of political reformation [and] to lose faith in the potency of the ballot or the protection of the law for the poor." Parsons wrote this after his turn to anarchism and just before being hanged by the neck for his alleged part in the murder of seven policemen by a handmade dynamite bomb in an alley off Haymarket Square.

3. Haymarket

"Socialism in America is an anomaly, and Chicago is the last place on the continent where it would exist were it not for the dregs of foreign immigration which find lodgement here." In 1886, the year this *Chicago Daily News* editorial appeared, Chicago was the capital of American radicalism, with the country's most visible and highly mobilized anarchist movement, led by German-American immigrants. It was also the center of the American trade-union movement, with over sixty thousand workers in labor organizations (25 percent of the city's workforce), almost a third of them Germans.

The Irish were heavily represented in Chicago's organized-labor movement, but there were not many Irish socialists in the city. The Irish used aggressive political and economic tactics for advancement within the system, which they made work for themselves. Irish radicalism was targeted not against American capitalism but against British imperialism. Even the city's Irish-Catholic clergy supported extremist groups like the secret Clan-na-Gael, which was committed to home-country independence by means of terror and sabotage, the very weapons that German anarchists proposed to use against America's "money kings" and "factory lords."

The Chicago press attributed the growth of German working-class militancy in the 1880s to the arrival of revolutionaries driven out of the fatherland by Bismarck's sweeping antisocialist laws. But conditions in Chicago, not back in Germany, were most responsible for the rise of German-American anarchism.

Germans were nineteenth-century Chicago's—and nineteenth-century America's—largest ethnic group. Their proportion of the city's population never dropped below 25 percent between 1840 and World War I. They settled in tightly concentrated enclaves on the North Side, the Northwest Side, and along the branches of the Chicago River, an area of tremendous industrial activity. Rich and poor, Catholic and Lutheran, Bavarian and Prussian, Germans lived together in these virtually self-sufficient urban villages, where German was the language of common discourse.

Germans were more ethnically conscious in Chicago and other heavily German midwestern cities than they were back in the home country, which had only recently been united. In the United States, as historian Kathleen Neils Conzen points out, Germans "invented an ethnicity for themselves" and "helped also to invent ethnicity itself as a category within American society." Members of the first generation, especially, saw assimilation as a collective or group experience in which they would not have to give up their German identity or their traditional way of socializing. They established neighborhood-based immigrant aid societies to help German émigrés adjust to American life, building and loan societies to help German families buy their first house, paramilitary self-defense units—"workingmen's militias"—to prevent the authorities from breaking up German labor demonstrations, and innumerable voluntary organizations for the promotion of Teutonic culture—singing, dance, and theater societies, hiking and debating clubs, and gymnastic associations—*Turnvereine*—to promote physical culture and German nationalism.

Germans seemed to do everything together, and on warm-weather Sundays they would gather in festive beer gardens within the German colony or march together, hundreds and sometimes thousands of them, to picnic grounds on the edge of the city. Carter Harrison II recalled these regular Sunday occasions: "Out on Madison Street the procession would move, with band playing and flags flying; the leaders on horseback, the well-to-do, the women and children in open barouches, buggies or rockaways, *hoi polloi* on foot, trudging vigorously to get up a good thirst. Bayern or Schwaben, Singing Society or Turngemeinde, the procession would move to the distant garden where the day would be spent in a round of singing, laughter, eating, drinking, and dancing, with a few speeches interpolated in memory of the Fatherland beyond the seas."

This ethnic unity carried over into the labor movement. German workers experienced oppression together and united against it as a community. While Germans of every profession and economic class immigrated to Chicago, the majority of newcomers were of the working class, and as late as 1900, two-thirds of German households in the city were still working-class. Most German workers arrived in this country trained in a trade. They were carpenters and printers, metalworkers and cigar makers, cabinetmakers and butchers, bakers and brewmasters, and their skills gave them easy entry into the flourishing local economy. But that economy began to change radically in the 1870s and 1880s, with devastating results for many artisans and skilled workers.

With the introduction of steam-powered, labor-saving machinery and new ways of organizing production, work was progressively segmented and deskilled, as seen in the case of the stockyards. There, master butchers became highly specialized and less well paid "splitters," while in the German community, small tradesmen and artisans—bakers, furniture makers, and printers—were unable to compete with factory operations producing what they did for half the cost. These structural changes took place over the course of two long economic downturns, one between 1873 and 1879 and the other between 1882 and 1886. In 1884 thirty thousand Chicagoans were unemployed, and a state-sponsored study of a group of German households found nearly half of them struggling to fight off ruin. "I never saw [back home] such real suffering from want as I have seen in this country," declared a German radical leader. Chicago's more militant German papers played on the differences between immigrants' expectations and American realities and began to call for unity and strong action to correct the disparity.

That was the message of Johann Most, the anarchist "Voice of Terror." He arrived in Chicago in 1882 on a nationwide organizational drive after serving a prison sentence in London for applauding the assassination of Czar Alexander II in an article entitled "At Last!" Chicago was a place ready-made for his incendiarism. Nowhere in America was the division between rich and poor greater; nowhere were the enemies of labor more solidly united; nowhere was nativism more pronounced. Most's spectacular speeches inspired great numbers of Chicago socialists to become fellow revolutionaries. "An end is to be made," he thundered, "to the mockery of the ballot. . . . The best that one can do with such fellows as Jay Gould and Vanderbilt is to hang them on the nearest lamp-post."

The anarchist organization he helped to form in this country, the International Working People's Association (I.W.P.A.), abjured electoral politics and demanded a war to the death with capitalism and the replacement of all organized government by a loose association of voluntary producers' cooperatives. But the Chicago anarchists, the largest group in the I.W.P.A., were never explicit about how they hoped to engineer a social revolution. Instead of sharpening their ideology, they concentrated on the politics of "the deed," winning the support of twenty-six of the city's most aggressive craft unions—all of them threatened by labor-saving mechanization—and organizing confrontational parades and rallies to arouse the city's workers and terrify "the capitalists and bourgeois politicians."

•

In 1883 there were only a few hundred anarchists in Chicago. Three years later there were over twenty-five hundred, with some twenty thousand sympathetic supporters in the union movement, according to Albert Parsons, the leader of the American Group in the I.W.P.A. and editor of its paper, the *Alarm*.

Parsons was an unlikely radical. A slender, dashingly handsome former Confederate cavalryman, he was descended from a family that arrived in Plymouth Colony on the second voyage of the *Mayflower*. Born in Alabama, where his father had a prosperous leather factory, he was five when his parents died, and he was sent to live with his eldest brother in Texas. Looking for adventure, he joined the Confederate cause at thirteen, riding with a group of volunteers known as the Lone Gray Stars. After the war, he was too embarrassed by his participation in the fight to save slavery to face his "Aunt" Esther, a former black slave who had raised him. But after being reunited with her—a turning point in his life—he joined the Radical Republicans and launched a newspaper in Waco, Texas, that campaigned for political rights for freedmen. Around this time he married a beautiful former slave, Lucy Gathings, a woman as committed as he was to human rights. Threatened by the local Klan, he and Lucy escaped to Chicago in 1873, where he took a job as a typesetter and became first a socialist, a leader in the Great Strike of 1877, and then, after the brutal suppression of that uprising and his defeat at the polls by ballot stuffing, an anarchist.

Parsons's closest associate in the movement was August Spies, a German-American editor who was as brilliantly convincing a writer as Parsons was a speaker. Together they mobilized massive demonstrations within the German community that drew upon traditional Old Country customs to broaden the movement's appeal. They helped turn the German community into a haven for revolutionary politics, a place where the system was questioned, members were recruited, and strategy was planned. Anarchist-sponsored picnics at Ogden's Grove opened with traditional German music performed by local bands and singing societies and ended with beer drinking and dancing that went on far into the night. These occasions made anarchism less frightening to many Germans, although the great majority of Chicago's German workers continued to vote Democratic and to remain active in labor unions dedicated to achieving "bread and butter" gains. At the height of its influence, the I.W.P.A. never had more than five thousand members. The impact of the anarchist movement, however, was impressively greater than its size. That influence was due to its extremist rhetoric and tactics, which emboldened its supporters and struck fear in its enemies.

Parsons and Spies took the fight straight to the capitalists. On Thanksgiving Day, 1884, anarchists wearing crimson sashes and carrying tremendous black flags—the symbols of hunger—marched up Prairie Avenue in a freezing drizzle, encouraging hoboes they recruited to ring the doorbells of the "robber classes" and demand jobs and bread. Passing by a prestigious downtown club, the marchers screamed and shook their fists at the members gathered at the windows to get a look, said an anarchist paper, at "their future executioners," a scene that might have reminded one or two Old Settlers in the club's dining room of the final Chicago war dance of the Potawatomi in front of the Sauganash Hotel. The next year, when the anarchists marched around the new Board of Trade Building on the occasion of its opening, the local militia, funded and armed by Marshall Field and the Citizens' Association, practiced street-riot drills nearby.

These demonstrations and the fiery rhetoric of anarchist newspapers put the propertied classes in a tense, confrontational mood. Articles calling for street rioting and supporting European comrades who assassinated public officials appeared in the local anarchist press alongside technical essays on how to build and use hand grenades, small bombs, and dynamite packages. Dynamite, the recent invention of the Swedish pacifist Alfred Nobel, had an electric appeal to the oppressed. Inexpensive and easy to carry and obtain, it was, as the writer Floyd Dell said, "a wonderful new substance which made one poor man the equal of an army. It seemed created as a sign to the oppressors of earth that their reign was not forever to endure." Only a few of Chicago's anarchists made bombs, and even fewer were prepared to use them, but "bomb-talking" became a way of drawing attention to a weak movement and exaggerating its strength. To shock inquiring reporters, August Spies kept a piece of gas pipe that was supposed to be a bomb on his desk at the *Arbeiter-Zeitung*, the leading German-language anarchist paper. That reckless display of bravado would later haunt him.

While no anarchist threw a bomb in Chicago before the Haymarket Riot, Spies and Parsons's encouragement of "dynamite talking" contributed to the public atmosphere that would result in the smashing of their movement by an aroused community. "These missives," Gen. Phil Sheridan described the small bombs anarchists were supposedly manufacturing at secret dynamite factories all over Chicago, "could be carried around in one's pocket with perfect safety" and used to destroy "whole armies and cities." There would soon be "an armed conflict," the general predicted, "between Capital and Labor. They will oppose each other not with words and arguments, but with shot and shell, gunpowder and cannon. The better classes are tired of the insane howlings of the lowest strata and they mean to stop them." Yet it was, ironically, the decision of Chicago's anarchists to join the city's nonradical labor organizations in a peaceful demonstration for moderate reform that set in motion the series of events that provoked the conflict Sheridan eagerly anticipated.

•

Eighteen eighty-six is known in American labor history as the year of the great uprising. In that year, there were more than fifteen hundred strikes and lockouts nationwide involving over six hundred thousand workers, most of them fighting for the eight-hour day. This campaign was pushed with surprising vigor by the Federation of Organized Trades and Labor Unions (the forerunner of the American Federation of Labor) in an effort to stop the alarming loss of its members to the Noble Order of the Knights of Labor, whose locals grew fantastically after a successful strike in 1885 against Jay Gould's railroad system, making the Knights the largest labor organization in the country. Just after this big victory by its most powerful rival, the Federation of Organized Trades, led by Samuel Gompers, an English-born cigar maker, called for a nationwide strike by all workers on May 1, 1886, to achieve the shorter workweek—ten hours' pay for eight hours' work. It was little more than a "publicity stunt," Gompers's biographer wrote, for Gompers's organization was almost moribund, but the results were dramatic, with almost a quarter of a million workers joining the cause.

At first, both anarchist leaders and Terrence V. Powderly, Grand Master of the Knights, opposed the eight-hour campaign, preferring to press for more fundamental social changes. But as May Day approached, they saw in the greatly growing power of the movement an opportunity to enlist fresh recruits for their own organizations. The result of this convergence of opportunism was the largest, most broadly based coalition of workers ever assembled—however briefly—on this continent.

With Carter Harrison publicly supporting the eight-hour cause, Chicago became the center of the crusade, and the anarchists assumed leadership of a movement they had only recently dismissed as "a sort of soothing syrup for babies." In a big lakefront rally in preparation for May first, their leaders proclaimed that this was the beginning of the final crisis of capitalism, and to demonstrate their resolve, anarchist organizations offered free rifle instruction at German beer halls on the North Side.

May first broke bright and beautiful in Chicago. After August Spies led a parade of eighty thousand workers up Michigan Avenue, some eighty-five thousand workers laid down their tools, part of a nationwide general strike of some three hundred thousand laborers, the first general strike in the history of the international labor movement. "No smoke curled up from the tall chimneys of the factories and mills," said a Chicago paper, "and the city took on a Sabbath-like appearance." The nerves of the city were stretched tight as people prepared for a repeat of the labor riots of 1877, and perhaps something far worse. Pinkertons and militia watched the anarchist-led parade from the roofs of business buildings, and troops armed with Gatling guns stood at the ready. The day went by without violence, but on May third there was a brief, explosive battle between police and workers in front of the McCormick Reaper Works that ignited the most sensational labor incident of the nineteenth century. "Take all history, search all its pages," a London paper wrote a year after the Haymarket Affair, "you will find nothing like what we saw that time in America."

•

The Reaper King had died in 1884, and his son, Cyrus H. McCormick II—whose mother pulled him out of Princeton to run the company—was determined to break the iron molders' union his father had grudgingly tolerated because the men's skills were thought to be indispensable. State-of-the-art pneumatic molding machines could now do the work of these proud iron craftsmen, and cold steel did not organize or complain. The first time young McCormick had tried to lay off skilled Irish workers, he was forced to surrender when Irish police refused to protect scabs or attack demonstrators outside the plant. McCormick, however, used his family's influence within the business community and the local Democratic Party to force the appointment of Capt. John Bonfield as police inspector, a large, powerfully built man known as "Black Jack" for his brutal suppression of a city trolley strike in 1885, when he had defied Carter Harrison's orders and issued a "shoot to kill" directive. This time, when McCormick locked out his iron molders and the "trouble makers" who made cause with them, he armed his strikebreakers with pistols and used Pinkertons—backed up by Bonfield's men—to crack the skulls of protesters who tried to stop them from entering "Ft. McCormick," as anarchists called the plant.

It was at this point that the strike at the McCormick Reaper Works merged with the eight-hour struggle in the city. On May third, August Spies was addressing a large open-air gathering of striking lumber shovers at a place called the Black Road when the shift bell tolled at the nearby McCormick plant, the signal for McCormick strikers on the fringe of the crowd to head for the factory gate to heckle and rough up scabs leaving work. The protesters drove the strikebreakers back into the plant and began smashing windows. Then, in an instant, two hundred of Bonfield's "clubbers" were on them, swinging their nightsticks wildly and firing their pistols. A short distance away, August Spies, who had heard the shots and raced to the scene, looked on in horror and then headed for the office of the *Arbeiter-Zeitung* and penned a "Revenge Circular," calling on workers to "destroy the hideous monster that seeks to destroy you." This was followed by a separate call by other anarchists for a meeting in Haymarket Square the next night to protest the killing of two workers by Bonfield's men.

Chicagoans of property feared that this demonstration would trigger the bombing campaign the anarchists had been threatening for some time, and as a precaution, Harrison stationed 167 riot-trained police, under Bonfield, at the Des Plaines Street Station, a half block from the Haymarket. Some anarchists expected over twenty thousand people, but only about twenty-five hundred showed up, causing Spies to move the meeting to an alley just off the Haymarket. Standing in the crowd as Spies began speaking from the bed of an empty delivery wagon was Carter Harrison, who struck match after match, as if to relight his cigar, in an effort to draw attention to his presence. "I want the people to know their mayor is here," he told a friend standing with him who feared that extremists in the crowd might spot him and attack him. Harrison left after Spies and Parsons spoke and stopped by the Des Plaines Street station house to tell Bonfield that the meeting was peaceful and that he should send home his reinforcements. But Bonfield was looking for a confrontation.

When Harrison rode home on his mare, Bonfield sent in his columns of riot police, even though the meeting had begun to break up as a rainstorm approached. As Bonfield's men marched with their revolvers drawn through the three hundred or so stragglers listening to the conclusion of Samuel Fielden's speech, a dark object trailing sparks appeared in the night sky and landed in the front ranks of the policemen. There was a blinding flash and an earsplitting explosion that Carter Harrison heard at his home as he prepared to climb into bed. Police went down like tenpins, and those not hit began firing in every direction, their shots returned by workers who carried pistols for protection. Seven police were killed and sixty injured, a great many of them by friendly fire, in what the papers described as two or three minutes of wild carnage. There was an indeterminate number of civilian casualties, probably as many as the police suffered.

"Now It Is Blood," screamed a Chicago headline the next morning. "The city went insane," recalled Mother Jones, the labor organizer, "and the newspapers did everything to keep it like a madhouse." Radicals of every stripe were rounded up and held without specific charges, in America's first Red Hunt; and all foreign-born workers were placed under suspicion. As the *Chicago Times* proclaimed, the "enemy forces" were not Americans. They were "rag-tag and bobtail cutthroats of Beelzebub from the Rhine, the Danube, the Vistula, and the Elbe." Local capitalists fueled the nativist revenge, funding the raids and raising money for the prosecution. Marshall Field led a movement within the Commercial Club to donate money to the federal government for the building of an army post thirty miles north of the city, later named Fort Sheridan. Field and his Prairie Avenue neighbors also hired Burnham and Root to design a formidable stone armory, "an engine of defense," not far from their homes, and smaller armories were built in working-class neighborhoods.

All efforts at social repression or class reconciliation in Chicago in the years immediately before the Columbian Exposition—from the building of armories to the creation of new museums and settlement houses—can be best understood against the background of Haymarket, "the chief tragedy," a Chicagoan called it, "of the closing years of the nineteenth century." And it was hardly coincidental that the city that staged, in 1893, the century's most impressive demonstration of civic order was the one that was shaken by the century's most terrifying single outburst of urban disorder.

•

"No event in the city's history," said a Chicago writer, "took stronger hold on the emotions than the ensuing murder trial." Although the person who threw the bomb was never caught, seven anarchists stood in the dock on June 21, to be joined later that day—in a sensational appearance—by Albert Parsons, who had fled the city after the bombing and returned on his own to stand trial with his comrades.

Before the trial State's Attorney Julius S. Grinnell had discussed with friends the difficulty of convicting eight men as accessories when the murderer could not be found. But Melville E. Stone, editor of the *Chicago Daily News,* had the answer. "I at once took the ground," he later wrote in his memoirs, "that the identity of the bombthrower was of no consequence, and that inasmuch as Spies and Parsons and Fielden had advocated over and over again the use of violence against the police and had urged the manufacture and throwing of bombs, their culpability was clear." This became the core of the state's case. The defendants would be prosecuted, as Henry Demarest Lloyd protested, "for the violent insanity of [their] public speeches."

It was perhaps the most dramatic trial in the history of American jurisprudence and easily one of the most unjust. In a sense, it was not a trial at all but a panicky prelude to a community lynching presided over by a judge, Joseph E. Gary, who allowed men on the jury, including the jury foreman—a salesman for Marshall Field—who were convinced the defendants were guilty. Not a single juryman was an industrial worker, and as Governor Altgeld said later, Judge Gary conducted the proceedings with "malicious ferocity." The leader of the defense team, William Perkins Black, a decorated Civil War veteran and distinguished corporate lawyer, demonstrated that all eight men had airtight alibis and that only two of them were on the scene when the bomb was thrown—and that these two were on the speakers' platform, in plain view of the police. Carter Harrison also testified that the demonstration was orderly, with the wives and children of anarchists sprinkled throughout the crowd. But Grinnell waved all this aside, striking the telling note for the prosecution at the dramatic conclusion of the two-month-long trial. "Law is on trial," he declared. "Anarchy is on trial. These men have been selected, picked out by the grand jury and indicted because they were leaders. They are no more guilty than the thousands who follow them. Gentlemen of the jury, convict these men, make examples of them, hang them and you save our institutions, our society."

The jury took only three hours to reach a verdict: death by hanging for seven of the defendants and a fifteen-year prison term for August Neebe. Not a defendant's face showed a hint of alarm as the verdict was read. Parsons was standing near an open window and tied the cords of the window shade into a noose to let the crowd below know the verdict. The mob began cheering wildly. "The Scaffold Waits," the *Tribune* headline read the next morning, "Seven Dangling Nooses for the Dynamite Fiends."

That day Lucy Parsons began a fight to have the convictions overturned, aided by Nina Van Zandt, a Vassar-educated Chicago socialite who married August Spies by proxy after attending the trial out of curiosity. Independently, Henry Demarest Lloyd, who had married a daughter of *Tribune* owner William Bross, began a national campaign for clemency, and Lyman J. Gage, later U.S. Secretary of the Treasury, called together a group of fellow bankers and businessmen to try to convince them that clemency would greatly help future labor-management relations. Moderates like Potter Palmer and Charles Hutchinson agreed, but Marshall Field was unmoved, and that settled it. A number of businessmen at the meeting told Gage later that they favored clemency but did not dare go up against the most powerful man in the city.

Appeals to the Illinois Supreme Court and the U.S. Supreme Court failed, leaving only the slender hope of the governor's intervention. Samuel Gompers wrote to Gov. Richard J. Oglesby saying that a country "great and magnanimous enough to grant amnesty to Jeff Davis" should do the same for these men. Even Judge Gary wrote to the governor requesting a commutation of the sentences of the two prisoners who had officially asked for mercy, Samuel Fielden and Michael Schwab. On the evening of the scheduled execution, Oglesby commuted the sentences of Fielden and Schwab to life imprisonment but said he was prevented from pardoning the other prisoners because they had not officially asked for clemency, as required by state law.

Just hours before the governor's statement, the most intransigent of the prisoners, Louis Lingg, who had sat through the trial with an unlit cigar in his mouth and a sneer on his face, blew off part of his face with a dynamite cartridge he had calmly placed in his mouth and lit, cheating the hangman with the help of a visiting friend who had planted the cigar bomb in his cell. His body was dumped into an iron tub, to be kept there until the other prisoners were executed.

The next morning, November 11, 1887, a heavy police guard ringed the Cook County prison, expecting trouble. Anarchists had earlier threatened to blow up the courthouse and kill everyone who took part in the prosecution and had sent letters written in red ink to the wives of Stone, Grinnell, and Gary, warning that their children would be kidnapped and their homes destroyed by dynamite. Ropes were stretched across the streets leading to the jail, and behind them were police with Winchester rifles. The homes of everyone involved with the prosecution were put under guard, and important capitalists left town. The journalist Charles Edward Russell saw a gun store still open at ten o'clock on the eve of the hangings, "crowded with men buying revolvers." "A cloud of apprehension lowered over the city," recalled Melville Stone. "There was a hush, and men spoke in whispers. . . . I have never experienced quite the like condition." But there would be no violence. The anarchists about to be hanged had urged restraint.

Albert Parsons, August Spies, George Engel, and Adolph Fischer went to their deaths with quiet dignity before 170 witnesses. Their faces were covered, their ankles were bound with leather straps, and they were clothed in white shrouds, open at the neck so that the nooses could be placed and set. As they stood on the hangman's platform, there was a moment of eerie silence, and then Spies spoke from behind his hood. "The day will come when our silence will be more powerful than the voices you are throttling today." Fischer and Engel then yelled, "Hurrah for anarchy!" As Parsons struggled to speak—"Will I be allowed to speak, O men of America? . . . Let me speak . . ."—the trap doors snapped open, and the four hooded and bound figures plunged, not to death immediately—for their necks were not broken by the fall—but to ghastly torture. Twitching and jerking horribly, the last of them died seven minutes and forty-five seconds later.

"Dropped to Eternity" was the jubilant *Tribune* headline the next day. In Galesburg, Illinois, a nine-year-old boy heard one railroad worker say to another as they passed each other quickly, "Well, they hanged 'em." There was no need to say more. Everyone in America knew what was to happen that Black Friday. "Like the Dreyfus case in France, it was one of those episodes," writes Paul Avrich in his riveting history, *The Haymarket Tragedy*, "that divide a nation, arousing deep-seated emotions, defining loyalties, and spawning a literature of social criticism and protest." That literature would include, years later, a stirring poem by Carl Sandburg, the kid by the railroad tracks in Galesburg.

They were buried at Waldheim Cemetery, near the German village of Forest Park, on the far West Side. It was the largest funeral Chicago had seen up to that time. Over twenty thousand mourners marched behind the burial carriages and past hushed crowds estimated at more than two hundred thousand, a quarter of the city's population. "Who that saw it can ever forget that Sunday funeral procession," wrote Charles Edward Russell. "The sobering impression of the amnesty of death, the still more sobering question whether we had done right."

The police prohibited the carrying of banners or flags. There was to be no singing or speechmaking and no music except funeral dirges. The order was obeyed with but one exception. As the procession began to make its way down Milwaukee Avenue—"Lunch Pail Avenue," as it was known to German workers—an army veteran in uniform stepped in front of the first row of marchers and unfurled a small American flag bordered in black crepe. A policeman tried to pull him from the procession but was knocked down by a group of workers. The veteran carried the flag at the front of the marchers all the way to the Wisconsin Central Station, where special trains waited to carry the scarlet-decorated coffins and more than ten thousand mourners to the cemetery. Captain Black spoke at the graves. Witnesses said it was the most stirring funeral oration they had ever heard.

•

Two years after the anarchists were put in the ground, a monument to the slain police was unveiled in Haymarket Square. During the Columbian Exposition, the policeman who modeled for the statue was stationed by it to explain to visitors what had happened there in May 1886. Several years later, this same policeman, Thomas J. Birmingham, was charged with trafficking with stolen goods and thrown off the force. This was after Bonfield had to leave the force in disgrace for taking bribes and then arresting the editors of the newspaper, the only pro-Harrison organ in the city, that broke the story. In his book *Chicago: City on the Make,* the novelist Nelson Algren argues that it was Haymarket that gave Chicago its permanent reputation as the "town of the hard and bitter strikes and the trigger-happy cops." In 1970, Algren paid tribute to Louis Lingg, whose defiant address to the court before he was hanged—"I despise your order, your laws, your force-propped authority. Hang me for it!"—typified for Algren a certain kind of Chicago toughness, and Algren applauded the radicals who blew up the Haymarket monument in 1970. Today the rebuilt statue stands in a protected spot at the Chicago Police Training Center.

The Haymarket bomb thrower has never been identified and probably never will be. Captain Black suspected the missile was hurled by a Pinkerton provocateur in a desperate attempt to break up the eight-hour movement. But evidence unearthed by Paul Avrich suggests that it was indeed an anarchist and probably a German. The man who made these claims, an anarchist named Dyer Lum, a close confidant of Albert Parsons known for personal rectitude, went to his grave with his secret, for he saw the assassin as a hero and wanted to protect him. Lum tried to explain the assassin's silence: Even if he had confessed, the lives of his comrades would not have been saved. He would have been just another lamb for the slaughter. Lum said that none of the eight defendants knew who threw the bomb at the time of the incident and that only two (probably Fischer and Engel) ever found out. The bomb thrower "was never mentioned in the trial and is today unknown to the public," Lum wrote two years before his suicide in 1893.

In June of that year—the day after the unveiling of a Haymarket monument in Waldheim Cemetery in the presence of eight thousand persons, many of them foreigners attending the' fair—Governor Altgeld unconditionally pardoned Fielden, Schwab, and Neebe, denouncing the trial, and Judge Gary especially, in the most extreme language. No matter how fanatical their beliefs, the anarchists, Altgeld declared, "were entitled to a fair trial, and no greater damage could possibly threaten our institutions than to have the courts of justice run wild or to give way to popular clamor."

The pardon made Altgeld the most hated man in America. Newspapers from New York to Los Angeles charged him with encouraging "anarchy and the overthrow of American institutions." And his foreign birth—he had been brought to America from Germany as an infant—became an issue. He had not "a drop of true American blood in his veins," steamed the *Tribune*. "He does not reason like an American, nor feel like one, and consequently does not behave like one."

It was one of the most courageous acts ever taken by an American politician, and Altgeld himself refused to answer the wild attacks on his character. "I saw my duty and I did it," he would say later.

•

Haymarket weakened but did not break the Chicago labor movement. The movement for the eight-hour day was smashed, and the Chicago anarchists never recovered. Neither did the Knights of Labor, although its sudden decline had more to do with the emergence of Samuel Gompers's new American Federation of Labor, formed in the year of the Haymarket incident. An organization of craft unions dedicated to realizable reforms, it excluded nonskilled workers, Gompers arguing that they could easily be replaced by employers in strike situations, weakening the federation's negotiating position. Gompers's "pure-and-simple" unionism mirrored labor's sobered post-Haymarket mood, and a number of the American Federation of Labor's affiliates in Chicago began discussions with moderate businessmen brought together by Lyman Gage to hammer out "no strike" agreements in exchange for wage increases and job security.

The use of lockouts, spies, Pinkertons, and blacklists by more intransigent employers made this brief labor peace, if it can be called that, extremely precarious. Instead of being intimidated by the post-Haymarket red hunts, many radicals took inspiration from the men hanged in the Cook County jail. Emma Goldman, leader of a resurgence of anarchism in cities outside Chicago, claimed that her radical "awakening" occurred on November 11, 1887, and Eugene V. Debs visited the anarchists' graves the day he ended his prison sentence for defying a federal injunction during the 1894 Pullman Strike. The Chicago martyrs were, he proclaimed, the "avant couriers of a better day." While Henry Demarest Lloyd could not agree with that, the Haymarket tragedy drove him into an alliance with American labor and into public affairs as a leading writer on social issues and author of *Wealth Against Commonwealth,* a blistering indictment of Standard Oil and the whole system of monopoly capitalism. As historian John Thomas writes, "The Haymarket tragedy was the central symbolic event for Lloyd's generation of reformers, . . . convincing them that class division threatened the very fabric of the American republic." "I only wish Marx could have lived to see it!" Friedrich Engels wrote to Florence Kelley, "the breaking out of class war in [bourgeois] America."

The economic prosperity that followed in the wake of the eight-hour agitation was a time of uneasiness and uncertainty in the entire country. Americans wondered whether the nation was headed toward a new era of labor peace or perhaps toward a "cataclysm of fire and blood." The atmosphere could not have been anything but uneasy, for the great economic divisions behind the labor troubles of the 1880s continued to widen. "Upon the one side," said Chicago socialist George Schilling, "we find the propertied classes. . . . They are in possession of the earth. Upon the other side we find a large army of workmen who have nothing on earth except their labor." Only time would tell what lay ahead for the worker who "had to sell his labor or go under."

It was Schilling, a leader in the amnesty movement, who had the final word on Haymarket. "At Waldheim sleep five men," he wrote Lucy Parsons, "among them your beloved husband—who died in the hope that their execution might accelerate the emancipation of the world. Blessed be their memories." But the world, he said, would never judge their methods either "wise or correct. They worshiped at the shrine of force; wrote it and preached it; until finally they were overpowered by their own Gods and slain in their own temple. . . . When you terrorize the public mind and threaten the stability of society with violence, you create the conditions which place the Bonfields and Garys in the saddle, hailed as the saviors of society."

4. It's Harrison Again

Haymarket almost destroyed Carter Harrison's political career. He had nearly lost the previous election when elite-led citizens' groups mounted an all-out campaign against him after public disclosures of massive fraud in the 1884 elections by some of his key Democratic lieutenants. (Only 7 of 171 precincts failed to show violations of the election laws.) And his conduct in the Haymarket Affair further damaged his standing with the business groups that were heading this clean-government campaign. The *Chicago Tribune* was their stalking horse, Joseph Medill assailing Harrison for not suppressing the anarchists' "madness long before it bore fruit in bombs." Many militant German, Irish, and Bohemian workers, meanwhile, deserted Harrison to form their own labor party, believing he could not protect their rights as strongly as he once had.

Harrison tried to get the new Union Labor Party to fuse with the Democrats. When its leaders refused and it became apparent to Harrison that he would probably lose the election, he declined his party's nomination and took off on a sixteen-month world tour, leaving the Democrats without a candidate against John Roche, a law-and-order Republican who was a member of a secret anti-Catholic organization. Faced with the possibility of a "socialist" victory, the Democrats panicked and merged with the Republicans against the United Labor Party. It was one of the lowest moments in the party's history, and it looked as though Harrison were finished as a Chicago politician. Without its charismatic standard-bearer, some Republican papers gleefully predicted, the Democratic Party in Chicago was heading for its demise.

But the Democrats came back fast and strong. DeWitt Cregier defeated Roche in the very next election, and Harrison recovered almost as quickly as his party. He returned from his world tour rejuvenated and eager for action. When the Democrats refused to nominate him for mayor in 1891, preferring to stick with Cregier, a mayor even more accommodating to the local machines than Harrison had been, he bolted the party and ran as an independent, losing the election by fewer than four thousand votes to Republican Hempstead Washburne. His strong showing convinced him that he had lost none of his old political magic, and as 1893 approached, he let his supporters know that his single remaining ambition was to be mayor of "the greatest city in the world" at the greatest moment in its history.

•

It was the most ferociously fought election in the city's history. Harrison entered it without the support of any newspapers, other than the one he had bought to promote his own candidacy, or of any organized groups, including his own party. To get his party's nomination, he had to go up against his old friend Washington Hesing, a prominent German publisher who was being backed by a new, fast-rising Irish machine led by John Hopkins and Roger Sullivan. Sullivan and Hopkins were ruthlessly efficient businessmen-politicians who saw in the city's recent annexation of new territory unprecedented opportunities for boodle, and they had already begun to sell lucrative franchises to electric and gas companies they owned.

Roger Sullivan would eventually become the undisputed leader of Chicago's Democratic Party, but in 1893, Johnny Powers's pro-Harrison "Irish Gang"—Sullivan and Hopkins's rival in the business of selling franchises—still controlled the party, and they packed the galleries at the nominating convention in Central Music Hall. When Hesing tried to address the delegates, he was shouted down by raucous Harrison supporters, and fistfights broke out all over the hall. It was "the most disorderly and riotous [convention] in the history of the city," declared the *Tribune*. Unable to speak, trembling with rage,

Hesing stormed out of the hall, and Harrison was nominated on the first ballot by what the papers called a "disgraceful mob."

The Republicans tried to get one of the city's capitalist luminaries to go up against Harrison, but when both Philip Armour and Lyman Gage refused to run, they had to settle for lackluster Samuel W. Allerton, a millionaire stockyards magnate and pork trader from an old eastern family. "I'm a businessman," Allerton defended his flat platform style, "not a politician." And that's the card Medill and the party played. If elected, Allerton declared, he would govern Chicago, "the second largest . . . business enterprise . . . in the country," like a corporate executive. Allerton promised to give Chicago clean streets and clean government, with only business and professional leaders of the "highest standing" appointed to office. At a revival-like political rally in April, he used the White City, then being brought to completion by some of his closest friends and supporters, as a harbinger of the kind of government Chicago could have. The world had never seen anything quite like Burnham's city, he said, and yet it had cost less to build than New York's new city hall. "Why is this? Because the White City has been built by businessmen" and New York's city hall by Tammany hacks. "One is business. The other is politics. Which do you want?"

The real choice in this election, Allerton proclaimed, was between "the slums" and the men who had made modern Chicago. Behind his candidacy were Lyman Gage, Philip Armour, Harry Selfridge, Charles Hutchinson, Franklin MacVeigh, Harlow Higinbotham, and the lumber king, Turlington Harvey, president of the Chicago Bible Society and builder of Harvey, Illinois, a temperance town in the Chicago suburbs Harvey hoped to turn into a Christian utopia. "Back of Carter Harrison is all the immorality of the city."

Allerton had a platform—civil service reform, better city services, lower taxes—but ideas were subordinated to slander in his campaign. "The bitterness and acrimony of the campaign," wrote Willis J. Abbot, "exceeded anything ever known in Chicago politics." Harrison was made responsible for all of Chicago's problems; the Christian evangelists even linked his support of Sunday openings with the Haymarket bombing. "Sunday traffic, Sunday excursions, Sunday newspapers . . . Sunday theaters, open saloons on Sunday, and suspected Anarchists' meetings at which treason is preached . . . then surprise and whines when the red flag explodes its bomb." Vote against this man, who was supported by dram sellers and Sabbath desecrators, ministers exhorted their congregations, "lest the wrath of God fall upon the city."

The Republicans ran a campaign of unhinged denunciation and disparagement because much of their platform, as even the *Tribune* would admit after the election, was virtually indistinguishable from the urban reforms their opponent had backed as mayor. Carter Harrison had greatly increased the number of paved streets and sidewalks downtown, strengthened the size and efficiency of the fire department, forced utility companies operating in the Loop to bury their unsightly wires, fought the Illinois Central's right to the lakefront, worked to convince railroad leaders to begin a program of track elevation downtown, and tried to push measures through the city council to have locomotives, steamships, and tugs burn anthracite and to get the city to build new and longer intake pipes for the public water system.

When Republicans attacked Harrison's "deplorable" record on street cleaning and garbage collection, he answered—with some justification—that he had done all he could, given state-imposed limitations on the city's taxing powers. Harrison at least campaigned for reform of a tax assessment system that had allowed Charles Yerkes to escape taxation on all but four thousand dollars of his personal property, while Republicans pressed for a pie-in-the-sky combination of lower taxes and expanded urban services, insisting that ten civil service appointees could do the work of a hundred of Harrison's patronage flunkies, saving the city money while upgrading its services.

To the ethnic press, it was the Republican reformers' insistence on lowering rather than equalizing taxes that exposed them for what they were—men of property who entered politics merely to advance their own interests. Harrison made all he could of this issue: "There are men in this city who pose as reformers who regularly permit the assessors to value their whole property for less than they paid for the pictures on their walls; who cheat the city, then thank God they are not thieves, like the aldermen." This hypocrisy, Harrison pointed out, extended to their campaign of moral uplift, which was a thinly disguised effort to deny the city's non-Protestant immigrants the right to govern until proper values had been beaten into them.

Unlike the Republican reformers, Harrison accepted Chicago for what it was, a battleground of competing classes and ethnic groups, each with its own share of power. To keep this divided city running well, a mayor, he believed, had to be a deal maker, not a moral dictator. It was, in the end, Harrison's cheerful willingness to bargain and compromise—often with utterly odious characters—and to give "the great unwashed" a voice in government that most offended the city's Protestant commercial establishment—and that made him almost unbeatable in most of the ethnic neighborhoods. A German newspaper summed up feelings in many of the immigrant-dominated wards: "This must be a city in which the peculiar habits of life of all the nationalities from the blending of which the future American national existence is to be formed must be recognized in all their full distinctiveness."

Medill and the "reformers" spoke of a new Chicago, but Carter Harrison had his own ideas on this. The new Chicago he spoke of would be a city not just of great architecture but also of great opportunity, a Chicago that would provide the greatest privilege a city can offer: a person's right to decide what he would be. Chicagoans, he believed, would have to continue to come together in the future to promote gigantic urban projects like the fair and the Sanitary Canal, and immigrants would have to learn to be urban patriots, not just American patriots, if Chicago was to be governable, safe, and orderly. But the city's strength, Harrison believed further, was in its neighborhoods. "Good government," Republican style, would have meant less, not more, power for struggling Poles, Italians, Jews, and Germans. For the Irish, especially, to have given way to business reformers would have meant surrendering most of what they had fought for since arriving on these shores, over violently pitching seas, in famine ships reeking of vomit and piss. It had to be Harrison.

•

On the morning of election day, both parties were confident. Speaking for Allerton, the *Tribune* predicted an overwhelming victory, made possible by massive defections from Harrison in the German wards, where Hesing was popular. Harrison, leaving nothing to chance, galloped from polling post to polling post on his splendid mare, urging his precinct captains to "push forward to victory." Toward evening, the downtown streets began to fill up with the supporters of both candidates, who huddled around blazing bonfires. The *Tribune* put a screen high across Madison Street to display the returns as they came in, and when Allerton conceded, a wild celebration broke out.

Harrison supporters, led by blaring bands and carrying torchlights, began marching through the streets of the Loop. As the paraders passed by the *Tribune*, "every hat was doffed and in slow and solemn step, the crowd went by," wrote one of that paper's own reporters, "to the lugubrious music of a dirge. Once past the corner on Madison Street the band broke into the swinging, jolly chorus of 'The Bowery.'"

It was a landslide, Harrison by over twenty-one thousand votes, his biggest victory margin ever, and in celebration the saloons ran full blast all night long. Throughout the evening the newsboys "cried their 'extry peppers,' and it was early this morning," the *Tribune* reported, "before Chicago went to sleep, ready, when it wakens, to throw politics aside and prepare for the opening of the Columbian Exposition."

Carter Harrison would be the city's representative at the World's

Fair, but the fair itself would be the civic elite's show, their ideal Chicago for all the world to see. Passing from the clotted ugliness of the city, fairgoers would see what American urban life could be like if planned and run, in the words of the *Tribune*, by "men of brains, wealth, and standing in the community." As it turned out, however, it was Carter Harrison's Chicago, not Daniel Burnham's city of ordered magnificence, that was a more accurate presentiment of the nation's urban future.

14

1893

1. The Fair

"THE world's greatest achievement of the departing century was pulled off in Chicago," wrote George Ade. "The Columbian Exposition was the most stupendous, interesting and significant show ever spread out for the public." The fair drew an estimated 27 million people, 14 million from outside the United States, making it the greatest tourist attraction in American history. And it was a cultural phenomenon of profound importance. Richard Harding Davis, the leading correspondent of the day, called it "the greatest event in the history of the country since the Civil War." The exposition that was to celebrate—one year late—the four hundredth anniversary of Columbus's discovery of the New World marked America's emergence from the carnage and bitterness of the war as a reunified nation of unrivaled power and wealth. The imperial architecture of the exposition's pavilions, the full-scale replica of the battleship *Illinois* at the fair's Naval Pier, and the astonishing exhibits of American advances in science, technology, and the world-transforming arts of mass production and merchandising announced that the approaching century would be indisputably ours.

American families mortgaged their farms and houses, borrowed money on their life insurance, or trimmed their Christmas budgets to save up for a summer week in Chicago, convinced there would be nothing like the fair for at least another century. Few who went regretted their sacrifices. "Well, Susan," a gray-bearded farmer said to his wife as they left the Court of Honor, "it paid, even if it did take all the burial money."

But if this was America's fair, it was even more so Chicago's. At no other world's fair, then or after, was there a closer identification between the host city and the show it put on. Almost on its own, Chicago financed and built the fair, and it remains, for many Chicagoans, the seminal event in their city's history. It was Chicago's "fete day," wrote the novelist Robert Herrick, "when it proclaimed to everybody that in spite of . . . [its] haste and ugliness and makeshift character . . . it had preserved its love of the ideal, of beauty and could accomplish it too— could achieve anything!"

The most "marvelous thing" about the fair, Charles Dudley Warner told a *Hartford Courant* reporter, was not its alabaster "palaces" and machine-age exhibits but "the short time it was erected in. It is safe to say that no other community in all history except the Chicago community could have done it. In no other city in the United States is there the requisite public spirit, generosity, and headlong energy." But Chicago almost didn't do it. Through the late winter and spring of 1893, newspapers all over the country had been expressing deep doubts that the fair would open on time, a delay that would have badly embarrassed the country. Director of Works Daniel Burnham and his "organized army," however, overcame enormous obstacles to save, in Warner's words, "the national honor."

That winter, one of the severest in Chicago history, as Burnham drove his crews furiously to get the fair ready for its May first opening, immense roofs caved in under heavy snows and high winds blew away smaller buildings. In the midst of final preparations, Henry Codman died suddenly following an appendectomy, leaving the enfeebled Frederick Law Olmsted, who rushed out from Boston, without an assistant to complete the work on the canals, lagoons, and basins. Accidents and labor problems further slowed down the work as mules and men slogged through spring mud more than a foot deep.

On the eve of the opening, F. Herbert Stead, brother of William T. Stead, arrived to cover the event. It had been raining hard for a week, and as he made his way around the partially flooded site, everything seemed to be in a state of "gross incompleteness." But when he returned to Jackson Park the next morning, the litter-strewn construction site had been cleaned up overnight, and hundreds of unloaded railroad cars had been drawn back into temporary sheds. The rain stopped shortly after dawn, and when President Grover Cleveland, Mayor Harrison, Daniel Burnham, and Bertha Palmer, "the queen of the occasion," arrived in open carriages just before noon, they were greeted by the cheers of a crowd of 200,000 persons packed together in front of the speaker's stand at the Administration Building. The president gave a blessedly short address and then pressed a gilded "electric button," setting in motion the machinery that powered the exhibition. In one instant the shroud fell from Daniel Chester French's statue of the *Republic* in the Great Basin, fountains sprayed water a hundred feet into the air, flags unfurled from a thousand standards, warships in the harbor fired thunderous salutes, and hundreds of lake craft sounded their steam whistles. "Buffalo Bill" Cody, in town for the summer with his Wild West Show, waved his immense white hat from his prominent position in front of the crowd, while Jane Addams, caught somewhere in the crush, felt someone snatch her purse.

As the terrific noise subsided, the band struck up "America the Beautiful," there being no official national anthem. And in the pride of the moment, the crowd seemed to forget that the buildings were unfinished, that the morning papers were reporting bank failures and panic trading on Wall Street, and that they were standing in mud and water up to their ankles.

Most fairgoers went out to Jackson Park by cable car, by Charles Yerkes's new fast-flying "El" train, or in one of the Illinois Central's open "cattle cars," which made the trip from the Loop to the fairgrounds in twelve minutes. But all the guidebooks agreed that the most delightful way to go was by lake steamer. The World's Fair Steamship Company ran a fleet of twenty-five steamers from its midtown dock, and for a fifteen-cent fare, passengers were treated to band music and a "continuous panoramic picture [of] the best built and busiest city in the world."

The boats landed at a pier reaching half a mile into the lake, where most passengers lingered for a while to take in the grounds. A movable sidewalk ran from one end of the pier to the other, carrying more than five thousand people at a time (when it was working) to the sculpture-decked Peristyle that formed the lakefront entrance to the Court of Honor. As the fairgoers passed through the Peristyle's Water-Gate, "the whole beauty of the Exposition broke upon the newcomer." Straight ahead on the horizon rose the golden-ribbed dome of Richard Morris Hunt's Administration Building, and around the basin was a continuous composition of architecture, sculpture, water, and esplanade. Pennants and flags snapped in the breeze from the towers of the buildings, and in the reflecting basin were the two main sculpture pieces of the exposition, French's *Republic* and Frederick William MacMonnies's *Columbian Fountain*. A canal led off from the basin to

Olmsted's terraced lagoons, and from the bridge that crossed it, visitors could see the other exhibition halls, all of them white except for Louis Sullivan's multicolored Transportation Building, with its high-arching Golden Doorway, the only experimental building on the grounds.

The buildings might have been imitations of the ancients—a derivative architecture, critics scoffed—but many people reported feeling a surge of "Americanism" on entering the Court of Honor and gazing upon architectural symbols of the country's greatness. They saw the architecture as a return not to the Rome of the Caesars but to the chaste classicism of Thomas Jefferson, "a return to our better selves." Then, too, French's sixty-five-foot-high *Republic* bore an uncanny resemblance to the Statue of Liberty, while the Administration Building looked strikingly like the Capitol in Washington. It was an American Forum to rival Rome's, one patriot enthused, and its popularity hastened the spread of a neoclassic eclecticism that gave the country some of its handsomest civic buildings, including New York's Pennsylvania Station and Joseph M. Huston's Capitol building in Harrisburg, Pennsylvania.

But the White City was more than an architectural stage set. It was a nearly complete miniature city equipped with its own sewage, water, and electric-power plants; fire, police, street cleaning, and governing bodies; and the most advanced urban transportation system in the world. Writing at the time, John Coleman Adams, a prominent clergyman and author of religious books, suggested it as an answer to "the blot and failure of modern civilization, the great city of the end of the century." It was designed, he pointed out, with the pedestrian in mind and was planned to handle large crowds without the push and congestion of big-city streets. The spacious exhibition halls were arranged in sympathy with their natural surroundings and were conveniently interconnected by picturesque walkways and two and a half miles of watercourse. At almost every major point on the grounds, footsore sightseers could climb aboard a "swift and silent" electric launch or flag down a smaller battery-run boat—like hailing a cab—and head to the next spot on their guidebook agenda. The railroad that circled the grounds was the first in America to operate heavy, high-speed trains by electricity, and it ran on elevated tracks, posing no danger to pedestrians at a time when trains, trolleys, and cable cars killed more than four hundred people a year on the streets of Chicago.

The streets and pavements of the White City were free of refuse and litter and patrolled by courteous Columbian Guards, drilled and uniformed like soldiers in the Prussian army; there was also a secret service force of two hundred men headed by "Black Jack" Bonfield of Haymarket fame. Every water fountain was equipped with a Pasteur filter, and the model sanitary system Burnham's engineers installed worked flawlessly, converting sewage into solids and burning it, the ashes being used for road cover and fertilizer. There were no garish commercial signs, and with concessionaires licensed and monitored, fairgoers walked the grounds free from the nuisance of peddlers and confidence men, yet with the myriad pleasures of metropolitan life near at hand. The pavilions were vast department stores stocked with the newest consumer products, and in the course of a crowded day of sightseeing, visitors could stop at courteously staffed coffee shops, teahouses, restaurants, and beer gardens located at ground level or on rooftop terraces. The White City seemed to suggest a solution to almost every problem afflicting the modern city, even its notoriously corrupt system of government.

The fair was built and administered without scandal or "jobbery" by a committee of public-minded businessmen, architects, and engineers. Machine-style politicians, as Samuel Allerton had emphasized in his mayoralty campaign against Carter Harrison, had no part in it. For once "the best were called upon to produce the best," rejoiced John Coleman Adams. This self-anointed urban elite had, as we have seen, a deep faith in the transforming power of good surroundings. "Take the roughest man," George Pullman said, "and bring him into a room elegantly carpeted and furnished and the effect upon his bearing is immediate." Burnham and Olmsted saw civic architecture and landscaped urban spaces operating to the same effect. Never, Adams said, had he seen such "well-behaved" public crowds; never had he felt more safe in a crowded urban place. Burnham and his fellow planners had shown that it was possible for even common working people to "have a good time," Adams marveled, "without boisterousness or disorder."

The summer city Burnham and Olmsted built on a bare, wind-torn beach in a mere two years was the most ambitious privately planned endeavor in Chicago up to that time, its only equal, perhaps, the town of Pullman located just south of it. Unlike Pullman, it was not built primarily to make money, but it was designed, as that earlier model city had been, as an antidote to social disorder.

•

The fair took place at a critical juncture in the nation's history. Many Americans saw their country's future bound up with the future of its industrial cities, and these cities appeared to be flying apart even as they were built ever larger. The city is "the storm center" of civilization, wrote Josiah Strong in his sensationalist polemic *Our Country*. "Here is heaped the social dynamite; here roughs, gamblers, thieves, robbers, lawless and desperate men of all sorts, congregate; men who are ready on any pretext to raise riots for the purpose of destruction and plunder." Strong spoke for growing numbers of his countrymen who feared that the unsettling changes urban growth had brought with it—socialism and labor unrest, spreading slums, waves of desperately poor Catholic and Jewish immigrants, and a new and freer morality—would tear apart the old Protestant republic. The Haymarket bombing, the sudden rise of agrarian radicalism, and the violent steel strike at Carnegie's mills in Homestead, Pennsylvania, in 1892 lent support to Strong's conviction that the nation was in deep crisis.

America was brewing "like a witches' kettle," wrote Frederick Jackson Turner, a young University of Wisconsin history professor. In a landmark essay he first read at a meeting of historians at the Chicago fair, "The Significance of the Frontier in American History," Turner added greater uncertainty to an already grave situation, announcing the closing of the frontier of free land, the nurturing source of American democracy and economic opportunity and a "safety-valve" for urban discontent. But this was also a decade of confidence and exuberant expansionism, and Burnham's celestial city—clean, orderly, safe, and spacious—was a reassuring expression of faith in the nation's future, a prophecy to millions who saw it of a new American Age, when all the large cities of the country would be made over in its image.

Even Turner ended his essay on the closing of the frontier on an uplifting note, befitting the theme of the exposition. "Since . . . the fleet of Columbus sailed into the waters of the New World, America has become another name for opportunity," and it would be "rash," he declared, to presume that the vitalizing characteristics of national life had run their course with the exhaustion of free lands. American energy would continue to demand "a wider field for its exercise."

To urban idealists like Daniel Burnham, that fresh territory of opportunity was the industrial city, the despair but also the great hope of American democracy. The White City symbolized the Chicago elite's conviction that industrial cities could be saved not by socialist planners or settlement-house reformers but by the civic-spirited leaders who had built them. "It's the Chicago business man's fair," exclaims a La Salle Street banker in Will Payne's novel *Mr. Salt*. "The business man—he did this!"

•

Another reason the White City was so reassuring to John Coleman Adams and others anxious about urban changes was that its architecture, like the majestic public buildings in the utopian city of Edward Bellamy's hugely popular novel *Looking Backward*, was traditional and familiar—what almost everyone thought a great city should look like. Yet while the emphasis was on formal order and ancient grandeur on the outside, on display inside the crowded main pavilions were the newest inventions of "an epoch of invention and progress" that the *Scientific American* called "unique in the history of the world."

This was the dawning of the Electric Age, and in the Electricity Building on the Court of Honor could be seen the work of the "wizards" who were inventing the future. "Light and power here reach their greatest development since the world began," declared the fair's chief electrician, Chicago's John P. Barrett. There were electric kitchens and calculating machines, electric brushes for relieving headaches, electric incubators for hatching chickens, electric chairs for "humane" executions, and what sightseers considered two of the marvels of the age by two of its technological heroes: Elisha Gray's telautograph for transmitting facsimile writing or drawings by telegraph—Victorian America's fax machine—and Thomas A. Edison's Kinetoscope, a peep-show device for viewing motion pictures on celluloid film. (That April, Edison had opened the world's first nickelodeon in Manhattan.) Fairgoers could see demonstrations of long-distance calls over Bell Telephone lines, and as they walked about the building, they were treated to live orchestra music transmitted over wires from New York and broadcast through a "mammoth telephone" suspended from the roof.

These inventions and discoveries were arranged to demonstrate the commanding social conceit of the age, the Idea of Progress. The popular orator John J. Ingalls described that idea perfectly: Walking through the exhibition sheds, "the most obtuse observer cannot fail to perceive that the path of humanity has been upward from the beginning; that every century has been better than that which preceded; . . . that man has advanced further and more rapidly in the last fifty years, than in the previous fifty centuries; . . . and that we are living in the best age of history and the most favored portion of the globe. We stand on the summit of time."

In Burnham's model city, tradition and change, order and innovation, were in perfect harmony, suggesting to people that they could enjoy all the benefits and conveniences of the coming technological age without changing their settled values and habits. Edison had invented the incandescent lightbulb in 1879, but to many fairgoers from farms and small towns electricity remained a mysterious, even frightening, force. In one of the dozens of novels inspired by the fair, Charles M. Stevens's *The Adventures of Uncle Jeremiah and Family at the Great Fair,* a farmer goes screaming mad and has to be arrested by security guards when he sees the Edison Tower of Light in the Electricity Building with its zigzagging, flashing bulbs "produc[ing] a pillar of fire" that looked to him like lightning torn from the sky. By giving the uninitiated a chance to examine the new electric devices up close and in action, the fair demystified electricity and helped create greater demand for its use. It soothed fears that ungoverned science was rushing mankind toward ruin, as Henry Adams argued after visiting the hall that housed the low-humming dynamos that provided electric current for the fair, three times the electric lighting power in use in Chicago at the time. "I used to be afraid that the government was all a goin' to pieces and that my fighting for Uncle Sam at Gettysburg was of no use," says Uncle Jeremiah, "but I ain't any more afraid of the world bustin' up. People that made the machinery that I've seen . . . have too much sense."

Sightseers who stayed on the grounds into the evening received an unforgettable display of the splendors of electricity in the nighttime illumination of the Court of Honor. The symmetrical outlines of the ghostly palaces were "etched in fire against the blackness of the night," one writer described the scene, while giant searchlights swept the basin and settled on the electric fountains, which shot up illuminated jets of colored water. A fireworks display lit the sky over the Peristyle, and electric boats, strung with lines of lights, streaked across the waters of the lagoon like swarms of fireflies. When the "millions of lights were suddenly flashed on, all at one time . . . [it] was like getting a sudden vision of Heaven," Hilda Satt of Halsted Street recalled the magical evening her father took the family to the fair, just a year after they arrived from Poland. That night, they were never prouder of America, "where all these wonderful things were happening."

In the crowd on one of these summer evenings was twenty-two-year-old Theodore Dreiser, who was covering the fair for a St. Louis newspaper. As the "black and motionless mass" of sightseers watched the water and light show, three Viking ships came drifting across the lagoon. "They were filled with singers," Dreiser wrote, "and as they neared the flaring waters their voices were uplifted in song." It was pure kitsch, but Dreiser and the crowd were completely taken by it. It was only when a whistle wailed announcing the lateness of the hour that the collective spell was broken. "Then the great enthusiastic mass tramped its way out and rejoiced that it had been fortunate enough of all the world's children to have seen such a display."

The crowds that lined the banks of the lagoons on these summer evenings were seeing more than an interesting entertainment. The show transported them to the Electric City of the approaching age, where "a blaze of lights" would banish the "fearful mysteries of darkness," one writer predicted, giving back the city's streets to decent folk. In the coming years, electricity would run America's factories and trains and heat its houses and businesses, said an engineer interviewed at the fair, clearing the air in its cities of grime and coal smoke.

•

This prophet was a thirty-four-year-old bridge designer from Pittsburgh named George Washington Gale Ferris. His big steel wheel on the Midway Plaisance, the exposition's commercially run entertainment strip, was the fair's only rival in popular appeal of the nighttime illumination and a foretaste of how technology would usher in a new industry of mass entertainment.

" 'What on earth is that?' is the first astonished inquiry that every passenger on the Illinois Central, the 'L,' and the steamship liner on the lake makes as soon as he gets his first sight of the Ferris Wheel," said the *Chicago Tribune*. "And he asks it from afar off, for the wheel is the landmark of the Fair."

Ferris got the inspiration for his invention from Daniel Burnham's challenge to American engineers to create something to outdo the Eiffel Tower, the chief exhibit at the Paris world's fair in 1889. Plans came in for a Tower of Babel forty stories high, with a different language spoken on each floor, for an aerial island supported by six giant hot-air balloons, for a replica of Dante's Hell, and for a range of man-made mountains, but Ferris was the only engineer to submit something both new and technically audacious, a proposal, as someone at the time described it, to put Eiffel's observatory on a pivot and set it in motion. He built his wheel in five months with his own money and assembled it in Jackson Park in June. When the 140-foot-high towers were anchored in concrete, the forty-five-ton axle—the largest piece of steel forged up to that time—was lifted into the sockets of the towers, and acrobatic construction workers pieced together the spiderweb of steel rods that held the wheel in perfect tension. When the 250-foot-diameter wheel was finished, it was ringed with three thousand electric bulbs.

Ferris took the first ride with his wife, Mayor Harrison, Bertha Palmer, the entire city council, and a forty-piece band. At the top of the wheel's revolution, a point higher than the crown of the Statue of Liberty, they could see the gray Gothic buildings of the University of Chicago and, in the distance, the tops of the skyscrapers of Chicago rising out of the smog and smoke.

"The World's Greatest Ride" was a carnival attraction to beat them all. More than 1.4 million riders paid fifty cents apiece for two revolutions in one of its thirty-six wood-veneered cabins, each larger than a Pullman Palace Car. But skeptics were persuaded of the wheel's strength and safety only when it withstood hurricane winds of a hundred miles per hour. Ferris, his wife, and a reporter rode out the gale in one of the cars. The windows shook, the blasts were deafening, but the wheel barely shivered as it made its slow, majestic orbit.

When the fair closed, the Ferris wheel appeared at two other sites before it was dynamited and sold for scrap metal. The forerunner of all entertainment wheels, it helped usher in the age of the amusement park. After visiting the fair on his honeymoon, George C. Tilyou ordered a wheel half the size of Ferris's and built his Coney Island Steeplechase Park around it. "We Americans," he told a journalist, "want either to be thrilled or amused, and are ready to pay well for either sensation."

•

The mile-long Midway was a place of eye-catching wonders. There was the exotic, the informative, and the just plain ridiculous—mosques and pagodas, German and Irish villages, Hindu jugglers, a young escape artist named Harry Houdini, boxing exhibitions by Gentleman Jim Corbett—the man who beat John L. Sullivan—an exhibit featuring a two-headed pig, an ostrich farm and an adjoining restaurant where the specialty of the house was an ostrich-egg omelet (made, actually, from the freshest midwestern chicken eggs), an International Beauty Show, Hagenbeck's Trained Animal Show, a giant panorama of the Swiss Alps, a dwarf elephant thirty-five inches high, and a model of Blarney Castle, where, for a charge, a customer could kiss a piece of the Blarney stone, which turned out to be a segment of Chicago paving block.

The Court of Honor was a pictorial and passive experience. In it you were a spectator—a student in a lecture hall—and many earnest sightseers sat on benches and took notes. The Midway, on the other hand, was a rousing urban drama, with fairgoers playing the parts of both actor and audience. People could play the clown on a camel in the Streets of Cairo exhibit, the fool in an Indian palanquin, or the child on the Ferris wheel, and observers spoke of a "Midway spirit," a sensation of "reason desert[ing] you when you entered the Plaisance."

It was "everyone with the brakes off," and it was an especially exciting place for children, none of whom was more thrilled to be there than eleven-year-old Franklin Delano Roosevelt, who made the trip to Chicago with his parents in his father's private railroad car.

The Court of Honor was too stiff and didactic for many of Chicago's working-class people, and the exhibits of modern machinery seemed too uncomfortably close to their lives. When Dreiser took his German-born father to the fair, the sullen and broken old man came to life only when they arrived on the Midway. Walking briskly, supported by a "stout stick," he exclaimed again and again, "By crackie! That is now beautiful!" The place he liked the most was the German village, where he had coffee and cakes with caraway seeds on them and "fell into a conversation with a buxom German frau who had a stand there and hailed from some part of Germany about which he seemed to know."

Burnham and the fair's Director of Decoration, Frank Millet, tried to counter the pull of the Midway by enlivening the White City. Frustrated by his failure to draw crowds of exhausted sightseers to his classical concerts in the stately "echo chamber" Charles Atwood had designed for his Exposition Orchestra, Theodore Thomas resigned as the fair's musical director in early August, recommending that for "the remainder of the Fair music shall not figure as an art at all but be treated merely on the basis of an amusevent." The exposition's directors were only too willing to oblige. Additional open-air concerts featuring the rousing military marches of John Philip Sousa were staged in the Court of Honor, and there were gondola regattas and swimming contests in the lagoon, tugs-of-war between various nationalities, donkey races, parachute drops, and tightrope-walking performances. But nothing rivaled the animation of the Midway, where a black pianist named Scott Joplin played a new kind of music called ragtime.

The impresario of the Midway was Sol Bloom, a twenty-one-year-old Polish-Jewish immigrant who had worked for Carter Harrison's election as World's Fair mayor shortly after arriving in the city from San Francisco, convinced that Harrison "personified Chicago" to the world. Originally, the Midway was to be a serious archaeology exhibit under the direction of Frederick Ward Putnam, director of the Peabody Museum at Harvard. But when Bloom was put in charge of installing the exhibits, he used his theater experience to turn it into the world's first amusement park, with Putnam's ethnological displays in a subordinate position. Putting Putnam in charge of the Midway, Bloom said many years later, was like making "Albert Einstein manager of the Ringling Brothers and Barnum and Bailey Circus."

Bloom loved Middle Eastern exotica and placed his Algerian Village and related exhibits in the most prominent places on the Midway, where they competed, to his delight, with other, more prosaic entertainments. Bloom's featured performers were North African women who performed the *danse du ventre*. "When the public learned that the literal translation was 'belly dance,'" Bloom recalled, "they delightedly concluded that it must be salacious and immoral. The crowds poured in. I had a gold mine."*

To combat such lasciviousness, the revivalist Dwight Moody organized a massive evangelical campaign that drew tens of thousands of fairgoers to his tent tabernacles, which spread out around Jackson Park like the camp of a besieging army.

•

The venerable black leader Frederick Douglass found something more seriously objectionable about the fair's exhibits: their near total exclusion of the accomplishments of over 8 million African Americans. Douglass attended the fair as the official representative of Haiti, where he had recently served as American minister, but except for the Haitian pavilion, the only spot on the grounds where blacks were in a prominent place was the Midway, where there was a grass-hut village of half-naked Dahomeyans on display as part of Putnam's ethnography project. The exposition's directors apparently wanted black Americans to be represented by the "barbaric rites [of] . . . African savages brought here to act the monkey," Douglass charged. In his anger he helped a young friend, Ida B. Wells, write and publish a pamphlet, *The Reason Why the Colored American Is Not in the World's Columbian Exposition.*

Ida B. Wells was one of the most remarkable Americans of her time. The daughter of slaves (her father was his master's son), she was born during the Civil War in Holly Springs, Mississipi, and educated in a missionary school run by northern abolitionists, her mother attending with her so that she could learn to read the Bible. When her parents and an infant brother were struck down by yellow fever, Wells, only sixteen at the time, took over the care and rearing of her five surviving brothers and sisters, lengthening her dresses to look older so that she could get a job in a country school six miles away. In 1882 she moved with her family to the home of a widowed aunt in Memphis and landed a better-paying job in that city's school system, writing a column for a small Negro magazine in her spare time.

*The famous entertainer "Little Egypt, the Darling of the Nile," did not, as some historians argue, appear on the Midway. She made her debut later at Coney Island.

Wells's political awakening came early and with sensational suddenness. Riding in the ladies' coach of a train, as she was accustomed to, she was asked by the conductor to move to the smoker, the car that local railroads were beginning to reserve for "colored folk." When Wells refused, she was dragged from her seat by three railroad men and carried out of the car, to the applause of the white passengers. Only twenty-one, she sued the railroad and won five hundred dollars in damages, but the decision was overturned by the state supreme court, part of a fast-building campaign of hate, terror, and apartheid that would persuade thousands of the South's best-educated young black people—the so-called Talented Tenth—to move to the North.

After this, Wells fearlessly fought injustice wherever she found it. In 1891 she became the editor and co-owner of the *Memphis Free Speech and Headlight,* the voice of the city's black community. The next year, when three of her friends were pulled from a jail cell and lynched by a mob for opening a grocery store in competition with a white-owned grocery, Wells organized a boycott of the city's new electric trolley system. Then she did the unthinkable, writing an editorial suggesting that many white women who were allegedly raped by black men—the standard southern excuse for lynching—had real feelings for these men. A mob destroyed her newspaper office, and Wells learned that a price had been put on her head. Exiled from the South and fearing for her life, she bought a pistol and made it known that if attacked, she would take down at least one of her assailants.

In her new position as staff writer for the *New York Age,* a prominent African-American publication, Wells organized a nationwide campaign against lynching. Determined to "give to the world the first inside story of Negro lynching," she had ten thousand copies of an explosive article she wrote in the *New York Age* distributed throughout the country. It gave names, exact dates, and places and prompted Frederick Douglass to organize a speaking tour for her in the Northeast. The following spring, Wells took her antilynching crusade to Great Britain, a slender, sharp-featured woman speaking to packed houses with unflappable composure, depending for effect on the facts themselves. On her return home, she went directly to Chicago to join Douglass, her new patron, with the idea of publishing a pamphlet protesting the exclusion of African-Americans from the greatest national celebration of the nineteenth century. When Douglass asked her where the money for the pamphlet would come from, conservative black leaders having condemned the idea, Wells said they would raise it in the Chicago Negro community.

•

The Great Migration of blacks from the Deep South to northern cities would not begin in earnest until World War I, but blacks had been living in Chicago since there was a Chicago. The black trader Jean Baptiste Point du Sable was probably the first non–Native American to settle on the site of Chicago, and when Chicago was incorporated as a town, a few blacks were among its first citizens. By the time the Illinois and Michigan Canal was opened, Chicago had an African-American community of fifty or so settlers, most of them fugitive slaves or free blacks from the East. On the eve of the Civil War this community had grown to about a thousand, its leaders active in the antislavery movement, offering their homes and churches as safe havens, or "stations," on the underground railroad.

Black migration to Chicago from the border states increased after the Civil War, but as late as 1890 there were only about fifteen thousand blacks in the city, a little over 1 percent of the population. Before the war, black Chicagoans had no civil rights that whites were obliged to respect. By the 1870s, however, blacks were voting for Republican candidates—electing their community's leader, the prosperous tailor John Jones, to the Cook County Board of Commissioners—and attending the newly desegregated public schools. In 1884 the Illinois legislature outlawed racial discrimination in public accommodations. Although blacks continued to be discriminated against in employment, housing, and, irregularly, in public accommodations, there was as yet no clearly demarcated black ghetto. Blacks lived in small neighborhood pockets, most of them on the South Side, close to yet apart from the white people the majority of them worked for as household or personal servants—or as janitors, porters, waiters, and dishwashers in such white establishments as the Palmer House. Because of their small numbers, they were not seen as a threat to community stability, nor did black laborers compete with whites for jobs in industry. Such jobs were reserved for whites only.

In their monumental work *Black Metropolis*, St. Clair Drake and Horace R. Cayton divide Chicago's end-of-the-century black community into three broad groups: "The 'respectables'—church-going, poor or moderately prosperous, and often unrestrained in their worship"; the "'refined people,' who, because of their eduction and breeding, could not sanction the less decorous behavior of their racial brothers"; and the "'riffraff,' the 'sinners'—unchurched and undisciplined," who were shunned by the two other groups. Most of the "refined people" traced their family histories back to the abolitionist movement, and many of them had been living in Chicago for some time and were of racially mixed heritage. Self-consciously genteel and educated at predominantly white schools, they were concentrated in the clergy and the professions and were integrationist in their politics, aggressively pushing for equal rights and racial assimilation. Their leaders were men like Dr. Daniel Hale Williams, the nationally known surgeon who was instrumental in founding Chicago's first black medical facility, Provident Hospital, and Ferdinand L. Barnett, a lawyer and journalist who founded Chicago's first black newspaper, the *Conservator,* in 1878. A militant crusader for black rights, Barnett was less condescending toward the "respectables" than others in Chicago's black elite. "Race elevation can be attained," he declared, "only through race unity."

It was to the women's church organizations of this Negro elite that Wells went for help in launching her protest pamphlet. She was received enthusiastically, for they had waged a spirited, albeit fractious, campaign to have black women represented on the fair's Board of Lady Managers, only to have the formidable Bertha Palmer appoint a white woman from Kentucky to "represent the colored people." With the five hundred dollars they raised, Wells and Douglass printed and distributed twenty thousand copies of their booklet. As Wells personally handed them out to visitors at the Haitian pavilion, she let it be known that over 235 blacks had been lynched the previous year, and not just in the South.

In 1893 the *Chicago Tribune* ran front-page stories of lynchings in the southern part of the state, and in the spring of that year, Chicago nearly had its first lynching. A black man involved in a fight on a streetcar with a white man, a fellow worker on the construction crew of the Columbian Exposition, was rushed by a mob and hanged by his neck from a lamppost in broad daylight in front of hundreds of witnesses, many of them screaming, "Lynch him, lynch the nigger." At that point, two Chicago policemen clubbed their way through the frenzied mob, firing their pistols in the air, and rescued the man. When they carried him to a nearby drugstore, the mob rushed the store and tried to smash through the door. Only when a patrol wagon filled with officers arrived on the scene did the crowd scatter.

•

Wells considered Frederick Douglass the greatest leader in American history, but she fiercely protested his decision to take part in organizing a special Colored People's Day at the fair, claiming it was being staged to ridicule Negroes, a claim given force when twenty-five hundred watermelons were provided for the crowd. Wells boycotted Colored People's Day, but Douglass, seventy-five years old and in failing health, stayed on the grounds and used the occasion to lash out at the U.S. government for its failure to protect blacks from discrimination and lynching. As he began to read his address, he was heckled by a gang of whites. His hands shook, his voice faltered, and he seemed about to succumb to the August heat. Then he pulled himself together, flung down his notes, and began speaking in his deep platform voice, "drowning out the catcalls, as an organ would a pennywhistle," a witness wrote later. "Men talk of the Negro problem," Douglass thundered. "There is no Negro problem. The problem is whether the American people have . . . honor enough, patriotism enough, to live up to their own Constitution. . . . We Negroes love our country. We fought for it. We ask only that we be treated as well as those who fought against it."

After reading about his speech in the morning papers, Ida Wells rushed to the Haitian pavilion to beg Douglass's forgiveness. He had done more to bring the concerns of black people to the attention of white Americans, she said later, than "anything else that happened during the fair."

In 1895, the year of Douglass's death, Ida Wells married Ferdinand Barnett, settled in Chicago, and took over her husband's newspaper so that he could enter politics. She attacked the accommodationist policies of Booker T. Washington and joined the fight against housing segregation in Chicago, which became more rigid after 1900. Her aim in life, she wrote just before she died in Chicago in 1931, was to "educate the white people out of their two hundred and fifty years of slave history."

To Ida Wells and Frederick Douglass, the fair represented a moral reversal, the reconciliation of North and South at the expense of black people. Douglass called the fair a "whited sepulcher," and that analogy carried over into areas other than its mistreatment of black people. Frederick Putnam organized impressive exhibits on the Midway of Native American life and handicrafts, but one of his staff, Emma Sickles, was fired when she publicly protested that the exhibits had been "used to work up sentiment against the Indian by showing that he is either savage or can be educated only by Government agencies. . . . Every means was used," she said, "to keep the self-civilized Indians out of the Fair." The federal government's Indian Bureau set up a model Indian school on the fairgrounds in an effort to dramatically contrast the image of the "long haired, blanket Indians" of Putnam's Midway encampments with the uniformed and Americanized Indian students of the government school.

The only place Native American participants in the fair had a chance to be anything like themselves was in Buffalo Bill's Wild West

Show, located in a covered area accommodating eighteen thousand spectators just outside the fair's gates. William Cody, as the Native American historian Vine Deloria, Jr., argues, treated the Indians in his show with respect and gave them a chance to escape reservation oppression and display their equestrian skills in the show's re-creations of warfare on the plains.

Inside the fairgrounds, however, more than a few of the estimated 8 million persons who attended Buffalo Bill's show read the caption for an Indian exhibit on the Midway, yet another expression—this one in racial terms—of the century's Idea of Progress. "The Winnebagoes from Wisconsin live in a house of bark and mat; the Penobscots of Maine have used birch-bark, and there are skin tepees, hogans, and other dwellings belonging to the various Western tribes. They are all in amazing contrast to the white palaces stretching away to the north, that evidence the skill and prosperity of their successors in this western domain." In a play on the same theme, the *Chicago Tribune* reported the return to the city of smoke and skyscrapers of a ragged group of Potawatomi whose ancestors had been expelled from Chicago only sixty years before. The story ran under the headline "Return as Freaks."

The impressive works of art, industry, and science on show in the Woman's Building "signalizes the emancipation of woman, who from her ancient condition of disgraceful servitude, has risen to be the equal and co-laborer of her former master," wrote Marian Shaw, a small-town reporter. The fair did give strong impetus to the women's movement, whose leaders played a critical role in pressuring Congress to create a Board of Lady Managers and to commission a separate Woman's Building designed by a woman architect. But the exhibits on display in Sophia G. Hayden's classically proportioned building emphasized woman's traditional roles as educator, housekeeper, and minister of the afflicted.

At the congresses on various world topics held throughout the summer in the future building of the Art Institute on Michigan Avenue, some of the country's leading reformers spoke, among them Susan B. Anthony, Jane Addams, Elizabeth Cady Stanton, Clarence Darrow, Henry George, and Samuel Gompers. But to suppress controversy, no questions from the audience were permitted, nor were speakers permitted to address each other. And in a fair that purported to present an urban utopia there were only two isolated examples of model workers' housing and no exhibits on the contributions of Hull-House, the country's leading laboratory for urban reform. In the White City, urban problems appeared only in the form of their proposed solutions, and the solutions were only for problems that could be "solved" by architecture and the industrial arts. That summer, Chicago itself gave visitors a vastly different picture of the urban prospect.

2. The "Gomorrah of the West"

"Chicago will be the main exhibit at the Columbian Exposition of 1893," Julian Ralph had predicted. "No matter what the aggregation of wonders there, . . . the city itself will be the most surprising presentation." In the time available to them, fairgoers took in what they could of this endless metropolis, shopping at its palatial department stores, taking "lightning" elevators to the tops of the tallest buildings in the world, riding out on the open-air trolleys to the Palmer Castle, flying along the boulevards and out along the blue-green lake—as Dreiser did—in a rented tally-ho, or taking bunting-decked excursion trains to the Union Stock Yards or to George Pullman's model town. For a pocketful of change, one could see almost everything of great interest in Chicago, and many of those who couldn't afford the "electrics" or the grip cars explored the city on foot.

Carl Sandburg of Galesburg, Illinois, did not get to see "the city of his destiny" until three years after the fair, when he was eighteen, but that first three-day visit, on his own, must have been something like the unrecorded visits to Chicago in 1893 of countless prairie boys like him who had never been more than fifty miles from home. Sandburg "walked miles and never got tired of the roar of the streets, the trolley cars, the teamsters, the drays, buggies, surreys, and phaetons." He walked every block in the Loop and stopped in front of the immense buildings of the *Daily News*, the *Tribune*, and the *Inter Ocean*. From the street he could feel the vibrations of the tremendous presses that were pouring out hundreds of thousands of papers for the long lines of delivery wagons waiting outside. "I had carried and sold so many of their papers," he later recalled, "that I wanted to see where they were made." He walked through the department stores on State Street he had heard so múch about and "dropped in at the Board of Trade and watched the grain gamblers throwing fingers and yelling prices." And he walked out to the Des Plaines Street police station and traced the route from there to where Bonfield's men were killed by an "'anarchist bomber.'" Standing on the site of the new police monument, he "wondered whether they would ever find out who threw the bomb."

He couldn't resist the Eden Musée on a shabby stretch of State Street, where he saw in wax Jesse James and several other desperadoes and a gruesome exhibit of what syphilis "does to your face." He ate mostly at Pittsburgh Joe's in the Loop, stacks of breakfast pancakes with piping-hot coffee for a nickel, steaming bowls of meat stew with all the bread you could eat for a dime. In the evenings he went to the vaudeville shows, sitting in the top gallery, where the seats were the cheapest.

The afternoon of his last day in the city he went to a taproom advertising a free lunch and helped himself to a big baloney-and-cheese sandwich, washing it down with a five-cent draft. "I didn't care much for the beer then, but I had heard so much about Chicago saloons and their free lunches and funny doings that I wasn't going to leave Chicago without seeing the inside of a saloon." As he was busy eating, a hard-faced young woman asked him if he was "lookin fer a good time?" Leaning closer, she told him she would be pleased to "polish" his "nailhead" for him. Pulling himself together, he told her he had only two nickels and that they wouldn't do her much good. With that, she cheerily jumped to the next table. "What those last two nickels were for I don't remember. I had seen Chicago on a dollar and a half."

•

For visitors to the fair with more cash and less traveler's courage than young Carl Sandburg, there were guidebooks offering point-by-point tours of the "Wonder City of the West." Most were works of mint-pure boosterism, but even these warned visitors to steer clear of certain unsavory neighborhoods and to be on the alert for slickers, pickpockets, footpads, and counterfeiters, who would be lying in wait for the innocent and the unwary at Chicago's tumultuous train stations. Papers carrying stories of crime and mayhem in Chicago went out by express mail trains to hinterland hamlets, giving expectant fairgoers who already considered Chicago the "Gomorrah of the West" more reason to heed the warnings of the guidebook writers. "If Old Carter Harrison's elected mayor," said an Indiana man, "I'm goin' to Chicago to the Fair, but I'm goin' to wear nothing but tights and carry a knife between my teeth and a pistol in each hand."

"The World's Fair was a gold mine for me and my friends during the years 1892 and 1893," recalled May Churchill, a prostitute and petty thief known as "Chicago May." "The first of those years we nicked the builders, the second the visitors. And what dreadful things were done by some of the girls! It always made me sick even to think of them." Chicago May was seventeen when she left the city the year after the fair closed, having completed what she proudly called her "high school in crime."

Hundreds of people who went to the Chicago fair were never heard from again, and police traced the trail of at least fifty missing women to the doors of a South Side rooming house run by an ordinary-looking doctor named Herman W. Mudgett, alias H. H. Holmes—forger, bigamist, swindler, and the most monstrous murderer in Chicago's history. Two years after the fair, during a sensational trial in Philadelphia, where police finally caught up with him, Holmes confessed to murdering twenty-seven people, and police close to the case believed he had killed as many as a hundred more women and children in 1893 at the Holmes Castle, the battlemented hotel he himself had designed. When police searched the place, they found trapdoors and hidden stairways, asbestos-lined crematoria chambers with gas pipes leading into them, fragments of human hair and clothing in the chimney flue, piles of human bones in basement graves, vats of acid and quicklime, a dissecting table with a box containing several human skeletons under it, and a mysterious-looking apparatus, apparently built by this man turned monster, that looked like a medieval torture rack. Another search located the bodies of two asphyxiated girls in a trunk. "Chicago, in the mind of the country, stands notorious for violent crime," wrote vice reporter George Kibbe Turner.

•

During the Columbian summer, many wary visitors stayed close to their hotels when they were not on the grounds of the exposition, some of them venturing only as far as the nearest camp meeting run by the urban evangelists of Dwight Moody, or perhaps by the rotund revivalist himself, the former Chicago salesman turned Christian huckster. Moody drew crowds of up to 150,000 people a week—most of them World's Fair visitors—to his circus-tent tabernacles on the lakefront and in the new wood-frame hotel district adjoining Jackson Park. At those meetings, solemn-faced, black-bonnetted women passed out pamphlets published by Frances Willard's Woman's Christian Temperance Union warning visitors away from Chicago's "Dark Places," which were luridly described. More than a few high-spirited country boys went to Moody's revivals just to get their hands on one of these unintended guides to the city's underworld. For maturer men who had come to Chicago expressly to taste its pleasures, there were guidebooks for sale at newsstands containing all the information anyone needed for an interesting evening on the town.

Harold Vynne's *Chicago by Day and Night* claimed that in the "Paris of America . . . all tastes may be promptly satisfied, all preferences catered to." Vynne, however, went no further than recommending a few tame—by Chicago standards—dance clubs, massage parlors, and racy theaters. The real guide to the city's fleshpots and sin centers was the anonymously authored *Sporting and Club House Directory*. Armed with a copy, a "gentleman" could find his way to "first class" sporting houses where he could expect to be entertained by plumed and perfumed women without fear of being rolled and robbed. That was the only reason most visitors needed a guidebook to Chicago's night life—to find out which places were "safe," for almost the entire vice trade was conspicuously concentrated in the Levee, a run-down neighborhood of low wooden and brick buildings between South State Street and the river, in the shadow of the city's skyscrapers. There "sex-starved men, from all parts of America," reporter Theodore Dreiser wrote, prowled the street from dark until dawn.

Chicago "makes a more amazingly open display of evil than any other city known to me," observed a London reporter. "Other places hide their blackness out of sight; Chicago treasures it in the heart of the business quarter and gives it a veneer." In the year of the fair, "there was no place in Chicago or the whole country which could compare with [the Levee] in depravity," declared Clifton R. Wooldridge, a Chicago detective who wrote a popular book about the hundreds of arrests he had made there. In a section called Hell's Half Acre, almost every paintless building and rotting shack was a saloon, a bordello, or a dice parlor, and "games of every description were conducted openly and in defiance of the law." Even police would not walk alone in this part of the Levee, where a notorious band of black female footpads, "Amazonian in physique," said Vynne, patrolled the alleys looking for "guileless" hicks. "Entering the district at midnight," Dreiser wrote of another section of the Levee called Little Cheyenne, "and wandering along the broken wooden pavements, ill-lighted by lamps and avoided by the police," a person would "tremble at the threatening appearance of the whole neighborhood." Dreiser's next story was of the place where hundreds of unwary visitors to this neighborhood wound up, the county morgue, temporary home of the "unknown dead."

Little Cheyenne and Hell's Half Acre were on the fringe of the Levee. The heart of the district was crowded, gaslit, and well patrolled by police, both the vice monarchs and the city having a stake in making it safe for free-spending out-of-towners. Detective Wooldridge described the circuslike atmosphere there during the summer of 1893: "Here at all hours of the day and night women could be seen at the doors and windows, frequently half-clad, making an exhibition of themselves and using vulgar and obscene language." Some houses of ill fame had extensions that had been built out into the streets so that the painted harlots could hang out of big swinging windows and exhibit themselves, playfully seizing the hats of men as they went by. "In these houses," wrote Wooldridge, "could be found every low and demoralizing phase of life that the human mind could think of. Many of these women were even lower than brutes."

Mary Hastings ran the most depraved houses in the Levee (she had four of them), advertising that no man could imagine an act of perversion that one of her girls would not perform. Hers were five-dollar houses, which only "heavy-hitters" could afford. The one- and two-dollar places were frequented by "simple horny" guys with "dusty shoes and derbies," a prostitute working at a typical cheap house wrote in her published memoirs. "They were Mamma and Papa fuckers, doing it mostly the straight and traditional American way, as they had been raised. . . . The Italian way, entering through the rear, was kind of a joke carried over from farm boys experimenting on themselves and each other, considered a sign of depraved city sinning."

It was in these kinds of places that a "john" was most likely to be robbed. Many of them were so-called panel houses. A customer would enter a prostitute's room, bare except for a bed and a single chair set against the wall. He would naturally hang his clothes on the chair, and when he was at the peak of preoccupation, a "creeper," peeking through a hole in the wall, would slide open a hidden panel just above the chair and pick his wallet and watch. Women employed by these houses also worked in teams with male hustlers at the badger game. A customer drinking alone in a bar would be given a knockout special (later called a "Mickey Finn" after a tough little Chicago saloonkeeper who would rob his customers after lacing their drinks with chloral hydrate and snuff water). He would then be carried, or escorted wobbly-legged, to a nearby flophouse. The woman would undress him and jump into bed with him. Minutes later an irate man would storm into the room claiming he was the husband and threatening violence or a lawsuit. Calming down, he would let it be known that he might be mollified by a financial consideration. Some prostitutes worked on their own. Chicago May would lure a "sucker" into a hotel room and, when he was undressed, steal his "wad," toss his pants out the window, and fly down the stairs.

The big out-of-town spenders and Prairie Avenue "sports" only frequented the safe and expensive New Orleans–style bordellos, arriving and leaving in brilliant carriages, as many as twenty of them at a time parked in one block of the Levee. The best of these gilded houses was Carrie Watson's. For the fair, Watson remodeled her converted mansion on South Clark Street and doubled the number of women on her payroll. Her house had five luxurious parlors and twenty bedrooms of rococo elegance, the walls hung with expensive paintings and tapestries, the floors covered with thick Belgian carpeting. Guests were served chilled wine in silver goblets by silk-gowned women, while a small orchestra played discreetly in the background; there was a billiard room and, in the basement, a bowling alley and shower baths. There were no blinking red lights over the door, no evidence whatsoever on the outside that this was anything but a regal men's club. But the expensive-looking proprietress did have a sense of humor, parking near the door a caged parrot trained to say, "Carrie Watson's. Come in, gentlemen."

•

There was something for everyone in the Levee, a teeming bazaar of sin. For those who couldn't afford even the one-dollar houses, there were squalid basement bagnios, twenty-five-cent "cribs," and free-lancing streetwalkers. A surprising number of street solicitors were "occasional" prostitutes, young women mostly, who lived alone or with other single women in the new furnished rooming houses that began to replace family-style boardinghouses, with their communal parlors, common meals, and house curfews. These "casual" prostitutes worked in knitting mills, shoe factories, and department stores by day and "hustled" several nights a week, often with their roommates, to help meet living expenses and buy some of the fine clothing and jewelry they made or sold for wages of five and six dollars a week.

Most of these street seducers took their customers to a cheap hotel, charging them for the room plus a dollar or so for a quick sexual fix, but a number of them worked on commission for houses of prostitution. In a large department store in the Loop, the head of the dress-making department was the manager of a parlor house in the Levee, recruiting the seamstresses who worked for her to sell themselves at night.

"Occasional" prostitution was the product of massive urban change. In the last two decades of the nineteenth century, the number of women in Chicago's workforce grew to approximately three times the national rate of increase, peaking at the time of the Columbian Exposition. In 1893 nearly every incoming train brought young women from small towns seeking lives for themselves in the city; women like Sister Carrie and Rose of Dutcher's Coolly probably outnumbered young men like Dreiser and Garland from these same towns. Roughly one in five of Chicago's working women lived apart from family and relatives, "women adrift," moral reformers began calling them. "Industrialism," wrote Jane Addams, "has gathered together multitudes of eager young creatures from all quarters of the earth as a labor supply for the countless factories and workshops, upon which the present industrial city is based. Never before in civilization have such numbers of young girls been suddenly released from the protection of the home and permitted to walk unattended upon the city streets and to work under alien roofs."

These homeless young women became objects of concern for settlement workers and moral crusaders. "Little Lost Sisters," they were supposedly driven cityward and into a life of sin by family destitution, broken homes, and abusive husbands and fathers. Hardships or abuse did cause some young women to enter a life of prostitution, and there were cases of women who were lured or kidnapped into the trade by procuresses like Mary Hastings and their "cadets," who worked the trains and towns of the Midwest. Some of these young women were locked in rooms and "broken in," a process that often involved rape and other forms of physical brutalization. But the evidence compiled by vice crusaders suggests that the "vast majority of women entered prostitution more or less voluntarily," as historian Ruth Rosen argues, seeing prostitution as an "easier" and more lucrative way of surviving in the city than working behind a store counter or a typewriter. Most prostitutes who talked with Chicago vice investigators posing as whores or customers insisted that they had voluntarily chosen their profession, however limited their employment options may have been. They refused to see themselves, as the moral reformers did, as innocent victims or urban "orphans." They enjoyed the freedoms and pleasures of the city, and there were worse forms of exploitation for women, some of them said, such as being married to a wife beater. Many of the women "find [prostitution] more pleasing and preferable to their married lives," claimed a Clark Street madam.

The fortunate prostitutes landed in the finer houses, where they were paid as much as three times what a salesclerk working twice as many hours a week earned and where they could dream of someday becoming a madam. Before the trade began to be taken over in the early 1900s by male pimps and organized crime, a successful Chicago madam ran a high-priced house much like the manager of a small business, recruiting the women herself or through procuresses, setting and enforcing the terms of employment, paying doctor and hospital bills, keeping the books, hiring and managing cooks and housekeepers, paying off the police and aldermen with money and house "markdowns," and counseling the girls, some of whom called her Mother. The better assignation houses were run by professionals in a disciplined and discreet fashion. Vina Fields, a black woman, had the biggest brothel in Chicago, employing over seventy prostitutes in 1893, "all colored, but all for white men." Her rules and regulations—

posted in every room—"enforce decorum and decency," wrote an impressed William T. Stead, who interviewed her at her place, "with pains and penalties which could hardly be more strict if they were drawn up for the regulation of a Sunday school." Carrie Watson, "the capitalist of her class," rode around town in a white carriage with bright yellow wheels, driven by a black coachman in scarlet livery, and she had a higher tax assessment than some of the members of the Board of Trade who frequented her place.

But Watson and Vina Fields, who supported her daughter in an expensive convent school, were the exceptions—as were their well-paid and pampered girls. Some broken-down prostitutes earned as little as three to five dollars a week and were regularly roughed up, robbed, and raped by police and street thugs. "These vile . . . prostitutes . . . who infested [Little Cheyenne] all led a strident if beggarly or horrible life," Dreiser wrote, describing them, as many others did, as "sows and termagants—wretched, filthy, greasy, swining things." In perhaps the majority of cases, the outcome of a life of prostitution was death, death from venereal disease or a butchered abortion operation, from physical mistreatment, drinking, murder, suicide, or drug addiction.

Prostitutes were likely to become alcoholics, drug addicts, or both. Cocaine, opium, and morphine (heroin was not discovered until 1898) could be obtained over the counter in drugstores and tobacco shops, and even through mail-order catalogs—fifty cents for enough opium to keep an addict supplied for up to three weeks. Streetwalkers would "shoot up" cocaine with a long hypodermic needle, called a gun, right out in the open in the Levee, and along its streets were basement opium dens where a pipeful of the drug could be obtained for a quarter or a fast sexual favor. Opium smoking was believed at the time to be the particular pastime of the Chinese, but Detective Wooldridge claimed that around 65 percent of the "criminal classes, both men and women, black and white, either smoke or use the drug in one form or another." Even the women in the plush parlor houses would spend their mornings drinking coffee laced with morphine or "opium cordials," which were regularly prescribed by physicians to all classes of patients, even children, for headaches and colds. The serious drinking and drug consumption began after nightfall and ran on until four or five in the morning.

Selling sex was not a crime in Chicago or in any other American city in the 1890s. Police were paid off by madams not to protect an illegal business but to refrain from raiding a legal one on a trumped-up charge, such as running a "disorderly house." Chicago's crusading newspapers rarely mentioned prostitution. After 1900, reformers,

ministers, and moralists would mount a tremendous nationwide campaign against prostitution aimed at "annihilating" it, a campaign fueled by lurid, wildly exaggerated reports of "white slavery." But
prostitution was quietly tolerated in the 1890s because it strangely
complemented Victorian morality. It was seen as a necessary evil,
"necessary," as a writer put it in 1892, "in ministering to the passions
of men who otherwise would be tempted to seduce young ladies of
their acquaintance." A man's powerful sexual drive, it was argued,
could not be eradicated, and if suppressed, was likely to manifest itself in dangerous ways. A segregated vice district "is really a protection," claimed one vice report, "to the morality of the womanhood of
the city, for without it rape would be common and clandestine immorality would increase." In this view, the prostitute was a "protector
of the home," accommodating male sexual needs that no respectable
woman could or would.

Gambling was another matter. It was illegal, and the purifiers went
after it hard. Under heavy public pressure, Carter Harrison ordered
well-publicized raids on dice halls and faro houses before the fair
opened. Later that summer, however, the raids stopped (except for a
few against places not protected by Harrison's political loyalists) when
fairgoers began flocking to the Levee. Interviewed by a *Tribune* reporter after one of the mayor's earlier symbolic raids, a gambling-
house proprietor spoke for most of his colleagues in crime: "It's only
one of the 'Old Man's' bluffs. We have arranged to do a good business
during the World's Fair and nothing can prevent us." Gamblers could
speak with such confidence because that summer they enjoyed the
protection of a new syndicate organized by two shrewd opportunists
who would remain the "Lords of the Levee" into the era of Al Capone:
"Bathhouse" John Coughlin and Michael "Hinky Dink" Kenna.

•

Chicago's First Ward, embracing the Loop, the Levee, and Prairie
Avenue, was the "overwhelming influence in Chicago politics," said
Sol Bloom, who stayed in the city after the fair to lay the groundwork
for his fortune. "The wealth of the city was concentrated there. So was
the underworld. The men who controlled the First Ward controlled
Chicago." That was not exactly right. Kenna and Coughlin would
never run Chicago, but in controlling the First Ward for almost half a
century, they controlled what Bloom correctly called one of the "richest municipal loot-bag[s] in the land."

Coughlin and Kenna started their climb to power in 1893, just when
it appeared that Coughlin's budding career in politics had come to a
disastrous close. A florid, bull-necked native of County Roscommon,

John Joseph Coughlin was brought up in a tough Irish settlement just east of the Chicago River, where he joined a gang headed by Billy Lorimer. The Great Fire wiped out his immigrant father's grocery business, forcing Coughlin to get a job to help support the family, a change in circumstance he claimed he never regretted. "I'm glad that fire came along and burned the store," he is reported to have declared on one of the anniversaries of the Great Fire. "Say, if not for that bonfire I might have been a rich man's son and gone to Yale—and never amounted to nothing!"

Early in life, he landed a job as a rubber in a Clark Street Turkish bath frequented by politicians, gamblers, jockeys, and touts, the kind of men who were likely to spend the entire night there after a roaring time on the Levee. Although a bit slow-witted, Coughlin was amiable and eager to please, and with the help of a well-connected First Ward saloonkeeper, he opened his own bathhouse in 1882, with steam cabinets, tin-lined tubs, rows of cast-iron cots, and a staff of rubbers and attendants. Through talking with customers, he developed a lively interest in politics, and his political friends, in turn, saw him as a "comer." He was a man of his word, he could keep a secret, and he never forgot a name. "Chesterfield" Joe Mackin, the flamboyantly corrupt First Ward boss, appointed him as one of his precinct captains, and he rose to become president of the neighborhood Democratic Club. He bought his first racehorse and began dining at expensive restaurants. And with new power and prosperity, he put on weight, waxed the tips of his mustache, combed his hair in a high, glistening pompadour, and began wearing the outlandishly loud attire of the racetrack crowd—lavender silk shirts and hats, crimson ties, checkered swallowtail coats, pink gloves, and yellow patent-leather pumps, outfits, in Dreiser's words, that were "almost a blare of sound." One night at Billy Boyle's chophouse, a gathering place of Democratic deal makers, he met Rep. (later U.S. senator) William Mason, who passed on to him advice he would live by: Never take big money. Stick to the "small stuff." It's safer.

A man on the rise, "he was impressive to behold, he was popular and he was dumb enough," said Sol Bloom, "to do what he was told without thought (of which he was incapable) or questions (which would never have occurred to him)." After years of faithful service to the First Ward Democratic machine, he was put up for alderman in 1892 by the gang at Billy Boyle's, his election virtually assured by the organization.

Coughlin would represent his ward for forty-six years, but in 1893 his freshly fashioned career nearly came crashing down when he made the worst political mistake of his life, opposing Carter Harrison in the mayoralty race, believing the old warrior was finished in politics. After the election, when Harrison began raiding the gambling places that counted on Coughlin for protection, a helpless and distraught "Bathhouse" considered quitting politics. A visit to the Workingmen's Exchange, the combination saloon and dice parlor of his acquaintance Michael Kenna, changed his mind.

"He is a compact, upright little man, with iron-gray hair, a clear blue eye, and a dry manner," H. G. Wells described Kenna after visiting his saloon, where he was served the largest schooner of beer he had ever seen. Although Wells claimed he "would as soon go to live in a pen in a stock-yard as into American politics," he found the poker-faced, tight-lipped Kenna "a straight man, the sort of man one likes and trusts at sight."

Kenna and Coughlin had much in common. They had grown up not far from one another, two hardscrabble kids who had to earn their keep and who entered politics as underlings of Joe Mackin, reputedly the first to introduce the saloon free lunch to Chicago. And both were, as young Chicago reporter Harold Ickes noted, "cash value realists. Politics was their living, their fortune—yes, their very lives." But whereas Coughlin "was bumbling and inept, [Kenna] was adroit," said Bloom. "Where John was loudmouthed, Hinky Dink was discreetly silent. Where John jumped in with both feet, [Kenna] walked on tiptoe. Together they were almost unbeatable."

When Kenna summoned Coughlin to his barnlike saloon in the late spring of 1893, he presented him with a proposition. Kenna was already on good terms with Harrison, and if Coughlin could make peace with the mayor, Kenna told him, the two ward leaders might be able to form a syndicate to provide protection from Harrison's raids.

After Coughlin personally declared his loyalty to Harrison, the raids stopped. Tourism was the real reason, but Kenna and Coughlin, having ideally timed their partnership, took full credit. Then they moved quickly to bring together the First Ward's brothel keepers and vice lords and establish, under their control, a defense fund—a pool of protection money that would be made available to any of the partners to the agreement who fell into trouble with the law. For this protection, saloonkeepers and brothel managers were forced to buy their property insurance, liquor, and groceries from companies controlled by Coughlin and Kenna and, after Kenna was also elected to the city council, to contribute heavily to the two aldermen's campaign chests.

In return for their loyalty to Harrison—and later to his son when he was mayor—Kenna and Coughlin were given freedom to run their rackets without a hint of discretion. In the course of their long control over the First Ward, they were accused of illegal activities by nearly every newspaper in Chicago and every reform organization that appeared after 1893. But they were never prosecuted. They knew too many big fish, both inside and outside government, and they had followed Billy Mason's advice to leave the "big stuff" alone.

Writing at the end of a long life, Ben Hecht gave his theory as to why Chicago exhibited such "epic indifference" to its villainous politicians: "The good-citizen majority looked on the wrongdoers as a sort of vaudeville, more entertaining than harmful. They watched these vaudevillians bilk the town, batten on its vices, and their virtuous citizen hearts applauded furtively. The parlors and bedrooms in which honest folk lived were (as now) rather dull places. It was pleasant, in a way, to know that outside their windows, the devil was still capering in a flare of brimstone."

3. Stories of the Streets and of the Town

Chicago's reporters were as enthralled as their readers with the low life of the Levee. Ben Hecht covered the First Ward for the *Journal,* the "spectacle" reminding him of autopsies he had watched in the coroner's office. "Here . . . were the insides of the body politic, with all its interlocking evils visible, and its diseased tissues on display." George Ade and his journalistic partner John T. McCutcheon lived in a seedy rooming house not far from Little Cheyenne, and the two of them liked to get together with Clifton Wooldridge, a spectacular braggart, to hear about his exploits as a crime smasher. When Lincoln Steffens came to Chicago in 1903 looking for a big story for *McClure's Magazine,* he went directly to the Workingmen's Exchange, where Kenna and Coughlin "launched into tirades against the reformers who were messing up everything in Chicago." Steffens would write a career-making piece about these new-style reformers, as tough as the bosses they battled, but left Chicago thinking he might have covered the wrong story. "The wide-openness of protected crime and vice fascinated my bulging eyes," he wrote in his famous autobiography. "How our readers would have liked the stuff I was seeing! The New York Tenderloin was a model of order and virtue compared with the badly regulated, police-paid criminal lawlessness of the Chicago Loop and its spokes."

Ade and other young reporters found in the city hundreds of characters and hidden-away dramas that no American had written about realistically before the 1890s. "If you want to keep tabs on the human race," Ade said of his move from rural Indiana to Chicago, "you must go where the interesting specimens are assembled." The World's Fair was "grand, glorious," Ray Stannard Baker wrote his father in St. Croix Falls, Wisconsin, but behind its "gilded glories" was a tale of discontent and desperation, of upstanding families that had to steal coal to stay alive. He was beginning to write that more important story, he told his conservative father, a former army officer who had directed the pursuit of John Wilkes Booth. "Any one could write of what was going on at the World's Fair," he observed later; "few took the trouble to describe what was going on behind the scenes."

For Baker's generation of writers, the city *was* reality, and the deepest reality was its underreported underside. It was to the city that young writers went for what Stephen Crane called their "artistic education," and the best place to get a close-up view of urban life, while preparing for a literary career, was the big-city newsroom, one of the most interesting places in the world at the end of the nineteenth century. Fast-rising reporters like Crane, Baker, Steffens, Dreiser, Ade, Jack London, Frank Norris, and Jacob Riis gave the country its first true picture of the most compelling of all creations of the nineteenth century, the wildly expanding industrial metropolis.

•

When Ray Stannard Baker arrived in Chicago in the summer of 1892 after dropping out of the University of Michigan's law school, he was nearly overpowered by the brutal vitality of the place. Wearing a brand-new suit and carrying his suitcase so tightly his hand hurt, he made his way from the train station to North State Street, where he rented a hall bedroom for three dollars a week. It was not much larger than the closets of his family's home, and the single gas lamp was placed so high on the wall that he had to stand on a chair to read by its dim light. But none of this mattered to him, "for this 'was The City: the dirty, clamorous, uncomfortable, wicked, fascinating city I had heard so much about. This was the real thing!"

He had come to Chicago expecting to land a job on Victor Lawson's *News-Record,** the best-written paper in the city, but when he went to the paper's offices, he was told by the city editor that Chicago was overrun by young reporters eager to make their reputations by cover-

---

*This paper was the morning edition of the *Chicago Daily News,* owned and operated by Victor Lawson. Its name had been changed from the *Morning News* to the *News-Record* in May 1892. Soon after, the name was changed to the *Chicago Record.*

ing the World's Fair. In desperation, Baker pulled out his diploma from Michigan Agricultural College and unrolled it on the editor's desk. Big, crusty Harry Yount disdainfully waved it away with a sweep of his hand but advised him to hang around the city room to see if anything opened up. Baker got assignments covering weddings for the society editor and went to fires and murder scenes with the reporters he respected, "eager to help them, still more eager to watch what they did and how they did it."

He could hardly have had a better learning experience. Lawson's paper had the most talented group of reporters in the city, perhaps the country. Finley Peter Dunne and George Ade were just coming into prominence, as were Brand Whitlock, afterward a successful novelist, mayor of Toledo, and minister to Belgium under Woodrow Wilson; Frank Vanderlip, who became a powerful figure on Wall Street; Will Payne, the novelist; and Charles Seymour, widely respected for his courage in the Indian Wars on the Great Plains.

"The most famous of them all" and the man he most wanted to meet was Eugene Field, a gaunt, glum-looking eccentric who dressed in wrinkled sack suits and wore open-backed bedroom slippers around the office. After Baker began to get regular work on the paper, he got to know his literary hero. Both were book lovers, given to browsing in secondhand shops looking for rare finds on dull, rainy days. Their favorite place was McClurg's, run by Gen. Alexander C. McClurg, a scholar and Civil War veteran whose wife was the niece of William Ogden. Field went there almost every day at noon to sit and talk with a group of friends in a cozy area he dubbed the Saints and Sinners' Corner; and in the evenings, Baker would see him at Billy Boyle's chophouse, where Field liked to hobnob with gamblers.

The two never became friends, however. Field was in failing health and held himself separate, and Baker was then a dim "asteroid" in the "editorial firmament" of which Field was "the bright particular star." Several years later, Baker would attend Field's funeral and write his memorial article in the *Record.*

Field had been a regular at the Press Club, formed by Melville Stone, Victor Lawson's original partner, as a place to swap newspaper gossip and play poker. By the time Baker arrived in town, the Press Club had given way to the Whitechapel Club, which was made up mostly of younger reporters and editors like Dunne, Seymour, Whitlock, Ade, McCutcheon, Charles H. Dennis, Baker's managing editor at the *Record,* and Opie Read, an enormous, disheveled character who published his humorous weekly *The Arkansas Traveler* in Chicago. Baker was not well established enough when Dennis hired him full-time in late 1892 to be invited to join, but he heard plenty about what Opie Read called "the world's most fantastic institution."

Named after the London site of Jack the Ripper's murders, the club met in rented rooms in Newspaper Alley, behind the *Daily News* building. The club's front room had a bar that appeared to be a coffin, and the walls were decorated with grisly trophies—human skulls donated by an alienist at the county insane asylum, murder weapons and hangmen's ropes passed on by Chicago policemen, and blood-drenched blankets that Charles Seymour brought back from his coverage of the Sioux Wars. What little light there was in the rooms came from gas jets placed inside the skulls hanging on the walls. After a member's initiation, he was served a quart of ale in a silver-lined skull.

The members liked to play pranks on famous out-of-town guests like Theodore Roosevelt, but their most outrageous spoof was the cremation on the shores of Lake Michigan of Morris Allen Collins, a rum-soaked, would-be poet who was the sole member of his own Suicide Club. When Collins eventually did himself in with an overdose of morphine, a group of Whitechapelers claimed his body at the morgue, placed it in a pine box, and escorted it by train to the Indiana Dunes. There they built a twenty-foot-high pyre for Collins's body, lit it with torches, and marched around it in hooded black robes, chanting dirges. Not far away a group of folks from Miller, Indiana, looked on in bewildered silence. The money for the coffin, the rail tickets, and the liquor that enlivened the evening had come from James W. Scott, editor of the *Chicago Herald,* in return for exclusive rights to the story. The next day, the story covered the entire front page of his Sunday edition and made the front page of the *New York Times* as well.

George Ade called the Whitechapel Club "a little group of thirsty intellectuals who were opposed to everything." Though mostly young in years, they had seen enough of big-city life to be able to report it without cant or sentimentality in tough, spare language. Newswriting that preached or instructed or lapsed into the melodramatic was viciously attacked by Whitechapel "sharpshooters," the best of whom was Finley Peter Dunne. After club members scorched one of Opie Read's folksy novels, he stormed out and never returned. The late-night talk around the club's coffin-shaped bar became a testing field for some of the best reporting in the city as club members began writing more for the approval of each other than for their city editors. And Ade recalled picking up leads for his column in these spirited conversations, talk "of the streets and of the town, stories of Chicago life."

The club's bloodcurdling decor symbolized its members' mental immunity to the shocks of urban life, almost an occupational necessity for a big-city reporter. As Ray Stannard Baker began covering slum life and murders, he noticed a change in his outlook, "[a] strange detachment even under the most horrifying or shocking circumstances." Covering a grisly murder in a German neighborhood on the West Side, he found himself inspecting the slaughterhouse-like crime scene with the hardened indifference of the police, examining the mangled body and the pools of blood on the floor and talking without emotion to a distraught witness. Only after the story was published—and this became a pattern with him—did he begin to feel something about what he had seen and been able to describe with cold clarity.

Chicago's toughness turned Harold Ickes—later one of the most powerful men in the country under Franklin Roosevelt—into "a realist," he wrote of his journalistic apprenticeship. "I became cynically wise to the selfishness and meanness of men when their appetites are involved." In *Newspaper Days*, Dreiser's story of his life as a reporter, he drew a distinction between the "moralistic" point of view that reigned in the editorial offices of the Chicago papers and the "pagan or unmoral character" of the newsrooms. "People make laws for other people to live up to," he remembered his news editor, John Maxwell, telling him, "and in order to protect themselves in what they have got. They never intend those laws to apply to themselves or to prevent them from doing anything that they want to do." This was a view that Dreiser came to share.

Chicago's reporters were part of a newspaper revolution. Breakthroughs in printing, communication, and transportation—larger and faster presses, the introduction of the linotype machine, photoengraving, the typewriter, the telephone, the reduction of postal rates and the growth and improvement of the nation's rail system—made it possible to gather the news, print it, and get it out to half a million readers in twenty-four hours. Newspapers also became bigger, with daily editions of up to a hundred pages and fat Sunday editions that were the print sensation of the 1890s. They also became better. "There are better reporters in America than anywhere else in the world," said an English journalist in 1893.

Only a century after all newspapers were printed on wooden presses, American metropolitan newspapers were big businesses, the rivals in influence and reach of the age's gigantic industrial combinations. Their operations were housed in multistory downtown buildings whose electric lights burned through the night and whose giant presses roared like thunder. The size, tempo, and clamor of these great high-speed operations mirrored that of the city itself, and everything about the urban newspaper became enormous except the price of a copy, two cents in 1893, a penny two years later.*

Behind these changes in newspaper production and distribution was a greatly enlarged and more diverse urban readership. Only 223,000 of Chicago's population of just over a million in 1890 were children of native-born white parents. To capture a share of this potential audience, newspapers had to be lively and entertaining as well as accurate, and they had to appeal to a bewildering range of tastes and preferences and to a large body of readers who were not yet fully American or confidently modern. The great urban dailies of the late nineteenth century contained society as well as self-improvement columns, sports coverage and coverage of the financial markets, reviews of popular theater and of the symphony, and an exploding number of human-interest and advice departments.

It was through their daily paper that many immigrants learned the English language—and learned how to be American. "A gr-great panorama in life is th' daily press," says Mr. Dooley. "Here ye' can meet kings, imp'rors, an' prisidents, . . . an' larn to tak th' knife be th' handle, not the blade, whin 'atin' spinach." As the city became incomprehensively large, the newspaper—which began covering everything that happened in town—replaced gossip as the chief source of information about community life. "He who is without a newspaper," declared P. T. Barnum, "is cut off from his species."

Newcomers to Chicago wanted stories about provincials like themselves struggling to push ahead in the devouring city. They wanted stories dealing with the familiar features of neighborhood life and with the scaled-back dreams of plain Joes and Janes who lugged their lunch to work. They wanted stories told with animation and humor. And what they wanted they got. "Unlike our competition," declared Melville Stone, a pioneer of the new journalism, "we must with single-mindedness accept as our masters, our readers."

This led to what Ray Stannard Baker called the "pick-up story," a glimpse of everyday city life, often told in story form, with a mixture of light and sober reporting. To collect material for these urban sketches, reporters—the foot soldiers of the new journalism—had to get out into parts of the city they had rarely covered before, and when they brought

---

*The *Chicago Daily News* had been selling for a penny a copy since the paper was launched in 1876. Other Chicago papers did not follow its example until 1895. The one-penny policy was part of a circulation war in Chicago, and it lasted there for only three years.

back their stories, they had to fight late-breaking news for space in the paper sheerly on the basis of the quality of what they wrote. The best practitioners of the new art of urban portraiture, chief among them Field, Ade, and Dunne, were given columns of their own on the editorial page. These features were almost exclusively of Chicago. That is what made them interesting to ordinary readers—and to more than one aspiring urban novelist.

Later in his life, Dreiser recalled the powerful pull of Eugene Field's "Sharps and Flats" column: "These trenchant bits on local street scenes, institutions, characters, functions all moved me as nothing hitherto had. For to me Chicago at this time had a peculiarly literary or artistic atmosphere." In 1890 nineteen-year-old Dreiser was working as a collection agent for a merchant dealing in lampshades, clocks, and shoddy bric-a-brac, and as he walked around the city, he dreamed of making wonderful word pictures of it: "Its smoke pall, fogs, rains, snows, blizzards—with people bending their bodies low against shrieking winds!" That, too, was the secret dream of another Eugene Field disciple, Ray Stannard Baker, who saw his work as a local reporter as preparation for the writing of a novel that would "present a complete picture of American life" as it had "burst upon" him since he arrived in Chicago from rural Michigan.

When Dreiser finally found work as a cub reporter at age twenty, a lean, bespectacled lad dressed in a new spring coat, his hair combed in a pompadour, he saw cards pasted on the walls of the newsroom shouting: Accuracy, Accuracy! Who? What? When? Where? How? He learned soon enough, however, that editors wanted more than the bare facts. They wanted stories with the authenticity and atmosphere of the best modern fiction. "Write it strong, clear, definite. Get in touches of local color, if you can," and remember Dickens and Hugo, Zola and Balzac, for "scenery" and "descriptive force," Dreiser remembered one of his city editors barking at him.

After Dreiser wrote his story on Little Cheyenne for the *Daily Globe*, John Maxwell told him that he might be cut out to be a "writer and not just an ordinary newspaper man. . . . A hell of a fine novel is going to be written about some of these things one of these days," Maxwell added. Dreiser would write that Chicago novel. But before *Sister Carrie* appeared in 1900, George Ade and Finley Peter Dunne gave back their city exactly as they had experienced it in the 1890s, creating—in a wonderful string of stories—some of the first Chicago literary characters that are completely alive. Dreiser, Ade, and Dunne were able to get the city right because, as city walkers, they had seen every part of it. "I knew my Chicago twenty-five years ago," Ade wrote at age fifty, "and it was some laboratory!"

•

George Ade was drawn to Chicago as if by destiny. His earliest memory of life in Kentland, Indiana, a town of six hundred with four saloons, was of sitting on a fence on an October night and staring at "a blur of illumination in the northern sky." It was Chicago, eighty miles away, "burning up in a highly successful manner."

Nineteen years later, at the age of twenty-four, he left his job as an advertising writer for a Corn Belt patent-medicine firm to join John T. McCutcheon, his Purdue fraternity brother, on the staff of Victor Lawson's morning paper. His trial assignment was reporting on the weather, and he went at it with the exuberance of someone covering the archbishop's elopement with a call girl. Blessed with a sharp eye and what McCutcheon called "an X-ray insight into motives and men," he was soon doing front-page stories—the Homestead Strike, the Democratic Convention of 1892, and the John L. Sullivan–James J. Corbett fight in New Orleans, "the fight of the century," San Francisco's "Gentlemen Jim" knocking out "the Boston Strongboy" in the twenty-first round. One month after his sensational "you are there" account of the fight, he was assigned by Charles Dennis to cover the World's Fair, beginning with its October dedication. He was to have his own column, "All Roads Lead to the Fair," to be illustrated with pen-and-ink drawings by McCutcheon. When the fair closed, Ade and McCutcheon were given their own permanent column, which appeared on the same page of the *Record* as Field's "Sharps and Flats."

They were Chicago's first roving reporters, at loose in the city, free to cover anything that excited their interest. "Tagging along after George, he chronicled and I illustrated," McCutcheon recalled, "almost every phase of Chicago's life and activities," making a faithful record of these things for the "future historian."

In "Stories of the Streets and of the Town," Ade experimented with a number of literary forms: dialogue, the short story, light verse, and fables, writing by hand on big yellow sheets, never using a "galloping typewriter." The best of the stories fused genial satire—usually the playful deflation of rural ignorance and big-city pretensions—with sharply etched portraiture of places and people as precisely detailed as a Flemish painting. And the writing was clean and compact. No other American of that time wrote about so many aspects of city life. Ade's subjects were Pullman porters, Prairie Avenue coachmen, and Polish immigrants, waiters, detectives, peanut vendors, millionaires, tugboat captains, office clerks, architects, household maids, shopgirls, and barbershop bootblacks. He wrote about boardinghouse life and the lives of freaks in State Street's dime museums, about Chinese laundries and the Jewish junk shops of Canal Street. His particular genius, however, was in capturing that parcel of humanity he knew best: small-town hopefuls trying to push their way up in the big town.

Like Balzac, Ade loved simple subjects, and he was a gifted social historian because he took a stronger interest in what makes people common than in what makes them uncommon—and because of that painter's proclivity for pinpoint detail. He held a mirror up to Chicago, and his readers saw themselves in it. He introduced these same readers to their own city. His stories became so popular that the *Record* published eight editions of them in paperback form.

It was one of these collections that caught the attention of William Dean Howells, who thought it the best study of city life in the American West he had yet read. For a time, Howells believed George Ade might be the one to produce the "great American novel," but Ade squandered his promise by going after the money. In 1900 he left the *Record*, where he made sixty dollars a week, and began writing fables in slang for a syndicate "wizard," earning over a thousand dollars a week as his "share of the conspiracy." He became further sidetracked when he began writing successful dramatic and musical comedies for the Broadway stage. "The show shops had me hooked," he wrote, "and the syndicate wouldn't let go of me, and between the two I was constantly incited and urged to do the most dreadful things to the English language." Then, in 1905, the chronicler of Chicago life moved to a four-hundred-acre estate, Hazelden Farm, fifteen miles from Kentland; a blanket Indian, he referred to himself, returning to the reservation. He loved his life there, throwing big fried-chicken picnics on football afternoons for his old Purdue classmates and playing golf on his gorgeous private course. In his advancing years, he admitted, without rancor or envy of others, that he had fallen short. "While some of us have been building chicken coops, or possibly, bungalows, Mr. Dreiser," he hailed the writer who stole a scene from one of his Chicago stories for the opening of *Sister Carrie*, "has been creating skyscrapers."

Ade was being far too modest. As a Chicago reporter he had been a pioneering urban realist, with a magnificent ear for the American language as he heard it spoken by ordinary people on the city's streets. His friend "Pete" Dunne, who would become the most widely read and quoted journalist of his time, had the same gift. Ade focused his camera lens on the middle walks of life, his characters feeling "their sense of difference from the mass, the great unwashed," James T. Farrell remarked, "as a quality of their own self-esteem," while Dunne was the first American to transform part of "the great unwashed"—Chicago's Irish—into the subject of literature. He was the biographer of Bridgeport, "the Boswell of the Sixth Wa-ard," his paper called him.

•

Finley Peter Dunne—he added his mother's name after her death—was the wonder boy of Chicago journalism, rising from cub reporter to city editor by the age of twenty-two. He and Ade were nearly opposites in temperament and appearance. Ade was genial and soft-spoken; Dunne, vindictive and explosive. Ade dressed neatly but simply; Dunne wore beautifully tailored suits and smoked flat Turkish cigarettes. Ade was temperate; Dunne, a prodigious drinker. They shared, however, an antipathy, in Ade's words, for "social show-offs, bigots on religion, fanatics on total abstinence, and all persons who take themselves seriously." And Dunne, too, saw himself as a chronicler of the "inconsequential."

"I know histhry isn't thrue," Mr. Dooley teels Hennessy, his favorite customer, "because it ain't like what I see ivry day in Halsted Sthreet. If any wan comes along with a histhry iv Greece or Rome that'll show me th' people fightin', gettin' dhrunk, makin' love, gettin' marrid, owin' th' grocery an' bein' without hard-coal, I'll believe they was a Greece or Rome, but not befure. Historyans is like doctors. They are always lookin' f'r symptoms. Those iv them that writes about their own times examines th' tongue an' feels th' pulse an' makes the wrong dygnosis. Th' other kind iv histhry is a post-mortem examination. It tells ye what a counthry died iv. But I'd like to know what it lived iv."

Dunne was a Chicagoan to the bone, born and brought up in the city. Once, when asked if he was a Roman Catholic, he replied, no, he was a Chicago Catholic. The child of famine-generation immigrants, he grew up on the West Side, under the steeple of St. Patrick's Church, where his uncle Dennis had been the first pastor. His father made a solid living in the lumber trade, and his bedridden mother would read aloud to him from Dickens, Thackeray, and Scott. He took no interest in school, however, and graduated last in his high school class. In despair, his father helped him get a job as a copyboy for a small Chicago paper. Street-smart and terrifically bright, he was rapidly promoted to police reporter. Four years later, after working briefly at the *Daily News,* he became a city editor at the *Times,* the youngest newspaperman to hold such a position in the history of Chicago journalism. He worked on other papers, always moving up, writing "picturesque stories," a colleague recalled, "that were a mirror of Chicago life." In

1892, as an editor on the *Chicago Evening Post,* he wrote his first story in Irish dialect.

His main character, Col. Malachi McNeery, was modeled on James McGarry, the round, rosy-faced owner of a public house frequented by reporters, athletes, and actors, "the best club in town," McGarry used to say, "not exclusive minje but refined." But when McGarry complained to Dunne's publisher, also a regular, that he was being ridiculed in Dunne's hilarious acount of McNeery at the fair, Dunne shipped the colonel back to Ireland, moved the liquor shop from the Loop to Bridgeport, and in the fall of 1893, just as Ade was beginning to write his "Stories of the Streets and of the Town," introduced the wisest fool in American writing.

Stout, balding Martin J. Dooley follows in the newspapers the successes of the lace-curtain Irish, the kind of people, as he would have said, who have fruit in the house when no one is sick. But his neighbors and customers are gas workers and cops, precinct captains and slag shovelers, people bound to the village ways of Bridgeport, with its yearly round of parish fairs, St. Patrick's Day parades, and baseball matches and brawls at the local dump. The Bridgeport of his taproom tales is the first imaginatively realized Irish-American neighborhood in American literature. A deep-dyed fatalist, sentimental yet cynical—"Trust everybody," he is fond of saying, "but cut the cards"—his running history of his Chicago tribe is a struggle of clan and family survival, with little help from outsiders. What the city really needs, he tells Hennessy, is a "social colony" like Hull-House built near the Board of Trade to bring rich bankers in contact with "poor an' honest people," not a settlement house to teach the poor how to behave like polite plutocrats.

Martin Dooley is Irish from cap to toe but is realistic enough to see the need for ethnic coexistence. He complains about the invasion of the "Huns" and brags about getting even with a "Polacker" by rolling a keg of beer at him and breaking his leg, but in a conversation at the bar about the Pullman Strike, he proudly tells of a struggling Irish family that gives a loaf of bread and a ham to Polish neighbors who are even worse óff than they are. "But what's it all to Pullman," Mr. Dooley declares as he rotates his rag on the bar. "He cares no more f'r thim little matthers in life an' death than I do f'r O'Conner's tab. 'Th' women an' childhren is dyin' iv hunger,' they sa-ays. 'They've done no wrong,' they sa-ays. 'Will ye not put out ye'er hand to help thim?' they sa-ays. 'Ah, what th' ell,' says George. 'What th' ell,' he sa-ays. 'James,' he sa-ays, 'a bottle iv champagne an' a piece iv crambree pie. What th' ell, what th' ell, what th' ell.'"

After the typesetter had run off the proof of this column, he passed it around the composing room. When Dunne stepped into the room, the typesetters began drumming their sticks on their cases. Dunne remembered it was the most moving experience of his life.

His Mr. Dooley column allowed Dunne to say things in print he could not say in another part of the paper. John R. Walsh, the banker who owned both the *Chicago Herald* and the *Evening Post,* was "nervous about libel suits and loans at banks that were interested in the franchises for sale in the council," Dunne later explained why he began writing in Irish dialect. "It occurred to me that while it might be dangerous to call an alderman a thief in English no one could sue if a comic Irishman denounced the statesman as a thief. . . . My victims did not dare to complain. They felt bound to smile and treat these highly libelous articles as mere humorous skits."

The purpose of a newspaper, Mr. Dooley declares, "should be to comfort the afflicted and afflict the comfortable." He then tells why the newspapers are "a gr-reat blessing" to him: "[The] papers opens up life to me, an' gives me a speaken' acquaintance with th' whole wur-ruld." A crucial part of that world outside Bridgeport for Dooley and his taproom regulars is the rising and falling fortunes of their local heroes, the Chicago White Stockings.

•

Chicago went "baseball crazy" in the 1880s, when the local nine, led by player-manager Adrian "Cap" Anson, the most feared slugger of the nineteenth century, won five National League pennants in seven years. The stands were packed for nearly every game, hundreds of amateur clubs were organized, makeshift diamonds were marked out in chalk on the wooden streets of ethnic neighborhoods, and the likeness of Mike "King" Kelley, the fleet-footed outfielder and "fancy man" who loved the nightlife on the Levee, appeared in saloons and pool halls all over the city. In the winter of 1888–89, the club went on a barnstorming world tour with a group of all-stars, playing one game in the drifting sands in front of the great pyramids, with several hundred Egyptians looking on and pouncing on every ball that came near them. The players left Chicago as the first "foreign apostle[s]" of the Columbian Exposition. On their return they were met at Union Station by a "howling, yelling mob" and led by a thousand bicyclists—the night sky lit up with bursting rockets and Roman candles—to a civic celebration at the Palmer House.

At a New York City banquet honoring the touring Chicago team, Mark Twain declared that baseball "is the very symbol, the outward and visible expression of the drive and push and rush and struggle of the raging, tearing, booming nineteenth century." The sport became even more popular in 1893 when the National League introduced Sunday baseball. This allowed factory and office workers on six-day schedules to get out to the park. That year, Chicago opened a new ball-park on the West Side, seven minutes from the Loop, with a double-deck grandstand with folding armchairs, a row of fifty-six private boxes for club officials and dignitaries, and five thousand uncovered seats, at a quarter a seat, for mill hands and office clerks in brown derbies and shirtsleeves.

The White Stockings were an expression of the forces that were making Chicago a great city. Baseball, like Chicago, was made possible by the railroad, which linked competing cities together; the telegraph and the telephone, which put fans in touch with their teams through the daily newspapers; and cable cars and electric trolleys, which brought fans from all over the spread-out city to the park. The White Stockings were run, as was Chicago itself, by prominent capitalists; two of the biggest of them—Potter Palmer and George Pullman—were original backers of the team. The Chicago club and the league it belonged to were largely the creations of William A. Hulbert, a prominent coal dealer. Hulbert's partner and successor as club president, the team's former player-manager, Albert Goodwill Spalding, called him "a typical Chicago man. He never spoke of what *he* would do, or what *his* club would do, but it was always what *Chicago* would do." As he once told Spalding: "I would rather be a lamp-post in Chicago than a millionaire in any other city."

Hulbert and Spalding ran their club as George Pullman ran his company town, part of their plan to make baseball "respectable," "honorable," and morally elevating. Under the terms of the reserve clause, proposed by them and adopted by the entire league, a player's services were "reserved" for his entire career by the team that "owned" him. Players were seen as commodities to be bought and sold and exploited whenever possible. When Spalding took complete control of the team after Hulbert's death in 1882, he hired detectives to shadow his players to make sure they stayed out of saloons and out of trouble with women or the law. "In fighting the encroachments of drink upon the efficiency of individual players," he told a reporter in 1887, "we are simply striving to give our patrons the full measure of entertainment and satisfaction to which they are entitled." That same year, he required the entire team to sign Frances Willard's temperance pledge. Two years later, he established a "salary cap" of twenty-five hundred dollars.

Players who refused to follow club policy were fired and blacklisted, their careers ruined. When rebellious players seceded from the National League and formed a players' league, club owners labeled them "anarchists," and Spalding led a swift and successful effort to crush the league and preserve the reserve clause. "Baseball as at present conducted," Cap Anson said at the conclusion of his career in 1897, "is a gigantic monopoly, intolerant of opposition and run on a grab-all-there-is-in-sight basis."

By that time, A. G. Spalding was baseball's "Big Mogul," as the press called him. He also owned a Chicago-based sporting-goods business that made him a millionaire. Spalding was a typical Chicago success story, an Illinois country boy who became the greatest pitcher in the game, and then, by his own accounting, "the father of American baseball." He ran both his team and the National League with an iron hand. In his private box above home plate in Chicago's new stadium, he had a gong to summon servants and a telephone, linked with the dugout, so he could call down instructions to Cap Anson. His personal motto—"Everything is possible to him who dares"—could have been Chicago's as well.

In the spring of 1887 Finley Peter Dunne had been assigned by the *Daily News* to cover the White Stockings. He was only twenty years old, but his reports transformed American sports journalism. Up to that time, most newspapers simply printed the box scores of games or, at best, dry-as-dust accounts of them. Dunne, along with Charles Seymour of the *Herald*, his road companion, filed stories that thundered to life—play-by-play accounts filled with picturesque lingo, slang, and simile, colorful and humorous reports about the on-and-off-the-diamond antics of the players.

Dunne helped make players like Cap Anson into America's first sports heroes and is credited with coining the expression "southpaw," for in Chicago's park, a left-handed pitcher delivered the ball to the plate from the south side. Soon all Chicago papers were following the lead of the *News* and the *Herald*. By 1893, nearly every paper in the city had a sports editor with a small staff, usually made up of apprentice reporters right out of college. One of them, Harold Ickes, got his start covering the football games of his alma mater, the University of Chicago.

Dunne and Ade made their reputations as reporters covering sports and the fair, but it is in Dunne's columns that we find the first embracement in American writing of big-city living. Ade saw the city perfectly but could never feel completely comfortable in it. His uprooted prairie folk find their only satisfaction in Chicago in small settings and situations that are redolent of home. "The dentist was in the city, but not of it," he writes also of himself. "The Indiana part of him insisted that any woman who drank a glass of beer in a public garden thereby degraded herself." Dunne's Bridgeporters, on the other hand, are, as he was, inalterably urban. Bridgeport might be a little piece of Ireland, but Martin Dooley has no desire to return to the home soil. "We live in th' city," he says of his family, "where they burn gas an' have a polis foorce to get on to. We're no farmers. . . . We belong to th' industhreel classes," people who are awakened in the morning by the milkman, not by the sun or a servant.

A number of young writers who read Dunne's column, Dreiser among them, thought that he might be the one to write the great Chicago novel. Those who knew him well, however, knew he never would. Ray Stannard Baker described his friend after Dunne left Chicago in 1898 for New York to turn Mr. Dooley into a commentator on national affairs: "He loved to talk—if the company was right. He loved so much to talk that he was likely to talk away all he had to say and it was with difficult and infinite procrastination that he got anything down on paper." Lincoln Steffens, who worked with both Baker and Dunne on the staff of *The American Magazine,* was more direct. "I never knew a writer who made such a labor of writing; he seemed to hate it; he certainly ran away from it whenever he could." And money seduced him, as it did George Ade. Both writers began to be paid too much for their "fables in slang" and Irish witticisms to give them up. "He was like me," Ade wrote of his friend, "in that popularity was thrust upon him, and he was marked for all time as a specialist in the production of a certain freak sort of 'humor.'"

So Dunne remained a sprinter, whereas Dreiser went on to become a long-distance runner. Yet they were alike in small but interesting ways. Both gained their first real education on Chicago's streets and in its newsrooms and both found poetry in the most unlikely places. One of Dreiser's finest newspaper pieces is an appreciation of the foul-smelling Chicago River—"the smallest river doing the largest business in the world." He loved to stand on its iron bridges and watch the soot-covered tugs pass under him, their propellers tearing the water into "splattering fragments." So did Peter Dunne. "Manny's th' time I've set on th' bridge . . . watchin' th' light iv th' tugs dancin' in it like stars," he has Mr. Dooley speak for him. "'Twas th' prettiest river f'r to look at that ye'll iver see." People claimed it was unhealthy, Dooley goes on, but "th' Chicago river niver was intinded as a dhrink. It didn't go ar-round advertisin' itself as a saisonable beverage! . . . It had other business more suited to it."

When Dunne and Ade and Dreiser covered the fair, their reportage mirrored what they found most striking in the city itself. They were more interested in the crowds than in the buildings, in the reaction of ordinary people—"thim that was n't annybody,"—to the vast spectacle and "wonderland." Ade's stories are about straw-hatted rural families on holiday, many of them for the first time; Dunne's columns are about McNeery and his cronies riding the Ferris wheel and drinking beer at the Irish Village; Dreiser's dispatches to the *St. Louis Republic* describe gondola parties on the lagoons and an evening at Buffalo Bill's Wild West Show.

Long after the fair closed, Mr. Dooley would reflect on its significance to the people from his part of town. He had heard, he tells Hennessy, that the fair gave a great impetus to architecture. "Ivrybody that was annybody had to go to live in a Greek temple with an Eyetalian roof an' bay-windows." But the people he knew had all but forgotten the Court of Honor, "an' whin ye say annything to thim about th' fair, they say: 'D'ye raymimber th' night I see ye on th' Midway? Oh, my!'"

•

The fair had been built at a time of rising hope and prosperity, but its final act took place in an atmosphere of economic crisis and labor upheaval. In the fall of 1893, as the nationwide depression that had begun earlier that year deepened, thousands of the unemployed demonstrated for bread and jobs outside the exposition grounds, on the downtown lakefront, and in front of the Board of Trade building. Club-wielding police cleared the lakefront parks of homeless drifters, and a special detachment of plainclothesmen was ordered to arrest "toughs and thugs" walking the streets at night in an effort to check an alarming rise in holdups. At a labor meeting on the lakefront attended by over twenty-five thousand protesters, Samuel Gompers, Henry George, and Clarence Darrow demanded that the city provide jobs and relief to the hungry. Carter Harrison tried to blunt the impact of the lengthening depression with public works spending, hiring men at a dollar a day to sweep the streets. The greatest Chicago public works project was the fair itself, and Harrison petitioned Congress to keep it open into November and to reopen it the following spring for another season.

Speaking on "All Cities Day," the second-to-last day of the fair, Harrison declared it a disgrace that millions of Americans would not get to see "the greatest of all world's fairs." It almost sickened him, he said, "to think that it will be allowed to crumble into dust." It was his last public appearance. Later that day, he was murdered by the "wild-looking" man Ray Stannard Baker had seen the year before creating a disturbance at a meeting of the Chicago Single Tax Club. "His name is

Prendergast, " Baker was told as he turned to look at him at the back of the hall, "we can't keep him out." Sometime later, Baker would witness his hanging.

Out of respect for the mayor's memory, the pageantry scheduled for the fair's final day was canceled. At sunset on October 30, a cannon salute and the lowering of a weatherworn American flag signaled the official closing of the World's Columbian Exposition.

Harvard's Charles Eliot Norton gave the fair its epitaph: It was the "United States on show, both in its real aspects and in its potentialities." It mirrored its beauty and its vulgarity, its order and its confusion, its unity and its gaping divisions, its industry and its artistic imagination, its present perils and its prospects. In 1893 the fair and Chicago itself symbolized all that the country was and could be. Both were expressions of American civilization at a time of crisis and opportunity.

15

After the Fair

1. If Christ Came to Chicago!

THE day after the official closing of the fair, over seventy-five thousand people came to Jackson Park for one last look at the grounds. In the crowd was William T. Stead, who had arrived in the city from London that very morning. The most celebrated reporter and moral reformer in the world in 1893, he had come to America to study its newspapers. His stop in Chicago changed his plans and ultimately the city itself.

The Court of Honor amazed him; never, he said, had he seen anything more magnificent than its "great palaces of staff." When he learned that they would be torn down, he swung into action. Told by city officials it would be too expensive to save them, he went to see Ernest R. Graham, Burnham's chief assistant, and Graham assured him that it would cost a mere twenty-five thousand dollars to physically preserve the main pavilions as "architectural monuments." Stead took his findings to the papers and began a campaign to save the exhibition halls and to move the largest of them, the Manufactures Building, to a vacant downtown site along the lake and transform it into a People's Palace, a center for conventions, public exhibits, and civic pageants. Stead's efforts to save the White City drew him into a larger cause, nothing less than the "civic and social regeneration" of the "Black City."

Stead found Chicago the most interesting city in the New World. "It is the only [American] city which has had anything romantic about its recent history. The building of the city, and still more its rebuilding, are one of the romances which light up the somewhat monotonous materialism of Modern America." He had never encountered a city with greater promise—or problems. The civic reformers who had done so much to refashion the physical and cultural environment of Chicago had passed over the immense social problems that the current economic depression was compounding, making Chicago, in his view, a cesspool of corruption and human misery. Stead proposed to change that, with the help of the churches, the labor unions, and the "syndicate of millionaires" that ran Chicago and had, up to now, neglected its Christian duty to the poor. To incite action, Stead searched for facts to back his jeremiads. They were not hard to find. Chicago was a city about to explode.

"What a spectacle!" Ray Stannard Baker wrote of Chicago during that terrible November. "What a human downfall after the magnificence and prodigality of the World's Fair. . . . Heights of splendor, pride, exaltation, in one month: depths of wretchedness, suffering, hunger, cold, in the next." It was a public emergency that reminded older Chicagoans of the one that followed the Great Fire.

The fair had helped to hold off the full impact of the depression, but when it closed, the floor fell out of the local economy. "Furnaces went out of blast, smelters shut down. Mills closed for repairs and never opened," Will Payne wrote in his novel *Mr. Salt.* The army of workers that had built and run the fair were "thrown back into the trades" when the economy was collapsing and there was no place for them. Thousands of them roamed the streets, unable, on some nights, to afford a urine-soaked mattress in a ten-cent flophouse. As a night reporter, Baker saw the conditions on the wintry streets long after comfortable Chicagoans had slipped into their beds. The depression, he wrote dispassionately, "gave me overwhelming material." He interviewed policemen assigned to guard mountains of heating coal from the marauding poor, Italian women who were evicted from their Halsted Street tenements and forced to put their babies into county orphanages, and sullen men, their collars turned up, their shoulders hunched, who walked the streets in an aimless search for temporary work or a handout.

Late one bitterly cold night he followed some of these men to city hall, which the government had made available as a refuge for the homeless. As he stepped into the dimly lit corridor, he was "all but overwhelmed by a rush of hot, heavy, fetid air." Stopping just inside the door, he saw that "every inch" of the stone floor of the corridor was covered with men sleeping on newspapers, their wet shoes serving as pillows. With the heat turned up, their unwashed bodies gave off an odor worse than that of the stockyards. Several blocks away, at the Harrison Street police station, William Stead, on a nocturnal investigation of his own, came upon a similar scene, slumbering men "pigged together literally like herrings in a barrel, . . . a pavement of human bodies" in a dark basement corridor that separated two long rows of jail cells. By day, these tramps were "like the frogs in the Egyptian plague," Stead wrote. "You could not escape [them], go where you would."

Robert Herrick described that desolate winter: "The city's huge garment was too large for it; miles of empty stores, hotels, flat-buildings, showed its shrunken state. Tens of thousands of human beings, lured to the festive city by abnormal wages, had been left stranded, without food or a right to shelter in its tenantless buildings." It would turn out to be the worst depression up to that time in the country's history. Unemployment rose to 3 million, by one estimate, and over 150 railroads and sixteen thousand other businesses, including the Illinois Steel Company, shut down. In Chicago, 20 percent of the workforce was laid off in the winter of 1892–93, and at least 10 percent of the population was pushed to the brink of starvation every day, many families saved only by fleet-footed children who were sent out, sometimes in gangs, to steal fuel and food. Every week, "Hinky Dink" Kenna fed thousands of men in his Workingmen's Exchange, knowing that the favor would be repaid up the line. Stead visited Kenna's saloon and a number of others and came away convinced that, whatever their motives, the saloonkeeper-politicians of Chicago, unlike the "predatory rich" and most of the city's churches, were practicing the "fundamental principle of human brotherhood which Christ came to teach."

When the *Record*'s city editor learned of Stead's investigations in the slums, he sent Ray Stannard Baker to cover him. "He was a fiery orator," Baker wrote, "with strong religious convictions, a virile, sturdy man with a bushy red beard and unusually large blue eyes, set widely apart." Baker was impressed by his fervor and investigative tenacity but found his repeated references to religion annoying. "What would you say if Christ came to Chicago?" Stead asked him in one of their meetings, a note of vehemence in his voice. "And what do you think He would do? . . . What do you think He would say and do if He walked down through Custom House place and saw the houses of ill-fame in that neighborhood?" And what would He say about the rich who refused to hear the cries of the starving poor? These questions were the themes of a remarkable civic meeting Stead convened at his own expense on November 12, 1893.

"Such a gathering Chicago had never seen before and is not likely to see again," reported Graham Taylor, a professor at Chicago Theological Seminary. The floor and galleries of the Central Music Hall were "thronged by men and women of all grades, races, sects and conditions." On the stage, corporate kings sat shoulder to shoulder with labor leaders—one of them Samuel Fielden, the recently pardoned Haymarket anarchist. There were women temperance reformers and saloonkeepers, judges and gambling bosses, "matrons of distinguished families and notorious 'madames' from houses of ill fame," all of them there at Stead's invitation. "Some of the women who came in quietly and took their places had not been to Sunday services in a long time," observed Baker.

Stead, the son of a Congregationalist minister, announced that he had called the meeting to discuss "whether if Christ came to Chicago he wouldn't find anything in Chicago he would have altered?" The answer was in the question, and Stead proceeded to assail nearly every person and institution of consequence in the city. He even attacked the churches and the temperance groups. He had been in the Levee district until 3:00 A.M. that morning talking with saloonkeepers and madams, and he declared that if he were a homeless wanderer he would rather take his "chances" with these people "than with some persons in your churches and chapels." Listening from his seat onstage, Graham Taylor felt that Stead, "at white heat, denouncing preventable evils, . . . [rose] to the stature of one of the Hebrew prophets."

When Stead finished, the hot-tempered socialist leader Thomas J. Morgan took the podium and thundered: "If you well-to-do people do not listen [to] . . . the pleadings of editor Stead . . . may someone blow you out with dynamite." At that, the audience rose as one, some persons cheering wildly, but most of the others hissing and shaking their fists at Morgan for daring to raise the specter of another Haymarket. It took all of Stead's persuasiveness to quiet the hall and secure the passage of a resolution designating a committee, which included Jane Addams and the millionaire temperance reformer Turlington W. Harvey, to form a Civic Federation to drive Satan from Chicago, as Stead put it. The model for this reform organization, Stead declared, should be none other than Tammany Hall. "The work for Christ must be done with as much astuteness and shrewdness as is used in the political intrigues of New York politicians." Stead then ended the meeting by leading a rousing chorus of "America, the Beautiful."

At this revival-like gathering, Stead had spoken of the need for "a comprehensive report of the conditions of evil in Chicago," the text to serve as the platform of the new civic coalition. The next day, he caught a train to Toronto, intending to leave Chicago for good, but returned a short time later to write the bill of indictment he had called for from the stage of the Central Music Hall. He finished his five-hundred-page book in February 1894 in a room in the Auditorium Building.

The publication of *If Christ Came to Chicago!* rocked the city. "Existing evils are exposed fearlessly," wrote the *New York World*, "and the chief abettors are named without regard to persons or consequence." It was, the paper said, "the most sensational book of the decade. The cover was perhaps even more controversial than the contents. It was a reproduction of a painting of an angry Jesus driving the money changers from the temple. The faces of the money changers were transformed, however. One of them was that of Charles T. Yerkes, another was the face of the leader of the local gas trust, a bag of coins under his arm, and the other faces were recognizable caricatures of some of the biggest political and business leaders of Chicago. "There are plenty more who ought to have gone in," Stead told Baker, "but we didn't have room for them." To add to the public outrage that greeted the appearance of the book, its frontispiece was a map of the Levee district, color-coded to indicate saloons, pawnbrokers, and brothels; and in the appendix Stead boldly listed the addresses, proprietors, and tax-paying owners of property in the city used for indecent purposes. For days before the book was published, news of its cover, its "map of sin," and its list of vice landlords swept through the city, Baker recalls, "like another Chicago fire." Seventy thousand copies of the book the *Tribune* said was "too vile a thing to be touched by the fingers of decency" were grabbed up on publication day.

If Christ Came to Chicago!, a fantastic and ultimately frightening fusion of radical religion and politics, became the catalyst—although not the blueprint—for a movement to clean up Chicago. Most of the book's demands were too ill defined or far reaching to become the foundation for a realistic reform movement. In the book's final chapter, Stead presents a gleaming vision of twentieth-century Chicago, "the model city of the world." An "oceanic canal" has connected the St. Lawrence River to the Mississippi, making Chicago "the greatest seaport in the world," and the canal waters descending from the lake provide power for enormous turbines that drive all the machinery in the city. The air over the city is clean, and the lakefront has been laid out as an aquatic park and promenade, a fitting site for the white-marble buildings that are being readied for the imminent transfer of the federal government to "the continental center."

The city council is run by the "best citizens," skyscrapers have been turned into cooperative housing projects, railroad grade crossings have been eliminated, and utilities, and even department stores, have been socialized—reforms set in motion by the city's first twentieth-century mayor, Bertha Honoré Palmer. White-uniformed sanitation crews scrub the streets every evening, every ward in the city has its Hull-House, and saloons have been replaced by government-run cafés serving only beer and light wine. Most remarkable of all, the churches of the city have become branches of a central "Church of Chicago," which acts as the community's moral arbiter. "If any spiritual or moral evil occurs . . . the whole of the massed force of the associated churches can be depended upon to assist in its removal." In working-class neighborhoods, these churches have stained-glass concert rooms, where "grimy, brawny" workers, eating out of lunch pails, listen to organ recitals. No citizen in the moralized city need worry about crime or public avarice, less because of legal punishment or religious censure than because of the universal spread of a single civic and moral code—Stead's own.

Even before his book was published, several newspapers attacked Stead as a demagogue. "I'd much rather be a demagogue than a Brahmin," he shot back, for a demagogue was at least in touch with the people. "It is only necessary that the demagogue should be moved by right ideas." But Chicagoans of influence were less interested in Stead's reform ideas than they were in his suggestion that the civic movement be led by the "best men and women in the town." In the end, Chicago was not converted. Indifference did give way to action, but the new Civic Federation was made up of municipal-minded millionaires and the ministers and reformers they were used to working with, with the labor unions left out. It was a coalition not likely to overthrow a social system Stead found rotten to the core. The organization's first president was Lyman Gage, and its leaders were Marshall Field, Jane Addams, Ellen Henrotin, Melville Stone, Franklin MacVeagh, Willian Rainey Harper, Jenkins Lloyd Jones, Rev. Frank Gunsaulus, Cyrus McCormick, Jr., Harlow Higinbotham, Graham Taylor, and, of course, Bertha Palmer.

The Chicago elite had its own "right ideas" about reform, and it wouldn't have William Stead around to complain that they were too timid. On the day his book appeared, the great journalist was on his way back to London, a dozen and more battles ahead of him. He was last seen on April 15, 1912, a doomed character in a human drama he would have given anything to have covered, loading women and children into lifeboats on the *Titanic*.

•

Stead, however, would have approved of at least part of the federation's "plan of salvation for Chicago." One of its first acts was to declare unconditional war on the gambling houses. Not trusting local police, the federation brought in justices of the peace from the dry suburb of Evanston to serve warrants on the big Clark Street gambling "hells." By the end of 1894, they were gone from Chicago for good.

Kenna and Coughlin were able to keep open the brothels and smaller gambling operations they controlled or protected, but the year Stead went down on the *Titanic*, Carter Harrison II gave in to mounting pressure from moral reformers and ordered police raids that closed down the Levee. These police sweeps were preceded by a march of twelve thousand Christians into the Levee, their leaders, in the spirit of Stead, calling on the paraders to reclaim it for Christ.

Prostitution continued to flourish, but it would never again be concentrated in an open, accessible area. The closing of the Levee resulted in the dispersal of the prostitution trade all over the city. In its decentralized form, it eventually came under the control of gangland Neanderthals like Johnny Torrio and Al Capone. As Walter Reckless put it in *Vice in Chicago*, his famous 1933 study, "Community vice was not eliminated by the closing of the red light district but has persisted under different marketing conditions."

"It is by politics," Stead had insisted, "that the work of redemption must be wrought." Political reform became the chief aim of the Civic Federation and its offshoot, the Municipal Voters' League. Under the near dictatorial direction of pint-sized, fiery-eyed George E. Cole, a "little, sawed-off giant of reform," the Municipal Voters' League organized itself like a political machine, as Stead had suggested, and dedicated itself to a single objective: the election to city council of its handpicked candidates, Republicans or Democrats.

Most of the work was done in the neighborhoods. "Each ward was separately studied, the politics of each was separately understood, and separately each ward was fought," Lincoln Steffens wrote of the league's *modus operandi*, which was similar to that of the corrupt city machines he had exposed in his muckraking essays for *McClure's*.

Using teams of ward and precinct workers and working closely with the Chicago press, the league investigated and publicized the records of all candidates for city council. "We're going to publish the records of the thieves that want to get back at the trough," declared Cole. The league then backed the cleanest candidates, using handbills, door-to-door canvassing, mass meetings, and torchlight parades.

Finley Peter Dunne and William Kent, a millionaire turned reformer, "joined in the wolf hunt," recalled Ernest Poole, "toured the saloons where they had many friends and came back chuckling to report to Cole the fast-deepening alarm of the boys in all the boodler wards." In the 1896 elections, twenty of the twenty-six council candidates the league opposed were defeated, and by 1900, only six or seven known grafters remained as aldermen, among them Powers, Kenna, and Coughlin. Laws creating a municipal civil service and regulating primary elections were also enacted. Every city in the country, Steffens wrote in a 1903 article, "Chicago: Half Free and Fighting On," had something to learn from Chicago's successful battle against the bosses. In Chicago he had seen, he said, "real reform."

This might be the most famous article ever written on Chicago politics, but Steffens would later express embarrassment that it had come from his pen. The Municipal Voters' League wrested control of the city council from ethnic bosses beholden, in the league's opinion, to the "cheap and nasty elements of the community"—but only for a short time, and without substituting social benefits for the benefactions of the bosses. Given the league's makeup, Steffens should not have been surprised by what it failed to accomplish. "Boss Cole" might have been, as he described himself to Steffens, a "second-class business man," but his organization was dominated by expensively educated bankers, corporate chieftains, and lawyers. There were no workers, union leaders, or Catholics in the organization and only a handful of Jews, none of them of Eastern European origin; nor were there many Democrats, despite the league's claim to being completely nonpartisan.

"I was seeing, and I noted in my report," Steffens would admit later, "the beginnings of the end, without realizing that those beginnings were to be the end." Chicago's businessmen-reformers were not interested in uncovering or challenging "sources of privilege." All they did was use their new power, as Steffens wrote in his autobiography, "to persuade, or if need be, force the business interests that had come to [them] . . . to get their privileges, to make open terms with and render some service to [the] . . . city." It was exactly the kind of government businessmen told Steffens they wanted, "not this so-called representative, but good government." This was the not surprising result of William T. Stead's suggestion for a "ring," or organization, of "the better elements of the town."

Steffens and Finley Peter Dunne were not the only hard-boiled reporters to be drawn in by the crusading vigor of Chicago's businessmen reformers. Ray Stannard Baker, who later claimed in his autobiography never to have been a "reformer," wrote enthusiastic accounts of the victories of bandy-legged George Cole over the most venal political bosses. It was a time of enormous political turmoil and confusion in the country, when few people had a clear understanding, as Baker himself later wrote, of "what the fundamental conditions really were, or the difficulties of meeting them." And Chicago's political reformers were at least hard-nosed, practical, and, for a time, excitingly effective, unlike the decade's great dreamers, Henry George and Edward Bellamy.

By the time Lincoln Steffens arrived in Chicago to collect material for his *McClure's* piece on the new-style reformers, the Civic Federation had long since abandoned Stead's original social objective for the organization: to reach out and help the needy. "I was a member of the committee of five appointed to carry out the suggestions [Stead] made in [his] . . . remarkable meeting," Jane Addams recalled in her autobiography, "and our first concern was to appoint a committee to deal with the unemployed." Relief stations were opened, money was raised for temporary shelters, and employment bureaus were set up to give sewing to women and road sweeping and shoveling jobs to men; "Stead's Brigades," these street crews were called. Over the course of the winter of 1893–94, the federation processed twenty-eight thousand applications for relief, impressive, perhaps, but less than one-half the number of men fed each day by the city's saloonkeepers.

Fear of class violence, not Stead's castigations, had awakened the elite's interest in public relief, but the magnitude of the economic crisis overwhelmed the federation's meager resources. And the tremendous industrial strike that broke out in Chicago in the summer of 1894 exposed the impossibility of achieving another of the organization's original aims: the promotion—in the most politically violent city in the country—of class conciliation through the arbitration of labor disputes.

As summer approached, "all the sores of the social system swelled and began to break," wrote Robert Herrick. "The first sore to break, ironically enough, was in the 'model industrial town' of Pullman." It was a dispute "over the question of a living wage."

2. Regeneration

The week he returned from his coverage of Jacob S. Coxey's protest march of the unemployed on the nation's capital from Massillon, Ohio, Ray Stannard Baker was sent by his paper to the town of Pullman to "see what the trouble was." He had never been there before but had written a glowing account of George Pullman as an American visionary. He regarded the experiment on the banks of the Calumet as one of the most promising social initiatives of the time and hoped someday to meet the man who was behind it. "He might be the Messiah of a new age."

Stepping off the suburban train, he found the town in a state of wild confusion. "Three thousand men," he wrote in his story of May 12, 1894, "stopped making palace cars for George M. Pullman yesterday forenoon and spent the day in discussing their wrongs in the streets of the 'model city.'" The strike had been called by the workers when three members of their grievance committee were fired following a meeting with management to discuss their complaints, and Baker was eager to learn who was at fault.

Pullman officials said that the company had been losing great amounts of money during the depression and had kept the shops open "only to keep the workingmen busy." The workers had a different story. While continuing to pay dividends to its stockholders, the company had cut the workforce dramatically and reduced the wages of remaining workers by 30 percent, without reducing the cost of rent or utilities in the town, putting residents in a cruel survival squeeze. Rent payments were automatically deducted from workers' paychecks, leaving some employees with little more than two dollars to support their families over the course of two weeks. The strike, they said, was also about Pullman tyranny. It was directed against "a slavery worse than that of negroes of the South," the workers declared in a petition for help to the people of Chicago. "They, at least, were well fed and well cared for, while the white slaves of Pullman . . . [can]not earn enough . . . to keep body and soul together."

Baker learned that the workers had organized and were affiliated with the new American Railway Union (ARU), headed by thirty-eight-year-old Eugene Victor Debs, who was one of the most brilliant labor organizers in the country. He had just led his union in a successful strike against James J. Hill's powerful Great Northern Railroad. Forbidden to meet in Pullman, the workers held turbulent all-night sessions in neighboring Kensington, where liquor flowed freely at forty-six saloons. Traveling back to Chicago on the night train, Baker wrote in his notes that he felt "in the very air a sternness of purpose, a deadly determination" that had been lacking in either of the two movements he had just seen—Stead's or Coxey's. "These men meant business! This was war!"

All that summer, Baker covered little else but the "Debs Rebellion," as the strike came to be called. Debs turned a local incident into a nationwide conflagration that tied up the country's rail system from Chicago to the Golden Gate. "It was one of the greatest industrial conflicts in the history of the country," Baker wrote a half century later, "perhaps the most important of all in its significance." It added a new weapon—the blanket federal injunction—to capital's already formidable arsenal and brought into being an unprecedented partnership between the federal government and big business for the purpose of suppressing strikes and boycotts. And it led eventually to the formation of the Socialist Party of America, on whose ticket Debs would make five runs for the presidency.

Baker first met Debs that June, when Debs arrived in Chicago from his home in Indiana for the convention of the ARU. "I . . . liked him almost on sight, for I felt his unselfish devotion to the cause he was interested in. It was not primarily unionism, the organization, that absorbed him, as it did Gompers, but the human problems of the workingman." Debs had recently jettisoned Gompers's strategy of craft organization and established the ARU as an organization open to all white-skinned railroad workers regardless of their skill level. He was, Baker described him, a warmhearted, animated man with a lively sense of humor and "a gift of explosive profanity."

Debs did not want to pit his still-fragile union against the amassed power of George Pullman and his railroad allies, who were united in the General Managers Association, an organization representing twenty-four railroad companies headquartered or terminating in Chicago. He was given no choice, however. Moved by the impassioned pleas of the Pullman workers, the convention delegates overruled him and called for the strangulation of the "Pullman monopoly." Debs gave George Pullman five days to settle the strike. When Pullman refused to budge, declined even to meet with a delegation sent by his friends in the Civic Federation to arbitrate the dispute, the battle began. Just before it did, George Pullman left town for his summer estate on the New Jersey shore, placing guards around his mansion and locking valuables in the vaults of his downtown office skyscraper.

On June 26, Debs ordered all Pullman cars cut from trains and sidetracked, initiating what the *New York Times* called "a struggle between the greatest and most powerful railroad labor ogranization and the en-tire railroad capital." His union was not to handle or service Pullman rolling stock. When ARU workers were fired for following these in-structions, the union shut down entire lines and virtually sealed off the city of Chicago, causing food shortages and a disruption of the federal mails. Debs agreed to move the mails if Pullman cars were not at-tached to trains, but management put mail cars on almost every train going in and out of Chicago, hoping to draw in the federal government on its side and crush the union completely. By the end of June, 125,000 workers had joined a sympathetic boycott that the *Tribune* was now calling an "insurrection." When railroad managers brought in scabs and protected them with Pinkertons and unruly gangs of dep-utized marshals, rioting broke out, despite Debs's repeated pleas to his men to remain orderly.

The worst violence occurred in early July when the U.S. attorney general, Richard Olney, who served on the boards of several railroads, including one involved in the strike, convinced President Grover Cleveland to send in federal troops to move the mails and to open in-terstate commerce, over the irate opposition of Governor Altgeld. The army regulars, commanded by Gen. Nelson A. Miles, the grand mar-shal of the civic parade that had opened the Columbian Exposition, ar-rived by train from Fort Sheridan and set up their encampment within sight of the buildings of the Court of Honor. They were soon joined there by troops from other parts of the country.

With the lakefront covered with the white tents of the troops and tensions running high in the city, a mob of ten thousand, many of them young ruffians out to cause trouble, attacked the Union Stock Yards and fanned out over the South Side, destroying hundreds of thousands of dollars of railroad property. "All southern Chicago seemed afire," Baker recalled. "I saw long freight trains burning on side-tracks. I saw Pullman cars that had been gutted by fire. I saw attacks by strikers on non-union men, and fierce conflicts between strikers and the police and deputies."

Baker continued to sympathize with the starving workers of Pull-man, but what he saw threw him into confusion. "Could such anarchy be permitted in a civilized society?" Should wild mobs be allowed to put the torch to industrial property and attack and physically harm nonunion workers? He could not make up his mind.

His uncertainty reflected a more dramatic shift of opinion in the city, brought on by exaggerated newspaper accounts of the violence. The public and the press had strongly supported the initial action of the Pullman workers against a cold and arrogant autocrat, but the strike had devolved into industrial warfare, with the city itself its main battleground. If the violence continued, "Dictator Debs" and his "drunken followers," the *Tribune* screeched, "will be fired upon, they will be bayoneted, will be trampled under foot by cavalry, and mowed down by artillery." "I believe in the free application of rifle balls, grape and canister to mobs," Baker's father wrote him, expressing the sentiments of many in the city who feared the disturbance had swung dangerously out of control.

Early Sunday morning, July 8, Baker went to Hammond, Indiana, an important railroad junction point for Chicago, anticipating a battle between troops and strikers. Troops with orders to shoot at anyone obstructing the tracks had started to ride "shotgun" on trains bringing mail and food into Chicago. The slouch-hatted soldiers, the *Tribune* reported, were perched on the cowcatchers, "their rifles loaded and their mouths filled with cartridges, which protruded like steel tusks."

By the time Baker arrived, the trouble had already begun. Crowds were burning boxcars and Pullman coaches, twisting rails, and spiking switches. He watched as a gang of a hundred and more men—most of them toughs from Chicago, not strikers—tugged at ropes and shouted, "Heave Ho! Heave Ho!" as they tried to turn over a Pullman car and block the tracks. At that moment, shooting broke out, and a man standing next to Baker went down, blood spurting from his chest, and died instantly. Another man fell, and Baker looked up the track and saw "a locomotive moving slowly down upon the mob. Blue-clad soldiers covered the fender, and the running boards, and the top of the cab. They had rifles lifted and were firing directly at us.

"Instantly there was a panic, men running and women screaming." In all, four persons were shot down.

The battle at Hammond broke the strike, Baker wrote in his paper. But it had already been dealt a death blow by an encompassing injunction Olney obtained in the courts forbidding ARU leaders from taking any action to aid the boycott; they were not even allowed to answer questions about it. When Debs ignored the injunction, as the government expected he would, he was jailed for contempt. He was released on bail, but the arrayed power of the railroad kings, the courts, the army, and the federal government bore down on and crushed the ARU. By the end of the month the troops were gone, and George Pullman had begun rehiring workers who had not been "disloyal" to him. At least thirty-four persons were killed and an unknown number of others seriously injured in the bloodiest labor action in Chicago's history.

That August, Pullman workers and their families "continued, more or less forgotten, to starve in their model houses," Baker wrote, without any help from the man who had said he loved his town like one of his own children. "If ye be ill, or poor, or starving, or oppressed, or in grief," wrote Eugene Field, "your chances for sympathy and for succor from E. V. Debs are one hundred where your chances with G. M. Pullman would be the little end of nothing whittled down." Field helped Baker organize a relief fund at their paper, and Baker hired a wagon and brought salt pork, beans, and coffee to the homes of the distressed people of Pullman, whose plight he publicized in the *Record*. Riding over to Pullman from Kensington, where he bought the supplies, he felt "like a kind of benevolent king. . . . What crowds gathered, and followed, and cheered!"

It was a costly victory for George Pullman. It cost him his reputation, his town, and, some said, his life. President Cleveland appointed a commission to investigate the strike, and its exhaustive report—"a roast," said the *Tribune*, not a report—condemned George Pullman for refusing to bargain with his workers and for charging exorbitant rates for town sevices. "The aesthetic features are admired by visitors, but have little money value to employees, especially when they lack bread." Even Pullman's friends could not understand his "pigheadedness." Trying to get to the deeper causes of the strike, the commission concluded that "men, as a rule, even when employees, prefer independence to paternalism."

After the publication of the strike commission's report, the Illinois attorney general filed suit to force the Pullman Palace Car Company to divest itself of its residential properties, claiming that in building a town it had exceeded the terms of its corporate charter. Pullman lined up his lawyers to fight the state of Illinois, but, his health weakened by the strike, he died of heart failure in 1897. One year later, the case was decided against his company, and the town of Pullman began its slow transformation into an ordinary industrial neighborhood. Company towns like Pullman, said the court, were "opposed to good public policy and incompatible with the theory and spirit of our institutions."

Pullman's tomb in Graceland is marked by a towering Corinthian column, the last thing Solon S. Beman designed for his patron. To prevent labor terrorists from vandalizing the body, the family had the lead-lined casket encased in a pit of reinforced concrete and bolted-together steel rails. Pullman was buried at night, under heavy security. The work of filling the grave took two days. Today, on a clear morning, you can stand on the Pullman family plot and see the obelisk that is the tomb of Gov. John P. Altgeld, an irony George Pullman would not have appreciated.

•

After serving a six-month sentence at Woodstock Prison, fifty miles from Chicago, Eugene Debs was pushed by his rising frustration with capitalism to organize a political party sworn to its overthrow, by peaceful means if possible. "The time has come," he declared, "to regenerate society—we are on the eve of universal change." Florence Kelley agreed and became one of the first members of the new Socialist Party of America.

Her friend Jane Addams, however, remained committed to the peaceful settlement of labor disputes and the fundamental correctness of capitalism itself. She had been a disappointed member of the delegation sent by the Civic Federation to try to convince George Pullman to meet with his striking workers, but most capitalists, she continued to believe, were not as intransigent as Pullman. They could be reasoned with. She knew; she had worked with many of them. The violence and destruction of the Pullman strike, she argued, was due largely to the "personal will" of a proud, all-controlling employer and the "temperament" of a stubborn "strike leader." No one in the union movement, however—not even Samuel Gompers, who had refused to join the strike against the Pullman Company—could agree with her. Not many capitalists could, either. In 1894, the country had crossed a divide, many Americans were convinced. Two gigantic forces, capital and labor, had formed, each stronger than they had ever been before. The future would surely be marked by blood and struggle.

To Florence Kelley, the Pullman strike was a "touchstone," forcing people to reconsider their views on the labor question. While Addams and other moderates called for legislation to prevent further conflicts of this scale—laws, for example, providing for industrial arbitration—others called for more power to crush labor radicals. The artist Frederic Remington, who had covered the Pullman strike for *Harper's Weekly*, described the strikers as a "malodorous crowd of anarchistic foreign trash," speaking "Hungarian, or Polack, or whatever the stuff is." They were "vicious wretch[es]" with "no blood circulating above [their] ears" and deserved, he said, every bayonet charge that had been sent at thém, every bullet fired into their midst. "There must be some shooting, men must be killed," an infuriated eastern minister agreed, "and then there will be an end to this defiance of law and destruction of property."

Those urging caution and those urging coercion seemed to agree, however, that the city itself was the poisoned source of the problems that had led to the Pullman strike. "One of the best remedies against all strikes," a Chicago churchman told the Pullman Strike Commission, "will be for the people to move out into the country and cultivate the land. There are too many people in the city." After reading his son's articles on the homeless of Chicago, Joseph Stannard Baker, a sod buster in his youth, wrote to him: "Why don't they get out of Chicago? There's plenty of room in the West. All they've got to do is to use their brains—and little at that—with some elbow-grease." Even Jane Addams, as we have seen, supported a scheme for the colonization of Chicago's Italian immigrants in the Deep South, and prominent labor leaders joined reactionaries in calling for immigration restriction.

In "What's the Matter with Chicago?," an essay written not long after he became a socialist, Eugene Debs argued that the two historical factors most responsible for Chicago's growth—geography and cupidity—had made the city "unfit for human habitation." Chicago was built on a "vast miasmic swamp," he wrote, an impossible place to live but a "prize location for money-making. . . . A thousand sites infinitely preferable for a city could have been found in close proximity, but they lacked the 'Commercial' advantages which are of such commanding importance in the capitalist system." From the day the lakeside site was gridded and put up for sale, "everything that entered into the building of the town and the development of the city was determined purely from profit considerations and without the remotest concern for the health and comfort of human beings who were to live there, especially those who had to do all the labor and produce all the wealth."

Monstrous commercial cities like Chicago, with their poisoned air and water, their corrupted politics and morals, their sweatshops and slums, were, Debs insisted, beyond reforming. "Regeneration will only come with depopulation—when Socialism has relieved the congestion and released the people and they spread out over the country and live close to the grass."

But those who continued to speak for the frontier did not realize— or refused to admit—that the city had become the new American frontier of opportunity. Mr. Dooley was not prepared to give up on the city; nor was Dreiser's Sister Carrie; nor were George Ade's transplanted villagers. Nor, most emphatically, were the nation's business barons. Rockefeller, Carnegie, Morgan, Field, Pullman, Armour, and others had made their fortunes in the city and located their corporate empires there, hiring architects and engineers to design for them daunting urban works of power and imagination, skyscrapers and bridges, great mills and mansions.

In 1894 a number of Chicago capitalists were living outside the city in pleasant railroad suburbs. In that year, the iron master William H. Winslow moved his family into a prophetic River Forest house designed by his Oak Park neighbor Frank Lloyd Wright. The prairie houses Wright built after this were inspired, some believe, by the stringently simple Japanese temple, the Ho-o-den, the architect visited on a wooded island Olmsted had designed on the grounds of the Columbian Exposition. They were suburban retreats, "safe," in Wright's words, "from the poisons of the great city," privatized versions of Olmsted's planned community on the banks of the Des Plaines. But businessmen and professionals who lived in Riverside, Oak Park, and River Forest—or, like Daniel Burnham, along the wooded ridge of the North Shore—were drawn every working day into the swirling center of Chicago.

Even Frank Lloyd Wright was for a time, until he could make a stronger name for himself. When Sullivan fixed him in 1893 for working nights on independent commissions to supplement his income, he opened a practice in the Schiller Building. It was in his plain-walled skyscraper office in the heart of the Loop that Wright met his first prominent surburban clients—Winslow, Nathan Moore, Chauncey Williams, and Edward Carson Waller, the real estate mogul who had helped bankroll the construction of the Home Insurance Building, the Rookery, and the Monadnock.

Men like Waller, Winslow, and Burnham could not abandon the city, as Wright eventually would, because their business interests continued to be centered there. With the fair as their inspiration, they were bold enough to believe, however, that they could remake the entire city, turning it into a place of planned order and stately beauty. After the Pullman strike, the commercial classes of Chicago were ready for urban "regeneration," but not the kind preached by Stead or Debs. Led by this invincibly confident metropolitan elite, Chicago stood poised in the crisis summer of 1894 to reinvent itself yet again. And as before, disaster was seen as the prelude to heroic civic action.

•

At sunset on July 5, as police battled incendiaries in the vast rail yards of the South Side, first one person then another in the roving bands of rioters began to look off to the southeast, where the entire lower sky was glowing fiery orange. It looked as if the town of Pullman were burning, but the mob quickly realized that it was the remains of Chicago's other model city that was going up in flames.

William Stead had not been able to save the buildings of the White City as architectural monuments, but neither had they been torn down. Not knowing what to do with them, the city had simply neglected them.

Visiting the grounds in January 1894, a Chicago reporter found the noble buildings disfigured by coal dust, with great patches of plaster peeling from their façades. Groups of unemployed men had taken refuge in the Court of Honor, now a "gray and grimy" city of the homeless. A week later, a fire destroyed the Peristyle and its flanking buildings. The city then hired a salvage company to tear down what remained, but the unknown "fire fiends" of July beat the wreckers to it.

As word of the blaze spread through the city on the evening of July fifth, people went to the top stories of the downtown skyscrapers to see the great tongues of flames shooting in the air, and more than a hundred thousand Chicagoans gathered in Jackson Park to watch a three-hour holocaust that "exceeded anything of the kind that had occurred since the Great Fire of 1871." The orderly crowd looked on in silence as if it were watching a fireworks display of the previous summer. "There was no regret; rather a feeling of pleasure that the elements and not the wrecker should wipe out the spectacle of the Columbian season," the *Tribune* reported. It was, said the paper, "a grand, a glorious ending" to the most "splendid [and] beautiful thing Chicago had ever created."

Like the Great Fire, the burning of the White City was seen by many Chicagoans as an opportunity for a fresh start. That summer, Daniel Burnham began conceiving plans for a series of civic improvements that would transform Jackson Park and the downtown lakeshore that Gurdon Hubbard had helped save for the city into a spectacular public pleasure ground, the landscape centerpiece of his Chicago Plan of 1909, the greatest civic project to come out of the fair. Serious work began on it, and serious support for it in the business community appeared as soon as the city emerged from the long depression of the mid-1890s, and "a current of splendid vitality began to throb," in Robert Herrick's words.

Chicago owes its peerless lakefront and the boulevard character of Michigan Avenue to Burnham's plan, the first comprehensive effort to discipline Chicago's unruly growth. But that plan—like the City Beautiful improvements he fashioned for Cleveland, San Francisco, and Washington, D.C.—made no provision for the needs of ethnic and black neighborhoods, the worlds of Jane Addams's Italian immigrants, Mr. Dooley's Bridgeporters, or Richard Wright's Bigger Thomas, who utters the epitaph of Burnham's White City vision: "Goddammit, look! We live here and they live there. . . . They got things and we ain't."

The White City's richest legacy is the confidence of its builders in the possibilities of urban life, their unassailable belief that the modern metropolis, with its enormous and multiplying problems, could be made over into a conscious work of art. But a great city is not a work of inspired scene painting, static and splendid. It is a living drama with a huge and varied cast and a plot filled with conflict, tension, spectacle, and significance. And a big city's diversity and explosive energy—the very factors Burnham and the civic elite hoped to tame and control—enliven the drama and "bring the performers," as Lewis Mumford wrote, "up to the highest pitch of skilled, intensely conscious participation."

Chicago's visionary White City planner failed, in the end, to heed the lessons his own tumultuous city provided in 1893: that a city's greatness is the result of an uneasy balance between order and energy, planning and privatism, diversity and conformity, vice and reform, art and enterprise, high culture and low culture, the smart and the shabby, the permanent and the temporary. Interesting cities are places of stimulating disparity and moral conflict where crudity and commerce are often accompanied by memorable advances in the arts. And like Aristotle's Athens, a city of filthy streets, chaotic markets, and scandalous sanitary facilities, they specialize in the making and remaking of interesting human beings—like the bright products of Chicago's railway hinterland, Theodore Dreiser, Hamlin Garland, Jane Addams, George Ade, Ida B. Wells, William Rainey Harper, Ray Stannard Baker, Frank Lloyd Wright, and countless others.

The industrial metropolis, we tend to forget, was an absolutely new thing to this generation, its culture nothing short of revolutionary. To them it was as strange, exotic, and thrillingly new as Burnham's city of wonders in Jackson Park.

"Chicago," wrote Dreiser, "was like no other city in the world, . . . a city which had no traditions but which was making them." Recalling those "furnace days" of his and Chicago's life, he said that "it was something wonderful . . . to see a world metropolis spring up under your eyes." Florence "in its best days must have been something like this to young Florentines."

ABBREVIATIONS USED IN NOTES

AND BIBLIOGRAPHY

AA:1   Andreas, Alfred T. *A History of Chicago from the Earliest Period to the Present, vol. 1—Ending with the Year 1857.* Chicago: A. T. Andreas, 1884.

AA:2   Andreas, Alfred T. *A History of Chicago from the Earliest Period to the Present, vol. 2—From 1857 until the Fire of 1871.* Chicago: A. T. Andreas, 1885.

AA:3   Andreas, Alfred T. *A History of Chicago from the Earliest Period to the Present, vol. 3—From the Fire of 1871 until 1885.* Chicago: A. T. Andreas, 1886.

AJS   *American Journal of Sociology*

AM   *Atlantic Monthly*

AR   *Architectural Record*

CDD   *Chicago Daily Democrat*

CDN   *Chicago Daily News*

CEP   *Chicago Evening Post*

CH   *Chicago History*

CHS   Chicago Historical Society

CR   *Chicago Record*

CT   *Chicago Tribune*

DAB   *Dictionary of American Biography*

GG   Poole, Ernest. *Giants Gone: Men Who Made Chicago.* New York: McGraw-Hill, 1943.

HC:1   Pierce, Bessie Louise. *The Beginning of a City, 1673–1848.* Vol. 1 of *A History of Chicago.* New York: Knopf, 1937.

HC:2   Pierce, Bessie Louise. *From Town to City, 1848–1871.* Vol. 2 of *A History of Chicago.* New York: Knopf, 1940.

HC:3   Pierce, Bessie Louise. *The Rise of the Modern City, 1871–1893.* Vol. 3 of *A History of Chicago.* New York: Knopf, 1957.

HW   *Harper's Weekly*

IA   *Inland Architect* [also identifies *The Inland Architect and Building News* and *The Inland Architect and News Record,* as the title changed over the years]

ICCC   Stead, William T. *If Christ Came to Chicago!* 1894. Reprint, Chicago: Chicago Historical Bookworks, 1990.

IO   Chicago *Inter Ocean*

JAH   *Journal of American History*

JSAH   *Journal of the Society of Architectural Historians*

JISHS   *Journal of the Illinois State Historical Society*

JWR   Monroe, Harriet. *John Wellborn Root.* Boston: Houghton Mifflin, 1896.

LS   Sullivan, Louis H. *Autobiography of an Idea.* 1924. Reprint, New York: Dover, 1956.

NAR   *North American Review*

NEM   *New England Magazine*

NYT   *New York Times*

OM   Bourget, Paul. *Outre-mer: Impressions of America.* New York: Charles Scribner's Sons, 1895.

SC   Dreiser, Theodore. *Sister Carrie.* 1900. Reprint, New York: Viking Penguin, 1987.

SOC   Kirkland, Joseph. *The Story of Chicago.* Vol. 1. Chicago: Dibble Publishing Co., 1892–94.

TG   *The Graphic*

otes

Preface

PAGE

15　*"This is"*: Quoted in Robert Cromie, *The Great Chicago Fire* (1958), 8.

15　*"the burning"*: Frederick Law Olmsted, "Chicago in Distress," *The Nation* 13 (Nov. 9, 1871): 303.

15　*"For three"*: Quoted in Alfred L. Sewell, *"The Great Calamity!"*: *Scenes, Lessons and Incidents of the Great Fire* (1871), 27.

16　*"In the midst"*: *CT*, Oct. 11, 1871.

17　*"the first"*: Henry B. Fuller, "Chicago's Book of Days," *Outlook* 69 (Oct. 5, 1901): 293.

17　*"[is] the very embodiment"*: "The Civic Life of Chicago: The Impressions of an Observant Englishman," *Review of Reviews*, Aug. 1893, 182.

17　*"the purest kind"*: Jacques Hermant in Henri Loyrette, "Chicago: A French View," in John Zukowsky, ed., *Chicago Architecture, 1872–1922, Birth of a Metropolis* (1987), 126.

17　*"All around"*: Frank Norris, *The Pit: A Story of Chicago* (1903; reprint, 1928), 55, 58.

17　*"the only great city"*: Henry B. Fuller, *With the Procession* (1895), 248.

18　*"queen and guttersnipe"*: George W. Steevens, *The Land of the Dollar* (1897), 144.

18　*"it is given"*: Theodore Dreiser, *Newspaper Days*, ed. T. D. Nostwich (1991), 3.

18　*"natural history"*: Lewis Mumford, "The Natural History of Urbanization," in William L. Thomas, ed., *Man's Role in Changing the Face of the Earth* (1956), 383–439.

19　*"A product of nature"*: Robert Park, "The City: Suggestions for the Investigation of Human Behavior in the Urban Environment," in Richard Sennett, ed., *Classic Essays on the Culture of Cities* (1969), 91.

PART I

Introduction: City of Dreamers and Doers

24　*"The place"*: LS, 200–201. All subsequent quotations in LS, 196, 241–44, 319.

Chapter One: Discovery

28　*"that far-away corner of the world"*: "The Pageant of 1671," in Louise Phelps Kellogg, ed., *Early Narratives of the Northwest, 1634–1699* (1917), 217; Reuben Gold Thwaites, *The Jesuit Relations and Allied*

PAGE

   *Documents: Travels and Explorations of the Jesuit Missionaries in New
   France, 1610–1791*, vol. 4 (1899), 105–15, hereafter cited as Thwaites,
   Relations; Saint Lusson was sent to the West to also locate copper mines
   in the Lake Superior region and find a waterway to the "Sea of the
   South"; see also Louise Phelps Kellogg, *The French Régime in Wisconsin
   and the Northwest* (1925; reprint, 1968), 179–90.

28   *"the voice"*: Kellogg, ed., "The Pageant of 1671," 218–28; see also Fran-
     cis Parkman, *La Salle and the Discovery of the West* (1891; 1893 edition),
     40–47; and Bernard DeVoto, *The Course of Empire* (1952), 122–32.

28   *"the most solemn ceremony"*: Kellogg, ed., "Pageant of 1671," 217.

29   *"of Lakes Huron"*: Ibid., 218.

29   *"he was whose standard"*: Ibid., 220.

29   *the escutcheon:* James A. Clifton, *The Prairie People: Continuity and
     Change in Potawatomi Indian Culture, 1665–1965* (1977), 73; Nicolas
     Perrot's description of the ceremony of annexation is contained in his
     Memoir, translated in Emma Helen Blair, ed., *The Indian Tribes of the
     Upper Mississippi Valley and the Region of the Great Lakes*, vol. 1 (1911),
     220–25.

30   *the Canadian-born Joliet:* I have used the modern spelling (Joliet) of Jol-
     liet's name. For Joliet, see Virginia Louise Eifert, *Louis Jolliet: Explorer
     of Rivers* (1961); Jean Delanglez, *Life and Voyages of Louis Jolliet
     (1645–1700)* (1948); and Timothy Severin, *Explorers of the Mississippi*
     (1967), 66–91.

30   *Marquette was younger:* For Marquette see, Joseph P. Donnelly, *Jacques
     Marquette, S. J., 1637–1675* (1968). This is the most current and reliable
     biography. For a short study of Marquette, see Raphael N. Hamilton, *Fa-
     ther Marquette* (1970). See also the somewhat dated Reuben Gold
     Thwaites, *Father Marquette* (1902). For an exhaustive examination of the
     written sources of the Marquette-Joliet expedition, see Hamilton's *Mar-
     quette's Explorations: The Narratives Reexamined* (1970).

30   *"a figure evoked"*: Parkman, *La Salle*, 29, 73; see also Parkman's *The Je-
     suits of North America in the Seventeenth Century* (1893).

31   *"horrible monsters"*: Thwaites, *Relations*, vol. 59, 95–119. All subsequent
     quotations from Marquette's journal are from Thwaites, *Relations*, vol. 59.
     The *Jesuit Relations* are reports from the Jesuits in New France back to
     France of their missionary activities. They were not the official reports of
     the superior of Jesuit missions in New France, but were intended to be
     read by a wide audience. They seem to have had two main purposes: to in-
     spire men to volunteer for mission service in New France and to encour-
     age the laity to contribute financially to that mission work. They are the
     best source for the activities of the Jesuits in New France. For a descrip-
     tion of the purposes and nature of the *Relations*, see Joseph P. Donnelly,
     Thwaites Jesuit Relations: Errata and Addenda (1967), 1–26. This work
     also contains an excellent bibliography of the Jesuits in New France.

33   *"the courage"*: This quote is from Dablon's introduction to Marquette's
     journal, Thwaites, *Relations*, 59: 87.

33   *"with all Our energy"*: Thwaites, *Relations*, 59: 115.

34   *"Master of Ceremonies"*: Ibid., 123; all subsequent quotes from Mar-
     quette's journal are from ibid., 123–41.

34   *"a torrent"*: Parkman, *La Salle*, 60.

34   *"floating islands"*: Thwaites, *Relations*, 59: 141.

34   *"held their way"*: Parkman, *La Salle*, 60.

35   *"to the southern sea"*: Thwaites, *Relations*, 59: 141; all subsequent
     quotes from Marquette's journal are from ibid., 147–61.

PAGE
36 *"What now remains"*: Parkman, *La Salle,* 43–44; for Parkman, see Howard Doughty, *Francis Parkman* (1962), and Mason Wade, *Francis Parkman: Heroic Historian* (1942).
37 *"We have seen nothing"*: Thwaites, *Relations,* 59: 161.
37 *"There are [great] prairies"*: Ibid., 58: 107.
37 *"solitary island"*: LS, 196.
38 *Illinois prairie:* Thwaites, *Relations,* 58: 105; James Parton, "Chicago," *AM* 19 (Mar. 1867): 325–45; W. J. Beecher, "The Lost Illinois Prairie," *CH* 2 (Spring-Summer 1973): 166–72; Lauren Brown, *Audubon Nature Society: Grasslands* (1985); For the prairie lands of North America, see also Victor E. Shelford, *The Ecology of North America* (1963); Edith M. Poggi, *The Prairie Province of Illinois: A Study of Human Adjustment to Natural Environment* (1934); and Betty Flanders Thomson, *The Shaping of America's Heartland: The Landscape of the Middle West* (1977).
38 *"grain of all kinds"*: Thwaites, *Relations,* 58: 107.
38 *"to instruct them"*: Ibid., 59: 161.
38 *"floating masses of ice"*: Ibid., 59: 165–71.
39 *"as an angel from Heaven"*: Ibid., 59: 189; The phrase "received as an angel from heaven" is Claude Dablon's. Marquette's journal stops after he left the portage. Dablon prepared "An Account of the Second Voyage and the Death of Father Jacques Marquette" for the Jesuit *Relations* after gathering evidence from Marquette's companions on the journey.
   There is a controversy about the authorship of Marquette's journals. Francis B. Steck and Jean Delanglez question Marquette's authorship of the journals, but their revisionist work has been overturned effectively, I believe, by the massive research of Raphael N. Hamilton (see his *Marquette's Explorations*). Donnelly's biography of Marquette, which appeared just before the publication of Hamilton's book, is in agreement with Hamilton's conclusion that the journal was from the hand of Marquette.
39 *"handled and carried about like a child"*: Thwaites, *Relations,* 59: 193; all subsequent quotes from *Relations,* 59: 193, 199, 201; see also Hamilton, *Marquette,* 75–7; Raphael N. Hamilton, "Marquette Death Site: The Case for Ludington," *Michigan History* 49 (1965): 228–48.
40 *Marquette's grave:* Hamilton, *Marquette's Explorations,* 195; John G. Shea, "Romance and Reality of the Death of Marquette and the Recent Discovery of his Remains," *The Catholic World* 26 (1877): 267–81.
41 *"the patron saint"*: J. Seymour Currey, *Chicago: Its History and Its Builders: A Century of Marvelous Growth,* vol. 1 (1908), 14; Mary C. Arth, "Marquette Memorials," *Mid-America* 13 (Apr. 1930): 291–303; Walter Nursey, *The Legend and Legacy of Père Marquette* (1897).
   In 1893, just after the Columbian Exposition closed, the Chicago architectural firm of William Holabird and Martin Roche began work on a steel-frame skyscraper at 140 S. Dearborn Street, in the heart of the downtown. One of its owners was Owen Aldis, the city's leading promoter of high-rise office buildings and a passionate admirer of Père Marquette, whose journal he had translated for his own reading pleasure. Aldis named the building, still one of Chicago's handsomest landmarks, after his hero and had Edward Kemeys, Herman A. MacNeil, and J. A. Holzer design a splendid memorial rotunda with glass mosaics and bronze reliefs depicting incidents in the life of Marquette.
41 *"all danger seemed over"*: Delanglez, *Jolliet,* 57–58; See also Delanglez, "The Jolliet Lost Map of the Mississippi," *Mid-America* 28 (1946): 67–144; Delanglez, "Louis Jolliet, Early Years, 1645–1674," *Mid-America* 28 (1945): 3–29.

PAGE

42   *"secured [Marquette's] fame":* Kellogg, *Narratives,* 225.

42   *"Except for this shipwreck":* Quoted in Eifert, *Jolliet,* 125–26. Delanglez scrutinizes this letter, dated Oct. 10, 1674, in *Jolliet,* 55–6.

42   *"the first recorded Chicago resident":* SOC, 18.

42   *Chicagoua:* John F. Swenson, "Chicagoua/Chicago: The Origins, Meaning, and Etymology of a Place Name," *Illinois Historical Journal* 84 (Winter 1991): 235–48; Henri Joutel, *Relation de Henri Joutel,* in Pierre Margry, ed., *Découvertes et établissments des Français dans . . . l'Amerique septentrionelle, 1614–1754,* vol. 3 (1876–1886), 91–534; part of Joutel's journal has been translated and reprinted in Milo M. Quaife, ed., *The Development of Chicago, 1678–1914, Shown in a Series of Contemporary Narratives* (1916), 22; Milo M. Quaife in *Checagou: From Indian Wigwam to Modern City, 1673–1835* (1933), 17–20, conjectures, unconvincingly, that the meaning of the Indian place name was "anything great or powerful"; for a pre-Swenson discussion of the controversy surrounding Chicago's name, see Virgil J. Vogel, "The Mystery of Chicago's Name," *Mid-America* 40 (July 1958): 163–74.

42   *shaping of its physical environment:* My account of the geology and geography of Chicago and its hinterland is based primarily on the following sources: Harold M. Mayer, "The Launching of Chicago: The Situation and the Site," *CH* 9 (Summer 1980), 68–79; Mayer, *Chicago: City of Decisions* (1955); J. Paul Goode, *The Geographic Background of Chicago* (1926); Douglas C. Ridgley, *The Geography of Illinois* (1921); J. Harlen Bretz, *Geology of the Chicago Region* (1964); Irving Cutler, *Chicago: Metropolis of the Mid-Continent* (1976), 5–13; Jack L. Hough, *The Geology of the Great Lakes* (1958); Patrick Walter Bryan, "The Cultural Landscape of Chicago," in P. W. Bryan, *Man's Adaptation of Nature: Studies of the Cultural Landscape* (1933); Carl O. Sauer, *Geography of the Upper Illinois Valley and History of Development* (1916); and Rollin D. Salisbury and William C. Alden, *The Geography of Chicago and Its Environs* (1990)

45   *"a very great and important advantage":* Thwaites, *Relations,* 58: 105–7; Joliet understated the length of the portage, which in dry seasons became as long as nine miles.

46   *"proposed ditch":* The letter in which La Salle outlines his objection to Joliet's canal plan is reproduced in AA:1, 45, 64.

46   *"lowest point":* Quoted in Hobart C. Chatfield-Taylor, *Chicago* (1917), 118.

46   *other explorers:* See "The Narrative of Joutel, 1687–88," and the report by Jean Buisson de St. Cosme, both reprinted in Quaife, ed., *Development of Chicago.*

46   *Frontenac was not interested:* Delanglez, *Jolliet,* 130–251; The best accounts of the Canadian frontier and of French policy in North America in these years are works by W. J. Eccles: *Canada Under Louis XIV, 1663–1701* (1964); *The Canadian Frontier, 1534–1760* (1969); and *France in America* (1972); Eccles's work is a useful corrective to Parkman's strong belief in the superiority of Anglo-American institutions and the inevitability of their triumph over France's. See also Clarence W. Alvord, *The Illinois Country, 1673–1818* (1920; reprint, 1987), 54–141; and Kenneth McNaught, *History of Canada* (1970), 1–44.

46   *He died in 1700:* Delanglez, *Jolliet,* 130–251. Delanglez examines all the extant Joliet documents pertaining to his voyage with Marquette; Severin, *Explorers,* 90–91.

Chapter Two: Didn't Expect No Town

PAGE

48 *"and led the way"* and *"Nothing of interest"*: Gurdon Saltonstall Hubbard, *The Autobiography of Gurdon Saltonstall Hubbard: Pa-Pa-Ma-Ta-Be, "The Swift Walker"* (1911), 25–32, 63, 142. Hubbard began writing his autobiography in 1870. After his manuscript was destroyed in the Great Chicago Fire, his second, and still uncompleted, manuscript was published in a limited edition by Rand McNally & Company in 1888. It was edited by his nephew Henry E. Hamilton and entitled *Incidents and Events in the Life of Gurdon Saltonstall Hubbard.*

Hubbard kept a diary, but it has been lost. In the introduction to the Lakeside Press edition of his autobiography, the publishers claim that Hubbard's diary was then in the possession of the Chicago Historical Society (CHS), but they were mistaken. Hamilton's text and the Lakeside Press edition of the autobiography follow, with some changes, the 104 manuscript pages composed by Hubbard in 1881 and found in his papers at the CHS in a volume entitled *Reminiscences and Scrap-book of Gurdon Hubbard.* The archivists at the CHS believe that this is the record that was mistaken for the lost diary.

The Gurdon S. Hubbard Papers at the CHS (hereafter cited as Hubbard MSS) were my principal source of information on Hubbard; see also Lloyd Wendt, *"Swift Walker": An Informal Biography of Gurdon Saltonstall Hubbard* (1986), 7–8, 62–63, 489. This "biography" is based largely on original sources but contains fictionalized dialogue, and there are some inaccuracies in quoted material. It is the only modern biography of Gurdon Hubbard and is true to the spirit of the man. Scholars, however, should exercise caution in using it.

50 *"True to his Indian training"*: Henry R. Hamilton, *The Epic of Chicago* (1932), 354. Hamilton, the son of Henry E. Hamilton, wrote this book—part biography of Hubbard and part autobiography—when he was seventy-two years old. His grandfather Judge Richard Hamilton was a close friend of Hubbard's, and the Judge's children and grandchildren considered Hubbard their "uncle."

50 *"four and a half houses"*: Hubbard to his mother, Aug. 1818, Hubbard MSS; see also Clint Clay Tilton, "Gurdon Saltonstall Hubbard and Some of His Friends," *Illinois State Historical Society Transactions* 40 (1933): 177; and *CT* article "The Original Chicagoan," May 3, 1886, in Hubbard's scrapbook in the Hubbard MSS; the Old Settlers Society was founded in 1855. Eligibility was restricted to pre-1837 arrivals. Hubbard and John Harris Kinzie were among its first officers.

50 *"The congregation"*: *Chicago Times*, Sept. 18, 1886; Hamilton's *Incidents* contains a number of memorials to Hubbard; see also Tilton, "Gurdon Staltonstall Hubbard," 175; and Henry R. Hamilton, *Biographical Sketch of Gurdon Saltonstall Hubbard* (1908); there are obituaries of Hubbard in the *Harpel Scrapbook*, 1888 edition, at the CHS.

50 *"time [I met him in 1835]"*: John Dean Caton to Mrs. Gurdon S. Hubbard, Aug. 14, 1888, in Paul Angle, "One Pioneer, by Another," *CH* 1 (Winter 1945–46): 35.

50 *"is the history of Chicago"*: Grant Goodrich, "Gurdon S. Hubbard; A Settler of Chicago in 1818," (Read before the CHS, Nov. 16, 1886) in Edward G. Mason, ed., *Early Chicago and Illinois* (1890), 26.

50 *"Only a single man"*: Quoted in Caroline M. McIlvaine's introduction to Hubbard's *Autobiography*, xiii.

PAGE

51 *"a defiant middle finger":* Jacqueline Peterson, "'Wild' Chicago: The Formation and Destruction of a Multiracial Community on the Midwestern Frontier, 1816–1837," in Melvin G. Holli and Peter d'A. Jones, eds., *The Ethnic Frontier: Essays in the History of Group Survival in Chicago and the Midwest* (1977), 52; see also Peterson, "Goodbye, Madore Beaubien: The Americanization of Early Chicago Society," *CH* 9 (Summer 1980): 98–111.

51 *Frederick Jackson Turner:* Frederick Jackson Turner, "The Significance of the Frontier in American History," in *Annual Report of the American Historical Association for the Year* 1893 (1894), 197–227.

52 *"and we, in our holiday attire":* Hubbard, *Autobiography,* 1–30.

53 *"swollen and inflamed":* Ibid., 41–43, 89–90; see also Hamilton, *Epic,* 96–97.

53 *trader in the Illinois country:* Hubbard, *Autobiography,* 58–64; Lowell A. Dearinger, "Trader Hubbard," *Outdoor Illinois* 8 (July-Aug. 1969): 8–17, 44; Gurdon S. Hubbard, "Journey of Gurdon S. Hubbard," *Pioneer Collections: Report of the Pioneer Society of the State of Michigan* 3 (1881): 125–27.

53 *"I passed over":* Quoted in Mrs. John H. Kinzie, *Wau-Bun: The "Early Day" in the North-West* (1856; reprint, 1948), 143, note.

55 *"the village":* William H. Keating, *Narrative of an Expedition to the Source of St. Peter's River . . . 1823 . . . Under the Command of Stephen Long, U.S.T.E.; Compiled from the Notes of Major Long, messrs. Say, Keating and Calhoun,* vol. 1 (1824), 162–67; see also Henry Row Schoolcraft, *Narrative Journal of Travels Through the Northwestern Regions of the United States . . . to the Sources of the Mississippi . . . in the Year 1820* (1821), 384; and Charles Butler, *Journal,* Aug. 2, 1833, in Charles Butler Papers, CHS (hereafter cited as Butler MSS).

55 *The Canadian-born Kinzie:* John Kinzie Papers and Accounts, CHS, was my principal source of information on Kinzie; Ramsay Crooks to John Kinzie, Nov. 1, 1821, American Fur Company Account Books, CHS. There are some copies of Letter Books of the American Fur Company in the American Fur Company Papers, CHS; Quaife, *Checagou,* 102–7; accounts of the massacre are in the Fort Dearborn Papers, CHS; for a biographical sketch of John Kinzie, see AA:1, 72–76.

55 *John Kinzie returned in 1816:* Quaife, *Checagou,* 156–74; for Indian life and the development of the fur trade in the region, see Jacqueline Louise Peterson, "The Peoples in Between: Indian-White Marriage and the Genesis of a Metis Society and Culture in the Great Lakes Region, 1680–1830" (Ph.D. diss., Univ. of Illinois at Chicago, 1981); for a masterful account of the interactions among Europeans and Indians of the Great Lakes regions, see Richard White, *The Middle Ground: Indians, Empires, and Republics in the Great Lakes Regions, 1650–1850* (1991); for the American Fur Company, see especially John D. Haeger, "The American Fur Company and Chicago of 1812–1835," JISHS (Summer 1968): 117–39.

55 *He had no chance:* Kinzie's *Account Books* (CHS) reflect the falloff of his trade; Ramsay Crooks to John Kinzie, Nov. 1, 1821, American Fur Trading Company Account Books, CHS.

55 Wau-Bun: Mrs. Kinzie, *Wau-Bun,* 143, 148; for the legend of Kinzie, see also *SOC,* 88; James Ryan Haydon, "John Kinzie's Place in History," *Transactions of the Illinois State Historical Society* 39 (1932): 183–89; Eleanor Lytle Kinzie Gordon, *John Kinzie, The "Father of Chicago": A Sketch* (1910); and Juliette A. Kinzie [Mrs. John H. Kinzie], *Mark Logan, the Bourgeois* (1887). The latter book was written in 1870, the year Mrs.

PAGE

Kinzie died when a druggist mistakenly gave her morphine instead of quinine.

56 *Point du Sable:* Milo M. Quaife, ed., "Property of Jean Baptiste Point du Sable," *Mississippi Valley Historical Review* 15 (June 1928): 89–92; Thomas A. Meehan, "Jean Baptiste Point du Sable: The First Chicagoan," JISHS 56 (Autumn 1963): 439–53; Augustin Grignon, "Seventy-two Years' Recollections of Wisconsin," *Collections of the State Historical Society, Wisconsin* 3 (1856): 292; AA:1, 70–77.

56 *one historian speculates:* Milo M. Quaife conjectured that du Sable was a baseborn descendant of the Dandonneau dit du Sable family, from Bourges, France. Quaife, *Checagou,* 31–36; The first book that disputed Mrs. Kinzie's account of Chicago's founding, Milo M. Quaife's *Chicago and the Old Northwest,* published in 1913, might have gone unnoticed had not the *CT* run a feature story on the CHS's refusal to publish it when it was offered to them. See *CT,* Aug. 16, 1912.

56 *Mark Beaubien:* AA:1, 84–85, 106–7; Frank Beaubien, "The Beaubiens of Chicago," *Illinois Catholic Historical Review* 2 (July 1919): 96–105 and (Jan. 1920): 348–64; Peterson, "'Wild' Chicago," 37–38; "Beaubiens of Chicago," Frank Gordon Beaubien Papers, CHS; Charles Cleaver, *Early-Chicago Reminiscences* (1882), 5–12; information on the Beaubiens, Billy Caldwell, and early Chicago can be found in the Beaubien Family Papers, the Billy Caldwell Papers, and the Madore Beaubien Papers, all at the CHS.

56 *Billy Caldwell:* For Billy Caldwell, see Clifton, *Prairie People,* 322–26, and James A. Clifton, "Billy Caldwell's Exile in Early Chicago," *CH* 6 (Winter 1977-78): 218–28.

56 *These taverns: Chicago Democrat,* July 8, 1835, Aug. 23, 1843; Cleaver, *Reminiscences,* 4–10; John Wentworth to Lydia Wentworth, Nov. 10, 1836, John Wentworth Papers, CHS; Edwin O. Gale, *Reminiscences of Early Chicago and Vicinity* (1902), 32.

57 *"a jolly good fellow":* Isaac N. Arnold quoted in Frank Beaubien, "The Beaubiens of Chicago," 361–62.

57 *"I plays de fiddle":* Undated MSS, Beaubien Family Papers, CHS.

57 *"Oh them was fine times":* Quoted in Frank Beaubien, "The Beaubiens of Chicago," 361.

57 *"a mighty lonesome":* Interview with Madore Beaubien, *Chicago Times,* May 16, 1882.

58 *"Didn't expect no town":* Quoted in Peterson, "'Wild' Chicago," 64.

58 *"I have been unsuccessful":* Gurdon Hubbard to Elizabeth Hubbard, Apr. 5, 1827, Hubbard MSS.

58 *"[my] true honest friends":* Hubbard, "Recollections of Gurdon S. Hubbard," Address Before Danville's Old Settlers Association (1880), 2, Hubbard MSS.

59 *"knew who owned it":* Wendt, *"Swift Walker",* 357.

59 *canal to the East:* James William Putnam, *The Illinois and Michigan Canal: A Study in Economic History* (1918), 10–18; Ninian Edwards to Henry Clay, July 18, 1825, Ninian Edwards Papers, CHS; Thomas Ford, *History of Illinois, From Its Commencement as a State in 1818 to 1847* (1854), 179–80.

59 *moved his combination house and tavern:* Undated manuscripts, Beaubien Family Papers, CHS.

59 *"urban strategists":* Michael P. Conzen, "The Historical and Geographical Development of the Illinois and Michigan Canal National Heritage Corridor," in Conzen and Kay J. Carr, eds., *The Illinois and Michigan*

PAGE

Canal National Heritage Corridor: A Guide to its History and Sources (1988), 9–10.

59 *"love the hum":* Wilson Nicely, *The Great Southwest* (1867), as quoted in David Hamer, *New Towns in the New World: Images and Perceptions of the Nineteenth-Century Urban Frontier* (1990), 100; see also William Cronon, *Nature's Metropolis: Chicago and the Great West* (1991). There is a growing bibliography, which Cronon summarizes, on this theme.

60 *Black Hawk:* Stephen R. Beggs, *Pages from the Early History of the West and North-West* (1868), 97–101; John Reynolds to Andrew Jackson, August 15, 1831, in Everts B. Greene and Clarence W. Alvord, eds., *Governors' Letter-Books, 1818–1834* (1909), 183.

60 *Asiatic cholera:* James N. Hyde, *Early Medical Chicago* (1879), 18–19.

61 *writing a stirring autobiography:* Black Hawk, *An Autobiography,* ed. Donald Jackson (1833; reprint, 1955); for the Black Hawk War, see Anthony F. C. Wallace, "Prelude to Disaster: The Course of Indian-White Relations Which Led to the Black Hawk War of 1832," *Collections of the Illinois State Historical Library* 35 (1970): 1–51; and Roger L. Nichols, "The Black Hawk War in Retrospect," *Wisconsin Magazine of History* 65 (1982): 238–46.

61 *Great White Father's interest:* Charles J. Latrobe, *The Rambler in North America,* vol. 2 (1836), 203.

61 *"upstart village":* Ibid., 203–16; for a graphic description of Chicago at this time, see Patrick Shirreff, *A Tour Through North America* (1835), especially 227–28.

62 *"our Great Father":* Charles J. Kappler, *Indian Affairs: Laws and Treaties,* vol. 2 (1904): 402–5.

62 *"appalling confusion":* Latrobe, *Rambler,* 205–16; see also Reuben Gold Thwaites, "Narrative of Peter J. Vieau," *Wisconsin Historical Collections* 15 (1900): 460–63.

62 *"forcible Jacksonian discourse":* Latrobe, *Rambler,* 210.

62 *council fire:* Hamilton, *Epic,* 237; Clifton, *Prairie People,* 238–45.

63 *last great Indian cession: Treaty with the Chippewa, Ottawa, and Potawatomi Indians, 1833,* in General Records of the U.S. Government Record Group 11, Ratified Indian Treaties (M668), National Archives, Washington, D.C.; James A. Clifton, "Chicago, September 14, 1833: The Last Great Indian Treaty in the Old Northwest," *CH* 9 (Summer 1980): 86–97; Anselm J. Gerwing, "The Chicago Indian Treaty of 1833," *JISHS* 57 (1964): 117–42.

63 *"Chicago, like Carthage":* Edgar Lee Masters, *The Tale of Chicago* (1933), 65.

63 *"active axes":* Latrobe, *Rambler,* 205–10.

63 *"too poor for snakes":* Jacob Van Der Zee, "Episodes in the Early History of the Wisconsin Iowa Country," *Iowa Journal of History and Politics* 11 (1913): 340; see also Gerwing, "Chicago Indian Treaty," 140.

63 *"their eyes wild":* John Dean Caton, *The Last of the Illinois and a Sketch of the Pottawatomes, Read before the Chicago Historical Society, December 13, 1870* (1876), 1–30, 118–20.

64 *"was troubled with them":* Parton, "Chicago," 328; see also Clifton, *Prairie People,* 277–346.

64 *"a most woe-begone appearance":* AA:1, 128.

64 *"'all nations and kindred":* Colbee C. Benton, *A Visitor to Chicago in Indian Days, "Journal to the Far-Off West",* ed. Paul M. Angle and James R. Getz (1957), 70–77.

PAGE

64 *"Strict sobersides"*: Quoted in Melvin G. Holli, "French Detroit: The Clash of Feudal and Yankee Values," in Holli and Jones, *Ethnic Frontier*, 90; see also Haeger, "American Fur Company," 138.

64 *"passive endurance"*: Lewis Mumford, *The City in History: Its Origins, Its Transformations, and Its Prospects* (1961), 30.

65 *"The shriek"*: Quoted in Holli, "French Detroit," 92.

65 *"magical changes"*: Joseph N. Balestier, *The Annals of Chicago; A Lecture Delivered Before the Chicago Lyceum, January 21, 1840* (1840), 1–24.

Chapter Three: Ogden's Chicago

66 *"the smaller town"*: Quoted in Tilton, "Hubbard," 145; *Reminiscences and Scrap-book of Gurdon Hubbard,* Hubbard MSS.

66 *an important city:* Hubbard to Samuel and Edward A. Russell, Sept. 25, 1835, Hubbard MSS.

67 *"foreign peasantry"*: G. A. Troop to Addison Troop, June 3, 1847, Transcripts, CHS.

67 *"where it remained"*: Cleaver, *Reminiscences,* 13–14, 30.

68 *"mere shells"*: Charles Fenno Hoffman, *A Winter in the West: By a New-Yorker* (1835), 242–43; Cleaver, *Reminiscences,* 6–7.

68 *impossible to write:* Hoffman, *Winter,* 242.

68 *"we felt and knew"*: John Dean Caton, "Address to the Settlers of Chicago Prior to 1840, May 27, 1879," in Mabel McIlvaine, ed., *Reminiscences of Early Chicago* (1912), 158.

68 *Jefferson Davis: Reminiscences and Scrap-book of Gurdon Hubbard,* n.p.

68 *"worst . . . any great commercial city"*: [Caroline Kirkland], "Illinois in Spring-Time: With a Look at Chicago," *AM* 2 (Sept. 1858): 487.

68 *"sick in consequence"*: Henry G. Hubbard quoted in Hamilton, *Epic,* 262.

68 *Bronson:* Charles Butler to CHS, Dec. 17, 1881, Autograph Letters, vol. 31, CHS; see also Francis Hovey Stoddard, *The Life and Letters of Charles Butler* (1903), 131; a record of Bronson's Chicago investments is in the *Land Books* of Arthur and Frederic Bronson, Bronson Papers, CHS.

69 *"If I were a young man"*: Butler to CHS, Dec. 17, 1881, CHS; Butler to Eliza Butler, Aug. 4, 1833, Butler to Bowen Whitney, Aug. 7, 1833, Butler to editors of *Albany Argus,* entitled "The Far West—Internal Improvement—Trade and Intercourse with the State of New York," Aug. 1833; Charles Butler, "Diary of a Journey, 1833." All in Charles Butler Collection, Library of Congress (hereafter cited as Butler MSS); Stoddard, *Butler,* 140–48; John Denis Haeger, *The Investment Frontier: New York Businessmen and the Economic Development of the Old Northwest* (1981), 74–127.

69 *Bronson also saw possibilities:* Haeger, *Investment Frontier,* 88–92, 105–27. .

70 *so "wild"*: Hubbard to Samuel and Edward A. Russell, Jan. 3, 1834; Hubbard to E. Russell, July 5, Sept. 25, 1835, Hubbard MSS; a record of Hubbard's business transactions is in the Hubbard MSS; Hamilton, *Epic,* 234–44; AA:3, 137.

70 *"the only remaining link"*: Hoffman, *Winter,* 245.

70 *"[You have] been guilty"*: Quoted in Butler to CHS, Dec. 17, 1881 Butler MSS; see also Ogden to Charles Butler, July 21, 1836, William Butler Ogden Letter, Book I, William B. Ogden Papers, CHS (hereafter cited as Ogden MSS); Patrick E. McLear, "William Butler Ogden: A Chicago Pro-

PAGE

moter in the Speculative Era and the Panic of 1837," *JISHS* 70 (November 1977): 284; McLear, "'. . . And Still They Come'—Chicago from 1832–36," *Journal of the West* 7, no. 3 (1968): 397–404; William L. Downard, "William Butler Ogden and the Growth of Chicago," *JISHS* 75 (Spring 1982): 47–60; Rima Lunin Schultz, "The Businessman's Role in Western Settlement: The Entrepreneurial Frontier, Chicago, 1833–1872," (Ph.D. diss., Boston Univ., 1985).

71   *a hustler's town:* Nelson Algren, *Chicago, City on the Make* (1951; reprint, 1987), 10–11.

71   *"I never saw a busier place":* Harriet Martineau, *Society in America*, vol. 1 (1837), 259–61; Patrick E. McLear, "Land Speculators and Urban and Regional Development: Chicago in the 1830s," *The Old Northwest* 6 (Summer 1980): 137–51.

72   *"wild prophesy":* Chicago Democrat, July 4–6, 1836; *Chicago American*, July 4–5, 1836.

72   *rushed the Irishmen: Reminiscences and Scrap-book of Gurdon Hubbard*, n.p.; AA:1, 165–68; Wendt, *"Swift Walker,"* 265–68; Tilton, "Hubbard," 161.

72   *"we shall see Chicago":* Balestier, *Annals*, 10–24.

72   *"great city":* The legislator, Henry W. Blodgett, is quoted in Caroline M. McIlvaine, introduction to Hubbard, *Autobiography*, xix–xx; see also Hamilton, *Epic*, 346.

73   *"absolute faith":* Isaac N. Arnold, "William B. Ogden and Early Days in Chicago," in Isaac N. Arnold and J. Young Scammon, *William B. Ogden* (1882), 4–10.

73   *"I did not . . . come here":* Grant Goodrich in *Reception to the Settlers of Chicago Prior to 1840* (1879), 63–66.

73   *"the most splendid system":* Arnold, "Ogden," 9; Thomas Wakefield Goodspeed, "William Butler Ogden," in *The University of Chicago Biographical Sketches*, vol. 1 (1922), 36–37.

74   *"He could not forget":* J. Young Scammon, "William B. Ogden" in Arnold and Scammon, *Ogden*, 72.

74   *"the first born of Chicago"* and *"transient speculator":* Chicago American, Apr. 29, 1837.

74   *put their man in office:* Marion G. Scheitlin, "Chicago's First City Election," *Sunday Record-Herald*, Mar. 31, 1907, in CHS; for a perceptive analysis of Chicago's booster system of government, see Robin L. Einhorn, *Property Rules: Political Economy in Chicago, 1833–1872* (1991), chapter 2.

74   *"a faucet":* Goodspeed, "Ogden," 41; John Wentworth, *Early Chicago* (1876), 37.

75   *"Men exchanged lots":* Wentworth, *Early Chicago*, 37.

75   *"was a colony":* Haeger, *Investment*, 229.

75   *"wholly existential":* Jane Jacobs, *The Economy of Cities* (1970), 141–42, 144.

76   *"who built":* Quoted in Arnold, "Ogden," 25.

76   *"By God":* Quoted in Wayne Andrews, *Battle for Chicago* (1946), 12.

76   *"every man":* Joseph T. Ryerson, "Gleanings from a Family Memoir," in Caroline Kirkland, ed., *Chicago Yesterdays: A Sheaf of Reminiscences* (1919), 56.

77   *"made us what we are":* Quoted in Frederick Cople Jaher, *The Urban Establishment: Upper Strata in Boston, New York, Charleston, Chicago, and Los Angeles* (1982), 467.

PAGE

77   *William Hibbard:* Addie Hibbard Gregory, *A Great-Grandmother Remembers* (1940), 7.

77   *"Poor and vicious foreigners":* William Ogden to A. Bushnell, Nov. 24, 1840, Ogden MSS.

77   *"Long John" Wentworth:* John Wentworth, *The Wentworth Genealogy: English and American,* 3 vols. (1878).

77   *"in pursuit of fortune and fame":* Quoted in Don Fehrenbacher, *Chicago Giant: A Biography of "Long John" Wentworth* (1957), 3.

78   *"the shortest":* Carl Sandburg, "John Wentworth," in *DAB,* vol. 8, 562–65.

78   *In his retirement:* Clippings, John Wentworth Papers, CHS; *GG,* 29–44; Fehrenbacher, *Chicago Giant,* 104–220.

78   *He died:* McIlvaine, ed., *Reminiscences,* xxiv; Ann Steinbrecher Windle, "John Wentworth, His Contribution to Chicago," in *Papers in Illinois History and Transactions for the Year 1937* (1938), 1–17.

78   *"desolate . . . young bachelors":* Chicago American, May 27, 1837.

79   *"vulgar exhibition":* Arnold, "Ogden," 24.

79   *"with robes thrown":* Cleaver, *Reminiscences,* 40–41; see also Mary Drummond, "Long Ago," in Kirkland, ed., *Chicago Yesterdays,* 140; and Reyerson, "Gleanings," in Ibid., 60.

79   *"It is a remarkable thing":* Harriet Martineau, "Society in America," in McIlvaine, ed., *Reminiscences,* 30.

79   *"when we [bachelors]":* Wentworth, *Early Chicago,* 35.

79   *"The guest":* Arnold, "Ogden," 24.

79   *"in conversation":* George P. A. Healy, *Reminiscences of a Portrait Painter* (1894), 57–64.

80   *"gave to the neighborhood":* Arnold, "Ogden," 23.

80   *"cultivated mind":* CDD, quoted in Daniel Bluestone, *Constructing Chicago* (1991), 11.

80   *"turned the heads":* Arnold, "Ogden," 22; see also Ogden to Charles Butler, Dec. 8, 1840, Ogden MSS.

80   *"deceptive treachery":* Ogden to F. Vanderburgh, Dec. 12, 1840, Ogden to James Allen, Jan. 15, 1840, Ogden to J. Whitcombs, Oct. 18, 1837, Ogden MSS.

80   *"to trade":* Fredrika Bremer, *The Homes of the New World: Impressions of America,* vol. 1 (1853), 601–12; see also William A. White, "Tradition and Urban Development: A Contrast of Chicago and Toronto in the Nineteenth Century," *Old Northwest* 8, no. 3 (1982): 255.

80   *"To be busy":* Mrs. Abby (Farwell) Ferry, *Reminiscences of John V. Farwell By His Elder Daughter,* vol. 1 (1928), 128, 151–52.

81   *Romans used the grid:* Richard Sennett, *The Conscience of the Eye: The Design and Social Life of Cities* (1990), 46–48; see also, Joseph Rykwert, *The Idea of a Town: The Anthropology of Urban Form in Rome, Italy, and the Ancient World* (1988).

82   *"With a T-square":* Mumford, *City in History,* 422; see also Spiro Kostof, *The City Shaped: Urban Patterns and Meanings Through History* (1991), 127.

82   *"powers of conquest":* Sennett, *Conscience,* 48.

83   *"one of the shabbiest":* Bremer, *Homes,* 601–6.

83   *"privatism":* Sam Bass Warner, Jr. *The Private City: Philadelphia in Three Periods of Growth* (1968), x–xi.

83   *"as abstract units":* Mumford, *City in History,* 421.

83   *"Emigrants were coming":* Butler to CHS, Dec. 17, 1881, Butler MSS.

PAGE
83 *"a common-sense way"*: Daniel J. Boorstin, *The Americans: The National Experience* (1965; reprint, 1967), 148.

83 *"never have arisen"*: Solon Robinson quoted in George E. Woodward, *Woodward's Country Homes* (1865).

84 *the balloon frame:* Paul E. Sprague, "The Origin of Balloon Framing," *JSAH* 40 (Dec. 4, 1981): 311–19; Sigfried Giedion, *Space, Time and Architecture: The Growth of a New Tradition* (1941; reprint, 1978), 351–53; Walker Field, "A Re-Examination into the Invention of the Balloon Frame," *JSAH* 2 (Oct. 1942): 3–29. Field disputes Giedion's claim that Snow first used the technique of balloon framing to build St. Mary's Church in 1833. St. Mary's, he proves, was built by Taylor, and he goes on to argue that Taylor was therefore the originator of balloon framing. However, more recent research by Sprague verifies that it was Snow who originated balloon framing, but in 1832, not 1833, and in the erection of a warehouse, not a church.

84 *"To put together"*: Giedion, *Space*, 347.

84 *Alexis de Tocqueville:* Sennett, *Conscience*, 51–52.

85 *"the fronts of which"*: Van Osdel in AA:1, 504.

85 *"the day of retribution"*: Balestier, *Annals*, 1–20.

85 *"It fell"*: Goodspeed, "Ogden," 38–42.

85 *"the more land"*: Balestier, *Annals*, 5–18.

85 *"Inflammatory speeches"*: AA:1, 618.

86 *"courage of men"*: Reported in Scammon, "Ogden," 46–47.

87 A *"raw"* and *"slovenly"*: William Cullen Bryant, *Letters of a Traveler: Notes of Things Seen in Europe and America* (1850), 259–60.

88 *"Chicago really owes"*: Currey, *Chicago*, vol. 1, 219.

Chapter Four: The Great Chicago Exchange Engine

90 *"slab city"*: William Bross, *What I Remember of Early Chicago: A Lecture* (1876), 116–19; John Lewis Peyton, *Over the Alleghanies and Across the Prairies: Personal Recollections of the Far West* (1869), 325–27; Bross passed through Chicago in 1846 but didn't settle in the city until 1848; see also Luther Van Dorn, "A View of Chicago in 1848," *Magazine of Western History* 10 (1889): 41–46; and William Cronon, "To Be The Central City: Chicago, 1848–1857," *CH* 10, no. 3 (1981): 130–40; for Bross, see Charles A. Young, *William Bross, 1813–1890* (1940); for the role of boosters in Chicago's development, see Carl Abbott, *Boosters and Businessmen: Popular Economic Thought and Urban Growth in the Antebellum Middle West* (1981); for another important Chicago booster, see Lloyd Lewis, *John S. Wright: Prophet of the Prairies* (1941).

90 *"we would be a week"*: Bross, *What I Remember*, 120–22.

90 *"is as mean a spot"*: Edward L. Peckham, "My Journey Out West," *Journal of American History* 17, no. 3 (1923): 227–30; Bross, *What I Remember*, 123.

90 *"Queen of the Lakes"*: Bremer, *Homes*, vol. 1, 601–12.

90 *"wild, rough"*: Peyton, *Alleghanies*, 328; *Chicago Daily Journal*, Oct. 18, 1849.

91 *"restless activity"*: Peyton, *Alleghanies*, 327, 342–43.

91 *"The modern world"*: Nicholas Faith, *The World the Railways Made* (1990), 1; Albro Martin makes the same argument for the railroad's importance. It was, he writes, "the most significant invention or innovation in the rise of an industrial society." *Railroads Triumphant* (1992), 12; for

PAGE

an alternative view, deemphasizing the railroad's economic importance, see Robert W. Fogel, *Railroads and American Economic Growth: Essays in Econometric History* (1964).

91 *"The development of the [prairies]":* Quoted in Boorstin, *The Americans: The National Experience,* 102.

92 *"Chicago does not":* Chicago Times, Mar. 25, 1868.

92 *"There seems a natural":* Quoted in Boorstin, *The Americans: The National Experience,* 102.

92 *"space is killed":* Quoted in Faith, *World,* 42.

92 *"first great railroad man":* Stewart H. Holbrook, *The Story of American Railroads* (1947), 133.

93 *"no one else":* CT, Aug. 4, 1877.

93 *River and Harbor Convention:* Robert Fergus, comp., *Chicago River-and-Harbor Convention, an Account of its Origin and Proceedings . . .* (1882); Mentor L. Williams, "The Chicago River and Harbor Convention, 1847," *Mississippi Valley Historical Review* 35 (June 1948–Mar. 1949): 607–26; Williams, "The Background of the Chicago River and Harbor Convention, 1847," *Mid-America* 30 (Oct. 1948): 219–32.

94 *He found them still cautious:* Scammon, "William B. Ogden," 66–67.

94 *$350,000 worth of stock:* Stock Subscription Lists of the Galena and Chicago Union Railroad Company, Charles S. Hempstead Collection, CHS; Ogden to Hempstead, Aug. 25, 1848, Hempstead Collection.

94 *"the first of the mighty army":* SOC, 201; see also John H. White, Jr., *The "Pioneer": Chicago's First Locomotive* (1976), 5–18.

95 *"player with railroads":* Carl Sandburg, *The Complete Poems of Carl Sandburg* (1970), 3.

95 *"electrified":* Galena and Chicago Union Railroad Company, *Report of William B. Ogden, Esq., President of the Company, . . . April 5, 1848* (1848), 3–4; *Chicago Daily Journal,* Nov. 21, 1848; Patrick E. McLear, "The Galena and Chicago Union Railroad: A Symbol of Chicago's Economic Maturity," *JISHS* 73 (1980): 17–26.

95 *"great wheat feeder":* HC: 3, 51.

95 *"by driblets":* Joseph Nimmo, Jr., *Report on the Internal Commerce of the United States* (1877–81), 24.

95 *"lays tribute":* Ridgley, *Geography,* 262.

96 *environmental costs:* Cronon, *Nature's Metropolis,* passim.

97 *"followed by their wives":* John Dean Caton, "'Tis Sixty Years Since' in Chicago," *AM* 71 (May 1893): 591–92; see also Russell S. Kirby, "Nineteenth-Century Patterns of Railroad Development on the Great Plains," *Great Plains Quarterly* 3, no. 3 (1983): 157–70.

97 *"All is astir":* Lippincott wrote under the name Grace Greenwood. *New Life in New Lands: Notes of Travel* (1873), 7–20; see also James Stirling, *Letters from the Slave States* (1857), 1–3.

98 *"started":* Douglas, "Autobiographical Sketch," Sept. 1, 1838, Stephen A. Douglas, *Letters,* ed., Robert W. Johannsen (1961), 59.

98 *"It was as natural":* Quoted in Robert W. Johannsen, *Stephen A. Douglas* (1973), 23–24.

99 *"I have become a Western man":* Douglas to Julius N. Granger, Dec. 15, 1833, Douglas, *Letters,* 3; see also, Douglas letters to Granger, Nov. 14, July 13, 1834, and Nov. 9, 1835, Douglas, *Letters,* 8–21.

99 *"one of the most gigantic enterprises":* Douglas to the Citizens of Chicago, Oct. 1850, Douglas, *Letters,* 197; Johannsen, *Douglas,* 314; *Chicago*

PAGE

Journal, Oct. 15, 1850, June 16, 1851; Darius B. Holbrook to Douglas, June 17, 20, 1850, Stephen A. Douglas Papers, University of Chicago Library, Dept. of Special Collections; for Wright's role in the creation of the Illinois Central, see Lewis, *Wright,* 122–30.

99   *"colonizing":* Johannsen, *Douglas,* 317; Paul W. Gates, *The Illinois Central Railroad and Its Colonization Work* (1934) is the standard work on the subject; see also John F. Stover, *History of the Illinois Central Railroad* (1975).

101   *"by right belongs":* Daniel H. Burnham and Edward H. Bennett, *Plan of Chicago* (1909; reprint, 1969); the best history of the battle for the lakefront is Lois Wille, *Forever Open, Clear and Free: The Historic Struggle for Chicago's Lakefront* (1972).

101   *"particular benefits":* Robin L. Einhorn, "A Taxing Dilemma: Early Lake Shore Protection," *CH* 18 (Fall 1989): 34–51. Einhorn bases her conclusions on the Chicago City Clerk Files, which were thought to have been lost in the Great Fire but were discovered in 1984. There is now a catalog of these papers; see Robert Baily et al., *Chicago City Council Proceedings Files 1833–1871: An Inventory* (1987); see also Einhorn, *Property Rules.*

102   *"Railroads are* not *constructed":* Quoted in Einhorn, "Taxing," 46; see also Stover, *Illinois Central,* 43–45, 180–81.

102   *"pathless waves": SOC,* 221.

102   *"As we approach . . . Chicago":* William H. Russell, *My Diary, North and South,* vol. 2 (1863), 87.

103   *"Glistening like a knight":* Chicago *Daily Journal,* Mar. 31, 1851.

104   *"whole soul":* Quoted in Herbert N. Casson, *Cyrus Hall McCormick: His Life and Work* (1909), 58.

104   *labor-hungry:* William T. Hutchinson, *Cyrus Hall McCormick,* vol. 1 (1930), 3–35, 258–63; Cyrus McCormick, *The Century of the Reaper* (1931), 1–12; Ogden's business records are in the Ogden MSS. The partnership ended amicably.

105   *John Deere's steel plow:* Herbert A. Kellar, "The Reaper as a Factor in the Development of the Agriculture of Illinois, 1834–1865," *Transactions of the Illinois State Historical Society* 34 (1927): 105–14; Wayne G. Broehl, Jr., *John Deere's Company: A History of Deere & Company and Its Times* (1984), 1–65.

105   *"mowed and reaped":* Parton, "Chicago," 337.

105   *traditional practices of manufacture:* For a study of McCormick's rather traditional manufacturing methods, see David A. Hounshell, *From the American System to Mass Production, 1800–1932: The Development of Manufacturing Technology in the United States* (1984), 152–87; McCormick's sales records are in the McCormick Archives, State Historical Society of Wisconsin; his production figures are listed in Hounshell, *American System,* 161.

105   *One price to all:* Hutchinson, *McCormick,* vol. 2 (1935), 87, 492, 499; see also Alan L. Olmstead, "The Mechanization of Reaping and Mowing in American Agriculture, 1833–1870," *Journal of Economic History* 35 (1975): 327–52.

105   *"To sell, I must advertise": McCormick's Reaper's Centennial Source Material* ([1931]), 55.

105   *testimonials: Genesee Farmer,* July 1850, 173; for a shrewd analysis of the McCormick sales and production system, see Cronon, *Nature's Metropolis,* 313–18.

106   *"a great commercial Thor":* Casson, *McCormick,* 154.

PAGE

106 *"work, work!"*: Quoted in ibid., 187; see also 73, 143; and Hutchinson, *McCormick*, vol. 2, 755.

107 *"the American Ceres"*: Anthony Trollope, *North America*, ed. Donald Smalley and Bradford Allen Booth (1862; reprint, 1951), 163–65; see also Thomas D. Odle, "The American Grain Trade of the Great Lakes, 1825–1873," *Inland Seas* 7 (1951): 237–45; 8 (1952): 22–28; and "The Great Granaries of Chicago," *HW* 3 (Sept. 10, 1859): 580.

108 *"bursting bags"*: *Chicago Democratic Press*, Sept. 13, 1854.

108 *"the great item with commercial men"*: Allan R. Pred, *Urban Growth and City-Systems in the United States, 1840–1860* (1980), 151–56.

108 *categorizing wheat by "grade"*: *Chicago Weekly Democrat*, Sept. 19, 1848; the best history of the Chicago grain elevator system is Guy A. Lee, "History of the Chicago Grain Elevator Industry, 1840–1890," (Ph.D. diss., Harvard Univ., 1938). Lee summarizes his work in "The Historical Significance of the Chicago Grain Elevator System," *Agricultural History* 11 (Jan. 1937): 16–32; The best history of the grain trade is John G. Clark, *The Grain Trade in the Old Northwest* (1966), 88–89, 255–78; for Chicago, see especially Chicago Board of Trade, *Annual Statement of the Trade and Commerce of Chicago (1862)*, 12; and Cronon, *Nature's Metropolis*, 97–147.

109 *"Altar of Ceres"*: *CT*, Aug. 11, 1865; Jonathan Lurie, *The Chicago Board of Trade, 1859–1905: The Dynamics of Self Regulation* (1979), 24–25.

110 *"men who don't own"*: Morton Rothstein, "Frank Norris and Popular Perceptions of the Market," *Agricultural History* 56 (1982): 58; see also Henry Crosby Emery, *Speculation on the Stock and Produce Exchanges of the United States* (1896), 38–40; Charles H. Taylor, ed., *History of the Board of Trade of the City of Chicago*, vol. 1 (1917), 107–93; vol. 2 (1917). This three-volume work is the only history of the Board of Trade, and it is largely noncritical and filled with errors; Jeffrey C. Williams, "The Origin of Futures Markets," *Agricultural History* 56, no. 1 (1982): 306–16; Percy Tracy Dodlinger, *The Book of Wheat: An Economic History and Practical Manual of the Wheat Industry* (1919), 221–25; for futures contracts as a form of gambling, see Ann Fabian, *Card Sharps, Dream Books, and Bucket Shops: Gambling in Nineteenth-Century America* (1990).

110 *"Over these wires"*: Daniel S. Curtiss, *Western Portraiture and Emigrants' Guide* (1852), 334; Joel A. Tarr with Thomas Finholt and David Goodman, "The City and the Telegraph: Urban Telecommunications in the Pre-Telephone Era," *Journal of Urban History* 14, no. 1 (1987): 38–80.

110 *"a grand ring"*: Joseph Medill, representing the Fifty-eighth District, in *Debates and Proceedings of the Constitutional Convention of the State of Illinois* (1870), 1629.

111 *"one of the most purely capitalistic"*: Thomas C. Cochran, *Business in American Life: A History* (1972), 67; see also Chester M. Destler, "Agricultural Readjustment and Agrarian Unrest in Illinois, 1880–1896," *Agricultural History* 21 (1947): 104–16; Harold D. Woodman, "Chicago Businessmen and the 'Granger Laws,'" *Agricultural History* 36 (1962): 16–24.

111 *The Chicago lumber trade*: George W. Hotchkiss, *History of the Lumber and Forest Industry of the Northwest* (1898), 661–65; AA:1, 554–55; Clippings, Hubbard MSS.

112 *"Over . . . this great rich prairie"*: John Dean Caton, "John Dean Caton's Reminiscences of Chicago in 1833 and 1834," ed. Harry E. Pratt, *JISHS* 28 (1935): 5–25.

PAGE

112 *Peshtigo River:* Ogden's record books are in the Ogden MSS; Scammon, "Ogden," 55.

113 *"Scores of chimneys":* James J. Wirt, "The Lumber Interests of Chicago," *HW* 27 (Oct. 20, 1883): 666; see also "A Visit to the States: The Metropolis of the Lakes," *Times* (London), Oct. 21, 24, 1887: 727–30; *HC:*2, 70–71.

114 *"how largely the manufactures":* AA:1, 560.

114 *"The corn crop":* Samuel B. Ruggles quoted in Parton, "Chicago," 331.

114 *Chicago replaced Cincinnati:* Margaret Walsh, *The Rise of the Midwestern Meat Packing Industry* (1982), 56–92; Richard G. Arms, "From Dis-Assembly to Assembly; Cincinnati: The Birthplace of Mass Production," *Bulletin of the Historical and Philosophical Society of Ohio* 17 (1959): 195–203.

115 *"In dealing":* The poem is from *The American Elevator and Grain Trade* 7 (Oct. 15, 1888): 83.

115 *"The very word":* B. P. Hutchinson, "Speculation in Wheat," *NAR* 153 (1891): 414–19; *CT,* Sept. 25, 28, 29, 1888, Jan. 1, 1889. "Some Anecdotes of 'Old Hutch,'" Charles L. Hutchinson Papers, Newberry Library (hereafter cited as Hutchinson MSS); Edward J. Dies, *The Plunger: A Tale of the Wheat Pit* (1929), 11–12, 25–28, 44; William Ferris, "Old Hutch—The Wheat King," *JISHS* 41 (1948): 231–43.

115 *"It was my immediate purpose":* Quoted in Edward J. Dies, *Street of Adventure* (1935), 201.

116 *his luck changed:* "Scrapbooks," Hutchinson MSS; Ferris, "Old Hutch," 241–42; Hutchinson, "Speculation," 417–19.

116 *"My place":* Clipping, Hutchinson MSS; Dies, *The Plunger,* 68–69.

116 *stockyards:* The most complete account of the Union Stock Yards is Louise C. Wade, *Chicago's Pride: The Stockyards, Packingtown, and Environs in the Nineteenth Century* (1987); see also Jack Wing, *The Great Union Stock Yards of Chicago* (1865), 1–15; and W. Jos. Grand, *Illustrated History of the Union Stockyards* (1896).

117 *"Strangers visiting":* *CT,* Dec. 23, 1875.

117 *"the backbone":* Bertram B. Fowler, *Men, Meat and Miracles* (1952), 44.

117 *new era in meat packing:* Walsh, *Midwestern Meat,* 7, 71–92.

118 *"the mightiest works of mankind":* L. U. Reavis, *A Change of National Empire; or, Arguments in Favor of the Removal of the National Capital from Washington City to the Mississippi Valley* (1869), passim.

118 *a declaration of war on St. Louis's:* Wyatt Winton Belcher, *The Economic Rivalry Between St. Louis and Chicago, 1850–1880* (1947), 13, 114–17; for a revision of Belcher, see J. Christopher Schnell, "Chicago Versus St. Louis: A Reassessment of the Great Rivalry," *Missouri Historical Review* 71 (1977): 245–65; for urban and railroad rivalries, see Lawrence H. Larsen, "Chicago's Mid-West Rivals: Cincinnati, St. Louis, and Milwaukee," *CH* 5 (1976): 141–51; and Timothy R. Mahoney, "Urban History in a Regional Context: River Towns on the Upper Mississippi, 1840–1860," *JAH* 72 (Sept. 1985): 318–39.

119 *"Samson of the West,":* Henry Cobb quoted in Lloyd Lewis and Henry Justin Smith, *Chicago: The History of Its Reputation* (1929), 108.

119 *"central hall":* A. F. Burghardt, "A Hypothesis About Gateway Cities," *Annals of the Association of American Geographers* 61 (1971): 269–85; for an astute review and critique of Central Place theory, see Cronon, *Nature's Metropolis,* 279–95. The classic work on the subject is Johann Heinrich von Thünen, *Von Thünen's Isolated State,* trans. Carla M. Wartenberg, ed. Peter Hall (1966); for further critiques of Central Place

PAGE

theory, as well as alternative approaches to urbanization, see Eric E. Lampard, "The History of Cities in the Economically Advanced Areas," *Economic Development and Cultural Change* 3 (1955): 81–136; and Michael P. Conzen, "The American Urban System in the Nineteenth Century," in D. T. Herbert and R. J. Johnston, eds., *Geography and the Urban Environment: Progress in Research and Applications,* vol. 4 (1981), 295–347.

120   *"Never was a great city":* Everett Chamberlin, *Chicago and Its Suburbs* (1874; reprint, 1974), 170–71.

120   *"stupendous agent of":* Ibid., 102.

120   *"do not mind failures":* Quoted in Bessie Louise Pierce, ed., *As Others See Chicago: Impressions of Visitors, 1673–1933* (1933), 122–23.

121   *"culture, taste,":* Quoted in Byron York, "The Pursuit of Culture: Founding the Chicago Historical Society, 1856," *CH* 10 (Fall 1981): 141; In a study of over four hundred Chicago businessmen in the period between 1833 and 1872, Rima Lunin Schultz argues that over one-third of them suffered financial failure at least one time in their lives. Schultz, "The Businessman's Role in Western Settlement."

121   *"In the midst":* Quoted in Edwin C. Rozwenc, ed., *Ideology and Power in the Age of Jackson* (1964), 27.

121   *"the paradise of workers and speculators":* Homer Hoyt, *One Hundred Years of Land Values in Chicago: The Relationship of the Growth of Chicago to the Rise in Its Land Values, 1830–1933* (1933), 82.

Chapter Five: Empire City of the West

122   *"the death cart":* Elias Colbert, *Chicago: Historical and Statistical Sketch of the Garden City* (1868), 4, 8, 18–19; Chicago's death rate between 1849 and 1854 was 84.92 per 1,000. Chicago Department of Health, *Report of the Board of Health of the City of Chicago for 1867, 1868, and 1869* (1871), 37.

123   *"spectacular":* Charles E. Rosenberg, *The Cholera Years: The United States in 1832, 1849, and 1866* (1962), 2–3; AA:1, 594–98.

123   *caused by filthy water:* The "filth" theory of disease prevailed until germs were discovered later in the century; M. E. M. Walker, *Pioneers of Public Health: The Story of Some Benefactors of the Human Race* (1930), 115–25.

123   *"noisome quagmires":* Quoted in Louis P. Cain, *Sanitation Strategy for a Lakefront Metropolis, the Case of Chicago* (1978), 23.

123   *"leaving standing pools":* Bross, *Reminiscences,* 18, 63–70; *CDD,* May 17, 1849.

123   *"a liquid":* Parton, "Chicago," 336.

123   *"greasy to the touch":* *CT* quoted in Lewis and Smith, *Chicago,* 96.

123   *"The river":* Quoted in Daniel M. Bluestone, "Landscape and Culture in Nineteenth-Century Chicago," (Ph.D. diss., Univ. of Chicago, 1984), 18–19.

124   *"The sort of mixture":* Quoted in Abbott, *Boosters,* 25.

124   *angry editorials:* G. P. Brown, *Drainage Channel and Waterway* (1894), 50–53, 61.

124   *Ellis Sylvester Chesbrough:* "Ellis Sylvester Chesbrough," *Proceedings of the American Society of Civil Engineers* 15 (Nov.-Dec. 1889): 160–63; Ellis S. Chesbrough, *Report and Plan of Sewerage for the City of Chicago, Illinois* (1855); Louis P. Cain, "Ellis Sylvester Chesbrough and Chicago's First Sanitary System," *Technology and Culture* 13 (July

PAGE

1972): 353–72; James C. O'Connell, "Technology and Pollution: Chicago's Water Policy, 1833–1930," (Ph.D. diss., Univ. of Chicago, 1980).

124 *new brick sewers:* Ellis S. Chesbrough, *Chicago Sewerage: Report of the Results of Examinations Made in Relation to Sewerage in Several European Cities, in the Winter of 1856–7* (1858), 7–10; Joel A. Tarr, "The Separate vs. Combined Sewer Problem: A Case Study of Urban Technology Design Choice," *Journal of Urban History* 5 (May 1979): 308–39.

124 *river was dredged:* Ellis S. Chesbrough, "The Drainage and Sewerage of Chicago," *Papers and Reports of the American Public Health Association* 4 (1878): 18–19.

125 *town of "ups and downs":* Stirling, *Letters,* 2–3.

125 *"sidewalk oglers":* Emmett Dedmon, *Fabulous Chicago* (1953), 13.

125 *"men's feet":* SOC, 23.

125 *George Mortimer Pullman:* Liston Edgington Leyendecker, *Palace Car Prince: A Biography of George Mortimer Pullman* (1992), 29–36.

125 *Pullman's procedure: Chicago Press and Tribune,* May 17, 1859, Apr. 14, 1860; *CDD,* Mar. 24, 1860.

127 *"sporting in":* Bross, *Reminiscences,* 10–75.

127 *"Of course this was nonsense":* SOC, 230; in 1862, the city installed a screen at the pumping works to keep fish out of the water pipes.

127 *Noah Brooks toured the tremendous tunnel system:* P. J. Staudenraus, ed., "'The Empire City of the West'—A View of Chicago in 1864" [an edited version of Noah Brooks's descriptions of Chicago], *JISHS* 56 (Summer 1963): 340–49; Chicago, Board of Public Works, *Third Annual Report of Public Works of the City of Chicago* (1864), 119–25.

128 *"the water":* "Chicago Waterworks," *HW* 11 (Apr. 20, 1867): 551–52.

128 *"the wonder of America": Frank Leslie's Illustrated Newspaper,* Nov. 3, 1866.

129 *"castellated monstrosity":* Quoted in Ira J. Bach, ed., *Chicago's Famous Buildings* (1980), 106.

129 *Dr. John H. Rauch:* John H. Rauch, "Sanitary Problems of Chicago, Past and Present," *Public Health Papers and Reports* 4 (1877); Arthur R. Reynolds, "Three Chicago and Illinois Public Health Officers: John H. Rauch, Oscar C. DeWolf and Frank W. Reilly," *Bulletin of the Society of Medical History of Chicago* 1 (Aug. 1912): 87–134.

130 *use technology to attack:* Chicago. Board of Sewerage Commissioners, *Report of the Board of Sewerage Commissioners of the City of Chicago, For the Half Year Ending December 31, 1860* (1861), 9–14; Brown, *Drainage,* 55; O'Connell, "Technology and Pollution," 68–79.

130 *sewage farms:* O'Connell, "Technology and Pollution," 26.

130 *"some moments of indecision":* Greenwood [Lippincott], *New Life,* 17–20.

130 *"purifying the river":* Chicago Citizens, "Testimonial to Ellis S. Chesbrough, City Engineer," Nov. 28, 1867, CHS; Greenwood [Lippincott], *New Life,* 20.

130 *"monster sewer":* Greenwood [Lippincott], *New Life,* 10–20; Brown, *Drainage,* 8–61.

131 *Ogden-Wentworth Ditch:* Brown, *Drainage,* 320–71; Frank J. Piehl, "Chicago's Early Fight to 'Save Our Lake,'" *CH* 5, no. 4 (1976–77): 223–32.

131 *"The purifying power":* Chesbrough, "Drainage," 18–19.

131 *"I wish I could":* Quoted in Lewis and Smith, *Chicago,* 113.

131 *"Here on the shore":* Staudenraus, ed., "Empire City," 342.

PAGE

131 *"a merchant's beau ideal":* Henry Ward Beecher, *Eyes and Ears* (1864), 100.

132 *"The eagerness":* AA:2, 563.

132 *"Parvenu period":* Thomas E. Tallmadge, *Architecture in Old Chicago* (1941), 64–132.

132 *"Architecture appears":* Staudenraus, ed., "Empire City," 343.

132 *"To describe Chicago":* [Kirkland], "Illinois in Springtime," 487–88.

133 *"the thirst for more":* Ibid.

133 *"Marseilles":* Parton, "Chicago," 330.

133 *"no sooner discharge":* Staudenraus, ed., "Empire City," 344.

134 *"the only street fit to live in":* Peckham, "Journey," 227–30.

134 *"magical of all the enterprises":* Greenwood [Lippincott], *New Life,* 12–13.

134 *"Miserable hovels":* Peckham, "Journey," 227.

135 *"In all of Chicago":* Parton, "Chicago," 339; Chamberlin, *Chicago and Its Suburbs,* 170–72.

135 *one day in 1857: HC:*2, 6.

135 *"The street may be singled out":* CT, June 19, 1873.

135 *inequality problem:* Craig Buettinger, "Economic Inequality in Early Chicago, 1849–1850," *Journal of Social History* 11, no 3 (1978): 413–18; the manuscript tax rolls Buettinger bases his conclusions on are at the CHS, Manuscript Division; "Median Reported Real Estate and Personal Property for Selected Occupations. Businessmen, born in the United States, 1860 Census"; see also Edward Pessen, "Who Governed the Nation's Cities in the 'Era of the Common Man'?" *Political Science Quarterly* 4 (Dec. 1972): 613.

136 *"Go to the polls":* CT, Mar. 5, 1860.

136 *"the most beastly sensuality":* Ibid., July 3, 1865.

136 *"Thus this congregation":* Ibid., Mar. 21, 1857.

136 *vice district:* David R. Johnson, "A Sinful Business: The Origins of Gambling Syndicates in the United States, 1840–1887," in David H. Bayley, ed., *Police and Society* (1977), 17–47.

137 *Police occasionally hassled:* John J. Flinn, *History of the Chicago Police from the Settlement of the Community to the Present Time* (1887), 30–76; Richard C. Lindberg, *To Serve and Collect: Chicago Politics and Police Corruption from the Lager Beer Riot to the Summerdale Scandal* (1991), ix–xi, 1–12.

137 *Sunday closing laws:* Perry R. Duis, *The Saloon: Public Drinking in Chicago and Boston, 1880–1920* (1983), 7, 234; CT, Apr. 21, 1872.

137 *"We are beset":* Quoted in Herbert Asbury, *Gem of the Prairie: An Informal History of the Chicago Underworld* (1940; reprint, 1986), 62.

137 *Potter Palmer:* There is less written on Palmer than on any other of Chicago's leading figures. My principal sources of biographical information were the Potter Palmer Papers, CHS; and, Anon., "Potter Palmer: Five Biographical Sketches by Friends," MSS, CHS; see also Robert W. Twyman, *History of Marshall Field & Co., 1852–1906* (1954); Lloyd Wendt and Herman Kogan, *Give the Lady What She Wants!: The Story of Marshall Field & Co.* (1952); Ishbel Ross, *Silhouette in Diamonds: The Life of Mrs. Potter Palmer* (1960).

138 *"a man of quiet persistence":* "Five Biographical Sketches," n.p.; for Potter's State Street plan, see Richard Sennett, *Families Against the City: Middle Class Homes of Industrial Chicago, 1872–1890* (1970; reprint, 1974), 25–31.

PAGE
139   *"to take possession":* "Five Biographical Sketches," n.p.
139   *"embryonic":* Ibid.
139   *transformed the city's retail trade: Chicago Times,* Oct. 6, 1857; Robert
       W. Twyman, "Potter Palmer: Merchandising Innovator of the West," in
       Explorations of Entrepreneurial History 4 (Dec. 1951): 62–65.
140   *"without question or quibble":* Twyman, "Palmer," 62–65; *CT,* Nov. 9, 26,
       1861.
140   *"the grandest affair"* and *"For once":* Quoted in Wendt and Kogan, *Give
       the Lady,* 85–86, 89.
141   *Bertha Honoré:* Ross, *Silhouette,* 18–22; Clippings, Potter Palmer Pa-
       pers, CHS; "Five Biographical Sketches," n.p.
142   *"Good out of evil":* Elias Colbert and Everett Chamberlin, *Chicago and
       the Great Conflagration* (1871; reprint, 1971), 212, 319, 445–55.
142   *"Not only was there no tearing":* Ibid., 319, 445–55.
142   "a night of horror": *Chicago Post,* Oct. 9, 1871.

Chapter Six: My Lost City

143   *"Chicago was then built":* AA:2, 703. Andreas's excellent history of the
       fire includes many eyewitness accounts and excerpts from official reports
       and newspaper stories. The Chicago Fire was an instant news and histor-
       ical event. By early 1872, seven book-length histories of the fire had
       been published.
            My account of the fire is based primarily on the rich collection of
       letters, narratives, reminiscences, and reports by eyewitnesses that was
       assembled by the CHS, "Chicago Fire of 1871 Collection." One limita-
       tion of these narratives is that they tell little about the plight of the poor
       who were caught in the fire and were its chief victims.
            The fire department's official inquiry into the fire is also at the CHS in
       the Archives and Manuscript Collection. For an insightful account of the
       literary response to the Great Fire, see Carl Smith, *Urban Disorder and
       the Shape of Belief: The Great Chicago Fire, The Haymarket Bomb, and
       the Model Town of Pullman* (1995), 1–98.
143   *"the grave defects":* Chicago, Board of Police, *Report of the Board of Po-
       lice, in the Fire Department, to the Common Council of the City of Chicago*
       (1868), 57; ibid., (1870), 8, 89.
143   *"firetraps pleasing":* *CT,* Sept. 10, Oct. 9, 1871.
144   *fire department recommended: Report of the Board of Police* (1868),
       57–59; ibid., (1870), 8–9, 89–90; AA:2 703, 709–10; Andreas's account
       of the fire includes portions of the official investigation of the fire depart-
       ment, which has been lost. *Official Investigation of the Chicago Fire by
       the Board of Police in the Fire Department, November 23–December 4,
       1871.* Chicago newspapers gave extensive coverage to this report.
144   *"turning all":* Joseph Kirkland, "The Chicago Fire," *NEM* 6 (June 18,
       1892): 726.
145   *"The absence":* *CT,* Oct. 8, 1871; Cromie, *Fire,* 11; for an illustrated ac-
       count of the fire, see Herman Kogan and Robert Cromie, *The Great Fire,
       Chicago 1871* (1971).
145   *"struck consternation":* AA:2, 705.
145   *"The feast":* SOC, 187, 289; the most reliable account of the fire and the
       Chicago fire department at that time is H. A. Musham, "The Great
       Chicago Fire, October 8–10, 1871," in *Papers in Illinois History and
       Transactions for the Year 1940* (1941): 69–189.

PAGE

145 *"[Strike] it"*: Quoted in Cromie, *Fire*, 280; see also *Rules and Regulations of the Fire Department of the City of Chicago* (1867).

146 *"One pull"*: *Report of the Board of Police* (1879), 70–89; Musham, "Fire," 85.

146 *Matthias Schaffer:* Kirkland, "Chicago Fire," 728; Musham, "Fire," 85–87, 161.

146 *"thickly studded"*: Joseph E. Chamberlin, a twenty-year-old *CEP* reporter, quoted in Colbert and Chamberlin, *Conflagration*, 226–27.

147 *"cow story"*: AA:2, 708. Andreas reproduces testimony given at the official inquiry; see also *Chicago Evening Journal*, Oct. 9, 1871.

148 *"an illuminated snowstorm"*: J. Seymour Currey, *Manufacturing and Wholesale Industries of Illinois*, vol. 1 (1919), 252; for the early spread of the fire, see *CT,* Oct. 8, 1871; and Joseph Kirkland, "Notes on the Chicago Fire," Joseph Kirkland Papers, Newberry Library.

148 *Conley's Patch:* For the fire in Conley's Patch, see especially James W. Sheahan and George P. Upton, *The Great Conflagration: Chicago: It's Past, Present, and Future* (1872), 50–82.

148 *courthouse:* Kirkland, "Chicago Fire," 731; AA:2, 724–26.

149 *"the most grandly magnificent"*: Bross's account of the fire was dictated to a New York reporter and is reproduced in Mabel McIlvaine, ed., *Reminiscences of Chicago During the Great Fire* (1915), 78–91; see also H. R. Hobart, "The Flight for Life," *Lakeside Monthly* 7 (Jan. 1872): 40–42; *CT,* Nov. 4, 1871; and Frank J. Loesch, *Personal Experiences During the Chicago Fire, 1871* (1925), 10–12.

149 *"over the adamantine bulwarks:* All quotes from Chamberlin account in *CEP,* Oct. 17, 1871; see also Colbert and Chamberlin, *Conflagration*, 201–36.

149 *"forlorn creatures"*: Colbert and Chamberlin, *Conflagration*, 221.

149 *"their shrieks and moans"*: Kathy Rannalletta, "Illinois Cómmentary: 'The Great Wave of Fire,' at Chicago: The Reminiscences of Martin Stamm," *JISHS* 70 (June 1977): 149–60; see also Colbert and Chamberlin, *Conflagration*, 221.

150 *"dirty," "villainous" Negroes:* Sensationalist stories of the fire reported in *CEP,* Oct. 18, 1871; Colbert and Chamberlin, *Conflagration*, 216–17; see also letter of Philip C. Morgan, Oct. 11, 1871, CHS, Fire Narratives (hereafter cited as FN); and Alexander Frear, "Chicago: The Full Story of the Great Fire," *New York World,* Oct. 15, 1871.

150 *"There was little"*: Sewell, *"The Great Calamity!"*: 58–59; for the social threat posed by the fire, see two suggestive studies, Ross Miller, *American Apocalypse: The Great Fire and the Myth of Chicago* (1990), 46–47; and Karen Sawislak, *Smoldering City: Chicagoans and the Great Fire, 1871–1874* (Chicago: Univ. of Chicago Press, 1995).

150 *"a tornado of fire"*: Frear, "Chicago."

151 *"I confess"*: John R. Chapin, *HW* 15 (Nov. 4, 1871), reprinted in Paul Angle, ed., *The Great Chicago Fire of 1871: Three Illustrated Accounts from Harper's Weekly* (1969): 31–42; *Chicago Post,* Oct. 17, 1871; see also, "Chicago in Ashes," *HW* 15 (Oct. 28, 1871).

152 *"fiercest Tornado of Wind"*: William B. Ogden to Charles Benter, Oct. 11, 1871, FN; see also Samuel Stone to Rev. William Berry, Mar. 26, 1872, FN.

152 *H. A. Musham:* Musham, "Fire," 163–73; Henry J. Cox and John H. Armington, *The Weather and Climate of Chicago* (1914), 197.

152 *giving "the fires a spin"*: Norman Maclean, *Young Men and Fire: A True*

PAGE

Story of the Mann Gulch Fire (1992), 36, 136, 287; William J. Humphreys, *Physics of the Air* (1920), 5–16.

153 *"like a wild beast"*: *SOC*, 293.

153 *"wall of fire"*: Reproduced in *SOC*, 269–71; see also Ellis Chesbrough to son, Oct. 21, 1871, FN.

154 *"Like an immense drove"*: Sewell, *Calamity*, 32; see also George Higginson, FN; Eleanor T. Stevens, "Chicago Fire," n.d., FN; Kiler R. Jones, "Recollections of the Great Chicago Fire," Nov. 1879, FN; Jennie E. Counselman, "Reminiscences of the Chicago Fire and Some of My Girlhood Days," Mar. 1928, FN.

154 *"The cry was 'North!'"*: Mrs. Aurelia R. King to Friends, Oct. 21, 1871, FN; George Payson's narrative, Sept. 28, 1880, FN; Arthur M. Kinzie's narrative, n.d., FN.

154 *"lowliest vagabond"*: Colbert and Chamberlin, *Conflagration*, 286.

154 *"The lumberyard"*: Del Moore to Father and Mother, Oct. 14, 1871, FN.

155 *The rescue of Isaac Arnold:* Arnold's account of the incident is in Colbert and Chamberlin, *Conflagration*, 254–56; see also AA:2, 748–55.

157 *"My God"*: Mary Ann Hubbard, *Family Memories* (1912), 102–39.

157 *The Hubbards never saw:* Mrs. Alfred Hebard Narrative, n.d., FN; Hubbard, *Family Memories*, 120–39.

158 *"calmly awaiting"*: Bross, in McIlvaine, *Reminiscences*, 78–91.

158 *"This building"*: Quoted in Cromie, *Fire*, 219–20; see also Cromie's "Notes of the Chicago Fire," CHS.

158 *"I never felt"*: Mary Fales to her mother, Oct. 10, 1871, FN.

159 *"I was . . . left alone"*: This account is reproduced in Colbert and Chamberlin, *Conflagration*, 279–82; see also F. W. Wilke, "Among the Ruins," *The Lakeside Monthly* 7 (Jan. 1872): 51. An official map of the burned area was made. See Chicago Board of Public Works, *Eleventh Annual Report of the Board of Public Works of the City of Chicago* (1873); a number of novels were written about the fire, including Edward Payson Roe, *Barriers Burned Away* (1872); Martha J. Lamb, *Spicy: A Novel* (1873); and John McGovern, *Daniel Trentworthy: A Tale of the Great Fire of Chicago* (1889); for the fire as an American event, see John J. Pauly, "The Great Chicago Fire as a National Event," *American Quarterly* 36 (1984): 668–83.

159 *"Since yesterday"*: *New York Tribune*, Oct. 11, 1871.

159 *the "destroyer"*: see Edgar Johnson Goodspeed, *The Great Fires in Chicago and the West . . . By a Chicago Clergyman* (1871), 210.

159 *leaving no trace"*: David Swing, "Historic Moments: A Memory of the Chicago Fire," *Scribner's* Magazine 11 (Jan.-June 1892): 692; see also Musham, "Fire," 139; Chicago Board of Trade, *Annual Report of the Trade and Commerce of Chicago* (1871), 10–15, 46–61,

159 *morgue:* Chicago Relief and Aid Society, *Report of the Chicago Relief and Aid Society of Disbursement of Contributions for the Sufferers of the Chicago Fire* (1874), 10–12; C. H. Jordan and Company Funeral Homes Records, CHS.

160 *"It has been the greatest fire"*: Quoted in Harold M. Mayer and Richard C. Wade, *Chicago: Growth of a Metropolis* (1969), 117; see also Sewell, *Calamity*, 43; Frank Luzerne, *The Lost City! Drama of the Fire-Fiend! Or, Chicago, As It Was, and As It Is! And Its Glorious Future!* (1872); on the mythical status of the fire, see Miller, *American Apocalypse*.

160 *"I know of few scenes"*: Arnold, "Ogden," 32–33.

160 *"utterly indescribable scene"*: Ogden to Charles Benter, Oct. 11, 1871, FN.

PAGE
161   *Ogden found his brother:* Anna Ogden West, "Recollections of the Fire," FN; Paul Angle, "What Survived the Fire," *CH* 6 (Fall 1961): 137–38.
161   *"Millions will not cover":* Ogden to Benter, Oct. 11, 1871, FN.
161   *Ogden took a lake steamer to Green Bay:* Arnold, "Ogden," 33–34.
161   *"swirling blasts":* The *New York Tribune* reporter's account of the fire is reproduced in Sewell, *Calamity,* 94–99; see also Goodspeed, *The Great Fires;* and Stephen J. Pyne, *Fire in America* (1988).
162   *Ogden remained in Peshtigo:* William Ogden to Julia Wheeler, Oct. 19, 1871, copied in Anna Ogden West's "Recollections of the Fire," FN.
162   *John B. Drake:* Colbert and Chamberlin, *Conflagration,* 342; Cromie, *Fire,* 219–20.
162   *Chicago Relief and Aid Society:* Sheahan and Upton, *Great Conflagration,* 222–26; the best account of the Relief and Aid Society is in Sawislak, *Smoldering City;* see also Timothy J. Naylor, "Responding to the Fire: The Work of the Chicago Relief and Aid Society," *Science and Society* 39 (Winter 1975–76): 450–64.
162   *"starving, fierce, and lawless mob":* Sydney Howard Gay quoted in Smith, *Urban Disorder,* 72.
163   *"shelter houses":* Chicago Relief and Aid Society, *Report* (1874), 184–94, 222–80; *CT,* Oct. 11–31, 1871.
163   *"To see the lines":* Anna Higginson to Mrs. Mark Skinner, Nov. 10, 1871, FN.
163   *George Pullman:* U. S. Grant to George Pullman, Nov. 22, 1871; Pullman to Grant, n.d., 1871, both in Pullman Papers, CHS (hereafter cited as Pullman MSS).
163   *"did her full share":* Indiana Democrat,* quoted in Sewell, *Calamity,* 522.
163   *"abstract men":* John G. Shortall's narrative, n.d., FN; *CT,* Oct. 9, 1872; *NYT,* Oct. 10–31; Sewell, *Calamity,* 40; Clifford Neal Smith, "Reconstructing Chicago's Early Land Records," *Illinois State Genealogical Society Quarterly* 5 (Winter 1973): 217–21.
164   *"His resilience":* Quoted in Wendt, *"Swift Walker,"* 470; see also *Fourth Annual Insurance Report of the Auditor of Public Accounts of the State of Illinois, 1872,* pt. 1 (1872), 3–80; Robert S. Critchell, *Recollections of a Fire Insurance Man* (1909).
164   *"death shall be":* Pinkerton's "Order," CHS; Mayor Mason's "Order," Oct. 11, 1871, in AA:2, 724, 775; *CT,* Oct. 8–15, 1871.
164   *"the most absurd rumors":* Philip H. Sheridan, *Report to the Hon. W. W. Belknap, Chicago, December 20, 1871* (1871), 1, 8, 16.
164   *Gov. John M. Palmer:* John M. Palmer to R. B. Mason, Oct. 20, 1871; R. B. Mason to John M. Palmer, Oct. 21, 1871, in AA:2, 776.
164   *"Go to hell":* Quoted in Cromie, *Fire,* 274; *Chicago Times,* Oct. 22–24; *CT,* Oct. 14, 28, 1871, Apr. 17, 1872.
165   *Sheridan restationed:* Wirt Dexter et al. to P. H. Sheridan, Oct. 28, 1871; P. H. Sheridan to W. T. Sherman, Oct. 31, 1871, both in AA:2, 77.
165   *"Under the shadow":* Colbert and Chamberlin, *Conflagration,* 395–97.
165   *"an influential man":* *CT,* Oct. 22–25, 1871; AA:2, 776–80.
165   *Kate O'Leary: Chicago Times,* Oct. 18, 1871; Perry R. Duis and Glen E. Holt, "Kate O'Leary's Sad Burden," *Chicago* 27 (Oct. 10, 1978): 220–22.
165   *"it is probable":* Swing, "Historic," 691.
165   *"concocted the story":* John Kelly to Jim O'Leary, Oct. 9, 1911, and Kelly to Patrick O'Leary, Mar. 2, 1927, both in Chicago Fire of 1871 Collection. CHS.

PAGE

166 *"One great reason"*: Quoted in Cromie, *Fire,* 280; see also Musham, "Fire," 81, 178–79.

166 *"The city was carelessly"*: Colbert and Chamberlin, *Conflagration,* 367–69.

167 *"For a time"*: Olmsted, "Chicago," 303–5.

167 *"We are in ruins"*: Jonas Hutchinson to Mrs. Betsey Hutchinson, Oct. 9, 1871, FN.

167 *"not ask or be publicly known"*: Olmsted, "Chicago," 304–5.

168 *"were not accustomed to exposures"*: Chicago Relief and Aid Society, *Report* (1874), 196–200.

168 *"I for one do not expect"*: Anna E. Higginson to Mrs. Mark Skinner, Nov. 10, 1871, FN.

168 *"how the city is to recover"*: Olmsted, "Chicago," 305.

168 *"I will rebuild"*: Quoted in Colbert and Chamberlin, *Conflagration,* 342.

168 *John M. Van Osdel:* AA:2, 568.

169 *Cyrus McCormick:* Hutchinson, *McCormick,* vol. 2, 104.

169 *"The day of his power"*: Dies, *Street of Adventure,* 206–7.

169 *"Go to Chicago"*: *New York Tribune,* Oct. 14, 1871; William Bross, *History of Chicago* (1876), 100.

169 *"The wonder"*: *New York World,* Oct. 14, 1871.

169 *"sad feature"*: *St. Louis Republican,* reproduced in the appendix to Colbert and Chamberlin, *Conflagration.*

170 *Chicago "will be built up again"*: William Ogden to Julia Wheeler, Oct. 19, 1871, copied in Anna Ogden West's "Recollection of the Fire," FN.

170 *"What is done here"*: Arnold quoted in J. Seymour Currey, *Manufacturing and Wholesale Industries of Illinois,* vol. 1 (1919), 298–300; see also York, "The Pursuit of Culture," 141–50, 175.

171 *"a town of mere traders"*: Arnold quoted in Currey, *Manufacturing,* vol. 1, 298–300.

171 *"the great city of the interior"*: Ogden to Wheeler, Oct. 19, 1871, FN.

PART II

Introduction: Let Us Build Ourselves a City

176 *"dream plants"*: Thomas Hughes, *American Genesis: A Century of Invention and Technological Enthusiasm, 1870–1970* (1989), 1–52; for the nineteenth-century city, and Chicago especially, as a "triumph of technology," see Jon C. Teaford, *The Unheralded Triumph: City Government in America, 1870–1900* (1984), chapter 8.

178 *the rebuilding:* Pierce, ed. *As Others See Chicago,* 208–209. After the Great Fire, Chicago adopted the phoenix as its official symbol. For a discussion of the "phoenix response" to great American fires, see Margaret Hindlé Hazen and Robert M. Hazen, *Keepers of the Flame: The Role of Fire in American Culture, 1775–1925* (1992), 149–53.

Chapter Seven: That Astonishing Chicago

180 *"an excellent selection"*: *A Visit to the States: A Reprint of Letters from the Special Correspondent of the Times* (1887), 362–63; see also Louis Schick, *Chicago and Its Environs: A Handbook for the Traveler* (1891), 20; the Pennsylvania Railroad did not have direct entry into New York City until 1910.

PAGE

180 *"the dreaded journey"*: Quoted in Lucius Beebe, *Mr. Pullman's Elegant Palace Car* (1961), 140.

180 *"It is literally"*: *Visit to the States*, 364–66, 372; for nineteenth-century rail travel, see John R. Stilgoe, *Metropolitan Corridor: Railroads and the American Scene* (1983), 52–71.

181 *"a sky of soot"*: Waldo Frank, *Our America* (1919), 118.

181 *"spluttering"*: Dreiser, *The "Genius"* (1915; reprint, 1967), 37.

181 *"This was the age of cities"*: Hamlin Garland, *Rose of Dutcher's Coolly* (1895; reprint, 1969), 172.

182 *Grand Central Station:* "Grand Central Station," CHS; Armstrong Chinn, "Grand Central Station," *Bulletin—Railroad and Locomotive Historical Society* 18 (1938): 53–55; A. B. Olson, "Chicago Union Station Company," *Locomotive Historical Society Bulletin* 49 (1939): 101–4; Ira J. Bach and Susan Wolfson, *A Guide to Chicago's Train Stations, Present and Past* (1986), 3, 85.

182 *"We find ourselves"*: Quoted in Wolfgang Schivelbusch, *The Railway Journey: Trains and Travel in the 19th Century* (1979), 161.

182 *"the greatest in the world"*: Julian Ralph, *Harper's Chicago and the World's Fair* (1893), 96.

184 *"No other great city"*: ICCC, 193–94.

184 *"the railroad officials"*: Julian Ralph, *Our Great West* (1893), 26.

185 *"hear the obscure thunder"*: Garland, *Rose*, 185–87, 192.

185 *"murderously actual"*: Frank Lloyd Wright, *An Autobiography* (1943), 63–66; Wright was born on June 8, 1867—not 1869, as he claimed.

185 *"A born New-Yorker"*: Ralph, *Our Great West*, 1.

185 *"money through their noses"*: Rudyard Kipling, *American Notes: Rudyard Kipling's West*, ed. Arrell Morgan Gibson (1981), 139–49.

185 *"a new circle in the Inferno"*: Eliot Gregory, "A Nation in a Hurry," *AM* 85 (May 1900): 609–10.

186 *"The civilized man"*: ICCC, 187.

186 *"Chicago never seems to go to bed"*: Martindale C. Ward, *A Trip To Chicago: What I Saw, What I Heard, What I Thought* (1895), 52; John Kendall, *American Memories: Recollections of a Hurried Run Through the United States During the Late Spring of 1896* (1896), 184.

186 *"With the prairie breezes"*: William Archer, *America To-day: Observations and Reflections* (1900), 87–89.

186 *"Boyington had done it"*: Wright, *Autobiography*, 66; for other reactions to the building, see *JWR*, 130–34; "Architectural Aberrations," *AR* 3 (July–Sept. 1893): 96–100.

186 *"Upon the broad"* and *"a tumult"*: *Visit to the States* 384–85; Norris, *The Pit*, 91.

187 *"the débris"*: Norris, *The Pit*, 98.

187 *"a great hotel"*: *Rand McNally & Co.'s Pictoral Chicago* (1896), 53–54; see also, John Leng, *America in 1876* (1877), 73–75.

187 *"news exchange"*: *Visit to the States*, 383–89.

188 *Travelers going west from Chicago:* See, for example, Willa Cather, *The Song of the Lark* (1915; reprint, 1978), 218.

188 *"Our menu"*: Lady Duffus Hardy, *Through Cities and Prairie Lands* (1881), 75–79.

188 *"There is in history"*: Charles Dudley Warner, "Studies of the Great West, III—Chicago," *Harper's New Monthly Magazine* 76 (Dec. 1887–May 1888): 870, 872.

188 *"We struck the home trail"*: Mark Twain, *Life on the Mississippi* (1883; reprint, 1965), 292.

PAGE
188   *"the concentrated essence"*: "City of Chicago," *The Inland Monthly Magazine* 10 (1877): 1184, 1189.

189   *"the great English cities"*: Quoted in Henri Loyrette, "Chicago: A French View," in Zukowsky, ed., *Chicago Architecture* (1987), 126–27.

189   *"in a manner at once foolish"*: Paul de Rousiers, *American Life* (1892), 73–74; see also Newton Dent, "The Romance of Chicago," *Munsey's Magazine* 37 (1907): 4, 20.

189   *"city of young men"*: Ralph, *Our Great West*, 10–11; Jaher, *Urban Establishment*, 492–98.

189   *Mamie*: Carl Sandburg, *Chicago Poems* (1916), 35.

189   *"The business section"*: Hamlin Garland, *A Son of the Middle Border* (1925), 271.

190   *"a world of hope"*: Dreiser, *The "Genius,"* 38.

190   *"the hetaerae of the city"*: Dreiser, *Newspaper Days*, 20–21; Dreiser's early newspaper writings are brought together in Theodore Dreiser, *Newspaper Writings, 1892–1895*, vol. 1 of *Journalism*, ed. T. D. Nostwich (1988); for novelists' reaction to Chicago life, see Carl Smith, *Chicago and the American Literary Imagination, 1880–1920* (1984).

190   *"the drag"*: SC, 23.

190   *"a new world"*: Dreiser, *The "Genius,"* 37–38.

190   *"I have struck"*: Kipling, *American Notes*, 139–49; see also, William S. Peterson, "Kipling's First Visit to Chicago," *JISHS* 63 (Fall 1970): 290–301; for reaction to Kipling's Chicago visit, see Louis Cornell, "The American Venture," in John Gross, comp., *The Age of Kipling* (1972), 72–79.

191   *"most American of cities"*: Hermant quoted in Loyrette, "Chicago," 128; for Chicago as a city of contrasts, see Steevens, *Land of the Dollar*, 144–52; Julian Street, *Abroad at Home* (1921), 141; and James Fullarton Muirhead, *America, The Land of Contrasts* (1898).

191   *"All America"*: Frederic Trautmann, "Arthur Holitischer's Chicago: A German Traveler's View of an American City," *CH* 12, no. 2 (1983): 42.

191   *Chicago "embraces"*: Archer, *America To-day*, 87–88.

191   *"spoke of a"* and *"the snarling"*: Dreiser, *The "Genius,"* 38; Kipling, *American Notes*, 139–49.

191   *"the new energies"*: Henry Adams, *The Education of Henry Adams* (1918; reprint, 1961), 343–45.

192   best *"symbolized"* America: Bourget, "A Farewell to the White City," *Cosmopolitan* 16 (Dec. 1893): 135–38; *OM*, 2–17, 110–58; Mark Twain wrote a wickedly funny critique of *OM*, "What Paul Bourget Thinks of Us," *NAR* 160 (1895): 48–62.

192   *"One's first visit"*: *OM*, 114–15.

192   *"the foundation of the world"*: Ibid., 115.

192   entering a walled medieval stronghold: A. J. Liebling, *Chicago: The Second City* (1952), 8–9.

192   *"some impersonal power"*: *OM*, 112–20.

193   *"hell with the lid taken off"*: Quoted in Franklin Toker, *Pittsburgh, An Urban Portrait* (1986), 10.

193   The *"whole powerful city"*: Quoted in Edward Shils, "The University, the City, and the World: Chicago and the University of Chicago," in Thomas Bender, ed., *The University and the City* (1988), 219.

193   *"We reached Chicago"*: L. de Cotton's account of his Chicago visit in *A travers le dominion et la Californie* is translated in Georges J. Joyaux, "A Frenchman's Visit to Chicago in 1886," *JISHS* 47 (1954): 45–56.

195   *"reeks of coal smoke"*: Trautmann, "Holitischer's Chicago," 42–44.

PAGE

195   *"huge red brick buildings"*: de Cotton in Joyaux, "Frenchman's," 47–48.
195   *"immense originality"*: *OM*, 158.
195   *"Toward what goal"*: Bourget, "Farewell," 135–37.
195   *"most perfect presentation"*: H. G. Wells, *The Future in America: A Search After Realities* (1906), 58–64; for Wells's American trip see David Smith, *H. G. Wells: Desperately Mortal: A Biography* (1986), 183–84.
196   *"the prospector's camp"*: Wells, *The Future in America*, 60–63; on this theme, see also Edward G. Mason, "Chicago," *AM* 70 (July 1892): 38–39.
196   *"the directing powers"*: Alexis de Tocqueville, *Journeys to England and Ireland*, ed. J. P. Mayer (1968), 45–96; Friedrich Engels, *The Condition of the Working Class in England in 1844* (1887), transl. by Florence Kelley (1887), 68–123.
196   *"The dark disorder"*: Wells, *The Future in America*, 58.

Chapter Eight: The Chicago Machine

198   *"You shall find"*: Kipling, *American Notes*, 115.
198   *"never a hill"*: Upton Sinclair, *The Jungle* (1906; reprint, 1985), 31.
199   *"order and death"*: Theodore Dreiser, "Great Problems of Organization, III: The Chicago Packing Industry," *Cosmopolitan* 25 (Oct. 25, 1895): 616; Dreiser, I have found, plagiarized most of this article from P. J. O'Keefe, "The Chicago Stock Yards," *NEM* 6 (May 1892): 358–71; Louise Carroll Wade, "Burnham and Root's Stockyards Connection," *CH* 4 (Feb. 1975): 139–47; The best study of the meat industry is Rudolf A. Clemen's *The American Livestock and Meat Industry* (1923).
199   *"at the crook of a finger"*: *OM*, 122–23.
199   *"greatest aggregation"*: Charles Edward Russell, *The Greatest Trust in the World* (1905), 147.
199   *"it was a thing"*: Sinclair, *The Jungle*, 51.
199   a workforce: Chicago Board of Trade, *Annual Report of the Trade and Commerce of Chicago* (1893), 42; by 1900 daily capacity at the Yards was 75,000 cattle, 80,000 sheep, and 300,000 hogs.
199   *"In Chicago"*: Sigfried Giedion, *Mechanization Takes Command: A Contribution to Anonymous History* (1948), 218.
200   *"they did it straight"*: Norman Mailer, *Miami and the Siege of Chicago* (1968), 90.
200   *"butchering of the hogs"*: Quoted in Loyrette, "Chicago," 124.
200   No one *"can be said"*: "Hog Killing at the Chicago Stock Yards," *Scientific American* 65 (Nov. 7, 1891): 291.
201   *"by the throat"*: and subsequent Bourget quotes in *OM*, 120–23.
201   *"this is the carrier"*: Dreiser, "Chicago Packing Industry," 620.
201   *"red-headed giant"*: *OM*, 123–28.
201   *"and then another"*: Sinclair, *The Jungle*, 44–45; *OM*, 124–28.
202   *"by a thread"* and *"as if a demon"*: Kipling, *American Notes*, 146–49; Sinclair, *The Jungle*, 45–46; for the system of pork packing, see *Directory and Hand-Book of the Meat and Provision Trade and Their Allied Industries for the United States and Canada* (1895), 290–380; for an excellent account of labor in the industry, see James R. Barrett, *Work and Community in the Jungle: Chicago's Packinghouse Workers, 1894–1922* (1987); for a description of each job in the packing plant, see United States Department of Labor, *Bulletin* (1919): 1075–1114.
202   *"where a stranger"*: Sinclair, *The Jungle*, 46.
202   *"sort of human chopping machine"*: Frederick Law Olmsted, *A Journey*

PAGE

Through Texas: Or, A Saddle-Trip on the Southwestern Frontier (1857; reprint, 1978), 9.

202 *"death struggle"*: OM, 125–26; O'Keefe, "Chicago Stock Yards," 364–65; Kipling, *American Notes*, 148–49; Sinclair, *The Jungle*, 48–50.

203 *"If the pig men"*: Kipling, *American Notes*, 149.

203 *"furious intensity"*: Sinclair, *The Jungle*, 49.

204 *"It will arrive"*: OM, 126.

204 *"discern the intellectual significance"*: Ibid., 127–28.

204 *"It was all so very businesslike"*: Sinclair, *The Jungle*, 44.

204 *"I had expected"*: de Rousiers, *American Life*, 65; for suggestive ideas on mass production work, see especially Harry Braverman, *Labor and Monopoly Capital: The Degradation of Work in the Twentieth Century* (1974); and David Montgomery, *Workers' Control in America: Studies in the History of Work, Technology, and Labor Struggles* (1979).

204 *"Of all the large industries"*: "Productivity of Labor in Slaughtering and Meat Packing and in Petroleum Refining," *Monthly Labor Review* 13 (Nov. 1926): 31.

204 *"Even when dead"*: Giedion, *Mechanization*, 93–94; see also Arms, "From Dis-Assembly," 195–203; Henry Ford claims the idea of the auto assembly line evolved from the slaughtering process in Chicago plants. Henry Ford, *My Life and Work* (1923), 81.

205 *"That marvelous speed"*: A. M. Simons, *Packingtown* (1899), 24; for machines made of human parts, see Lewis Mumford, "The First Megamachine," *Diogenes* (Fall 1960): 1–5.

205 *"grand seigneurs"*: OM, 124–58; de Rousiers, *American Life*, 70–172.

205 *"The cautious rentier"*: Giedion, *Mechanization*, 226–27.

205 *"a map of his business"*: Dent, "Romance of Chicago," 13.

206 *"Wild West Scheme"*: Louis Swift, with Arthur Van Vlissingen, Jr., *The Yankee of the Yards: The Biography of Gustavus Franklin Swift* (1927); Thomas Wakefield Goodspeed, "Gustavus Swift, 1839–1903," *University of Chicago Record* 7 (Apr. 1921): 91–97; Helen Swift, *My Father and My Mother* (1937), 3–43; Wade, *Chicago's Pride*, 92–93, 155–56, 221; Louise A. Neyhart, *Giant of the Yards* (1952), 1–33.

207 *"an eye for waste"*: Swift and Van Vlissingen, *Yankee*, 6–8; Howard C. Hill, "The Development of Chicago as a Center of the Meat Packing Industry," *Mississippi Valley Historical Review* 3 (Dec. 1923): 253–73; for a thrilling account of the great cattle drives, see Andy Adams, *The Log of a Cowboy: A Narrative of the Old Trail Days* (1903; reprint, 1964).

207 *"Commercial history"*: Russell, *Greatest Trust*, 24; the most comprehensive account of Swift's development and utilization of the refrigerator car is Mary Yeager Kujovich, "The Refrigerator Car and the Growth of the American Dressed Beef Industry," *Business History Review* 44 (Winter 1970): 460–82; George Hammond, the Detroit packer, was the first to experiment with the refrigerator car. In the late 1860s he sent beef to Boston in a freight car fitted out as an ice box. See Rudolph A. Clemen, *George H. Hammond (1838–1886): Pioneer in Refrigerator Transportation* (1946).

207 *Andrew S. Chase:* Harper Leech and John Charles Carroll, *Armour and His Times* (1938), 129–30.

208 *"without being removed"*: HW, Oct. 21, 1882, 663.

208 *Swift's distribution problems:* Chicago Board of Trade, *Annual Report* (1885), 105; Kujovich, "Refrigerator Car," 462–66; in 1899, four local companies controlled over 90 percent of the beef slaughtered in Chicago. Chicago Board of Trade, *Annual Report* (1889), 140; U.S. *Eleventh Cen-*

sus, 1890, "Manufacturing Industries," pt. 1, "Totals for States and Industries," 392–93, pt. 2, "Statistics of Cities," 140–41. After 1900 Chicago's importance as a meatpacking center slowly declined as the industry moved westward, closer to sources of supply, to cities such as Omaha, Kansas City, and Sioux City, Iowa. After World War II, Chicago's decline as a meat center was dramatic, and in 1970 the stockyards closed. See, "Armour, Swift, Wilson: Why the Old Brands Are Fading," *NYT*, Dec. 21, 1980.

209   *"no young man":* Swift and Van Vlissingen, *Yankee*, 9, 190, 199; Goodspeed, "Swift," 110.

209   *first vertically integrated business corporation:* Alfred D. Chandler, Jr., *The Visible Hand: The Managerial Revolution in American Business* (1977), 299.

209   *"How he wore down":* Swift and Van Vlissingen, *Yankee*, 9; see also Kujovich, "Refrigerator Car," 467–68.

209   *"sell a superior 'cut'":* Swift and Van Vlissingen, *Yankee*, 10–50; J. Ogden Armour, *The Packers, the Private Car Lines, and the People* (1906), 24; for a valuable study of branch houses, see Glenn Porter and Harold C. Livesay, *Merchants and Manufacturers: Studies in the Changing Structure of Nineteenth-Century Marketing* (1971). Even federal investigators critical of concentration in the industry concluded that the big packers gave the consumer better quality meat. United States Federal Trade Commission, *Report on the Meat-Packing Industry* (1919), 138.

209   *"If you're going to lose money":* Swift and Van Vlissingen, *Yankee*, 67.

210   *"cunning in cooperation":* Leech and Carroll, *Armour*, 189; United States Congress, Select Committee on the Transportation and Sale of Meat Products, *Testimony Taken by the Select Committee of the United States Senate on the Transportation and Sale of Meat Products* (1889), 4–16, 131–83, 213–328; United States Federal Trade Commission, *Report on the Meat Packing Industry*; by 1900, the Big Five packers were Swift, Armour, Morris, Michael Cudahy—an associate of Armour's until 1887— and the New York firm of Schwarzschild and Sulzberger. G. H. Hammond and Co., one of the giants of the industry in the 1880s, declined after Hammond's death in 1886

210   *"The causes of oligopoly":* Mary Yeager, *Competition and Regulation: The Development of Oligopoly in the Meat Packing Industry* (1981), 241. An expansion of her earlier study of the refrigerator car, this is the best study of the rise of oligopoly in the meatpacking industry.

210   *"the growth of the West":* Quoted in Theodore Dreiser, "Life Stories of Successful Men, No. 10," *Success* 1 (Oct. 1898): 3–4; see also Carter H. Hepburn, "Phillip D. Armour," *Munsey's Magazine* 9 (1893): 57.

210   *"Swift and Company":* Quoted in Andrews, *Battle for Chicago*, 101.

211   *"Father was very happy":* Swift, *My Father*, 58.

211   *"You must all stand together"* and *"We brothers":* Both quoted in Andrews, *Battle for Chicago*, 93.

211   *"Ogden was impressed":* Quoted in Leech and Carroll, *Armour*, 82.

211   *"in carrying his business cares":* Ibid., 81.

211   *"At sixty"* and *"You can always tell":* Hepburn, "Armour," 56–57.

211   *"in a manner":* John J. Flinn, *Chicago: The Marvelous City of the West: A History, and Encyclopedia and a Guide* (1891), 496–97.

212   *"Such a mobilization":* Dreiser, "Life Stories," 3–4; Frank W. Gunsaulus, "Philip D. Armour: A Character Sketch," *North American Monthly Review of Reviews* 23 (1901): 174.

212   *A long line of callers:* Arthur Warren, "Philip D. Armour: His Manner of

PAGE

Life, His Immense Enterprises in Trade and Philanthropy," *McClure's Magazine* 2 (1893–94): 263–70.

212   *"before the boys"*: Quoted in Andrews, *Battle for Chicago,* 87–88; Gunsaulus, "Armour," 167–75.

212   *"Give me plenty of work"*: Quoted in Leech and Carroll, *Armour,* 24, 66; Warren, "Armour," 263–67; Jaher, *Urban Establishment,* 491–98; *CT,* Oct. 12, 1886.

213   *"I never think"*: Quoted in Dreiser, "Life Stories," 3–4.

213   *"You have your pile"*: *ICCC,* 79.

213   *"He had eyes"*: *GG,* 139; Gunsaulus, "Armour," 169.

213   *"working night and day"*: *OM,* 129.

213   best represented *"your Western life"* and *"Chicago man"*: Warren, "Armour," 260; Hepburn, "Armour," 57.

214   *"Through the wages"*: Quoted in *GG,* 139. In 1890, Armour employed twice as many people at his stockyards operation than Andrew Carnegie did at his Homestead Steel Works. In 1890 total Packingtown employment was twenty-five thousand, and its manufactures counted for 30 percent of Chicago's total. *Eleventh Census,* 1890, vol. 6, Manufacturing Industries, pt. 2, 143.

214   *"Oneida is for those"*: Quoted in Andrews, *Battle for Chicago,* 88; for Armour's life, see Leech and Carroll, *Armour;* for a brief corporate history of Armour and Company, see N. S. B. Gras and Henrietta M. Larson, eds., *Casebook in American Business History* (1939), 623–44; The Armour and Company records (in the Grayhound Tower, Phoenix, Arizona) are very incomplete for the nineteenth century.

214   *"Chicago was the place"*: Swift, *My Father,* 127.

214   *"scientific business methods"*: Gunsaulus, "Armour," 172.

215   *"It is the aim"*: Quoted in Leech and Carroll, *Armour,* 46.

215   *"I pack . . . everything"*: Quoted in Gunsaulus, "Armour," 172; see also Rudolf A. Clemen, *By-Products in the Packing Industry* (1927).

215   *"dumped into the hoppers"*: Sinclair, *The Jungle,* 164; Thomas H. McKee, "The Failure of Government Inspection," *World's Work* 12 (May 1906): 7510–14.

215   *"Like all great industries"*: Mary McDowell, "Beginnings," 6, Mary McDowell Papers, CHS (hereafter cited as McDowell MSS).

216   *"They get all the blood"*: Antanas Kaztauskis [Ernest Poole], "From Lithuania to the Chicago Stockyards," *Independent* 57 (Aug. 4, 1904): 241–48. The "author" Kastauskis was created by Ernest Poole, the real writer of the essay, from his talks with a number of immigrant workers during the strike of 1904 organized by the Amalgamated Meat Cutters and Butcher Workmen.

216   *"Sometimes, in the haste"*: Sinclair, *The Jungle,* 138; Charles J. Bushnell, *The Social Problem at the Chicago Stock Yards* (1902), 26–27.

217   *"some-policemen"*: Kaztauskis, "Lithuania," 241–48; Sinclair, *The Jungle,* 98–99.

217   *"have neither the face"*: Guiseppe Giacosa, "The Nature of Waste," in Oscar Handlin, *This Was America: True Accounts of People & Places, Manners & Customs* (1949), 390–402.

217   *"These are not packing plants"*: Upton Sinclair, *The Autobiography of Upton Sinclair* (1962), 110. In 1894, 320 children under sixteen years old worked in the Chicago meatpacking industry. Armour employed the most children. See Illinois Office of Inspector of Factories and Workshops, *Annual Report of the Factory Inspectors of Illinois,* vol. 3 (1895), 10–12. By 1900, common laborers accounted for about two-thirds of the

PAGE

    workforce in packing plants. Black workers were employed in increasing numbers between 1910 and 1920. In 1910 there were only 186 blacks in Chicago's packing plants. By 1918, there were 6,510. In 1890 only 1.6 percent of Chicago's packinghouse workers were women; by 1920, 12.6 percent. See Barrett, *Work and Community,* 44–46, 51. During the strikes of 1894 and 1904, the companies hired women to do jobs formerly reserved for men. See Sophonisba P. Breckenridge and Edith Abbott, "Women in Industry: The Chicago Stockyards," *Journal of Political Economy* 19 (Oct. 1911): 641.

217   *"a lordly collection":* Giacosa, in Handlin, *This Was America,* 401–2.

218   *"Back of the Yards":* Andrew Vogler, "From an Old Timer Back of the Yards," McDowell MSS; Dominic A. Pacyga, *Polish Immigrants and Industrial Chicago: Workers on the South Side, 1880–1922* (1991), 63–64. This is the best work on the subject.

218   *"No other neighborhood":* Sophonisba P. Breckenridge and Edith Abbott, "Housing Conditions in Chicago, III: Back of the Yards," *AJS* 16 (Jan. 1911): 433–35.

218   *"as bad as any in the world":* Robert Hunter, *Tenement Conditions in Chicago: Report by the Investigating Committee of the City Homes Association* (1901; reprint, 1970), 12–14.

218   *"only "remedy":* CT, Mar. 6, 1918.

219   *"a place segregated":* Mary McDowell, "Social Science in Chicago," *The University Record* 9 (Oct. 9, 1923): 300; *Report of the Chicago Department of Health,* City of Chicago, 1894; Caroline M. Hill, comp., *Mary McDowell and Municipal Housekeeping: A Symposium* (1939), 2; McDowell, "The Settlement Comes to Town of Lake," 7–9; and McDowell, "Beginnings," 1–4, both in McDowell MSS.

219   *"A worker ill-nourished":* Caroline Hedger, "The Unhealthfulness of Packingtown," *World's Work* 12 (May 1906): 7507–9; see also Hedger, "Health—Summer of 1908," McDowell MSS.

219   *"The cold":* Sinclair, *The Jungle,* 101.

219   *"In the night":* and subsequent McDowell quotes in Mary McDowell, "Beginnings," 1–4, McDowell MSS.

220   *"Cattle and hogs":* Frank, *Our America,* 480–81.

220   *"fortress of oppression":* Sinclair, Autobiography, 109.

221   *"I am just a butcher":* Quoted in Wade, *Chicago's Pride,* 221.

221   *"Take youth":* Quoted in Warren, "Armour," 276.

221   *"I don't care":* Quoted in Gunsaulus, "Armour," 174.

221   *"that the labor problem":* Ibid., 170.

222   *"rubb[ing] out the line":* CT, Oct. 15, 1893; Philip Armour to Frank W. Gunsaulus, Dec. 5, 1893, Armour Institute of Technology Papers, John Crerar Library, Illinois Institute of Technology. The Armour Institute evolved into the Illinois Institute of Technology, whose campus was designed by Ludwig Mies van der Rohe.

222   *"An American captain of industry":* Clifford L. Snowden, "The Armour Institute of Technology," *NEM* 16 (May 1897): 371.

222   *"which will fit them":* Quoted in Warren, "Armour," 272–73.

222   *"Always keep at it":* Quoted in *GG,* 156.

222   *"Dii Majores":* ICCC, 72.

222   *"Old Man Armour":* Quoted in Ernest Poole, *The Bridge: My Own Story* (1940), 97–99; the 1904 strike was led by the Amalgamated Meat Cutters and Butcher Workmen of North America, founded in 1897.

223   *"As long as we are heads":* Quoted in Wade, *Chicago's Pride,* 123; see also David Brody, *The Butcher Workmen: A Study of Unionization* (1964), 35.

PAGE

223   *"that tended to ruthlessness"*: Sinclair, *The Jungle*, 376.

223   *"more hopeless"*: McDowell, "Beginnings," 7–12; McDowell, "Beginnings of the University of Chicago Settlement," Feb. 10, 1914, both in McDowell MSS.

223   *studying wage conditions*: John C. Kennedy et al., *Wages and Family Budgets in the Chicago Stockyards District* (1914), 1–23, 65–80.

223   *"You must get money"*: Kaztauskis, "Lithuania," 48.

223   *open shop*: For information on immigrant workers in the industry in the early 1900s, see United States Immigration Commission, *Slaughtering and Meat Packing*, vol. 13 of *Immigrants in Industries* (1911), 202–60; and "Wages and Hours of Labor in the Slaughtering and Meat-Packing Industry," *Bulletin of United States Labor Statistics* 252 (Aug. 1917): 1076.

224   *"We want to make"*: Quoted in Warren, "Armour," 275; see also Leech and Carroll, *Armour*, 218.

224   *"that stopped or set"*: Thomas J. Morgan quoted in Wade, *Chicago's Pride*, 226.

224   *"[It was] certainly very good"*: *Chicago Times*, Aug. 12, 1888; see also, "Nora's Stock-Yards Fun," *CT*, Nov. 25, 1888, written by Nora Marks, a reporter investigating the Libby plant in Chicago; and Francis L. Lederer II, "Nora Marks, Investigative Reporter," *JISHS* 68 (Sept. 1975): 306–18.

224   *"It must be realized"*: Hedger, "The Unhealthfulness," 7509.

224   *"The working people"*: George M. Pullman Testimony, United States Strike Commission, *Report on the Chicago Strike of June-July, 1894* (1895), 529 (hereafter cited as *Report on Chicago Strike*).

224   *"No place in the United States"*: *A Visit to the States*, 395.

225   *"an abnormally healthy place"*: Ibid., 395–98; There was a wide disparity in the quality of housing in Pullman, ranging from three-story blockhouse tenements containing flats of two to four rooms, with some families sharing the same toilet, to attractive nine-room cottages for management. Duane Doty, "Homes of Operatives" (clipping), Pullman Collection, Pullman Branch Library, Pullman, Illinois.

225   *"kept in perfect repair"*: Pullman Testimony, *Report on Chicago Strike*, 530; *TG* 7 (June 17, 1893): 399–403; Another reason for Pullman's low death rate, aside from its cleanliness, was the company's policy of hiring mostly younger, healthy workers. See Virgil J. Vogel, Introduction to William H. Carwardine, *The Pullman Strike* (1894; reprint, 1973), vii.

225   *sports facilities*: [Duane Doty], *The Story of Pullman* (1893), 22–25; Wilma J. Pesavento, "Sport and Recreation in the Pullman Experiment, 1880–1900," *Journal of Sport History* 9, no. 2 (1982): 38–62. Although records of the Pullman Company for the founding years were discarded in 1957, there is material on the town and the company in the Pullman Company papers and scrapbooks at the Newberry Library, Chicago, Illinois, and in the Pullman Papers at the Historic Pullman Foundation, Pullman, Illinois. See also, Fred Leavitt and Nancy Miller, *Pullman: Portrait of a Landmark Community* (1981); the best history of the town is Stanley Buder, *Pullman: An Experiment in Industrial Order and Community Planning, 1880–1930* (1967).

225   *"The most perfect"* and *"distressed socialists"*: *Pall Mall Budget*, Apr. 6, 1883; *TG*, June 17, 1893, 403.

226   *"stands related"*: Theodore Dreiser, "The Town of Pullman," *Ainslee* 3 (Mar. 1899): 191.

226   *"The manufacturing interests"*: George Pullman to Stockholders of Pull-

PAGE

man Palace Car Co., entered in the minutes of "Stockholders Special Meeting," Feb. 1, 1882, "Record Book A," pp. 394–95, Pullman Collection, Newberry Library (hereafter cited as Pullman Coll.); Records of the Pullman Land Association, Pullman Coll.

226 *"probably the best known Chicago name":* A Visit to the States, 390; George Pullman Obituary, News Clipping Collection, 1897–1898, Pullman Coll.

226 *"example of high-principled":* de Rousiers, *American Life,* 176–83.

226 *"rows of tenement houses:* CT, Sept. 21, 1881; *Chicago Journal of Commerce,* Apr. 7, 1886, Pullman Scrapbooks, Pullman Coll.; Almont Lindsey, *The Pullman Strike: The Story of a Unique Experiment and of a Great Labor Upheaval* (1942), 61.

227 *"where so much":* Hugh Dalziel Duncan, *Culture and Democracy* (1965; reprint, 1988), 167.

227 *"the Olympus":* ICCC, 71–72; *CT,* June 22, 1893.

227 *"The story of Pullman":* [Doty], *Story of Pullman,* 18.

228 *"wonderfully neat":* New York World, Dec. 25, 1892; see also "New Building of Pullman's Palace Car Company in Chicago," *The Railway Age* (May 15, 1884): 318.

228 *"He was one of the most frigid":* Quoted in GG, 197.

228 *time away from home:* George M. Pullman to Harriet S. Pullman, Feb. 19, 1892, Mrs. C. Philip Miller Collection, CHS (hereafter cited as Miller Coll.).

228 *origins of his gigantic railroad company:* TG, June 17, 1893, 403; Joseph Husband, *The Story of the Pullman Car* (1917; reprint, 1974), 24; Horace Porter, "Railway Passenger Travel: 1825–1880," *Scribner's Magazine,* Sept. 4, 1888, 303–4; August Mencken, *The Railroad Passenger Car* (1957), 55–74; Theodore T. Woodruff, the leader in the field before Pullman, was building sleeping cars in the 1850s.

229 *"Mr. Pullman's car":* Boston Daily Globe, March 5, 1888, 65, clipping in Pullman Coll.; Leyendecker, *Palace Car Prince,* 77–78.

230 *"were those who were grumbling":* Husband, *Story of the Pullman Car,* 42–43.

230 *"[The] principle":* TG, June 17, 1893, 403.

230 *"luxury in travel":* Giedion, *Mechanization,* 452.

230 *"We know now":* [Doty], *Story of Pullman* 5.

230 *"the educational":* Quoted in Buder, *Pullman,* 43; see also Mrs. Duane Doty, *The Town of Pullman: Its Growth with Brief Accounts of Its Industries* (1893), 23.

230 *"attention to detail":* TG, June 17, 1893; *New York World,* December 25, 1892.

230 *"paper wheels":* "Paper Car Wheels—How They Are Made," *Western Manufacturer,* July 15, 1880, 136.

231 *"The development":* A Visit to the United States, 391.

231 *The site Pullman chose:* The Pullman Company kept the location of its new plant secret until after the land was purchased in order to keep the price of the land from being inflated by its sellers. See Pullman Parlor Car Co., "Record Book A," 349–51, Pullman Coll.

231 *Put Yourself in His Place:* Charles Reade, *Put Yourself in His Place* (1870).

231 *"breaking down":* Quoted in Kostof, *City Shaped,* 169.

231 *example of Saltaire:* In 1882, a reporter for the *Boston Herald* claimed that he had been told by an unnamed close friend of Pullman's that Pullman was powerfully influenced by Reade's novel. *Boston Sunday Herald,*

PAGE

Jan. 15, 1882, from Pullman Coll.; see also Thomas B. Grant, "Pullman and Its Lessons," *American Journal of Politics* 5 (1894): 190–204.

232 *"TERROR'S REIGN":* Quoted in Richard Schneirov, "Chicago's Great Upheaval of 1877," *CH* 9 (Spring 1980): 3–17; for newspaper coverage of the strike, see also Robert V. Bruce, *1877: Year of Violence* (1959; reprint, 1970), 237–53; and Philip Foner, *The Great Labor Uprising of 1877* (1977), 9, 139–56.

232 *"Squelch them out":* IO, July 22, 24, 25, 1877; *CT,* July 24, 1877; *Chicago Times,* July 27, 1877; Foner, *Great Labor Uprising,* 141–55.

233 *"bummers, ruffians":* NYT, July 26, 1877; Bruce, *1877,* 314.

233 *"The Social Revolution":* Parsons quoted in Schneirov, "Chicago's Great Upheaval," 17.

233 *"The railroad strike":* Gompers quoted in Bruce, *1877,* 318.

233 *Citizens' Association: CT,* July 28–30, 1877.

233 *Solon Spencer Beman:* S. S. Beman, Architectural Scrapbooks, Solon S. Beman Papers, CHS; Beman worked for the famous father-son firm of Richard and Richard M. Upjohn and did most of his work for Richard M. Upjohn. For Beman's life and career see Thomas J. Schlereth, "Solon Spencer Beman, Pullman, and the European Influence on and Interest in his Chicago Architecture," in Zukowsky, ed. *Chicago Architecture,* 172–87; Richard Schermerhorn, Jr., "Nathan Franklin Barrett, Landscape Architect," *Landscape Architect* 10 (Apr. 1920): 109–10.

234 *"The building of Pullman":* Duncan, *Culture and Democracy,* 163.

234 *"watched the dream"* and *"a captain":* Graham Taylor, *Satellite Cities: A Study of Industrial Suburbs* (1915; reprint, 1970), 30; *ICCC,* 87.

234 *"caught fire":* Marian T. Beman, "Selling a Dream," July 1959, 2–24, Solon S. Beman Papers, CHS; Irving K. Pond, "Pullman: America's First Planned Industrial Town," *Illinois Society of Architects Monthly Bulletin,* June–July 1934, 8.

234 *"Mr. Beman's association":* Louis Sullivan, "Tribute to Solon S. Beman," in Robert Twombly, ed., *Louis Sullivan: The Public Papers* (1988), 208–11.

235 *"This is the best sanitary system":* "Arcadian City of Pullman," *Agricultural Review* 3 (Jan. 1883): 77–78; "Sewage Purification in America: Pullman, Illinois," *Engineering News* 29 (Jan. 12, 1893): 26–28.

235 *George Pullman himself hired: Chicago Times,* Nov. 10, 1880; The initial construction of the new town is beautifully detailed in a map prepared by the Pullman Company, dated Apr. 11, 1881, "The Town of Pullman, Illinois," Ryerson and Burnham Libraries, Chicago Art Institute; a fascinating account of the industrial and technological aspects of Pullman and its shops was prepared for the Historic American Engineering Record and the Historic Pullman Foundation, a local preservation organization, by Donald Jackson and Carol Poli Miller, "Historic American Engineering Record Report On: Pullman, Illinois," (1976–1977). I am indebted to Donald Jackson for sharing this report with me.

235 *"were light":* Roger H. Grant, ed., "A Wonderfully Busy Place," *CH* 20, nos. 1 and 2 (Spring–Summer 1991): 60. This is an edited account of a Detroit man's visit to Chicago in 1881; Burgett Meakin, *Model Factories and Villages: Ideal Conditions of Labour and Housing* (1905), 285–89.

235 *"Everything is done":* de Rousiers, *American Life,* 173.

236 *"formidable written examination":* Chicago Herald, Feb. 21, 1886; Pullman Testimony, *Report on Chicago Strike,* 529.

236 It *"was to the employer's":* New York Sun, Dec. 9, 1883.

236 *"below the angels":* William Adelman, *Touring Pullman* (1972), 12.

PAGE

236 *"profit" not "purification"*: "Sewage Purification," 27–28.

237 *"the moral and spiritual disorder"*: *ICCC*, 89.

237 *"We will not sell"*: *CT*, Aug. 16, 1881.

237 *"run the risk"*: de Rousiers, *American Life*, 180–81.

237 *"un-American"*: Warner, "Studies of the Great West," 127.

238 *"distinctive type"*: de Rousiers, *American Life*, 174–83.

238 *"all humbug"*: Charles H. Eaton, "Paternalism and Pullman," *The American Journal of Politics* 5 (1899): 579.

238 *"it will be strange"*: *IO*, Jan. 10, 1883.

238 *"all pervading air"*: Richard T. Ely, "Pullman: A Social Study," *Harper's Monthly* 70 (1885): 457–66; see also Ely, *Ground Under Our Feet: An Autobiography* (1938), 168; Testimony of Thomas W. Heathcoate, *Report on Chicago Strike*, 425.

239 *"nobody," a local dissident minister said:* Carwardine, *The Pullman Strike*, 15–26; Testimony of Carwardine, *Report on Chicago Strike*, 444–54; Buder, *Pullman*, 81–85.

239 *"A large number of home owners"*: Ely, "Pullman," 464; for a perceptive analysis of Pullman's behavior toward his workers, see Jane Addams, "A Modern Lear," *Survey* 29 (Nov. 1912): 131–37.

239 *"true and only master" and "but desired"*: de Rousiers, *American Life*; Ely, "Pullman," 466.

239 *"the establishment"*: Ely, "Pullman," 466.

239 *"In dreams"*: Kostof, *City Shaped*, 207.

240 *"the zero hour"*: *LS*, 308–12.

240 *"flaring with"*: Sinclair, *The Jungle*, 245–48.

241 *"wild and animal-like"*: Hamlin Garland, "Homestead and Its Perilous Trades," *McClure's Magazine* 3 (June 1894): 3–20; for the role of steel in the development of America, see Thomas J. Misa, *A Nation of Steel: The Making of Modern America, 1865–1925* (1995).

241 *"full of something white"*: Sinclair, *The Jungle*, 246–48.

241 *Chicago entered the steel age:* AA:3, 471–500.

243 *Illinois Steel:* George W. Cope, *The Iron and Steel Interests of Chicago* (1890), 1–18, 23–53; for Chicago's iron empire, see David A. Walker, *Iron Frontier: The Discovery and Early Development of Minnesota's Three Ranges* (1979).

243 *"The tendency"*: *CT*, Jan. 1, 1884; *Manufacturing and Wholesale Industries of Illinois*, vol. 1 (1919), 304, 399–400.

243 *two types of industries:* Chicago Commerce, *Manufactures, Banking and Transportation Facilities* (1884), 1–110; David R. Meyer, "Midwestern Industrialization and the American Manufacturing Belt in the 19th Century," *Journal of Economic History* 49 (1989): 921–37; Harold L. Platt, *The Electric City: Energy and the Growth of the Chicago Area, 1880–1930* (1991), 6–10.

243 *second largest manufacturing center:* Cope, *Iron and Steel*, 53–64.

244 *"a web of steel"*: Quoted in Jon C. Teaford, *Cities of the Heartland: The Rise and Fall of the Industrial Midwest* (1993), 51; Census Office, *Compendium of the Eleventh Census 1890* (1894), 705–12.

244 *Aaron Montgomery Ward:* Boris Emmet and John E. Jeuck, *Catalogues and Counters: A History of Sears, Roebuck & Company* (1950), 1–45; for an account of Ward's origins in the mail-order business, see also, Louis E. Asher and Edith Heal, *Send No Money* (1942).

246 *the catalog business:* For Ward's contribution to American merchandising, see Daniel J. Boorstin, "A. Montgomery Ward's Mail-Order Business," *CH* 2 no. 3 (1973): 142–52.

PAGE
246   *"Dead-Beats": CT,* Nov. 8, 1873; A. Montgomery Ward & Company, *Catalogue,* 1875; Cecil C. Hoge, *The First Hundred Years Are the Toughest: What We Can Learn from the Century of Competition Between Sears and Ward's* (1988), 8–22; Emmet and Jeuck, *Catalogues and Counters,* 21, 39.

246   *"alarming amount[s] of insanity": Northwest Illustrated Monthly Magazine,* quoted in Boorstin, "A. Montgomery Ward's," 142.

247   *"As you advertise":* Quoted in Daniel J. Boorstin, *The Americans: The Democratic Experience* (1973; reprint, 1974), 123–24.

248   *Chicago Tribune* compared: *CT,* Nov. 19, 1883; Ira R. Bartky, "The Invention of Railroad Time," *Railway History,* no. 148 (Spring 1983): 13–33.

248   *"the Cheapest":* Sears, Roebuck & Co., *Catalogue,* 1893, 1894, 1898; Emmet and Jeuck, *Catalogues and Counters,* 23–25, 33.

248   *"a vast department store": Atlanta Constitution,* quoted in Asher and Heal, *Send No Money,* 50.

248   *"generous spirit":* Edward A. Duddy, "Richard Warren Sears," *DAB,* vol. 16, 540.

249   *"Honesty":* Gordon L. Weil, *Sears, Roebuck, USA: The Great American Catalog Store and How It Grew* (1977), 1–25; *Sears, Roebuck & Co. Catalogue,* no. 104 (1897; reprint, 1968); Hoge, *The First Hundred Years,* 3–30; Donald R. Katz, *The Big Store: Inside the Crisis and Revolution at Sears* (1987), 10.

249   *"as good as": New York People's Home Journal* quoted in Asher and Heal, *Send No Money,* 50; Katz, *Big Store,* 10.

249   *"Tell us":* Quoted in Weil, *Sears, Roebuck, USA,* 25.

249   *"examined at express office": Montgomery Ward & Co. Catalogue,* 1893.

249   *"the greatest revolution":* Boorstin, "A. Montgomery Ward's," 149–151.

249   *Alvah Roebuck sold out:* Asher and Heal, *Send No Money,* 12; John Steele Gordon, "No Respect," *American Heritage* 44 (Sept. 1993): 14–16.

250   *"compendium of everything":* "Holitischer's Chicago," 46–47.

250   *"according to our plans":* Sears, Roebuck & Company, Mail Order Housing Ad, 1900, Library of Congress.

250   *"the greatest efficiency":* "Holitischer's Chicago," 47.

250   *"Mail-order":* Quoted in Asher and Heal, *Send No Money,* 72; for the rise of mass distribution, see Chandler, *Visible Hand,* 232–39.

251   *"Are you a salesman?":* Quoted in Twyman, *Marshall Field,* 88–90.

251   *"cut of a striped and crossed pattern": SC,* 5–6.

251   *"No place":* Quoted in Perry R. Duis, "Life of a Salesman," *Chicago,* May 1985, 10; see also Timothy B. Spears, "A Grip on the Land," *CH* 17 (Fall–Winter 1988–89): 4–25.

252   *"modern commercial architecture":* Talbot F. Hamlin, "Henry Hobson Richardson," *DAB,* vol. 15, 568.

252   *Louis Sullivan thought:* Louis H. Sullivan, *Kindergarten Chats and Other Writings,* ed. Isabella Athey (1947), 28; see also John Edelmann, "Pessimism of Modern Architecture," *The Engineering Magazine* 3 (Apr.–Sept. 1892): 44–54.

252   *"largest and best arranged":* John J. Flinn, *The Standard Guide to Chicago* (1894), 510–12.

252   *"Probably under no one roof":* Ibid., 511; Wendt and Kogan, *Give the Lady,* 194–96.

253   *"where members of the order":* Neil Harris, "Shopping—Chicago Style," in Zukowsky, ed., *Chicago Architecture,* 138–39.

Chapter Nine: The Streetcar City

PAGE

254   *"The nature":* SC, 22.

254   *"the highest monoliths":* Marshall Field and Company (1913), a guide-book published by the firm and located in the Field Archives, Chicago, Illinois; John Dennis, Jr., "Marshall Field, A Great Mercantile Genius," *Everybody's Magazine* 14 (Mar. 1906): 293–97; Samuel Hopkins Adams, "The Department Store," *Scribner's Magazine* 21 (Jan. 1897): 4–27.

256   *"found herself in fairyland":* Thomas Wakefield Goodspeed, "Marshall Field," *University of Chicago Biographical Sketches,* vol. 1, 26–28.

256   *"call of thrift":* Katherine G. Busbey, *Home Life in America* (1910), 151.

256   *"the modern woman's paradise":* Anna Steese Richardson, "The Modern Woman's Paradise," *Woman's Home Companion* 38 (Sept. 1911): 22.

256   *Field . . . saw his company's future in urban retail:* "Marshall Field & Co.," *Fortune Magazine* 14 (Oct. 1936): 83; for an insightful history of the department store and American consumerism, see William Leach, *Land of Desire: Merchants, Power, and the Rise of a New American Culture* (1993); my analysis of the world of the department store profited greatly from Elaine S. Abelson's *When Ladies Go A-Thieving: Middle-Class Shoplifters in the Victorian Department Store* (1989; reprint, 1992).

256   *"the block of probity":* CT, Jan. 17, 1906.

257   *"All of Mr. Field's money":* Quoted in Goodspeed, "Field," 26.

257   *"He had the merchant instinct":* Quoted ibid., 7.

257   *"money and advance":* Field quoted in Harold Irwin Cleveland, "Fifty-five Years in Business: The Life of Marshall Field," *System,* 10 (July 1906): 563.

257   *"the old-timers' tricks":* Quoted in Wendt and Kogan, *Give the Lady,* 50–51.

257   *"I was determined":* Dreiser, "Life Stories of Successful Men, No. 12," *Success* 1 (Dec. 8, 1898): 7–8.

257   *"you were never forced to listen":* Hobart C. Chatfield-Taylor, *Cities of Many Men: A Wanderer's Memories of London, Paris, New York, and Chicago During Half a Century* (1925), 255–56.

257   *"At work":* Andrews, *Battle for Chicago,* 4.

258   *"reflection of the man":* Dennis, "Marshall Field," 299; Goodspeed, "Field," 25.

258   *"merit did not have to wait":* Dreiser, "Life Stories No. 12," 7–8; Marshall Field, *Elements of Success* (1896), 2–6.

259   *"Over all is a covering":* Dennis, "Marshall Field," 298–302; S. H. Ditchett, *Marshall Field and Company: The Life Story of a Great Concern* (1922), 70–75; Twyman, *Marshall Field,* 17–25.

259   *"I have never believed":* Dreiser, "Life Stories No. 12," 7–8.

259   *"the store and the stock":* Farwell quoted in Cleveland, "Fifty-five Years," 564.

259   *The Fair:* Forrest Crissey, *Since 40 Years Ago: An Account of the Origin and Growth of Chicago and Its First Department Store* (1915); see also "The World's Largest Store," *Chicago Dry Goods Reporter* 28 (Jan. 1, 1898): 53.

261   *"a fountain of spectacular":* Tom Mahoney and Leonard Sloane, *The Great Merchants: America's Foremost Retail Institutions and the People Who Made Them Great* (1966), 124; Joseph Siry, *Carson Pirie Scott: Louis Sullivan and the Chicago Department Store* (1988), chapter 1.

261   *"streetcars of the mind":* Boorstin, *The Americans: The Democratic Experience* (1974), 106; see also, Twyman, *Marshall Field,* 105–10.

PAGE

261 *"long talked of experiment"*: Platt, *Electric City*, 3.

262 *"fire and light would never again be identical"*: David E. Nye, *Electrifying America: Social Meanings of a New Technology, 1880–1940* (1990), 2.

262 *Edison's lamps*: Platt, *Electric City*, 34–37; Mark Jansen Bouman, "Luxury and Control: The Urbanity of Street Lighting in Nineteenth-Century Cities," *Journal of Urban History* 14 (Nov. 1987): 7–37.

262 *"They walked north"*: *SC*, 76.

262 *"be suspended in air"*: *CT*, Oct. 2, 1892, 2.

263 *"shop girls"*: *SC*, 23, 76.

263 *"It does not say"*: Quoted in Leach, *Land of Desire*, 3.

263 *democratized shopping*: Emile Zola, *Au bonheur des dames* (1884); Rachel Bowlby, *Just Looking: Consumer Culture in Dreiser, Gissing, and Zola* (1985), chapter 4; Margaret Walsh, "The Democratization of Fashion: The Emergence of the Women's Dress Pattern Industry," *JAH* 66 (Sept. 1979): 299–313.

264 *"starvation wages"*: Annie M. MacLean, "Two Weeks in Department Stores," *AJS* 4 (May 1899): 721–41.

264 *on "the streets, in horsecarts" and "so much more down-towny"*: E. L. Godkin, "Stewart's," *The Nation* 34 (Apr. 20, 1882): 332; Henry James, *A Small Boy and Others* (1913), 66.

264 *"the awful prevalence"*: *NYT*, June 13, 1881.

264 *"acknowledged the call"*: Busbey, *Home Life*, 119; Abelson, *When Ladies Go A-Thieving*, 29–41; for an interesting social novel on the new consumer city, see Margaret Bohme, *The Department Store: A Novel of Today* (1912).

265 *"it was a long way"*: Robert J. Casey, *Chicago Medium Rare: When We Were Both Younger* (1952), 123.

265 *"All of the principal street car lines"*: Theodore Dreiser, *Dawn* (1931; reprint, 1965), 530.

266 *"The man who has no business"*: Charles Henry White, "Chicago," *Harper's Monthly Magazine* 118 (Apr. 1909): 730; see also Brian J. Cudahy, *Destination: Loop: The Story of Rapid Transit Railroading In and Around Chicago* (1982), 9; Mayer and Wade, *Chicago*, 138; and Robert David Weber, "Rationalizers and Reformers: Chicago Local Transportation in the Nineteenth Century," (Ph.D. diss., Univ. of Wisconsin—Madison, 1971), 9–10. This is the most exhaustive account of Chicago's nineteenth-century transit system. It offers a revisionist account of Charles T. Yerkes as a farsighted transit builder.

266 *"neutral land"*: Hobart C. Chatfield-Taylor, *Chicago* (1917), 26–27.

266 *horse-drawn streetcars*: *CT*, Aug. 30, 1896, 44; Weber, "Rationalizers," 10–15; for maps and photographs of Chicago's transit system, see James D. Johnson, *A Century of Chicago Streetcars 1858–1958: A Pictorial History of the World's Largest Street Railway* (1964).

267 *fifteen thousand horses*: Joel A. Tarr, "Urban Pollution: Many Long Years Ago," *American Heritage* 22 (Oct. 1971): 66–68.

267 *cable cars*: *CT*, July 13, 1881.

267 *"The street cars are propelled"*: Grant, ed., "A Wonderfully Busy Place," 59–63.

268 *"shopping hours are confined"*: Quoted in Siry, *Carson*, 37–38.

269 *"Streetcars, he knew,"*: Dreiser, *The Titan*, 12; for Yerkes, see Charles Edward Russell, "Where Did You Get It, Gentlemen?" *Everybody's Magazine* 17 (Sept. 1907): 349–50; Josiah G. Leach, *Chronicle of the Yerkes Family with Notes on the Leech & Rutter Families* (1904), 190–91; Sid-

PAGE

ney I. Roberts, "Portrait of a Robber Baron: Charles T. Yerkes," *Business History Review* 35 (Autumn 1961): 344–71.

269   *"Death in the Air"*: *CT*, Apr. 21, May 11, Nov. 26, 1893; "New Charge Against the Trolly," *Street Railway Gazette* 10 (May 10, 1894): 213.

269   *"the deadly trolley"*: *CT*, Oct. 10, 1892.

270   *"prevented the normal development"*: Quoted in Connie Fletcher, "The Loop El: Love It or Lose It," *Chicago* (Nov. 1977): 192–205.

270   *"a fellow who uses Chicago"*: Quoted in Johnson, *Century*, 11; *CT*, Jan. 8, 1893, Dec. 30, 1905; for Yerkes's telescope, see Pamela D. Hodgson, "The Scoundrel and the Scientist," *CH* 19 (Fall–Winter 1990–91): 83–96.

271   *"He had no friends"*: Fuller, *Cliff-Dwellers*, 38–39; When preparing to create his fictional character Cowperwood, Dreiser did exhaustive research into Yerkes's life; still, his novels should not be relied on as factual accounts of Yerkes's life, for he freely changed characters and events or made them up entirely, as his biographer Richard Lingeman points out, to serve his own "heroic conception of him." See Lingeman, *Theodore Dreiser: An American Journey, 1908–1945* (1990), 60–100. For newspaper reaction to Yerkes, see Weber, "Rationalizers," 309.

271   packed to *"the guards"*: *CT*, Dec. 18, 1893, Sept. 7, Dec. 4–5, 1895.

271   *"It is the people"*: Quoted in Roberts, "Portrait," 352–54.

271   *"The secret of success"*: Quoted in Burton J. Hendrick, *The Age of Big Business: A Chronicle of the Captains of Industry*, vol. 39, *Chronicles of America Series*, Allan Johnson, ed. (1919), 126.

271   *"His bookkeeping methods"*: Roberts, "Portrait," 348.

271   *Philadelphia backers:* Burton J. Hendrick, "Great American Fortunes and their Making: Street-Railway Financiers," *McClure's* 30 (1908): 33–48.

272   *"Mr. Yerkes is not a safe man"*: Quoted in Roberts, "Portrait," 353.

272   *"Whatever I do"*: *Chicago Journal*, Jan. 29, 1898.

272   *an exposé:* Lloyd Wendt and Herman Kogan, *Bosses in Lusty Chicago: The Story of Bathhouse and Hinky Dink* (originally published as *Lords of the Levee*, 1943; reprint, 1967), 37.

272   *"revolutions"*: *CT*, May 19–31, 1897, Dec. 12–15, 1898.

273   *repealed the Allen Bill:* *CT*, Apr. 21–23, 1897; Elizabeth T. Kent, *William Kent: Independent: A Biography* (1950), 155–56; *Council Proceedings*, 1898–99, 49–51, 1171–72, 1197–98.

273   *"in Oriental splendor"*: *CT*, Dec. 30–31, 1905.

273   *"celebrating the coming of cholera"*: [Finley Peter Dunne], *CEP*, Oct. 9, 1897.

273   *"Mr. Yerkes was not ambitious"*: *CT*, Dec. 30, 1905.

273   *"Its streets and houses"*: *SC*, 16.

273   *Chicago had annexed:* Michael P. McCarthy, "The New Metropolis: Chicago, The Annexation Movement and Progressive Reform," in Michael H. Ebner and Eugene M. Tobin, eds., *The Age of Urban Reform: New Perspectives on the Progressive Era* (1977), 43–54.

274   *"place of inferior, debased"*: Quoted in Robert Fishman, *Bourgeois Utopias: The Rise and Fall of Suburbia* (1987), 3–38.

274   *"the word suburb suggested"*: Kenneth T. Jackson, *Crabgrass Frontier: The Suburbanization of the United States* (1985), 3–11. The most perceptive account of the changing geographical form of the city is Michael P. Conzen, "Analytical Approaches to the Urban Landscape," in Karl W.

Butzer, ed., *Dimensions of Human Geography: Essays on Some Familiar and Neglected Themes* (1978), 128–65.

274   *"inside out":* Joel Schwartz, "Evolution of the Suburbs," in Phillip C. Dolce, ed. *Suburbia: The American Dream and Dilemma* (1976), 1–36.

276   *municipal guarantee:* Chamberlin, *Chicago and Its Suburbs,* 188–223; the best early study of the suburb is Adna Ferrin Weber, *The Growth of Cities in the Nineteenth Century: A Study in Statistics* (1899; reprint, 1967); a modern work of equal excellence is John Stilgoe, *Borderland: Origins of the American Suburb, 1820–1939* (1988), 139–50.

276   *Baron Georges-Eugène Haussmann:* Fishman, *Bourgeois,* 103–16.

277   *"The fact is thoroughly established":* Chamberlin, *Chicago and Its Suburbs,* 188.

277   *Affluent New Yorkers:* Elizabeth Hawes, *New York, New York: How the Apartment House Transformed the Life of a City (1869–1930)* (1993), 5–12.

277   *"into those terrible tenement houses":* Laborer's resolution quoted in Christine M. Rosen, *The Limits of Power: Great Fires and the Process of City Growth in America* (1986), 101.

277   *"no room":* Quoted in Carroll W. Westfall, "The Golden Age of Chicago's Apartments," *IA* 24 (1980): 20–39.

277   *"women with lovers":* Edith Wharton, *The Age of Innocence* (1920; reprint, 1993), 28.

278   *"upon the front 'stoop,'":* Norris, *The Pit,* 116.

278   *"Once out of the thicket":* Ralph, *Our Great West,* 18–21; see also Montgomery Schuyler, "Glimpses of Western Architecture: Chicago," *Harper's Magazine* 83 (Aug. 1891): 395–406; 83 (Sept. 1891): 554–70.

278   *"flocking into the suburbs":* Chamberlin, *Chicago and Its Suburbs,* 188.

278   *"their tens of thousands":* Joseph Kirkland, "Among the Poor of Chicago," in Robert Woods et al., *The Poor in Great Cities* (1895), 195–239.

279   *"great wooden signs":* Dreiser, *Jennie Gerhardt* (1911; reprint, 1989), 326.

279   *Gross:* Emily Clark and Patrick Ashley, "The Merchant Prince of Cornville," *CH* 21 (Dec. 1992): 4–19; Miles L. Berger, *They Built Chicago: Entrepreneurs Who Shaped a Great City's Architecture* (1992), 113–18.

279   *"Only let me know":* Quoted in Mayer and Wade, *Chicago,* 138.

279   Home Primer: S. E. Gross Collection, CHS.

280   *"the major architectural work":* Mumford, in Museum of Modern Art, *Modern Architecture: International Exhibition* (1932), 179.

280   *"which but for him":* Quoted in Clark and Ashley, "Merchant Prince," 9–19; see also Ann Durkin Keating, *Building Chicago: Suburban Developers and the Creation of a Divided Metropolis* (1988), 27–28, 70–71, 87–88, 192.

280   *"Beer and whiskey":* Kirkland, "Among the Poor," 213.

281   *"I foresee a time":* John S. Wright, *Chicago: Past, Present, Future Relations to the Great Interior and to the Continent* (1868), 281.

281   *"to go out into the country":* Ade, "The Intellectual Awakening in Burton's Row," in *Stories of the Streets and of the Towns: From the Chicago Record, 1893–1900,* ed. Frank J. Meine (1941), 40; for Chicago's park building programs, see Bluestone, *Constructing Chicago,* chapters 1 and 2; and Glen E. Holt, "Private Plans for Public Spaces: The Origins of Chicago's Park System, 1850–1875," *CH* 8 (Fall 1979): 173–84. As Holt points out, little land was added to the park system after 1880, and by

PAGE

1909 Chicago had dropped from second to thirty-second among American cities in the amount of parkland it provided each inhabitant.

282 *Cornell arrived in Chicago:* Paul Cornell to Herman K. Hopkins, May 31, 1848, Paul Cornell Papers, CHS.

282 *Hyde Park:* Paul Adrien Cornell, "Biographical Sketch of Paul Cornell," 1–4, CHS; *CT,* Mar. 25, 1900, Mar. 4, 1904; *Chicago Herald,* Mar. 4, 1904; Jean F. Block, *Hyde Park Houses: An Informal History, 1865–1910* (1978), 1–10; Glen E. Holt and Dominic A. Pacyga, *Chicago: A Historical Guide to the Neighborhoods: The Loop and the South Side* (1979), 72–85.

284 *"people's garden":* Simon Andreas, *Chicago, The Garden City: Its Magnificent Parks, Boulevards, and Cemeteries* (1893), 43.

284 *"contaminating" air:* John H. Rauch, *Public Parks: Their Effects Upon the Moral, Physical and Sanitary Condition of the Inhabitants of Large Cities; with Special Reference to the City of Chicago* (1869), 6–7, 30–31, 80–83; Frederick Law Olmsted, "Public Parks and the Enlargement of Towns," *Journal of Social Science* 2 (1871): 28, 34.

284 *park bill became law: CT,* Mar. 23, 1869; H. W. S. Cleveland to Olmsted, July 25, 1888, Frederick Law Olmsted Papers, Manuscript Division, Library of Congress, Washington, D.C. (hereafter cited as Olmsted MSS); Galen Cranz, *The Politics of Park Design: A History of Urban Parks in America* (1982), 165–68.

285 *"the Greatest American Suburb":* Walter L. Creese, *The Crowning of the American Landscape: Eight Great Spaces and their Buildings* (1985), 233–35.

285 *"an unsatisfactory means of communication":* Olmsted, Vaux and Company, *Preliminary Report Upon the Proposed Suburban Village at Riverside, Near Chicago,* (1868), 3–16, 23–29; see also Riverside Improvement Company, *Riverside in 1871, with a Description of Its Improvements* (1871), 21.

286 *"Give us straight": CT,* Apr. 29, 1869.

286 *"leisure, contemplativeness":* Olmsted and Vaux, *Preliminary Report,* 3–29.

286 *"None of the planning":* Mumford, *City in History,* 497.

286 *Jenney:* Theodore Turak, *William Le Baron Jenney: A Pioneer of Modern Architecture* (1986), 72–76; Creese, *Crowning of American Landscape,* 223–24; Carl Abbott, "'Necessary Adjuncts to its Growth': The Railroad Suburbs of Chicago, 1854–1875," *JISHS* 73 (Summer 1980): 121–23.

287 *"superficially opposed":* Raymond Williams, *The Country and the City* (1973), 124.

287 "ruralizing of all": Quoted in Fishman, *Bourgeois Utopias,* 128–29.

287 *"withdraw like a monk":* Mumford, *City in History,* 486.

288 *"little by little":* Olmsted and Vaux, *Preliminary Report,* 3–29; *CT,* Feb. 25, 1900; Turak, *Jenney,* 98–100; for a suggestive account of Riverside's influence, or lack of, on other suburbs, see Leonard Eaton, "The American Suburb: Dream and Nightmare," *Landscape* 13 (Winter 1963– 64): 12–26.

288 *"limitless expanse of lake":* Olmsted, Vaux and Company, *Report Accompanying Plan for Laying Out the South Park* (1871), 1–54.

288 *Washington Park:* Olmsted, "Public Parks," 22–23; Olmsted to Charles Loring Brace, Aug. 1, 1853, in *The Papers of Frederick Law Olmsted,* vol. 2, *Slavery and the South, 1852–1857,* ed. Charles E. Beveridge, Charles Capen McLaughlin, and David Schuyler (1981), 232–36; Victoria Post

PAGE

Ranney, *Olmsted in Chicago* (1972), 26–28; Geoffrey Blodgett, "Frederick Law Olmsted: Landscape Architecture as Conservative Reform," *JAH* 62 (Mar. 1976): 869–89.

289 *"unoccupied for the most part"*: H. W. S. Cleveland, *The Public Grounds of Chicago: How to Give Them Character and Expression* (1869), 11–15.

289 *Horace Cleveland:* Horace William Shaler Cleveland, "Landscape Architect's Report," in *Report of the South Park Commission to the Board of County Commissioners of Cook County, from Dec. 1st., 1872, to Dec. 1st., 1873,* 10–20; *CT,* Dec. 17, 1876.

289 *West Side:* "Report of Jenney, Schermerhorn and Bogart, Architects and Engineers," in *Second Annual Report of West Chicago Park Commission for Year Ending 28 February, 1871* (1871), 1–81; Turak, "William Le Baron Jenney: Pioneer of Chicago's West Parks," *IA* 25 (Mar. 1981): 40–42.

290 *"paddled by gentlemen"*: Willie, *Forever,* 43.

290 *"No Chicago millionaire"*: George Ade, "The Advantages of Being 'Middle Class,'" *Stories,* 79.

290 *alien territory:* Steven A. Riess, *City Games: The Evolution of American Urban Society and the Rise of Sports* (1989), 129–31; Perry R. Duis and Glen E. Holt, "Chicago's Green Crown: The Parks," *Chicago* (Aug. 1977): 84–86.

290 *"jam is such"*: H. W. S. Cleveland to Olmsted, July 11, 1874, Olmsted MSS; for a marvelous sketch of the world of the avenues, see *Tally-Ho!: Coaching Through Chicago's Parks and Boulevards* (1888).

291 *"to merit the approval"*: Hobart C. Chatfield-Taylor, "The Yesterday of the Horse," in Kirkland, ed., *Chicago Yesterdays,* 274.

291 *"Smart daughters"*: Dreiser, *The Titan,* 24.

291 *Washington Park Race Club:* Mrs. B. F. Ayer, "Old Hyde Park," in Kirkland, ed., *Chicago Yesterdays,* 188–89.

292 *"the refuse acres"*: Herrick, *Web of Life,* 59–87, 198–201.

293 *"Political meetings"*: Block, *Hyde Park Homes,* 17–46.

293 *"the suburb served"*: Mumford, *City in History,* 494.

293 *"the dangerous classes"*: Charles Loring Brace, *The Dangerous Classes of New York and Twenty Years Work Among Them* (1872).

293 *"It is more pleasant"*: Quoted in Stanley Buder, "The Future of the American Suburbs," in Dolce, ed., *Suburbia,* 197; the best study of Chicago's North Shore is Michael H. Ebner, *Creating Chicago's North Shore: A Suburban History* (1988).

294 *"queer conglomerate mass"*: Jacob Riis, *How the Other Half Lives: Studies Among the Tenements of New York* (1901; reprint, 1971), 19.

294 *"speeding sightseeing platforms"*: Nye, *Electrifying America,* 106.

295 *"a gypsy"*: Ade, "Sophie's Sunday Afternoon," in *Stories,* 135–40.

295 *"an ardent Wagnerite"*: LS, 208.

295 *"youths from the country towns"*: Masters, *Tales of Chicago,* 242.

296 *"Quite every Sunday"*: Dreiser, *Dawn* (1931; reprint 1965), 512–14.

296 *"Why is it"*: Ade, "The Advantages of Being 'Middle Class,'" in *Stories,* 75–79.

297 *"wheeling"*: George D. Bushnell, "When Chicago Was Wheel Crazy," *CH* 4 (Fall 1975): 167–75; Richard Harmond, "Progress and Flight: An Interpretation of the American Cycle Craze of the 1890s," *Journal of Social History* 5 (Winter 1971): 238–40.

297 *"This club"*: Casey, *Medium Rare,* 77.

297 *"whin a woman's"*: Finley Peter Dunne, "The Divided Skirt," in *Mr. Doo-*

PAGE

      ley: In the Hearts of his Countrymen, the Chicago Journal, 1898 (1899; reprint, 1969), 154–57.

297   *New York Times reported:* Reported in *CT,* July 1, 1893; Frances Elizabeth Willard, *A Wheel Within a Wheel: How I Learned to Ride a Bicycle* (1895).

298   *"the only amusement park":* [Harold Richard Vynne] *Chicago by Day and Night: The Pleasure Seeker's Guide to the Paris of America* (1892), 27–41.

299   *"all classes of men and women":* Ibid., 43–49.

299   *"The phenomenon of the CBD":* Spiro Kostof, *The City Assembled: The Elements of Urban Form Through History* (1992), 101.

299   *"an array of wonders":* Casey, *Medium Rare,* 22–23.

300   *"flaunting flaps":* Masters, *Tale of Chicago,* 232.

300   *"gaze for hours":* Casey, *Medium Rare,* 16.

Chapter Ten: Stories in Stone and Steel

301   *"When I came from Sweden":* Henry Ericsson, *Sixty Years a Builder: The Autobiography of Henry Ericsson* (1942), ix.

301   *"The skyscraper is":* Col. W. A. Starrett, *Skyscrapers and the Men Who Build Them* (1928), 1.

302   *"The [tall] office building":* Barr Ferree, "The Modern Office Building: Part I," *IA* 27, no. 1 (Feb. 1896): 4.

302   *"faith in the dollar":* Montgomery Schuyler, "The Evolution of the Skyscraper," *Scribner's Magazine* 46 (Sept. 1909): 258; Schuyler's work is brought together in Montgomery Schuyler, *American Architecture and Other Writings,* ed. William H. Jordy and Ralph Coe, 2 vols. (1961).

302   *"exclusively" of skyscrapers:* Schuyler, "Glimpses of Western Architecture," 395–466, (Sept. 1891): 554–70; Schuyler, "Architecture in Chicago: Adler and Sullivan," *AR* 4, Special Series (Dec. 1895): 3.

302   *"It all started":* Quoted in John Summerson's Commentary, in "The Chicago School of Architecture: A Symposium—Part II," *The Prairie School Review* 9 (1972): 35; Barr Ferree, "The High Building and Its Art," *Scribner's Magazine* 15 (Mar. 1894): 314.

302   *"preexisting":* John Wellborn Root, "A Great Architectural Problem," *IA* 15 (June 1890): 67–70.

303   *"It is noticeable":* Quoted in Kostof, *City Shaped,* 281.

303   *"The towers of Zenith":* Sinclair Lewis, *Babbitt* (1922; reprint, 1980), 5.

303   *"so tall":* Carl Sandburg, "The People Yes," *The Complete Poems of Carl Sandburg* (1970), 491.

303   *"At no time in the history":* John Wellborn Root, "The City House in the West," *Scribner's Magazine* 8 (Oct. 1890): 416.

304   *"and who took":* Schuyler, "Glimpses," 395–96.

304   *"completely junking":* Tallmadge, *Architecture in Old Chicago,* 135.

304   *a fireproof city:* Peter Wight, "Recent Fireproof Building in Chicago," *IA* 5 (1885): 52–53; Gerald R. Larson, "Fire, Earth, and Wind—Part I," *IA* 25 (Sept. 1981): 20–29; and Larson, "Fire, Earth, and Wind—Part II," *IA* 27 (Jan.–Feb. 1983): 31–37.

304   *"no established traditions":* Henry-Russell Hitchcock, *Architecture: Nineteenth and Twentieth Centuries* (1977), 337.

305   *"this Florence":* Dreiser, *The Titan,* 13.

305   *"cruelty and culture":* Howard Mumford Jones, *Ideas in America* (1944), 140–46.

PAGE

305 *Florence:* Gene Brucker, *Renaissance Florence* (1983); Richard A. Goldthwaite, *The Building of Renaissance Florence: An Economic and Social History* (1980); John Hale, *The Civilization of Europe in the Renaissance* (1994), 259–81; Leonard K. Eaton, *Two Chicago Architects and Their Clients: Frank Lloyd Wright and Howard Van Doren Shaw* (1969), 6–7; Jakob C. Burckhardt, *The Civilization of the Renaissance in Italy* (1965).

306 *"No creation":* Ericsson, *Sixty Years*, 241–42.

306 *"[In] the repelling region":* Henry B. Fuller, "The Upward Movement in Chicago," *AM* 80 (Oct. 1897): 541.

307 *"Tear down":* Hoyt, *One Hundred Years*, 153.

307 *"the greed of 'improvement'":* George Ade, "A Breathing-Place and Play-Ground," in *Stories*, 85.

307 *"square-paned little windows"* and *"downtown confusion":* George Ade, "At the Green Tree Inn," 70–74; Ade, "After the Sky-Scrapers, What?" 104–8, both in *Stories*.

308 *"one could see Council Bluffs":* Quoted in David Lowe, *Lost Chicago* (1975; reprint, 1985), 146.

308 *"Not for many years":* Ade, "After the Sky-Scrapers," 104–8.

308 *"the individual is supreme":* J. Lincoln Steffens, "The Modern Business Building," *Scribner's Magazine* 22 (July 1897): 39–40.

308 *"Men passengers":* Ade, "After the Sky-Scrapers," 104–8.

309 *Chicago's first skyscraper quarter: CT,* June 24–26, 1881; Hoyt, *One Hundred Years,* 135–40.

309 *"awe-inspiring":* C. H. Blackall, "Notes of Travel: Chicago," *American Architect and Building News* 23 (Feb. 22, 1888): 88–91.

309 *"by the power of ascension":* Montgomery Schuyler, "'The Sky-Scraper' Up to Date," *AR* 8 (Jan.–Mar. 1899): 232.

310 *"All safe":* Quoted in Earle Shultz and Walter Simmons, *Offices in the Sky* (1959), 42.

310 *Elisha Graves Otis:* Otis Elevator Company, *The First One Hundred Years* (1953), 1–10.

310 *"Babylonian elegance":* Shultz and Simmons, *Offices in the Sky,* 44; see also Perry R. Duis, "Yesterday's City," *CH* (Summer 1987): 65–72.

311 *"the enterprise of business":* Steffens, "Modern Business Building," 37.

311 *"tentatives":* Schuyler, "Evolution of the Skyscraper," 262.

311 *"responsible for the modern office building":* Sullivan in Twombly, ed., *Sullivan: The Public Papers,* 220.

311 *"something new under the sun":* LS, 313.

311 *"one of the most concentrated bursts":* Carl W. Condit, *American Building Art: The Nineteenth Century* (1960), 50.

311 *"Not since man"* and *"inaccessible as a mountain-top":* Ferree, "High Building," 298–316; see also Ferree, "The Modern Office Building: Part 1," and "The Modern Office Building: Part II," *IA* 27 (Mar.–Apr. 1896): 4–5, 12–13, 23–25.

312 *"A great office building":* Ray Stannard Baker, "The Modern Sky-scraper," *Munsey's Magazine* 22 (Oct. 1899): 57–58.

312 *"It is a common remark":* Quoted in Condit, *American Building Art,* 63.

313 *"The 'modern office building'":* Louis Sullivan, "The Tall Building Artistically Considered," *Lippincott's* 57 (Mar. 1896): 403; LS, 310–14.

313 *"Within certain limits":* Dankmar Adler, "Tall Office Buildings—Past and Future," *Engineering Magazine* 3 (1892): 765–73.

314 *"He was never without a pencil":* "Alumni Who Are a Credit," *CT,* Dec. 29, 1895, 26; see also Daniel H. Burnham, "Biography of Daniel H.

PAGE

Burnham of Chicago, Notes from Editor," in Charles Moore Papers, Library of Congress, Washington, D.C.; Thomas S. Hines, *Burnham of Chicago: Architect and Planner* (1979), 1–11. This is the only modern biography of Burnham; Charles Moore, *Daniel H. Burnham, Architect, Planner of Cities,* 2 vols. (1921), is the work of a close friend and associate and contains excerpts from Burnham's diaries and correspondence.

315 *"the greatest architect":* Burnham to his mother, May 11, 1868, Daniel H. Burnham Papers, Ryerson and Burnham Libraries, Art Institute of Chicago (hereafter referred to as Burnham MSS).

315 *"There is a family tendency":* Burnham to John Goddard, Apr. 1, 1901, Burnham MSS.

315 *"roving disposition":* Burnham, "Biography," Moore Papers; Peter B. Wight, "A Paper Delivered at a Meeting Held at the Art Institute, Chicago, June 11, 1912," *AR* 32 (Aug. 1912): 176, 178.

315 *"original designs":* Peter B. Wight, "John W. Root as a Draftsman," *IA* 16 (Jan. 1891): 18.

315 *Root had never known failure: JWR,* 1–23; Theodore Starrett, "John Wellborn Root," *Architecture and Building* 44 (Nov. 1912): 429; Monroe's book is the only biography of Root. The best study of his architecture is Donald Hoffmann, *The Architecture of John Wellborn Root* (1973); Hoffman brings together Root's writings in John Wellborn Root, *The Meanings of Architecture: Buildings and Writings,* ed. Donald Hoffmann (1967).

316 *"[He] was essentially":* Wight, "Root as a Draftsman," 18.

316 *"His conversational powers":* Quoted in *JWR,* 264.

316 *"with such solemn slowness": JWR,* 26–27.

316 *" 'The Saloons Must Go' ":* Hoffmann, *Root,* 194.

316 *"arms of iron":* LS, 286–87.

317 *"the most ... iridescent":* Mrs. Henry Demarest Lloyd quoted in *JWR,* 44.

317 *"magnetic power": JWR,* 198.

317 *"He always lacked application":* Burnham's mother to Burnham, Nov. 22, 1867, Burnham MSS.

317 *"saved Root"* and *"My partner": JWR,* 25, 198; LS, 285.

317 *"With a couple of pencils":* Burnham, "Biography," Moore Papers; *JWR,* 25–27.

317 *"the best-designed residence":* LS, 285.

318 *"used to hang around":* Margaret Sherman Burnham to Burnham, record of conversation in Daniel H. Burnham, Jr., to Charles Moore, Feb. 21, 1918, Burnham MSS.

318 *"starving time":* Hines, *Burnham,* 21.

318 *concern about his son-in-law's drinking habits:* Margaret Burnham later told Charles Moore about her father's concerns about Burnham's drinking in the first years of their marriage; Burnham, "Biography," Moore Papers; Wade, "Burnham and Root's Stockyards Connection," 139–47.

318 *"and the work of": JWR,* 25.

318 *"He could really see it":* Quoted in *JWR,* 113.

319 *"Get the job":* Richardson quoted in Frank Lloyd Wright, *Genius and Mobocracy* (1949; reprint, 1971), 56.

319 *"No other man":* Quoted in *JWR,* 193–94.

319 *"Here our originality":* Quoted in Moore, *Burnham,* vol. 1, 24.

319 *"What Chartres":* Tallmadge, *Architecture in Old Chicago,* 142–44.

319 *"responsible for the modern office building":* Sullivan in Twombly, ed., *Sullivan, The Public Papers,* 220.

PAGE

319   *Aldis who convinced wary investment clients:* Aldis's case for the effi-
      ciency of the high-rise office is made most compellingly by Dankmar
      Adler in "Tall Office Buildings—Past and Future," 767–73.

321   *"Since the water hems in":* CT, Oct. 28, 1888; see also Shultz and Sim-
      mons, *Offices in the Sky,* 22.

321   *"Limited as to the ground":* Steffens, "Modern Business Building," 41.

321   *"if the earth":* The correspondence between Brooks and Aldis has been
      lost. Some of the correspondence is reproduced in Carl W. Condit, *The
      Chicago School of Architecture: A History of Commercial and Public
      Buildings in the Chicago Area, 1875–1925* (1964), and Shultz and Sim-
      mons, *Offices in the Sky.*

321   *"As an engineer":* JWR, 114.

321   *"made such great demands":* Corydon T. Purdy, "The Use of Steel in
      Large Buildings," *Engineering News Record* 31 (Feb. 1895): 207.

321   *"[are] probably not equalled":* Blackall, "Notes of Travel: Chicago," 147.

321   *"More buildings tumbled over":* Ericsson, *Sixty Years,* 209–10.

322   *"pier foundations":* Frederick H. Baumann, *The Art of Preparing Foun-
      dations for All Kinds of Buildings, with Particular Illustrations of the
      Method of Isolated Piers as Followed in Chicago* (1873).

322   *"great transverse":* Root, "A Great Architectural Problem," 68–70.

322   *"In carrying out":* Quoted in *JWR,* 115.

323   *"to persuade or to hoodwink":* Schuyler, "Architecture in Chicago: Adler
      and Sullivan," 3–14.

323   *"sugar-factory":* JWR, 134.

323   *"I prefer to have a plain structure":* Peter Brooks to Owen Aldis, Mar. 25,
      1881, July 23, 1881, in Condit, *Chicago School,* 52.

324   *artificial lighting:* Shultz and Simmons, *Offices in the Sky,* 129–31. The
      sun produces in the open, on a clear day, ten thousand foot-candles of il-
      lumination, whereas electric lights produce only three to four foot-
      candles of illumination, a foot-candle being the amount of illumination a
      candle will give to an area a foot square, placed a foot from a candle's
      flame.

324   *fireproofing iron:* Wight used a form of porous terra-cotta invented by
      Chicago's Sanford E. Loring; Wight, "Fireproof Construction and the
      Practice of American Architecture," *American Architect and Building
      News,* Aug. 19, 1893, 144; Wight, "Origin and History of Hollow Tile
      Fireproof Floor Construction—Part I," *Brickbuilder* 6 (Mar. 1897):
      54–55; between 1881 and 1891, Wright's Fireproof Company installed
      fireproof systems in over two hundred Chicago buildings, using many of
      his own fire-prevention inventions; for Wight's experience as a fireproof-
      ing contractor see Sarah Bradford Landau, *P. B. Wight: Architect, Con-
      tractor, and Critic, 1838–1925* (1981), 44–50.

325   *"From the hour that the ground":* Schuyler, "Architecture in Chicago:
      Adler and Sullivan," 4–16.

325   *"My idea":* Quoted in LS, 285–86.

326   *"one of the greatest businessmen":* Peter B. Wight, "Daniel Hudson Burn-
      ham, An Appreciation," *AR* 32 (Aug. 1912): 179, 184–85; see also
      Wight, "A Paper Delivered at a Meeting Held at the Art Institute,"
      176–78.

326   *"He was the dictator":* A. N. Rebori quoted in Moore, *Burnham,* 26.

326   *"There are men called 'high livers'":* Steffens, "Modern Business Build-
      ing," 44.

326   *Central Safety Deposit Company:* "Chicago," *American Architect* 25 (Feb.
      1889): 79; Ericsson, *Sixty Years,* 234–35.

PAGE

328 *"plain massiveness"*: Brooks quoted in Hoffmann, *Root*, 68.

328 *"architectural prevision"*: *JWR*, 111–13, 123.

328 *"like lightning"*: Starrett, "Root," 430–31.

328 *light-filled courtyard*: Henry Van Brunt, "John Wellborn Root," *IA* 16 (Jan. 1891): 87; even at night the room shone with a golden-white light from the carbon-filament lamps of two giant, floral-shaped electrolliers. Root had designed a large light court for the headquarters of the Chicago, Burlington & Quincy Railroad, but it is not nearly this sumptuous.

329 *"a landing in the sky"*: *JWR*, 268–74; for a shrewd analysis of the economic value of light, see Dankmar Adler, "Light in Tall Office Buildings," *Engineering Magazine* 4 (Nov. 1892): 171–86.

329 *"The real estate man"*: Steffens, "Modern Business Building," 53–61.

329 *"Build no second-class space"*: Quoted in Shultz and Simmons, *Offices in the Sky*, 33–34.

330 *"The truth is"*: Aldis letter of May 24, 1894, quoted in Shultz and Simmons, *Offices in the Sky*, 62.

330 *"trade palaces"*: Root, "What Are the Present Tendencies of Architectural Design in America?" in Root, *Meanings*, 208.

331 *"an achievement unsurpassed"*: Robert D. Andrews, "The Broadest View of Precedent," *AR* 2 (May 1893): 34–35.

331 *the architect rejected ornament*: Condit, *Chicago School*, 65–69.

331 *"brick box"*: *JWR*, 141; Harriet Monroe, *A Poet's Life: Seventy Years in a Changing World* (1938), 60–61. The story of the building of the Monadnock is told by Donald Hoffmann in "John Root's Monadnock Building," *JSAH* 26 (Dec. 1967): 269–77. I am grateful to Bill Donnell, who financed and supervised the restoration of the Monadnock, and two of the architects on the project, Myron Goldsmith and John Vinci, for discussing the building's construction and design with me. For the restoration of the building, see Donald L. Miller, "One Fine Building and a Few Good Men," *Chicago Magazine*, Mar. 1991, 140–47.

331 *"a new spirit of beauty"*: Root, "Broad Art Criticism," *IA* 11 (Feb. 1888): 3–5.

331 *"It was very ungrateful"*: Quoted in George A. Larson and Jay Pridmore, *Chicago Architecture and Design* (1993), 23.

332 *"by the careful study"*: Root, "A Few Practical Hints on Design." This manuscript, reproduced in Monroe, has been lost. *JWR*, 64–75.

332 *"The conditions of Chicago"*: *CT*, Nov. 2, 1879, 9.

332 *"There never was a picture"*: Root in *JWR*, 211–12.

332 *"enduring monuments"*: Root, "A Great Architectural Problem," 67–71; Root, "Style," in Root, *Meanings*, 162; Root in *JWR*, 63–75, 107.

333 *"should . . . by their mass"*: Root, "A Great Architectural Problem," 69–71.

333 *"grave and simple"*: Root, "Architectural Ornamentation," *IA* 5 (Apr. 1885): 54–55.

333 *"The value of plain surfaces"*: Root, "Style," in Root, *Meanings*, 162.

333 *"self-denial"*: Root, "A Great Architectural Problem," 67–71.

333 *"solidity and strength"*: Hoffmann, *Root*, 65–83, 155–76.

333 *"mercifully cloak"*: "The Art Critic and the Tall Building," *Scientific American* 80 (Jan. 28, 1899): 50.

333 *"refuses to give up"*: Aldis quoted in Hoffmann, *Root*, 157–60; Brooks needed to be nudged because the Monadnock was to be built in a lightly developed southern part of the Loop, near gambling halls, dime hotels, and clapboard shacks.

333 *Lunatic architecture*: *CT*, October 10, 1892.

PAGE
334   *"This is . . . the thing itself":* Montgomery Schuyler, "D. H. Burnham &
      Company," *AR* 5 (Dec. 1895): 56.
334   *"An amazing cliff of brickwork":* LS, 309.
335   *"a crisis":* Ibid., 311.
335   *"he gave young architects":* Giedion, *Space, Time and Architecture,* 370.
336   *"[will] read":* Jenney, "Architecture: Part I," *IA* 1 (Mar. 1883): 18–20.
336   *"The Major":* LS, 203.
336   *"the least of his draftsmen":* William Mundie, "Skeleton Construction, Its
      Origins and Development Applied to Architecture" (1932), unpublished
      MSS, Chicago Microfilm Project, Ryerson and Burnham Libraries, The
      Art Institute of Chicago, 167–68 (hereafter cited as Jenney MSS).
336   *"a lump of sugar":* Quoted in Turak, *Jenney,* 7.
336   *"not an architect":* LS, 203.
336   *"Today William Le Baron Jenney's":* Giedion, *Space, Time and Architec-
      ture,* 371.
337   *"I was obliged":* Jenney, "Autobiography of William Le Baron Jenney,"
      The Western Architect 10 (1907): 59–61; the original unpublished version
      of this autobiographical fragment is in the Chicago Microfilm Project of
      the Art Institute of Chicago. The published version is hereafter referred
      to as "Autobiography," and the unpublished as "Autobiography, MSS";
      Turak, *Jenney,* 11–24; for Jenney in Paris, see Theodore Turak, "The
      École Centrale and Modern Architecture: The Education of William Le
      Baron Jenney," *JSAH* 29 (1970): 40–47.
337   *"to draw":* Jenney, "Whistler and Old Sandy in the Fifties," *American Ar-
      chitect and Building News* 9 (1898): 4–5.
337   *"war is upon us":* Jenney, Autobiography, 62.
337   *siege of Vicksburg:* Jenney, "Personal Recollections of Vicksburg"
      (1883), Jenney MSS.
337   *"The engineering corps":* Jenney, "Autobiography, MSS," 9.
338   *"about as fast":* Quoted in Duncan, *Culture and Democracy,* 332; see also
      Theodore F. Upson, *With Sherman to the Sea,* ed. O. O. Winther (1958),
      113.
338   Principles and Practice of Architecture: Jenney and Sanford E. Loring,
      Principles and Practice of Architecture (1869), 10–32.
338   *Eugène Emmanuel Viollet-le-Duc:* Jenney, "Lectures on Architecture,"
      IA 1 (1883–84): 18–19; There is a brief, brilliant discussion of Viollet-
      le-Duc's ideas in David P. Billington, *The Tower and the Bridge: The New
      Art of Structural Engineering* (1983), 100–102.
338   *"weightless expression":* Kenneth Clark, *Civilisation: A Personal View*
      (1969), 60.
338   *"A practical architect":* Eugène-Emmanuel Viollet-le-Duc, *Entretiens sur
      l'architecture,* trans. Benjamin Buckall (1881), 8–135; John Summerson,
      Heavenly Mansions (1950), 135–58.
339   *"Bright":* Quoted in Clark, *Civilisation,* 50.
339   *"immense height":* Quoted in Spiro Kostof, *A History of Architecture: Set-
      tings and Rituals* (1985), 323.
340   *"largely influenced":* Peter B. Wight, "On the Present Conditions of Archi-
      tectural Art in the Western States," *American Art Review* 1 (1880), 138.
340   *"many times the height":* Quoted in Larson, "Fire, Earth and Wind—Part
      I," 25; see also Larson, "The Iron Skeleton Frame: Interactions Between
      Europe and the United States," in Zukowsky, ed., *Chicago Architecture,*
      38–55.
341   *"It was actually":* Meredith L. Clausen, "Frank Lloyd Wright, Vertical

Space, and the Chicago School's Quest for Light," *JSAH* 44 (Mar. 1985): 66–67.

341 *"maximum number"* and *"a size too small":* Jenney, "Autobiography," 66; Mundie, *Skeleton Construction,* 19–20; Jenney, "Castles in the Air," 2–3, Jenney MSS; Jenney, "The Construction of a Heavy Fireproof Building on a Compressible Soil," *IA* 6 (Dec. 1885): 100.

341 *"At that an inspiration":* Ericsson, *Sixty Years,* 217–18.

341 *the Philippines:* Mundie, "Skeleton Construction," 10–11; Jenney, "Architecture," *IA* 1 (1883–84): 18; Jenney, "The Steel Skeleton, or the Modern Skyscraper—the Engineering Problem," *IA* 34 (Jan. 1900): 2–8.

342 *"Where is there":* Jenney, "Autobiography," 66.

342 *"Here, for the first time":* Ericsson, *Sixty Years,* 219.

343 *"wrote against the sky":* Ibid., 221.

343 *"it was unquestionably":* Thomas E. Tallmadge, "Was the Home Insurance Building the First Skyscraper of Skeleton Construction?" *AR* 76 (1934): 113–18; for a dissenting opinion, see Irving K. Pond, "Neither a Skyscraper nor of Skeleton Construction," *AR* 76 (1934): 18. Pond, a member of the Field Committee called together to decide whether the Home Insurance Building was the world's first iron skeleton skyscraper, argues that the structure of the building was not an example of modern skeleton construction; for the dispute about who built the first skyscraper, see J. Carson Webster, "The Skyscraper: Logical and Historical Considerations," *JSAH* 18 (1959): 126–39.

343 *"Without the rigidity":* Gerald R. Larson and Roula Mouroudellis Geraniotis, "Toward a Better Understanding of the Evolution of the Iron Skeleton Frame in Chicago," *JSAH* 46 (Mar. 1987): 39–47.

343 *Frederick Baumann:* Frederick Baumann, "Improved Construction of High Buildings," *Sanitary News* 3 (Mar. 15, 1884): 123; Baumann, "Life, Reminiscences, and Notes," *Construction News* 4 (Jan. 15, 1916): 9.

343 *Baumann stole the idea:* Mundie, "Skeleton Construction," 10–41; Theodore Turak, "Remembrances of the Home Insurance Building," *JSAH* 44 , no. 1 (1985): 60–65.

344 *"This principle":* Quoted in Frank A. Randall, *History of the Development of Building Construction in Chicago* (1949), 106.

344 *"Mr. Jenney":* Mundie, "Skeleton Construction," 10.

344 *"simple engineering problem":* Jenney, "Autobiography," 66; Jenney, "Castles in the Air," 2–3.

344 *"the most extraordinary":* Mundie, Skeleton Construction, 10.

345 *"Disaster was predicted":* Starrett, *Skyscrapers,* 40.

345 *Holabird and Roche:* For an astute assessment of Holabird and Roche's work, see Robert Bruegmann, "Holabird & Roche and Holabird & Root: The First Two Generations," *CH* 9, no 3 (1980): 130–65.

345 *"The devices":* Quoted in *JWR,* 118–19.

346 *"absolutely trustworthy":* Root, "A Great Architectural Problem," 67–71; on Z-bar construction see William H. Birkmire, *Skeleton Construction in Buildings* (1894; reprint, 1972): 53–54; for an excellent essay on the technology of the first Chicago skyscrapers see Tom F. Peters, "The Rise of the Skyscraper From the Ashes of Chicago," *Invention and Technology,* Fall 1987, 14–22; see also, Peters, "The Relative Value of Invention and the History of Tall Buildings," and Carl W. Condit, "The Two Centuries of Technical Evolution Underlying the Skyscraper," both in Lyne S. Beedle, ed., *Second Century of the Skyscraper* (1988), 11–32.

346 *"The life of":* Quoted in Turak, *Jenney,* 267.

PAGE

346   *"We have entered":* Jenney, "An Age of Steel and Clay," *IA* 16 (1890): 77–79.

346   *Second Leiter Building: Industrial Chicago,* vol. 1 (1891), 205; Jenney, "A Few Practical Hints," *IA* 13 (1889): 8–9.

347   *"Fifteen years ago":* Flinn, *Chicago* (1890), 1–30; and Flinn, in Bruegmann, "Holabird & Roche," 152.

348   *"paper empire":* Thomas J. Schlereth, "The World and Workers of the Paper Empire," in Schlereth, *Victorian America: Transformations in Everyday Life, 1876–1915* (1991), 145–76.

348   *"bureaucratic rule and hierarchy":* Oliver Zunz, *Making America Corporate, 1870–1920* (1990), 106, 126–32, 202–3.

348   *new kind of factory:* Braverman, *Monopoly Capital,* 294–301; for Chicago clerical workers, see Lisa M. Fine, *The Souls of the Skyscraper: Female Clerical Workers in Chicago, 1870–1930* (1990); for an economic study with a wider focus, see Elyce J. Rotella, *From Home to Office: U.S. Women at Work, 1870–1930* (1981).

348   *"Smiles and tears":* Carl Sandburg, "Skyscraper," in *Chicago Poems,* 65–67.

349   *"new fangled writing machine":* Quoted in Margery W. Davies, *Woman's Place Is at the Typewriter: Office Work and Office Workers, 1870–1930* (1982), 35–36; see also Adrian Forty, *Objects of Desire: Design and Society, 1750–1890* (1986), 120–56.

349   *"Five years ago":* Quoted in Richard Current, *The Typewriter and the Men Who Made It* (1954), 110; see also Bruce Bliven, Jr., *The Wonderful Writing Machine* (1954), 30–62.

349   *first women typists:* Stenographic Efficiency Bureau, *Making the Body an Efficient Machine* (1916), 1–10; Current, *Typewriter,* 28–64; Phil Patton, *Made in USA: The Secret Histories of the Things That Made America* (1992), 76–82.

349   *"expecting the same" "flowers in the office"* and *"powder puffs":* Quoted in Fine, *Souls,* 7–8, 58; see also "Wanted—One Hundred Girls as Stenographers," *The Phonographic World,* Apr. 1910, 224 (reprint of a piece in the *Chicago Journal*); Jeanette Ballantyne, "Why Some Women Fail of Success in Court Reporters or Business Offices," *The Phonographic World,* Sept. 1887, 16.

349   *"In the cozy den"* and *"can live a consistent":* Quoted in Fine, *Souls,* 59; see also Marion Harland, "The Incapacity of Business Women," *NAR* 149 (1889): 707–12; and Joanne J. Meyerowitz's insightful study, *Women Adrift: Independent Wage Earners in Chicago, 1880–1930* (1988).

350   *women were in the office to stay:* Alba Edwards, *Comparative Occupational Statistics for the United States, 1870–1940* (1943), 91–94, 100; Ethel Erickson, "The Employment of Women in Offices," *U.S. Department of Labor, Women's Bureau, Bulletin,* no. 120 (1934): 10–13.

350   *"Ten-dollar-a-week stenographers":* Sandburg, "Skyscraper," 66.

351   *"especially suited as typists":* Rotella, *From Home to Office,* 158, 161.

351   *"should preferably be a man":* Lee Galloway, *Office Management: Its Principles and Practice* (1919), 156–57.

351   *new commercial schools:* Janice Weiss, "Educating for Clerical Work: The Nineteenth-Century Private Commercial School," *Journal of Social History* 14 (Spring 1981): 411–17.

351   *"energy,":* David Lockwood, *The Blackcoated Worker: A Study in Class Consciousness* (1958), 19.

352   *"The alienating conditions":* Mills quoted in Braverman, *Monopoly Capital.* 352.

PAGE
352 *the Autocrat:* Schlereth, "Paper Empire," 166–71.
353 *Filing cabinets in the sky:* Interview with Lewis Mumford, Amenia, N.Y., May 6, 1986.
353 *"an indefinite number":* Sullivan, "Tall Office," 403–5.
353 *"to keep buzzing":* George Ade, "From the Office Window," in *Stories,* 167–71.
353 *"sterile pile"* and *"[is] not a merchant":* Sullivan, *Kindergarten Chats and Other Writings,* 140; Sullivan, "Tall Office," 403–8.
353 *"coarse and strong city":* Sandburg, "Chicago," *Chicago Poems,* 3.

Chapter Eleven: Sullivan and Civic Renewal

354 *"something more than":* Schuyler, "Architecture in Chicago, Part I," 12–16.
354 *"make it something":* Henry B. Fuller, *With the Procession* (1895), 114.
355 *"to bring order":* Burnham and Bennett, *Plan of Chicago,* 1.
355 *"only one city":* Quoted in Ericsson, *Sixty Years,* 235.
356 *"to the faintest":* LS: 293; Dankmar Adler, "The Chicago Auditorium," *AR* Apr.–June 1892, 415. My account of the building's conception and construction is based on documents in the Roosevelt University Archives. These include the minutes of the Board of Directors and Executive Committee of the Auditorium Association. The Art Institute has a collection of working drawings of the building and a scrapbook of clippings compiled by the Auditorium Association. Edward R. Garczynski's *Auditorium* (1890) is an oddly interesting storehouse of information on the construction and physical characteristics of the building.
356 *meeting of the Commercial Club: CT,* June 13, 1886, Sept. 26, 1886.
356 *"older communities":* Franklin H. Head, "The Heart of Chicago," *NEM* 6 (July 1892): 559.
357 *"[These three young men]":* Thomas W. Goodspeed, clipping, Hutchinson MSS.
357 *"I, too, was part":* Robert Herrick, *The Memoirs of an American Citizen* (1905; reprint, 1963), 266.
358 *"The past shows plainly": IO,* Oct. 11, 1896.
358 *"a pleasant gentleman":* Quoted in David Van Zanten, "Sullivan to 1890," in Wim de Wit, ed., *Louis Sullivan: The Function of Ornament* (1986), 13; see also Minutes of Board of Directors, Chicago Auditorium Association, Dec. 21, 1886, Roosevelt University Archives.
358 *"dreamer for the populace":* Clipping, Auditorium Building Scrapbook, Art Institute of Chicago.
358 *"an art that will live":* Sullivan, "Tall Office Building," 409.
358 *"enormous, unprecedented work":* LS, 294.
358 *"was made":* Condit, *Chicago School,* 69.
358 *"There are many men":* Giorgio Vasari, *Lives of the Artists* (1965 edition), 133.
359 *"Only the heroic scale":* Albert Bush-Brown, *Louis Sullivan* (1960), 7.
359 *"see what architecture":* LS, 189.
359 *joined his parents:* Sullivan "Family Record," Louis Sullivan Collection, Ryerson and Burnham Libraries, the Art Institute of Chicago; the most recent and reliable biography of Sullivan is Robert Twombly's excellent *Louis Sullivan: His Life and Work* (1986; reprint, 1987); see also Hugh Morrison, *Louis Sullivan: Prophet of Modern Architecture* (1935); Willard Connely, *Louis Sullivan As He Lived: The Shaping of American Architecture: A Biography* (1960); and Mervyn Kaufman, *Father of Skyscrapers: A*

PAGE

Biography of Louis Sullivan (1969); for an aggressively critical yet richly suggestive account of Sullivan, see David S. Andrew, *Louis Sullivan and the Polemics of Modern Architecture: The Present Against the Past* (1985); perhaps the best way to approach Sullivan as an architect is through his drawings, which have been assembled and edited by Paul Sprague, *The Drawings of Louis Henry Sullivan* (1979); for a shrewd appraisal of Sullivan's architecture see John Szarkowski, *The Idea of Louis Sullivan* (1956); Frank Lloyd Wright wrote a brilliant, though sometimes badly inaccurate, account of Sullivan the architect, *Genius and Mobocracy;* the best place to begin a study of Sullivan's architectural philosophy is in his *Kindergarten Chats* and Twombly's *Sullivan: The Public Papers,* which brings together all of Sullivan's papers intended for a public audience.

359   *"headquarters":* LS, 189, 202–10; see also Sullivan, "Records," Avery Library, Columbia University; Donald D. Egbert and Paul E. Sprague, "In Search of John Edelmann," *AIA Journal* 45 (Feb. 1966): 35–41.

359   *"alone there":* LS, 234–35.

360   *"thunder-struck" Brunelleschi:* Vasari, *Lives of the Artists,* 139.

360   *"almost a pantheistic":* Bush-Brown, *Sullivan,* 10.

360   *"Imitation cannot":* Ralph Waldo Emerson, "An Address," in *Ralph Waldo Emerson: Essays and Lectures* (1983), 89.

360   *"The function of a building":* LS, 290; Sullivan to Claude Bragdon, July 25, 1904, in Bragdon, "Letters from Louis Sullivan," *Architecture* 6 (July 1931): 8.

360   *"who did things":* LS, 245–49.

360   *"to make an architecture":* Ibid., 257, 294, 303.

361   warehouse to house: Andrew, *Sullivan,* 86–88.

361   *"severe treatment":* Adler, "The Chicago Auditorium," 417–20.

363   *commanding campanile:* Adler was entirely responsible for the construction of the tower, a monumental engineering feat; Dankmar Adler, "Foundations of the Auditorium Building, Chicago," *IA* 11 (Mar. 1888): 31–32; Rochelle S. Elstein, "The Architecture of Dankmar Adler," *JSAH* 26 (Dec. 1967): 242–49; for Adler's theater architecture, see Charles E. Gregersen, *Dankmar Adler: His Theatres and Auditoriums* (1989).

363   *"professional brethren":* Schuyler, "Architecture in Chicago: Adler and Sullivan," 23.

363   *"dull, mellow gold":* Morrison, *Sullivan,* 103.

363   *"He may have been ridiculous":* Wright, *Genius and Mobocracy,* 72–78, 95. "Sound rode along to the listeners," Wright said of the Auditorium, "upon air-conditioning. Air-conditioning arrived as a carrier of sound!"; See also Carl W. Condit, "Sullivan's Skyscrapers as the Expression of Nineteenth Century Technology," *Technology and Culture* 1 (1960): 78–93; My thanks to Tim Samuelson and John Vinci for giving me on-site instruction on the decorative and engineering aspects of this great American building.

364   *"according to ancient usage"* and *"stupendous monument":* CT, Sept. 21, Oct. 3, 1889; *IO,* Oct. 3, 1889.

364   *"the most brilliant audience":* IO, Dec. 10, 1889.

365   *"A great genius":* Wright, *Genius and Mobocracy,* 66, 64; the CT printed a letter the next day from "one of the contractors" protesting the failure to recognize Sullivan by name the night before; Dec. 15, 1889.

365   *"temple of* practical *service":* IO, Dec. 8, 10, 1889.

365   *"not percent"* and *"the honor and glory":* CT, Dec. 10, 1889; *HW,* Nov. 9, 1889. Not expecting to make a profit, the sponsors of the Auditorium never did. The only dividend the stockholders ever received was for

1893, when visitors to the fair filled the hotel. See Gregersen, *Adler*, 67–68. The Auditorium Hotel is now home to Roosevelt University, while the theater is still used for civic performances.

365 *"Such a crowd"*: Norris, *The Pit*, 1–58.

366 *"A monument to trade"*: Sullivan, *Kindergarten Chats*, 30.

366 *"The Auditorium Building"*: Adler, "Chicago Auditorium," 415.

367 *"finest, purest thinking"*: LS, 297.

367 *"paid no attention to anyone"*: Wright, *Autobiography*, 96–103; Wright, *Genius and Mobocracy*, 61–63, 70–72; see also William Purcell, "Sullivan at Work," *Northwest Architect* 8 (Jan.–Feb. 1944): 11. Sullivan was married in 1899 to Mary Azona Hattabaugh, who called herself Margaret. She was twenty and he was forty-two at the time of the marriage. She left him in 1909 after he began drinking heavily when his career hit the skids.

368 *"essentially a technician"* and *"to the front"*: LS, 288, 257; see also Joan W. Saltzstein, "Dankmar Adler: Part One—The Man," *Wisconsin Architect*, July–Aug. 1967, 15–19.

368 *"in his own unique"*: Lewis Mumford, *The Brown Decades: A Study of the Arts in America, 1865–1895* (1931; reprint, 1971), 65.

368 *"wide windows," "adored" Whitman*, and *"Every building you see"*: Wright, *Genius and Mobocracy*, 70–71; Wright, *Autobiography*, 90–107; LS, 256–313; Sullivan, *Kindergarten Chats*, passim. Biographers of Wright have tended to underplay his adoration for Sullivan, but Sullivan had an undeniably strong influence on the young Wright, not so much on his ideas about architecture, perhaps, as on his vision of the architect as a cultural hero.

369 *"an equally revolutionary"*: LS, 298.

369 *"every inch of it tall"*: Sullivan, "Tall Office Building," 406.

369 *"masonry period"*: Sullivan to Claude Bragdon, Nov. 8, 1903, in Bragdon, "Letters," 9.

369 *"picturesque verticality"*: Wright, *Genius and Mobocracy*, 74–76.

370 *"poetic imagery"*: Sullivan, "Ornament in Architecture," 187–90; see also Sullivan, "Emotional Architecture as Compared with Intellectual: A Study in Objective and Subjective" (1894), reprinted in *Kindergarten Chats*, 191–201; Paul Goldberger has an astute appraisal of the Wainwright in *The Skyscraper* (1982), 18; for a thoughtful analysis of Sullivan's theory of ornament, see Lauren S. Weingarden, "Naturalized Technology: Louis H. Sullivan's Whitmanesque Skyscrapers," *The Centennial Review* 30 (Fall 1986): 480–95.

370 *"countenance"*: Wright, *Genius and Mobocracy*, 74–76. Wright believed he was the founder of true organic architecture. He drew his inspiration, he said, from music. "My father taught me that a symphony was an *edifice* of sound. I wanted to see, someday, a building continuously plastic from inside to outside and exterior from outside to inside." *Genius and Mobocracy*, 78.

370 *"dogma" of form follows function*: Frank Lloyd Wright, review of Hugh Morrison's *Louis Sullivan* in *Saturday Review of Literature* 13 (Dec. 14, 1935): 6.

370 *"one of the most beautiful"*: Barr Ferree, "High Building and Its Art," 312; see also Ferree, "The Modern Office Building, Part III," *IA* 27 (June 1896): 45. The building later became the Garrick Theater.

370 *"is in the same relation"*: Bannister Fletcher, "American Architecture Through English Spectacles," *Engineering Magazine* 7 (June 1894): 318; for astute appraisals of this building, see Carl W. Condit, "The

PAGE

Structural System of Adler and Sullivan's Garrick Theater Building,"
Technology and Culture 5 (Fall 1984): 523–40; and Paul E. Sprague,
"Adler and Sullivan's Schiller Building," *The Prairie School Review* 2
(Second Quarter 1965): 5–20. The greatest authority on the building was
the brilliant architectural photographer Richard Nickel, who supervised
the salvage of the ornamental work during demolition of the building.
Nickel was killed in 1972 while trying to save the last pieces of ornament
from the Chicago Stock Exchange when one of the final standing sections
of the building collapsed on him, the tragic end of a protracted struggle
by preservationists to save this building.

371 *"The High Building Question"*: Louis Sullivan, "The High Building
Question," *TG* 5 (Dec. 19, 1891): 405; see also Donald Hoffmann, "The
Setback Skyscraper City of 1891: An Unknown Essay by Louis H. Sulli-
van," *JSAH* 29 (May 1970): 181–87.

371 *"damp and dark basements"*: Ralph, *Harper's Chicago*, 4–15; Hoyt, *One
Hundred Years*, 153; *CT*, Jan. 13, June 9, 1889, Dec. 18, 1891, Feb. 17,
July 18, 1892.

371 *"canyonizing"*: "Deliberations of the Architects," *Economist* 6 (Nov. 21,
1891): 857–58; Lane, "High Buildings in Chicago," 853–56. The controversy about height restrictions continued in Chicago and New York
throughout the 1890s. See "Fire and the Modern Skyscraper," *Scientific
American* 80 (Jan. 1890): 39; Ernest Flagg, "The Dangers of High Buildings," *Cosmopolitan* 21 (May 1896): 70–79; on elevator fatalities, see
Duis, "Yesterday's City," 71.

371 *"prescribed limit"*: Sullivan, "High Building Question," 405.

372 *Odd Fellows Temple*: "Chicago—Proposed Odd Fellows Temple," *TG* 5
(Dec. 9, 1891): 404.

372 *"social menace"*: LS, 313.

372 *"license [to] . . . disregard"*: Sullivan, "High Building Question," 405.

373 *"untroubled by a social conscience"*: Wright, *Genius and Mobocracy*,
53, 54.

373 *"It is not my purpose"*: Sullivan, "Tall Office Building," 403.

373 *Spencerian faith"*: Sullivan read Spencer as early as 1877. See *Lotus
Club Notebooks*, 1872–82. Louis Sullivan Papers, Avery Library, Columbia University.

373 *"there was stir"*: LS, 202. For the romantic interpretation of Sullivan, see
especially Sherman Paul, *Louis Sullivan, An Architect in American
Thought* (1962). Sullivan's thought was shaped by transcendentalist-
democratic ideas, especially Emerson's idea of the poet as cultural hero,
but his interpretation of those ideas was idiosyncratic and often at vari-
ance with nineteenth-century American romantic ideas about democracy and individualism; for a more critical perspective on Sullivan
romanticism, see Morrison, *Sullivan*, and more recent studies: Narciso
G. Menocal, *Architecture as Nature: The Transcendentalist Idea of Louis
Sullivan* (1981), and Andrew, *Sullivan*. A more balanced interpretation of Sullivan as romantic-democratic poet is found in Twombly, *Sullivan*.

Twombly, in another place, argues quite correctly, I think, that Sullivan lost faith in the reformability of the businessman. "He feared that the
power of the very entrepreneurial class upon which his livelihood depended had gotten out of control" (Twombly, "Introduction," *Public Papers*, xxii). But it is not insignificant that his radical ideas about
capitalism and capitalists surfaced after business clients stopped bringing work to him with regularity following his split with Adler in 1895.

PAGE

374 *"To the artist":* Quoted in Justin Kaplan, *Walt Whitman: A Life* (1980), 168–69; see also John William Draper, *History of the Intellectual Development of Europe* (1876); LS, 329.

374 *his failing years:* For Sullivan's later and bitterly critical views of "the city," see especially *Kindergarten Chats,* 109–16. Scholars have gone to these later writings to argue that Sullivan was antiurban. "Seventy years ago it was a mudhole," Sullivan wrote in *Kindergarten Chats* of Chicago. "Today it is a human swamp" (109). Sullivan remembered the city much more fondly in his autobiography. Wright, who truly was anticity, saw Sullivan as a thoroughly urban man. "Neither knowledge of nor any desire for the warm simple ways of country life were ever seen in him," *Genius and Mobocracy,* 53.

374 *Adler's daring foundation work:* Adler, "Piling for Isolated Foundations Adjacent to Wall," *IA* 20 (Jan. 1893): 63–64; "Chicago Stock Exchange Building," *Ornamental Iron* 2 (July 1894): 7–13.

375 *"unleashed the ultimate":* Ericsson, *Sixty Years,* 233.

375 *limiting the height of buildings:* In 1900, the height limitation was raised to 260 feet, and in the 1920s height limitations virtually disappeared in Chicago allowing John Mead Howells and Raymond Hood to design the 450-foot-high Tribune Tower. See Shultz and Simmons, *Offices in the Sky,* 282–83; Bluestone, *Constructing Chicago,* 150; and John W. Stamper, *Chicago's North Michigan Avenue: Planning and Development* (1991), 27–39.

376 *"the future looked bright":* LS, 314–25

376 *"the appalling calamity":* LS, 321; for important discussions of neoclassical architecture see Paul R. Baker, *Richard Morris Hunt* (1980); and Richard Guy Wilson, *McKim, Mead & White, Architects* (1983).

Chapter Twelve: The New Chicago

378 *"a mate":* CT, Dec. 10, 1889.

378 *"was the first act":* Monroe, *A Poet's Life,* 109.

378 *"the Upward Movement":* Henry B. Fuller, "The Upward Movement in Chicago," *AM* 80 (Oct. 1897): 534–47.

379 *"The men":* CT, Aug. 2, 1889; see also Francis L. Lederer II, "Competition for the World's Columbian Exposition: The Chicago Campaign," *JISHS* 65 (1972): 382–88.

379 *fight between Chicago and New York:* CT, July 22, Sept. 26, 1889, Feb. 25, 1890; H. N. Higinbotham, *Report of the President of the Board of Directors of the World's Columbian Exposition* (1898), 9; *Three American Expositions, Arguments before the Quadri-Centennial Committee of the United States Senate in Support of Bills Nos. 1839 and 1135 . . .* (1890).

379 *"jumbo":* CT, Feb. 21, 25, Mar. 2, Apr. 4, 1890; Rossiter Johnson, ed., *A History of the World's Columbian Exposition,* vol. 1 (1897), 12.

379 *"Make it the Greatest":* P. T. Barnum, "What a Fair Should Be," *NAR* 150 (Mar. 1890): 400.

379 *"cattle show":* JWR, 218.

380 *"painter":* Daniel H. Burnham, *The Final Official Report of the Director of Works of the World's Columbian Exposition* (1894; reprint, 1989), vol. 1, 1–98; vol. 4, 1–63; Frederick Law Olmsted, "The Landscape Architecture of the World's Columbian Exposition," *IA* 12 (Sept. 1893), passim.

380 *"conspicuous buildings":* Daniel H. Burnham, "The Organization of the World's Columbian Exposition," *IA* (Aug. 1893): 5–6; Burnham and

Francis D. Millet, *World's Columbian Exposition, The Book of the Builders* (1894): 28–30.

381 *"a dream city":* Charles Moore, "Lessons of the Chicago World's Fair: An Interview with the Late Daniel H. Burnham," *AR* 33 (Jan. 1913): 39–40; Daniel H. Burnham, "Report to the Committee on Grounds and Buildings," *Century Illustrated Monthly Magazine* 44 (1892): 83.

381 *"splendor which an exposition":* Burnham to E. L. Corthell, Oct. 4, 1890, Burnham MSS.

381 *group of local designers:* Titus M. Karlowicz, "D. H. Burnham's Role in the Selection of Architects for the World's Columbian Exposition," *JSAH* 29 (Oct. 1970): 247–54.

382 *"Do you mean"* and *"team-work":* Moore, "Lessons," 39–46.

382 *"I have worked":* Quoted in Monroe, *A Poet's Life,* 114.

382 *"Beaux-Arts boys":* Sally Chappell, "Beaux-Arts Architecture in Chicago," *IA* 24 (Oct. 1980): 23.

382 *"Look here":* Moore, "Lessons," 42; Burnham to James Windrim, Feb. 7, 1891; McKim, Mead, and White to Burnham, Jan. 7, 1891, both in Burnham MSS.

382 *Construction of the White City:* Burnham, *First Official Report,* vol. 1, 1–98, vol. 4, 1–63; H. C. Bunner, "The Making of the White City," *Scribner's Magazine* 12 (Oct. 1892): 398–418.

383 *"one of those magnificent":* Monroe, *A Poet's Life,* 114.

384 *"Guarded by sentries":* Walter A. Wyckoff, *The Workers: An Experiment in Reality: The West* (1898), 247–49.

384 *Burnham drove his crews relentlessly: Chicago Record's History of the World's Fair* (1893), 10–15; Burnham to Lyman J. Gage, Feb. 14, 1891, Burnham MSS; "Organized Labor and the World's Fair," *IA* 17 (June 1891): 54.

385 *"in matters of order":* Charles Moore, *The Life and Times of Charles Follen McKim* (1929), 115; Charles Follen McKim to Burnham, Oct. 26, 1892, Burnham MSS.

385 *Charles Lawrence Hutchinson: Annual Report of the Trustees of the Art Institute of Chicago, June 5, 1890* (hereafter cited as *Trustees*); *Trustees,* June 7, 1892; *CT,* Oct. 12, 1890; on the building of the Art Institute, see Linda S. Phipps, "The 1893 Art Institute Building and the 'Paris of America': Aspirations of Patrons and Architects in Late Nineteenth-Century Chicago," *Museum Studies* 14, no. 1 (1988): 28–45; and John Zukowsky, "The Art Institute of Chicago: Constructions, Concepts, and Queries," *Threshold* 3 (Autumn 1985): 60–85.

386 *New York architect predicted:* Bluestone, *Constructing Chicago,* 183.

386 *"The Art Institute"* and *"gray ghosts":* Frank Lloyd Wright, "Chicago Culture," 1918 speech, reprinted in Bruce Brooks Pfeiffer, ed., *Frank Lloyd Wright Collected Writings, vol. 1, 1894–1930* (1992), 154–61.

386 *The Art Institute's design:* Minutes of the Jan. 7, 1892, meeting of the Board of Trustees of the Art Institute, in Meeting Minutes 1891–present, Office of the Secretary, the Art Institute; Proceedings of Chicago Library Board, Sept. 26, 1891, Chicago Public Library.

387 *"We have built": Chicago Herald,* Nov. 20, 1887; "Cheers on Young Men," report on speech by Hutchinson, Dec. 2, 1905, clipping in *Scrapbook, 1899–1920,* n.p., Hutchinson MSS; for an appraisal of America's "cultural capitalists," see Paul Dimaggio, "Cultural Entrepreneurship in Nineteenth-Century Boston: The Creation of an Organized Base for High Culture in America," *Media, Culture and Society* 4 (1982): 33–50; and Dimaggio, "Cultural Entrepreneurship in Nineteenth-Century Boston,

PAGE

Part II: The Classification and Framing of American Art," ibid., 303–22. My interpretation of the role of Chicago's Art Institute is more in line with that of Neil Harris in "The Gilded Age Revisited: Boston and the Museum Movement," *American Quarterly* 14 (Winter 1964): 545–66.

387   *"the expression and the product"*: Quoted in Goodspeed, "Hutchinson," 76; Resolution Adapted at a Special Meeting of the Chicago Clearing House Association, Oct. 10, 1924, Hutchinson MSS.

388   *Charles Hutchinson:* Goodspeed, "Hutchinson," 50–76; see also Charles Hutchinson, "Notebook with Special References to Church Activities," Hutchinson MSS; and Thomas J. Schlereth, "Big Money and High Culture: The Commercial Club and Charles L. Hutchinson," *The Great Lakes Review* 3 (Summer 1976): 15–27.

388   *"in his youth"*: Goodspeed, "Hutchinson," 55.

388   *"Everybody should"*: Hutchinson, "The Democracy of Art," *The American Magazine of Art* 7 (Aug. 1916): 399.

389   *"In the deepest sense"*: Tribute to Charles L. Hutchinson, Art Institute of Chicago, 1925, Charles L. Hutchinson Papers, CHS.

389   *"We live"*: Hutchinson, "Art: Its Influence and Excellence in Modern Times," Mar. 31, 1888, Hutchinson MSS; Lorado Taft, "Charles L. Hutchinson and the Art Institute," in *In Memorium: Charles Hutchinson, 1854–1924* (1925), 11, Charles L. Hutchinson Papers, CHS.

389   *"The real work"* and *"organized effort"*: Hutchinson, Notebook report as Sunday School Superintendent [n.d.], 2–4, Hutchinson MSS; Hutchinson, "Right Conception of Art in Rochester," Memorial Art Gallery Scrapbook, 1922, Charlotte Whitney Allen Library, University of Rochester.

390   *"keen trader"*: Andrews, *Battle for Chicago,* 156.

390   *"The princess"*: *CT,* July 3, 1890; *IO,* June 7, 1890; Hutchinson Diary, 1890, Hutchinson MSS: for Ryerson as a collector, see Patricia Erens, *Masterpieces: Famous Chicagoans and Their Paintings* (1979), 34–47; for the early years of the Art Institute, see W. M. R. French, *The Art Institute of Chicago: Historical and Descriptive* (1901).

390   *"corkers"* and *"probably paid"*: *New York Press,* July 4, 1890; *Chicago Times,* Nov. 8, 1890, both clippings in *Art Institute Scrapbooks.*

390   *"We have made"*: Quoted in Elia W. Peattie, "The Artistic Side of Chicago," *AM* 84 (Dec. 1899): 833.

391   *"the Institute should be measured"*: Quoted in Jahr, *Urban Establishment,* 524.

391   *"Workmen"*: Quoted in Kathleen D. McCarthy, *Noblesse Oblige: Cultural Philanthropy in Chicago, 1849–1929* (1982), 87–88; *Trustees,* June 4, 1889; Charles Hutchinson, "Notebook with Special Reference to The Art Institute of Chicago," Hutchinson MSS.

391   *"I want all Chicago here"* and *"three-ring circus"*: Quoted in *GG,* 272; and Taft, "Charles L. Hutchinson," 16–18.

391   *"a Community House"*: Taft, "Charles L. Hutchinson," 18; Peter C. Marzio, "A Museum and a School: An Uneasy but Creative Union," *CH* 8 (Spring 1979): 20–52; Hamlin Garland, *A Daughter of the Middle Border* (1922), 4–6.

391   *"Time and again"*: *GG,* 274; see also Charles L. Hutchinson Diary, May 1881 to Mar. 22, 1911, Hutchinson MSS.

392   *"Terribly fond"*: Quoted in *GG,* 275.

392   *"I could write a book"*: Quoted in Goodspeed, "Hutchinson," 71–72; Frances Kinsley Hutchinson, *Our Country Life* (1912) 3–30.

PAGE

392   *"in no other city":* Quoted in Jahr, *Urban Establishment,* 524; see also
       Trustees, 1905–1906.

393   *"I love to lie here": GG,* 276.

393   *"Like the cathedral":* Wright, "Chicago Culture," 158.

393   *"Gentlemen":* Robert Morss Lovett, *All Our Years: The Autobiography of
       Robert Morss Lovett* (1948), 60; Lovett was the assistant who walked
       alongside Harper as he bicycled; Thomas Wakefield Goodspeed, *A His-
       tory of the University of Chicago: The First Quarter-Century* (1916), 133;
       for Harper, see Goodspeed, *William Rainey Harper, First President of the
       University of Chicago* (1928); the two best accounts of the early history of
       the university are Goodspeed and Richard J. Storr, *Harper's University:
       The Beginnings: A History of the University of Chicago* (1966); Jean F.
       Block, *The Uses of Gothic: Planning and Building the Campus of the
       University of Chicago, 1892–1932* (1983), is a splendid account of the
       physical planning and architecture of the university; for the university
       and the city, see Steven J. Diner, *A City and Its Universities: Public Pol-
       icy in Chicago, 1892–1919* (1980).

393   *"A short, broad man":* Robert Herrick, "Memoirs," Robert Herrick's Pa-
       pers, University of Chicago Library, Dept. of Special Collections [here-
       after cited as Herrick MSS], 46–49.

394   *"on both sides":* Block, *Gothic,* 2–5.

394   *"witness to a still higher":* Quoted in Block, *Gothic,* 5.

395   *"The whole thing":* Herrick, "Memoirs," 46–49.

395   *"a passport to heaven":* Lovett, *All Our Years,* 58; Storr, *Harper's Univer-
       sity,* 3–52.

395   *"If some Christian":* Quoted in Block, *Hyde Park Houses,* 59.

395   *"to save the undertaking":* Goodspeed, "Hutchinson," 64–65.

396   *Goodspeed went to Marshall Field:* Goodspeed, *University of Chicago,*
       173–77; Hutchinson to William Rainey Harper, Feb. 18, 27, 1892, Uni-
       versity President's Papers, 1889–1925, University of Chicago Library,
       Dept. of Special Collections.

396   *"with smoldering eyes":* Lovett, *All Our Years,* 69.

397   *"moral health"* and *"I've tried":* Harper and Veblen quoted in John P.
       Diggins, *The Bard of Savagery: Thorstein Veblen and Modern Social The-
       ory* (1978), 32–41, 169–85.

397   *"If the higher learning":* Thorstein Veblen, *The Higher Learning in Amer-
       ica: A Memorandum on the Conduct of Universities by Business Men*
       (1918), 11, 75, 85, 92, 241, 265–67; for Edward Teller Crane on higher
       education, see *CT,* Jan. 9, 10, 16, 1912.

397   *"direction of the pursuit":* Veblen, *Higher Learning,* v–134.

398   *"No one can testify":* Lovett, *All Our Years,* 60.

398   *"bastard antique":* Veblen, *Higher Learning,* 142–47.

399   *Hutchinson and Ryerson's preference for Gothic:* Hutchinson to William
       Rainey Harper, Apr. 4, 1900, University President's Papers, *University of
       Chicago Weekly* 1 (Oct. 1, 1892): 12.

399   *"wonderful contrast":* Quoted in Neil Harris introduction to Block,
       Gothic, xiii.

399   *"survive as one":* Neil Harris, "University of Chicago Quadrangles," in
       AIA Guide to Chicago, ed. Alice Sinkevitch (1993), 425.

400   *"I cannot conceive":* Quoted in Storr, *Harper's University,* 47.

400   *"mankind wherever mankind is":* Quoted in ibid., 194.

400   *"to comfort and edify":* Veblen, *Higher Learning,* 192.

400   *"the cultural redemption":* Storr, *Harper's University,* 196–98.

PAGE

401   *"hire learning"*: Quoted in Lovett, *All Our Years*, 62.

401   *"Titanic-looking"*: *IO*, Apr. 21, 1895.

402   *"Dr. Harper . . . unfolded"*: Harper to Stagg, Oct. 21, 1890, University President's Papers; see also Stagg's account of the meeting with Harper in Stagg, *Touchdown!*, as told by Coach Amos Almzo Stagg to Wesley Winans Green (1927), 134–44; Robin Lester, "The Rise, Decline, and Fall of Intercollegiate Football at the Univ. of Chicago, 1890–1940" (Ph.D. diss., University of Chicago, 1974), 13–16.

402   *"spread the gospel"*: *CT*, Sept. 20, 1893, Oct. 2, 1892.

402   *"the university of Chicago believes in football"* and *"If Chicago University"*: Quoted in Lester, "Football," 18, 23. Years later, the university eliminated all varsity sports.

403   *"Harper's Bazaar"*: J. Laurence Laughlin to Mrs. George Palmer, Aug. 9, 1896, Herrick Collection; Herrick wrote a satire of Harper's university, *Chimes* (1926); for the University's policy on coeducation see Marion Talbot, *More than Lore: Reminiscences of Marion Talbot, Dean of Women, the University of Chicago, 1892–1925* (1936).

403   *"an absolutely sexless"*: Robert Herrick, "The University of Chicago," *Scribner's Magazine* 18 (Oct. 1895): 413–17.

403   *"[But] there were bigger things"*: Herrick, "Memoirs," 50–51.

404   *"His death"*: Lovett, *All Our Years*, 101.

404   *"FREE PUBLIC LIBRARY"*: "Will of Walter Newberry," Newberry Library.

404   *William Frederick Poole*: William Landram Williamson, *William Frederick Poole and the Modern Library Movement* (1963), 39–60; "Chicago Public Library," *TG*, May 21, 1892, 380–81.

405   *"satisfy the wants"*: Quoted in Paul Finkelman, "Class and Culture in Late-Nineteenth-Century Chicago: The Founding of the Newberry Library," *American Studies* 16, no. 1 (1975): 6–7; see also Lawrence W. Towner, *An Uncommon Collection of Uncommon Collections: The Newberry Library* (1985), 10–14.

405   *The Newberry's architecture*: William Frederick Poole, *The Construction of Library Buildings* (1881), 8–16; Houghton Wetherold, "The Architectural History of the Newberry Library," *The Newberry Library Bulletin* 6 (Nov. 1962): 3–23; Horowitz, *Culture*, 72.

405   *"decent people"* and *"the better and cleaner classes"*: Edith Wharton and *Chicago Times* quoted in Finkelman, "Newberry," 17, 19.

406   *"dirty French novels"*: "The Librarian," *The John Crerar Library* (n.d.), 1–34; *The Newberry Library: Trustees, Officers, and Committees; By-Laws* (1894), 18.

406   *"social defense of caste"*: E. Digby Baltzell, *The Protestant Establishment: Aristocracy and Caste in America* (1964), 109–21.

406   *"to produce the greatest"*: *NYT*, Nov. 7, 1890; *CT*, Mar. 22, 1891; Theodore Thomas, *Theodore Thomas: A Musical Autobiography*, ed. George P. Upton 1 (1905; reprint, 1964): 1–50, 100; C. Norman Fay, "The Theodore Thomas Orchestra," *The Outlook*, Jan. 22, 1910, 159–69; Ezra Schabas, *Theodore Thomas: America's Conductor and Builder of Orchestras, 1835–1905* (1989), 181.

406   *father of American symphonic music*: Rose Fay Thomas, *Memoirs of Theodore Thomas* (1911), 22–29, 52–100, 246; Charles Edward Russell, *The American Orchestra and Theodore Thomas* (1927), 1–104.

407   *"the sons of God"*: Robert McColley, "Classical Music in Chicago and the Founding of the Symphony, 1850–1905," *Illinois Historical Journal* 78, no. 4 (1985): 289–302; Lawrence W. Levine, *Highbrow/Lowbrow: The*

PAGE

Emergence of Cultural Hierarchy in America (1988), 112–19; Philo
Adams Otis, *The Chicago Symphony Orchestra: Its Organization, Growth
and Development, 1891–1924* (1924; reprint, 1972), 15–16.

407 *"the only cool place"*: Fay, "Thomas," 162.

407 *"Shut your eyes"*: *GG*, 283.

407 *"a music merchant"* and *"I would go to hell"*: Quoted in Fay, "Thomas,"
     159–69.

407 *"lifelong campaign"* and *"All my life"*: Rose Fay Thomas, *Memoirs*, 356;
     Thomas, *Musical Autobiography*, vol. 1, 73–99.

408 *"Sullivan, nothing comes back"*: Quoted in McColley, "Classical Mu-
     sic," 298.

408 *"The seating capacity"*: Rose Fay Thomas, *Memoirs*, 365.

409 *"missionary work"*: Rose Fay Thomas, *Memoirs*, 26–61, 238.

409 *"Mr. Thomas is here"*: Rose Fay Thomas to Frances Glessner, May 3,
     1892, Glessner Journals, CHS; for a rich discussion of Thomas and "the
     disciplining of spectatorship," see the chapter of that title in John F. Kas-
     son, *Rudeness and Civility: Manners in Nineteenth-Century Urban Amer-
     ica* (1990).

409 *"When you play"*: Quoted in Teaford, *Cities of the Heartland*, 86; see also
     CT, May 31, 1884.

409 *"We had to take"*: Fay, "Thomas," 164; see also C. Norman Fay to
     Charles Hutchinson, Feb. 1, 1894, Hutchinson MSS.

409 *"He not only disciplined"*: Rose Fay Thomas, *Memoirs*, 562.

410 *"If you do not like it now"*: "The Chicago Orchestra," *Dial* 22 (1897):
     270; Little Room membership list, 1903, Little Room Papers, Newberry
     Library; for the Little Room group, see especially Bernard I. Duffey, *The
     Chicago Renaissance in American Letters: A Critical History* (1954),
     51–57; for Chicago's women writers, see Sidney H. Bremer, "Willa
     Cather's Lost Chicago Sisters," in *Women Writers and the City: Essays in
     Feminist Literary Criticism*, Susan Merrill Squier, ed. (1984), 210–29.

410 *"The rise of Chicago"*: Hamlin Garland, *Crumbling Idols: Twelve Essays
     on Art Dealing Chiefly with Literature, Painting, and the Drama* (1891;
     reprint, ed. Jane Johnson, 1960), 114–17.

410 *"to art and song"*: Garland, *Daughter*, 1–5.

410 *"sweat and do not wear socks"*: Eugene Field, "Sharps and Flats," *CDN*,
     July 13, 1893.

411 *"sufferer"* and *"except as a hair tonic"*: Henry Fuller, "The Downfall of
     Abner Joyce," in *Under the Skylights* (1901), 77–83.

411 *"wraith in pantaloons"*: Quoted in Jean Holloway, *Hamlin Garland: A Bi-
     ography* (1960), 110.

411 *"carried himself"*: Hamlin Garland, *Roadside Meetings* (1930), 265–75;
     Fuller's two European novels are *The Chevalier of Pensieri-Vani* (1891)
     and *The Chatelaine of La Trinité* (1892).

411 *"What an awful thing"*: Fuller, *The Cliff-Dwellers*, 236–37.

412 *"kept up"*: Garland, *Roadside*, 270–71.

412 *"who led the van"*: Quoted in Jay Martin, *Harvests of Change: American
     Literature, 1865–1914* (1967), 249.

412 *"pomp and luxury"*: Fuller, "Downfall of Abner Joyce," 88, 136–39; see
     also Bernard R. Bowron, Jr., *Henry B. Fuller of Chicago: The Ordeal of a
     Genteel Realist in Ungenteel America* (1974), 204.

412 *"to raise this dirt pile"*: Fuller to William Dean Howells, quoted in Mar-
     tin, *Harvests*, 249.

413 *"the most desirable"*: Fuller, *With the Procession*, 70, 109, 114–15, 159,
     175. 199.

PAGE

413   *"as a Society Queen":* Fuller, "Downfall of Abner Joyce," 15–16.

414   *"a community where":* Anonymous commentary on Potter Palmer's life, CHS.

414   *"the Age of Pericles"* and *"sumptuous and abominable":* quoted in Ross, *Silhouette in Diamonds,* 53.

414   *"The more you put on":* Quoted in Dedmon, *Fabulous Chicago,* 127; see also "Entries," Potter Palmer Ledger, Potter Palmer Papers, CHS.

414   *Palmer's art collection:* Sara T. Hallowell to Potter Palmer, July 8, 9, 1891, Jan. 21, Dec. 12, 1892, Sara T. Hallowell to Bertha Palmer, undated letter (1892), Camile Claudel to Bertha Palmer, Sept. 15, 1892, all in Mrs. Potter Palmer Letters, Ryerson and Burnham Libraries, Art Institute of Chicago; for women and the Art Institute see Kathleen D. McCarthy, *Women's Culture: American Philanthropy and Art, 1830–1930* (1991), 102–5, 130–35.

415   *"ideals":* Mrs. Reginald De Koven, *A Musician and His Wife* (1926), 83, 102.

415   *The daughter:* Addie Hibbard Gregory, *A Great-Grandmother Remembers* (1940), 63, 108–23.

415   *"I once heard":* De Koven, *A Musician,* 101.

416   *"He'll need the money":* Quoted in Erens, *Masterpieces,* 31.

416   *a feminist:* Jeanne Madeline Weimann, *The Fair Women* (1981), 8–9.

416   *"the Mother of woman's":* Ralph, *Our West,* 41.

416   *"I have said":* Marie Thérèse de Solms Blanc, *The Condition of Women in the United States: A Traveler's Notes* (1895; reprint, 1972), 43–46. Under the pseudonym Th. Bentzon, Marie Thérèse de Solms Blanc wrote popular novels in France.

417   *"the free public bath":* Marilyn Thornton Williams, *Washing "The Great Unwashed": Public Baths in Urban America, 1840–1920* (1991), 85; McCarthy, *Noblesse Oblige,* 49–76, 114; McCarthy maintains, correctly I think, that Chicago women, despite their advances, remained at "the periphery of the [city's] decision making process"(50).

417   *"I had been brought up":* Louise de Koven Bowen, *Growing Up With a City* (1926), 10–110.

417   *"had sympathy":* Ibid., 81. The best account of Addams's life and mission remains her autobiography, *Twenty Years at Hull-House,* published in 1910. All my citations are from the New American Library edition, 1981; see also Addams, *The Second Twenty Years at Hull-House* (1930).

Jane Addams historiography has become an academic industry. The best account of her life and work remains Allen F. Davis, *American Heroine: The Life and Legend of Jane Addams* (1973). See also Davis, *Spearheads For Reform: The Social Settlements and the Progressive Movement, 1890–1914* (1967); and Davis and Mary Lynn McCree Bryan, eds., *One Hundred Years at Hull-House* (1989).

The presence of Jane Addams can still be felt at what remains of Hull-House, on the sprawling campus of the University of Illinois at Chicago. Some of those responsible for maintaining Hull-House have pieced together a brief anthology of essays that serves as an introduction to the history of the settlement, *Opening New Worlds: Jane Addams's Hull-House* (1989).

For Addams, see also the dated but still useful James Weber Linn, *Jane Addams: A Biography* (1935). For a suggestive critique of Addams as a feminist, see, Jill Conway, "Women Reformers and American Culture, 1870–1930," *Journal of Social History* 5, no. 2 (1971–72): 164–77.

PAGE
417 *"doglike devotion"* and *"filled with shame"*: Addams, *Twenty Years*, 1–59, 90–100.

418 *"picture parties"*: Quoted in Davis, *Spearheads*, 8.

418 *"The dependence of classes"*: Mary Lynn McCree, "The First Year of Hull-House, 1889–1890, In Letters By Jane Addams and Ellen Gates Starr," *CH* 1 (1970): 101–14.

419 *"more for the benefit"*: Jane Addams to Anna Haldeman Addams, May 9, 1899, Jane Addams Memorial Collection, University of Illinois at Chicago, hereafter cited as Addams MSS.

419 *"uselessness"*: Addams, *Twenty Years*, 94.

419 *"that shame"*: Elia W. Peattie, *The Precipice* (1914; reprint, 1989), 49.

419 *"Twenty years ago"*: Quoted in Davis, *Spearheads*, 37.

419 *"Probably no young matron"*: Addams, *Twenty Years*, 78; see also Jane Addams to Alice Haldeman, Oct. 8, 1889, Addams MSS.

419 *"clean, bright"*: Blanc, *Condition of Women*, 67.

420 *"The solicitude:* Thorstein Veblen, *The Theory of the Leisure Class* (1899; reprint, 1959), 224.

420 *"the residents consist"*: David A. Shannon, ed., *Beatrice Webb's American Diary, 1898* (1963), 108; see also Kathryn Kish Sklar, "Hull House in the 1890s: A Community of Women Reformers," *Signs* 10 (Summer 1985): 660.

420 *"queenly looking"*: Hilda Satt Polacheck, *I Came a Stranger: The Story of a Hull-House Girl*, ed. Dena J. Polacheck Epstein (1989), 102.

420 *"line of thought and action"*: Jane Addams, "Hull-House: A Social Settlement," 207, in *Hull-House Maps and Papers: A Presentation of Nationalities and Wages in a Congested District of Chicago, Together with Comments and Essays on Problems Growing out of the Social Conditions* (1895; reprint, 1970).

421 *"better elements"*: Ellen Gates Starr, "Art and Labor," *Hull-House Maps and Papers*, 165–77; see also Addams, "Hull-House," *Hull-House Maps and Papers*, 210–15; Jane Addams, "The Art Work Done at Hull-House, Chicago," *Forum* 19 (July 1895): 614–17.

421 *"The blessings"*; Addams, *Twenty Years*, 92.

421 *"helpful to the life"* and *"an elevated tone"*: Addams, "Hull-House," 210–11; Addams, "Art Work," 614–17.

422 *"musical taste"*: Addams, "Hull-House," 210–23.

422 *"a fragile, ethereal"*: Polacheck, *Stranger*, 66–68.

422 *"The one thing"*: Addams, *Twenty Years*, 98.

423 *"May we not say"*: Quoted in Williams, *Washing'"The Great Unwashed,"* 82–83; see also Marlene Stein Wortman, "Domesticating the Nineteenth Century City," *Prospects*, 3 (1977), 531–72.

423 *"genius for inclusiveness"*: Peattie, *The Precipice*, 27, 48, 105–6, 39.

424 *"The smoke nuisance"*: *CT*, July 28, 1893, Aug. 4, 1893.

424 *"The World's Fair city"*: "A Burning Issue," *TG* in "Scrapbooks Supposedly Compiled by J. C. Ambler for Citizens' Association of Chicago," vol. 70, CHS; see also Christine M. Rosen, "Chicago's Society for the Prevention of Smoke," unpublished paper, July 1989.

424 *"They were the first objects"*: Addams, *Twenty Years*, 200.

425 *"shocked"*: Ibid., 204.

425 *"They can balance"*: Lincoln Steffens, *The Shame of the Cities* (1904; reprint, 1967), 163.

425 *"absolute necessity"*: Theodore Dreiser, "The Chicago Drainage Canal," *Ainslee* 3 (Feb. 1899): 53–61.

PAGE
425   *"sickness and death"* and *"stink herself"*: Both quotes in Wade, *Chicago's Pride,* 132–33.

426   *Citizens' Association:* Citizens' Association of Chicago, *Report of the Committee on the Main Drainage and Water Supply of Chicago* (1885); Lyman E. Cooley, *The Lakes and Gulf Waterway as Related to the Chicago Sanitary Problem* (1891), 4, 21–25; the story of the origins of the sanitation canal is told in Cain, *Sanitation Strategy,* 59–83; and Robert Isham Randolph, "The History of Sanitation in Chicago," *Journal of the Western Society of Engineers* 44 (Oct. 1939): 236.

427   *highest death rate from typhoid:* Isaac D. Rawlings et al., *The Rise and Fall of Disease in Illinois,* vol. 2 (1927), 332, 339.

427   *"I have heard":* Quoted in Brown, *Drainage,* 434.

427   *"the great leveler":* *CT,* July 23, 1893.

428   *"The Chicago Drainage Canal":* "The Chicago Drainage Canal," *HW* 38 (Sept. 1, 1894): 827; Currey, *Chicago,* vol. 1, 120–28.

428   *"The thirty-eight saloons":* *CT,* June 6–15, July 23, 1893.

428   *"Though it was accomplished":* *CT,* Jan. 3–4, 1893.

428   *St. Louis still took Chicago to court:* Cain, *Sanitation Strategy,* 81.

429   *"The achievements":* Teaford, *Unheralded,* 217.

429   *"Mighty Engineer":* Quoted in Brown, *Drainage,* 448.

430   *The city's water was the cleanest:* *CT,* June 1, 1893; Rawlings, *Rise and Fall of Disease,* vol. 2, 332; Chicago Department of Health, *Annual Report* (1892), 9.

430   *blame for the spread of typhoid:* Chicago Department of Health, *Annual Report* (1892), 8–9.

430   *revolution in medicine:* Rawlings, *Rise and Fall of Disease,* vol. 2, 342–45; Thomas Neville Bonner, *Medicine in Chicago, 1850–1950: A Chapter in the Social and Scientific Development of a City* (1991), 33–68.

430   *William S. MacHarg:* Burnham, *Official Report,* vol. 2, 65–85; for fair officials' efforts to create a disease-free exposition, see Michael P. McCarthy, "Should We Drink the Water? Typhoid Fever Worries at the Columbian Exposition," *Illinois Historical Journal* 86 (Spring 1993): 2–14.

431   *clean water policy:* *CT,* Aug. 20, 1983; Burnham, *Official Report,* vol. 2, 70–85.

432   *"If the great pyramid":* Johnson, *Columbian Exposition,* vol. 3, 406; see also Donald Hoffmann, "Clear Span Rivalry: The World's Fairs of 1889–1893," *JSAH* 29 (Mar. 1970): 48–50.

432   *"It took nerve":* *CT,* May 13, 1893.

432   *"the greatest ceremonial":* Burnham to Edward F. Lawrence, July 11, 1891, Burnham MSS.

433   *"blare of patriotic":* *Chicago Record's History,* 8–15.

433   *"This would be a good time":* Polacheck, *Stranger,* 22–39.

433   *"rising with a flutter":* Monroe, *A Poet's Life,* 128–30; see also Higinbotham, *Report of the President,* 156–65, 211–12.

433   *"the day of days":* *CT,* Oct. 21, 1893.

434   *"first in violence":* Steffens, *Shame,* 163.

434   *"greatest glory":* Fuller, "Upward Movement," 534.

Chapter Thirteen: The Battle for Chicago

436   *"I never knew a man":* *CT,* Oct. 20, 1893.

436   *"For a moment":* *CR,* Nov. 2, 1893.

PAGE

437   *"was given that quick":* Ibid.; *CT,* Nov. 2, 1893.

437   *"We kept her":* Quoted in *GG,* 177.

437   *Joseph Medill:* David L. Protess, "Joseph Medill: Chicago's First Modern Mayor," in Paul M. Green and Melvin Holli, eds., *The Mayors: The Chicago Political Tradition* (1987), 1–15; and Joel A. Tarr, *A Study in Boss Politics: William Lorimer of Chicago* (1971), 26.

438   *"magnetic man":* Los Angeles Times, Oct. 31, 1893.

438   *"Born a Kentucky gentleman":* Charles E. Merriam, Introduction to Claudius O. Johnson, *Carter Henry Harrison I: Political Leader* (1928), viii–ix; no major work on Harrison has been published since Johnson's book.

438   *"personified in himself":* Chicago Globe, Oct. 28, 1893.

439   *"My acquaintance":* Los Angeles Times, Oct. 31, 1893.

439   *"I was born":* Scrapbooks, Carter Harrison Papers, Newberry Library (hereafter cited as Harrison MSS); *CT,* Oct. 30–31, Nov. 8, 1893, July 1, Oct. 1, 1897.

440   *"destined to be":* Chicago Times, Nov. 5, 1893; Carter H. Harrison II, *Growing Up With Chicago* (1944), 258–59.

440   *"He would work":* Quoted in *GG,* 160; see also Harrison II, *Growing Up,* 22, 259; Carter H. Harrison II, "A Kentucky Colony," in *Chicago Times,* Nov. 5, 1893; Carter H. Harrison, *A Race With the Sun* (1889).

440   *"It's my idea of happiness":* CT, Oct. 30–31, 1893; see also Willis John Abbot, *Carter Henry Harrison: A Memoir* (1895), 1–31.

440   *"He made himself the center":* Los Angeles Times, Oct. 31, 1893; Willis John Abbot, "The Harrison Dynasty in Chicago," *Munsey's Magazine,* Sept. 1903, 809–15; *CT,* Oct. 30–31, 1893.

441   *"business-style" mayor:* Abbot, *Harrison,* 58–151.

441   *The Irish came to Chicago:* For Irish emigration, see especially Kerby A. Miller, *Emigrants and Exiles: Ireland and the Irish Exodus to North America* (1985); for the Irish in Chicago, see Lawrence J. McCaffrey, Ellen Skerrett, Michael F. Funchion, and Charles Fanning, *The Irish in Chicago* (1987); Paul Michael Green, "Irish Chicago: The Multiethnic Road to Machine Success," in Holli and Jones, *Ethnic Chicago;* Joseph Hamzik, "Gleanings of Archer Road" (1961), Local Community Research Committee, "Chicago Communities," vol. 3, Document 23 CHS; and John T. McEnnis, "The Irish in Illinois," *CDN,* May 30–July 2, 1889.

442   *largest Scandinavian settlement:* Odd S. Lovall, *A Century of Urban Life: The Norwegians in Chicago Before 1930* (1988), 155–61; Anita R. Olson, "A Community Created: Chicago Swedes, 1880–1950," in Holli and Jones, *Ethnic Chicago,* fourth ed. (1995), 110–20; Ulf Beijbom, *Swedes in Chicago: A Demographic and Social Study of the 1846–1880 Immigration* (1971); Philip S. Friedman, "The Americanization of Chicago's Danish Community, 1850–1920," *CH* 9 (Spring 1980): 36, 38.

442   *A person could not be a papist:* CT, Dec. 23, 1853.

443   *"Ten o'clock":* Quoted in William F. Shannon, *The American Irish: A Political and Social Portrait* (1963), 18.

443   *fourth-largest Irish city:* U.S. Tenth Census, 1880, "Population," 538–41; *U.S. Eleventh Census,* 1890, "Population," Part 1, 670–73.

443   *neighborhood-based organizations:* Michael F. Funchion, "Irish Chicago: Church, Homeland, Politics, and Class—The Shaping of an Ethnic Group, 1870–1900," in Holli and Jones, *Ethnic Chicago,* 15–24; Ellen Skerrett, "The Development of Catholic Identity Among Irish Americans in Chicago, 1880 to 1920," in Timothy J. Meagher, ed., *From Paddy to*

PAGE

Studs: Irish-American Communities in the Turn of the Century Era, 1880–1920 (1986), 117–23. On the Irish American community in Chicago see Charles Fanning, Ellen Skerrett, and John Corrigan, *Nineteenth Century Catholic Irish: A Social and Political Portrait* (1980).

444   *Harrison's labor policy: Chicago Times,* Nov. 5, 1893; Richard Schneirov, "The Knights of Labor in the Chicago Labor Movement and Municipal Politics, 1877–1887" (Ph.D. diss., Northern Illinois Univ., 1984), 311–57, 373–74.

444   *Carter Harrison:* Johnson, *Harrison,* 84, 125, 262; *CT,* Oct. 31, 1893.

445   *"Marse Catah: IO,* Apr. 5, 1885; Abbot, *Harrison,* 177; Johnson, *Harrison,* 188–95.

445   *"On St. George's Day": CT,* Mar. 29, 1893.

445   *Protestant pietists:* Large numbers of "unchurched" Swedes and Danes voted Democratic, however, whenever temperance or any other kind of sabbath restrictions were electoral issues. See Tarr, *Boss Politics,* 18–19; and Richard Oestreicher, "Urban Working-Class Political Behavior and Theories of American Electoral Politics, 1870–1940," *JAH* 74 (Mar. 1988): 1275–76.

445   *"The Live and Let-Livers"* and *"A Republican":* Algren quoted in John D. Buenker, "Chicago's Ethnics and the Politics of Accommodation," *CH* 3 (Fall 1974): 94; Coughlin quoted in Buenker, *Urban Liberalism and Progressive Reform* (1973), 98.

446   *ethnic treason:* For the relationship between culture and politics at this time, see John M. Allswang, *A House for All Peoples: Ethnic Politics in Chicago, 1890–1936* (1971).

446   *"to meet their social needs":* E. C. Moore, "The Social Function of the Saloon," *AJS* 3 (July 1897): 1–12.

446   *The saloon's daily routine:* Royal L. Melendy, "The Saloon in Chicago," *AJS* 6 (1900–1901): 289–306, 433–64; Jon M. Kingsdale, "The 'Poor Man's Club': Social Functions of the Urban Working-Class Saloon," *American Quarterly* 25 (Oct. 1973): 255–83; For a perceptive social history of the saloon, see Perry Duis, *The Saloon: Public Drinking in Chicago and Boston: 1880–1920* (1983).

447   *"The saloon is a very wholesome":* Quoted in Norman Haymer, "The Effect of Prohibition in Packingtown" (M.A. thesis, Univ. of Chicago, 1920), 17; see also Moore, "Social Function," 8; and Klaus Easslen, "German-American Working-Class Saloons in Chicago," in Hartmut Keil, ed., *German Workers' Culture in the United States, 1850 to 1920* (1988), 164–66.

447   *Saloonkeepers:* Melendy, "Saloon," 290–306, 433–50; Moore, "Social Function," 1–12.

448   *"the easiest business":* Quoted in Duis, *Saloon,* 47.

448   *"While much has been said":* Quoted in Ibid., 115; see also Charles E. Merriam, *Chicago: A More Intimate View of Urban Politics* (1929), 90–101.

449   *"consistently held that the masses":* Abbot, "Harrison Dynasty," 814.

449   *"no meaningful difference":* Oestreicher, "Working-Class," 1275.

449   *"The Republican Party":* Quoted in Bruce C. Nelson, *Beyond the Martyrs: A Social History of Chicago's Anarchists, 1870–1900* (1988), 208.

449   *"You can't make people moral":* Quoted in Abbot, *Harrison,* 113; *CT,* July 3, 1893.

449   *delegation of ministers:* Richard Lindberg, "The Evolution of an Evil Business," *CH* 22 (July 1993): 38–53.

449   *Michael Cassius McDonald: Chicago Record-Herald,* Aug. 18, 1907; for

PAGE

an insider's account of gambling in the Harrison era, see John Philip
Quinn, *Fools of Fortune* (1892).

450   *"ruled the city": Chicago Record-Herald*, Aug. 18, 1907.

450   *"virtually the dictator": HC*:3, 305.

450   *"a close friend":* Asbury, *Gem*, 142.

450   *"Boss Croker":* Wendt and Kogan, *Bosses in Lusty Chicago*, 27; *IO*, Mar.
28, 1893.

451   *"feudal" structure:* Merriam, *Chicago*, 90–98.

451   *"a greater obstacle":* Paul Michael Green, "The Chicago Democratic
Party, 1840–1920: From Factionalism to Political Organization" (Ph.D.
diss., Univ. of Chicago, 1975), 89, 94; see also Merriam, *Chicago*,
90–98.

451   *"He knew the whole town":* Abbot, "Harrison Dynasty," 809.

452   *"ain't bean bag": CR*, Oct. 31, 1893.

452   *mayors came from old stock American families:* Donald S. Bradley and
Mayer N. Zald, "From Commercial Elite to Political Administration: The
Recruitment of the Mayors of Chicago," *AJS* 71 (Sept. 1965): 154,
160–62.

452   *"Your saloon's on fire!":* Steffens, *Shame*, 23.

452   *"During lulls":* Quoted in Teaford, *Unheralded*, 23–39; see also *CT*, Apr.
4, 1892, Apr. 10, 1894.

452   *"Anybody who goes into politics":* Quoted in Bill and Lori Granger, *Lords
of the Last Machine: The Story of Politics in Chicago* (1987), 6.

453   *"If he speaks":* Ray Stannard Baker, "Hull-House and the Ward Boss,"
The Outlook 58 (Mar. 26, 1898): 769–71.

453   *"Rayformers": CEP*, Sept. 25, 1897.

453   *"never about":* Baker, "Hull-House," 769–71.

453   *"Will I wake them?":* Quoted in Ginger, *Altgeld's America*, 94.

453   *"better [to] send back":* Quoted in Charles Fanning et al., *Nineteenth-
Century Chicago Irish: A Social and Political Portrait* (1980), 16.

454   *"We soon discovered":* Addams, *Twenty Years*, 222.

454   *"The people come cheap":* Lincoln Steffens, "New York: Good Government in Danger" (1903) reprinted in William L. Riordan, ed., *Plunkitt of
Tammany Hall* (1994), 129.

454   *"shocking a genuine sentiment":* Addams, "Ethical Survivals," *International Journal of Ethics* 8 (Apr. 1898): 273–91. A shorter version of this
essay appeared in *The Outlook* 68 (Apr. 2, 1898): 879–82, under the title
"Why the Ward Boss Rules."

454   *"Votes, like babies":* Quoted in Buenker, *Urban Liberalism*, 5; see also
Humbert S. Nelli, *Italians in Chicago, 1880–1930: A Study in Ethnic
Mobility* (1970), 98; and Nelli, "John Powers and the Italians: Politics in
a Chicago Ward, 1896–1921," *JAH* 57 (June 1970): 67–84.

454   *"We had election polls":* Ernest Poole interviewed this unnamed woman,
a worker at Hull-House for most of her life. *GG*, 220–34; for Addams's
two electoral campaigns against Powers, see Davis, *American Heroine*,
121–25; after the defeat of her candidate in 1898, Addams decided it
was not worth the effort to continue to try to defeat Powers.

455   *converted to socialism:* Florence Kelley, *The Autobiography of Florence
Kelley, vol. 1, Notes of Sixty Years*, ed. Kathryn Kish Sklar (1986), 1–89;
Sklar, *Florence Kelley and the Nation's Work: The Rise of Women's Politi-
cal Culture, 1830–1900* (1995), 1–167.

456   *"Nowhere else in the Western world":* Sklar, *Kelley*, 237; see also Abraham
Bisno, *Abraham Bisno, Union Pioneer* (1967); 148–50. Bisno was one of
Kelley's factory inspectors.

PAGE

456 Hull-House Maps and Papers: Kelley, "The Illinois Child Labor Law," *AJS* 3 (Jan. 1898): 492–95; Josephine Goldmark, *Impatient Crusader: Florence Kelley's Life Story* (1953), 1–50; Mary Jo Deegan, *Jane Addams and the Men of the Chicago School, 1892–1918* (1988), 10–11. Deegan documents the failure of Chicago socialists to acknowledge their deep debt to Hull-House's sociological investigations while imitating their methods.

456 *Robert Hunter:* Hunter, *Tenement,* 1–14, 26–41, 70–74, 94; Agnes Sinclair Holbrook, "Map Notes and Comments," in *Hull-House Maps and Papers,* 5–14.

457 *"look dwarfed and ill-fed":* Holbrook, "Map Notes and Comments," in *Hull-House Maps and Papers,* 6.

457 *Hunter's exhaustive investigations:* Hunter, *Tenement,* 63, 94, 108–17.

458 *"The condition of the sweaters'":* Kelley, "The Sweating-System," in *Hull-House Maps and Papers,* 41.

458 *"pathetic stupidity":* Addams, *Twenty Years,* 170; Kelley, *Autobiography,* 86–88. The colonizing scheme was the brainchild of Hull-House associate Alessandro Masto-Valerio. See his "Remarks Upon the Italian Colony in Chicago," in *Hull-House Maps and Papers,* 131–35.

459 *"utter servility":* Bayard Holmes, "The Sweat-Shops and Smallpox in Chicago," *Journal of American Medical Association* 23 (Sept. 15, 1894): 422.

459 *"conspiracy of silence":* Kelley, *First Special Report of the Factory Inspectors of Illinois on Small-Pox in the Tenement House Sweatshops of Chicago* (1894), 6–40; Arthur R. Reynolds, "History of the Chicago Smallpox Epidemic in 1893, 1894, and 1895, With Side Lights and Reflections," in Rawlings, *Rise and Fall of Disease,* vol. 1, 316–20; John B. Hamilton, "The Epidemic of Chicago," *Bulletin of the Society of Medical History of Chicago,* 1 (Oct. 1911): 83–86; over 1,200 persons died in the two-and-a-half-year epidemic.

459 *"Labor is property":* CT, Mar. 15, 16, 1895; "Opinion of Supreme Court of Illinois, Filed March 18, 1895, Ritchie vs. the People," 129–30.

460 *Robert Hunter's report:* Hunter, *Tenement,* 165–79.

460 *code reforms were passed:* Thomas Lee Philpott, *The Slum and the Ghetto: Neighborhood Deterioration and Middle-Class Reform, Chicago, 1880–1930* (1978), 5.

460 *"the ghetto":* Louis Wirth, *The Ghetto* (1928), 225–26; for a critical assessment of Hull-House's failure to play more than "a limited role" in the immigrant community, see Rivka Shpak Lissak, *Pluralism and Progressives: Hull-House and the New Immigrants, 1890–1919* (1989), 2–30, 79–82, 122.

460 *Americanize immigrants:* Addams, "Americanization," *American Sociological Review* 14 (1919): 210. Hull-House envisioned a two-stage process of Americanization: temporary segregation followed by the breakup of the ethnic colony.

461 *two fatherlands:* Pacyga, *Polish Immigrants,* 145.

461 *"like a swarm of bees":* Quoted in Rudolph J. Vecoli, "Contadini in Chicago: A Critique of the Uprooted," *JAH* 51 (Dec. 1969): 408; see also Dominic Candeloro, "Chicago Italians: A Survey of the Ethnic Factor, 1850–1990," in Holli and Jones, *Ethnic Chicago,* 4th ed., 229–59.

461 Jewish community: Hyman L. Meites, ed., *History of the Jews of Chicago* (1924; reprint, 1990), 175–82. There were almost 80,000 Jews in Chicago by 1900, of whom approximately 52,000 were from Eastern Europe. Although census data on Jews is unreliable, by 1930 there were about 275,000 Jews in the city, 80 percent of them Eastern European.

PAGE

   See Edward Mazur, "Jewish Chicago: From Shtetl to Suburb," in Holli and Jones, *Ethnic Chicago*, 77.

461   *"No one was safe"*: Bernard Horwich, *My First Eighty Years* (1939), 126.

461   *"with the people from one village"* and *"Emigrating"*: Addams and Italian writer quoted in Vecoli, "Contadini," 408.

462   *"A Landsmannschaft"*: Wirth, *Ghetto*, 223.

462   *"personal or business need"*: Meites, *History of the Jews*, 190–91.

463   *homeownership:* Pacyga, *Polish Immigrants*, 74–80, 107; the most comprehensive analysis of the early Polish-American experience is the multivolume analysis by William I. Thomas and Florian Znaniecki, *The Polish Peasant in Europe and America*, which is now in an abridged form, edited by Eli Zaretsky (1984); see also, Edward Kantowicz, *Polish-American Politics in Chicago, 1888–1940* (1975); Joseph John Parot, *Polish Catholics in Chicago, 1850–1920* (1981). Poles settled in two separate parts of Chicago, and by 1910 Chicago had approximately 210,000 Polish-American residents (by 1930 there were 401,316), more Poles than in any other city in the nation. Today they are the largest ethnic group in Chicago.

463   *"Pullman spirit"*: Philpott, *Slum and Ghetto*, 82.

463   *"truly democratic"*: Meites, *History of the Jews*, 186.

463   *"It is a startling fact"*: Thomas A. Faulkner, *From the Ballroom to Hell* (1894), 14–15.

464   *"a hard, constructive animality"*: Dreiser, *Newspaper Days*, 21.

464   *"Ours is a cosmopolitan city"*: Undated clipping, Harrison MSS.

464   *"The Alderman is really elected"*: Addams, "Why the Ward Boss Rules," 879–82.

465   *"It got so"*: Quoted in Tarr, *Boss Politics*, 14.

465   *"more nearly right"*: Brand Whitlock, *Forty Years of It* (1925), 202–5, 246–27.

465   *Hibernianization:* Funchion, "Irish Chicago," in Holli and Jones, *Ethnic Chicago*, 28–30; U.S. *Twelfth Census*, 1900, "Special Reports: Occupations," 516–20.

466   *Democratic Party nominated twenty-one Irish-Americans:* Funchion, "Irish Chicago," 28–30; Green, "Irish Chicago," 413–31, both in Holli and Jones, *Ethnic Chicago*.

466   *"Rainbow Coalition" thesis:* For a critique of the "Rainbow Coalition" theory, see especially Steven P. Erie, *Rainbow's End: Irish-Americans and the Dilemmas of Urban Machine Politics, 1840–1985* (1988). Although Erie does not deal with the nineteenth-century Chicago Irish "machines," my findings support his argument that Irish big-city machines tended to offer limited opportunities to other ethnic groups.

466   *"the four-dollar-a-day"*: Quoted in Nelli, *Italians*, 89.

466   *Italian opposition to Johnny Powers:* CT, Jan. 26, 1898; Municipal Voters' League of Chicago, *The Municipal Campaign, 1898* (1898), 6.

466   *"liquid reward"*: Duis, *Saloon*, 135.

466   *"Floaters"*: George Ade, "Some Instances of Political Devotion," in *Stories*, 45–50.

466   *elections of 1883: IO*, June 16, 1883; Bruce Grant, *Fight for a City: The Story of the Union League Club of Chicago and Its Times, 1880–1955* (1955), 67–79.

466   *"Who took it"*: Harrison II, *Growing Up*, 271.

467   *"Th' lads"*: Quoted in Fanning, "The Irish Presence," 160.

467   *"You had to have"*: *Chicago Herald and Examiner*, June 5, 1924.

PAGE

467   *"who wore a clean collar": CT,* Apr. 4, Nov. 20, 1894; Robert M. Fogelson, *Big-City Police* (1977), 33.

467   *"We [are] fully justified":* Quoted in Harmut Keil, "The German Immigrant Working Class of Chicago, 1875–90: Workers, Labor Leaders, and the Labor Movement," in Dirk Hoerder, ed., *American Labor and Immigration History, 1877–1920s: Recent European Research* (1983), 162.

467   *"to realize":* Lucy E. Parsons, ed., *Life of Albert R. Parsons* (1903), xxviii; see also William Adelman, *Haymarket Revisited* (1976), 8.

467   *Haymarket:* The two best histories of the Haymarket Affair are Paul Avrich, *The Haymarket Tragedy* (1984), which takes a biographical approach and is vividly written; and Henry David, *The History of the Haymarket Affair: A Study in the American Social-Revolutionary and Labor Movements* (1936).

468   *"Socialism in America": CDN,* Jan. 14, 1886.

468   *Irish radicalism:* Funchion, "Irish Chicago," in Holli and Jones, *Ethnic Chicago,* 23; for Irish nationalism, see especially Michael F. Funchion, *Chicago's Irish Nationalists, 1881–1890* (1976); in the 1880s, most Irish who joined unions joined Anglo-American–dominated organizations affiliated with the city's Trades and Labor Assembly.

468   *settled in tightly concentrated enclaves:* Hartmut Keil, "Immigrant Neighborhoods and American Society: German Immigrants on Chicago's Northwest Side in the Late Nineteenth Century," in Keil, *German Workers' Culture,* 25–58; In 1890, first- and second-generation Germans made up 33 percent of Chicago's population; the native born of native stock, 24 percent; the Irish, 18 percent; Scandinavians, 8 percent; immigrants from the British Isles (Welsh, Scottish, and English), 5 percent; Bohemians, 5 percent; Poles, 4 percent; French, 1 percent; blacks, 1 percent; and the remaining groups, less than 1 percent. *The People of Chicago* (1976), 21–22; for first-hand accounts of German working-class culture in Chicago, see Hartmut Keil and John B. Jentz, eds., *German Workers in Chicago: A Documentary History of Working-Class Culture from 1850 to World War I* (1988).

468   *"invented an ethnicity":* Kathleen Neils Conzen, "German-Americans and the Invention of Ethnicity," in Frank Trommler and Joseph McVeigh, eds., *America and the Germans: An Assessment of a Three-Hundred-Year History,* vol. 1, *Immigration, Language, Ethnicity* (1985), 133, 138–39.

469   *"Out on Madison street":* Carter Harrison, II, "Kentucky," 172; Historians David Ward and Sam Bass Warner, Jr., argue that ethnic concentration was not as prevalent as older historians of immigration claim. See David Ward, "The Emergence of Central Immigrant Ghettoes in American Cities, 1840–1920," *Annals of the Association of American Geographers* 38 (1968): 343–59; and Sam Bass Warner, Jr., and Colin B. Blake, "Cultural Change and the Ghetto," *Journal of Contemporary History* 4 (Oct. 1969): 173–87. For a corrective to Warner and Ward, see Kathleen Neils Conzen, "Immigrants, Immigrant Neighborhoods, and Ethnic Identity: Historical Issues," *JAH* 66, no. 3 (1979): 603–15. Although individual members of ethnic groups that settled in cities were not trapped in ghettoes, the ghetto model still applies to most Southern and Eastern European immigrants and "some Germans," Conzen writes (608).

470   *"I never saw":* Quoted in Hartmut Keil and Heinz Ickstadt, "Elements of German Working-Class Culture in Chicago, 1880–1890," in Keil, *German Workers' Culture,* 87; "Earnings, Expenses, and Conditions of Workingmen and Their Families," Illinois Bureau of Labor Statistics, *Third*

PAGE

Biennial Report (1884), 135–391; "Chicago Project, Analysis of the Lower Middle Class According to Occupation and Generation for Chicago's German Population in 1900, Sample of 1,532 German Households," *U.S. Census of Population 1900.*

470 *unity and strong action:* "How Wages Are Depressed," *Chicagoer Arbeiter-Zeitung,* Mar. 9, 1883, reprinted in Keil and Jentz, eds., *German Workers in Chicago,* 57.

470 *"At Last!":* Friedrich Sorge, *Friedrich A. Sorge's Labor Movement in the United States,* ed. Philip Foner, (1977), 71; Heimer Becker, "Johann Most," in Dave Roediger and Franklin Rosemont, eds., *Haymarket Scrapbook* (1986), 137–39.

470 *"An end is to be made":* Johann Most, *Beast and Monster: The Beast of Property and the Social Monster* (1973), 3–15.

470 *Chicago anarchists:* Some Chicago anarchists were actually revolutionary socialists. Parsons claimed it was the capitalist press that "began to stigmatize us as Anarchists, and to denounce us as enemies to all law and government." In response, "we began to allude to ourselves as anarchists . . . and to defend [that name] with pride." Quoted in Nelson, *Beyond,* 154.

470 *Albert Parsons:* Philip Foner, ed., *The Autobiographies of the Haymarket Martyrs* (1969), 27–30, 55; Carolyn Ashbaugh, *Lucy Parsons: American Revolutionary* (1976), 12–14, 267–68; Alan Calmer, *Labor Agitator: The Story of Albert R. Parsons* (1937), 6–24.

471 *August Spies:* August Spies, *August Spies' Auto-Biography: His Speech in Court and General Notes* (1887), 1–35; *CT,* Apr. 5, 1886; on the role of ethnic enclaves in promoting labor solidarity, see Eric L. Hirsch, *Urban Revolt: Ethnic Politics in the Nineteenth-Century Chicago Labor Movement* (1990), 207. In 1886, Chicago employed approximately 250,000 wage workers. Approximately forty thousand wage earners were organized, barely 12 percent of the workforce. Illinois Bureau of Labor Statistics, *Fourth Biennial Report, 1886,* 221–26.

472 *"their future executioners":* The Alarm, Nov. 29, 1884, May 2, 1885.

472 *"a wonderful new substance":* Floyd Dell, "Socialism and Anarchism in Chicago," in *Chicago,* ed. Currey, vol. 2, 361–405.

472 *"These missives":* Quoted in *The Alarm,* June 13, 1885.

473 *"publicity stunt":* Harold C. Livesay, *Samuel Gompers and Organized Labor in America* (1978), 79; *The Knights of Labor* 1 (Jan. 29, 1887): 5.

473 *"a sort of soothing syrup":* Quoted in Avrich, *Haymarket,* 182.

473 *"No smoke curled up":* Quoted in Calmer, *Labor Agitator,* 79.

474 *"Take all history":* Quoted in Avrich, *Haymarket,* 457. The CHS has an excellent collection of Haymarket material, including letters, police reports, and a complete trial manuscript ("Official Court Record of the Haymarket Trial, 1887"), as well as a two-volume abridgement.

474 *McCormick locked out his iron molders:* Robert Ozanne, *A Century of Labor-Management Relations at McCormick and International Harvester* (1967), chapter 1; Charles Edward Russell, *These Shifting Scenes* (1914), 81. While there is no direct surviving evidence of McCormick's efforts to get Bonfield appointed, he became a Carter Harrison supporter after Harrison had broken the iron molders' union (Ozanne, *McCormick,* 27).

475 *"destroy the hideous monster":* CT, May 4, 1886; Spies, *Auto-Biography,* 42–43. Spies said he himself did not write the word "revenge" on the circular. This, he claimed, was the idea of a worker at the newspaper who

thought it would make an electrifying headline; "People's Exhibit 6," *Haymarket Exhibits*, 1887, CHS.

475 *"I want the people to know"*: Haymarket Trial, "K," 44–5, "L," 28–45, CHS.

475 *casualties*: George Brown, "The Police Riot: An Eyewitness Account," in *Haymarket Scrapbook*, 75; one police officer died instantly, and six others died over the next several weeks. An eighth died on June 13, 1888, from a lingering illness attributed to a bullet wound received at the Haymarket.

475 *"Now It Is Blood": IO*, May 5, 1886.

475 *"The city went insane"*: Mary Harris Jones, *The Autobiography of Mother Jones* (1925; reprint, 1974), 21.

476 *"enemy forces": Chicago Times*, May 5, 1886.

476 *"an engine of defense"*: Citizens' Association, *Annual Report*, 1886, 33–6; Michael J. Schaack, *Anarchy and Anarchists* (1889), 380–84. Schaack was a police officer heavily involved in the case against the anarchists; Nina B. Smith, "'This Bleak Situation': The Founding of Fort Sheridan, Illinois," *Illinois Historical Journal* 80, no. 1 (1987): 13–22. The architects of the fort were Holabird and Roche. They were hired by William Holabird's father, who was quartermaster general. "Holabird Diary," Samuel Beckley Holabird Collection, CHS.

476 *"the chief tragedy"*: George Schilling quoted in Avrich, *Haymarket*, 436.

476 *"No event"*: Frederick Rex, *The Mayors of Chicago from March 4, 1837 to April 13, 1933* (1985), 66.

476 *"I at once took the ground"*: Melville E. Stone, *Fifty Years a Journalist* (1921), 173.

476 *"for the violent insanity"*: Quoted in John L. Thomas, *Alternative America: Henry George, Edward Bellamy, Henry Demarest Lloyd and the Adversary Tradition* (1983), 208.

477 *"malicious ferocity"*: John Peter Altgeld, *Reasons for Pardoning Fielden, Neebe and Schwab* (1893; reprint, 1986), 1–34.

477 *William Perkins Black*: Samuel P. McConnell, "The Chicago Bomb Case: Personal Recollections of an American Tragedy," *Harper's Monthly* 168 (May 1934): 730–39.

477 *"Law is on trial"*: Haymarket Trial, "I," 75–86, "K," 408–09, 438, "L," 70, 150–235, CHS.

477 *"The Scaffold Waits": CT*, Aug. 21, 1886.

477 *Lyman J. Gage*: Gage, *Memoirs of Lyman J. Gage* (1937), 69–71.

478 *"great and magnanimous"*: Samuel Gompers, *Seventy Years of Life and Labor: An Autobiography*, vol. 2 (1925), 178–80.

478 *Even Judge Gary*: Joseph E. Gary, "The Chicago Anarchists of 1886; The Crime, the Trial, and the Punishment," *The Century Magazine* 45 (Apr. 1, 1893): 803–37.

478 *"crowded with men"*: Charles Edward Russell, "The Haymarket and Afterwards: Some Personal Recollections," *Appleton's Magazine* 10 (Oct. 1907): 410–11.

478 *"A cloud of apprehension"*: Stone, *Fifty Years*, 175–77.

478 *"The day will come"*: "Bulletin of the Haymarket Riot Execution," MSS, CHS.

479 *"Dropped to Eternity": CT*, Nov. 12, 1887.

479 *"Well, they hanged 'em"*: Carl Sandburg, *Always the Young Strangers* (1953), 133–34.

479 *"Like the Dreyfus case"*: Avrich, *Haymarket*, xii; for a fresh account of the

Haymarket riot's impact on the city of Chicago, see Smith, *Urban Disorder*, part 2.

479   *stirring poem:* Sandburg, "Government," in Sandburg, *Complete Poems*, 71–72.

479   *"Who that saw it":* Russell, "The Haymarket and Afterwards," 411.

479   *funeral oration:* Captain William P. Black, "Eulogy at Waldheim," 121, in *Haymarket Scrapbook;* after the trial, Black lost many of his corporate clients and his income plummeted.

480   *"town of the hard":* Algren, *Chicago*, 64.

480   *Algren paid tribute* and *"I despise": The Famous Speeches of the Eight Chicago Anarchists in Court* (1886; reprint, 1910), 35–36; "Nelson Algren and Louis Lingg" in *Haymarket Scrapbook*, 239.

480   *"was never mentioned":* Quoted in Avrich, *Haymarket*, 442–43; in an essay published after his book on Haymarket, Avrich argues that while the evidence is inconclusive, there is "a strong possibility" the Haymarket bomber was George Meng, a militant, German-born anarchist. "The Bomb-Thrower: A New Candidate," in *Haymarket Scrapbook*, 71–73.

480   *"were entitled to a fair trial": CT,* June 25–30, 1893.

480   *"a drop of true American":* Ibid.; *New York Tribune,* July 9, 1893.

481   *"I saw my duty":* Quoted in Avrich, *Haymarket*, 427.

481   *anarchists never recovered:* For the plight of Chicago labor immediately after Haymarket, see Barbara Wayne Newell, *Chicago and the Labor Movement* (1961); for the Chicago anarchist movement after Haymarket, see Nelson, *Beyond*, chapters 9 and 10.

481   *"awakening":* Quoted in Avrich, *Haymarket*, 433–34.

481   *"avant couriers":* Quoted in *Haymarket Scrapbook*, 185.

481   *"The Haymarket tragedy":* Thomas, *Alternative*, 217.

481   *"I only wish Marx":* Quoted in Sklar, *Kelley*, 120.

482   *"cataclysm": HC:*3, 299.

482   *"Upon the one side":* George Schilling, "The Lessons of the Homestead Troubles," *The Sunset Club Yearbook,* 1892–93, 15.

482   *"At Waldheim sleep five men":* Quoted in Avrich, *Haymarket*, 455.

482   *"madness long before": CT,* Mar. 1, 24, Apr. 3, 1893.

483   *United Labor Party: Chicago Times,* Apr. 13, 1887; HC:3, 365; Roche belonged to the United Order of Deputies.

483   *"the greatest city":* Abbot, *Harrison*, 192–93.

483   *"the most disorderly"* and *"disgraceful mob": CT,* Oct. 29–30, 1892, Mar. 15–16, 1893; Johnson, *Harrison*, 144.

484   *"I'm a businessman"* and *"the second largest . . . business enterprise": CT,* Feb. 16, Mar. 10, 15, 16, 28, 1893.

484   *"Why is this?": CT,* Apr. 4, 1893.

484   *"Back of Carter Harrison":* Ibid.; see also *CT,* Mar. 16, 25, 28, Apr. 3, 1893.

484   *"The bitterness and acrimony":* Abbot, *Harrison*, 205–6.

484   *"Sunday traffic": The Christian Advocate* quoted in Adelman, *Haymarket*, 18.

484   *"lest the wrath": CT,* Oct. 30, 1893.

485   *Harrison's "deplorable" record:* Willis John Abbot, *Watching the World Go By* (1933), 105–7; *CT,* Feb. 24, Mar. 13, June 19, July 8, 1893; for an analysis of the reform agendas of Chicago newspapers, see David Paul Nord, "The Public Community: The Urbanization of Journalism in Chicago," *Journal of Urban History* 11 (Aug. 1985): 411–41; and Nord, *Newspapers and New Politics: Midwestern Municipal Reform, 1890–1900* (1981), chapters 3 and 4; for businessmen-reformers, see Michael Mc-

PAGE

Carthy, "Businessmen and Professionals in Municipal Reform: The Chicago Experiment, 1877–1920" (Ph.D. diss., Northwestern Univ., 1970); on the elite background of Chicago businessmen reformers, see Joan S. Miller, "The Politics of Municipal Reform in Chicago During the Progressive Era: The Municipal Voters' League as a Test Case, 1896–1920" (master's thesis, Roosevelt Univ., 1966), 25–43.

485   *"There are men in this city"*: Clipping, n.d., Harrison MSS.

485   *"the great unwashed"*: HC:3, 357.

485   *"This must be a city"*: Quoted in *CT*, Nov. 6, 1873; see also Samuel P. Hays, "The Politics of Reform in Municipal Government in the Progressive Era," *Pacific Northwest Quarterly* 55 (1964): 157–69. Although Hays does not write of Chicago in this influential essay, the end-of-the-century reform movement in that city fits his characterization of reform movements in a number of other cities. "The movement for reform in municipal government . . . constituted an attempt by upper-class, advanced professional and large business groups to take formal political power from the previously dominant lower- and middle-class elements so that they might advance their own conceptions of desirable public policy. These two groups came from entirely different urban worlds, and the political system fashioned by one was no longer acceptable to the other." For an excellent interpretive review of this and other more recent literature on bosses and reformers, see Terrance J. McDonald, "The Problem of the Political in Recent American Urban History: Liberal Pluralism and the Rise of Functionalism," *Social History* 10 (1985): 323–45; for an insightful study of the role of power elites in American cities, see David C. Hammack, "Problems in the Historical Study of Power in the Cities and Towns of the United States, 1800–1960," *American Historical Review* 83 (1978): 323–49.

486   *"every hat was doffed"*: CT, Apr. 5, 1893.

486   *"cried their 'extry peppers'"*: Ibid.

487   *"men of brains"*: *CT* quoted in Nord, "The Public Community," 425.

Chapter Fourteen: 1893

488   *"The world's greatest achievement"*: Quoted in Fred C. Kelly, *George Ade: Warmhearted Satirist* (1947), 106.

488   *"the greatest event"*: Richard Harding Davis, "The Last Days of the Fair," *HW* 37 (Oct. 21, 1893), 1002.

489   *"Well, Susan"*: Alice Freeman Palmer, "Some Lasting Results of the World's Fair," *Forum* 16 (Dec. 1893): 519.

489   *"fete day"*: Robert Herrick, "Memoirs," 8, Herrick MSS.

489   *"marvelous thing"*: Reprinted in *CT*, July 30, 1893.

489   *"gross incompleteness"*: F. Herbert Stead, "An Englishman's Impressions at the Fair," *Review of Reviews* 8 (July 1893): 30–34.

489   *"the queen of the occasion"*: CT, Apr. 18, May 1–4, 1893; [Moses Handy], *The Official Directory of the World's Columbian Exposition* (1893), 67–70; Ginger, *Altgeld's America*, 18–19.

490   *"continuous panoramic picture"*: Rand McNally & Co.'s *A Week at the Fair* (1893), 37–41.

491   surge of *"Americanism"*: Charles Mulford Robinson, "The Fair as Spectacle," in Johnson, *Columbian Exposition*, vol. 1, 494; see also Marian Shaw, *World's Fair Notes: A Woman Journalist Views Chicago's 1893 Columbian Exposition* (1992), 23.

491   *"a return to our better selves"*: Moore, *Burnham*, vol. 1, 91; see also John

PAGE

J. Flinn, *Official Guide to the World's Columbian Exposition* (1893), 24–25; and Barr Ferree, "Architecture," *Engineering Magazine* 5 (June 1893): 393–97.

491 *"the blot and failure":* John Coleman Adams, "What a Great City Might Be—A Lesson From the White City," *NEM* 14 (Mar. 1896): 3–13.

491 *"swift and silent":* Murat Halstead, "Electricity at the Fair," *Cosmopolitan* 15 (Sept. 1893): 577–83.

492 *vast department stores:* Russell Lewis, "Everything Under One Roof: World's Fairs and Department Stores in Paris and New York," *CH* 12 (Fall 1983): 28–47.

492 *"the best were called":* Adams, "Great City," 6–13.

492 *"Take the roughest man":* Quoted in Doty, *Town of Pullman,* 23. This utopian theme was carried over into the photography of C. D. Arnold, the fair's official photographer. In his highly formalized photographs all is orderly and beautiful; even the weather is always perfect. His photographs also reflect a common characteristic of utopian fiction: The people are absolutely lifeless. In Arnold's photographs, as in utopian fiction, background, not life itself, is everything. For Arnold, see Peter B. Hales, *Constructing the Fair: Platinum Photographs by C. D. Arnold of the World's Columbian Exposition* (1993).

492 *"well-behaved" public crowds:* Adams, "Great City," 16.

493 *"the storm center":* Josiah Strong, *Our Country: Its Possible Future and Its Present Crisis* (1891; reprint, 1963), 171–86.

493 *"like a witches' kettle":* Frederick Jackson Turner, "The Problem of the West," *AM* 78 (1896): 289–97.

493 *"safety-valve":* Turner, "Frontier," 197–227.

493 *a prophecy:* See, for example, the reaction of William Dean Howells, "Letters of an Altrurian Traveler," *Cosmopolitan* 16 (Dec. 1893): 219.

493 *"Since . . . the fleet":* Turner, "Frontier," 199–226.

493 *"It's the Chicago business man's":* Will Payne, *Mr. Salt: A Novel* (1903), 54–55.

494 *"unique in the history":* Edward W. Byrn, "The Progress of Invention During the Past Fifty Years," *Scientific American* 75 (July 25, 1896): 82–83.

494 *"Light and power":* *CT,* June 2, 1893.

494 "mammoth telephone": Johnson, *Columbian Exposition,* vol. 2, 296–97; John P. Barrett, *Electricity at the Columbian Exposition* (1894).

494 *"the most obtuse observer":* John J. Ingalls, "Lessons of the Fair," *Cosmopolitan* 16 (Dec. 1893): 141.

495 *"produc[ing] a pillar":* Quondam [Charles M. Stevens], *The Adventures of Uncle Jeremiah and Family at the Great Fair: Their Observations and Triumphs* (1893), 72–75; see also J. R. Cravath, "Electricity at the World's Fair," *Review of Reviews* 8 (July 1893): 35–39; For Henry Adams at the fair, see Paul C. Nagel, "Twice to the Fair," *CH* 14 (1985–86): 4–19.

495 *"etched in fire":* *CT,* May 9, June 14, 1893.

495 *"millions of lights":* Polacheck, *Stranger,* 40.

495 *"black and motionless mass":* Dreiser's articles on the fair for the *St. Louis Republican* are collected in Nostwich, ed., *Newspaper Writings,* 121–37.

496 *"a blaze of lights":* Murray Melbin, "Night as Frontier," *American Sociological Review* 43 (Feb. 1978): 3–22; Carl Snyder, "Engineer Ferris and His Wheel," *Review of Reviews,* Sept. 1893, 272–76; in 1893 thirty-two-year-old Samuel Insull, an English immigrant, arrived in Chicago to

PAGE

head the Chicago Edison Company and began building a system to produce low-cost energy for a mass market. By the 1920s, he had created
the greatest electrical empire in the world. On Insull's start in Chicago,
see Platt, *Electric City,* chapter 4.

496   *"What on earth": CT,* June 18, 1893.

496   *Ferris:* George W. Ferris to L. V. Rice, Dec. 12, 1892, George W. Ferris
Papers, CHS; Denton J. Snider, *World's Fair Studies* (1895), 25; *CT,* June
15, 1890, Oct. 17, 1891; Robert Jay, "Taller than Eiffel's Tower: The
London and Chicago Tower Projects, 1889–1894," JSAH 46, no. 2 (June
1987): 145–56. Ferris was never modest about his invention. He believed
(and some historians of technology back him up) that it was superior as
an engineering breakthrough to Eiffel's Tower, which demonstrated no
new engineering principle beyond the idea that steel framing could be
carried to unprecedented heights. Ferris's invention was a totally new
kind of structure, a wheel that was held in a perfect circle not by heavy
rigid spokes but by light steel rods in tension.
    Four years after building his great wheel, Ferris died of tuberculosis at
the age of thirty-seven. His fascination with Chicago had never left him.
In his spare time, he had helped construct an exact model of the
Columbian Exposition, which was put on display at later fairs; and on his
drawing board at the time of his death was a plan to convert Chicago into
a seaport by using compressed air instead of water in canal locks to lift
and carry large oceangoing vessels; see John A. Kouwenhoven, "The Eiffel Tower and the Ferris Wheel," *Arts Magazine* 54 (Feb. 8, 1980):
170–73.

497   *"We Americans":* Quoted in John F. Kasson, *Amusing the Million: Coney
Island at the Turn of the Century* (1978): 58.

497   *Midway:* [M. P. Handy], World's Columbian Exposition, *Official Catalogue* (1893), 10–20.

497   *"Midway spirit"* and *"reason desert[ing]":* Robinson, "Fair," in Johnson,
Columbian Exposition, vol. 4, 503–04.

498   *"everyone with the brakes off":* Edward F. Tilyou, "Human Nature with
the Brakes Off—Or: Why the Schoolma'am Walked into the Sea," *American Magazine* 94 (July 1922): 19–21, 86. The best description of this
Midway spirit is in Theresa Dean, *White City Chips* (1895), 331–34.
Dean covered the Fair for the *Inter Ocean.*

498   *"stout stick":* Dreiser, *Newspaper Days,* 315.

498   *"the remainder of the Fair":* Quoted in Schabas, *Thomas,* 208; see also
Thomas, *Memoirs,* 412–14; and *CT,* Aug. 4, 12, 1893.

498   *"personified Chicago":* Sol Bloom, *The Autobiography of Sol Bloom*
(1948), 106, 132–37, 199–215. Bloom claimed that the *danse du ventre*
was actually "a masterpiece of rhythm and beauty." After the fair, however, it was widely imitated in amusement parks in what he called a
"debased and vulgarized" form known as the "Hootchy-Kootchy." *Autobiography,* 135.

499   *"barbaric rites": CT,* Aug. 6, 1893; Ida B. Wells, Frederick Douglass,
Garland I. Penn, Ferdinand L. Barnett, *The Reason Why the Colored
American Is Not in the World's Columbian Exposition* (1893).

500   *Wells's political awakening:* Ida B. Wells, *Crusade for Justice: The Auto-
biography of Ida B. Wells,* ed. Alfreda M. Duster (1970), 1–20; see also
Ida B. Wells-Barnett Diary, 1930, Ida B. Wells Papers, Univ. of Chicago
Library, Dept. of Special Collections.

500   *had real feelings for these men:* Wells, *Crusade,* 35–71. The three men
were taken from their cells by a mob and shot to death on the outskirts of

the city; Wells, "Lynch Law in All Its Phases," *Our Day*, May 1893; David M. Tucker, "Miss Ida Wells and Memphis Lynching," *Phylon* 32 (Summer 1971): 115–16.

500 *"campaign against lynching"*: Wells, *Crusade*, 69–71, 84; Ida Wells to Frederick Douglass, Oct. 17, 1892, Frederick Douglass Papers, Library of Congress, Manuscript Division, Washington, D.C.

500 *raise it in the Chicago Negro community*: Wells, *Crusade*, 116–17.

501 *"The 'respectables'"*: St. Clair Drake and Horace R. Cayton, *Black Metropolis: A Study of Negro Life in a Northern City* (1945), 32–45, 48–51.

502 *"Race elevation"*: Barnett quoted in Allan H. Spear, *Black Chicago: The Making of a Negro Ghetto, 1890–1920* (1967), 60; In Chicago in 1900, approximately 65 percent of Negro men and 80 percent of Negro women worked as domestic and personal servants. See Estelle Hill Scott, *Occupational Changes Among Negroes in Chicago* (1939), 18–20.

502 *"represent the colored people"*: F. L. Barnett to Bertha Palmer, Dec. 20, 1891, Bertha Palmer Board of Lady Managers Records, CHS; see also Ann Massa, "Black Women in the 'White City,'" *Journal of American Studies* 8 (1974): 319–37.

502 *235 blacks had been lynched*: Wells, *Crusade*, 117; August Meier, *Negro Thought in America, 1880–1915* (1968), 20.

502 *"Lynch him"*: *CT*, Apr. 18, 1893. In the summer of 1893 a black man was lynched near Cairo, Illinois, after being falsely accused of a double murder (*CT*, June 8, 1893); another black man was lynched in Decatur, Illinois, beneath an electric streetlight on a prominent corner (*CT*, June 4, 1893). Later that summer, a wealthy black man from Lawrence County, Illinois, was hanged by a mob for allegedly performing a criminal abortion (*CT*, July 15, 1893).

502 *she fiercely protested*: Wells, *Crusade*, 72.

503 *"drowning out the catcalls"*: Paul Dunbar quoted in William S. McFeely, *Frederick Douglass* (1992), 357–72.

503 *"Men talk of"*: Douglass quoted in ibid., 371.

503 *"anything else"*: Wells, *Crusade*, 416–19. Historians who have studied the issue claim that black visitors did not experience discrimination at the restaurants and amusements on the exposition grounds. See Elliot M. Rudwick and August Meier, "Black Man in the 'White City': Negroes and the Columbian Exposition, 1893," *Phylon* 26 (Winter 1965): 357.

503 *"educate the white people"*: Quoted in Spear, *Black Chicago*, 59.

503 *"whited sepulcher"*: Quoted in Rudwick and Meier, "Black Man," 361.

503 *"used to work up sentiment"*: Quoted in Robert W. Rydell, *All the World's a Fair: Visions of Empire at American International Expositions, 1876–1916* (1984), 63.

503 *"long haired, blanket Indians"*: L. G. Moss, "Indians on the Midway: Wild West Shows and the Indian Bureau at World's Fairs, 1893–1904," *South Dakota History* 21 (1991): 206–29.

504 *Vine Deloria, Jr. argues*: Vine Deloria, Jr., "The Indians," in *Buffalo Bill and the Wild West*, (1981); Raymond D. Fogelson, "The Red Man in the White City," in David Hearst Thomas, ed., *Columbian Consequence*, vol. 3 (1991): 73–90.

504 *"The Winnebagoes"*: Quoted in Fogelson, "Red Man," 81.

504 *"Return as Freaks"*: *CT*, July 1, 1893.

504 *"signalizes the emancipation"*: Shaw, *Woman Journalist*, 61–62.

505 *"Chicago will be"*: Ralph, *Harper's Chicago*, 1.

PAGE

505   *"the city of his destiny":* Penelope Niven, *Carl Sandburg, A Biography* (1991), 27.

505   *"walked miles":* Sandburg, *Strangers,* 378–81.

506   *"Gomorrah of the West": CR,* Nov. 30, 1892.

506   *"If Old Carter":* Quoted in Lewis and Smith, *Chicago,* 178.

506   *"The World's Fair":* May Churchill Sharpe, *Chicago May: Her Story* (1928), 37–44.

507   *H. H. Holmes:* David Franke, *The Torture Doctor* (1975); Herman W. Mudgett [H. H. Holmes], *Holmes' Own Story* (1895).

507   *"Chicago, in the mind":* George Kibbe Turner, "The City of Chicago: A Study of the Great Immoralities," *McClure's* magazine 28 (1907): 575–92.

507   *Chicago's "Dark Places": Chicago's Dark Places: Investigations by a Corps of Specially Appointed Commissions* (1891); *CT,* June 19, Oct. 31, Nov. 1, 1893; for a fascinating account of Moody's Chicago crusade of 1893, see Gilbert, *Perfect Cities,* chapter 6.

507   *"the Paris of America":* [Harold Richard Vynne], *Chicago by Day and Night: The Pleasure Seeker's Guide to the Paris of America* (1892), 1–56.

508   Sporting and Club House Directory: *The Sporting and Club House Directory, Chicago, Containing a Full and Complete List of All First Class Club and Sporting Houses* (1889).

508   *"sex-starved men":* Dreiser, *Dawn,* 407–8.

508   *"makes a more amazingly open display":* Quoted in Dedmon, *Fabulous Chicago,* 251.

508   *"there was no place":* Clifton R. Wooldridge, *Hands Up! In the World of Crime or 12 Years a Detective* (1906), 312–15.

508   *"Amazonian in physique":* [Vynne], *Chicago By Day and Night,* 153–57.

508   *"Entering the district":* Dreiser, "Cheyenne, Haunt of Misery and Crime" and "Fate of the Unknown," reprinted in Nostwich, ed., *Newspaper Writings,* 4–6. Both stories first appeared in the *Chicago Globe* in the summer of 1892.

508   *"Here at all hours":* Wooldridge, *Hands Up!,* 482–84.

509   *Mary Hastings:* Asbury, *Gem,* 118–19.

509   *"simple horny":* Nell Kimball, *Her Life as an American Madame* (1970), 109.

509   *badger game:* Wooldridge, *Hands Up!,* 42–45.

509   *Chicago May:* Sharpe, *Chicago May,* 37–44.

510   *"Carrie Watson's": Sporting,* 145.

510   *"occasional"* prostitutes: The Vice Commission of Chicago, *The Social Evil in Chicago: A Study of Existing Conditions with Recommendations* (1911). The commission interviewed a large number of Chicago prostitutes; *ICCC,* 245, 254.

510   *"women adrift":* U.S. Commission of Labor, *Working Women in Large Cities: Fourth Annual Report* (1888); Illinois Bureau of Labor Statistics, *Seventh Biennial Report, 1892, pt. 1: Working Women in Chicago* (1893); *Twelfth Census 1900, Population,* vol. 2, 126–28; U.S. Bureau of Census, *Statistics of Women at Work* (1907), 198–228. Basing her conclusions on the changing sex ratio in Chicago among young adults, Meyerowitz, in *Women Adrift,* argues that "among the native-born migrants to Chicago in the late-nineteenth and early-twentieth centuries, young women seem to have outnumbered young men."

510   *"Industrialism":* Jane Addams, *The Spirit of Youth and the City Streets* (1915), 5.

PAGE

511 *"Little Lost Sisters":* Virginia Brooks, *Little Lost Sister* (1914); "The Girl Who Comes to the City: A Symposium," *Harper's Bazaar,* Jan. 1908, 54.

511 *"vast majority of women":* Ruth Rosen, *The Lost Sisterhood: Prostitution in America, 1900–1918* (1982), xiv.

511 *prostitutes who talked with Chicago vice investigators:* Robert O. Harland, *The Vice Bondage of a Great City or the Wickedest City in the World* (1912).

511 *"find [prostitution]":* Quoted in *ICCC,* 248.

511 *"all colored," "enforce decorum,"* and *"the capitalist of her class":* ICCC, 247, 250.

512 *"These vile":* Dreiser, *Newspaper Days,* 78–79.

512 *"criminal classes":* Wooldridge, *Hands Up!,* 210–11; Wooldridge claims there were five hundred opium dens in Chicago in 1885.

512 *"opium cordials":* Walter Clarke, "Prostitution and Alcohol," *Journal of Social Hygiene* 3 (1917–18): 75–90; William Rosser Cobbe, *Doctor Judas: A Portrayal of the Opium Habit* (1895), 3–14.

513 *"annihilating" it:* Vice Commission, *The Social Evil in Chicago* (1911), 25; U.S. Department of Commerce and Labor, Office of the Secretary, *Arrest and Deportation of Prostitutes and Procurers of Prostitutes,* Department Circular #156, 1907.

513 *"necessary," "is really"* and *"protector of the home":* Quoted in Rosen, *Lost Sisterhood,* 5; see also Mark Thomas Connelly, *The Response to Prostitution in the Progressive Era* (1980), 11–12.

513 *"It's only one of the 'Old Man's'":* CT, Apr. 20, 1893.

513 *"overwhelming influence":* Bloom, *Autobiography,* 124–25.

514 *"I'm glad that fire":* Quoted in Wendt and Kogan, *Bosses,* 13.

514 *"almost a blare of sound":* Dreiser, *Newspaper Days,* 79.

514 *"he was impressive":* Bloom, *Autobiography,* 124–26.

515 *"He is a compact":* Wells, *Future in America,* 129–31.

515 *"cash value realists":* Harold Ickes, *The Autobiography of a Curmudgeon,* (1943), 33.

515 *"was bumbling and inept":* Bloom, *Autobiography,* 126.

515 *form a syndicate:* Wendt and Kogan, *Bosses,* 7–84; see also Green, "Irish Chicago," 424–25, and Asbury, *Gem,* 277–80.

516 *"epic indifference":* Hecht, *Gaily,* 213.

516 *"Here . . . were the insides":* Hecht, *Gaily,* 213.

516 *George Ade:* Kelly, *Ade,* 82–83.

516 *"launched into tirades":* Lincoln Steffens, *The Autobiography of Lincoln Steffens* (1931), 423–25.

517 *"If you want":* Quoted in Finis Farr, *Chicago: A Personal History of America's Most American City* (1973), 253.

517 *"grand, glorious":* Ray Stannard Baker to J. Stannard Baker, Aug. 5, 1893, Ray Stannard Baker Papers, Library of Congress (hereafter cited as Baker MSS.)

517 *"Any one":* Baker, *Native American: The Book of My Youth* (1941), 319–22.

517 *"artistic education":* Quoted in Justin Kaplan, *Lincoln Steffens: A Biography* (1974), 53.

517 *for this was The City":* Baker, *Native American,* 259–60.

518 *"eager to help them":* Baker, *Native American, 261–309;* Ray Stannard Baker, *American Chronicle: The Autobiography of Ray Stannard Baker* (1945), 1.

518 *"the most famous"* and *"asteroid":* Baker, *Native American,* 268–70;

PAGE

Baker's memorial article is partly reprinted in Charles H. Dennis, *Eugene Field's Creative Years* (1924), 328–30.

518 *"the world's most fantastic":* Opie Read, *I Remember* (1930), 232.

519 *cremation:* *NYT,* July 18, 1892; undated newspaper clipping, Wallace Rice Scrapbook, CHS; Read, *I Remember,* 232–40; Paul T. Gilbert, "Whitechapel Nights," *Townsfolk* 36 (Feb. 1947): 16, 31; Wallace Rice, "Whitechapel Club Dedicates Its New Clubhouse," *IO,* Mar. 6, 1892.

519 *"a little group"* and *"of the streets":* Ade quoted in Kelly, *Ade,* 100; and *Stories,* xxv; the club disbanded in 1895 when its chief financial supporter, James W. Scott, editor of the *Chicago Herald,* died.

520 *"[a] strange detachment":* Baker, *Native American,* 302–4.

520 *"a realist":* Ickes, *Autobiography,* 33.

520 *"moralistic":* Dreiser, *Newspaper Days,* 81–83, 184.

520 *"Newspaper revolution":* Bernard A. Weisberger, *The American Newspaperman* (1961), 122–26.

520 *"There are better reporters":* *New Review,* June 1893, 655.

521 *"A gr-great panorama":* Finley Peter Dunne, *Mr. Dooley at His Best,* ed. Elmer Ellis (1938), 205.

521 *"He who is without":* P. T. Barnum, *The Life of P. T. Barnum* (1888), 506; for an incisive analysis of the new metropolitan press, see Barth, *City People,* chapter 3; for insiders' accounts of the Chicago newspaper revolution, see Stone, *Fifty Years a Journalist;* Charles H. Dennis, *Victor Lawson: His Time and His Work* (1935); and Willis J. Abbot, "Chicago Newspapers and their Makers," *Review of Reviews* 6 (Jan. 1895): 646–65; for a history of Chicago journalism in these years, see Norman Howard Simms, "The Chicago Style of Journalism," (Ph.D. diss., University of Illinois at Urbana-Champaign, 1979).

521 *"Unlike our competition":* Undated clipping, Baker MSS.

521 *"pick-up" story:* Baker, *Native American,* 291.

522 *"These trenchant":* Dreiser, *Newspaper Days,* 3.

522 *"Its smoke":* Dreiser, *Dawn,* 333.

522 *"present a complete picture":* Baker, *American Chronicle,* 2.

522 *"Write it strong":* Dreiser, *Newspaper Days,* 43–80, 260–61.

522 *"A writer":* Ibid., 89.

523 *"I knew my Chicago":* George Ade, "Looking Back from Fifty," *The American Magazine,* Feb. 1917, 7–9, 60–61.

523 *"a blur of illumination":* Ade, "Autobiography of George Ade," Ade Papers, Newberry Library; Kelly, *Ade,* 15–40, 109–10.

523 *"an X-ray insight":* John T. McCutcheon, "George Ade," *Appleton's Magazine,* Nov. 1907, 541; George Ade, ed., *Letters of George Ade,* ed. Terence Tobin (1973), 2.

523 *their own permanent column:* Charles H. Dennis to Franklin J. Meine, July 2, 1940, in *Stories,* xii–xvii.

523 *"Tagging-along":* McCutcheon to Franklin Meine, Nov. 11, 1944 in *Stories,* xvii.

523 *"galloping typewriter":* Ade, "Looking Back," 60–63; see also Ade, "They Simply Wouldn't Let Me Be a High-Brow," *The American Magazine,* Dec. 1920, 50.

524 *"great American novel":* William Dean Howells, "Certain of the Chicago School of Fiction," *NAR* 176 (1903): 739–46.

524 *syndicate "wizard"* and *"The show shops":* Ade, "They Simply," 50–51.

524 *"While some of us":* Ade to Editor, *Herald Tribune,* Sept. 8, 1926, in Tobin, ed., *Letters,* 110.

PAGE
524   *"their sense of difference"*: Quoted in Sims, "Chicago Style," 165.

525   *"the Boswell"*: *CEP,* Dec. 10, 1898.

525   *"social show-offs"* and *"inconsequential"*: Ade, "Autobiography"; Philip
      Dunne, "Commentary," in Finley Peter Dunne, *Mr. Dooley Remembers:
      The Informal Memoirs of Finley Peter Dunne,* ed. Philip Dunne (1963),
      165–82.

525   *"I know histhry"*: Dunne, *Mr. Dooley at His Best,* 201–5.

525   *"picturesque stories"*: Clipping, *CT,* Wallace Rice Scrapbooks, CHS;
      Philip Dunne, "Commentary" in *Mr. Dooley Remembers,* 152–82; for
      Dunne's life see Elmer Ellis, *Mr. Dooley's America: A Life of Finley Peter
      Dunne* (1941); and Charles Fanning, *Finley Peter Dunne and Mr. Dooley:
      The Chicago Years* (1978).

526   *"the best club"*: Dunne, *Mr. Dooley At His Best,* xxi–xxvi; Dunne's
      Chicago columns are collected in Charles Fanning, ed., *Mr. Dooley and
      the Chicago Irish: The Autobiography of a Nineteenth-Century Ethnic
      Group* (1976; reprint, 1987).

526   *"Trust everybody"* and *"social colony"*: Dunne, *Mr. Dooley Remembers,*
      303; *CEP,* Jan. 15, 1898.

526   *"But what's it all"*: *CEP,* Aug. 25.

527   *drumming their sticks:* Ellis, *Mr. Dooley's,* 86.

527   *"nervous about libel suits"*: Dunne, *Mr. Dooley,* xxiii.

527   *"should be to comfort"*: Quoted in Sims, "Chicago Style," 238; for Doo-
      ley's views about newspapers, baseball, and all other manner of things,
      see Schaaf, *Mr. Dooley's Chicago.*

527   *"foreign apostle[s]"* and *"howling, yelling mob"*: *CT,* Mar. 17, 1889;
      Adrian C. Anson, *A Ball Player's Career: Personal Experiences and Rem-
      iniscences* (1900), 283–84; Albert G. Spalding, *America's National Game*
      (1911; reprint, 1991), 157–62; *CT,* Mar. 17, Apr. 20, 1889; Arthur
      Bartlett, *Baseball and Mr. Spalding: The History and Romance of Base-
      ball* (1951), 174–99; Anson, a flagrant racist, refused to have his team
      play on the same field as black players.

527   *"is the very symbol"*: Quoted in Anson, *Ball Player's Career,* 278.

528   *new ballpark: Sporting News,* Apr. 23, 1893.

528   *"a typical Chicago man"* and *"I would rather be"*: Spalding, *America's
      National Game,* 128.

528   *make baseball "respectable"*: Spalding, *America's National Game,* 130;
      Anson, *Ball Player's Career,* 287–306; Harold Seymour, *Baseball: Vol. 1,
      The Early Years* (1960), 82–84, 105, 128–29; Chadwick Scrapbook,
      Spalding Collection, New York Public Library.

528   *"In fighting the encroachments"*: Quoted in Peter Levine, *A. G. Spalding
      and the Rise of Baseball: The Promise of American Sport* (1986 edition), 43.

529   *"Baseball as at present conducted"*: Chadwick Scrapbook.

529   *"Everything is possible"*: Quoted in Levine, *Spalding,* xiv.

529   *cover the White Stockings: CDN,* Aug. 8, July 11, 1887.

529   *"southpaw"*: Ellis, *Mr. Dooley's America,* 27; Ickes, *Autobiography,* 27;
      for the new sports journalism, see also Barth, *City People,* 164; and John
      R. Betts, "Sporting Journalism in Nineteenth-Century America," *Ameri-
      can Quarterly* 5 (Spring 1973): 41–50.

529   *"The dentist"*: Quoted in Larzer Ziff, *The American 1890s: Life and Times
      of a Lost Generation* (1968), 58.

530   *"We live in th' city"*: Quoted in Schaaf, *Mr. Dooley's Chicago,* 98; see also
      CEP, Sept. 4, 1897.

530   *"He loved to talk"*: Baker, *American Chronicle,* 225.

530   *"I never knew"*: Steffens, *Autobiography,* 537.

530 *"He was like me":* Ade quoted in Franklin P. Adams, "Foreword," to Dunne, *Mr. Dooley,* xvii.

530 *"the smallest river"* and *"splattering fragments":* Dreiser, "The Smallest and Busiest River in the World," *Metropolitan* 7 (Oct. 1898): 355–63; Dreiser, *The "Genius,"* 48.

530 *"Manny's th' time":* Chicago Journal, Jan. 13, 1900.

531 *"Ivrybody that was annybody":* Dunne, *Mr. Dooley's Opinions* (1901), 140.

531 *unemployed demonstrated: CT,* Aug. 26, Sept. 1–11, Oct. 28, 29, Nov. 18, 1893.

531 *"the greatest of all world's fairs": CT,* Oct. 9–11, 28–31, Nov. 1–3, 1893.

531 *"wild-looking" man:* Baker, *Native American,* 285.

532 *"United States on show":* Quoted in Moore, *Burnham,* vol. 1, 87.

Chapter Fifteen: After the Fair

533 *"great palaces of staff"* and *"civic and social regeneration":* Stead, "My First Visit to America: An Open Letter to My Readers," *Review of Reviews* 9 (Jan.–June 1894): 414–17; *CR,* Nov. 10–12; *CT,* Nov. 10, 13, 1893; the only biography of Stead is Frederick Whyte, *The Life of W. T. Stead,* 2 vols. (1925; reprint, 1971); see also, Joseph O. Baylen, "A Victorian's 'Crusade' in Chicago, 1893–1894," *JAH* 51 (Dec. 1964): 418–34; and Dennis B. Downey, "William Stead and Chicago: A Victorian Jeremiah in the Windy City," *Mid-America* 68, no. 3 (Jan. 1986): 161–68.

533 *"It is the only":* Stead, "First Visit," 415–16.

534 *"What a spectacle!":* Baker, *American Chronicle,* 2.

534 *"Furnaces went":* Payne, *Mr. Salt,* 95–96.

534 *"gave me overwhelming material":* Baker, *Native American,* 310–36; Baker, *American Chronicle,* 1–25.

534 *"all but overwhelmed":* Baker, *Native American,* 325–26.

535 *"pigged together"* and *"like the frogs": ICCC,* 17, 21.

535 *"The city's huge garment":* Herrick, *Web of Life,* 135.

535 *worst depression: CT,* Sept. 6–12, 1893; Charles Hoffman, "The Depression of the Nineties," *Journal of Economic History* 16 (June 1956): 137–52.

535 *"predatory rich"* and *"fundamental": ICCC,* 107, 68.

535 *"He was a fiery orator":* Baker, *American Chronicle,* 27–29.

536 *"Such a gathering":* Graham Taylor, *Pioneering on Social Frontiers* (1930), 28–33.

536 *"Some of the women": CR,* Nov. 13, 1893.

536 *"whether if Christ":* Ibid.; *CT,* Nov. 13, 1893.

536 *"at white heat":* Taylor, *Pioneering,* 73.

536 *"If you well-to-do":* Quotes on Stead's meeting from the *CR,* Nov. 13–14, 1893.

537 *"Existing evils":* Stead published some of the reviews of his book in his study of the Pullman Strike, *Chicago To-Day: The Labour War in America* (1894; reprint, 1969), 275–87. By the fall of 1894, the book had sold approximately 120,000 copies.

537 *"There are plenty more":* Baker, *American Chronicle,* 29–30; Baker reviewed Stead's book in the Mar. 3, 1894. issue of the *CR.*

537 *"too vile":* Quoted in Stead, *Chicago,* 277.

537 *"the model city": ICCC,* 421–42.

538 *"I'd much rather": CT,* Nov. 12, 1893.

PAGE
538   *new Civic Federation:* Franklin MacVeagh, "A Program for Municipal
      Reform," *AJS* 1 (Mar. 1896): 562; see also Albion W. Small, "The Civic
      Federation of Chicago: A Study in Social Dynamics," *AJS* 1 (July 1895):
      88–89.

539   *closed down the Levee:* Clifford W. Barnes, "The Story of the Committee
      of Fifteen in Chicago," *Social Hygiene* 4 (Apr. 1918): 145–56; Barratt
      O'Hara, "The Work of the Illinois State Vice Commission," *The Light* 19
      (May-June 1916): 3–11.

539   *"Community vice":* Walter Reckless, *Vice in Chicago* (1933; reprint,
      1969), 8–31.

539   *"It is by politics":* ICCC, 324–442; *CT,* Nov. 12–13, 1893.

539   *"little, sawed-off":* Douglas Sutherland, *Fifty Years on the Civic Front: A
      History of the Civic Federation's Dynamic Activities* (1943), 1–75; see
      also Hoyt King, *Citizen Cole of Chicago* (1931).

539   *"Each ward":* Steffens, *Shame,* 162–94; Steffens, *Autobiography,*
      422–29.

540   *"We're going to publish":* Quoted in Steffens, *Autobiography,* 428; see
      also George Cole, Circular Letter, Dec. 1896, The Municipal Voters'
      League Papers, CHS; Sidney I. Roberts, "The Municipal Voters' League
      and Chicago's Boodlers," *JISHS* 53 (1960), 131–48.

540   *"joined in the wolf hunt":* GG, 246.

540   *"real reform":* Steffens, *Shame,* 162–94; Executive Committee Minutes,
      Feb.–Mar. 1896, Municipal Voters' League Papers, CHS.

540   *"cheap and nasty":* Quoted in Tarr, *Boss Politics,* 68, 70.

540   *"second-class business man":* Steffens, *Autobiography,* 427; Miller, "Pol-
      itics of Municipal Reform," 37–43.

540   *"I was seeing":* Steffens, *Autobiography,* 429.

541   *a "ring":* CT, Nov. 12, 1893; Victor Lawson to Ralph Easley, Aug. 3,
      1895, Lawson to Lyman Gage, May 29, 1896, Victor Lawson Papers,
      Newberry Library, Chicago; Joel A. Tarr, "William Kent to Lincoln Stef-
      fens: Origins of Progressive Reform in Chicago," *Mid-America* 47 (Jan.
      1965): 55.

541   *a "reformer":* Baker, *Native American,* 334; see also Baker, "The Civic
      Federation of Chicago," *The Outlook* 52 (July 27, 1895): 133.

541   *"what the fundamental conditions":* Baker, *American Chronicle,* 32.

541   *"I was a member":* Addams, *Twenty Years,* 122.

541   *the federation processed:* Louise C. Wade, *Graham Taylor, Pioneer for So-
      cial Justice, 1851–1938* (1964), 75.

541   *"all the sores":* Herrick, *Web of Life,* 135, 137.

542   *"see what the trouble was":* Baker, *American Chronicle,* 34–35.

542   *"Three thousand men":* CR, May 12, 1894.

542   *"only to keep":* Baker, *American Chronicle,* 36.

542   *"a slavery":* Reprinted in Stead, *Chicago,* 178.

543   *"in the very air":* Baker, *American Chronicle,* 36; *CR,* May 12–June 1,
      1894; Baker to J. S. Baker, June 27, 1894, Baker MSS.

543   *"It was one of the greatest":* Baker quotes in *American Chronicle,* 36–38.

543   *"Pullman monopoly":* Ibid., 38; *CR,* June 15–30, 1894.

543   *"a struggle":* NYT, June 27, 1894.

544   *"insurrection":* CT, June 27–29, 1894; for the strike, see Lindsey, *Pull-
      man;* and Nick Salvatore, *Eugene V. Debs: Citizen and Socialist* (1982),
      114–46.

544   *"All southern Chicago":* Baker, *American Chronicle,* 38–39.

545   *"Dictator Debs":* CT, July 5, 1894.

545   *"I believe":* J. S. Baker to R. S. Baker, July 10, 1894, quoted in Robert C.

PAGE

Bannister, Jr., *Ray Stannard Baker: The Mind and Thought of a Progressive* (1966), 51.

545 *"their rifles loaded"*: CT, July 9, 1894.

545 *"Heave Ho!"*: Baker, *American Chronicle*, 39–40.

545 *broke the strike:* CR, July 9–30, 1894; CT, July 9–30, 1894.

545 *"continued, more or less forgotten"*: Baker, *American Chronicle*, 41–43.

546 *"If ye be ill"*: Quoted in Ray Ginger, *Eugene V. Debs: A Biography* (1966), 187.

546 *"like a kind of a benevolent king"*: Baker, *American Chronicle*, 43.

546 *"a roast"*: CT, Nov. 13, 1894.

546 *"The aesthetic features," "pig-headedness"* and *"men, as a rule"*: Report on Chicago Strike, xxii, xxxviii; Lindsey, *Pullman*, 229–44.

546 *"opposed to good"*: Reports of Cases at Law and in Chancery Argued and Determined in the Supreme Court of Illinois 175 (1899): 150–59.

546 *Pullman was buried at night:* CT, Oct. 24, 1897.

547 *"The time has come"*: Quoted in Salvatore, *Debs*, 162.

547 *Florence Kelley:* Kelley probably met Debs in June 1893. For her relationship with him, see Sklar, *Kelley*, 269–75.

547 *"personal will"*: Addams, *Twenty Years*, 158–61.

547 *Samuel Gompers:* Samuel Gompers, "The Lessons of the Recent Strikes," NAR 159 (Aug. 1894): 204.

547 *"touchstone"*: Kelley to Henry Demarest Lloyd, Aug. 15, 1894, quoted in Buder, *Pullman*, 189; Addams, *Twenty Years*, 158.

547 *"malodorous crowd"*: Frederic Remington, "Chicago Under the Mob," HW 38 (July 21, 1894): 280–88.

547 *"There must be some shooting"*: Quoted in Ginger, *Debs*, 161.

547 *"One of the best remedies"*: Quoted in Smith, *Urban Disorder*, 261.

548 *"Why don't they get out"*: Quoted in Baker, *Native American*, 322.

548 *"unfit for human habitation"*: Debs, "What's the Matter with Chicago?" in *Debs: His Life, Writings, and Speeches* (1908), 319–24. This essay originally appeared in the *Chicago Socialist*, Oct. 25, 1902.

549 *"safe," in Wright's words:* Wright, *Autobiography*, 79.

549 *Wright met his first prominent suburban clients:* Eaton, *Two Architects*, 67–74, 91–95; Grant Manson, *Frank Lloyd Wright to 1910: The First Golden Age* (1958), 34–40, 46–48, 62–68; William Cronon gives a fresh reading of Wright's reaction to the Ho-o-den exhibit in "Inconstant Unity: The Passion of Frank Lloyd Wright," in Terrance Riley, ed., *Frank Lloyd Wright, Architect* (1994), 21–23.

550 *"gray and grimy"*: Dean, *White City Chips*, 424.

550 *"exceeded anything"*: CT, July 6–7, 1894.

550 *"a current of splendid vitality"*: Herrick, *Web of Life*, 331; a character in Will Payne's novel *Mr. Salt* describes this fire as the beginning of a new order, 138–39; see also, H. H. Van Meter's poem "The Vanishing Fair," (1894).

550 *"Goddammit, look!"* Richard Wright, *Native Son* (1940), 23.

551 *"bring the performers"*: Mumford, *City in History*, 116.

551 *"Chicago"*: Dreiser, *Newspaper Days*, 3–5.

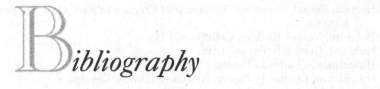
Bibliography

Manuscript Collections

Addams, Jane. Memorial Collection. University of Illinois at Chicago.
Ade, George. Papers. Newberry Library. Chicago.
American Fur Company. Papers. CHS.
Anonymous Commentary on Potter Palmer's Life. CHS.
Armour Institute of Technology. Papers. John Crerar Library. Illinois Institute of Technology.
Art Institute Scrap Books, 1889–1910. Ryerson and Burnham Libraries. Art Institute of Chicago.
Baker, Ray Stannard. Papers. Library of Congress. Washington, D.C.
Beaubien Family. Papers. CHS.
Beaubien, Frank Gordon. Papers. CHS.
Beaubien, Madore. Papers. CHS.
Beman, Solon S. Papers. CHS.
Bronson Papers. CHS.
Burnham, Daniel H. Papers. Ryerson and Burnham Libraries. Art Institute of Chicago.
Butler, Charles. Collection. Library of Congress. Washington, D.C.
Butler, Charles. Papers. CHS.
C. H. Jordan and Company Funeral Homes. Records. CHS.
Caldwell, Billy. Papers. CHS.
Chicago Auditorium Building Papers. Roosevelt University Archives. Chicago.
Chicago Fire of 1871 Collection. CHS.
Chicago Microfilm Project. Ryerson and Burnham Libraries. Art Institute of Chicago.
Chicago Surface Collection. CHS.
Cornell, Paul. Papers. CHS.
Douglas, Stephen A. Papers. University of Chicago Library, Dept. of Special Collections.
Douglass, Frederick. Papers. Library of Congress. Washington, D.C.
Dreiser, Theodore. Collection. Van Pelt Dietrich Library Center, University of Pennsylvania, Philadelphia, Pa.
Edwards, Ninian. Papers. CHS.
Ferris, George W. Papers. CHS.
Fire Narratives. CHS.
Fort Dearborn Papers. CHS.
Glessner, Frances M. Journals. CHS.
Gross, S. E. Collection. CHS.
Harpel Scrapbooks. CHS. 1888.
Harrison, Carter. Papers. Newberry Library. Chicago.
Haymarket Papers. CHS.
Hempstead, Charles S. Collection. CHS.

Herrick, Robert. Collection. University of Chicago Library, Dept. of Special Collections.

Holabird, Samuel Beckley. Collection. CHS.

Hubbard, Gurdon S. Papers. CHS.

Hutchinson, Charles L. Papers. CHS.

Hutchinson, Charles L. Papers. Newberry Library. Chicago.

Kinzie, John. Papers and Accounts. CHS.

Kirkland, Joseph. Papers. Newberry Library. Chicago.

Lawson, Victor. Papers. Newberry Library. Chicago.

Little Room Papers. Newberry Library. Chicago.

Local Community Documents. CHS.

McCormick Archives. State Historical Society of Wisconsin.

McDowell, Mary. Papers. CHS.

Meeting Minutes, 1891–Present. Office of the Secretary. Ryerson and Burnham Libraries. Art Institute of Chicago.

Memorial Art Gallery Scrapbook, 1922. Charlotte Whitney Allen Library. University of Rochester.

Miller, Mrs. C. Philip. Collection. CHS.

Moore, Charles. Papers. Library of Congress. Washington, D.C.

Municipal Voters' League. Papers. CHS.

Ogden, William B. Papers. CHS.

Olmsted, Frederick Law. Papers. Library of Congress. Washington, D.C.

Palmer, Bertha. Board of Lady Managers Records. CHS.

Palmer, Potter. Papers. CHS.

Palmer, Mrs. Potter. Letters. Ryerson and Burnham Libraries. Art Institute of Chicago.

Pullman, George. Papers. CHS.

Pullman Collection. Newberry Library. Chicago.

Pullman Collection. Pullman Branch Library. Pullman, Ill.

Rice, Wallace. Scrapbook. CHS.

Spalding Collection. New York Public Library.

Sturges Collection. CHS.

Sullivan, Louis. Collection. Ryerson and Burnham Libraries. Art Institute of Chicago.

Sullivan, Louis. Papers. Avery Library. Columbia University.

University President's Papers. University of Chicago Library, Dept. of Special Collections.

Wells, Ida B. Papers. University of Chicago Library, Dept. of Special Collections.

Wentworth, John. Papers. CHS.

World's Columbian Exposition Papers. CHS.

Books and Official Reports

Abbot, Willis John. *Carter Henry Harrison: A Memoir.* New York: Dodd, Mead & Co., 1895.

———. *Watching the World Go By.* Boston: Little, Brown, 1933.

Abbott, Carl. *Boosters and Businessmen: Popular Economic Thought and Urban Growth in the Antebellum Middle West.* Westport, Conn: Greenwood Press, 1981.

Abelson, Elaine S. *When Ladies Go A-Thieving: Middle-Class Shoplifters in the Victorian Department Store.* 1989. Reprint, New York: Oxford Univ. Press, 1992.

Adams, Andy. *The Log of a Cowboy: A Narrative of the Old Trail Days.* 1903. Reprint, Lincoln: Univ. of Nebraska Press, 1964.

Adams, Henry. *The Education of Henry Adams.* 1918. Reprint, New York: Little, Brown, 1961.

Addams, Jane. *A New Conscience and an Ancient Evil.* New York: Macmillan, 1912.

———. *The Second Twenty Years at Hull-House.* New York: Macmillan, 1930.

———. *The Spirit of Youth and the City Streets.* New York: Macmillan, 1915.

———. *Twenty Years at Hull-House.* 1910. Reprint, New York: New American Library, 1981.

Ade, George. *Letters of George Ade.* Ed. Terence Tobin. West Lafayette, Ind.: Purdue Univ. Studies, 1973.

———. *Stories of the Streets and of the Town: From the Chicago Record, 1893–1900.* Ed. Frank J. Meine. Chicago: Caxton Club, 1941.

Adelman, William. *Haymarket Revisited.* Chicago: Illinois Labor History Society, 1976.

———. *Touring Pullman.* Chicago Illinois Historical Society, 1972.

AIA Guide to Chicago. Ed. Alice Sinkevitch. New York: Harcourt, Brace, 1993.

Algren, Nelson. *Chicago, City on the Make.* 1951. Reprint, Chicago: Univ. of Chicago Press, 1987.

Allswang, John M. *A House for All Peoples: Ethnic Politics in Chicago, 1890–1936.* Lexington: Univ. Press of Kentucky, 1971.

Altgeld, John Peter. *Reasons for Pardoning Fielden, Neebe, and Schwab.* 1893. Reprint. Chicago: C. H. Kerr, 1986.

Alvord, Clarence W. *The Illinois Country, 1673–1818.* 1920. Reprint, Urbana: Univ. of Illinois Press, 1987.

Andreas, Alfred T. *History of Chicago from the Earliest Period to the Present Time.* 3 vols. Chicago: Alfred T. Andreas, 1884–86.

———. *History of Cook County, Illinois from the Earliest Period to the Present Time.* Chicago: Alfred T. Andreas, 1884.

Andreas, Simon. *Chicago, the Garden City: Its Magnificent Parks, Boulevards, and Cemeteries.* Chicago: The F. Gindele Printing Co., 1893.

Andrew, David S. *Louis Sullivan and the Polemics of Modern Architecture: The Present Against the Past.* Urbana: Univ. of Illinois Press, 1985.

Andrews, Wayne. *Battle for Chicago.* New York: Harcourt, Brace & Co., 1946.

Angle, Paul, ed. *The Great Chicago Fire of 1871: Three Illustrated Accounts from Harper's Weekly.* Ashland, Ore.: L. Osborne, 1969.

Annual Report of the American Historical Association for the Year 1893. Washington, D.C.: GPO, 1894.

Annual Report of the Trustees of the Art Institute of Chicago. Chicago: The Art Institute of Chicago, 1890–1899.

Anson, Adrian C. *A Ball Player's Career: Personal Experiences and Reminiscences.* Chicago: Era Publishing Co., 1900.

Archer, William. *America To-day: Observations and Reflections.* London: Heinemann, 1900.

Armour, J. Ogden. *The Packers, the Private Car Lines, and the People.* Philadelphia: Henry Altemus, 1906.

Arnold, Isaac N., and J. Young Scammon. *William B. Ogden.* Chicago: Fergus Printing Co., 1882.

Asbury, Herbert. *Gem of the Prairie: An Informal History of the Chicago Underworld.* 1940. Reprint, DeKalb: Northern Illinois Univ. Press, 1986.

Ashbaugh, Carolyn. *Lucy Parsons: American Revolutionary.* Chicago: C. H. Kerr, 1976.

Asher, Louis E., and Edith Heal. *Send No Money.* Chicago: Argus Books, 1942.

Avrich, Paul. *The Haymarket Tragedy.* Princeton, N.J.: Princeton Univ. Press, 1984.

Bach, Ira J., ed. *Chicago's Famous Buildings*. Chicago: Univ. of Chicago Press, 1980.

Bach, Ira J., and Susan Wolfson. *A Guide to Chicago's Train Stations, Present and Past*. Athens: Ohio Univ. Press, 1986.

Badger, Reid. *The Great American Fair: The World's Columbian Exposition and American Culture*. Chicago: N. Hall, 1979.

Baily, Robert, et al. *Chicago City Council Proceedings Files 1833–1871: An Inventory*. Springfield: Illinois State Archives, 1987.

Baker, Nina. *Big Catalogue: The Life of Aaron Montgomery Ward*. New York: Harcourt, Brace, 1956.

Baker, Paul R. *Richard Morris Hunt*. Cambridge, Mass.: MIT Press, 1980.

Baker, Ray Stannard. *American Chronicle, The Autobiography of Ray Stannard Baker*. New York: Charles Scribner's Sons, 1945.

———. *Native American: The Book of My Youth*. New York: Charles Scribner's Sons, 1941.

Balestier, Joseph N. *The Annals of Chicago; A Lecture Delivered Before the Chicago Lyceum, January 21, 1840.* Chicago: H. Rudd, printer, 1840.

Baltzell, E. Digby. *The Protestant Establishment: Aristocracy and Caste in America*. New York: Random House, 1964.

Bannister, Robert C., Jr. *Ray Stannard Baker: The Mind and Thought of a Progressive*. New Haven, Conn.: Yale Univ. Press, 1966.

Barker-Benfield, G. L. *The Horrors of the Half-Known Life: Male Attitudes toward Women and Sexuality in Nineteenth Century America*. New York: Harper & Row, 1976.

Barnum, P. T. *The Life of P. T. Barnum*. Buffalo: Courier Co., 1888.

Barrett, James R. *Work and Community in the Jungle: Chicago's Packinghouse Workers, 1894–1922*. Urbana: Univ. of Illinois Press, 1987.

Barrett, John P. *Electricity at the Columbian Exposition*. Chicago: R. R. Donnelley & Sons, 1894.

Barth, Gunther. *City People: The Rise of Modern City Culture in Nineteenth Century America*. New York: Oxford Univ. Press, 1982.

Bartlett, Arthur. *Baseball and Mr. Spalding: The History and Romance of Baseball*. New York: Farrar, Straus and Young, 1951.

Baumann, Frederick H. *The Art of Preparing Foundations for All Kinds of Buildings, with Particular Illustrations of the Method of Isolated Piers as Followed in Chicago*. Chicago: J. M. Wing, 1873.

Bayley, David H., ed. *Police and Society*. Beverly Hills, Calif.: Sage Publications, 1977.

Beebe, Lucius. *Mr. Pullman's Elegant Palace Car*. Garden City, N.Y.: Doubleday, 1961.

Beecher, Henry Ward. *Eyes and Ears*. Boston: Ticknor & Fields, 1864.

Beedle, Lynn S., ed. *Second Century of the Skyscraper*. New York: Van Nostrand Reinhold, 1988.

Beggs, Stephen R. *Pages from the Early History of the West and North-West*. Cincinnati: Ohio: Methodist Book Concern, 1868.

Beijbom, Ulf. *Swedes in Chicago: A Demographic and Social Study of the 1846–1880 Immigration*. Stockholm: Laromedelsforlaget, 1971.

Belcher, Wyatt Winton. *The Economic Rivalry between St. Louis and Chicago, 1850–1880*. New York: Columbia Univ. Press, 1947.

Bender, Thomas, ed. *The University and the City*. New York: Oxford Univ. Press, 1988.

Benson, Susan Porter. *Counter Cultures: Saleswomen, Managers, and Customers in American Department Stores, 1890–1940*. Urbana: Univ. of Illinois Press, 1986.

Benton, Colbee C. *A Visitor to Chicago in Indian Days, "Journal to the Far-Off West."* Ed. Paul M. Angle and James R. Getz. Chicago: Caxton Club, 1957.

Berger, Miles L. *They Built Chicago: Entrepreneurs Who Shaped a Great City's Architecture.* Chicago: Bonus Books, 1992.

Berkow, Ira. *Maxwell Street: Survival in a Bazaar.* Garden City, N.Y.: Doubleday, 1977.

Billington, David P. *The Tower and the Bridge: The New Art of Structural Engineering.* New York: Basic Books, 1983.

Birkmire, William H. *Skeleton Construction in Buildings.* 1894. Reprint, New York: Arno Press, 1972.

Bisno, Abraham. *Abraham Bisno, Union Pioneer.* Madison: Univ. of Wisconsin Press, 1967.

Black Hawk. *An Autobiography.* 1833. Reprint, Ed. Donald Jackson. Urbana: Univ. of Illinois Press, 1955.

Blair, Emma Helen, ed. *The Indian Tribes of the Upper Mississippi Valley and the Region of the Great Lakes.* 2 vols. Cleveland: Clark, 1911–12.

Blanc, Marie Therèse de Solms. *The Condition of Women in the United States: A Traveller's Notes.* 1895. Reprint, New York: Arno Press, 1972.

Bliven, Bruce, Jr. *The Wonderful Writing Machine.* New York: Random House, 1954.

Block, Jean F. *Hyde Park Houses: An Informal History, 1856–1910.* Chicago: Univ. of Chicago Press, 1978.

———. *The Uses of Gothic: Planning and Building the Campus of the University of Chicago, 1892–1932.* Chicago: Univ. of Chicago Press, 1983.

Bloom, Sol. *The Autobiography of Sol Bloom.* New York: G. P. Putnam's Sons, 1948.

Bluestone, Daniel. *Constructing Chicago.* New Haven, Conn.: Yale Univ. Press, 1991.

Bohme, Margaret. *The Department Store: A Novel of Today.* New York: D. Appleton, 1912.

Bonner, Thomas Neville. *Medicine in Chicago, 1850–1950: A Chapter in the Social and Scientific Development of a City.* Urbana: Univ. of Illinois Press, 1991.

Boorstin, Daniel J. *The Americans: The Democratic Experience.* 1973. Reprint, New York: Vintage, 1974.

———. *The Americans: The National Experience.* New York: Knopf, 1965. Reprint, New York: Vintage, 1967.

Borris, Emmet, and John E. Jeuck. *Catalogues and Counters: A History of Sears, Roebuck and Company.* Chicago: Univ. of Chicago Press, 1950.

Bourget, Paul. *Outre-mer: Impressions of America.* New York: Charles Scribner's Sons, 1895.

Bowen, Louise de Koven. *Growing Up With a City.* New York: Macmillan, 1926.

Bowlby, Rachel. *Just Looking: Consumer Culture in Dreiser, Gissing, and Zola.* New York: Methuen, 1985.

Bowron, Bernard R. Jr., *Henry B. Fuller of Chicago: The Ordeal of a Genteel Realist in Ungenteel America.* Westport, Conn.: Greenwood Press, 1974.

Brace, Charles Loring. *The Dangerous Classes of New York and Twenty Years Work Among Them.* New York: Wynkoop & Hallenbeck, 1872.

Braverman, Harry. *Labor and Monopoly Capital: The Degradation of Work in the Twentieth Century.* New York: Monthly Review Press, 1974.

Bremer, Fredrika. *The Homes of the New World: Impressions of America.* 2 vols. New York: Harper & Bros., 1853.

Bretz, J. Harlen. *Geology of the Chicago Region.* Urbana: Illinois State Geological Survey, 1964.

Brody, David. *The Butcher Workmen: A Study of Unionization.* Cambridge, Mass.: Harvard Univ. Press, 1964.

Broehl, Wayne G., Jr. *John Deere's Company: A History of Deere & Company and its Times.* New York: Doubleday, 1984.

Brooks, Virginia. *Little Lost Sister.* Chicago: Gazzdo & Ricksen, 1914.

Bross, William. *Chicago and the Sources of Her Past and Future Growth.* Chicago: Jansen, McClurg, 1880.

———. *History of Chicago.* Chicago: Jansen, McClurg, 1876.

———. *What I Remember of Early Chicago: A Lecture.* Chicago: Jansen, McClurg, 1876.

Brown, G. P. *Drainage Channel and Waterway.* Chicago: R. R. Donnelley & Sons Co., 1894.

Brown, Lauren. *Audubon Nature Society: Grasslands.* New York: Knopf, 1985.

Bruce, Robert V. *1877: Year of Violence.* 1959. Reprint, Chicago: Quadrangle Books, 1970.

Brucker, Gene. *Renaissance Florence.* Berkeley: Univ. of California Press, 1983.

Bryan, Mary Lynn McCree, and Allen F. Davis, eds. *100 Years at Hull-House.* Indianapolis: Indiana Univ. Press, 1990.

Bryan, P. W. *Man's Adaptation of Nature: Studies of the Cultural Landscape.* New York: Henry Holt & Company, 1933.

Bryant, William Cullen. *Letters of a Traveler: Notes of Things Seen in Europe and America.* New York: George P. Putnam, 1850.

Buder, Stanley. *Pullman: An Experiment in Industrial Order and Community Planning, 1880–1930.* New York: Oxford Univ. Press, 1967.

Buenker, John D. *Urban Liberalism and Progressive Reform.* New York: Charles Scribner's Sons, 1973.

Buffalo Bill and the Wild West. Brooklyn: Brooklyn Museum; distributed by the Univ. of Pittsburgh Press, 1981.

Buisseret, David. *Historic Illinois from the Air.* Chicago: Univ. of Chicago Press, 1990.

Burckhardt, Jakob C. *The Civilization of the Renaissance in Italy.* Oxford: Phaidon, 1965.

Burg, David F. *Chicago's White City of 1893.* Lexington: Univ. Press of Kentucky, 1976.

Burnham, Daniel H. *The Final Official Report of the Director of Works of the World's Columbian Exposition.* 1894. Reprint, New York: Garland Publishing Co., 1989.

Burnham, Daniel H., and Edward H. Bennett. *Plan of Chicago.* 1909. Reprint, New York: De Capo Press, 1969.

Burnham, Daniel H., and Francis D. Millet. *World's Columbian Exposition: The Book of the Builders.* Chicago: Columbian Memorial Publication Society, 1894.

Burt, Nathaniel. *Palaces for the People: A Social History of the American Art Museum.* Boston: Little, Brown, 1977.

Busbey, Katherine G. *Home Life in America.* New York: Macmillan, 1910.

Bush-Brown, Albert. *Louis Sullivan.* New York: G. Braziller, 1960.

Bushnell, Charles J. *The Social Problem at the Chicago Stock Yards.* Chicago: Univ. of Chicago Press, 1902.

Business History Conference. *Business and Economic History.* Ed. Jeremy Atack. Urbana-Champaign: Bureau of Economic & Business Research, College of Commerce and Business Administration, Univ. of Illinois, 1981–87.

Butzer, Karl W., ed. *Dimensions of Human Geography: Essays on Some Familiar and Neglected Themes.* Chicago: Univ. of Chicago, Dept. of Geography, 1978.

Cain, Louis P. *Sanitation Strategy for a Lakefront Metropolis, the Case of Chicago.* DeKalb: Northern Illinois Univ. Press, 1978.

Calmer, Alan. *Labor Agitator: The Story of Albert R. Parsons.* New York: International Publishers, 1937.

Carwardine, William H. *The Pullman Strike.* 1894. Reprint, Chicago: C. H. Kerr, 1973.

Casey, Robert J. *Chicago Medium Rare: When We Were Both Younger.* Indianapolis: Bobbs-Merrill, 1952.

Casey, Robert J., and W. A. S. Douglas. *Pioneer Railroad: The Story of the Chicago and North Western System.* New York: Whittlesey House, 1948.

Casson, Herbert N. *Cyrus Hall McCormick: His Life and Work.* Chicago: A. C. McClurg, 1909.

Cather, Willa. *The Song of the Lark.* Boston: Houghton Mifflin, 1915.

Caton, John Dean. *The Last of the Illinois and a Sketch of the Pottawatomies. Read before the Chicago Historical Society, December 13, 1870.* Chicago: Fergus Printing, 1876.

Chamberlin, Everett. *Chicago and Its Suburbs.* 1874. Reprint, New York: Arno Press, 1974.

Chandler, Alfred D., Jr. *The Visible Hand: The Managerial Revolution in American Business.* Cambridge, Mass.: Harvard Univ. Press, 1977.

Chatfield-Taylor, Hobart C. *Chicago.* New York: Houghton Mifflin Co., 1917.

————. *Cities of Many Men: A Wanderer's Memories of London, Paris, New York, and Chicago During Half a Century.* New York: Houghton Mifflin Co., 1925.

Chesbrough, Ellis S. *Chicago Sewerage: Report of the Results of Examinations Made in Relation to Sewerage in Several European Cities, in the Winter of 1856–7.* Chicago: Board of Sewerage Commissioners, 1858.

————. *Report and Plan of Sewerage for the City of Chicago, Illinois.* Chicago: Charles Scott, 1855.

Chicago. Board of Police. *Report of the Board of Police, in the Fire Department, to the Common Council of the City of Chicago.* 1867–1879.

Chicago. Board of Public Works. *Third Annual Report of Public Works of the City of Chicago.* Chicago: Jameson & Morse, 1864.

————. *Eleventh Annual Report of the Board of Public Works of the City of Chicago.* Chicago: Jameson & Morse, 1873.

Chicago. Board of Sewerage Commissioners. *Report of the Board of Sewerage Commissioners of the City of Chicago, For the Half Year Ending December 31, 1860.* Chicago: Board of Sewerage Commissioners, 1861.

Chicago. Department of Development and Planning. *The People of Chicago.* Chicago: Department of Development and Planning, 1976.

Chicago. Department of Health. *Annual Report.* 1892–1894.

————. *Report of the Board of Health of the City of Chicago for 1867, 1868, and 1869.* Chicago: Lakeside Printing & Publishing Co., 1871.

Chicago Board of Trade. *Annual Report of the Trade and Commerce of Chicago.* 1871–1893.

————. *Annual Statement of the Trade and Commerce of Chicago.* Chicago: Chicago Tribune Book & Job Printing, 1862.

Chicago Commerce, Manufactures, Banking and Transportation Facilities. Chicago: S. Ferd Howe, 1884.

The Chicago Railway Terminal Problem. Reports of the Chicago Terminal Commission to the Mayor and Common Council of the City of Chicago. New York: Jenkins & McGowan, 1892.

The Chicago Record's History of the World's Fair. Chicago: Chicago Daily News Co., 1893.

Chicago Relief and Aid Society. *Report of the Chicago Relief and Aid Society of Disbursement of Contributions for the Sufferers of the Chicago Fire.* Chicago: Riverside Press. 1874.

Chicago's Dark Places: Investigations by a Corps of Specially Appointed Commissions. Chicago: Craig Press, 1891.

Citizens' Association of Chicago, Committee on Main Drainage and Water Supply. *Report of the Committee on the Main Drainage and Water Supply of Chicago, September, 1885.* Chicago: K. Hazlitt & Co., Printers, 1885.

The Civic Federation: What It Has Accomplished in Its First Year. Chicago: 1895.

Clark, John G. *The Grain Trade in the Old Northwest.* Urbana: Univ. of Illinois Press, 1966.

Clark, Kenneth. *Civilisation: A Personal View.* New York: Harper & Row, 1969.

Cleaver, Charles, *Early-Chicago Reminiscences.* Chicago: Fergus Historical Series, no. 19, Fergus Printing Company, 1882.

Clemen, Rudolf A. *The American Livestock and Meat Industry.* New York: Ronald Press Co., 1923.

———. *By-Products in the Packing Industry.* Chicago: Univ. of Chicago Press, 1927.

———. *George H. Hammond (1838–1886): Pioneer in Refrigerator Transportation.* New York: Newcomen Society, 1946.

Cleveland, H. W. S. *The Public Grounds of Chicago: How to Give them Character and Expression.* Chicago: C. D. Lakey, 1869.

Clifton, James A. *The Prairie People: Continuity and Change in Potawatomi Indian Culture, 1665–1965.* Lawrence: Regents Press of Kansas, 1977.

Cobbe, William Rosser. *Doctor Judas: A Portrayal of the Opium Habit.* Chicago: S. C. Griggs and Company, 1895.

Cochran, Thomas C. *Business in American Life: A History.* New York: McGraw-Hill, 1972.

Colbert, Elias. *Chicago: Historical and Statistical Sketch of the Garden City.* Chicago: P. T. Sherlock, 1868.

Colbert, Elias, and Everett Chamberlin. *Chicago and the Great Conflagration.* 1871. Reprint, New York: Viking Press, 1971.

Condit, Carl W. *American Building Art: The Nineteenth Century.* New York: Oxford Univ. Press, 1960.

———. *The Chicago School of Architecture: A History of Commercial and Public Building in the Chicago Area, 1875–1925.* Chicago: Univ. of Chicago Press, 1964.

Connelly, Mark Thomas. *The Response to Prostitution in the Progressive Era.* Chapel Hill: Univ. of North Carolina Press, 1980.

Connely, Willard. *Louis Sullivan as He Lived: The Shaping of American Architecture, a Biography.* New York: Horizon Press, 1960.

Conzen, Michael P., and Kay J. Carr, eds. *The Illinois and Michigan Canal National Heritage Corridor: A Guide to its History and Sources.* DeKalb: Northern Illinois Univ. Press, 1988.

Cooley, Lyman E. *The Lakes and Gulf Waterway as Related to the Chicago Sanitary Problem.* Chicago: Press of J. W. Weston, 1891.

Cope, George W. *The Iron and Steel Interests of Chicago.* Chicago: Rand McNally, 1890.

Cox, Henry J., and John H. Armington. *The Weather and Climate of Chicago.* Chicago: Univ. of Chicago Press, 1914.

Cranz, Galen. *The Politics of Park Design: A History of Urban Parks in America.* Cambridge, Mass.: MIT Press, 1982.

Creese, Walter L. *The Crowning of the American Landscape: Eight Great Spaces and their Buildings.* Princeton, N.J.: Princeton Univ. Press, 1985.

Crissey, Forrest. *Since 40 Years Ago: An Account of the Origin and Growth of Chicago and its First Department Store.* Chicago: The Fair, 1915.

Critchell, Robert S. *Recollections of a Fire Insurance Man.* Chicago: Author, 1909.

Cromie, Robert. *The Great Chicago Fire.* New York: McGraw-Hill, 1958.

Cronon, William. *Nature's Metropolis: Chicago and the Great West.* New York: W. W. Norton & Company, 1991.

Cudahy, Brian J. *Destination: Loop: The Story of Rapid Transit Railroading In and Around Chicago.* Brattleboro, Vt.: S. Greene Press, 1982.

Current, Richard. *The Typewriter and the Men Who Made It.* Urbana: Univ. of Illinois Press, 1954.

Currey, J. Seymour. *Chicago: Its History and Its Builders: A Century of Marvelous Growth.* 5 vols. Chicago: S. J. Clarke Publishing Co., 1908–1912.

———. *Manufacturing and Wholesale Industries of Illinois.* 3 vols. Chicago: Thomas B. Poole, 1919.

Curtiss, Daniel S. *Western Portraiture and Emigrants' Guide.* New York: J. H. Colton, 1852.

Cutler, Irving. *Chicago: Metropolis of the Mid-Continent.* Dubuque, Iowa: Kendall/ Hunt, 1976.

Cutler, Irving, ed. *The Chicago Metropolitan Area: Selected Geographic Readings.* New York: Simon & Schuster, 1970.

David, Henry. *The History of the Haymarket Affair: A Study in the American Social-Revolutionary and Labor Movements.* New York: Farrar and Rinehart, 1936.

Davies, Margery W. *Woman's Place is at the Typewriter: Office Work and Office Workers, 1870–1930.* Philadelphia: Temple Univ. Press, 1982.

Davis, Allen F. *American Heroine: The Life and Legend of Jane Addams.* New York: Oxford Univ. Press, 1973.

———. *Spearheads for Reform: The Social Settlements and the Progressive Movement, 1890–1914.* New York: Oxford Univ. Press, 1970.

Dean, Theresa. *White City Chips.* Chicago: Warren Publishing Co., 1895.

Debates and Proceedings of the Constitutional Convention of the State of Illinois. Springfield, Ill.: E. L. Merritt & Bros., 1870.

Dedmon, Emmett. *Fabulous Chicago.* New York: Random House, 1953.

Deegan, Mary Jo. *Jane Addams and the Men of the Chicago School, 1892–1918.* New Brunswick, N.J.: Transaction Books, 1988.

De Koven, Mrs. Reginald. *A Musician and His Wife.* New York: Harper & Bros., 1926.

Delanglez, Jean. *Life and Voyages of Louis Jolliet (1645–1700).* Chicago: Institute of Jesuit History, 1948.

Dennis, Charles H. *Eugene Field's Creative Years.* Garden City, N.Y.: Doubleday, Page & Co., 1924.

———. *Victor Lawson: His Time and His Work.* 1935. Reprint, New York: Greenwood Press, 1968.

de Rousiers, Paul. *American Life.* New York: Firmin-Didot, 1892.

DeVoto, Bernard. *The Course of Empire.* Boston: Houghton Mifflin, 1952.

de Wit, Wim, ed. *Louis Sullivan: The Function of Ornament.* New York: W. W. Norton, 1986.

The Dictionary of American Biography. 22 vols. New York: Charles Scribner's Sons, 1946–58.

Dies, Edward J. *The Plunger: A Tale of the Wheat Pit.* New York: Corvici-Friede, 1929.

———. *Street of Adventure.* Boston: Stratford Company Publishers, 1935.

Diggins, John P. *The Bard of Savagery: Thorstein Veblen and Modern Social Theory.* New York: Seabury Press, 1978.

Diner, Steven J. *A City and Its Universities: Public Policy in Chicago, 1892–1919.* Chapel Hill: Univ. of North Carolina Press, 1980.

Directory and Hand-Book of the Meat and Provision Trade and Their Allied In-dustries for the United States and Canada. New York: National Provisioner Publishing Co., 1895.

Ditchett, S. H. *Marshall Field and Company: The Life Story of a Great Concern.* New York: Dry Goods Economist, 1922.

Dodlinger, Percy Tracy. *The Book of Wheat: An Economic History and Practical Manual of the Wheat Industry.* New York: Orange Judd, 1919.

Dolce, Phillip C., ed. *Suburbia: The American Dream and Dilemma.* Garden City, N.Y.: Anchor Press/Doubleday, 1976.

Donnelly, Joseph P. *Jacques Marquette, S.J., 1637–1675.* Chicago: Loyola Univ. Press, 1968.

———. *Thwaites Jesuit Relations: Errata and Addenda.* Chicago: Loyola Univ. Press, 1967.

Dorfman, Joseph. *Thorstein Veblen and His America.* New York: Viking Press, 1934.

[Doty, Duane]. *The Story of Pullman.* Chicago: Blakely & Rogers, 1893.

Doty, Mrs. Duane. *The Town of Pullman: Its Growth with Brief Accounts of its In-dustries.* Pullman: T. P. Struhsacker, 1893.

Doughty, Howard. *Francis Parkman.* New York: Macmillan, 1962.

Douglas, Stephen A. *Letters.* Ed. Robert W. Johannsen. Urbana: Univ. of Illinois Press, 1961.

Drake, St. Clair, and Horace R. Cayton. *Black Metropolis: A Study of Negro Life in a Northern City.* New York: Harcourt, Brace & Company, 1945.

Draper, John William. *History of the Intellectual Development of Europe.* 2 vols. New York: Harper, 1876.

Dreiser, Theodore. *Dawn.* 1931. Reprint, New York: Fawcett, 1965.

———. *The "Genius."* 1915. Reprint, New York: New American Library, 1967.

———. *Jennie Gerhardt.* 1911. Reprint, New York: Viking Penguin, 1989.

———. *Newspaper Days.* Ed. T. D. Nostwich. Philadelphia: Univ. of Pennsylva-nia Press, 1991.

———. *Newspaper Writings, 1892–1895.* Vol. 1 of *Journalism.* Ed. T. D. Nost-wich. Philadelphia: Univ. of Pennsylvania Press, 1988.

———. *Sister Carrie.* 1900. Reprint, New York: Viking Penguin, 1987.

———. *The Titan.* 1914. Reprint, New York: New American Library, 1965.

Duffey, Bernard I. *The Chicago Renaissance in American Letters: A Critical His-tory.* East Lansing: Michigan State College Press, 1954.

Duis, Perry. *Chicago: Creating New Traditions.* Chicago: CHS, 1976.

———. *The Saloon: Public Drinking in Chicago and Boston, 1880–1920.* Ur-bana: Univ. of Illinois Press, 1983.

Duncan, Hugh Dalziel. *Culture and Democracy.* 1965. Reprint, New Brunswick, N.J.: Transaction Books, 1989.

Dunne, Finley Peter. *Mr. Dooley and the Chicago Irish: The Autobiography of a Nineteenth-Century Ethnic Group.* Ed. Charles Fanning. 1976. Reprint, Washington, D.C.: Catholic University of America Press, 1987.

———. *Mr. Dooley at His Best.* Ed. Elmer Ellis. New York: Charles Scribner's Sons, 1938.

———. *Mr. Dooley Remembers: The Informal Memoirs of Finley Peter Dunne.* Ed. Philip Dunne. Boston: Little, Brown, 1963.

———. *Mr. Dooley's Opinions.* New York: R. H. Russell, 1901.

Dyos, H. J., and Michael Wolff, eds. *The Victorian City: Images and Realities.* 2 vols. Boston: Routledge & Kegan Paul, 1973.

Eaton, Leonard K. *Two Chicago Architects and Their Clients: Frank Lloyd Wright and Howard Van Doren Shaw.* Cambridge, Mass.: MIT Press, 1969.

Ebner, Michael H. *Creating Chicago's North Shore: A Suburban History.* Chicago: Univ. of Chicago Press, 1988.

Ebner, Michael H., and Eugene M. Tobin, eds. *The Age of Urban Reform: New*

Perspectives on the Progressive Era. Port Washington, N.Y.: Kennikat Press, 1977.

Eccles, W. J. *Canada Under Louis XIV, 1663–1701.* London: McClelland and Stewart Limited, 1964.

———. *The Canadian Frontier, 1534–1760.* New York: Holt, Rinehart and Winston, 1969.

———. *France in America.* New York: Harper & Row, 1972.

Edwards, Alba. *Comparative Occupational Statistics for the United States, 1870–1940.* Washington, D.C.: Government Printing Office, 1943.

Eifert, Virginia Louise. *Louis Jolliet: Explorer of Rivers.* New York: Dodd, Mead & Company, 1961.

Einhorn, Robin L. *Property Rules: Political Economy in Chicago, 1833–1872.* Chicago: Univ. of Chicago Press, 1991.

Ellis, Elmer. *Mr. Dooley's America: A Life of Finley Peter Dunne.* New York: Knopf, 1941.

Ely, Richard T. *Ground Under Our Feet: An Autobiography.* New York: Macmillan, 1938.

Emerson, Ralph Waldo. *Essays and Lectures.* New York: Library of America 1983.

Emery, Henry Crosby. *Speculation on the Stock and Produce Exchanges of the United States.* New York: Columbia Univ. Press, 1896.

Emmet, Boris, and John E. Jeuck. *Catalogues and Counters: A History of Sears, Roebuck & Company.* Chicago: Univ. of Chicago Press, 1950.

Engels, Friedrich. *The Condition of the Working Class in England in 1844.* Trans. by Florence Kelley. New York: J. W. Lovell Co., 1887.

Erens, Patricia. *Masterpieces: Famous Chicagoans and Their Paintings.* Chicago: Review Press, 1979.

Erickson, Ethel. *The Employment of Women in Offices.* U.S. Department of Labor, Women's Bureau, *Bulletin,* no. 120, 1934.

Ericsson, Henry. *Sixty Years a Builder: The Autobiography of Henry Ericsson.* Chicago: A. Kroch & Son, 1942.

Erie, Steven P. *Rainbow's End: Irish-Americans and the Dilemmas of Urban Machine Politics, 1840–1985.* Berkeley: Univ. of California Press, 1988.

Fabian, Ann. *Card Sharps, Dream Books, and Bucket Shops: Gambling in Nineteenth-Century America.* Ithaca, N.Y.: Cornell Univ. Press, 1990.

Faith, Nicholas. *The World the Railways Made.* New York: Carroll & Graf, 1990.

The Famous Speeches of the Eight Chicago Anarchists in Court. Chicago: Lucy E. Parsons, 1886. Reprint, 1910.

Fanning, Charles. *Finley Peter Dunne and Mr. Dooley: The Chicago Years.* Lexington: Univ. Press of Kentucky, 1978.

Fanning, Charles, Ellen Skerrett, and John Corrigan. *Nineteenth Century Chicago Irish: A Social and Political Portrait.* Chicago: Center for Urban Policy, Loyola Univ. of Chicago, 1980.

Farr, Finis, *Chicago: A Personal History of America's Most American City.* New Rochelle, N.Y.: Arlington House, 1973.

Faulkner, Thomas A. *From the Ball Room to Hell.* Chicago: Henry Brothers & Co., 1894.

Federal Writers Project. *The WPA Guide to Illinois.* 1939. Reprint, New York: Pantheon Books, 1983.

Fehrenbacher, Don. *Chicago Giant: A Biography of "Long John" Wentworth.* Madison, Wis.: American History Research Center, 1957.

Fergus, Robert, comp. *Chicago River-and-Harbor Convention, an Account of its Origin and Proceedings . . .* Fergus Historical Series, no. 18, Chicago: Fergus Printing Company, 1882.

Ferris, William G. *The Grain Traders: The Story of the Chicago Board of Trade.* East Lansing: Michigan State Univ. Press, 1988.

Ferry, Mrs. Abby (Farwell). *Reminiscences of John V. Farwell By His Elder Daughter.* 2 vols. Chicago: Ralph Seymour Fletcher Publisher, 1928.

Field, Marshall. *Elements of Success.* Chicago: privately printed, 1896.

Fine, Lisa M. *The Souls of the Skyscraper: Female Clerical Workers in Chicago, 1870–1930.* Philadelphia: Temple Univ. Press, 1990.

Fishman, Robert. *Bourgeois Utopias: The Rise and Fall of Suburbia.* New York: Basic Books, 1987.

Fitzpatrick, Ellen. *Endless Crusade: Women Social Scientists and Progressive Reform.* New York: Oxford Univ. Press, 1990.

Flinn, John J. *Chicago: The Marvelous City of the West: A History, an Encyclopedia and a Guide.* Chicago: Standard Guide Company, 1891.

———. *History of the Chicago Police from the Settlement of the Community to the Present Time.* Chicago: Under auspices of police book fund, 1887.

———. *Official Guide to the World's Columbian Exposition.* Chicago: Columbian Guide Co., 1893.

———. *The Standard Guide to Chicago.* Chicago: Standard Guide Company, 1894.

Fogel, Robert W. *Railroads and American Economic Growth: Essays in Econometric History.* Baltimore, Md.: Johns Hopkins Univ. Press, 1964.

Fogelson, Robert M. *Big-City Police.* Cambridge, Mass.: Harvard Univ. Press, 1977.

Foner, Philip. *The Great Labor Uprising of 1877.* New York: Monad Press, 1977.

———, ed. *The Autobiographies of the Haymarket Martyrs.* New York: Published for A.I.M.S. by Humanities Press, 1969.

Ford, Henry. *My Life and Work.* Garden City, N.Y.: Doubleday, Page & Co., 1923.

Ford, Thomas. *History of Illinois, From Its Commencement as a State in 1818 to 1847.* Chicago: S. C. Griggs & Co., 1854.

Forty, Adrian. *Objects of Desire: Design and Society, 1750–1980.* London: Thames & Hudson, 1986.

Fourth Annual Insurance Report of the Auditor of Public Accounts of the State of Illinois, 1872. 1872.

Fowler, Bertram B. *Men, Meat and Miracles.* New York: Julian Messner, 1952.

Frank, Waldo. *Our America.* New York: Boni and Liveright, 1919.

Franke, David. *The Torture Doctor.* New York: Hawthorn Books, 1975.

French, William R. *Historical Sketch and Description of the Art Institute of Chicago.* Chicago: W. P. Dunn Co., 1904.

Fuller, Henry B. *The Cliff-Dwellers.* 1893. Reprint, New York: Irvington Publishers, 1981.

———. *Under the Skylights.* New York: D. Appleton & Co., 1901.

———. *With the Procession.* New York: Harper Bros., 1895.

Funchion, Michael F. *Chicago's Irish Nationalists, 1881–1890.* New York: Arno Press, 1976.

Gage, Lyman J. *Memoirs of Lyman J. Gage.* New York: House of Field, Inc., 1937.

Gale, Edwin O. *Reminiscences of Early Chicago and Vicinity.* Chicago: Revell, 1902.

Galena and Chicago Union Railroad Company. *Report of William B. Ogden, Esq., President of the Company, together with Reports of the Engineer, Secretary, and Treasurer, read at the Annual Meeting of the Stockholders, April 5, 1848.* Chicago: Stewart, Wheeler & Ellis, job printers, 1848.

Galloway, Lee. *Office Management: Its Principles and Practice.* New York: Ronald Press, 1919.

Garczynski, Edward R. *Auditorium.* New York: Exhibit Publishing Co., 1890.

Garland, Hamlin. *Crumbling Idols: Twelve Essays on Art Dealing Chiefly with Literature, Painting, and the Drama.* 1894. Reprint, ed. Jane Johnson. Cambridge, Mass.: The Belknap Press of Harvard Univ. Press, 1960.

————. *A Daughter of the Middle Border.* New York: Macmillan, 1922.

————. *Roadside Meetings.* New York: Macmillan, 1930.

————. *Rose of Dutcher's Coolly.* 1895. Reprint, Lincoln: Univ. of Nebraska Press, 1969.

————. *A Son of the Middle Border.* New York: Macmillan, 1925.

Gates, Paul. W. *The Illinois Central Railroad and Its Colonization Work.* Cambridge, Mass.: Harvard Univ. Press, 1934.

Giedion, Sigfried. *Mechanization Takes Command: A Contribution to Anonymous History.* New York: Oxford Univ. Press, 1948.

————. *Space, Time and Architecture: The Growth of a New Tradition.* Cambridge, Mass.: Harvard Univ. Press, (1941) 1978 edition.

Gilbert, James Burkhart. *Perfect Cities: Chicago's Utopias of 1893.* Chicago: Univ. of Chicago Press, 1991.

Ginger, Ray. *Altgeld's America: The Lincoln Ideal Versus Changing Realities.* 1958. Reprint, Chicago: Quadrangle Books, 1965.

————. *Eugene V. Debs: A Biography.* New York: Macmillan, 1966.

Goldberger, Paul. *The Skyscraper.* New York: Knopf, 1981.

Goldmark, Josephine. *Impatient Crusader: Florence Kelley's Life Story.* Urbana: Univ. of Illinois Press, 1953.

Goldthwaite, Richard A. *The Building of Renaissance Florence: An Economic and Social History.* Baltimore, Md.: Johns Hopkins Univ. Press, 1980.

Gompers, Samuel. *Seventy Years of Life and Labor: An Autobiography.* Vol. 2. New York: E. P. Dutton, 1925.

Goode, J. Paul. *The Geographic Background of Chicago.* Chicago: Univ. of Chicago Press, 1926.

Goodrich, Grant. *Reception to the Settlers of Chicago Prior to 1840.* Chicago: Calumet Club, 1879.

Goodspeed, Edgar Johnson. *History of the Great Fires in Chicago and the West.* Chicago: J. W. Goodspeed, 1871.

Goodspeed, Thomas Wakefield. *A History of the University of Chicago: The First Quarter Century.* Chicago: Univ. of Chicago Press, 1916.

————. *The University of Chicago Biographical Sketches.* 2 vols. Chicago: Univ. of Chicago Press, 1922.

————. *William Rainey Harper, First President of the University of Chicago.* Chicago: Univ. of Chicago Press, 1928.

Gordon, Eleanor Lytle Kinzie. *John Kinzie, The "Father of Chicago": A Sketch.* [Savannah?, Ga.], 1910.

Grand, W. Jos. *Illustrated History of the Union Stockyards.* Chicago: Thos. Knapp, 1896.

Granger, Bill, and Lori Granger. *Lords of the Last Machine: The Story of Politics in Chicago.* New York: Random House, 1987.

Grant, Bruce. *Fight for a City: The Story of the Union League Club of Chicago and Its Times, 1880–1955.* Chicago: Rand McNally, 1955.

Gras, N. S. B., and Henrietta M. Larson, eds. *Casebook in American Business History.* New York: F. S. Crofts & Co., 1939.

Green, Paul M., and Melvin G. Holli. *The Mayors: The Chicago Political Tradition.* Carbondale: Southern Illinois Univ. Press, 1987.

Greene, Everts B., and Clarence W. Alvord, eds. *Governors' Letter-Books, 1818–1834.* Springfield: Trustees of the Illinois State Historical Society, 1909.

Greenwood, Grace [Mrs. Sara Jane Lippincott]. *New Life in New Lands: Notes on Travel.* New York: J. B. Ford & Co., 1873.

Gregersen, Charles E. *Dankmar Adler: His Theatres and Auditoriums*. Athens, Ohio: Swallow Press, 1989.

Gregory, Addie Hibbard. *A Great-Grandmother Remembers*. Chicago: A. Kroch & Son, 1940.

Gross, John, comp. *The Age of Kipling*. New York: Simon & Schuster, 1972.

Haeger, John Denis. *The Investment Frontier: New York Businessmen and the Economic Development of the Old Northwest*. Albany: State Univ. of New York Press, 1981.

Hale, John. *The Civilization of Europe in the Renaissance*. New York: Harper-Collins, 1994.

Hales, Peter B. *Constructing the Fair: Platinum Photographs by C. D. Arnold of the World's Columbian Exposition*. Chicago: Art Institute of Chicago, 1993.

Hamer, David. *New Towns in the New World: Images and Perceptions of the Nineteenth-Century Urban Frontier*. New York: Columbia Univ. Press, 1990.

Hamilton, Henry R. *Biographical Sketch of Gurdon Saltonstall Hubbard*. Chicago: Chicago Historical Society, 1908.

———. *The Epic of Chicago*. Chicago: Willett, Clark & Co., 1932.

Hamilton, Raphael N. *Father Marquette*. Grand Rapids, Mich.: William B. Eerdmans, 1970.

———. *Marquette's Explorations: The Narratives Reexamined*. Madison: Univ. of Wisconsin Press, 1970.

Handlin, Oscar. *This Was America: True Accounts of People & Places, Manners & Customs*. Cambridge, Mass.: Harvard Univ. Press, 1949.

[Handy, Moses]. *The Official Directory of the World's Columbian Exposition*. Chicago: W. B. Conkey Co., 1893.

———. *World's Columbian Exhibition: Official Catalogue*. Chicago: W. B. Conkey Co., 1893.

Hardy, Lady Duffus. *Through Cities and Prairie Lands*. New York: R. Worthington, 1881.

Harland, Robert O. *The Vice Bondage of a Great City or the Wickedest City in the World*. Chicago: Young People's Civic League, 1912.

Harper, William Rainey. *The Trend in Higher Education*. Chicago: Univ. of Chicago Press, 1905.

Harrison, Carter H. *A Place with the Sun; or, a Sixteen Months' Tour from Chicago around the World*. New York: G. P. Putnam's Sons, 1889.

Harrison, Carter H., II. *Growing Up with Chicago*. Chicago: R. F. Seymour, 1944.

Hawes, Elizabeth. *New York, New York: How the Apartment House Transformed the Life of a City (1869–1930)*. New York: Knopf, 1993.

Hazen, Margaret Hindle, and Robert M. Hazen. *Keepers of the Flame: The Role of Fire in American Culture, 1775–1925*. Princeton, N.J.: Princeton Univ. Press, 1992.

Healy, George P. A. *Reminiscences of a Portrait Painter*. Chicago: A. C. McClurg & Co., 1894.

Hecht, Ben. *Gaily, Gaily*. Garden City, N.Y.: Doubleday, 1963.

Hendrick, Burton J. *The Age of Big Business: A Chronicle of the Captains of Industry*. Vol. 39 of *Chronicles of America Series*. Ed. Allan Johnson. New Haven, Conn.: Yale Univ. Press, 1919.

Herbert, D. T., and R. J. Johnston, eds. *Geography and the Urban Environment: Progress in Research and Applications*. 5 vols. New York: Wiley, 1978–82.

Herrick, Robert. *The Gospel of Freedom*. New York: Macmillan, 1898.

———. *The Memoirs of an American Citizen*. 1905. Reprint, Cambridge, Mass.: Harvard Univ. Press, 1963.

———. *The Web of Life*. New York: Macmillan, 1900.

Higinbotham, H. N. *Report of the President of the Board of Directors of the World's Columbian Exposition*. Chicago: Rand McNally, 1898.

Hill, Caroline M., comp. *Mary McDowell and Municipal Housekeeping: A Symposium.* Chicago: Millar Publishing Co., 1939.

Hines, Thomas S. *Burnham of Chicago: Architect and Planner.* Chicago: Univ. of Chicago Press, 1979.

Hirsch, Eric L. *Urban Revolt: Ethnic Politics in the Nineteenth-Century Chicago Labor Movement.* Berkeley: Univ. of California Press, 1990.

Hitchcock, Henry-Russell. *Architecture: Nineteenth and Twentieth Centuries.* New York: Penguin Books, 1977.

Hoerder, Dirk, ed. *American Labor and Immigration History, 1877–1920s: Recent European Research.* Urbana: Univ. of Illinois Press, 1983.

Hoffman, Charles Fenno. *A Winter in the West: By a New-Yorker.* New York: Harper & Bros., 1835.

Hoffmann, Donald. *The Architecture of John Wellborn Root.* Baltimore, Md.: Johns Hopkins Univ. Press, 1973.

Hofmeister, Rudolf A. *The Germans of Chicago.* Champaign, Ill.: Stipes Publishing Co., 1976.

Hoge, Cecil C. *The First Hundred Years are the Toughest: What We Can Learn from the Century of Competition Between Sears and Ward's.* Berkeley, Calif.: Ten Speed Press, 1988.

Holbrook, Stewart H. *The Story of American Railroads.* New York: Crown Publishers, 1947.

Holli, Melvin G., and Peter d'A. Jones. *Ethnic Chicago.* Grand Rapids, Mich.: William B. Eerdmans Publishing Co., 1984.

———, eds. *The Ethnic Frontier: Essays in the History of Group Survival in Chicago and the Midwest.* Grand Rapids, Mich.: William B. Eerdmans Publishing Co., 1977.

Holloway, Jean. *Hamlin Garland: A Biography.* Austin: Univ. of Texas Press, 1960.

Holt, Alfred Hubbard. *Hubbard's Trail.* Chicago: Erie Press, 1952.

Holt, Glen E., and Dominic A. Pacyga. *Chicago: A Historical Guide to the Neighborhoods: The Loop and the South Side.* Chicago: CHS, 1979.

Horowitz, Helen Lefkowitz. *Culture and the City: Cultural Philanthropy in Chicago from the 1880s to 1917.* Lexington: Univ. Press of Kentucky, 1976.

Horwich, Bernard. *My First Eighty Years.* Chicago: Argus, 1939.

Hotchkiss, George W. *History of the Lumber and Forest Industry of the Northwest.* Chicago: G. W. Hotchkiss & Co., 1898.

Hough, Jack L. *The Geology of the Great Lakes.* Urbana: Univ. of Illinois Press, 1958.

Hounshell, David A. *From the American System to Mass Production, 1800–1932: The Development of Manufacturing Technology in the United States.* Baltimore, Md.: Johns Hopkins Univ. Press, 1984.

Hoyt, Homer. *One Hundred Years of Land Values in Chicago: The Relationship of the Growth of Chicago to the Rise in Its Land Values, 1830–1933.* Chicago: Univ. of Chicago Press, 1933.

Hubbard, Gurdon Saltonstall. *The Autobiography of Gurdon Saltonstall Hubbard: Pa-Pa-Ma-Ta-Be, "The Swift Walker."* Chicago: Lakeside Press, 1911.

Hubbard, Mary Ann. *Family Memories.* [Chicago?]: 1912.

Hughes, Thomas. *American Genesis: A Century of Invention and Technological Enthusiasm, 1870–1970.* New York: Viking, 1989.

Hull-House Maps and Papers: A Presentation of Nationalities and Wages in a Congested District of Chicago, Together with Comments and Essays on Problems Growing out of the Social Conditions. 1895. Reprint, New York: Arno Press, 1970.

Humphreys, William J. *Physics of the Air.* Philadelphia: J. B. Lippincott Co., 1920.

Hunter, Robert. *Tenement Conditions in Chicago: Report by the Investigating Committee of the City Homes Association.* 1901. Reprint, New York: Garrett Press, 1970.

Husband, Joseph. *The Story of the Pullman Car.* 1917. Reprint, Chicago: A. C. McClurg & Co., 1974.

Hutchinson, Frances Kinsley. *Our Country Life.* Chicago: A. C. McClurg, 1912.

Hutchinson, William T. *Cyrus Hall McCormick.* 2 vols. New York: Century Co., 1930 & 1935.

Hyde, James N. *Early Medical Chicago.* Chicago: Fergus Printing Co., 1879.

Ickes, Harold. *The Autobiography of a Curmudgeon.* New York: Reynal and Hitchcock, 1943.

Illinois. Bureau of Labor Statistics. *Biennial Reports.* 1884–92.

Illinois. Office of Inspector of Factories and Workshops. *Annual Report of the Factory Inspectors of Illinois.* Vol. 3. Chicago: 1895.

Industrial Chicago. 6 vols. Chicago: Goodspeed, 1891–94.

Jackson, Kenneth T. *Crabgrass Frontier: The Suburbanization of the United States.* New York: Oxford Univ. Press, 1985.

Jacobs, Jane. *The Economy of Cities.* 1969. Reprint, New York: Vintage, 1970.

Jaher, Frederick Cople. *The Urban Establishment: Upper Strata in Boston, New York, Charleston, Chicago, and Los Angeles.* Urbana: Univ. of Illinois Press, 1982.

James, Henry. *A Small Boy and Others.* New York: Charles Scribner's Sons, 1913.

Jenney, William Le Baron, and Sanford E. Loring. *Principles and Practice of Architecture.* Chicago: Cobb, Pritchard & Co., 1869.

Johannsen, Robert W. *Stephen A. Douglas.* New York: Oxford Univ. Press, 1973.

Johnson, Claudius O. *Carter Henry Harrison I: Political Leader.* Chicago: Univ. of Chicago Press, 1928.

Johnson, James D. *A Century of Chicago Streetcars 1858–1958: A Pictorial History of the World's Largest Street Railway.* Wheaton, Ill.: Traction Orange Co., 1964.

Johnson, Rossiter, ed. *A History of the World's Columbian Exposition.* 4 vols. New York: D. Appleton, 1897.

Jones, Howard Mumford. *Ideas in America.* Cambridge, Mass.: Harvard Univ. Press, 1944.

Jones, Mary Harris. *The Autobiography of Mother Jones.* Chicago: C. H. Kerr, 1925. Reprint, 1974.

Kantowicz, Edward R. *Polish-American Politics in Chicago, 1888–1940.* Chicago: Univ. of Chicago Press, 1975.

Kaplan, Justin. *Lincoln Steffens: A Biography.* New York: Simon & Schuster, 1974.

Kappler, Charles J. *Indian Affairs: Laws and Treaties.* 2 vols. Washington, D.C.: Government Printing Office, 1904.

Kasson, John F. *Amusing the Million: Coney Island at the Turn of the Century.* New York: Hill & Wang, 1978.

———. *Rudeness and Civility: Manners in Nineteenth-Century Urban America.* New York: Hill & Wang, 1990.

Katz, Donald R. *The Big Store: Inside the Crisis and Revolution at Sears.* New York: Viking Press, 1987.

Kaufman, Mervyn. *Father of Skyscrapers: A Biography of Louis Sullivan.* Boston: Little, Brown, 1969.

Keating, Ann Durkin. *Building Chicago: Suburban Developers and the Creation of a Divided Metropolis.* Columbus: Ohio State Univ. Press, 1988.

Keating, William H. *Narrative of an Expedition to the Source of St. Peter's River . . . 1823 . . . Under the Command of Stephen Long, U.S.T.E.; Com-*

piled from the Notes of Major Long, Messrs. Say, Keating and Calhoun. 2 vols. Philadelphia, 1824.

Keil, Hartmut, ed. *German Workers' Culture in the United States, 1850 to 1920.* Washington, D.C.: Smithsonian Institution Press, 1988.

Keil, Hartmut, and John B. Jentz, eds. *German Workers in Chicago: A Documentary History of Working-Class Culture from 1850 to World War I.* Urbana: Univ. of Illinois Press, 1988.

Kelley, Florence. *First Report of the Factory Inspectors of Illinois on Small-Pox in the Tenement House Sweatshops of Chicago.* Springfield, Ill.: H. W. Rokker, State Printer & Binder, 1894.

———. *Notes of Sixty Years: The Autobiography of Florence Kelley.* Ed. Kathryn Kish Sklar, Chicago: C. H. Kerr, 1986.

Kellogg, Louise Phelps. *The French Régime in Wisconsin and the Northwest.* 1925. Reprint, New York: Cooper Square Publishers, 1968.

———. ed. *Early Narratives of the Northwest, 1634–1699.* New York: Charles Scribner's Sons, 1917.

Kelly, Fred C. *George Ade: Warmhearted Satirist.* Indianapolis: Bobbs-Merrill Co., 1947.

Kendall, John. *American Memories: Recollections of a Hurried Run Through the United States During the Late Spring of 1896.* Nottingham, Eng.: W. Burrows, 1896.

Kennedy, John C., et al. *Wages and Family Budgets in the Chicago Stockyards District.* Chicago: Univ. of Chicago Press, 1914.

Kent, Elizabeth T. *William Kent, Independent: A Biography.* n.p., 1950.

Kimball, Nell. *Nell Kimball: Her Life as an American Madame.* New York: Macmillan, 1970.

King, Hoyt. *Citizen Cole of Chicago.* Chicago: Horder's, 1931.

Kinzie, Juliette A. *Mark Logan, the Bourgeois.* Philadelphia: Lippincott, 1887.

Kinzie, Mrs. John H. *Wau-Bun, The "Early Day" in the North-West.* 1856. Reprint: ed. Louise Phelps Kellogg. Chicago: Lakeside Press, 1948.

Kipling, Rudyard. *American Notes: Rudyard Kipling's West.* Ed. Arrell Morgan Gibson. Norman: Univ. of Oklahoma Press, 1981.

Kirkland, Caroline, ed. *Chicago Yesterdays: A Sheaf of Reminiscences.* Chicago: Daughaday & Co., 1919.

Kirkland, Joseph. *The Story of Chicago.* 2 vols. Chicago: Dibble Publishing Co., 1892–94.

Kogan, Herman, and Robert Cromie. *The Great Fire: Chicago, 1871.* New York: Putnam, 1971.

Kostof, Spiro. *The City Assembled: The Elements of Urban Form Through History.* Boston: Bulfinch Press, 1992.

———. *The City Shaped: Urban Patterns and Meanings Through History.* Boston: Little, Brown, 1991.

Lamb, Martha J. *Spicy: A Novel.* New York: D. Appleton, 1873.

Landau, Sarah Bradford. *P. B. Wight: Architect, Contractor, and Critic, 1838–1925.* Chicago: The Art Institute of Chicago, 1981.

Larson, George A., and Jay Pridmore. *Chicago Architecture and Design.* New York: H. N. Abrams, 1993.

Lasch, Christopher, ed. *The Social Thought of Jane Addams.* New York: Bobbs-Merrill, 1965.

Latrobe, Charles J. *The Rambler in North America.* 2 vols. London: R. B. Seeley & W. Burnside, 1836.

Leach, Josiah G. *Chronicles of the Yerkes Family with Notes on the Leech & Rutter Families.* Philadelphia: J. B. Lippincott, 1904.

Leach, William. *Land of Desire: Merchants, Power, and the Rise of a New American Culture.* New York: Pantheon Books. 1993.

Leavitt, Fred, and Nancy Miller. *Pullman: Portrait of a Landmark Community.* Chicago: Historic Pullman Foundation, 1981.

Leech, Harper, and John Charles Carroll. *Armour and His Times.* New York: D. Appleton-Century, 1938.

Leng, John. *America in 1876.* Dundee, Scotland: Dundee Advertiser Office, 1877.

Levine, Peter. *A. G. Spalding and the Rise of Baseball: The Promise of American Sport.* New York: Oxford Univ. Press, 1986.

Levine, Lawrence W. *Highbrow/Lowbrow: The Emergence of Cultural Hierarchy in America.* Cambridge, Mass.: Harvard Univ. Press, 1988.

Lewis, Lloyd. *John S. Wright: Prophet of the Prairies.* Chicago: Prairie Farmer, 1941.

Lewis, Lloyd, and Henry Justin Smith. *Chicago: The History of Its Reputation.* New York: Harcourt, Brace & Co., 1929.

Lewis, Sinclair. *Ann Vickers.* New York: P. F. Collier & Son, 1933.

————. *Babbitt.* 1922. Reprint, New York: New American Library, 1980.

Leyendecker, Liston Edgington. *Palace Car Prince: A Biography of George Mortimer Pullman.* Niwot: Univ. Press of Colorado, 1992.

Liebling, A. J. *Chicago: The Second City.* New York: Knopf, 1952.

Lindberg, Richard C. *To Serve and Collect: Chicago Politics and Police Corruption from the Lager Beer Riot to the Summerdale Scandal.* New York: Praeger, 1991.

Lindsey, Almont. *The Pullman Strike: The Story of a Unique Experiment and of a Great Labor Upheaval.* Chicago: Univ. of Chicago Press, 1942.

Lingeman, Richard R. *Theodore Dreiser: An American Journey, 1908–1945.* New York: Putnam, 1990.

————. *Theodore Dreiser: At the Gates of the City, 1871–1907.* New York: Putnam, 1986.

Linn, James Weber. *Jane Addams: A Biography.* New York: Appleton-Century Co., Inc., 1935.

Lissak, Rivka Shpak. *Pluralism and Progressives: Hull-House and the New Immigrants, 1890–1919.* Chicago: Univ. of Chicago Press, 1989.

Livesay, Harold C. *Samuel Gompers and Organized Labor in America.* Boston: Little, Brown, 1978.

Lockwood, David. *The Blackcoated Worker: A Study in Class Consciousness.* London: Allen & Unwin, 1958.

Loesch, Frank J. *Personal Experiences During the Chicago Fire, 1871.* Chicago, 1925.

Lovall, Odd S. *A Century of Urban Life: The Norwegians in Chicago Before 1930.* [Northfield, Minn.]: Norwegian-American Historical Association; distributed by Univ. of Illinois Press, Champaign, Ill., 1988.

Lovett, Robert Morss. *All Our Years: The Autobiography of Robert Morss Lovett.* New York: Viking Press, 1948.

Lowe, David. *Lost Chicago.* Boston: Houghton Mifflin, 1975. Reprint, New York: American Legacy Press, 1985.

Lurie, Jonathan. *The Chicago Board of Trade, 1859–1905: The Dynamics of Self Regulation.* Urbana: Univ. of Illinois Press, 1979.

Luzerne, Frank. *The Lost City! Drama of the Fire-Fiend! Or, Chicago, As It Was, and As It Is! And Its Glorious Future!* New York: Wells & Co., 1872.

Maclean, Norman. *Young Men and Fire: A True Story of the Mann Gulch Fire.* Chicago: Univ. of Chicago Press, 1992.

Mahoney, Tom, and Leonard Sloane. *The Great Merchants: America's Foremost Retail Institutions and the People Who Made Them Great.* New York: Harper & Row, 1966.

Mailer, Norman. *Miami and the Siege of Chicago.* New York: World Pub. Co., 1968.

Manson, Grant. *Frank Lloyd Wright to 1900: The First Golden Age.* New York: Van Nostrand Reinhold, 1958.

Margry, Pierre, ed. *Découvertes et établissments des Français dans . . . l'Amerique septentrionelle, 1614–1754.* 3 vols. Paris: D. Jouaust, 1876–1886.

Martin, Albro. *Railroads Triumphant.* New York: Oxford Univ. Press, 1992.

Martin, Jay. *Harvests of Change: American Literature, 1865–1914.* Englewood Cliffs, N.J.: Prentice-Hall, 1967.

Martineau, Harriet. *Society in America.* 3 vols. London: Saunders & Otley, 1837.

Mason, Edward G., ed. *Early Chicago and Illinois.* Chicago: Fergus Printing Co., 1890.

Masters, Edgar Lee. *The Tale of Chicago.* New York: G. P. Putnam's Sons, 1933.

Mayer, Harold M. *Chicago: City of Decisions.* Chicago: Geographic Society of Chicago, 1955.

———. *The Railway Pattern of Metropolitan Chicago.* Chicago: University of Chicago Department of Geography, 1943.

Mayer, Harold M., and Richard C. Wade. *Chicago: Growth of a Metropolis.* Chicago: Univ. of Chicago Press, 1969.

McCaffrey, Lawrence J. *The Irish Diaspora in America.* Bloomington: Indiana Univ. Press, 1976.

——— et al. *The Irish in Chicago.* Urbana: Univ. of Illinois Press, 1987.

McCarthy, Kathleen D. *Noblesse Oblige: Cultural Philanthropy in Chicago, 1849–1929.* Chicago: Univ. of Chicago Press, 1982.

———. *Women's Culture: American Philanthropy and Art, 1830–1930.* Chicago: Univ. of Chicago Press, 1991.

McCormick, Cyrus. *The Century of the Reaper.* Boston: Houghton Mifflin, 1931.

McCormick's Reaper's Centennial Source Material. Chicago: International Harvester, [1931].

McFeely, William S. *Frederick Douglass.* New York: Simon & Schuster, 1992.

McGovern, John. *Daniel Trentworthy: A Tale of the Great Fire of Chicago.* Chicago: Rand McNally, 1889.

McIlvaine, Mabel, ed. *Reminiscences of Early Chicago.* Chicago: Lakeside Press, 1912.

———. *Reminiscences of Chicago During the Great Fire.* Chicago: Lakeside Press, 1915.

McNaught, Kenneth. *History of Canada.* New York: Praeger, 1970.

Meagher, Timothy J., ed. *From Paddy to Studs: Irish-American Communities in the Turn of the Century Era, 1880–1920.* Westport, Conn.: Greenwood Press, 1986.

Meakin, Burgett. *Model Factories and Villages: Ideal Conditions of Labour and Housing.* Philadelphia: G. W. Jacobs, 1905.

Meeker, Arthur. *Chicago, With Love: A Polite and Personal History.* New York: Knopf, 1955.

Meier, August. *Negro Thought in America, 1880–1915, Racial Ideologies in the Age of Booker T. Washington.* Ann Arbor: Univ. of Michigan Press, 1968.

Meites, Hyman L., ed. *History of the Jews of Chicago.* 1924. Reprint, Chicago: Chicago Jewish Historical Society; Wellington Pub., 1990.

Mencken, August. *The Railroad Passenger Car.* Baltimore, Md.: Johns Hopkins Univ. Press, 1957.

Menocal, Narciso G. *Architecture as Nature: The Transcendentalist Idea of Louis Sullivan.* Madison: Univ. of Wisconsin Press, 1981.

Merriam, Charles E. *Chicago: A More Intimate View of Urban Politics.* New York: Macmillan, 1929.

Meyerowitz, Joanne J. *Women Adrift: Independent Wage Earners in Chicago, 1880–1930.* Chicago: Univ. of Chicago Press, 1988.

Miller, Kerby A. *Emigrants and Exiles: Ireland and the Irish Exodus to North America.* New York: Oxford Univ. Press, 1985.

Miller, Ross. *American Apocalypse: The Great Fire and the Myth of Chicago.* Chicago: Univ. of Chicago Press, 1990.

Miller, William, ed. *Men in Business.* Cambridge, Mass.: Harvard Univ. Press, 1952.

Misa, Thomas J. *A Nation of Steel: The Making of Modern America, 1865–1925.* Baltimore: Johns Hopkins Univ. Press, 1995.

Moers, Ellen. *Two Dreisers.* New York: Viking Press, 1969.

Monroe, Harriet. *John Wellborn Root: A Study of his Life and Work.* Boston: Houghton Mifflin & Co., 1896.

————. *A Poet's Life: Seventy Years in a Changing World.* New York: Macmillan, 1938.

Montgomery, David. *Workers' Control in America: Studies in the History of Work, Technology, and Labor Struggles.* New York: Cambridge Univ. Press, 1979.

Moore, Charles. *Daniel H. Burnham, Architect, Planner of Cities.* 2 vols. Boston: Houghton Mifflin, 1921.

————. *The Life and Times of Charles Follen McKim.* Boston: Houghton Mifflin, 1929.

Morrison, Hugh. *Louis Sullivan: Prophet of Modern Architecture.* New York: W. W. Norton & Co., 1935.

Moses, John, and Joseph Kirkland, eds. *The History of Chicago.* 2 vols. Chicago: Munsell & Co., 1895.

Most, Johann. *Beast and Monster: The Beast of Property and the Social Monster: Two Essays on Anarchism.* Tucson, Ariz.: The Match!, 1973.

Mr. Dooley: In the Hearts of his Countrymen, the Chicago Journal, 1898. 1899. Reprint, New York: Greenwood Press, 1969.

Mudgett, Herman W. [Holmes, H. H.]. *Holmes' Own Story.* Philadelphia: Burk & McFetridge Co., 1895.

Muirhead, James Fullarton. *America, the Land of Contrasts.* New York: J. Lane, 1898.

Mumford, Lewis. *The City in History: Its Origins, Its Transformations, and Its Prospects.* New York: Harcourt, Brace & World, 1961.

————. *Sticks and Stones: A Study of American Architecture and Civilization.* New York: Boni & Liveright, 1924.

————. *The Brown Decades: A Study of the Arts in America, 1865–1895.* 1931. Reprint, New York: Dover, 1971.

Nelli, Humbert S. *Italians in Chicago, 1880–1930; A Study in Ethnic Mobility.* New York: Oxford Univ. Press, 1970.

Nelson, Bruce C. *Beyond the Martyrs: A Social History of Chicago's Anarchists, 1870–1900.* New Brunswick, N.J.: Rutgers Univ. Press, 1988.

The Newberry Library: Trustees, Officers, and Committees By-Laws. 1894.

Newell, Barbara Warne. *Chicago and the Labor Movement.* Urbana: Univ. of Illinois Press, 1961.

Neyhart, Louise A. *Giant of the Yards.* Boston: Houghton Mifflin, 1952.

Nimmo, Joseph, Jr. *Report on the Internal Commerce of the United States.* Washington, D.C.: United States Treasury Department, Bureau of Statistics, 1877–81.

Niven, Penelope. *Carl Sandburg, A Biography.* New York: Charles Scribner's Sons, 1991.

Nord, David Paul. *Newspapers and New Politics: Midwestern Municipal Reform, 1890–1900.* Ann Arbor, Mich.: UMI Research Press, 1981.

Norris, Frank. *The Pit: A Story of Chicago.* 1903. Reprint, Garden City, N.Y.: Doubleday, Doran, 1928.

Nursey, Walter. *The Legend and Legacy of Père Marquette*. Chicago: Marquette Publishing Co., 1897.

Nye, David E. *Electrifying America: Social Meanings of a New Technology, 1880–1940*. Cambridge, Mass.: MIT Press, 1990.

Olmsted, Frederick Law. *A Journey Through Texas: Or, A Saddle-Trip on the Southwestern Frontier*. 1857. Reprint, Austin: Univ. of Texas Press, 1978.

———. *Slavery and the South; 1852–1857*. Vol. 2 of *The Papers of Frederick Law Olmsted*. Ed. Charles E. Beveridge, Charles Capen McLaughlin, and David Schuyler. Baltimore, Md.: Johns Hopkins Univ. Press, 1981.

Olmsted, Vaux, and Company. *Preliminary Report Upon the Proposed Suburban Village at Riverside, Near Chicago*. New York: Sutton, Bowne, 1868.

———. *Report Accompanying Plan for Laying Out the South Park*. Chicago: Evening Journal, Book & Job Printing House, 1871.

Olson, Ernest W. *History of the Swedes in Illinois*. Chicago: Engberg-Holmberg Pub. Co., 1908.

Opening New Worlds: Jane Addams's Hull-House. Chicago: Univ. of Illinois at Chicago, 1989.

Otis, Philo Adams. *The Chicago Symphony Orchestra: Its Organization, Growth, and Development, 1891–1924*. 1924. Reprint, Freeport, N.Y.: Books for Libraries Press, 1972.

Otis Elevator Company. *The First One Hundred Years*. New York: The Company, 1953.

Ozanne, Robert. *A Century of Labor-Management Relations at McCormick and International Harvester*. Madison, Wis.: Univ. of Wisconsin Press, 1967.

Pacyga, Dominic A. *Polish Immigrants and Industrial Chicago: Workers on the South Side, 1880–1922*. Columbus: Ohio State Univ. Press, 1991.

Papers in Illinois History and Transactions for the Year 1937. Springfield: Illinois State Historical Society, 1938.

Papers in Illinois History and Transactions for the Year 1940. Springfield: Illinois State Historical Society, 1941.

Parkman, Francis. *The Jesuits of North America in the Seventeenth Century*. Boston: Little, Brown & Co., 1893.

———. *La Salle and the Discovery of the West*. Boston: Little, Brown & Co., 1891, 1893 edition.

Parot, Joseph John. *Polish Catholics in Chicago, 1850–1920*. DeKalb: Northern Illinois Univ. Press, 1981.

Parsons, Lucy E., ed. *Life of Albert R. Parsons*. Chicago: L. E. Parsons, 1903.

Patton, Phil. *Made in U.S.A.: The Secret Histories of the Things That Made America*. New York: Grove Weidenfeld, 1992.

Paul, Sherman. *Louis Sullivan: An Architect in American Thought*. Englewood Cliffs, N.J.: Prentice-Hall, 1962.

Payne, Will. *Mr. Salt: A Novel*. New York: Houghton, Mifflin Co., The Riverside Press, 1903.

Peattie, Elia W. *The Precipice*. 1914. Reprint, Urbana: Univ. of Illinois Press, 1989.

Peavy, Linda, and Ursula Smith. *Women Who Changed Things*. New York: Charles Scribner's Sons, 1983.

Peterson, Virgil W. *Barbarians in our Midst: A History of Chicago Crime and Politics*. Boston: Little, Brown & Co., 1952.

Peyton, John Lewis. *Over the Alleghanies and Across the Prairies: Personal Recollections of the Far West*, London: Simpkin Marshall, 1869.

Pfeiffer, Bruce Brooks, ed. *Frank Lloyd Wright Collected Writings*. 5 vols. New York: Rizzoli, Frank Lloyd Wright Foundation, 1992–95.

Philpott, Thomas Lee. *The Slum and the Ghetto: Neighborhood Deterioration and*

Middle-Class Reform, Chicago, 1890–1930. New York: Oxford Univ. Press, 1978.

Pierce, Bessie Louise. *A History of Chicago.* 3 vols. New York: Knopf, 1937–1957.

————, ed. *As Others See Chicago: Impressions of Visitors, 1673–1933.* Chicago: Univ. of Chicago Press, 1933.

Platt, Harold L. *The Electric City: Energy and the Growth of the Chicago Area, 1880–1930.* Chicago: Univ. of Chicago Press, 1991.

Poggi, Edith M. *The Prairie Province of Illinois: A Study of Human Adjustment to Natural Environment.* Urbana: Univ. of Illinois Press, 1934.

Polacheck, Hilda Satt. *I Came a Stranger: The Story of a Hull-House Girl.* Ed. Dena J. Polacheck Epstein. Urbana: Univ. of Illinois Press, 1989.

Poole, Ernest. *The Bridge: My Own Story.* New York: Macmillan, 1940.

————. *Giants Gone: Men Who Made Chicago.* New York: McGraw-Hill, 1943.

Poole, William Frederick. *The Construction of Library Buildings.* Washington, D.C.: Government Printing Office, 1881.

Porter, Glenn, and Harold C. Livesay. *Merchants and Manufacturers: Studies in the Changing Structure of Nineteenth-Century Marketing.* Baltimore, Md.: Johns Hopkins Univ. Press, 1971.

Pred, Allan R. *Urban Growth and City-Systems in the United States, 1840–1860.* Cambridge, Mass.: Harvard Univ. Press, 1980.

Putnam, James William. *The Illinois and Michigan Canal A Study in Economic History.* Chicago: Univ. of Chicago Press, 1918.

Pyne, Stephen J. *Fire in America: A Cultural History of Wildland and Rural Fire.* Princeton, N.J.: Princeton Univ. Press, 1988.

Quaife, Milo M. *Checagou: From Indian Wigwam to Modern City, 1673–1835.* Chicago: Univ. of Chicago Press, 1933.

————. *Chicago and the Old Northwest.* Chicago: Univ. of Chicago Press, 1913.

————. *Pictures of Illinois One Hundred Years Ago.* Chicago: R. R. Donnelley, 1918.

————, ed. *The Development of Chicago, 1678–1914, Shown in a Series of Contemporary Narratives.* Chicago: Caxton Club, 1916.

Quinn, John Philip. *Fools of Fortune.* Chicago: Anti-Gambling Association, 1892.

Quondam [Charles M. Stevens]. *The Adventures of Uncle Jeremiah and Family at the Great Fair: Their Observations and Triumphs.* Chicago: Laird & Lee, 1893.

Ralph, Julian. *Harper's Chicago and the World's Fair.* New York: Harper & Bros., 1893.

————. *Our Great West.* New York: Harper & Bros., 1893.

Rand McNally & Co.'s A Week at the Fair. Chicago: Rand McNally, 1893.

Rand McNally & Co.'s Pictoral Chicago. Chicago: Rand McNally, 1896.

Randall, Frank A. *History of the Development of Building Construction in Chicago.* Urbana: Univ. of Illinois Press, 1949.

Ranney, Victoria Post. *Olmsted in Chicago.* Chicago: R. R. Donnelley & Sons, 1972.

Rauch, John H. *Public Parks: Their Effects Upon the Moral, Physical and Sanitary Condition of the Inhabitants of Large Cities; with Special Reference to the City of Chicago.* Chicago: S. C. Griggs, 1869.

Rawlings, Isaac D., et al. *The Rise and Fall of Disease in Illinois.* 2 vols. Springfield, Ill.: Schnepp and Barnes, 1927.

Reckless, Walter. *Vice in Chicago.* 1933. Reprint, Montclair, N.J.: Patterson Smith, 1969.

Read, Opie. *I Remember.* New York: R. R. Smith, 1930.

Reade, Charles. *Put Yourself in His Place.* New York: Harper & Bros., 1870.

Reavis, L. U. *A Change of National Empire; or, Arguments in Favor of the Removal of the National Capital from Washington City to the Mississippi Valley.* St. Louis: J. F. Torrey, 1869.

Report of the South Park Commission to the Board of County Commissioners of Cook County, From Dec. 1st, 1872, to Dec. 1st, 1873.

Rex, Frederick. *The Mayors of Chicago from March 4, 1837 to April 13, 1933.* Chicago: Municipal Reference Library, 1934; reprint, 1985.

Ridgley, Douglas C. *The Geography of Illinois.* Chicago: Univ. of Chicago Press, 1921.

Riess, Steven A. *City Games: The Evolution of American Urban Society and the Rise of Sports.* Urbana: Univ. of Illinois Press, 1989.

Riis, Jacob. *How the Other Half Lives: Studies Among the Tenements of New York.* 1901. Reprint, New York: Dover, 1971.

Riley, Terence, ed. *Frank Lloyd Wright, Architect.* New York: Museum of Modern Art, 1994.

Riordan, William L., *Plunkitt of Tammany Hall: A Series of Very Plain Talks on Very Practical Politics.* Ed. Terrance J. McDonald. Boston: Bedford Books of St. Martin's Press, 1994.

Riverside Improvement Company, *Riverside in 1871. With a Description of its Improvements.* Chicago: D. & C. H. Blakely, Printers, 1871.

Roe, Edward Payson. *Barriers Burned Away.* New York: Dodd & Mead, 1872.

Roediger, Dave, and Franklin Rosemont, eds. *Haymarket Scrapbook.* Chicago: C. H. Kerr, 1986.

Root, John Wellborn. *The Meanings of Architecture: Buildings and Writings.* Ed. Donald Hoffmann. New York: Horizon Press, 1967.

Rosen, Christine M. *The Limits of Power: Great Fires and the Process of City Growth in America.* New York: Cambridge Univ. Press, 1986.

Rosen, Ruth. *The Lost Sisterhood: Prostitution in America, 1900–1918.* Baltimore, Md.: Johns Hopkins Univ. Press, 1982.

Rosenberg, Charles E. *The Cholera Years: The United States in 1832, 1849, and 1866.* Chicago: Univ. of Chicago Press, 1962.

Ross, Ishbel. *Silhouette in Diamonds: The Life of Mrs. Potter Palmer.* New York: Harper, 1960.

Rotella, Elyce J. *From Home to Office: U.S. Women at Work, 1870–1930.* Ann Arbor, Mich.: UMI Research Press, 1981.

Rozwenc, Edwin C., ed. *Ideology and Power in the Age of Jackson.* New York: Anchor Books, 1964.

Rules and Regulations of the Fire Department of the City of Chicago. 1867.

Russell, Charles Edward. *The American Orchestra and Theodore Thomas.* Garden City, New York: Doubleday, Page & Co., 1927.

————. *The Greatest Trust in the World.* New York: Ridgeway-Thayer, 1905.

————. *These Shifting Scenes.* New York: Houghton & Stoughton, 1914.

Russell, William H. *My Diary, North and South.* 2 vols. London: Bradbury & Evans, 1863.

Rydell, Robert W. *All the World's a Fair: Visions of Empire at American International Expositions, 1876–1916.* Chicago: Univ. of Chicago Press, 1984.

Rykwert, Joseph. *The Idea of a Town: The Anthropology of Urban Form in Rome, Italy, and the Ancient World.* Cambridge, Mass.: MIT Press, 1988.

Salisbury, Rollin D., and William C. Alden. *The Geography of Chicago and Its Environs.* Chicago: Rand McNally & Co. for the Geographic Society of Chicago, Bulletin no. 1, 1990.

Salvatore, Nick. *Eugene V. Debs: Citizen and Socialist.* Urbana: Univ. of Illinois Press, 1982.

Salzman, Jack, ed. *Prospects: An Annual of American Cultural Studies.* 14 vols. New York: Burt Franklin & Co.. 1975–89.

Sandburg, Carl. *Always the Young Strangers.* New York: Harcourt, Brace, 1953.
————. *Chicago Poems.* New York: Henry Holt, 1916.
————. *The Complete Poems of Carl Sandburg.* New York: Harcourt Brace Jovanovich, 1970.

Sauer, Carl O. *Geography of the Upper Illinois Valley and History of Development.* Urbana: Illinois State Geological Survey, 1916.

Sawislak, Karen. *Smoldering City: Chicagoans and the Great Fire, 1871–1874.* Chicago: Univ. of Chicago Press, 1995.

Schaack, Michael J. *Anarchy and Anarchists.* Chicago: F. J. Schulte, 1889.

Schabas, Ezra. *Theodore Thomas: America's Conductor and Builder of Orchestras, 1835–1905.* Urbana: Univ. of Illinois Press, 1989.

Schaff, Barbara C. *Mr. Dooley's Chicago.* Garden City, N.Y.: Anchor Press, 1977.

Schick, Louis. *Chicago and Its Environs: A Handbook for the Traveler.* Chicago: L. Schick, 1891.

Schivelbusch, Wolfgang. *The Railway Journey: Trains and Travel in the 19th Century.* New York: Urizen Books, 1979.

Schlereth, Thomas J. *Victorian America: Transformations in Everyday Life, 1876–1915.* New York: HarperCollins, 1991.

Schoolcraft, Henry Row. *Narrative Journal of Travels Through the Northwestern Regions of the United States . . . to the Sources of the Mississippi . . . in the Year 1820.* Albany: E & E Hosford, 1821.

Schuyler, David. *The New Urban Landscape: The Redefinition of City Form in Nineteenth-Century America.* Baltimore, Md.: Johns Hopkins Univ. Press, 1986.

Schuyler, Montgomery. *American Architecture and Other Writings.* Ed. William H. Jordy and Ralph Coe. 2 vols. Cambridge, Mass.: Harvard Univ. Press, 1961.

Scott, Estelle Hill. *Occupational Changes Among Negroes in Chicago.* [Chicago], 1939.

Scudder, Janet. *Modeling My Life.* New York: Harcourt, Brace, 1925.

Second Annual Report of West Chicago Park Commission for Year Ending 28 February, 1871. 1871.

Seeger, Eugene. *Chicago: The Wonder City.* Chicago: 1893.

Sennett, Richard. *The Conscience of the Eye: The Design and Social Life of Cities.* New York: Knopf, 1990.

————. *Families Against the City: Middle Class Homes of Industrial Chicago, 1872–1890.* 1970. Reprint, New York: Vintage Books, 1974.

————, ed. *Classic Essays on the Culture of Cities.* Englewood Cliffs, N.J.: Prentice-Hall, 1969.

Severin, Timothy. *Explorers of the Mississippi.* London: Routledge & K. Paul, 1967.

Sewell, Alfred L. *"The Great Calamity!": Scenes, Lessons and Incidents of the Great Fire.* Chicago: A. L. Sewell, 1871.

Seymour, Harold. *Baseball.* Vol. 1, *The Early Years.* New York: Oxford Univ. Press, 1960.

Shannon, William F. *The American Irish: A Political and Social Portrait.* New York: Macmillan, 1963.

Sharpe, May Churchill. *Chicago May: Her Story.* New York: Macaulay Co., 1928.

Shaw, Marian. *World's Fair Notes: A Woman Journalist Views Chicago's 1893 Columbian Exposition.* St. Paul: Pogo Press, 1992.

Sheahan, James W., and George P. Upton. *The Great Conflagration: Chicago: Its Past, Present, and Future.* Chicago: Union, 1872.

Shelford, Victor E. *The Ecology of North America.* Urbana: Univ. of Illinois Press, 1963.

Sheridan, Philip H. *Report to the Hon. W. W. Belknap, Chicago, December 20, 1871.* Chicago: 1871.

Shirreff, Patrick. *A Tour Through North America.* Edinburgh: Oliver & Boyd, 1835.

Shultz, Earle, and Walter Simmons. *Offices in the Sky.* Indianapolis: Bobbs-Merrill Co., 1959.

Simons, A. M. *Packingtown.* Chicago: C. H. Kerr, 1899.

Sinclair, Upton. *The Autobiography of Upton Sinclair.* New York: Harcourt, Brace & World, 1962.

———. *The Jungle.* 1906. Reprint, New York: Penguin, 1985.

Siry, Joseph. *Carson Pirie Scott: Louis Sullivan and the Chicago Department Store.* Chicago: Univ. of Chicago Press, 1988.

Sklar, Kathryn Kish. *Florence Kelley and the Nation's Work: Vol. 1, The Rise of Women's Political Culture, 1830–1900.* New Haven, Conn.: Yale Univ. Press, 1995.

Smith, Carl. *Chicago and the American Literary Imagination, 1880–1920.* Chicago: Univ. of Chicago Press, 1984.

———. *Urban Disorder and the Shape of Belief: The Great Chicago Fire, The Haymarket Bomb, and the Model Town of Pullman.* Chicago: Univ. of Chicago Press, 1995.

Smith, David. *H. G. Wells: Desperately Mortal: A Biography.* New Haven, Conn.: Yale Univ. Press, 1986.

Snider, Denton J. *World's Fair Studies.* Chicago: Sigma Publishing Co., 1895.

Sorge, Friedrich. *Friedrich A. Sorge's Labor Movement in the United States: a History of the American Working Class from Colonial Times to 1890.* Trans. Brewster Chamberlin and ed. Philip Foner. Westport, Conn.: Greenwood Press, 1977.

Spalding, Albert G. *America's National Game.* 1911. Reprint, San Francisco: Halo Books, 1991.

Spear, Allan H. *Black Chicago: The Making of a Negro Ghetto, 1890–1920.* Chicago: Univ. of Chicago Press, 1967.

Spies, August. *August Spies' Auto-Biography: His Speech in Court and General Notes.* Chicago: Nina Van Zandt, 1887.

The Sporting and Club House Directory, Chicago, Containing a Full and Complete List of All First Class Club and Sporting Houses. Chicago: Ross & St. Clair, 1889.

Sprague, Paul, ed. *The Drawings of Louis Sullivan.* Princeton, N.J.: Princeton Univ. Press, 1979.

Squier, Susan Merrill, ed. *Women Writers and the City: Essays in Feminist Literary Criticism.* Knoxville: Univ. of Tennessee Press, 1984.

Stagg, Amos Alonzo. *Touchdown!* New York: Longmans, Green, 1927.

Stamper, John W. *Chicago's North Mighican Avenue: Planning and Development.* Chicago: Univ. of Chicago Press, 1991.

Starrett, Col. W. A. *Skyscrapers and the Men Who Build Them.* New York: Charles Scribner's Sons, 1928.

Stead, William T. *Chicago To-Day: The Labour War in America.* 1894. Reprint, New York: Arno Press, 1969.

———. *If Christ Came to Chicago!* 1894. Reprint, Chicago: Chicago Historical Bookworks, 1990.

Steevens, George W. *The Land of the Dollar.* New York: Dodd, Mead, 1897.

Steffens, Lincoln. *The Autobiography of Lincoln Steffens.* New York: Harcourt, Brace, 1931.

———. *The Shame of the Cities.* 1904. Reprint, New York: Hill & Wang, 1967.

Stenographic Efficiency Bureau, Making the Body an Efficient Machine. 1916.

Stilgoe, John R. *Borderland: Origins of the American Suburb, 1820–1939.* New Haven, Conn.: Yale Univ. Press, 1988.

———. *Metropolitan Corridor: Railroads and the American Scene.* New Haven, Conn.: Yale Univ. Press, 1983.

Stirling, James. *Letters from the Slave States.* London: John W. Parker & Son, 1857.

Stoddard, Francis Hovey. *The Life and Letters of Charles Butler.* New York: Charles Scribner's Sons, 1903.

Stone, Melville E. *Fifty Years a Journalist.* Garden City, N.Y.: Doubleday, Page & Co., 1921.

Storr, Richard J. *Harper's University: The Beginnings; A History of the University of Chicago.* Chicago: Univ. of Chicago Press, 1966.

Stover, John F. *History of the Illinois Central Railroad.* New York: Macmillan, 1975.

Street, Julian. *Abroad at Home: American Ramblings, Observations, and Adventures of Julian Street, with Pictorial Sidelights.* Garden City, N.Y.: Garden City Publishing Co., 1921.

Strong, Josiah. *Our Country: Its Possible Future and Its Present Crisis.* Ed. Jurgen Herbst. 1891. Reprint, Cambridge, Mass.: Harvard Univ. Press, 1963.

Sullivan, Louis H. *The Autobiography of an Idea.* 1924. Reprint, New York: Dover Publications, 1956.

———. *Democracy: A Man-Search!* With an introduction by Elaine Hedges. Detroit: Wayne State Univ. Press, 1961.

———. *Kindergarten Chats and Other Writings.* Ed. Isabella Athey. New York: Wittenborn Art Books, 1947.

———. *A System of Architectural Ornament According With a Philosophy of Man's Powers.* New York: Press of the American Institute of Architects, Inc., 1924.

Summerson, John. *Heavenly Mansions.* New York: Charles Scribner's Sons, 1950.

The Sunset Club: Yearbook. Chicago: Sunset Club, 1892.

Sutherland, Douglas. *Fifty Years on the Civic Front: A History of the Civic Federation's Dynamic Activities.* Chicago: Civic Federation, 1943.

Swift, Helen. *My Father and My Mother.* Chicago: Lakeside Press, 1937.

Swift, Louis, with Arthur Van Vlissingen, Jr. *The Yankee of the Yards: The Biography of Gustavus Franklin Swift.* New York: A. W. Shaw Co., 1927.

Szarkowski, John. *The Idea of Louis Sullivan.* Minneapolis: Univ. of Minnesota Press, 1956.

Talbot, Marion. *More than Lore: Reminiscences of Marion Talbot, Dean of Women, the University of Chicago, 1892–1925.* Chicago: Univ. of Chicago Press, 1936.

Tallmadge, Thomas E. *Architecture in Old Chicago.* Chicago: Univ. of Chicago Press, 1941.

———. *The Story of Architecture in America.* New York: W. W. Norton, 1927.

Tally-Ho! Coaching Through Chicago's Parks and Boulevards. Chicago: J. P. Craig, 1888.

Tarr, Joel A. *A Study in Boss Politics: William Lorimer of Chicago.* Urbana: Univ. of Illinois Press, 1971.

Taylor, Charles H., ed. *History of the Board of Trade of the City of Chicago.* 3 vols. Chicago: Robert O. Law, 1917.

Taylor, George R., ed. *The Turner Thesis Concerning the Role of the Frontier in American History.* Boston: Heath, 1949.

Taylor, Graham. *Pioneering on Social Frontiers.* Chicago: Univ. of Chicago Press, 1930.

———. *Satellite Cities: A Study of Industrial Suburbs.* 1915. Reprint, New York: Arno Press. 1970.

Teaford, Jon C. *Cities of the Heartland: The Rise and Fall of the Industrial Midwest.* Indianapolis: Indiana Univ. Press, 1993.

————. *The Unheralded Triumph: City Government in America, 1870–1900.* Baltimore, Md.: Johns Hopkins Univ. Press, 1984.

Tebbel, John. *The Marshall Fields: A Study in Wealth.* New York: E. P. Dutton, 1947.

Terkel, Studs. *Chicago.* New York: Pantheon Books, 1985.

Thomas, David Hearst, ed. *Columbian Consequences. Vol. 3.* Washington, D.C.: Smithsonian Institution Press, 1991.

Thomas, John L. *Alternative America: Henry George, Edward Bellamy, Henry Demarest Lloyd and the Adversary Tradition.* Cambridge, Mass.: Harvard Univ. Press, 1983.

Thomas, Rose Fay. *Memoirs of Theodore Thomas.* New York: Moffat, Yard, 1911.

Thomas, Theodore. *Theodore Thomas: A Musical Autobiography. Vol. 1.* Ed. George P. Upton. 1905. Reprint, New York: DeCapo Press, 1964.

Thomas, William I., and Florian Znaniecki. *The Polish Peasant in Europe and America.* 1900. Ed. Eli Zaretsky. Urbana: Univ. of Illinois Press, 1984 edition.

Thomas, William L., ed. *Man's Role in Changing the Face of the Earth.* Chicago: Univ. of Chicago Press, 1956.

Thompson, Mildred I. *Ida B. Wells-Barnett: An Exploratory Study of an American Black Woman, 1893–1930.* Brooklyn: Carlson Pub., 1990.

Thomson, Betty Flanders. *The Shaping of America's Heartland: The Landscape of the Middle West.* Boston: Houghton Mifflin, 1977.

Three American Expositions, Arguments before the Quadri-Centennial Committee of the United States Senate in Support of Bills Nos. 1839 and 1136 . . . Washington, D.C.: GPO, 1890.

Thwaites, Reuben Gold. *Father Marquette.* New York: D. Appleton & Co., 1902.

————. *The Jesuit Relations and Allied Documents: Travels and Explorations of the Jesuit Missionaries in New France, 1610–1791.* 73 vols. Cleveland: Burrows Bros. Co., 1896–1901.

Tocqueville, Alexis de. *Journeys to England and Ireland.* Ed. J. P. Mayer. Garden City, N.Y.: Anchor Books, 1968.

Toker, Franklin. *Pittsburgh, An Urban Portrait.* University Park: Pennsylvania State Univ. Press, 1986.

Towner, Lawrence W. *An Uncommon Collection of Uncommon Collections: The Newberry Library.* Chicago: Newberry Library, 1985.

Trachtenberg, Alan. *The Incorporation of America: Culture and Society in the Gilded Age.* New York: Hill and Wang, 1982.

Treaty with the Chippewa, Ottawa, and Potawatomi Indians, 1833. In General Records of the U.S. Government Record Group 11, Ratified Indian Treaties (M668). Washington, D.C., National Archives.

Trollope, Anthony. *North America.* 1862. Ed. Donald Smalley and Bradford Allen Booth. New York: Knopf, 1951.

Trommler, Frank, and Joseph McVeigh, eds. *America and the Germans: An Assessment of a Three-Hundred-Year History. Vol. 1: Immigration, Language, Ethnicity.* Philadelphia: Univ. of Pennsylvania Press, 1985.

Turak, Theodore. *William Le Baron Jenney: A Pioneer of Modern Architecture.* Ann Arbor, Mich.: UMI Research Press, 1986.

Twain, Mark. *Life on the Mississippi.* 1883. Reprint, New York: Airmont Publishing Co., 1965.

Twombly, Robert. *Louis Sullivan: His Life and Work.* 1986. Reprint, Chicago: Univ. of Chicago Press, 1987.

————, ed. *Louis Sullivan: The Public Papers.* Chicago: Univ. of Chicago Press, 1988.

Twyman, Robert W. *History of Marshall Field & Co., 1852–1906*. Philadelphia: Univ. of Pennsylvania Press, 1954.

United States. Department of Commerce and Labor. Office of the Secretary. *Arrest and Deportation of Prostitutes and Procurers of Prostitutes*. Department Circular #156. 1907.

United States. Department of Labor. *Bulletin*. 1919.

―――. *Working Women in Large Cities*. Washington, D.C., 1889.

United States. Federal Trade Commission. *Report on the Meat-Packing Industry*. Washington, D.C.: GPO, 1919.

United States. Immigration Commission. *Slaughtering and Meat Packing*. Vol. 13 of *Immigrants in Industries*. Washington, D.C.: GPO, 1911.

United States. Strike Commission. 1894. *Report on the Chicago Strike of June–July, 1894*. Washington, D.C.: GPO, 1895.

United States Senate. Select Committee on the Transportation and Sale of Meat Products. *Testimony Taken by the Select Committee of the United States Senate on the Transportation and Sale of Meat Products*. Washington, D.C.: GPO, 1889.

Unrivaled Chicago; Containing an Historical Narrative of the Great City's Development, and Descriptions of Points of Interest. Chicago: Rand McNally, 1896.

Upson, Theodore F. *With Sherman to the Sea*. Ed. O. O. Winther. Bloomington: Indiana Univ. Press, 1958.

Vasari, Giorgio. *Lives of the Artists*. Middlesex, England: Penguin Books, 1965.

Veblen, Thorstein. *The Higher Learning in America: A Memorandum on the Conduct of Universities by Business Men*. 1918. Reprint, New York: Hill & Wang, 1962.

―――. *The Theory of the Leisure Class*. 1899. Reprint, New York: New American Library, 1953.

Vice Commission of Chicago. *The Social Evil in Chicago: A Study of Existing Conditions with Recommendations*. Chicago: Gunthorp-Warren Printing Co., 1911.

Vinci, John. *The Art Institute of Chicago: The Stock Exchange Trading Room*. Chicago: The Art Institute, 1977.

Visit to the States. A Reprint of Letters from the Special Correspondent of the Times. London: G. E. Wright, 1887.

von Thünen, Johann Heinrich. *Von Thünen's Isolated State*. Trans. Carla M. Wartenberg and ed. Peter Hall. New York: Pergamon Press, 1966.

[Vynne, Harold Richard]. *Chicago by Day and Night: The Pleasure Seekers Guide to the Paris of America*. Chicago: Thomson & Zimmerman, 1892.

Wade, Louise C. *Chicago's Pride: The Stockyards, Packingtown, and Environs in the Nineteenth Century*. Urbana: Univ. of Illinois Press, 1987.

―――. *Graham Taylor, Pioneer for Social Justice, 1851–1938*. Chicago: Univ. of Chicago Press, 1964.

Wade, Mason. *Francis Parkman: Heroic Historian*. New York: Viking Press, 1942.

Walker, David A. *Iron Frontier: The Discovery and Early Development of Minnesota's Three Ranges*. St. Paul: Minnesota Historical Society Press, 1979.

Walker, M. E. M. *Pioneers of Public Health: The Story of Some Benefactors of the Human Race*. New York: Macmillan, 1930.

Walsh, Margaret. *The Rise of the Midwestern Meat Packing Industry*. Lexington: Univ. Press of Kentucky, 1982.

Ward, Martindale C. *A Trip to Chicago: What I Saw, What I Heard, What I Thought*. Glasgow, Scotland: A. Malcolm, 1895.

Warner, Charles Dudley. *Studies in the South and the West with Comments on Canada*. New York: Harper & Brothers, 1889.

Warner, Sam Bass, Jr. *The Private City: Philadelphia in Three Periods of Growth.* Philadelphia: Univ. of Pennsylvania Press, 1968.

————. *The Urban Wilderness: A History of the American City.* New York: Harper & Row, 1972.

Webb, Beatrice Potter. *American Diary, 1898.* Ed. David Shannon. Madison: Univ. of Wisconsin Press, 1963.

Weber, Adna Ferrin. *The Growth of Cities in the Nineteenth Century: A Study in Statistics.* 1899. Ithaca, N.Y.: Cornell Univ. Press, 1967.

Weil, Gordon L. *Sears, Roebuck, USA: The Great American Catalog Store and How It Grew.* Briarcliff Manor, N.Y.: Stein & Day, 1977.

Weimann, Jeanne Madeline. *The Fair Women.* Chicago: Academy, 1981.

Weisberger, Bernard A. *The American Newspaperman.* Chicago: Univ. of Chicago Press, 1961.

Weisman, Winston. "A New View of Skyscraper History." In Edgar Kaufman, Jr., ed. *The Rise of an American Architecture.* New York: Praeger, 1970.

Wells, H. G. *The Future in America: A Search After Realities.* New York: Chapman & Hall, 1906.

Wells, Ida B. *Southern Horrors: Lynch Law in All Its Phases.* New York: New Age Print, 1892.

Wells, Ida B., Frederick Douglass, Garland I. Penn, and Ferdinand L. Barnett. *The Reason Why the Colored American Is Not in the World's Columbian Exposition.* Chicago: Ida B. Wells, 1893.

Wells, Ida B. *Crusade for Justice: The Autobiography of Ida B. Wells.* Ed. Aldreda M. Duster. Chicago: Univ. of Chicago Press, 1970.

Wendt, Lloyd. *"Swift Walker": An Informal Biography of Gurdon Saltonstall Hubbard.* Chicago: Regnery Books, 1986.

Wendt, Lloyd, and Herman Kogan. *Bosses in Lusty Chicago: The Story of Bathhouse John and Hinky Dink.* 1943. Reprint, Bloomington: Indiana Univ. Press, 1967.

————. *Give the Lady What She Wants!: The Story of Marshall Field & Co.* Chicago: Rand McNally, 1952.

Wentworth, John. *Early Chicago.* Chicago: Fergus Printing Co., 1876.

————. *The Wentworth Genealogy: English and American.* 3 vols. Boston: Little, Brown, 1878.

Wharton, Edith. *The Age of Innocence.* 1920. Reprint, New York: Macmillan, 1992.

White, John H., Jr. *The "Pioneer": Chicago's First Locomotive.* Chicago: Chicago Historical Society, 1976.

White, Richard. *The Middle Ground: Indians, Empires, and Republics in the Great Lakes Regions, 1650–1850.* New York: Cambridge Univ. Press, 1991.

Whitlock, Brand. *Forty Years of It.* New York: D. Appleton & Co., 1925.

Whyte, Frederick. *The Life of W. T. Stead,* 2 vols. 1925. Reprint, New York: Garland Press, 1971.

Willard, Frances Elizabeth. *A Wheel Within a Wheel: How I Learned to Ride a Bicycle.* Chicago: F. H. Revell Co., 1895.

Wille, Lois. *Forever Open, Clear and Free: The Historic Struggle for Chicago's Lakefront.* Chicago: Henry Regnery Co., 1972.

Williams, Marilyn Thornton. *Washing "The Great Unwashed": Public Baths in Urban America, 1840–1920.* Columbus: Ohio State Univ. Press, 1991.

Williams, Raymond. *The Country and the City.* New York: Oxford Univ. Press, 1973.

Williamson, William Landram. *William Frederick Poole and the Modern Library Movement.* New York: Columbia Univ. Press, 1963.

Wilson, Richard Guy. *McKim, Mead & White, Architects.* New York: Rizzoli, 1983.

Wing, Jack. *The Great Union Stock Yards of Chicago*. Chicago: Religio-
    Philosophical Publishing Association, 1865.
Wirth, Louis. *The Ghetto*. Chicago: Univ. of Chicago Press, 1928.
Woodward, George E. *Woodward's Country Homes*. New York: G. E. Woodward,
    1865.
Woods, Robert, et al. *The Poor in Great Cities*. New York: Charles Scribner's
    Sons, 1895.
Wooldridge, Clifton R. *Hands Up! In the World of Crime: or 12 Years a Detective*.
    Chicago: C. C. Thompson Co., 1906.
World's Columbian Exposition, Chicago, 1893, Midway Plaisance. *Official Cata-
    logue of the Exhibits on the Midway Plaisance*. Chicago: Conkey, 1893.
Wright, Frank Lloyd. *An Autobiography*. New York: Duell, Sloan & Pearce, 1943.
————. *Genius and Mobocracy*. 1949. Reprint, New York: Horizon Press, 1971.
Wright, Gwendolyn. *Moralism and the Model Home: Domestic Architecture and
    Cultural Conflict in Chicago, 1873–1913*. Chicago: Univ. of Chicago Press,
    1980.
Wright, John S. *Chicago: Past, Present, Future Relations to the Great Interior and
    to the Continent*. Chicago: [Horton & Leonard, printers], 1868.
Wright, Richard. *Native Son*. New York: Harper & Row, 1940.
Wyckoff, Walter A. *The Workers; An Experiment in Reality: the West*. New York:
    Charles Scribner's Sons, 1898.
Yeager, Mary. *Competition and Regulation: The Development of Oligopoly in the
    Meat Packing Industry*. Greenwich, Conn.: JAI Press, 1981.
Young, Charles A. *William Bross, 1813–1890*. Lake Forest, Ill.: Lake Forest Col-
    lege, 1940.
Ziff, Larzer. *The American 1890s: Life and Times of a Lost Generation*. New York:
    Viking, 1968.
Zola, Emile. *Au bonheur des dames*. 1884.
Zukowsky, John, ed. *Chicago Architecture, 1872–1922, Birth of a Metropolis*.
    Chicago: Art Institute of Chicago, 1987.
Zunz, Oliver. *Making America Corporate, 1870–1920*. Chicago: Univ. of Chicago
    Press, 1990.

Articles

Abbott, Carl. "'Necessary Adjuncts to its Growth': The Railroad Suburbs of Chi-
    cago, 1854–1875." *JISHS* 73 (Summer 1980).
Abbot, Willis J. "Chicago Newspapers and Their Makers." *Review of Reviews* 6
    (June 1895).
————. "The Harrison Dynasty in Chicago." *Munsey's Magazine*, Sept. 1903.
Adams, John Coleman. "What a Great City Might Be—A Lesson From the White
    City." *NEM* 14 (Mar. 1896).
Adams, Samuel Hopkins. "The Department Store." *Scribner's Magazine* 21 (Jan.
    1897).
Addams, Jane. "Americanization." *American Sociological Review* 14 (1919).
————. "The Art Work Done at Hull-House, Chicago." *Forum* 19 (July 1895).
————. "Ethical Survivals." *International Journal of Ethics* 8 (Apr. 1898).
————. "A Modern Lear." *Survey* 29 (Nov. 1912).
————. "Why the Ward Boss Rules." *The Outlook* 68 (Apr. 2, 1898).
Ade, George. "Looking Back from Fifty." *The American Magazine*, Feb. 1917.
————. "They Simply Wouldn't Let Me Be a High-Brow." The *American Maga-
    zine* 90 (Dec. 1920).
Adler, Dankmar. "The Chicago Auditorium." *AR*, Apr.–June, 1892.
————. "Chicago's Stock Exchange Building." *Ornamental Iron* 26 (July 1894).
————. "Foundations of the Auditorium Building, Chicago." *IA* 11 (Mar. 1888).

————. "Light in Tall Office Buildings." *Engineering Magazine* 4 (Nov. 1892).

————. "Piling for Isolated Foundations Adjacent to Wall." *IA* 20 (Jan. 1893).

————. "Tall Office Buildings—Past and Future." *Engineering Magazine* 3 (1892).

Andrews, Robert D. "The Broadest View of Precedent." *AR* 2 (May 1893).

Angle, Paul. "One Pioneer, by Another." *CH* 1 (Winter 1945–46).

————. "What Survived the Fire." *CH* 6 (Fall 1961).

"Arcadian City of Pullman." *Agricultural Review* 3 (Jan. 1883).

"Architectural Aberrations." *AR* 3 (July–Sept. 1893).

Arms, Richard G. "From Dis-Assembly to Assembly; Cincinnati: The Birthplace of Mass Production." *Bulletin of the Historical and Philosophical Society of Ohio* 17 (1959).

"The Art Critic and the Tall Building." *Scientific American* 80 (Jan. 28, 1899).

Arth, Mary C. "Marquette Memorials." *Mid-America* 13 (Apr. 1930).

Babcock, Kendric C. "The Scandinavians in the Northwest." *The Forum* 14 (Sept. 1892).

Baker, Ray Stannard. "The Civic Federation of Chicago." *The Outlook* 52 (July 27, 1895).

————. "Hull-House and the Ward Boss." *The Outlook* 58 (Mar. 26, 1898).

————. "The Modern Skyscraper." *Munsey's Magazine* 22 (Oct. 1899).

Ballantyne, Jeannette. "Why Some Women Fail of Success in Court Reporters or Business Offices." *The Phonographic World*, Sept. 1887.

Barnes, Clifford W. "The Story of the Committee of Fifteen in Chicago." *Social Hygiene* 4 (Apr. 1918).

Barnum, P. T. "What a Fair Should Be." *NAR* 150 (Mar. 1890).

Bartky, Ira R. "The Invention of Railroad Time." *Railway History*, no. 148 (Spring 1983).

Baumann, Frederick. "Improved Construction of High Buildings." *Sanitary News* 3 (Mar. 15, 1884).

————. "Life, Reminiscences, and Notes." *Construction News* 4 (Jan. 15, 1916).

Baylen, Joseph O. "A Victorian's 'Crusade' in Chicago, 1893–1894." *JAH* 51 (Dec. 1964).

Beaubien, Frank. "The Beaubiens of Chicago." *Illinois Catholic Historical Review* 2 (July 1919) and (Jan. 1920).

Beecher, W. J. "The Lost Illinois Prairie." *CH* 2 (Spring–Summer 1973).

Betts, John R. "Sporting Journalism in Nineteenth-Century America." *American Quarterly* 5 (Spring 1973).

Blackall, C. H. "Notes of Travel: Chicago." *American Architect and Building News* 23 (Feb. 22, 1888).

Blodgett, Geoffrey. "Frederick Law Olmsted: Landscape Architecture as Conservative Reform." *JAH* 62 (Mar. 1976).

Booney, C. C. "The Chicago of the Publicist." *Lakeside Monthly*, Oct. 1873.

Boorstin, Daniel J. "A. Montgomery Ward's Mail-Order Business." *CH* 2, no. 3 (1973).

Bouman, Mark Jafisen. "Luxury and Control: The Urbanity of Street Lighting in Nineteenth-Century Cities." *Journal of Urban History* 14 (Nov. 1987).

Bourget, Paul. "A Farewell to the White City." *Cosmopolitan* 16 (Dec. 1893).

Bradley, Donald S., and Mayer N. Zald. "From Commercial Elite to Political Administration: The Recruitment of the Mayors of Chicago." *AJS* (Sept. 1965).

Bragdon, Claude. "Letters from Louis Sullivan." *Architecture* 64 (July 1931).

Breckenridge, Sophonisba P., and Edith Abbott. "Housing Conditions in Chicago, III: Back of the Yards." *AJS* 16 (Jan. 1911).

————. "Women in Industry: The Chicago Stockyards." *Journal of Political Economy* 19 (Oct. 1911).

Brown, M. Craig, and Charles N. Halaby. "Machine Politics in America, 1870–1945." *Journal of Interdisciplinary History* 17, no. 3 (1987).

Bruegmann, Robert. "Holabird & Roche and Holabird & Root: The First Two Generations." *CH* 9, no. 3 (1980).

Buenker, John D. "Chicago's Ethnics and the Politics of Accommodation." *CH* 3 (Fall 1974).

Buettinger, Craig. "Economic Inequality in Early Chicago, 1849–1850." *Journal of Social History* 11, no. 3 (1978).

Bunner, H. C. "The Making of the White City." *Scribner's Magazine* 12 (Oct. 1892).

Burghardt, A. F. "A Hypothesis About Gateway Cities." *Annals of the Association of American Geographers* 61 (1971).

Burnham, Daniel H. "The Organization of the World's Columbian Exposition." *IA*, Aug. 1893.

———. "Report to the Committee on Grounds and Buildings." *Century Illustrated Monthly Magazine* 44 (1892).

Bushnell, George D. "When Chicago Was Wheel Crazy." *CH* 4 (Fall 1975).

Byrn, Edward W. "The Progress of Invention During the Past Fifty Years." *Scientific American* 75 (July 25, 1896).

Cain, Louis P. "Ellis Sylvester Chesbrough and Chicago's First Sanitary System." *Technology and Culture* 13 (July 1972).

Caton, John Dean. "Reminiscences of Chicago in 1833 and 1834." Ed. Harry E. Pratt. *JISHS* 28 (1935).

———. "'Tis Sixty Years Since' in Chicago." *AM* 71 (May 1893).

Chappell, Sally. "Beaux-Arts Architecture in Chicago." *IA* 24 (Oct. 1980).

Chesbrough, E. S. "The Drainage and Sewerage of Chicago." *Papers and Reports of the American Public Health Association* 4 (1878).

"Chicago." *American Architect* 25 (Feb. 1889).

"The Chicago Drainage Canal." *HW* 38 (Sept. 1, 1894).

"Chicago in Ashes." *HW* 15 (Oct. 28, 1871).

"The Chicago Orchestra." *Dial* 22 (1897).

"Chicago—Proposed Odd Fellows Temple." *TG* 5 (Dec. 9, 1891).

"Chicago Public Library." *TG*, May 21, 1892.

"The Chicago School of Architecture: A Symposium—Part II," *The Prairie School Review* 9 (1972).

"Chicago Waterworks." *HW* 11 (Apr. 20, 1867).

"Chicago's Higher Evolution." *The Dial* 13 (Oct. 1, 1892).

Chinn, Armstrong. "Grand Central Station." *Bulletin—Railroad and Locomotive Historical Society* 18 (1938).

"City of Chicago." *The Inland Monthly Magazine* 10 (1877).

"The Civic Life of Chicago: The Impressions of an Observant Englishman." *The Review of Reviews*, Aug. 1893.

Clark, Emily, and Patrick Ashley. "The Merchant Prince of Cornville." *CH* 21 (Dec. 1992).

Clarke, Walter. "Prostitution and Alcohol." *Journal of Social Hygiene* 3 (1917–18).

Clausen, Meredith L. "Frank Lloyd Wright, Vertical Space, and the Chicago School's Quest for Light." *JSAH* 44 (Mar. 1985).

Cleveland, Harold Irwin. "Fifty-five Years in Business: The Life of Marshall Field." *System* 9 (June 1906); 10 (July 1906).

Clifton, James A. "Billy Caldwell's Exile in Early Chicago." *CH* 6 (Winter 1977–78).

———. "Chicago, September 14, 1833: The Last Great Indian Treaty in the Old Northwest." *CH* 9 (Summer 1980).

Condit, Carl W. "The Structural System of Adler and Sullivan's Garrick Theater Building." *Technology and Culture* 5 (Fall 1984).

———. "Sullivan's Skyscrapers as the Expression of Nineteenth Century Technology." *Technology and Culture* 1 (1959).

Conway, Jill. "Women Reformers and American Culture, 1870–1930." *Journal of Social History* 5, no. 2 (1971–72).

Conzen, Kathleen Neils. "Immigrants, Immigrant Neighborhoods, and Ethnic Identity: Historical Issues." *JAH* 66, no. 3 (1979).

Conzen, Michael P. "A Transport Interpretation of the Growth of Urban Regions: An American Example." *Journal of Historical Geography* 1 (1975).

Cravath, J. R. "Electricity at the World's Fair." *The Review of Reviews* 8 (July 1893).

Cronon, William. "To Be the Central City: Chicago, 1848–1857." *CH* 10, no. 3 (1981).

Davis, Richard Harding. "The Last Days of the Fair." *HW* 37 (Oct. 21, 1893).

Dearinger, Lowell A. "Trader Hubbard." *Outdoor Illinois* 8 (July–Aug. 1969).

Delanglez, Jean. "The Jolliet Lost Map of the Mississippi." *Mid-America* 28 (1946).

———. "Louis Jolliet, Early Years, 1645–1674." *Mid-America* 28 (1945).

"Deliberations of the Architects." *Economist* 6 (Nov. 21, 1891).

Dennis, John, Jr. "Marshall Field, A Great Mercantile Genius." *Everybody's Magazine* 14 (Mar. 1906).

Dent, Newton. "The Romance of Chicago." *Munsey's Magazine* 37 (1907).

Destler, Chester M. "Agricultural Readjustment and Agrarian Unrest in Illinois, 1880–1896." *Architectural History* 21 (1947).

Di Gaetano, Alan. "The Rise and Development of Urban Political Machines," *Urban Affairs Quarterly* 24 (1988).

Dimaggio, Paul. "Cultural Entrepreneurship in Nineteenth-Century Boston: The Creation of an Organized Base for High Culture in America." *Media, Culture and Society* 4 (1982).

———. "Cultural Entrepreneurship in Nineteenth-Century Boston, Part II: The Classification & Framing of American Art." *Media, Culture and Society* 4 (1982).

Downard, William L. "William Butler Ogden and the Growth of Chicago." *JISHS* 75 (Spring 1982).

Downey, Dennis B. "William Stead and Chicago: A Victorian Jeremiah in the Windy City." *Mid-America* 68, no. 3 (1986).

Dreiser, Theodore. "The Chicago Drainage Canal." *Ainslee* 3 (Feb. 1899).

———. "Great Problems of Organization, III: The Chicago Packing Industry." *Cosmopolitan* 25 (Oct. 25, 1895).

———. "Life Stories of Successful Men, No. 10." *Success* 1 (Oct. 1898).

———. "Life Stories of Successful Men, No. 12." *Success* 1 (Dec. 1898).

———. "The Smallest and Busiest River in the World." *Metropolitan* 7 (Oct. 1898).

———. "The Town of Pullman." *Ainslee* 3 (Mar. 1899).

Duis, Perry R. "Life of a Salesman." *Chicago*, May 1985.

———. "Yesterday's City." *CH*, Summer 1987.

Duis, Perry R., and Glen E. Holt. "Chicago's Green Crown: The Parks." *Chicago*, Aug. 1977.

———. "Kate O'Leary's Sad Burden." *Chicago*, Oct. 1978.

Eaton, Charles H. "Paternalism and Pullman." *The American Journal of Politics* 5 (1899).

Eaton, Leonard. "The American Suburb: Dream and Nightmare." *Landscape* 13 (Winter 1963–64).

Edelmann, John. "Pessimism of Modern Architecture." *The Engineering Magazine* 3 (Apr.–Sept. 1892).

Egbert, Donald D., and Paul E. Sprague. "In Search of John Edelmann." *AIA Journal* 45 (Feb. 1966).

Einhorn, Robin L. "A Taxing Dilemma: Early Lake Shore Protection." *CH* 18 (Fall 1989).

"Ellis Sylvester Chesbrough." *Proceedings of the American Society of Civil Engineers* 15 (Nov.–Dec. 1889).

Elstein, Rochelle S. "The Architecture of Dankmar Adler." *JSAH* 26 (Dec. 1967).

Ely, Richard T. "Pullman: A Social Study." *Harper's Monthly 70* (1885).

Erickson, Ethel. "The Employment of Women in Offices." *U.S. Department of Labor, Women's Bureau, Bulletin,* no. 120 (1934).

Fay, C. Norman. "The Theodore Thomas Orchestra." *The Outlook,* Jan. 22, 1910.

Ferree, Barr. "Architecture." *Engineering Magazine* 5 (June 1893).

———. "The High Building and Its Art." *Scribner's Magazine* 15 (Mar. 1894).

———. "The Modern Office Building." Parts 1–3. *IA* 27, no. 1 (Feb. 1896), no. 2 (Mar. 1896), no. 3 (Apr. 1896), no. 5 (June 1896).

Ferris, William. "Old Hutch—The Wheat King." *JISHS* 41 (1948).

Field, Walker. "A Re-Examination into the Invention of the Balloon Frame." *JSAH* 2 (Oct. 1942).

Finkelman, Paul. "Class and Culture in Late Nineteenth-Century Chicago: The Founding of the Newberry Library." *American Studies* 16, no. 1 (1975).

"Fire and the Modern Skyscraper." *Scientific American* 80 (Jan. 1890).

Flagg, Ernest. "The Dangers of High Buildings." *Cosmopolitan* 21 (May 1896).

Fletcher, Bannister. "American Architecture Through English Spectacles." *Engineering Magazine* 7 (June 1894).

Fletcher, Connie. "The Loop El: Love It or Lose It." *Chicago,* Nov. 1977.

Friedman, Philip S. "The Americanization of Chicago's Danish Community, 1850–1920." *CH* 9 (Spring 1980).

Fuller, Henry B. "Chicago's Book of Days." *The Outlook* 69 (Oct. 5, 1901).

———. "The Upward Movement in Chicago." *AM* 80 (Oct. 1897).

Garland, Hamlin. "Homestead and Its Perilous Trades." *McClure's Magazine* 3 (June 1894).

Gary, Joseph E. "The Chicago Anarchists of 1886: The Crime, the Trial, and the Punishment." *The Century Magazine* 45 (Apr. 1, 1893).

Gerwing, Anselm J. "The Chicago Indian Treaty of 1833." *JISHS* 57 (1964).

Gilbert, Paul T. "Whitechapel Nights." *Townfolk* 36 (Feb. 1947).

"The Girl Who Comes to the City: A Symposium." *Harper's Bazaar,* Jan. 1908.

Godkin. E. L. "Stewart's." *The Nation* 34 (Apr. 20, 1882).

Gompers, Samuel. "The Lessons of the Recent Strikes." *NAR* 159 (Aug. 1894).

Goodspeed, Thomas Wakefield. "Gustavus Franklin Swift, 1839–1903." *University of Chicago Record* 7 (Apr. 1921).

Gordon, John Steele. "No Respect." *American Heritage* 44 (Sept. 1993).

Grant, Roger H., ed. "A Wonderfully Busy Place." *CH* 20, nos. 1 and 2 (1991).

Grant, Thomas B. "Pullman and Its Lessons." *American Journal of Politics* 5 (1894).

"The Great Granaries of Chicago." *HW* 3 (Sept. 10, 1859).

Gregory, Eliot. "A Nation in a Hurry." *AM* 85 (May 1900).

Griffin, Dick. "Opium Addiction in Chicago: The Noblest and the Best Brought Low." *CH* 6 (Summer 1977).

Grignon, Augustin. "Seventy-two Years' Recollections of Wisconsin." *Collections of the State Historical Society, Wisconsin* 3 (1856).

Gunsaulus, Frank W. "Philip D. Armour: A Character Sketch." *North American Monthly Review of Reviews* 23 (1901).

Haeger, John D. "The American Fur Company and Chicago of 1812–1835." *JISHS,* Summer 1968.

Halstead, Murat. "Electricity at the Fair." *Cosmopolitan* 15 (Sept. 1893).

Hamilton, John B. "The Epidemic of Chicago." *Bulletin of the Society of Medical History of Chicago* 1 (Oct. 1911).

Hamilton, Raphael N. "Marquette Death Site: The Case for Ludington." *Michigan History* 49 (1965).

Hammack, David C. "Problems in the Historical Study of Power in the Cities and Towns of the United States, 1800–1960." *American Historical Review* 83, no. 2 (1978).

Harland, Marion. "The Incapacity of Business Women." *NAR* 149 (1889).

Harmond, Richard. "Progress and Flight: An Interpretation of the American Cycle Craze of the 1890s." *Journal of Social History* 5 (Winter 1971).

Harris, Neil. "The Gilded Age Revisited: Boston and the Museum Movement." *American Quarterly* 14 (Winter 1964).

Haydon, James Ryan. "John Kinzie's Place in History." *Transactions of the Illinois State Historical Society* 39 (1932).

Hays, Samuel P. "The Politics of Reform in Municipal Government in the Progressive Era." *Pacific Northwest Quarterly* 55 (1964).

Head, Franklin H. "The Heart of Chicago." *NEM* 6 (July 1892).

Hedger, Caroline. "The Unhealthfulness of Packingtown." *World's Work* 12 (May 1906).

Hendrick, Burton J. "Great American Fortunes and their Making: Street-Railway Financiers." *McClure's Magazine* 30 (1908).

Hepburn, Carter H. "Philip D. Armour." *Munsey's Magazine* 9 (1893).

Herrick, Robert. "The University of Chicago." *Scribner's Magazine* 18 (Oct. 1895).

Hill, Howard C. "The Development of Chicago as a Center of the Meat Packing Industry." *Mississippi Valley Historical Review* 3 (Dec. 1923).

Hilton, George W. "Transport Technology and the Urban Pattern." *Journal of Contemporary History* 4 (1969).

Hobart, H. R. "The Flight for Life." *Lakeside Monthly* 7 (Jan. 1872).

Hodgson, Pamela D. "The Scoundrel and the Scientist." *CH* 19 (Fall–Winter 1990–91).

Hoffmann, Charles. "The Depression of the Nineties." *Journal of Economic History* 16 (June 1956).

Hoffmann, Donald. "Clear Span Rivalry: The World's Fairs of 1889–1893." *JSAH* 29 (Mar. 1970).

———. "John Root's Monadnock Building." *JSAH* 26 (Dec. 1967).

———. "The Setback Skyscraper City of 1891: An Unknown Essay by Louis H. Sullivan." *JSAH* 29 (May 1970).

"Hog Killing at the Chicago Stock Yards." *Scientific American* 65 (Nov. 7, 1891).

Holland, James P. "Chicago and the World's Fair." *The Chautauquan* 17 (May 1893).

Holmes, Bayard. "The Sweat-Shops and Smallpox in Chicago." *Journal of the American Medical Association* 23 (Sept. 15, 1894).

Holt, Glen E. "Private Plans for Public Spaces: The Origins of Chicago's Park System, 1850–1875." *CH* 8 (Fall 1979).

Horowitz, Helen. "The Art Institute of Chicago: The First Forty Years." *CH* 8 (Spring 1979).

Howells, William Dean. "Certain of the Chicago School of Fiction." *NAR* 176 (1903).

———. "Letters of an Altrurian Traveler." *Cosmopolitan* 16 (Dec. 1893).

Hubbard, Gurdon S. "Journey of Gurdon S. Hubbard." *Pioneer Collections: Report of the Pioneer Society of the State of Michigan* 3 (1881).

Hutchinson, B. P. "Speculation in Wheat." *NAR* 153 (1891).

Hutchinson, Charles L. "The Democracy of Art." *The American Magazine of Art* 7 (Aug. 1916).

Ingalls, John J. "Lessons of the Fair." *Cosmopolitan* 16 (Dec. 1893).

Jay, Robert. "Taller than Eiffel's Tower: The London and Chicago Tower Projects, 1889–1894." *JSAH* 46, no. 2 (1987).

Jenney, William Le Baron. "An Age of Steel and Clay." *IA* 16 (Dec. 1890).

———. "Architecture: Part I." *IA* 1 (Mar.–July 1883); 2 (Sept. 1883–Jan. 1884); 3 (Feb. 1884).

———. "Autobiography of William Le Baron Jenney." *The Western Architect* 10 (1907).

———. "The Chicago Construction, or Tall Building on a Compressible Soil." *IA* 18 (Nov. 1891).

———. "The Construction of a Heavy Fireproof Building on a Compressible Soil." *IA* 6 (Dec. 1885).

———. "A Few Practical Hints." *IA* 13 (Feb. 1889).

———. "Whistler and Old Sandy in the Fifties." *American Architect and Building News* 91 (1898).

———. "The Steel Skeleton, or the Modern Skyscraper—the Engineering Problem." *1A* 34 (Jan. 1900).

Joyaux, Georges J. "A Frenchman's Visit to Chicago in 1886." *JISHS* 47 (1954).

Karlowicz, Titus M. "D.H. Burnham's Role in the Selection of Architects for the World's Columbian Exposition." *JSAH* 29 (Oct. 1970).

Kaztauskis, Antanas [Ernest Poole]. "From Lithuania to the Chicago Stockyards." *Independent* 57 (Aug. 4, 1904).

Kellar, Herbert A. "The Reaper as a Factor in the Development of the Agriculture of Illinois, 1834–1865." *Transactions of the Illinois State Historical Society* 34 (1927).

Kelley, Florence. "The Illinois Child Labor Law." *AJS* 3 (Jan. 1898).

Kingsdale, Jon M. "The 'Poor Man's Club': Social Functions of the Urban Working-Class Saloon." *American Quarterly* 25 (Oct. 1973).

Kirby, Russell S. "Nineteenth-Century Patterns of Railroad Development on the Great Plains." *Great Plains Quarterly* 3, no. 3 (1983).

[Kirkland, Caroline]. "Illinois in Spring-Time: With a Look at Chicago." *AM* 2 (Sept. 1858).

Kirkland, Joseph. "The Chicago Fire." *NEM* 6 (June 18, 1892).

Kogan, Herman. "William Perkins Black: Haymarket Lawyer." *CH* 5 (Summer 1976).

Kouwenhoven, John A. "The Eiffel Tower and the Ferris Wheel." *Arts Magazine* 54 (Feb. 8, 1980).

Kujovich, Mary Yeager. "The Refrigerator Car and the Growth of the American Dressed Beef Industry." *Business History Review* 44 (Winter 1970).

Kwiat, Joseph E. "The Newspaper Experience: Crane, Norris, and Dreiser." *Nineteenth-Century Fiction* 7–8 (June 1952–Mar. 1954).

Lamoureaux, David. "Baseball in the Late Nineteenth Century: The Source of Its Appeal." *Journal of Popular Culture* 11 (Winter 1977).

Lampard, Eric E. "The History of Cities in the Economically Advanced Areas." *Economic Development and Cultural Change* 3 (1955).

Larsen, Lawrence H. "Chicago's Mid-West Rivals: Cincinnati, St. Louis, and Milwaukee." *CH* 5 (1976).

Larson, Gerald R. "Fire, Earth, and Wind." Parts I and II. *IA* 25 (Sept. 1981); 27 (Jan.–Feb. 1983).

Larson, Gerald R., and Roula Mouroudellis Geraniotis. "Toward a Better Understanding of the Evolution of the Iron Skeleton Frame in Chicago." *JSAH* 46 (Mar. 1987).

Lederer, Francis L., II. "Competition for the World's Columbian Exposition: The Chicago Campaign." *JISHS* 65 (1972).

———. "Nora Marks, Investigative Reporter." *JISHS* 68 (Sept. 1975).

Lee, Guy A. "Historical Significance of the Chicago Grain Elevator System." *Agricultural History* 11 (Jan. 1937).

Lewis, Russell. "Everything Under One Roof: World's Fairs and Department Stores in Paris and Chicago." *CH* 12 (Fall 1983).

Lindberg, Richard. "The Evolution of an Evil Business." *CH* 22 (July 1993).

MacLean, Annie M. "Two Weeks in Department Stores." *AJS* 4 (May 1899).

MacVeagh, Franklin. "A Program for Municipal Reform." *AJS* 1 (Mar. 1896).

Mahoney, Timothy R. "Urban History in a Regional Context: River Towns on the Upper Mississippi, 1840–1860." *JAH* 72 (Sept. 1985).

"Marshall Field & Co." *Fortune Magazine* 14 (Oct. 1936).

Marzio, Peter C. "A Museum and a School: An Uneasy but Creative Union." *CH* 8 (Spring 1979).

Mason, Edward G. "Chicago." *AM* 70 (July 1892).

Massa, Ann. "Black Women in the 'White City.'" *Journal of American Studies* 8 (1974).

Mayer, Harold M. "The Launching of Chicago: The Situation and the Site," *CH* 9 (Summer 1980).

———. "Urban Geography and the Chicago Region in Retrospect," *Annals of the Association of American Geographers* 69, no. 1 (1979).

McCarthy, Michael P. "Should We Drink the Water? Typhoid Fever Worries at the Columbian Exposition." *Illinois Historical Journal* 86 (Spring 1993).

McColley, Robert. "Classical Music in Chicago and the Founding of the Symphony 1850–1905." *Illinois Historical Journal* 78, no. 4 (1985).

McConnell, Samuel P. "The Chicago Bomb Case: Personal Recollections of an American Tragedy." *Harper's Monthly* 168 (May 1934).

McCree, Mary Lynn. "The First Year of Hull-House, 1889–1890, In Letters by Jane Addams and Ellen Gates Starr." *CH* 1 (1970).

McCutcheon, John T. "George Ade." *Appleton's Magazine*, Nov. 1907.

McDonald, Terrance J. "The Burden of Urban History: The Theory of the State in Recent American Social History." *Studies in American Political Development* 3 (1989).

———. "The Problem of the Political in Recent American Urban History: Liberal Pluralism and the Rise of Functionalism." *Social History* 10 (1985).

McDowell, Edward B. "The World's Fair Cosmopolis." *Frank Leslie's Popular Monthly* 36 (Oct. 1893).

McDowell, Mary. "Social Science in Chicago." *The University Record* 9 (Oct. 9, 1923).

McKee, Thomas H. "The Failure of Government Inspection." *World's Work* 12 (May 1906).

McLear, Patrick E. "'. . . And Still They Come'—Chicago from 1832 [to 18]36." *Journal of the West* 7, no 3 (1968).

———. "The Galena and Chicago Union Railroad: A Symbol of Chicago's Economic Maturity." *JISHS* 73 (1980).

———. "Land Speculators and Urban and Regional Development: Chicago in the 1830s." *The Old Northwest* 6 (Summer 1980).

———. "William Butler Ogden: A Chicago Promoter in the Speculative Era and the Panic of 1837." *JISHS* 70 (Nov. 1977).

Meehan, Thomas A. "Jean Baptiste Point du Sable: The First Chicagoan." *JISHS* 56 (Autumn 1963).

Melbin, Murray. "Night as Frontier." *American Sociological Review* 43 (Feb. 1978).

Melendy, Royal L. "The Saloon in Chicago." *AJS* 6 (1900–1901).

Meyer, David R. "Midwestern Industrialization and the American Manufacturing Belt in the 19th Century." *Journal of Economic History* 49 (1989).

Miller, Donald L. "Lewis Mumford: Urban Historian, Urban Visionary," *Journal of Urban History* 18 (May 1992).

———. "One Fine Building and a Few Good Men." *Chicago Magazine*, Mar. 1991.

Moore, Charles. "Lessons of the Chicago World's Fair: An Interview with the Late Daniel H. Burnham." *AR* 33 (Jan. 1913).

Moore, E. C. "The Social Function of the Saloon." *AJS* 3 (July 1897).

Moss, L. G. "Indians on the Midway: Wild West Shows and the Indian Bureau at World's Fairs, 1893–1904." *South Dakota History* 21 (1991).

Moss, Leonard, and Stephen C. Cappannari. "Patterns of Kinship, Comparaggio and Community in a Southern Italian Village." *Anthropological Quarterly* 33 (Jan. 1960).

Mumford, Lewis. "The First Megamachine." *Diogenes*, Fall 1960.

Nagel, Paul C. "Twice to the Fair." *CH* 14, no. 1 (1985–86).

Naylor, Timothy J. "Responding to the Fire: The Work of the Chicago Relief and Aid Society." *Science and Society* 39 (Winter 1975–76).

Nelli, Humbert S. "John Powers and the Italians: Politics in a Chicago Ward, 1896–1921." *JAH* 57 (June 1970).

Neufeld, Maurice. "The White City: The Beginnings of a Planned Civilization in America." *JISHS* 27 (Apr. 1934).

"New Building of Pullman's Palace Car Company in Chicago." *The Railway Age*, May 15, 1884.

"New Charge Against the Trolley." *Street Railway Gazette* 10 (May 10, 1894).

Nichols, Roger L. "The Black Hawk War in Retrospect." *Wisconsin Magazine of History* 65 (1982).

Nord, Paul David. "The Public Community: The Urbanization of Journalism in Chicago." *Journal of Urban History* 11 (Aug. 1985).

Odle, Thomas D. "The American Grain Trade of the Great Lakes, 1825–1873." *Inland Seas* 7 (1951); 8 (1952).

Oestreicher, Richard. "Urban Working-Class Political Behavior and Theories of American Electoral Politics, 1870–1940." *JAH* 74 (Mar. 1988).

O'Hara, Barratt. "The Work of the Illinois State Vice Commission." *The Light* 19 (May–June 1916).

O'Keefe, P. J. "The Chicago Stock Yards." *NEM* 6 (May 1892).

Olmstead, Alan L. "The Mechanization of Reaping and Mowing in American Agriculture, 1833–1870." *Journal of Economic History* 35 (1975).

Olmsted, Frederick Law. "Chicago in Distress." *The Nation* 13 (Nov. 9, 1871).

———. "The Landscape Architecture of the World's Columbian Exposition," *IA* 12 (Sept. 1893).

———. "Public Parks and the Enlargement of Towns." *Journal of Social Science* 2 (1871).

Olson, A. B. "Chicago Union Station Company." *Locomotive Historical Society Bulletin* 49 (1939).

"Organized Labor and the World's Fair." *IA* 17 (June 1891).

Palmer, Alice Freeman. "Some Lasting Results of the World's Fair." *Forum* 16 (Dec. 1893).

"Paper Car Wheels—How They Are Made." *Western Manufacturer*, July 15, 1880.

Parton, James. "Chicago." *AM* 19 (Mar. 1867).

Pauly, John J. "The Great Chicago Fire as a National Event." *American Quarterly* 36 (1984).

Peattie, Elia W. "The Artistic Side of Chicago." *AM* 84 (Dec. 1899).

Peckham, Edward L. "My Journey Out West." *Journal of American History* 17, no. 3 (1923).

Pesavento, Wilma J. "Sport and Recreation in the Pullman Experiment, 1880–1900." *Journal of Sport History* 9, no. 2 (1982).

Pessen, Edward. "Who Governed the Nation's Cities in the 'Era of the Common Man'?" *Political Science Quarterly* 4 (Dec. 1972).

Peters, Tom F. "The Rise of the Skyscraper from the Ashes of Chicago." *Invention and Technology,* Fall 1987.

Peterson, Jacqueline. "Goodbye, Madore Beaubien: The Americanization of Early Chicago Society." *CH* 9 (Summer 1980).

Peterson, William S. "Kipling's First Visit to Chicago." *JISHS* 63 (Fall 1970).

Phipps, Linda S. "The 1893 Art Institute Building and the 'Paris of America:' Aspirations of Patrons and Architects in Late-Nineteenth-Century Chicago," *Museum Studies* 14, no. 1 (1988).

Piehl, Frank J. "Chicago's Early Fight to 'Save Our Lake.'" *CH* 5, no. 4 (1976–77).

Piety, James W. "The Illinois and Michigan Canal and the Early Historical Geography of Chicago." *Geographical Perspectives* 47 (1981).

Pond, Irving K. "Neither a Skyscraper nor of Skeleton Construction." *AR* 76 (1934).

———. "Pullman: America's First Planned Industrial Town." *Illinois Society of Architects Monthly Bulletin,* June–July 1934.

Porter, Horace. "Railway Passenger Travel: 1825–1880." *Scribner's Magazine,* Sept. 4, 1888.

"Productivity of Labor in Slaughtering and Meat Packing and in Petroleum Refining." *Monthly Labor Review* 13 (Nov. 1926).

Purcell, William. "Sullivan at Work." *Northwest Architect* 8 (Jan.–Feb. 1944).

Purdy, Corydon T. "The Use of Steel in Large Buildings." *Engineering News Record* 31 (Feb. 1895).

Quaife, Milo M., ed. "Property of Jean Baptiste Point du Sable." *Mississippi Valley Historical Review* 15 (June 1928).

Randolph, Robert Isham. "The History of Sanitation in Chicago." *Journal of the Western Society of Engineers* 44 (Oct. 1939).

Rannalletta, Kathy. "Illinois Commentary: 'The Great Wave of Fire,' at Chicago: The Reminiscences of Martin Stamm." *JISHS* 70 (June 1977).

Rauch, John H. "Sanitary Problems of Chicago, Past and Present." *Public Health Papers and Reports* 4 (1877).

Reynolds, Arthur R. "Three Chicago and Illinois Public Health Officers: John H. Rauch, Oscar C. DeWolf, and Frank W. Reilly." *Bulletin of the Society of Medical History of Chicago* 1 (Aug. 1912).

Reynolds, Patrick. "'Fra Lorado,' Chicago's Master Sculptor." *CH* 14, no. 2 (1985).

Richardson, Anna Steese, "The Modern Woman's Paradise." *Woman's Home Companion* 38 (Sept. 1911).

Roberts, Sidney I. "The Municipal Voters' League and Chicago's Boodlers." *JISHS* 53 (1960).

———. "Portrait of a Robber Baron: Charles T. Yerkes." *Business History Review* 35 (Autumn 1961).

Root, John Wellborn. "Architectural Ornamentation." *IA* 5 (Apr. 1885).

———. "Broad Art Criticism." *IA* 11 (Feb. 1888).

———. "The City House in the West." *Scribner's Magazine* 8 (Oct. 1890).

———. "A Great Architectural Problem." *IA* 15 (June 1890).

Rothstein, Morton. "Frank Norris and Popular Perceptions of the Market." *Agricultural History* 56 (1982).

Rudwick, Elliot M., and August Meier. "Black Man in the 'White City': Negroes and the Columbian Exposition, 1893." *Phylon* 26 (Winter 1965).

Russell, Charles Edward. "The Haymarket and Afterwards: Some Personal Recollections." *Appleton's Magazine* 10 (Oct. 1907).

————. "Where Did You Get It, Gentlemen?" *Everybody's Magazine* 17 (Sept. 1907).

Salzstein, Joan W. "Dankmar Adler: Part One—The Man." *Wisconsin Architect*, July–Aug. 1967.

Sawislak, Karen. "Relief, Aid, and Order: Class, Gender, and the Definition of Community in the Aftermath of Chicago's Great Fire." *Journal of Urban History* 20 (Nov. 1993).

Schermerhorn, Richard, Jr. "Nathan Franklin Barrett, Landscape Architect." *Landscape Architect* 10 (Apr. 1920).

Schilling, George. "The Lessons of the Homestead Troubles," *The Sunset Club Yearbook*, 1892–93.

Schlereth, Thomas J. "Big Money and High Culture: The Commercial Club of Chicago and Charles L. Hutchinson." *The Great Lakes Review* 3 (Summer 1976).

Schneirov, Richard. "Chicago's Great Upheaval of 1877." *CH* 9 (Spring 1980).

Schnell, J. Christopher. "Chicago versus St. Louis: A Reassessment of the Great Rivalry." *Missouri Historical Review* 71 (1977).

Schuyler, Montgomery. "Architecture in Chicago: Adler and Sullivan." *AR*, Special Series, 4 (Dec. 1895).

————. "D.H. Burnham and Company." *AR* 5 (Dec. 1895).

————. "The Evolution of the Skyscraper." *Scribner's Magazine* 46 (Sept. 1909).

————. "Glimpses of Western Architecture: Chicago." *Harper's Magazine*, 83 (Aug. 1891); 83 (Sept. 1891).

————. "Last Words About the World's Fair." *AR* 3 (Jan.–Mar. 1894).

————. "'The Sky-Scraper' Up to Date." *AR* 8 (Jan.–Mar. 1899).

"Sewage Purification in America: Pullman, Illinois." *Engineering News* 29 (Jan. 12, 1893).

Shea, John G. "Romance and Reality of the Death of Marquette and the Recent Discovery of his Remains." *The Catholic World* 26 (1877).

Sklar, Kathryn Kish. "Hull-House in the 1890s: A Community of Women Reformers." *Signs* 10 (Summer 1985).

Small, Albion W. "The Civic Federation of Chicago: A Study in Social Dynamics." *AJS* 1 (July 1895).

Smith, Clifford Neal. "Reconstructing Chicago's Early Land Records." *Illinois State Genealogical Society Quarterly* 5 (Winter 1973).

Smith, Nina B. "'This Bleak Situation': The Founding of Fort Sheridan, Illinois." *Illinois Historical Journal* 80, no. 1 (1987).

Snowden, Clifford L. "The Armour Institute of Technology." *NEM* 16 (May 1897).

Snyder, Carl. "Engineer Ferris and His Wheel." *The Review of Reviews*, Sept. 1893.

Spears, Timothy B. "A Grip on the Land." *CH* 17 (Fall–Winter 1988–89).

Sprague, Paul E. "Adler and Sullivan's Schiller Building." *The Prairie School Review* 2 (Second Quarter 1965).

————. "The Origin of Balloon Framing." *JSAH* 40 (Dec. 4, 1981).

Starrett, Theodore. "John Wellborn Root." *Architecture and Building* 44 (Nov. 1912).

"The State Street Stores." *Economist* 15 (June 13, 1896).

Staudenraus, P. J., ed. "'The Empire City of the West'—A View of Chicago in 1864." *JISHS* 56 (Summer 1963).

Stead, F. Herbert. "An Englishman's Impressions at the Fair." *Review of Reviews* 8 (July 1893).

Stead, William T. "My First Visit to America: An Open Letter to My Readers." *Review of Reviews* 9 (Jan.–June 1894).

Steffens, J. Lincoln. "The Modern Business Building." *Scribner's Magazine* 22 (July 1897).

Sullivan, Louis. "The High Building Question." *TG* 5 (Dec. 19, 1891).

———. "The Tall Building Artistically Considered." *Lippincott's* 57 (Mar. 1896).

Swenson, John F. "Chicagoua/Chicago: The Origins, Meaning, and Etymology of a Place Name." *Illinois Historical Journal* 84 (Winter 1991).

Swing, David. "Historic Moments: A Memory of the Chicago Fire." *Scribner's Magazine* 11 (Jan.–June 1892).

Tallmadge, Thomas E. "Was the Home Insurance Building the First Skyscraper of Skeleton Construction?" *AR* 76 (1934).

Tarr. Joel A. "The Separate vs. Combined Sewer Problem: A Case Study of Urban Technology Design Choice." *Journal of Urban History* 5 (May 1979).

———. "Urban Pollution: Many Long Years Ago." *American Heritage* 22 (Oct. 1971).

———. "William Kent to Lincoln Steffens: Origins of Progressive Reform in Chicago." *Mid-America* 47 (Jan. 1965).

Tarr, Joel A., Thomas Finholt, and David Goodman. "The City and the Telegraph: Urban Telecommunications in the Pre-Telephone Era." *Journal of Urban History* 14, no. 1 (1987).

Thwaites, Reuben Gold. "Narrative of Peter J. Vieau." *Wisconsin Historical Collections* 15 (1900).

Tilton, Clint Clay. "Gurdon Saltonstall Hubbard and Some of his Friends." *Illinois State Historical Society Transactions* 40 (1933).

Tilyou, Edward F. "Human Nature with the Brakes Off—Or: Why the Schoolma'am Walked into the Sea." *American Magazine* 94 (July 1922).

Trautmann, Frederic. "Arthur Holitischer's Chicago: A German Traveler's View of an American City." *CH* 12, no 2 (1983).

Tselos, Dimitri. "The Chicago Fair and the Myth of the 'Lost Cause.'" *JSAH* 26 (Dec. 1967).

Tucker, David M. "Miss Ida Wells and Memphis Lynching." *Phylon* 32 (Summer 1971).

Turak, Theodore. "The École Centrale and Modern Architecture: The Education of William Le Baron Jenney." *JSAH* 29 (1970).

———. "Remembrances of the Home Insurance Building." *JSAH* 44, no. 1 (1985).

———. "William Le Baron Jenney: Pioneer of Chicago's West Parks." *IA* 25 (Mar. 1981).

Turner, Frederick Jackson. "The Problem of the West." *AM* 78 (1896).

Turner, George Kibbe. "The City of Chicago, A Study of the Great Immoralities." *McClure's* 28 (Apr. 7, 1907).

Twain, Mark. "What Paul Bourget Thinks of Us." *NAR* 160 (1895).

Twyman, Robert W. "Potter Palmer: Merchandising Innovator of the West." *Explorations in Entrepreneurial History* 4 (Dec. 1951).

Van Brunt, Henry. "Architecture at the World's Columbian Exposition, I." *The Century Magazine* 44 (May 1892).

———. "John Wellborn Root." *IA* 16 (Jan. 1891).

Van Der Zee, Jacob. "Episodes in the Early History of the Wisconsin Iowa Country." *Iowa Journal of History and Politics* 11 (1913).

Van Dorn, Luther. "A View of Chicago in 1848." *Magazine of Western History* 10 (1889).

Vecoli, Rudolph J. "Contadini in Chicago: A Critique of the Uprooted." *JAH* 51 (Dec. 1969).

Vogel, Virgil J. "The Mystery of Chicago's Name." *Mid-America* 40 (July 1958).

Wade, Louise Carroll. "Burnham and Root's Stockyards Connection." *CH* 4 (Feb. 1975).

"Wages and Hours of Labor in the Slaughtering and Meat-Packing Industry." *Bulletin of United States Labor Statistics* 252 (Aug. 1917).

Wallace, Anthony F. C. "Prelude to Disaster: The Course of Indian-White Relations Which Led to the Black Hawk War of 1832." *Collections of the Illinois State Historical Library* 35 (1970).

Walsh, Margaret. "The Democratization of Fashion: The Emergence of the Women's Dress Pattern Industry." *JAH* 66 (Sept. 1979).

"Wanted—One Hundred Girls as Stenographers." *The Phonographic World,* Apr. 1910.

Ward, David. "The Emergence of Central Immigrant Ghettoes in American Cities, 1840–1920." *Annals of the Association of American Geographers* 38 (1968).

Warner, Charles Dudley. "Studies of the Great West: III—Chicago." *Harper's New Monthly Magazine* 76 (May 1888).

Warner, Sam Bass, Jr., and Colin B. Blake. "Cultural Change and the Ghetto." *Journal of Contemporary History* 4 (Oct. 1969).

Warren, Arthur. "Phillip D. Armour: His Manner of Life, His Immense Enterprises in Trade and Philanthropy." *McClure's Magazine* 2 (1893–94).

Webster, J. Carson "The Skyscraper: Logical and Historical Considerations." *JSAH* 18 (Dec. 1959).

Weingarden, Lauren S. "Naturalized Technology: Louis H. Sullivan's Whitmanesque Skyscrapers." *The Centennial Review* 30 (Fall 1986).

Weisman, Winston. "A New View of Skyscraper History." In Edgar Kaufmann, Jr., ed. *The Rise of an American Architecture.* New York: Praeger, 1970.

———. "New York and the Problem of the First Skyscraper." *JSAH* 12 (1953).

Weiss, Janice. "Educating for Clerical Work: The Nineteenth-Century Private Commercial School." *Journal of Social History* 14 (Spring 1981).

Wells, Ida B. "Lynch Law in All Its Phases." *Our Day* (May 1893).

Westfall, Carroll W. "The Golden Age of Chicago's Apartments," *IA* 24 (1980).

———. "Home at the Top: Domesticating Chicago's Tall Apartment Buildings," *CH* 14 (1985).

Wetherold, Houghton. "The Architectural History of the Newberry Library." *The Newberry Library Bulletin* 6 (Nov. 1962).

White, Charles Henry. "Chicago." *Harper's Monthly* 118 (Apr. 1909).

White, William A. "Tradition and Urban Development: A Contrast of Chicago and Toronto in the Nineteenth Century." *Old Northwest* 8, no. 3 (1982).

Wight, Peter B. "Daniel Hudson Burnham, an Appreciation." *AR* 32 (Aug. 1912).

———. "Fireproof Construction and the Practice of American Architecture." *American Architect and Building News,* Aug. 19, 1893.

———. "John W. Root as a Draftsman." *IA* 16 (Jan. 1891).

———. "On the Present Conditions of Architectural Art in the Western States." *American Art Review* 1 (1880).

———. "Origin and History of Hollow Tile Fireproof Floor Construction—Part I." *Brickbuilder* 6 (Mar. 1897).

———. "A Paper Delivered at a Meeting Held at the Art Institute, Chicago, June 11, 1912." *AR* 32 (Aug. 1912).

———. "Recent Fireproof Building in Chicago." *IA* 5 (1885).

Wilke, F. N. "Among the Ruins," *The Lakeside Monthly* 7 (Jan. 1872).

Williams, Jeffrey C. "The Origin of Futures Markets." *Agricultural History* 56, no. 1 (1982).

Williams, Mentor L. "The Background of the Chicago River and Harbor Convention, 1847." *Mid-America* 30 (Oct. 1948).

———. "The Chicago River and Harbor Convention, 1847." *Mississippi Valley Historical Review* 35 (June 1948–Mar. 1949).

Wills, Garry. "Sons and Daughters of Chicago." *New York Review of Books* 41 (June 9, 1994).

Wirt, James J. "The Lumber Interests of Chicago." *HW* 27 (Oct. 20, 1883).

Wish, Harvey. "Governor Altgeld Pardons the Anarchists." *JISHS* 31 (Dec. 1938).

Woodman, Harold D. "Chicago Businessmen and the 'Granger Laws.'" *Agricultural History* 36 (1962).

Wortman, Marlene Stein. "Domesticating the Nineteenth Century City." *Prospects* 3 (1977).

"The World's Largest Store." *Chicago Dry Goods Reporter* 28 (Jan. 1, 1898).

Wright, Frank Lloyd. "Louis H. Sullivan—His Work." *AR* 56 (July 1924).

———. Review of *Louis Sullivan*, by Hugh Morrison. *Saturday Review of Literature* 13 (Dec. 14, 1935).

York, Byron. "The Pursuit of Culture: Founding the Chicago Historical Society, 1856." *CH* 10 (Fall 1981).

Zukowsky, John. "The Art Institute of Chicago: Constructions, Concepts, and Queries." *Threshold*, Autumn 1985.

Unpublished Articles, Dissertations, and Theses

Bluestone, Daniel M. "Landscape and Culture in Nineteenth-Century Chicago." Ph.D. diss., Univ. of Chicago, 1984.

Cierpik, Anne Felicia. "History of the Art Institute of Chicago from Its Incorporation on May 24, 1879, to the Death of Charles L. Hutchinson." Master's thesis, DePaul Univ., 1957.

Green, Paul Michael. "The Chicago Democratic Party, 1840–1920: From Factionalism to Political Organization." Ph.D. diss., Univ. of Chicago, 1975.

Haymer, Norman. "The Effect of Prohibition in Packingtown." Master's thesis, Univ. of Chicago, 1920.

Lee, Guy A. "History of the Chicago Grain Elevator Industry, 1840–1890." Ph.D. diss., Harvard Univ., 1938.

Lester, Robin D. "The Rise, Decline, and Fall of Intercollegiate Football at the University of Chicago, 1890–1940." Ph.D. diss., Univ. of Chicago, 1974.

McCarthy, Michael. "Businessmen and Professionals in Municipal Reform: The Chicago Experience, 1887–1920." Ph.D. diss., Northwestern Univ., 1970.

Miller, Joan S. "The Politics of Municipal Reform in Chicago During the Progressive Era: The Municipal Voters' League as a Test Case, 1896–1920." Master's thesis, Roosevelt Univ., 1966.

O'Connell, James C. "Technology and Pollution: Chicago's Water Policy, 1833–1930." Ph.D. diss., Univ. of Chicago, 1980.

Peterson, Jacqueline Louise. "The Peoples in Between: Indian-White Marriage and the Genesis of a Metis Society and Culture in the Great Lakes Region, 1680–1830." Ph.D. diss., Univ. of Illinois at Chicago, 1981.

Rosen, Christine M. "Chicago's Society for the Prevention of Smoke." Unpublished paper, July 1989.

Sawislak, Karen Lynn. "Smoldering City: Class, Ethnicity & Politics in Chicago at the Time of the Great Fire, 1867–1874." Ph.D. diss., Yale Univ., 1990.

Schneirov, Richard. "The Knights of Labor in the Chicago Labor Movement and Municipal Politics, 1877–1887." Ph.D. diss., Northern Illinois Univ., 1984.

Schultz. Rima Lunin. "The Businessman's Role in Western Settlement: The Entrepreneurial Frontier, Chicago, 1833–1872." Ph.D. diss., Boston Univ., 1985.

Sims, Norman Howard. "The Chicago Style of Journalism." Ph.D. diss., Univ. of Illinois at Urbana-Champaign, 1979.

Taft, Lorado. "Charles L. Hutchinson and the Art Institute." *In Memoriam: Charles L. Hutchinson, 1854–1924.* CHS, 1925.

Weber, Robert David. "Rationalizers and Reformers: Chicago Local Transportation in the Nineteenth Century." Ph.D. diss., Univ. of Wisconsin–Madison, 1971.

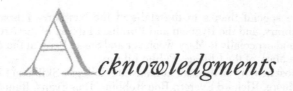

Acknowledgments

Not long after we met at his home in Amenia, New York, Lewis Mumford suggested that I write a book about a great American city, and to him I owe an enormous intellectual debt. His luminous work on the city and civilization, along with the urban fiction of Theodore Dreiser, drew me to city studies and provided inspiration throughout the telling of this Chicago story.

I decided to write about Chicago after walking its streets and experiencing its sights and scenes. It was the architecture that first took hold of me—that and the power and energy of the place. And my first guide to the city's secrets was Tim Samuelson. He and the architect John Vinci gave me an incomparable introduction to nineteenth-century Chicago's greatest surviving buildings. They encouraged me, as Mumford had, to see these buildings not as isolated masterworks but as living parts of the physical ecosystem of the city and as records—like the pages of a book—of its life and spirit.

Christine Newman of *Chicago Magazine* and Bill Mullen of the *Chicago Tribune* took an early interest in this project, and my conversations with them and other thirsty Chicago writers at Riccardo's enriched my understanding of the city. At Riccardo's I met Leonard Aronson, a writer and filmmaker who became my most enthusiastic supporter and toughest critic—and a wonderful guide to Chicago itself, then and now.

Bill Donnell, a Chicago real estate developer, and Byron Goldsmith, one of the city's most brilliant architects, shared with me their intimate knowledge of the construction and interworkings of a commercial skyscraper. And Bill Newman of the *Chicago Sun-Times* helped sharpen my notion that nineteenth-century Chicago bore some interesting similarities to fifteenth-century Florence, an idea that first came into my mind on a research trip in Florence sponsored by the Alfred P. Sloan Foundation.

I did most of my research at the Chicago Historical Society, the finest urban history library in the country. The staff was unfailingly helpful, especially Emily Clark and Archie Motley. They made me feel welcome and pointed me to important finds. Michael Ebner, a trustee at the historical society and an urban historian of note, invited me to give an earlier version of this work at the society's urban history seminar. It was there that I first met Harold M. Mayer, the distinguished urban geographer and historian and coauthor, with Richard C. Wade, of that magnificent pictorial history of Chicago, *Chicago: Growth of a Metropolis*. Harold invited me to join him for drinks and conversation after the seminar, and from that night until his untimely death he was a source of encouragement and insightful advice.

My thanks to other colleagues and friends who contributed to the book with readings, comments, and conversation: Jim Tiernan, David Johnson, John Cell, Alan Trachtenberg, John Thomas, Bob Bruegman, Bill Gapp, Debra Rosen, Richard Snow, Jim Daugherty, and my agent, Gina Maccoby, who has the eye and instincts of a first-rate editor.

I am thankful for the resources of the libraries listed in the bibliography and would like to give special thanks to the staffs of the Newberry Library, the Chicago Public Library, and the Ryerson and Burnham Library of the Art Institute of Chicago—and especially to Mary Woolever and Susan Perry at the Art Institute and Andrea Mark of the Chicago Public Library.

I came to rely most heavily on the staff at Lafayette College's Skillman Library, especially Betsy Moore, Richard Everett, Ron Robbins, Dan Evans, Rani Sinha, and the director, Neil McElroy. They helped locate materials essential to my work, often anticipating my needs.

A group of terrific undergraduate students helped with the research, under the sponsorship of Lafayette College's Excel Program: Sam Chapin, Tina Beth Pina, Kathleen Stewart, Deborah Marcus, Jennifer Biderman, and Kate Young, who worked three years on the project. A grant from the National Endowment for the Humanities allowed me to spend an uninterrupted year completing an early draft of this book, and my work was generously supported on a continuing basis by Lafayette College.

Kathleen Stewart was my typist and editorial assistant. I came to rely on her greatly and truly appreciate her highly professional help.

At Simon & Schuster, Bob Bender was the perfect editor. He made the writing of this long book an enlivening intellectual experience. His splendid assistant, Johanna Li, helped with all the essential details involved in turning a manuscript into a book. I also had the benefit of a superb team of copyeditors headed by Gypsy da Silva. I am particularly indebted to Theresa A. Czajkowska, who took a special interest in this book and helped make it better.

This book is dedicated to my nephew, Andrew Miller, and to my father, Donald L. Miller. Andy's fight against staggering odds was an inspiration to all who loved him, as was the uncrushable courage of his parents, Larry and Bernadette Miller. And my father, the patriarch of a big and noisy family, left an example of how a life ought to be lived. Bless them both.

Donald Miller
Easton, Pennsylvania

Index